INSURGENCY AND COUNTERINSURGENCY
IN SOUTH AFRICA

D1479186

DANIEL L. DOUEK

Insurgency and Counterinsurgency in South Africa

HURST & COMPANY, LONDON

First published in the United Kingdom in 2020 by
C. Hurst & Co. (Publishers) Ltd.,
41 Great Russell Street, London, WC1B 3PL

Printed in India

Distributed in the United States, Canada and Latin America by Oxford
University Press, 198 Madison Avenue, New York, NY 10016, United States
of America.

A Cataloguing-in-Publication data record for this book
is available from the British Library.

ISBN: 9781849048804

www.hurstpublishers.com

For Julia, more than ever

CONTENTS

ACKNOWLEDGEMENTS

First of all, no words can express my gratitude to the people in South Africa who made this book come true. Their belief in this project from the very start and the warmth of their welcome after knowing me for only a few hours will forever be engraved in my heart. Ronnie, you are noble and brave as a lion. Phumla, you made this all possible, I can never thank you enough. Eldridge, you are a magnificent friend. Endless thanks to the late Mama Koko for her hospitality; Mxwedisa, the late Baba Luvo, Makana, Lihle, Mangete, Junior, Lufuno, MaBoyz, Qoqo, the late Hani, Tzagane, and others too numerous to mention. Many thanks to uGan for sharing his love of Peter Tosh. Much love and respect to King Buyelekhaya and his family. Many thanks to the Molope family in Mabopane and Gauteng, especially Tumelo: you embody Ubuntu in so many ways.

I cannot name here most of my interviewees for this project, but I must emphasize how humbled I am by their hospitality and trust. Many of them went to great lengths, geographically and emotionally, to make themselves available. I will never forget my surprise when one former guerrilla commander who lived in a distant rural area, and whom I had given up all hope of reaching before my departure, came to meet me as I waited for my plane in the Mthatha airport lounge, where we conducted a captivating interview. MK veteran Barry Gilder encouraged me after attending my presentation on MK at the 2013 African Studies Conference in Baltimore, and generously sat for an interview afterwards.

ACKNOWLEDGEMENTS

I am much obliged to the Institute for Security Studies (ISS) in Tshwane for welcoming me during my stay in 2009. Cheryl Frank and Johan Burger were particularly helpful and generous with their time. Thanks to Sasha Gear, formerly at the Centre for the Study of Violence and Reconciliation in Braamfontein, for sending me her excellent reports. Thanks also to Fikile Hintsa of the King Sabata Dalindyebo Municipality Public Safety Department, to Mr Somkoko and Mr Sonamzi of Walter Sisulu University, and especially to Somadoda Fikeni for sparing two hours of his time to do an interview in a Tshwane hotel lobby. I also wish to thank warmly the staff at the South African History Archive (SAHA) in Braamfontein – you are a bulwark of democracy. At SAHA, Debra Matthews made it possible for me to do weeks' worth of archival research in mere hours.

Several people whom I have never met have helped me a lot with this book: I am so grateful to Danga Mughogho for repeatedly consulting archival sources in great depth on my behalf. Evelyn Groenink was kind and trusting enough to send me the manuscript of her excellent book before it was released. Jeffrey Haas, Susan Williams, Ellen Moodie, and J. Patrice McSherry provided encouragement and key insights. Chris Saunders' comments and feedback vastly improved this manuscript.

This book would not exist without the funding I received from the Province of Québec's Fonds de recherche sur la société et la culture (FQRSC); Canada's Social Sciences and Humanities Research Council (SSHRC); McGill University's Institute for the Study of International Development; and McGill's Department of Political Science.

Many thanks to Michael Dwyer of Hurst Publishers for inviting me to discuss with him the idea for my book, then backing me until its completion. He is the sort of editor most authors can only wish for. Thanks also to Russell Martin and Daisy Leitch.

I have been very fortunate to have Will Reno as friend and mentor. Will has offered so many insights on African conflicts and on navigating the shoals of academia. Thanks for inviting me to present my research at Northwestern University and to consult the Herskovits African Studies Library's massive collection. My deepest gratitude also to Juliet Johnson, a pillar of integrity and wisdom, for her support and advice. Aisha Ahmad has been a key friend and ally through thick and thin. Allen Stack's brilliance and enthusiasm have greatly helped to shape this book. Bill Minter was kind enough to take the time to discuss this project with me. Thanks also to Philip Gooding, Khalid Medani, Philip Oxhorn, Steve Saideman, and Rachel Sandwell at McGill, and to Frank Chalk, Amy Poteete and Leander Schneider at Concordia, for their helpful comments and suggestions, and to Andrew Davison, Luke Charles Harris, Ismail Rashid, and the late Constance Berkeley at Vassar College.

I am especially grateful to the McGill undergraduate students who have done excellent volunteer work for me as research assistants over the past few years, including Alexa Coleman, Darren Elias, Théophraste Fady, Pierre Gugenheim, Alexandra Harvey, Liam Kirkpatrick, Eric Krol, Sebastien Oudin-Filipecki, Sarah Pollack (who accessed the Mayibuye Archives on my behalf and endured a hair-raising train ride afterwards), Eliott Scharf, Quentin Thomas, Kelly Tragash, Maeve Williams, and Wong Wing: may you all enjoy much success going forward. Thanks to the countless other students I have taught over the years at Concordia and McGill who have inspired and challenged me.

Thanks also to Ginger DiGaetano, Sarah-Myriam Martin-Brulé, Theodore McLauchlin, Aviad Rubin, and Ora Szekely. Peace to Dave Acel, Mallar Chakravarty, Pablo Elliott, Leibish Hundert, Amos Joannides, Todd Jones, Daniel Nerenberg, John Randall, Arianne Shaffer, and the incomparable Yang Hai Sifu.

Above all, my gratitude goes to my family for their love and support: Pa, Oma, Jennifer, Benjamin, Motsumi, Siamela, Agi, Andy, Nikki, as well as Zosia, Dragan, Charlotte, Duncan, and Douglas, plus aunts, uncles, and cousins too numerous to mention. The memories of my beloved late mother Eva and my grandparents Leon, Frida, Miki, and Marica burn brightly against eternity; their proud example has kept me going. My kids, James and Eva, are the coolest and most wonderful – I love you both beyond measure. My wife Julia has been amazingly patient, gracious, and supportive, and the best partner in crime.

Montreal, 2020

ABBREVIATIONS

ACDP	African Christian Democratic Party
ADM	African Democratic Movement
ANC	African National Congress
APLA	Azanian People's Liberation Army (armed wing of the PAC)
ARAC	Africa Risk Analysis Consultancy (Pty) Ltd
AWB	Afrikaner Weerstandsbeweging
AZANLA	Azanian National Liberation Army (armed wing of the Black Consciousness Movement)
BAT	Boere Assault Troops
BCM	Black Consciousness Movement
BDF	Bophuthatswana Defence Force
BEE	Black Economic Empowerment
BMATT	British Military Advisory and Training Team
BOSS	Bureau of State Security (predecessor of the NIS)
BSI	Bureau of Security and Intelligence
CCB	Civil Cooperation Bureau (SADF MI death squad)
CDF	Ciskei Defence Force (the military of the Bantustan of Ciskei)
COSATU	Congress of South African Trade Unions

ABBREVIATIONS

CPR	Certified Personnel Registers
DCC	Directorate of Covert Collection (secret branch of SADF MI)
DESO	Defence Exports Services Organization
DP	Democratic Party
DSO	Directorate of Special Operations
FAPLA	Front African People's Liberation Army
FMLN	Farabundo Martí National Liberation Front
FRELIMO	Mozambique Liberation Front (Mozambican government since 1975)
GEAR	Growth, Employment, and Redistribution
IFP	Inkatha Freedom Party
IR-CIS	International Researchers-Ciskei Intelligence Services
JMCC	Joint Military Coordinating Council
JMS	Joint Management Centre
JSCI	Joint Standing Committee on Intelligence
KANU	Kenyan African National Union
KZP	KwaZulu Police
LLA	Lesotho Liberation Army (an apartheid proxy militia to destabilize Lesotho)
MHQ	Military Headquarters
MID	Military Intelligence Department
MK	Umkhonto we Sizwe (armed wing of the ANC)
MKMVA	Umkhonto we Sizwe Military Veterans' Association (founded in 2001)
MPLA	Popular Movement for the Liberation of Angola (Angolan government since 1975)
NAPPCRU	National Police and Public Civil Rights Union
NAT	Department of National Intelligence and Security

NCM	National Coordinating Mechanism
NEC	National Executive Committee
NIA	National Intelligence Agency (the post-apartheid successor to the NIS)
NICOC	National Intelligence Coordinating Committee
NIS	National Intelligence Service (the apartheid civilian spy agency)
NITU	National Investigating Task Unit
NLA	Natal Liberation Army
NP	National Party (the party that governed South Africa, 1948–94)
NPKF	National Peacekeeping Force
NSF	Non-Statutory Forces
NSMS	National Security Management System
OAS	Organisation de l'Armée Secrète
OLC	Overall Leadership Committee
PAC	Pan Africanist Congress
PAIGC	Partido Africano da Independência da Guiné e Cabo Verde (African Party for the Independence of Guinea and Cape Verde)
PAIIC	Pan-Afrik Industrial Investment Consultants
PIDE	Portuguese overseas secret police, active in Portugal's African colonies
PLAN	People's Liberation Army of Namibia
PMC	Politico-Military Council
PWV	Pretoria-Witwatersrand-Vereeniging (the former name for Gauteng province)
RDP	Reconstruction and Development Programme
RENAMO	National Resistance of Mozambique
SABC	South African Broadcasting Corporation

ABBREVIATIONS

SACP	South African Communist Party
SADF	South African Defence Force (the apartheid military)
SADF MI	South African Defence Forces Military Intelligence (also known as the Military Intelligence Directorate, or MID)
SAHA	South African History Archive
SAIMR	South African Institute for Maritime Research
SANDF	South African National Defence Force (South Africa's post-transition military)
SAP	South African Police (the apartheid-era police force)
SAPS	South African Police Service (South Africa's post-transition police force)
SAPU	South African Police Union
SASS	South African Secret Service (South Africa's post-transition foreign intelligence arm)
SB	Security Branch
SDECE	Service de Documentation Exteriéure et de Contre-Espionnage
SDUs	Self-Defence Units (ANC militias during the 1990–4 political violence)
SPUs	Self-Protection Units (IFP militias, counterparts of the SDUs)
SSC	State Security Council
SWAPO	South West Africa People's Organization (the Namibian liberation movement during apartheid South Africa's occupation)
TDF	Transkei Defence Force (the military of the Bantustan of Transkei)
TREWITS	Afrikaans acronym for Counter-Revolutionary Target Information Centre
UDF	United Democratic Front
UNITA	National Union for the Total Independence of Angola

UNTAG — United Nations Transition Assistance Group

UWUSA — United Workers' Union of South Africa

VAG — Verligte Aksie Groep (Enlightened Action Group)

WCCC — Western Cape Civic Committee

XWB — Xhosa Resistance Movement

ZANLA — Zimbabwe African National Liberation Army (ZANU-PF armed wing)

ZANU-PF — Zimbabwe African National Union – People's Front (Zimbabwe's main pro-independence faction and post-independence ruling party)

ZAPU — Zimbabwe African People's Union (breakaway faction of ZANU)

ZIPRA — Zimbabwe People's Revolutionary Army (armed wing of ZAPU)

INTRODUCTION

Reality never exists in isolation
                                    – Amilcar Cabral

In January 1994, months before the free-and-fair elections held on 27 April, guerrillas from the armed wing of the African National Congress (ANC), Umkhonto we Sizwe ('Spear of the Nation' in isiXhosa, commonly known as MK), were ordered to assemble at designated military bases for integration into the National Peacekeeping Force (NPKF), precursor to the post-apartheid security forces.

Several ex-guerrillas described to me a chilling situation awaiting them at the Wallmansthal base near Pretoria. Upon admission to the base they were immediately required to surrender their weapons, while being guarded by heavily armed South African Defence Force (SADF) soldiers, including the feared *askaris* (black guerrilla turncoats organized into apartheid death squads): 'we were fighting these people in the bush and we hit them hard. Now when we integrate, they were still bullying. They disarmed us, but they had guns and they were still parading, guiding us.'[1] The SADF knew the MK guerrillas' pseudonyms (or 'travelling names,' as they were known within MK), suggesting that certain MK officers had collaborated with the regime without their knowledge: 'But when we went there they called us with our pseudonyms, the names we were using outside. So, we are amazed, where did they get those names?'[2] The guerrillas took this as an ominous sign. Another ex-guerrilla explained that among the newly decommissioned guerrillas

1

swarmed many askaris 'all over. People who killed our comrades. It was not good [for us] to mingle with the same enemy, on the same *kraal* [camp], especially askaris, who were at the assembly points, and they had the advantage over us there – positions, monetary, surveillance, logistically, so we were just out, last in everything.'[3] The procedure was for the guerrillas to be interviewed individually, ostensibly to determine the rank that they would be offered in the integrated security forces, but as another ex-guerrilla explained, [the askaris] 'showed us that no, here you have been followed, you have been investigated, and they wanted to know who were the commanders.'[4] Several ex-combatants I interviewed mentioned that a number of MK guerrillas assembled at Wallmansthal, who had long been targeted by the regime, disappeared during these intake interviews, never to be heard from again: 'there were enemy agents, a lot of them. They were still active. They were screening, analysing individuals, categorizing people. Some people even vanished without a trace.'[5] Another ex-guerrilla described how askaris subjected the MK veterans assembled at Wallmansthal to questioning that was clearly intended to identify the key fighters within their units: 'They brought us in one by one, asked us who is in charge, which of us are the commanders, and so on. Some just disappeared, they were never heard from again. So we decided that no, here they will kill us one by one. We'd rather leave the army and demobilize. After that we just left the base. That was it.'[6]

Suspicions arose that the apartheid regime had recruited spies among top ANC and MK officials, which caused many guerrillas to decide against joining the post-transition security forces. As one explained: 'getting to understand that some of the top military brass were sellouts – it broke my morale, and that's when I said no, I am no more going to the army.' Many others who did join the post-apartheid military and police were marginalized by systematic identity-based discrimination. This episode, related by several ex-guerrillas and corroborated by archival documents, is emblematic of South Africa's 'hidden histories.'

This book focuses on the shadow war between guerrillas struggling to seize the South African state and the apartheid regime's counterinsurgency forces. It studies how insurgency and counterinsurgency shape post-transition democratic consolidation in highly negative ways that haven't been fully understood until now, focusing on the case of South Africa but producing findings that are more broadly applicable to cases of democratic transition and civil war resolution. Using extensive interview-based and archival field research, I have studied ex-guerrillas' 'hidden histories' to reveal dimensions of the struggle against apartheid, and the regime's violent response, which have thus far gone untold. These interviews and archival sources provide detailed narratives of MK guerrillas' experiences, on the one hand, and of apartheid counterinsurgency operations, on the other. They yield powerful evidence of the apartheid regime's clandestine violent strategy calibrated to shape South Africa's democratic transition, which began with the dismantling of apartheid laws in 1990 and ended with South Africa's first free-and-fair elections in April 1994, which brought the ANC to power. According to these sources, apartheid counterinsurgency operations, which intensified at the transition's onset, continued even beyond the ANC's rise to power, aiming to shape the post-transition security forces in ways that would preserve the apartheid security elites' power and influence.

Counterinsurgency legacies affect democratic transitions and consolidation in several key ways: they give authoritarian security elites ongoing power to shape post-transition institutions, especially the security forces, when they are unwilling to cede equal power in the institutions they control. The persistence of authoritarian security force elites, and limits on ex-rebels' integration into the post-transition police, military, and intelligence services, inhibit these forces' ability to enforce law and provide security. By marginalizing former rebels with high popular legitimacy, counterinsurgency disables democratic reform of the police, military, and intelligence services (the security sector), while preserving entrenched criminal networks and racist tendencies within them. Secondly, by fracturing social trust and flooding communities with weapons, these legacies have contributed to high levels of post-transition violence and instability. This perpetuates institutional illegitimacy and corruption and weakens state responses to waves of post-transition violence, thereby distorting democratic outcomes.

Counterinsurgency programmes have been an integral aspect of authoritarian regimes' attempts to violently thwart opposition movements, yet their impact on transitions from authoritarianism remains poorly understood and undertheorized. In the ambiguous period after the formal cessation of hostilities, the government has strong incentives to maintain counterinsurgency until the last possible moment and even after the transition. Even when negotiators have addressed security sector reform, this process can remain incomplete as the security forces seek to shape the political transition. In particular, government elites' control of the security institutions whose reform is being negotiated, and into which guerrillas will be integrated, gives them leverage over rebel groups. State elites will attempt to use this leverage to preserve key aspects of their power, especially their grip on the post-transition military and police, even as political office changes hands. The two main counterinsurgency strategies at this stage, I argue, are to co-opt select rebel leaders through intelligence recruitment, and to marginalize or kill guerrillas who cannot be co-opted during the negotiations and security-sector reform process.

The state's capacity to sustain clandestine violence during negotiations creates a crucial imbalance between government and rebels, heightening rebels' fears of being marginalized or 'sold out' by their leadership during the elite pacting process. This sharpens previous findings about civil war that emphasize the importance of 'credible commitment' from both sides but assume parity between state and rebels. Instead, the South African case indicates that counterinsurgency puts rebels at a distinct disadvantage during negotiations because state security elites will seek to exploit their advantage by using clandestine violence to renege on their commitments. Counterinsurgency also drives a wedge between rebel elites, whom the state will try to co-opt or recruit, and the rebels' rank and file, who are likely to become disgruntled with the elite pact and its provisions for security sector reform.

South Africa's democratic transition astounded the world for its relatively bloodless adoption of universal suffrage, multiparty democracy, and a comprehensive, progressive constitution. Post-transition elections have been regular, free, fair, and peaceful; South Africa has one of the most vibrant economies on the continent; a robust independent judiciary protects strong political and press freedoms; and the 1996–8 Truth and Reconciliation Commission

(TRC) held the previous regime more accountable than similar processes elsewhere. However, the lack of transformation of the state security sector and the prevalence of urban violence stand in stark contrast to post-transition accomplishments and compromise the quality of South Africa's democracy. Moreover, state institutions have had persistently low effectiveness and legitimacy since the transition. This book analyses these problems affecting South Africa's transition from apartheid to democracy and identifies the practices of insurgency and counterinsurgency in South Africa as key explanatory variables for the persistence of violence, insecurity, and unreformed security forces in this and other post-authoritarian contexts.

A growing body of literature on the security–development nexus explains how violent histories continue to shape social and economic development. Reforming the state's security agencies to become effective and legitimate is therefore central to providing a context of security in which democracy and development can flourish. Democracy and development in post-conflict settings depend critically upon a secure society free of violence. Without this, gains such as political rights and democratic institutions mean little and are easily reversed. Yet counterinsurgency remains undertheorized as a factor inhibiting democratic consolidation. Developing this variable promises to generate theoretical insights that are critical for explaining why some democratic transitions remain incomplete. This book demonstrates how South Africa's unreformed security forces have contributed to post-conflict violence, both by having a limited capacity to prevent the violence and, in some cases, by actively abetting it, thus distorting and subverting democratic change.

This book also contributes to the debate about whether and to what extent the apartheid state's highest echelons had authorized these 'Third Force' attacks. Some authors have argued that although various covert units of the apartheid security forces attacked the liberation movements' leadership and their supporters during the transition, they operated without centralized state control and without a unified objective.[7] Conversely, others have insisted that the 'Third Force' operated with the National Party government's knowledge and authorization, and that it appeared to operate with government connivance 'until late 1992.'[8] The evidence contained here reinforces this latter position, revealing an elaborate counterinsurgency strategy that aimed to undermine the ANC and the Pan Africanist Congress (PAC) and their respective armed wings, a strategy which seems to have been calculated not so much to derail negotiations as to shape them to the National Party's advantage. This perspective is reinforced by post-transition testimonies from key South African counterinsurgency operators themselves, who insisted that their operations were authorized at the highest levels. Though such claims were undoubtedly self-serving, it is crucial to consider that far from being the schemes of rogue units, the counterinsurgency operations comprised extensive planning, logistics, personnel, and intelligence networks, were often coordinated with civilian decision-makers, and lasted until at least 1994, the year of Nelson Mandela's election to power, and even afterwards.

Defining Insurgency and Counterinsurgency

'Insurgency' refers to a popular struggle aiming to topple and replace the incumbent government. Insurgencies typically encompass armed and unarmed actors, whose activities may vary in terms of how closely or loosely their activities are centralized and coordinated. Kilcullen defines 'counterinsurgency' as 'an umbrella term that describes the full range of measures that governments take to defeat insurgencies,' including 'political, administrative, military, economic, psychological, or informational, and these are almost always used in combination.'[9] Previous literature has distinguished between 'hard,' or armed (also known as 'kinetic') counterinsurgency strategies, and 'soft' strategies 'designed to win the hearts and minds (and sometimes debts) of local populations' through a blend of propaganda and patronage; historically, most campaigns have deployed both strategies simultaneously.[10] For the purposes of analysing counterinsurgency's impact on democratic transitions, however, I find it more useful to distinguish between its 'blunt' and 'sharp' ends, which are complementary rather than mutually exclusive: at the 'blunt' end, the state deploys conventional army and police forces to achieve overt (that is, not secret) objectives through such strategies as 'clear-and-hold' military campaigns and mass arrests of suspected insurgents.

As compared to the conventional military and police operations unfolding alongside it, counterinsurgency's 'sharp' end features a clandestine nexus of military, police, and intelligence services, which afford the state 'plausible deniability' for its actions. The units tasked with such operations are typically covert, and nebulous chains of command are calculated to ensure that their activities, if uncovered, cannot be conclusively traced to the top. They include death squads, and they often finance themselves through illicit channels that cannot be traced to state spending. In their study of death squads in El Salvador, Mason and Krane have noted that states will often initiate violence against civil society even when no armed insurgency yet exists by targeting defiant elements.[11] In a civil war context, the state will seek to 'turn' captured guerrillas or entice their leaders into collaborating with the state through bribery, blackmail, and torture, creating fear and suspicion of 'sellouts' within the rebel group and the larger population. This strategy has seen wide use, from the Italian security forces' fight against the Red Brigades in the 1970s,[12] to European colonial forces throughout Africa.

In the ambiguous period after the formal cessation of hostilities, the government has strong incentives to maintain counterinsurgency until the last possible moment, and even after the transition. Key counterinsurgency strategies at this stage are the co-optation of rebel leaders through intelligence recruitment, and the marginalization or assassination of guerrillas who cannot be co-opted during the negotiations and security-sector reform process. Even when negotiators have addressed security sector reform – the process of reforming the military, police, and intelligence services – this process can remain incomplete as elements of the old authoritarian regime within the security forces seek to shape the political transition. In particular, by controlling the security institutions whose reform is being negotiated, and into which guerrillas will be integrated, government elites gain leverage over rebel groups during the transition process. Leaving elites from the authoritarian regime in control of the security forces was a precondition for transition to civilian rule in Argentina in 1983 and in Chile in 1988; in the latter case, ex-dictator Pinochet not only received immunity from prosecution but retained de facto control over the military for a decade afterward. When authoritarian security elites

7

remain largely in control of the security forces after the transition, this also places them in a position to maintain aspects of their covert operations agenda.

State Formation, Security Forces, and Colonial Violence

If South Africa's transition to democracy was relatively successful, the high levels of violence that prevailed before, during and since have also exposed the tension between its state strengths, on the one hand, and its predatory history, on the other. South Africa is typical of the ongoing tension between what Musah characterizes as the 'Tillian' and 'Weberian' paths to state formation, with the former defined as state consolidation through protection racket mechanisms, and the latter defined as state consolidation through bureaucratic expansion.[13] Even as South Africa has established a set of solid political institutions, its violent colonial history continues to loom large, exposing the tension between South Africa's normatively 'Western' legal-rational state and its authoritarian functions. Indeed, as Mamdani argues, South African apartheid must be considered the blueprint for the African colonial state, rather than an extreme outlier.[14]

In his study of British and French colonial control of the Middle East during the 1920s to 1930s, Thomas identifies the centrality of intelligence gathering to the formation and policing of colonial states. Intelligence, he notes, aided not only in the formation of policy, but in the survival of the colonial state. The colonial intelligence apparatus relied upon indigenous collaboration, as the most valuable intelligence 'derived from locally recruited personnel who worked with security services in numerous ways as informants, interpreters, and covert operatives, or as soldiers and police deputies.' Citing French colonial repression in Algeria, Thomas notes that beyond social control, 'one logical, if appalling, endpoint of this repressive colonialism could be a descent into "state terror."'[15] Indeed, in many racist authoritarian regimes, intelligence was the spearhead for targeting activists of all stripes. In 1980, commenting on the Guatemalan army death squads that during the 1960s and 1970s killed 'lawyers, schoolteachers, journalists, peasant leaders, priests and religious workers, politicians, trade union organizers, students, professors, and others,' the liberal

Guatemala City mayor, Manuel Colom Argueta, said: 'you will see that every single murder is of a key person. They are not all of the same ideological orientation. They are simply the people in each sector or movement who have a capacity to organize around a cause.' A few days after speaking these words, Argueta himself was assassinated.[16]

In Guatemala, as in apartheid South Africa and other instances of state terror, the branch of the state security apparatus most capable of identifying and targeting dissidents has typically been the military intelligence corps. In an interview with a senior operative of the notorious Guatemalan military intelligence division G-2, scholar Jennifer Schirmer asked whether G-2 was 'the same thing as a death squad,' to which her informant replied: 'G-2 *is* a death squad; it is a squad directly for killing.'[17] The mechanisms for mass violence, then, were built into the colonial state and, in many instances of transition from authoritarianism, have proved difficult to reform.

The Shadow State

The shadow state, also known as the parallel state or deep state, refers to a semi-formal network of military and intelligence operatives that pervades state institutions and wields the power to deploy a range of coercive methods to subvert meaningful political change. The shadow state coexists with the formal, civilian state institutions in a variable relationship; in some instances, the shadow state will closely collude with the mainstream leadership to ensure its grip on power and inhibit reform, while in other instances it will clandestinely undermine the civilian leadership's agenda, especially when this tends toward allowing greater political freedom. Across the Global South, protracted periods of violence between colonial and anti-colonial forces galvanized a core network of military and civilian state operatives into shadow state networks whose political, economic and military goals persisted even after the mainstream government sought to bring violence to an end. These vestigial colonial extremists have possessed a rejectionist agenda focused on preserving the authoritarian regime they served and the economic privileges they enjoyed during wartime, while being steeped in counterinsurgency practices and connected via intelligence networks that persisted to varying degrees after the transition.

9

In the case of the French Organisation de l'Armée Secrète (OAS), born of the Algerian independence war, these rejectionists attempted to extend the war for colonial control of Algeria after the French government decided to withdraw, even plotting to kill French president, de Gaulle, for betraying the colonial cause. In Argentina and Chile, the military and intelligence services continued to wield a great degree of control over politics even after transition to democracy, and elements in the Argentine shadow state have been complicit in a variety of violent episodes since the transition.[18] During the Cold War, the intelligence services of various Latin American authoritarian regimes, trained and supplied by the United States' Central Intelligence Agency (CIA), launched the top-secret Operation Condor, which established a transnational network to monitor, arrest, torture and kill leftist dissidents throughout the region. Under Operation Gladio, secret, far-right European organizations with links to domestic and external intelligence agencies also constituted a shadow state within several NATO member countries, perpetrating several high-profile incidents such as the 1980 bombing of a train station in Bologna that killed 85, and the deaths of leftist Portuguese politicians in a plane crash the same year.[19] During the Cold War, Gladio forces within the Italian intelligence services, in alliance with right-wing terrorists, waged a 'secret and undeclared war' that destabilized Italy and compromised its democracy.[20] Meanwhile, even after civil war resolution and transition from military rule, shadowy forces continued to assassinate former rebel leaders and prominent leftist figures in El Salvador, Guatemala and other Latin American countries.

Across these various regimes, the shadow state 'tended to represent the interests of three very specific groups: the military hierarchy, the national economic elite, and the transnational corporations.'[21] The shadow state's existence and deployment were integral to counterinsurgency warfare, 'and the concept of the parallel state provides a frame of reference with which to understand the hidden apparatus of terror and social control.'[22] Like the forces behind Operation Condor, the apartheid 'Third Force,' which was in reality a better-hidden appendage of the regime's conventional security forces, embodied a branch of the state that served as an extension of its strategy of clandestine violence against progressive forces. This manifestation of the shadow state, just like its counterparts in Latin American dictatorships, enabled the state to surveil and kill dissidents while preserving the facade of normality for its legal-rational institutions of governance.

The shadow state's signature has been its ability to use violence while ensuring plausible deniability, so that the government's responsibility cannot be conclusively traced. The apartheid regime used the euphemistic term 'Strategic Communications,' or 'Stratcom,' to refer to its most secret counterinsurgency operations, ranging from disseminating disinformation to assassination. In remarks at a lecture he gave to South African security police in May or June 1990, after the apartheid government began negotiations with the ANC, Col. Johan Putter described Stratcom's ultimate objective as '[winning] the hearts and minds of the people' through disseminating propaganda and discrediting the opposition. Putter 'listed ways of sabotaging the enemy organizations using bribery, blackmail, fraud, and false operations,' and assured his audience, 'I just want to tell you that the lecture we are presenting to you was given to the [Army] General Staff and the minister of law and order [Adriaan Vlok], and what I am telling you now is officially the view of the police.' He noted: 'Assassination is a recognized strategic communications technique,' but emphasized that plausible deniability needed to be paramount when conducting assassinations. 'If you want to assassinate, you are never in your life going to use a firearm to kill a guy,' as shooting was regarded as a sure way of '[drawing] an investigation to yourself, and if you've drawn an investigation, you have bloody trouble. So, assassination technique is, a guy pulls out of his driveway one morning, and a big truck rides, boom! over him: an accident. Or the guy has a heart attack...' Col. Putter emphasized to his audience: 'These are the things the generals want us to perpetrate, but not in a stupid way, understand?'[23] This source, and others, underscore National Party law and order minister Vlok's intimate knowledge of such covert operations and his authorization of them. Indeed, former security policemen leaked the recording of Putter's lecture after apartheid ended in order to emphasize, amidst National Party ministers' strenuous denials, that the orders they received to carry out these 'dirty tricks' had originated at the top. Reached for comment in response to the tape's release, Vlok said: 'I cannot even remember Colonel Putter.'[24]

In the Cold War and colonial contexts, counterinsurgency forces have originated within the authoritarian regime's military and intelligence services, and then gone on to develop links with the private sector, insinuating themselves into the fabric of civil society. This is because private sector front companies and organizations provided ideal vehicles for outsourcing clandestine violence and establishing plausible deniability, and because counterinsurgency operatives sought to develop illicit self-financing channels that overlapped with the private sector. These forces have also attracted funding from private actors that have a stake in preserving the authoritarian regime, including arms manufacturers or wealthy landowners. In the context of the Salvadorean civil war, for example, this dynamic gave rise to a state counterinsurgency apparatus that was sponsored by the landowning and business classes as a means of safeguarding their property against FMLN rebels,[25] while the Guatemalan armed forces, after waging counterinsurgency warfare from 1965 with close support from the United States, had by the 1980s 'become a wealthy caste unto itself.'[26] In South Africa, the imperative to create untraceable sources of funding led the counterinsurgency forces to develop private funding streams, and they were often given the cover of private businesses or based at private properties. One of these, the Vlakplaas farm, lent its name to the notorious police death squad based there under the command of Colonel Eugene de Kock.

Unreformed shadow state networks become a potent source of post-authoritarian destabilization, as violent crime and intelligence intrigues continue to emanate from them. These networks remain embedded even as they become increasingly decentralized amid greater economic growth, privatization and urbanization, coming to resemble a series of nodes gathered around a centre instead of a conventional top-down ordering. This is often accompanied by the expansion of mercenaries, paramilitaries and other decentralized, privatized forms of organized violence that blur the line between politically motivated and profit-seeking violence.[27] Counterinsurgency strategies also include recruiting informers within insurgent movements and establishing, funding, and arming ostensibly independent or private actors, such as gangs, vigilante groups and death squads, in order to establish plausible deniability for state violence. As we shall see, clandestine state counterinsurgency strategies are often causally prior to individual motivations for engaging in civil war violence.

The persistence of violence in such post-authoritarian contexts has come to be defined by 'multiple equilibria' of socio-political violence in new democracies, violence that exists alongside processes of democratic transition and even consolidation.[28] In the South African case, both the apartheid state and the ANC rebels increasingly outsourced violence during the final years of the conflict,[29] and the profitability of violence during this era contributed directly to post-transition organized crime. Meanwhile, security forces' mutually profitable links with criminal networks often endure into the new era. In authoritarian regimes, security force chiefs have been able to circumvent conventional channels and to exert their influence directly on heads of state and other key political decision-makers.[30] Furthermore, security force elites have often secretly colluded with political elites in times of upheaval. For example, the KGB launched its failed 1991 coup attempt to reverse Gorbachev's reforms at the behest of old-guard politicians within the Soviet government; after the transition, KGB elements maintained important political influence and corruption networks.[31]

Insurgency, Ideology, and Legitimacy

Do insurgents target civilians because of endogenous structural constraints, such as access to resources, as some contend,[32] or are they driven by ideology? My study highlights the role of ideology in shaping MK's low levels of violence against civilians. MK's ideology aimed to counter apartheid with non-racialism, and to minimize civilian casualties while doing so. This ideology was crucial in creating a robust movement that withstood the depredations of a powerful and ruthless regime. The case of Umkhonto we Sizwe departs from findings that explain the degree of success of insurgent movements through the nature and level of the economic and social endowments they possess.[33] Scholars analysing civil war have argued that these factors in turn determine the extent to which insurgent movements use violence against local civilian populations. According to this formulation, insurgents refrain from preying on local populations when, constrained

13

by a lack of access to external resources, they are forced to rely upon those populations for material support. Instead, the South African case suggests that political ideology, and not just structural conditions, can be the single most important factor in determining how a guerrilla army interacts with a local population, and the degree to which it is willing to target civilians.

I define political ideology as a set of ideas that constitute a set of practices and actions in the political realm. As opposed to simplistic explanations of rebels' grievances,[34] ideology represents a system of knowledge characterized by an interactive dynamic between elites and masses, with elites interpreting mass grievance, and masses expressing their grievances to elites. Revolutionaries across a broad geographical spectrum, such as Mao Zedong, Ernesto 'Che' Guevara and Frantz Fanon, have all emphasized the importance of ideology in triggering and sustaining rebellion; although their explanations for rebellion are undoubtedly self-serving, the role of ideology in overcoming the collective action problems posed by rebellion needs to be taken seriously. Pointing to the instrumental motives that have driven rebels and their supporters, Kalyvas cautions: 'it is a grave mistake to infer the motivation of rank-and-file members from their leadership's articulation of its ideological messages.'[35] Yet my research indicates that MK's rank and file were generally well versed in the ideology of their struggle, and their primary motivations for joining the struggle derived from the ANC's ideology of combating apartheid's class and racial inequalities. This ideology was widely disseminated by both the ANC leadership based in exile and grassroots organizations nominally aligned with the ANC. During the anti-colonial struggle in southern Africa, and South Africa's anti-apartheid struggle in particular, ideologically motivated rebels won the day against a government possessing far greater economic and military capabilities.[36]

Security Sector Reform

One of the greatest challenges facing South African democracy has been reforming the state security institutions in order to make a clean break with apartheid's violent past. While there is much literature on the South African security forces' transition from authoritarianism to democracy,[37] and a proliferation of literature on post-apartheid security institutions, very little of this addresses either counterinsurgency and its legacies or the integration of former guerrillas into the security forces. Furthermore, these former guerrillas' voices, perspectives and experiences are virtually absent within the literature. This book addresses an undertheorized root cause of urban violence in South Africa, and also sheds light on the role that weak security sector institutions have played in the country's continuing urban violence crisis.

Counterinsurgency programmes' post-transition legacies include the stunting of state-security sector reform by preserving authoritarian tendencies and channels of corruption within these forces, thereby eroding their effectiveness and legitimacy. These compromised security institutions in turn contribute to high post-transition levels of urban violence, both through an inability to police effectively and by actively participating in certain types of crime and political control. This strongly distorts and subverts democratic change.

During the demobilization period of both sides' forces, strong states enjoy crucial advantages in power and resources over rebels, making it likely that the government will use clandestine means to tilt the playing field in its favour. The state can secretly renege on its commitments, thereby tainting the outcome of reform. For rebels, this causes an acute post-civil war security dilemma, making it crucial to establish secure cantonment points where guerrillas will not fear betrayal.[38] But security guarantees for rebels mean little because governments will try to use counterinsurgency for clandestine 'cheating,' aiming to infiltrate rebel movements, recruit spies, and marginalize or kill those who refuse co-optation.

Sustaining counterinsurgency operations during negotiations increases the importance of secrecy and plausible deniability, both to avert a showdown with the state's political leadership and to avoid international condemnation that could weaken the state's bargaining position. Security force elites are typically more radical than the moderate state leaders who negotiate with rebels. These elites may be concerned with both the country's political future and their own personal fates after reform, perpetuating authoritarian tendencies in post-conflict security institutions and compromising their ability to provide effective internal security. This prevents the 'new' security institutions from overcoming their reputations for violence and brutality, and from developing popular legitimacy.

Rocky Williams, himself an MK veteran, emphasizes 'the importance of ensuring that high levels of legitimacy ('buy-in') accrue' during security sector reform, and further stresses the importance of transforming 'the culture of the institution,' including its 'leadership, management, and administrative ethos.' Williams also warns that unless security sector 'transformation' 'initiatives are thoroughly indigenized and imbued with practical, local content, then African civil–military relations will be no more than a reflection of "imported" non-African systems.'[39] In the event, this is precisely what occurred in South Africa, where apartheid remained largely encoded in the post-transition security institutions.

South Africa's Post-Conflict Instability

South Africa has maintained soaring violent crime rates since its transition to democracy in 1994. In per capita and real terms, it has one of the highest rates of murder and rape in the world.[40] Urban violence has remained the biggest challenge to the state since its transition from apartheid, preoccupying and constraining state policy.[41] A broad spectrum of literature about the violence during and after South Africa's transition has adopted culturalist or behaviouralist explanations, emphasizing anomie and the deterioration of the social fabric, and ignoring the role of apartheid counterinsurgency in triggering and sustaining this violence.[42] Mamdani analyses the violence between Zulu hostel-dwellers loyal to the Inkatha Freedom Party (IFP) and Xhosa hostel-dwellers loyal to the ANC in South Africa's peri-urban black townships during the deadly 1990–4 transition years between apartheid and democracy. He explains this violence in terms of a traditional, rural ethnic identity that became politically mobilized in the context of urban, industrial modernity. Yet the origins of this violence can be understood properly only by examining the role of apartheid counterinsurgency forces in recruiting key members of the IFP's leadership, and then training, arming and abetting IFP militants before and during the outbreak of violence.

Counterinsurgency has also played a key role in creating and sustaining criminal gangs and vigilante outfits in many violent post-transition societies.[43] In the South African case, the apartheid counterinsurgency apparatus flooded African communities with weaponry; established and armed paramilitary community and youth organizations; empowered criminal gangs; recruited police informers on a broad scale; perpetrated widespread violence through the police, the very state institution normally tasked with stopping violence; and, through both conventional and secret branches of the security forces, killed African civilians in both targeted and random fashion, a strategy that originated decades before African unrest broke out, and that intensified as negotiations proceeded between the government and the ANC. All of these counterinsurgency strategies, in which the apartheid state invested tremendous resources and expertise, severely eroded bonds of social trust and undermined the fabric of African civil society. Counterinsurgency, then, must be considered as analytically prior to culturalist or behaviouralist explanations for post-colonial violence and lawlessness in African communities.

South Africa as a Paradigmatic Case

South Africa is a paradigmatic case for analysing counterinsurgency's impact on transitions from authoritarianism, for several key reasons. South Africa represents a case of successful civil war settlement, and its transition to democracy has, by most metrics, been very successful. Given the conditions and outcome, the effect of counterinsurgency on the transition should have been weak, yet my findings show that it nevertheless played a critical role. We can deduce that in other cases of transition from authoritarianism whose outcomes remain even less conclusive, counterinsurgency is likely to have had at least as strong an impact. In particular, the South African security forces' lack of reform[44] and low popular legitimacy,[45] along with the persistence of widespread urban violence, stand in contradistinction to the relative success of other post-authoritarian reforms, and point to these institutions' susceptibility to strategies of clandestine violence carried out by previous security elites.

South Africa's civil war and negotiated transition featured a contest between a government that espoused free-market ideals and aligned itself with the NATO countries, and an armed insurgency with a redistributive economic platform that was backed by the Warsaw Pact countries. Furthermore, South Africa is instructive as a case study because its history of colonialism, agricultural and industrial capitalism, resource exploitation, and a bureaucratic-authoritarian regime with close ties to international business interests and characterized by sharp racial disparities, all gave rise to particular patterns of insurgency and counterinsurgency strategies shaped by colonialism and the Cold War. The ANC insurgency was characterized by a socialist redistributive ethos, communist-inspired rhetoric, and support from the Soviet Union and its Warsaw Pact allies. In these regards it resembled to an important degree insurgent groups such as El Salvador's FMLN, Guatemala's Army of the Poor and other assorted rebel groups, Nicaragua's Sandinistas, as well as the gamut of southern African anti-colonial rebel groups and many other insurgent groups across the Cold War divide. On the regime's side, its counterinsurgency strategies were strongly shaped by the colonial blueprint for outsourcing violence; this included 'turning' former guerrillas, recruiting paramilitaries, and raising ethnic militias. In the Cold War context, the apartheid regime also benefited from NATO countries' support and enjoyed the backing of their military and intelligence forces. This unfolded against a broader context where colonial minority-rule governments in Africa and pro-free market authoritarian regimes throughout the Global South enjoyed support from NATO countries.

In order to fully understand the nature of 'low-intensity democracy,' we would do well to understand the low-intensity warfare that preceded it in many countries whose class and racial struggles were shaped by Cold War dynamics. Indeed, the very term 'low-intensity warfare' was itself coined by the US military to denote its counterinsurgency war in Vietnam; the term then was given to other wars in the Global South where the USA applied its 'lessons' from the Vietnam War. In this sense, we need to consider counterinsurgency's role in creating the 'low-intensity' quality of post-Cold War democracy in many of these countries that arose after their civil wars were resolved.

Previous literature has argued that transitions from authoritarianism are inherently path dependent because personnel, attitudes and practices in state institutions tend to endure for years after a democratic government has been elected.[46] The new state therefore retains many imprints of the old, including authoritarian legacies in civil–military relations.[47]Counterinsurgency shifts the political spectrum to the right by restricting democratic participation even as the state transitions away from authoritarianism. Levitsky and Way measure competitive authoritarian regimes' coercive capacity according to two indicators: 'scope,' defined by the security apparatus's 'effective reach'; and 'cohesion,' referring 'to the level of compliance within the state apparatus.' They also note that these regimes often exercise repression through covert 'low intensity coercion.'[48] Yet their focus on post-Cold War hybrid regimes does not consider prior institutional history, nor does it trace the continuity within these institutions across the democratic transition process. Most importantly, they examine the impact of security forces' coercion when it is wielded on behalf of the state, but not when it is wielded by security force elites to undermine the state. These institutions' propensity to contribute to post-transition violence has also manifested itself in a variety of post-conflict cases across Latin America.[49] In these contexts, ongoing crime and violence have been caused by myriad factors emanating both from state institutions and from civil society, including high levels of poverty and inequality, an abundance of illicit small arms, and disputes over land redistribution. Yet against this backdrop, counterinsurgency legacies remain a critical source of violence and insecurity.

Post-colonial and post-civil war democracies have also been shaped by a colonially derived class paradigm whose self-legitimating logic passed virtually unchanged through the post-Cold War transitions to democracy. In this context, one feature of 'low-intensity' democracy has been widespread violent crime and the privatized securitization of civil society,[50] as the state has lacked the capacity to contain urban violence, while elements within both state institutions and the private sphere have stood to profit from this chronic insecurity. At the same time, violence during South Africa's democratic transition resembles other cases throughout Africa that experienced different Cold War trajectories, but whose ethnic rivalries closely resemble

South Africa's during this period, being the common result of colonial counterinsurgency strategies, such as in Mozambique, and Zimbabwe. Furthermore, as Reno has noted, security forces in African states have established profitable networks, leavened by a 'creative tension' between different branches of the security forces within the same country.[51] Apartheid South Africa illustrates this pattern, as the various branches of its civilian and military intelligence agencies came to compete with each other to a certain degree by the late 1980s. This was overlaid with the heavily securitized bureaucratic authoritarian regime, and a thriving military-industrial complex. After the transition, this highly developed military and industrial base, combined with uneasy political–military relations, contributed to a lack of security force transformation which in turn hindered democratic consolidation.

Guerrilla Ethnography

> The study of the margins is important not only for communicating and interpreting the voices of less powerful people, but also because the knowledge produced in the margins may sometimes be, in the world of truth claims, more accurate than that generated in the center. People in the margins may have more than 'another perspective' to contribute: as actors close to local processes of political change, they sometimes have more detailed information about certain types of phenomena than do political and social elites…ethnography offers an opportunity not only for enriching our understanding of perspectives on politics, but also for identifying otherwise elusive causal mechanisms, for more firmly establishing what happened and why.[52]

The full extent and duration of a counterinsurgency programme often remain unclear long after the conflict's end, just as its planners intended. Decades after a counterinsurgency programme has ended, its historical trajectory and impact can still be difficult to identify and easy for its architects, agents and apologists to obscure and deny. The two best sources for researching counterinsurgency history are therefore archival documents and personal interviews, especially with those who were the programme's intended targets. Although the topic of apartheid counterinsurgency is well-ploughed terrain, existing literature has mostly ignored ex-guerrillas, who were the regime's intended targets, and many of whom are confined to South Africa's margins even today. Using extensive interview-based field research, I have drawn on insights from ethnographic methodology in my study of these ex-guerrillas' 'hidden histories.'

I have relied on over one thousand pages of primary source documents from the South African History Archive (SAHA) and the Mayibuye Archives, containing much information on apartheid clandestine operations during the transition and which surfaced only partially or not at all at the Truth and Reconciliation Commission. At its core, my study is based on material collected in interviews with 13 former members of the ANC's armed wing, Umkhonto we Sizwe. Over the course of two months, I interviewed these men in and around the city of Mthatha, in South Africa's Eastern Cape Province, and in Johannesburg. Three of these ex-guerrillas had been regional commanders, two others high-ranking officers, one had belonged to an elite unit within the guerrilla force, and most were well placed to offer important insights. These interviews shed new light on the apartheid counterinsurgency programme during South Africa's democratic transition, one of the bloodiest and most disputed periods in the country's history. Interviewing ex-guerrillas who fought apartheid and constructing a narrative of their struggle can be an imposing challenge. 'A strong theme that emerges in interviews and questionnaires [with MK veterans] is *the respondents' need to contain within themselves information that might damage them in some way if it were leaked.* Those who went through similar experiences might be the only ones trusted with such information.'[53] The ex-guerrillas' reluctance to speak openly about their experiences has largely been due to fear of the uncertain circumstances that are a legacy of the apartheid counterinsurgency programme, a fear borne out by the nature of the transition itself, as we shall see. For many ex-combatants, the fear of leaking damaging information is not merely a vestige of a career led in absolute secrecy. Many remain mistrustful of the South African state and its security forces to this day, precisely because of the incomplete nature of the transition within these institutions.

The relatively small sample of ex-guerrillas I interviewed is offset by the long duration of many of the interviews and the details provided therein. When notified of my plan to interview former guerrillas, several South African researchers warned me that locating ex-guerrillas would be a great challenge, that getting them to talk was likely to be very difficult, and that getting them to tell me anything of substance, even more so. Some ex-guerrillas were more guarded in what they chose to reveal, but most were quite candid, and some appeared relieved to be unburdening themselves of harrowing details they had rarely shared.

This is an inductive study in which the topic of counterinsurgency itself and the conclusions I draw about it derive from the people I met and the stories they told me, corroborated by archival sources. I conducted the field research for this study over two months in South Africa, mostly in Mthatha (whose official spelling prior to 1994 was Umtata), formerly the capital of the Bantustan of Transkei and today one of the largest cities in South Africa's Eastern Cape province, with an estimated population of between 600,000 and 800,000. Through a set of fortuitous circumstances, I came to befriend a group of former Umkhonto we Sizwe guerrillas who ran a private security company together. Within several hours of being introduced, I was invited by these men to move as a guest into their house for the duration of my stay. In addition to affording me the closest possible exposure to their lives and stories, living under their roof also protected me from the constant menace of urban South Africa. These former guerrillas were widely known and well respected in the community; nobody wanted to tangle with them.

As their guest, I was also able to maximize the 'snowball' technique of gathering interviews. The snowball method was integral not only in locating ex-guerrillas, but in gaining their trust so they could talk to me freely about their experiences. My hosts introduced me to other former guerrillas and vouched for my trustworthiness, opening doors that would otherwise have remained firmly shut even had I managed to find them. The distance that often separates the researcher from the researched, especially in a country so polarized along race and class lines, was closed considerably, though it would have been impossible to close it altogether. Because I had not expected to be able to interview ex-guerrillas in depth, my back-up field research plan consisted of archival research and interviews with academics and civil servants. I was fortunate that interviews with ex-guerrillas indeed became the main thrust of my research.

Living under the same roof as ex-guerrillas blurred the usual boundaries between researcher and subject, boundaries that tend to be all the more defined between a foreign white researcher and local African people in a country awash with apartheid legacies. This may seem problematic from the perspective of maintaining 'objectivity' in my research, since I became empathetic towards my interviewees and predisposed to absorbing their interpretations of the history they had lived through. Yet it is clear that otherwise my access to these data would have been severely restricted, if it were granted at all. Furthermore, the very data I sought on the histories and legacies of persecution and resistance in South Africa are located in the margins of the state, among those who were persecuted and excluded. 'Objectivity,' in this context, is precisely the scientific voice of what Lalu, following Guha, calls 'the colonial archive,' whose hegemonic narrative has continued to marginalize critical perspectives on apartheid history even after South Africa's transition to democracy.[54] Wherever possible I have used archival materials to corroborate the knowledge derived from interviews. In virtually all cases, the interviews and archival sources have complemented each other, dovetailing to shed new light on an extensive hidden history.

During my stay in Mthatha, I found myself in the unexpected role of gatekeeper to a realm of sensitive historical knowledge. An important local figure was charged with serious crimes; among those assembled to cover the trial was a photojournalist from Johannesburg. The photojournalist soon took a keen interest in some ex-guerrillas present at the trial, and, noticing my interactions with them, asked me whether these men in fact possessed the experience and credentials that they were reputed to have. I demurred and dodged the question. When I mentioned this later to my hosts, they expressed satisfaction that I had revealed nothing, since they believed this photojournalist was likely to 'distort information and cause confusion.' Although he was a black South African fluent in isiXhosa, whereas I was a white foreigner whose interactions with them were limited to English, the photojournalist failed to gain the ex-guerrillas' trust, and they remained suspicious of his motives.

Several interview subjects for this study had been captured and tortured by the apartheid security forces, and not all had recovered equally well. One man, who bore horrific scars on his torso from having been tortured by apartheid agents with a power drill, then left for dead in a trash dumpster, experienced severe flashbacks while talking to me. As he started to relate his story he suddenly began spiralling into the hell of his trauma, sobbing uncontrollably. I was shocked to realize that looking into my Caucasian face while I asked questions about the past had likely reminded him of his torturers, triggering the flashback. 'I saw faces,' he explained, after walking off into the yard for a while to regain his composure. He was determined to overcome the horror of memory and tell me his story. I later learned that this particular man was saved by homeless children who, while foraging for food, found him in the dumpster and brought him to hospital. The children would check on his progress during his hospital stay. However, he fled the hospital before his wounds had fully healed out of fear that the security forces would come there to find him. Indeed, during the struggle years, there were several documented instances of the apartheid forces coming to hospitals to find resistance fighters wounded in shootouts and murdering them in their beds. My hosts told me that since then, despite being destitute, this man has always given money to street children. Since the transition, he survives thanks to support from former comrades. Like many other MK veterans, he had never received any compensation from the ANC government.

Another ex-guerrilla who had been captured along with two comrades in the mid-1980s spoke of having been denied food in captivity for several weeks; his captors then inserted an electrical wire into his anus and switched on the current. 'Then, they would feed us,' he said, explaining that the pain of defecating after this torture was just as bad as the torture itself. In another interview during one of Mthatha's drizzly afternoons, the same ex-guerrilla, dissatisfied with the kerosene heater running at full blast right next to us, turned to give an employee some cash with instructions that he go out and buy a brand-new electric heater. 'They used to keep us naked for months in prison,' he explained. 'The floor was always wet with dirty water. Now, I don't like to be cold.'

Most of the ex-guerrillas told me I was the first researcher of any kind to ask them about their experiences in the struggle. I encountered barely any suspicion, but during one interview with an ex-guerrilla on a balmy evening in his Johannesburg backyard, I heard a nearby commotion going on in isiXhosa between his wife, her friend, and one of my friends. Amid the discussion, I heard my friend hotly invoke the late Joe Slovo, the most senior white ANC member and a onetime Umkhonto we Sizwe commander and South African Communist Party chief; this caught my attention. She later told me that the veteran's wife and her friend were incredulous that he was 'selling out' by discussing MK history with a white man. My friend upbraided them – 'that's Joe Slovo's son!' – to remind them of the ANC's non-racial ethos. Afterward we shared food and music, dissolving lingering tensions. Another former MK commander explained his motives for disclosing to me: 'Listen, we MK veterans now have nothing. That's why I helped to form the [MK] Veterans' Association, because most of us are living in poverty. So, I figure, now we have that freedom we fought so hard for, what is there for me to hide?'[55]

These episodes indicate that even after the advent of democracy in South Africa and the establishment of universal rights, the historical record of the anti-apartheid struggle remains largely safeguarded within the communities that waged it. Despite the public revelation of this secret history through such mechanisms as the Truth and Reconciliation Commission, and partial entry into the mainstream historical record, many who experienced apartheid have remained reluctant to openly reveal or share their experiences. Nor did these people necessarily assume, even fifteen years after South Africa's democratic transition, that a white interviewer's motives were benign.

For this study, I also interviewed Dr Somadoda Fikeni, an academic at the University of South Africa (Unisa) and well-known political commentator, in Tshwane (Pretoria), as well as Mr Somkoko and Mr Sonamzi, faculty members at Walter Sisulu University in Mthatha, and Johan Burger and Cheryl Frank, both senior researchers of the Institute of Strategic Studies in Tshwane.

The archival documents upon which I have drawn fall into two categories: documents from the South African History Archive in

Braamfontein, Johannesburg, and transcripts of interviews with MK cadres conducted in 1993 by Wolfie Kodesh, which belong to the Mayibuye Archives, housed at the University of the Western Cape near Cape Town. These sources provide some powerful insights, but constitute only a fragment of the total documentation gathered and stored by the apartheid regime, which systematically destroyed its own security forces' archives before the ANC was elected to power, and planted informers inside the successive state-appointed investigations into apartheid dirty tricks.

Methodology and Representativeness

All my informants granted me interviews on the condition that I maintain their confidentiality. Due to these limitations, it is not possible to identify these informants at length. The relatively small size of my sample must be considered in the light of the difficulty of locating ex-guerrillas and securing their consent to conduct and record interviews about the struggle years. To ensure confidentiality, I avoid attributing the quotes in this book to specific informants.

These ex-guerrillas represent both lower-ranking as well as higher-ranking former MK cadres. Some had achieved a degree of economic success since independence; others were barely getting by. Though there was a degree of correlation between the ex-combatants' rank in MK and their post-struggle level of income, some who had been high-ranking officers were poor, while some with low rank now lived comfortably.

Some had reached a greater level of formal education than others; most had joined the armed struggle around age 15 or 16 and had not subsequently had the opportunity to complete their studies. One informant had got a university degree while in exile in Zambia before joining MK. All spoke isiXhosa as a first language; and, like most South Africans, all spoke English. Some of the informants were willing to divulge virtually their entire personal histories as MK combatants. Others were more circumspect, particularly those currently working in the security forces; one ex-combatant working for the National Intelligence Agency (NIA) opened our interview by declaring: 'I won't give you any state secrets!'

There is an important range of variation among former MK combatants: they can be divided according to those who went 'into exile' from South Africa for more extensive training at MK bases and in Warsaw Pact countries, and those who received military training in crash courses in Lesotho and within South Africa proper. After MK was forced to close its Angolan bases in 1989, its cadres moved to bases in Zambia, Tanzania and Uganda, where the training was generally not as intensive. Thus, the informants in this study range across a spectrum of rank, combat experience and training within MK. Some informants were bitter towards the ANC because of their perceived marginalization during and after the transition, while others expressed pride in the ANC's accomplishments during and since the negotiated transition and thought that the ANC accommodated its cadres to the greatest extent possible during and after the transition. Thus, this sample reflects the political and social divisions, such as they are, within the ANC and MK.

Informant #1 had been a senior officer at an MK base. Belonging to an older generation of combatants than the rest of the informants, this man was among the first MK fighters to be deployed in Angola. He received overseas training, and also saw extensive combat during the 1970s and 1980s. Like many ex-guerrillas, he has not been able to secure steady employment since South Africa's independence.

Informant #2 was a high-ranking officer during the early to mid-1980s at an MK base, and so was informant #3. Informant #4 was a high-ranking officer at a different base, and all three saw extensive combat during that era. All three received advanced military training overseas. After independence in 1994, two of the men became self-employed, while one joined the post-transition security forces.

Informant #5 saw extensive training in MK camps before being sent overseas for further specialized training. During one incursion into South Africa, he was captured and tortured before managing to escape while in state custody, whereupon he fled and regrouped with MK formations. He found only sporadic employment after the transition.

Informant #6 was a youth activist with the Congress of South African Students (COSAS), and went on to join MK in Angola. After the transition he pursued a career in the post-transition security forces, and today remains active in the ANC.

Informant #7 was recruited into MK as a youth, undergoing a crash course and then serving as a liaison for guerrillas infiltrating from outside. He then went into exile under the ANC's auspices. Shortly before the transition began in 1990, he decided to join MK and received military training. After the transition he became a civil servant.

Informant #8 joined MK as a youth in the late 1970s, receiving training in a crash course. He served as a driver and courier for MK units throughout the 1980s, smuggling weaponry and messages, and arranging logistics for MK strike teams. After the transition, he found work with a private security company.

Informant #9 was heavily persecuted by the Bantustan regime in Transkei. In the mid-1980s he went into exile, receiving training at an MK base. Upon his return to South Africa after the transition, he worked in a traditional leadership role.

Informants #10, 11, 12, and 13 belonged to a younger generation of combatants compared to the other informants, joining MK as youths from 1989 onward. All four received crash-course training and were involved in missions inside South Africa.

1

UMKHONTO WE SIZWE'S ARMED LEGITIMACY

'The guerrilla wins if he does not lose'
— Henry Kissinger, US National Security Advisor, 1969

'Hamba kahle Umkhonto / Umkhonto we Sizwe'
('Go well, defender / defender of the nation')
— African National Congress protest song[1]

'Hamba kahle Umkhonto,' a popular refrain from the anti-apartheid struggle era, was ubiquitous in South Africa during mass actions, strikes and funerals from the 1960s onward, and remained popular even after independence in 1994. The song illustrates the degree to which Umkhonto we Sizwe penetrated black South African consciousness as the legitimate 'defender of the nation.' The lyrics also reveal how, in isiXhosa, the word 'spear' (which is how 'Umkhonto' is usually translated as part of the guerrilla movement's name) is interchangeable with 'defender,' underscoring MK's status as an armed group that broadly represented South Africa's oppressed during apartheid. In spite of the movement's weaknesses and shortcomings, MK guerrillas were the closest thing that African communities had in terms of a security force tasked with defending them, and the only personnel who enjoyed anything close to popular legitimacy among these communities, where they were for the most part lionized.[2] This chapter argues that it matters

29

what kind of armed insurgency a country experiences, especially because the nature of the insurgent movement contributes to shaping the transition from the civil war to the post-civil war era. In particular, this chapter highlights MK's effectiveness and legitimacy as a fighting force during the anti-apartheid struggle, which previous literature has underestimated,[3] as well as MK's emphasis on a policy of 'moral restraint,'[4] which involved mostly avoiding civilian targets. I argue that the reason a guerrilla army such as MK avoided targeting civilians in its military operations can be attributed primarily to ideology, a factor similar to what Wood, writing about FMLN guerrillas and their sympathizers in El Salvador, has described as 'pleasure in agency.'[5]

Previous literature has argued that rebel armies chart their strategies based on 'exogenous' structural factors such as the resource endowments available to them.[6] However, the MK example demonstrates that guerrilla armies may adopt a strategy based, at least in part, on an ideology of a 'just' liberation struggle. In MK's case, this was further rooted in what the movement itself proclaimed and considered to be 'democratic values.' These democratic values, then, matter for the type of state institutions that are forged during and after the transition to democracy. Kalyvas has argued that noble-seeming liberation ideologies espoused by top commanders are rarely the same factors that motivate a rebel army's rank and file, which are often driven by profit-seeking motives disconnected from their movement's grand narrative of struggle.[7] Several accounts have depicted some MK guerrillas as driven by greed: Kynoch argues that during South Africa's 1990–4 spike in political violence, many combatants claiming political motives were in fact motivated by profiteering opportunities.[8] Shubin recalls an MK trainee in the USSR who horrified his Soviet instructors by declaring that he now possessed the skills to rob banks back home.[9] However, the evidence about MK presented here echoes other scholars' findings about similar guerrilla armies in such countries as Namibia, El Salvador and Guatemala, where rebels of every rank joined the armed struggle primarily as a result of anti-colonial convictions. The power and relevance of this ideological component are borne out by the fact that unlike the apartheid regime's indiscriminate violence, MK forces generally avoided targeting civilians and used violence in more calibrated ways. The ANC leadership established a Code of

Conduct for MK that was notable for the high standards it set forth, and that was by all accounts largely adhered to in the guerrilla army's combat operations. The code proclaimed: 'Our armed struggle is a continuation of our political struggle by means that include armed force.' MK engaged in no forcible recruitment, and children who wished to join were given schooling until they were of an appropriate age to join the army. Assault, rape and cruelty were prohibited, as were 'bullying and intimidation, abuse of power, theft, or forcible seizure of goods; the use of drugs; and even insulting or obscene language.'[10] At the Truth and Reconciliation Commission (TRC) after apartheid's fall, it emerged that in 1981 MK had considered targeting State President PW Botha and his entire cabinet with a bomb during a mass celebration to be held in Bloemfontein; according to the ANC's submission to the TRC: 'The sketches of the venue and details on where a car-bomb could be placed to decimate the leadership of the NP government were drawn up.'[11] However, the ANC ultimately decided against this option because of the likelihood of mass civilian casualties, and because 'the obliteration of the NP cabinet could start to blur the distinction between legitimate and illegitimate targets.'

The apartheid security forces derided MK guerrillas as 'commuter bombers' who would plant explosives and flee, unable to challenge the regime's forces head-on.[12] Sanders writes that MK cadres' lives were typically 'nasty, brutish, and short,' and insists that MK's claims to have mauled the apartheid security forces were vastly overstated for propaganda purposes.[13] Yet MK, for all its flaws, was a guerrilla army resilient and savvy enough to endure until 1994, when it achieved its primary goal: to bring down the apartheid regime. Cherry calls MK one of the least successful guerrilla armies in history, citing the low number of deaths caused by MK operations during its existence. However, MK launched dozens of operations calculated to have a symbolic impact but not to kill; these included sabotaging infrastructure and bombing courthouses and other buildings when MK guerrillas knew they would be empty. For example, MK regarded its 1980 attack on the Soekmekaar police station as a success chiefly because thousands of police files on local activists were incinerated in the attack.[14]

Throughout the mid-to-late 1980s, there was an ever-increasing number of shootouts between guerrillas and apartheid forces that never made the headlines, in which the regime undoubtedly downplayed its casualties. One seasoned former guerrilla explained: 'As you know, always when there is contact with the enemy, propaganda prevails saying that no one was hurt, all that, as if we were just aiming [at] the air.'[15] An MK document similarly reported: 'In a lengthy analysis marked "secret" and dated April 1982, the CIA says...that their ally, the South African racists, are "deliberately suppressing reliable reports of successful guerrilla attacks to protect white morale."'[16] After the regime declared its 1985 State of Emergency and struggled to re-establish its governing structures in the townships in the face of widespread unrest, MK became instrumental in targeting and discrediting these structures, which, as Chris Hani described it, was a key goal of the ANC's 'People's War.'[17] Although MK was unable to match the apartheid security forces on the battlefield, it achieved a far greater degree of military success in rooting out the regime's collaborators within South African black communities, and in combat against apartheid proxy forces such as the Inkatha Freedom Party (IFP) and Angola's UNITA.

Throughout the apartheid era, MK guerrillas were more of a shadowy presence in South Africa than a visible army, more the object of secrets and rumours than a standing force situated within the community. Unlike other southern African liberation movements such as Zimbabwe's ZANU and ZAPU, Mozambique's FRELIMO, or Angola's MPLA, MK was, with few exceptions, unable to secure 'liberated zones' in which it could maintain a sustained, visible presence. Although this hindered its military capabilities and battlefield results, MK nonetheless waged a relatively successful strategy that inspired and politicized South Africa's population fighting against apartheid and forced the regime to devote ever-greater resources to security.

MK's recruitment was rooted in kinship networks. Although they grew best in traditional hinterlands such as the Bantustan of Transkei, these kinship networks were not static social institutions inseparable from their native soil. Rather, they often emerged even in the urban dislocation that was characteristic of apartheid South Africa's industrialized peri-urban core, which produced interlocking networks of solidarity and resistance ranging from union activities to armed struggle, generating a pan-African and anti-colonial culture of affinity and kinship. Such kinship ties resembled those that arose elsewhere during African anti-colonial struggles: they bound Zimbabwe African National Liberation Army guerrillas to local populations in eastern and central Rhodesia during Zimbabwe's Second Chimurenga liberation struggle;[18] and in Guinea-Bissau's villages, Amilcar Cabral's PAIGC rebels won hearts and minds on their way to defeating the Portuguese colonizers. In MK's case, this kinship often transcended regions and ethno-linguistic groups within South Africa. During MK's 1967 Wankie campaign, MK forces found that villagers in Rhodesia's Matabeleland region were willing to give them food and warn them of enemy forces' movements, despite the regime's harsh penalties for assisting 'terrorists.'[19]

MK's leadership was under no illusions of being able to defeat the apartheid regime's powerful war machine on the battlefield, and the ANC's president, Oliver Tambo, repeatedly declared that the movement's goal was to force the regime to the negotiating table.[20] This emphasis on using violence in the name of 'armed propaganda' was also a pragmatic admission of MK's weakness against South Africa's formidable military. Yet MK sought time and again to expose the weaknesses in apartheid's armour, and thereby to generate political leverage and popular support for the ANC. MK was instrumental in transmitting the ANC's leadership to communities within South Africa that otherwise could not be accessed directly; the armed struggle also strengthened ANC credibility both within South Africa and on the world stage, where the ANC's profile grew tremendously during apartheid's final decade.[21] The symbolic power of MK's armed struggle is embodied by four MK cadres facing the death penalty at their 1988 trial: the imprisoned guerrillas appeared in the courtroom dressed in their MK combat fatigues, complete with black berets bearing a gold five-pointed star, sending gasps through the packed courtroom audience.[22]

Because of apartheid South Africa's regional hegemony and its long military reach, MK was generally unable to secure forward operating bases closer to South African territory and was forced for most of its history to station and train its fighters thousands of miles from the South African border. The ANC still managed to infiltrate many of these fighters into South Africa on a variety of combat and intelligence missions. Some of these were successful, while many others were thwarted, leading to MK cadres' capture and often to their deaths.[23] These geo-strategic limitations, and particularly MK's near-total failure to establish any liberated zones within South African territory for most of its history, had a key impact in shaping the ANC's response to its fear of spy infiltration. This fear is characteristic of rebel groups that never managed to establish a liberated zone, and that are thus always on the run, facing threats to their very survival. As Reno has noted, the apartheid regime's relentless attacks on MK targets, and 'intimidation of neighbouring state governments, meant that the ANC found itself fighting for its survival in places that it originally planned would be its rear bases, not the forward areas of conflict.'[24] In this context, the ANC's well-founded paranoia about being infiltrated by apartheid spies led to widespread instances of human rights abuses against suspected informers, especially in the ANC's prison camps in Angola.

The ANC Develops an Armed Wing

Founded in 1912, the ANC only began its resort to violence after the apartheid state responded to five decades of political struggle with progressively more punitive and violent policies. The ANC founded MK in response to the killing by the South African Police of 69 unarmed Pan Africanist Congress (PAC) protesters and the wounding of 186 more at Sharpeville, near Johannesburg, on 21 March 1960, which convinced the ANC leadership that negotiating with the apartheid regime was futile. In response to Sharpeville, the smaller, racially constituted PAC also founded its own armed wing, Poqo ('the Steadfast,' later renamed the Azanian People's Liberation Army, or APLA). MK was integrated into the ANC as a military wing subordinate to the overall leadership, with Nelson Mandela as its commander. Its manifesto stated: 'Umkhonto we Sizwe will carry on the struggle for freedom and democracy by new methods, which are necessary to complement the actions of the established national liberation organizations... Umkhonto we Sizwe will be at the front line of the people's defence.'[25] Beginning on 16 December 1961, the first MK attacks were ineffectual sabotage bombings of government buildings and infrastructure that caused no casualties and revealed 'a large degree of amateurism.'[26] In 1962, MK suffered a blow when many of its founding operatives, including Mandela, were captured in a police raid on a farmhouse in the Johannesburg suburb of Rivonia, and sentenced to life imprisonment.[27]

The ANC established guerrilla training camps in Tanzania and Zambia, dispatching contingents to train in the USSR and other Warsaw Pact countries.[28] MK mingled with other African armed movements and trained at the same bases. For example, MK commander Raymond Mhlaba received military training in Algeria at the same time as Che Guevara, on his way to lead rebels in the Congo, who addressed and encouraged the MK guerrillas training there.[29] In Algeria MK trained alongside Mozambique's FRELIMO, and in Egypt alongside Palestinian militants.[30] At its Kongwa base in Tanzania, MK trained alongside FRELIMO, PLAN (the People's Liberation Army of Namibia), and ZIPRA (the Zimbabwean People's Revolutionary Army) under the auspices of the Organization of African Unity.[31]

MK's armed actions were envisioned as complementing the ANC's mass struggle, and the movement formally adopted a policy of non-racialism and moral restraint in its armed wing's recruitment and combat operations. By 1964, there were hundreds of trained MK soldiers in exile.[32] In 1967, MK launched the ill-fated Wankie Operation into Rhodesia alongside cadres from ZIPRA. The MK contingent, commanded by future MK chief of staff Chris Hani, was tasked with establishing forward operating bases on Rhodesian soil from which they could then infiltrate South Africa. Once it crossed from Zambia, the guerrilla force clashed repeatedly with Rhodesian military units reinforced by South African forces, inflicting heavy casualties on the Rhodesian forces and killing SADF anti-guerrilla warfare specialist Maj. Thomas Morgan Thomas, who had been the US Army's guest in Korea and Vietnam.[33] With dwindling rations and ammunition, and enemies in hot pursuit, the MK detachment's remnants crossed into Botswana and surrendered to the authorities there, who imprisoned them. Nearly 50 MK cadres were killed in the Wankie and subsequent Sipolilo campaigns, and the obstacles to establishing a forward operating base near South Africa proved insurmountable, but the combat experience of those who survived, especially Lennox Lagu and Chris Hani, provided the basis for leadership in the fighting against UNITA in Angola, and during the bloody years of Third Force violence.[34] As one former MK commander explained: 'We wanted that the Boers [Afrikaners] should feel that we are around. Because they said MK is dead.'[35] Further armed encounters in the open battlefield would be limited mainly to the Angolan theatre of operations, although by the late 1980s MK forces were increasingly confronting the regime in the border regions, as they did at the 1988 Battle of Mutale River.[36] Nonetheless, largely because of the regime's armed might, the ANC never achieved 'the one element central to a successful seizure of power – an armed, mass-based internal cadre' among South Africa's masses.[37]

MK Legitimacy and Recruitment

'The apartheid regime did all our recruiting for us,' recalled one former MK commander.[38] Indeed, from 1976 onward, the influx of South African youth hoping to join the armed struggle was more than the ANC could absorb. Ex-guerrillas described joining the armed struggle as a natural step in their progression towards political awareness and activism: 'As we grow, we are aware of the situation because you can see the police brutality, you witness it on a daily basis. Most of us were from families who affected by the system.'[39] Under apartheid, African communities typically had high infant and early childhood mortality rates, and several MK cadres reported having young siblings who died from lack of access to adequate care.[40] Another ex-guerrilla recalled how he resolved to take up arms against apartheid when one of his teenage schoolmates was pursued and killed by police after a student rally. One morning shortly thereafter, an MK cadre approached him and two of his friends as they practised karate drills on a hillside; all three eventually joined.[41] Many who had not been politically involved were motivated by ANC propaganda to join the struggle, including the ANC's Radio Freedom, broadcast from exile and banned in South Africa.[42] The ANC's non-racial message resonated widely, as one ex-guerrilla recalled:

> As I grew up, I joined the ANC, which was preaching non-racialism. The first step of your politicization is your conscientization, so that you

feel that it's good to be an African. Then, the next step is to develop to understand broader politics – that it's not about black and white. You can have a fellow black man who can be your enemy, much as we have white people who have died in our struggle.[43]

As one ex-guerrilla said, 'we were regarded in fact as super-heroes, because everybody was willing to assist even though everybody knew the price.' People 'caught harbouring an MK cadre' would be 'charged under the Terrorism Act,' yet even when guerrillas 'came in numbers, everybody welcomed us.'[44] Another ex-guerrilla explained MK guerrillas were 'loved and respected' within African communities. Emphasizing MK's reliance on mass support, he described how the regime fundamentally misunderstood their strategy:

> They thought that we guerrillas operate only from the bushes. You know what they did, right around the [Venda–Zimbabwe] border they chopped all those trees because they expected us to come through the forest, so they didn't know, because our strategy was to mobilize the masses inside and they were our forest because they are the ones who were hiding us, not the trees down there.[45]

The apartheid regime derided MK 'as a "phantom army"; but what it lacked in resources and personnel was offset by its powerful ideological presence,' and 'MK soldiers were heroized.'[46]

One former MK commander explained the ANC's success at attracting sympathizers and recruiting moles inside the regime: 'Even within the regime there were sympathizers and ANC people inside. Even in the South African government itself, police there, up! The Communist Party was there to recruit whites and did its job, too much.'[47] White MK guerrillas played integral roles in gathering intelligence and infiltrating apartheid forces, laying the groundwork for such spectacular MK operations as the 1980 SASOL oil refinery bombing and the 1983 Church Street bombing of South African Air Force headquarters in Pretoria.[48] According to one ex-MK commander: 'we were not fighting a racist war in the first place, not fighting whites. We had whites within MK and daring ones. And no one ever sold out from those guys.'[49] In its Angolan battles with UNITA, MK even absorbed several defectors, 'commandos, even from the [elite] South African reconnaissance unit... We trained mostly blacks, but also some whites.'[50] In 1988, Chris Hani announced that MK would be deploying teams of mixed ethnicity throughout South Africa to establish contact with local populations and reinforce the ANC's pan-ethnic 'national consciousness.' Although inter-African ethnic tensions occasionally cropped up within MK,[51] these never led to broader schisms, as occurred in other African liberation movements. And although there were several mutinies at MK's Angolan bases in the early 1980s and instances of officers abusing their power over the rank and file, the ANC experienced hardly any violent or enduring fragmentation, unlike so many other insurgent movements; indeed, the ANC was the only southern African liberation movement never to split during its thirty years in exile.[52]

Ideology and MK's Selective Use of Violence

Despite the wartime constraints imposed by a brutal, omnipresent enemy, MK exercised remarkable restraint. MK's declared intention was always to replace the apartheid police and military in a seizure of power, and thereby constitute a democratic security force that would represent the oppressed majority. It emphasized politicizing its cadres before deploying them. As one former MK commander explained: 'If you aren't politicized, you're a thug.'[53] Another former MK commander elaborated: 'With us, you couldn't give somebody a gun without politicizing him, you must first politicize him that he or she should know who the enemy is. Because giving somebody a gun who is not politicized is like giving a lunatic a gun.'[54] According to Reno, effective politicization is the line that distinguishes guerrilla armies that defend their communities from those that prey upon them.[55] To cultivate international solidarity, the ANC sought to distinguish itself in the eyes of the world from apartheid's brutality, and in 1980 it announced that MK would adhere to the Geneva Conventions, becoming the first non-state actor to do so.[56] The ANC was also 'remarkably willing to crack down on its own members for human rights violations, through two internal commissions in 1992 and 1993.'[57] MK was not the only African liberation movement to avoid targeting non-combatants: Amilcar Cabral's PAIGC was known throughout Guinea-Bissau for avoiding civilian casualties, such that even the Portuguese colonial army conscripts knew, in the words of one officer who defected to the guerrilla ranks, 'that most acts of terrorism and atrocities were committed by our forces, not the PAIGC.'[58] Cherry notes that MK 'acted with remarkable restraint, and in doing so prevented a bloody race war from engulfing South Africa in the 1980s.'[59] After MK's 1985–7 mine-laying campaign targeting border patrols killed and maimed several civilians, MK abandoned the exercise even though other rebel armies used anti-personnel mines indiscriminately.[60]

One ex-guerrilla emphasized the strict directives guiding the use of force: 'There was a standing order that said soft targets must be avoided at all costs.'[61] Another described how, when MK forces attacking a police station in Kokstad realized that the officers' families were on the premises, 'we called off the attack immediately and withdrew with harassing fire. Our mission wasn't to hurt small kids.'[62] As the ANC stepped up its efforts to recruit and train cadres inside the country, it inevitably diluted the level of training and political 'conscientization,' as well as oversight and centralized command and control. Yet even its crash-course trainees in the Self-Defence Units (SDUs) learned 'that when [a new recruit] handles any lethal weapon he must know the enemy. And they must not select targets without telling [regional MK leadership], so that we give a go-ahead, to avoid anarchy.'[63]

With few exceptions, the ANC refrained from operations it could have easily mounted to 'cause fear, panic amongst the white population. They were vulnerable, but we were no terrorists.'[64] The ANC's decision not to kill civilians 'limited their scope,' whereas in other revolutions 'when you have to bomb a bridge you bomb a bridge. When you have to kill you kill. Then it sends those shockwaves.'[65] The ANC considered how inflicting casualties might impact on the broader struggle, and by the late 1980s it was reluctant to undermine its 'recruitment drive within white communities' and 'within SADF itself.' The ANC used the regime's mandatory conscription of white males to the SADF as an opportunity to recruit sympathetic whites.[66] As one former MK commander recalled: 'we didn't just do as we like. We had to check first the political situation. Is it going to gain us for the revolution if we hit them? We knew that, no man, we are going to win the war, let's not destroy the country.'[67] The ex-guerrilla further emphasized: 'since we didn't use terrorist tactics, they thought we are not good enough, but we won the struggle, at the end of the day.'[68] Another ex-guerrilla recalled the 1980 Silverton bank shootout between guerrillas and police in which the former, fleeing arrest, seized hostages but sought to confront the security forces: 'it was whites only inside that bank [and the MK operatives could have killed many civilians], but those guys were fighting the police.'[69]

Internal Rifts and the ANC's Tenuous Unity

Significant divisions within the ANC and MK emerged in the 1960s and persisted into the era of negotiations with the National Party, and beyond. These divisions arose especially between rank-and-file cadres who envisioned armed revolution, and the ANC leadership, which never committed wholeheartedly to armed struggle, largely owing to the apartheid regime's military strength and the leaders' own reluctance to jeopardize Western sympathy for their cause. Many MK guerrillas regarded the ANC political elites in exile as being soft, admiring only those leaders, such as OR Tambo and Chris Hani, willing to endure the rigours of camp life alongside the cadres.[70]

Some MK leaders became habituated to the relative comfort of life in exile, which afforded apartheid intelligence recruitment opportunities. Corruption for personal gain closely overlapped with 'selling out' to the regime.

As the ANC leadership was setting up MK in the early 1960s, it sought to absorb 'thugs' from street gangs and criminal networks, such as gangsters from Alexandra and Sophiatown, as a way of organizing violence for a movement lacking personnel with military training.[71] In this way, the ANC recruited Joe Modise, who became overall commander of MK and, later, South African defence minister. Prior to joining MK, Modise was involved in a car-theft ring,[72] and his criminal background is significant when considering evidence that he may have been recruited by the South African Defence Force's Military Intelligence Directorate (SADF MI), using blackmail based on Modise's involvement in illicit smuggling networks, sometime during the transition period (see Chapter Six).

The first expression of this split between ANC elites and the MK rank and file arose in 1969 when Chris Hani, having jointly commanded the Wankie incursion and then served a prison term in Botswana, penned a document that became known as the Hani Memorandum. The document criticized members of the ANC leadership who had 'become professional politicians rather than professional revolutionaries.'[73] It described the 'opening of mysterious business enterprises' run by individuals within the ANC leadership in Zambia for their own profit, noting that 'more and more MK men' were 'being diverted' to these businesses at the expense of the armed struggle. The memorandum singled out Joe Modise, referred to by his pseudonym Thabo More, as being 'fully involved with these enterprises,' such that it was 'extremely doubtful that with his attention so divided he can do justice to the armed struggle in South Africa which should be his primary and absolute concern.'[74] The memorandum further criticized Modise for receiving payments from the ANC's External Mission, and for owning 'a posh, militarily irrelevant car.'[75] It accused the ANC in exile 'of having created a machinery that has become an end in itself and is completely divorced from the situation at home,' with cadres keeping automobiles and pocketing salaries, thus emerging as a middle class within the ANC.[76]

Hani's memorandum went on to identify worrisome security breaches in MK, including MK cadres in Tanzania flirting with volunteers from the Peace Corps, a suspected CIA front; and the employment of ANC member Vuyiswa Nokwe, wife of the ANC secretary-general and chief of security Duma Nokwe, by Amiran-Israel, an Israeli import-export firm regarded as a front for Israeli intelligence. The memorandum criticized the arbitrary and harsh punishments meted out at ANC camps against offenders within MK ranks, and 'secret trials and secret executions' of those accused of betraying the organization (a problem that would grow exponentially by the 1980s). The memorandum also condemned nepotism within the ANC and, in a telling passage, anticipated the divide between ANC elites and much of the MK rank and file after the fall of apartheid:

> The sending of virtually all the sons of the leaders to universities in Europe is a sign that these people are being groomed for leadership positions after the MK cadres have overthrown the fascists. We have no doubt that these people will just wait in Europe and just come home when everything has been made secure and comfortable for them.[77]

41

The ANC leadership in exile responded to Hani's memorandum by expelling him and the other dissenters. Modise – whom the memorandum had accused of carrying out secret executions – led a majority on the MK tribunal demanding that Hani and his co-signatories be executed for their insubordination.[78] It took ANC president OR Tambo's personal intervention to overturn the death sentence; Hani and the others were ultimately readmitted to MK.

After the ill-fated Wankie and Sipolilo missions, Joe Modise continued to insist on sending MK units into 'the meat grinder that Rhodesia has become,' to the disagreement of others in the MK High Command in Lusaka.[79] The trend of 'secret trials and executions' led by Modise, which the memorandum had criticized, would continue in the 1970s and 1980s, as MK cadres became aware that Modise was controlling a clique within the ANC Lusaka leadership that was executing cadres for arbitrary reasons.[80] In 1982, Modise refused to travel to Botswana to meet with MK cadres 'and discuss with [infiltrating] units about their needs and experiences,' and rebuffed Joe Slovo's attempt to meet them.[81] Ellis 'confirms that Modise was arrested in Botswana in March 1982 together with Cassius Maake, the chief of ordnance of MK.[82] In their possession, it is alleged that a sum of R60,000 in cash and illegal diamonds was found.' Modise's name was then 'removed from a "hit-list" that was compiled by the apartheid security forces targeting senior ANC leaders.'[83] Manong recounts having warned Modise about MK cadre Peter Mogoai's suspicious behaviour while they were both based in Botswana, but Modise did nothing about it, and Mogoai soon defected and became an askari.[84] According to 'Trish,' a former MK operative in Swaziland, Modise was widely 'hated' within the ANC's armed wing.[85]

There were more allegations about Modise's profitable ventures in subsequent years: the 1981 Shishita Report issued by the ANC's internal security apparatus alleged that Modise was skimming profits from an ANC-owned factory in Zambia and running other private businesses there, 'extracting rent from cadres who had been housed in the area of Chunga.'[86] The report also mentioned involvement by members of the ANC leadership in transnational drug and car-theft networks, with mandrax being smuggled into South Africa in exchange for stolen cars. Furthermore, according to MK cadre Sibusiso Madlala, Modise 'also had his own gangs [stealing cars and robbing banks] and reporting to him,' and allegedly sold a cache of weapons to a UNITA representative in the midst of fighting in Angola.[87] The divisions between Hani and Modise apparently gave rise to the emergence of two separate loci of MK power by the time its cadres began returning to South Africa from exile in 1990: one was located under Modise's command in Johannesburg, while the other was under Hani's command and rooted in Transkei.[88] Madlala recalled that both Hani and Joe Slovo suspected Modise of working for apartheid intelligence, noting that 'whoever got in Bra Joe's way tended to get caught by the Boers' security police on their next mission – everyone in the ANC was frightened of him. They knew he had killed people himself, that he was completely ruthless, and that he had presided over mass torture and executions in the MK punishment camps like Quatro.'[89]

Turning Point: The 1976 Soweto Uprising and Its Aftermath

The prospects of MK's armed struggle changed dramatically in 1975 when Portugal's military regime collapsed, and Angola and Mozambique gained their independence. The Portuguese had collaborated closely with the Rhodesians and South Africans, and as Portugal's colonies gained independence, MK established bases within striking distance of South Africa. The following year, the Soweto uprising, in which the apartheid regime killed hundreds of unarmed student protesters, politicized a generation of South African youth and persuaded them of the necessity of armed struggle. MK received a massive influx of young South Africans who fled into exile in hopes of joining the guerrillas.

Before 1976 there had been 1,000 ANC members in exile. After 1976, this increased to 9,000, and a further 4,000–5,000 left between 1984 and 1986.[90] The exact number of guerrillas in MK ranks by the end of the 1980s is unclear; during the struggle, MK avoided divulging its full strength. One former MK base commander in Angola estimated that he trained over 1,000 guerrillas yearly throughout the 1980s. Barrell estimated that by 1986, MK consisted of roughly 10,000 troops, 300 or 400 of whom were inside South Africa. Davis calculated total ANC forces at 9,000, 'of which 5,400 were MK members.'[91]

The years following this influx of recruits were some of the most successful in terms of spectacular MK attacks on South African targets. Until then, MK had focused on sabotage operations calculated to demonstrate restraint, as with a 1976 railway bombing in which the MK operative 'intended to cause damage insufficient to derail a train,' because he had been ordered 'only to show "the police and army how far we could penetrate if we were forced to do so and what our capabilities were."'[92] Such nuances were lost on the apartheid regime, which used violence indiscriminately and perceived its enemies' hesitation to do the same as a sign of weakness.

From 1976 to 1981, MK began 'armed attacks on the property of black "collaborators" such as councillors and policemen. For the first time there [were] armed attacks on police patrols and police stations, security force vehicles and property.'[93] These included attacks on the Booysens, Soweto and Soekmekaar police stations, as well as clashes with police in rural areas such as Derdepoort and Rustenburg.[94] After the ANC leadership's visit to Vietnam in 1979 to study insurgency techniques, MK began the transition from armed propaganda to People's War, rooted in a vision of mass mobilization. In 1979, MK founded its Special Operations unit, or 'Special Ops,' which answered directly to Joe Slovo, incorporating only highly trained cadres and maintaining a high level of secrecy to protect against spy infiltration. Special Ops launched 'sustained operations of a higher quality that [had] a strong political content' inside South Africa,[95] and also fought UNITA in Angola. The unit's missions inside South Africa were based on elaborate intelligence gathering, using agents to infiltrate highly guarded areas, and demonstrated its cadres' high level of training, 'raising the profile of the ANC and inspiring the masses.'[96]

The period from 1981 to 1983 brought a 'dramatic increase in the incidence of attacks on government targets, military and economic installations and infrastructure.'[97] These attacks were too spectacular for the regime to conceal from the press: MK's June 1980 bombing of the SASOL oil-from-coal plant, which burned for days, causing damage estimated at R66 million; the 1981 rocket attack on Voortrekkerhoogte military headquarters in Pretoria; a sabotage attack in the same year on the not-yet-operational nuclear power plant at Koeberg near Cape Town, causing extensive damage; and the 1983 bombing of South

African Air Force headquarters in downtown Pretoria, killing 19 and wounding 217, some of them military personnel.[98] In 1984, MK's 'Special Ops' unit also bombed the Mobil oil refinery in Durban, aiming to weaken the apartheid regime by striking at its infrastructure.[99]

Whereas MK's Angolan bases were located many hundreds of miles from South Africa, its positions in Mozambique afforded it unprecedented opportunities to infiltrate South Africa. PW Botha's government retaliated first with cross-border raids, and then with an ultimatum to the Mozambican government forcing it to close all MK bases and expel ANC personnel or face crippling economic sanctions and an escalation of the apartheid-backed RENAMO insurgency. Facing a threat to Mozambique's very survival, its government submitted to Botha's terms under the 1984 Nkomati Accord, leaving the ANC 'shocked and stunned.'[100] While Mozambique expelled all but a few ANC members, South Africa maintained its covert support for RENAMO until at least 1991, perpetuating Mozambique's devastating civil war.[101] The loss of Mozambique as a platform not only deprived MK of a launching point into South Africa, but also threw MK command-and-control networks into disarray.[102]

In 1983, the United Democratic Front (UDF) emerged across South Africa as an umbrella body for grassroots resistance to apartheid, following which MK sought to consolidate its own presence inside the country. In 1984, the ANC started to build Area Political Military Committees, which deployed trained combatants 'inside' to create a leadership and logistics framework that would facilitate guerrilla strikes.[103] MK cadres began crossing the Zambezi River by dinghy into Botswana; planted landmines along the roads used by border patrols; and infiltrated small, lightly armed units of MK operatives to bolster the mass protests against apartheid. The MK leadership envisaged this as the precursor to mass armed resistance against the regime and the establishment of a revolutionary army.[104] Meanwhile, MK continued to receive and train recruits at its camps in northern Angola, where its ranks swelled to around 8,000. MK also increasingly used Bantustans such as Bophuthatswana, Venda and Transkei as points of entry into South Africa.[105] Yet reluctance on the part of the independent 'Frontline' states bordering South Africa, combined with the SADF's oft-demonstrated ability to strike at ANC targets in these states, prevented MK from establishing bases near, or inside, South African territory. During the 1980s, an estimated 350 to 2,000 guerrillas operated inside South Africa at any given time.[106]

'People's War' and the Intensification of Armed Struggle

The period 1983–5 represented MK's transformation from a guerrilla war conducted by insurgents to a so-called 'People's War' featuring attacks against 'commercial and economic targets' to reinforce popular strikes and boycotts,[107] such as the May 1985 bombing of the Anglo American and Anglovaal mining houses in Johannesburg in support of a mining strike.[108] On 8 January 1985 Oliver Tambo issued his famous call to 'render South Africa ungovernable.' This was accompanied by the call for 'People's War' at the Kabwe conference later that same year. By waging 'People's War' the ANC could exert more direct influence on mass struggle within South Africa, bolstering the ANC's mass representation and legitimacy. The 'People's War' phase saw a twelve-fold increase 'in the killing of black collaborators such as black councillors, suspected informers, and policemen,' along with a three-fold 'increase in the number of shootouts between ANC guerrillas and police.'[109] MK increasingly targeted the South African and Bantustan political and security forces. MK units received orders from Chris Hani 'to infiltrate the RSA and to assassinate appropriate political opponents, especially "sell-outs" and police informers.'[110] MK leadership justified 'armed attacks in city centres, on civilian buildings containing SADF recruiting offices, police interrogation centres, and agents of the security management system.'[111] The year 1988 saw an unprecedented number of MK attacks; and the escalation of MK's armed actions during the period preceding the onset of negotiations suggests that MK was in a position to sustain its armed struggle even after the ANC lost its superpower patron with the Soviet Union's collapse. In two separate operations in 1989, MK forces struck the ultra-modern South African Air Force radar station at Klippan[112] and launched a mortar attack on the SADF's Slurry base near Ramatlabama, causing damage and inflicting several casualties.[113] In a January 1990 interview, Chris Hani emphasized: 'If armed struggle was ineffective South Africa would not have militarized itself in the way it has done. They have to build bases along the borders, they have had to patrol, they have had to pay, spend substantial amounts – billions, in fact – for defence. Defending against what if armed struggle has been ineffective?'[114] During this period, MK was also able to set up intelligence networks that included the recruitment of agents within the apartheid security forces, especially within the South African Police Security Branch and, by the mid-1980s, the National Intelligence Service (NIS).[115]

MK's Links to Mass Structures

Guerrillas moved among South Africa's black communities like Mao's proverbial fish among water, often relying on them for shelter, food, transportation, and other forms of support. Guerrillas sheltered in homes, workplaces, and university dormitories.[116] A former guerrilla explained MK's approach: 'The ANC never undermined the strength of the Army. Even in the [ANC leaders'] speeches, they recognized that South Africa has a big army, with all the money and all the stuff. But our struggle was based not on the military approach, because we used guerrilla tactics whereby you don't need to be many, and you have the support of the communities.'[117] MK sought to expand in communities where political and ethno-regional constraints had thus far limited its influence. Chris Hani described how in the Bantustan of Bophuthatswana, in a climate of severe political repression, 'the local population was sympathetic to the courageous cadres of the ANC… And there was a clear politicization of the black population in an area where the ANC was never really known.' Hani emphasized the propaganda power of MK's symbolic attacks: 'Bombs are also an active weapon in mobilizing our people, in reviving their hopes, in destroying despondency.' Operating under the UDF umbrella in many black townships, 'despite their initial weaknesses, people were experimenting with democratic institutions. Street committees, people's organs of power, people's courts.'[118] It was in this context that MK had come closest to establishing liberated zones on South African territory, 'in certain areas in the townships where police had difficulty penetrating because [MK cadres] with combat experience were coordinating the street committees and so forth.'[119] MK cadres infiltrated into South Africa trained *amabutho* units of locally organized, paramilitary fighters who mostly used makeshift weaponry as they sought to create no-go zones in the townships for the regime's forces.[120] Many of these structures were ultimately rolled back by the South African Police, while in other zones the ANC struggled to recruit followers.

During the mid-1980s a spate of unauthorized bombings by raw recruits at shopping malls, beaches and restaurants killed and wounded a number of white civilians, and the ANC was forced to awkwardly distance itself from these actions.[121] During this period, ANC members in South Africa's black townships also began manifesting their anger against suspected regime collaborators by killing them with tyres placed around their necks, doused with petrol, and set aflame – the infamous 'necklacing.' Again, the ANC disavowed such tactics that 'deviated from Congress policy' while acknowledging the extreme conditions that had pushed untrained activists to adopt them.[122] One ex-guerrilla contended that apartheid agents were the first to introduce necklacing as a tactic to spread fear and confusion within the UDF. He recounted how misinformation spread by the regime's agents sometimes caused SDU militants and MK fighters to mistakenly suspect or even kill their own comrades, who they would later learn were innocent: 'One unit from MK shot another comrade in Durban and they were hanged. But it was later realized that no, man, that was an enemy agent who sent that information.'[123] The necklacing of suspected informers gained widespread international media attention by the mid-1980s and showcased a horrific strain of 'black-on-black' violence that the regime relished. Yet Chris Hani insisted necklacing was 'not a weapon of the ANC. It is a weapon of the masses themselves.'[124] And as shocking as the 'necklacings' were, they 'quickly killed the security forces' sources of "grassroots intelligence."'[125]

In the increasingly lawless atmosphere of the black townships during the 1980s, gangsters sought to capitalize on ANC–UDF legitimacy by posing as political activists while profiting from criminal activities, so much so that a term was coined to describe them: *comtsotsis*, signifying gangsters ('tsotsis' in township slang) who posed as comrades.[126] One ex-guerrilla recalled how 'some people manipulated the process for their own gains,' abusing the struggle in order to gain revenge or profit.[127] Putting the question of discipline in a broader historical context, a former MK commander argued that it ultimately 'was successful, because at least we didn't have anarchists who just went to attack whites on racial lines.'[128] Although there were isolated incidents of such indiscriminate violence by MK fighters, the overall level of discipline was remarkable considering the intense grievances that fuelled MK recruitment.

MK's Legitimacy in Comparative Perspective

The struggle against apartheid saw the rise of several guerrilla armies in South Africa in the 1960s and 1970s, all of which were dissolved in the transition to democracy in 1994. MK was undoubtedly the largest and best known, followed by the PAC's armed wing, the Azanian People's Liberation Army (APLA), and the historically marginal Azanian National Liberation Army (AZANLA). MK was best positioned, in terms of its numerical strength, training and political leadership, to be directly involved in the negotiations. The PAC, by contrast, played a very marginal role in political negotiations, joining only a year before the 1994 elections, and only after extensive internal 'wrangling.'[129]

As opposed to MK's non-racial ideology, APLA was notorious for its racially charged slogan of 'One Settler, One Bullet.'[130] Whereas MK operatives generally avoided civilian targets and refrained from looting, APLA deliberately sought white civilian targets.[131] APLA cadres were responsible for the 1993 Heidelberg Tavern and St James Church massacres in Cape Town, which targeted white civilians. Jeffery alleges that the ANC was involved in planning APLA attacks on civilian targets and MK cadres participated in their execution.[132] However, there is no evidence of this, and the mainstream South African media sources she cites were almost certainly fed this disinformation by the apartheid regime (see Chapter Three). Indeed, Sparks points to evidence that the regime's own agents provocateurs had orchestrated these attacks on white civilian targets to polarize the country,[133] and APLA in particular was known to be heavily infiltrated by SADF MI.[134] In 1993, the PAC claimed credit for a robbery in Khayelitsha, Cape Town, in which a security guard was murdered, leaving MK officer Lerumo Kalako to speculate that the regime itself was responsible for the spike in PAC attacks: 'The government benefits a lot from the violence... I think the major orchestrators of this [spate of attacks by APLA on white civilians] are right inside the state apparatus.'[135] Finally, after the transition, former APLA director of operations Letlapa Mphahlele claimed sole responsibility for the Heidelberg Tavern and St James Church attacks, which he claimed to have ordered.[136]

APLA also systematically engaged in predatory behaviour, as it funded its armed operations through a 'robbery unit' that committed armed robberies.[137] During the period 1990–4, according to Mphahlele, the PAC lost more cadres trying to finance themselves through robberies than in actual combat operations.[138] MK, by contrast, largely refrained from such predation, both because its leadership prohibited it and because it received more international funding than did APLA.[139] The ANC enjoyed more support than the PAC across virtually all sectors of the South African population. After 1994, the PAC faded into insignificance.

Yet unlike other anti-colonial guerrilla groups that turned on each other despite sharing a common foe, such as ZANLA and ZIPRA in Zimbabwe or MPLA, UNITA and FNLA in Angola, MK and APLA cadres developed no overt rivalry, generally refrained from targeting each other both during and after the struggle,[140] and sometimes displayed pan-African solidarity. One former MK guerrilla who had spent six years in prison along with several members of his unit related how their apartheid captors placed MK and APLA cadres in separate cells to foment rivalry between them. One day in the prison yard, he approached the APLA men and 'broke the ice' by appealing to their shared African identity and common struggle goals. This served to establish camaraderie between the MK and APLA prisoners and blunted their captors' attempts to manipulate and divide them.[141] The ANC also had no intra-party mass executions, unlike many other southern African liberation movements.[142] Manong credits Oliver Tambo's leadership with preventing mass executions of mutineers or dissidents, 'which was the norm' in southern Africa's liberation movements, noting that the execution in 1984 of seven mutineers in Angola 'pales into insignificance when compared to the mass executions that took place within FRELIMO, ZANU, ZAPU, SWAPO, and our very own PAC in South Africa.'[143]

In 1988, after joint Cuban–Angolan forces outmanoeuvred SADF forces at the battle of Cuito Cuanavale in south-west Angola, the apartheid regime realized that if it carried out further military campaigns in Angola, South African forces would suffer unacceptable casualties.[144] Thereafter, South Africa became more committed to political negotiations, and a political solution to the international flashpoint emerged soon afterward. Under glasnost, southern Africa was no longer a Soviet foreign policy priority and Gorbachev pressed for negotiations, as did the United States, which hosted the proceedings in New York. In exchange for South Africa's withdrawal from Angola and Namibia, which gained its independence in 1989, Cuba withdrew its troops from African soil and Angola forced MK to close all bases on its territory.

By 1990, despite the collapse of its Soviet patron and the loss of its Angolan bases, MK had amassed vast quantities of light weapons ideal for urban guerrilla warfare: AK-47s, pistols, grenades, and limpet mines. According to one ex-guerrilla: 'All you needed was an AK and some grenades, with that you could cause havoc. It was just a question of knowing tactics, how to use them effectively.'[145] This is significant because it suggests that MK's operational capacity was largely insulated from the loss of its superpower patron. It also raises the possibility that, contrary to claims that the USSR's collapse eroded the ANC's strategic position vis-à-vis the apartheid regime, MK's military resources remained largely undiminished.

Although it was never able to achieve supremacy on the battlefield and never enjoyed the benefit of a rear base so crucial to successful guerrilla warfare, MK nevertheless managed to play an important role in motivating popular resistance to apartheid and in sapping the regime's strength. What it lacked in military might, the ANC's armed wing compensated for in a sophisticated and nuanced political programme which saw it capture the popular imagination of South Africa's oppressed communities, helping to pave the way for the popular uprisings of the 1980s, apartheid's final decade. Because of the discipline that was such an integral component of MK training, the movement largely adhered to its doctrine of avoiding civilian targets, despite the apartheid regime's indiscriminate violence. As a movement, MK's defining trait and greatest asset was its popular legitimacy, which it cultivated by recruiting from all sectors of South African society, and which was a crucial component of the ANC's popularity throughout South Africa.

2

THE COLONIAL ORIGINS OF
COUNTERINSURGENCY

'Why had so many people collaborated with the apartheid secret police? Was it fear, ambition, greed, jealousy, even hatred? It was just the same during the slave trade, where so many had collaborated in the selling of men and women, transforming their lives in an instant into an unrelenting nightmare.'
— Mongane Wally Serote, *Rumours* (2013)

'The enemy will never free itself from the basic contradiction of its dirty colonial war.'
— Amilcar Cabral, 'New Year's Message' (1973)

On the night of 9 December 1982, South African Defence Force (SADF) commandos raided ANC headquarters in Maseru, Lesotho's capital. The raiders were operating on the basis of detailed intelligence gathered by the apartheid regime's secret services. They targeted individual ANC members identified beforehand and whomever they encountered as they went from house to house; in all, forty ANC members and Lesotho citizens were killed, including five women and two children. Only a handful of the dead were actual MK guerrillas. Landlocked by South African territory, Lesotho's mountainous sovereign territory afforded MK unique opportunities

53

for recruitment, training, and planning cross-border operations. Among Maseru's important South African exile population, a great many were covertly affiliated with the ANC and MK. The raiders sought to kill MK regional commander Chris Hani, stationed in Maseru along with his family, but Hani was out of the country; as Hani's wife, Limpho, and their daughters cowered under a bed, a loyal watchman directed their would-be killers to a neighbour's flat instead, where the commandos slaughtered a terrified woman.[1] One former MK guerrilla recalls the raid as his first encounter with the regime's forces, at the age of 16: 'We were caught by surprise that time. I was unarmed when they came.' To save his life, he jumped into a sewerage trench running behind the ANC members' flats and lay still until the shooting stopped. 'After that, I lost my fear of the Boers. I would go out on a mission without fear.'[2]

Such cross-border raids were a key feature of apartheid counterinsurgency. SADF commandos struck at the ANC in Lesotho repeatedly; they hit an MK safe house at Matola on the outskirts of the Mozambican capital of Maputo in 1981, killing 12 MK operatives for the loss of two commandos;[3] an ANC way station for refugees in Gaborone, Botswana, in 1985; and many other targets. Throughout the 1970s and 1980s, SADF commandos also launched countless raids against targets in Angola, Zimbabwe, and other southern African states whose leaders were sympathetic to the ANC's liberation struggle; during apartheid's final years, the SADF also conducted many operations within South Africa. Its raids abroad complemented the web of intelligence-gathering networks and spies run by the apartheid intelligence services, and the operations of the South African Police (SAP), which played a key role in both domestic and foreign counterinsurgency operations, especially in Namibia and Swaziland.[4] In Angola, South Africa deployed special forces teams and mercenaries to assist its proxy, UNITA. SADF MI took over the coordination of RENAMO, a guerrilla army originally created by the Rhodesian intelligence services to destabilize neighbouring Mozambique, which had served as a rearguard for ZANU guerrillas, and which began to shelter the ANC after Zimbabwean independence. SADF also created and supported other surrogate groups to destabilize southern African states, including the Lesotho Liberation Army and 'Super-ZAPU' in

Zimbabwe.[5] The apartheid regime also recruited former Rhodesian agents as moles in post-independence Zimbabwe.[6] These operations were so extensive that according to one analysis from 1987, 'South Africa's Special Forces are now one of the dominant factors in the geopolitics of southern Africa.'[7]

The Evolution of Counterinsurgency

At the start of the Cold War, colonial subjugation techniques merged with Allied clandestine warfare methods from the Second World War to produce modern counterinsurgency strategies. Counterinsurgency specialists wrote manuals based on their experiences, such as David Galula's 1957 *Counterinsurgency Warfare: Theory and Practice*, Roger Trinquier's 1961 *Modern Warfare* on the French war in Algeria, and JJ McCuen's 1962 *Counterinsurgency Warfare*, all of which were widely read within SADF ranks.[8] Indeed, the apartheid regime's 'Total Strategy' of destabilizing neighbouring states while annihilating domestic resistance was borrowed from French General André Beaufre's book *An Introduction to Strategy*, based on French counterinsurgency in Algeria.[9] The regime's counterinsurgency doctrines derived 'directly from the British experiences in Malaya and Northern Ireland, the French in Algeria, and the US in Vietnam and El Salvador,'[10] as well as from the Israelis, Portuguese and Rhodesians. American weapons technology also reached South Africa through a covert network of arms smugglers, including CIA agents, who had tacit US government approval to circumvent international sanctions on South Africa.[11]

The SADF formed its Military Intelligence branch in 1960, and 'its officers were sent for advanced training in France, Germany, the UK, and USA.'[12] SADF officers, including future chief of staff and defence minister, Magnus Malan, went on an officer's course at the US Army War College and received '"on-the-job" training in the conduct and pursuit of counterinsurgency campaigns'; Malan, for example, was seconded 'to the French Army in Algeria for this purpose.'[13] The South African military's closest alliances, however, were with their fellow colonial regimes in southern Africa: the Portuguese counterinsurgency police, PIDE, and the Rhodesian intelligence and special forces. As the Portuguese colonies gained independence and

Rhodesia became Zimbabwe, the SADF Special Forces absorbed ex-Portuguese *flechas* and Rhodesian Selous Scouts,[14] as well as Angolan and Mozambican mercenaries.[15] After Zimbabwe's independence, South Africa launched Operation Winter, 'a scheme to recruit as many as possible of the Rhodesian Special Forces for the SADF,' overseen by SADF Special Forces commander Gen. Loots; hundreds of Rhodesian Special Forces 'came south, both black and white.'[16] The SADF's 3rd Reconnaissance Regiment (or 'Recce') would be staffed entirely with Rhodesian Special Forces veterans. Ex-special forces from NATO countries also joined the SADF. This was highlighted in the case of ANC intelligence operative Ronnie Watson, who in 1985 survived an assassination attempt in Gaborone when he overpowered and disarmed 'would-be assassin' Stephen Burnett, who had entered Watson's hotel room with a gun.[17] After his arrest, Burnett told a Botswana court he was a member of the British Special Air Service; Watson testified that Burnett had claimed to work for the apartheid regime. Burnett received a five-year sentence.[18]

South Africa also cultivated close military and intelligence ties with Latin American dictatorships, through visits by heads of state and government ministers and by military and intelligence personnel. Argentine officers, including the infamous torturer Alfredo Astiz, visited South Africa to exchange interrogation techniques,[19] and officers from the Guatemalan G2 military intelligence unit toured the Angolan front as guests of the South African military.[20] The 1977 killing of National Party MP Robert Smit was carried out by assassins with alleged links to Western and Latin American intelligence agencies, suggesting ties between the apartheid regime and such shadowy international death-squad networks as Operation Condor in Latin America and Operation Gladio in NATO member countries.[21] For their European operations, the apartheid regime's secret services were known to employ 'Mafia-types' and local 'ultra-right-wing organisations,' which concealed their direct involvement; nonetheless, evidence emerged that the regime had contracted the 1988 assassination in Paris of ANC representative Dulcie September to former French Foreign Legionnaires, and had helped to orchestrate the 1986 assassination of Swedish prime minister, Olof Palme.[22]

Perverse Kinship: Askaris and Mercenaries

Colonialism depended on the ability to rapidly deploy overwhelming violence to crush African resistance. This was achieved through the recruitment or conscription of black soldiers who could be paid a small fraction of white soldiers' wages, and whose deaths, unlike white combat deaths, incurred no domestic political cost. In some cases, recruitment among certain ethnic groups led to the formation of virtual warrior castes, facilitating the colonial imperative of divide and conquer. The British raised armies in East Africa by drafting Africans from northern Ugandan ethnic groups such as the Acholi, while Portugal sustained its African wars by relying on African conscripts, who did most of the fighting, and the dying, on behalf of their colonial masters.[23]

There were three forms of collaboration by African subjects with the colonial counterinsurgency forces: African troops recruited as part of the mainstream colonial security forces; African rebels captured and 'turned' into colonial special forces; and members of liberation movements recruited as spies. The apartheid regime used all three extensively, raising battalion-strength units of African conscripts from both South Africa and neighbouring countries. This included the SADF's notorious 32nd 'Buffalo' Battalion, composed of ethnic Angolan and Zambian soldiers, which formed the cutting edge of SADF operations in Angola. The apartheid regime also refined the tactic of 'turning' captured ANC and PAC guerrillas, and recruited spies extensively within the liberation forces' ranks. The regime nurtured or even helped to create proxy rebel groups which it deployed in order to destabilize neighbouring governments, as well as South Africa's own African communities. This form of outsourcing violence included the cultivation of the UNITA rebel group in post-independence Angola; of RENAMO in Mozambique; and the training of the Inkatha Freedom Party's militias in KwaZulu-Natal, along with other Third Force elements in South Africa. This strategy of outsourcing violence aimed to threaten the liberation movements' very existence and the Frontline States' viability as independent states. Janet Cherry describes 'different categories of betrayal: informers (those paid by the police for information); agents (spies infiltrated by the police into resistance organizations); collaborators (those who aligned themselves politically with institutions associated with the apartheid regime, such as the Homeland administrations or Black Local Authorities); and state witnesses (MK and ANC members who agreed to give state evidence – often after torture – in the trial of their comrades).'[24] Moreover, some straddled several categories; askaris, in particular, made dramatic appearances in court, wearing black masks to hide their identities while testifying against MK cadres.[25]

During the British counterinsurgency campaign against Kenya's Mau Mau uprising in the 1950s, 'askari,' the Swahili and Arabic word for 'soldier,' came to denote a captured guerrilla 'turned' into a collaborator. 'Turning' insurgents 'became a systematic feature of the southern African wars,' according to Minter, who describes British intelligence officer Frank Kitson's mix of threats and incentives for turning Kenyan guerrillas: 'the combination of carrots (employment, loot), sticks (execution) and a plausible rationale (cooperating with a powerful government is wiser than terrorism).'[26] The Rhodesian military adopted this tactic from the British, raising elite units such as the notorious, 1,800-strong Selous Scouts with 50 per cent black conscripts or higher, many of whom were captured from the military wings of ZANU and ZAPU. They taught these tactics in turn to the South Africans, who used askaris extensively against MK and APLA. Kitson's methods were adopted by SADF Maj. Gen. Jac Büchner, who boasted of his ability to 'turn' captured MK guerrillas throughout the 1980s.[27]

State military and intelligence formations subjected would-be sellouts to a combination of persuasion and coercion to make them switch allegiances. One former guerrilla explained askari recruitment:

> Everybody who gets arrested, chances are that they are recruited. They use all types of tactics, depending on what they think will work on you. Then they will maybe force you to shoot one of your comrades and once you do that, you can't go back to your comrades, you are part of them. So they had a small army from our people.[28]

Another former MK guerrilla, who was himself captured and tortured by the apartheid regime, related its methods for 'turning' guerrillas: 'When you are taken in, all sorts of things are used to frighten you. They break your heart, your morale. They make you feel useless, [wearing] not even your underwear, and you are always blindfolded. You are tortured, burned, cigarette butts, all sorts of things. So if you are not strong enough...' Although newer guerrilla recruits were most vulnerable, even 'some who were well-trained, politically mature, they would sell.'[29]

While MK recruited through kinship networks, the apartheid regime created its own network consisting of white officers commanding African informers, defectors, and collaborators. In this sense, colonial intelligence recruitment undermined kinship networks and the 'moral economy' of colonized societies: a form of perverse kinship. In Guinea-Bissau, Cabral referred to the Portuguese army's '"African commando companies" in which were included socially rootless elements and traitors to our people, recruited by some of the most faithful stooges of the Portuguese colonialists.'[30] Fanon echoed Cabral's characterization of such collaborators as being 'socially rootless':

> In Algeria, it is the *lumpen-proletariat* which furnished the *harkis* and the *messalists* [Algerian locals organized into French army units]; in Angola, it supplied the road-openers who nowadays precede the Portuguese armed columns; in the Congo, we find once more the *lumpen-proletariat* in regional manifestations in Kasai and Katanga, while at Leopoldville the Congo's enemies made use of it to organize 'spontaneous' mass meetings against Lumumba.[31]

In a 1988 interview, Chris Hani underscored this point, noting the South African regime's failure 'in building pro-regime organizations – except bandit organizations like askaris and a few vigilante groups. But these are mercenaries, people who do not enjoy any organized, structured support by the masses... In the South African context they have not even managed a [stooge resembling Rhodesia's Abel] Muzorewa.'[32]

Unable to build kinship networks of African collaborators, the regime sought instead to destroy African civil society by deploying death squads. The apartheid regime escalated its use of death squads during the 1976 Soweto uprising. In addition to regular police units, the regime also began deploying 'special hit squads. There was a black car just going in our areas shooting people at night. Just shooting people standing on corners... And that was some sort of a general pattern.'[33] Both the SAP's Special Branch and the SADF used black agents for such operations. By 1977–8, the SAP had brought into African townships near Port Elizabeth 'policemen from Natal' who were being deployed to raid areas loyal to the ANC, 'who were speaking Zulu and they were living in tents in the police station in New Brighton.'[34] The askari, Frank Msekwa (MK Gerald 'Casper' Pitje), 'accompanied the SADF troops and pinpointed the residences' of MK Special Ops soldiers during the 1981 Matola raid.[35] These death-squad techniques were refined throughout the 1980s. By 1990, the SAP death squad, unit C1 – known as 'Vlakplaas' after the police-owned farm where it was based – featured over 300 askaris under a white officer corps commanded by Colonel Eugene de Kock.[36]

Despite their deadliness, askaris faced discrimination like any other African under apartheid. The Vlakplaas commanders regularly beat askaris and killed several who performed poorly, wanted to leave, or knew too much. Brian Ngqulunga, a Vlakplaas askari who had participated in the murder of ANC lawyer, Griffiths Mxenge, was killed by his death squad comrades in July 1990.[37] Goodwill Sikhakhane was killed by Vlakplaas operatives in Durban in 1991 after SAP Gen. Bertus Steyn told them that Sikhakhane wanted to defect to the ANC. Yet after they killed Sikhakhane, the Vlakplaas men learned that the real reason for having him killed was to cover up SAP Col. Hentie Botha's killing of MK operatives Charles Ndaba and Mbuso Shabalala, which Sikhakhane knew about.[38] The askaris also enforced a grim code among themselves: Dandala, an askari who operated in the Eastern Cape, told the Truth and Reconciliation Commission (TRC) that his unit's members, while en route to a death squad assignment, had determined that if anyone 'does not take part in the mission,' his comrades 'would come back and kill the person.'[39]

The highest-ranking askari was Glory 'September' Sedibe, who had been the MK chief of intelligence for Transvaal, and who had received training in East Germany and the Soviet Union. Vlakplaas operatives abducted Sedibe from his jail cell in Swaziland where he had been imprisoned for his ANC activities.[40] With the intelligence gleaned from Sedibe, the apartheid regime was able to 'virtually wipe out' MK structures in Swaziland.[41] Sedibe repeatedly testified before police audiences and SABC TV cameras about the torture and killing of dissidents in the ANC's Angolan camps, while wearing a ski mask to conceal his identity. On one TV programme he claimed: 'I'm trained to kill and wreak havoc in South Africa. Cities must go up in flames and innocent people of all races must be killed. But fortunately, I came to other conclusions after spending years in ANC camps.'[42] Sedibe was the star state witness in the 1988 trial against three MK operatives; the judge in the case ordered that no photographs or drawings of Sedibe be published, and that he be referred to only as 'Mr X1.' In 1990, Sedibe testified in camera to the Harms Commission about alleged ANC 'death squad' operations. The TRC examined Sedibe's story over three days in 2000 at an Amnesty Committee meeting in Pretoria, but portrayed him purely as a victim of apartheid, without examining his motives for collaboration.[43] He died in April 1994 shortly before a scheduled meeting with ANC intelligence chief Joe Nhlanhla (see Chapter Nine).

With the exception of two white ex-MK guerrillas at Vlakplaas who had been captured and turned,[44] askaris were always African. However, their role also demonstrated the malleability of racial perceptions in the midst of war: for example, Vlakplaas commander Eugene de Kock regarded Sedibe so highly that he did not consider him to be an 'askari,' but regarded him as an equal.[45] De Kock told the TRC that like their white counterparts, askaris who distinguished themselves on their missions 'were congratulated many times, sometimes by the Minister [Vlok], also for people that they arrested, or ANC members that they recruited.' De Kock practised 'counter-intelligence' within Vlakplaas by having trusted askaris spy on the rest, and on each other: 'I had askaris who spied on askaris.'[46] MK Special Ops guerrilla Fumanikile Booi told the TRC that when it came to units tasked with 'tracking down MK cadres around the country and assassinating some high leadership members…we dubbed them all as askaris, because they were doing the same mission.'[47]

Askaris could infiltrate African communities and guerrilla movements in ways that white operatives never could, making them 'very, very dangerous,' a bigger threat to MK fighters than white soldiers and policemen.

If you are crossing the border from Lesotho on some trucks with two hundred labourers, who is going to identify you? The white policeman doesn't speak African languages, he thinks all blacks look the same. He won't recognize the signs. It's blacks who will identify you, then they will sell you out. Those bastards were everywhere. And they wanted to impress [their white commanders], so they were very arrogant. Very destructive. Very cruel.[48]

In his testimony to the TRC, Vlakplaas commander Eugene de Kock echoed this analysis, noting that white operatives 'didn't speak the language of the [MK] camp... They wouldn't know the songs which were sung in the camp, they wouldn't have the same form of speech and they wouldn't use the same form of reference, terminology, they wouldn't know the Commanding Officers and so forth, and that is why [askaris] were of cardinal importance.'[49] The Security Branch compiled an album with the names and photos of thousands of MK and APLA guerrillas for use in identifying suspects. One ex-guerrilla whose photograph appeared in the album described being detained at the Bophuthatswana–South Africa border in the late 1980s: a car with tinted windows pulled up and the askari inside identified him, leading to his imprisonment and torture.[50] De Kock told the TRC that 'before the [1994] election' the Security Branch's album had photos of 6,800 guerrillas, and had the names and identities of 2,500 more,[51] suggesting that this intelligence gathering continued well into the period of negotiations between the regime and the ANC.

Though headquartered at Vlakplaas, C1 had other detachments deployed in rural areas throughout the country, 'including at Camperdown and Elandskop, and the askari unit in Natal run by Colonel Andy Taylor.'[52] This was in addition to the Northern Transvaal Security Branch, which had its own death squad founded by C1 veteran Jac Cronje which included notorious askari Joe Mamasela. Askaris were also occasionally 'loaned out' to other SAP and Special Forces units. The threat posed by askaris and spies to the ANC is underscored by the high priority that MK accorded to their eradication: by 1988, Chris Hani had identified the 'elimination' of spies within the movement as MK's top operational priority, taking precedence over offensive operations.[53] To achieve this, Hani tasked 'Icing Units' with identifying and killing spies and collaborators.[54]

'Total Strategy' and Death Squads

After defence minister PW Botha stepped in as South Africa's prime minister in 1978, and then as president in 1984, he restructured the security establishment to secretly escalate the war on southern Africa's liberation movements. Botha and SADF chief Gen. Magnus Malan 'popularized the propaganda doctrine of a Soviet-led international "total onslaught" to legitimate the SADF's "Total Strategy," propagated in the 1977 Defence White Paper.'[55] Botha concentrated more power in SADF MI and downgraded its civilian rival, BOSS (which he renamed the National Intelligence Service, or NIS), to a secondary status. SADF MI was connected widely to clandestine commando units and death squads, which were given free rein to infiltrate, destabilize and hunt down any individual, movement or government, in South Africa or elsewhere, that resisted apartheid.[56] The military would use its full range of resources to conduct internal surveillance and repression.

'Total Strategy' entailed a reconfiguration of the intelligence services and 'most government departments under the security umbrella of the National Security Management System (NSMS).'[57] The term 'securocrats' emerged to describe state decision-makers as counterinsurgency became increasingly part of government bureaucracy. The NSMS 'had the power to intervene at every level of South Africa's civil administration. It was also the brain centre of a security network whose nerve ends reached into some five hundred regional, district, and local Joint Management Centres.'[58] The State Security Council directed the NSMS, with PW Botha himself as its chairman. It divided South Africa into security jurisdictions to facilitate rapid responses to anti-apartheid activism wherever it arose. Through the Joint Management Centres (JMCs), the apartheid state 'aimed at radically reshaping the moral, cultural, religious, political and material underpinnings of civil society in the black townships.'[59] The JMC's mid-level leadership was the counterinsurgency nerve centre where general guidelines for suppression, handed down from the top civilian and security force leadership, were implemented domestically through assassinations and bombings.[60]

A JMC might, for example, respond to a wave of protests through an integrated carrot-and-stick response that involved arresting or killing key activists while improving public works and housing to dampen local grievances and, in counterinsurgency parlance, 'win hearts and minds.'[61] One former combatant described NSMS surveillance in this way: 'there were street committees, police members from the community, so that each and every house is known: who stays there, who goes there. If something's wrong, they put that certain house under surveillance. That's when death squads started.'[62] According to this ex-guerrilla, this strategy of surveillance linked to death squads 'first appeared in Latin America.'[63] As an example of the State Security Council's (SSC) total reach, in March 1990 a spy ring was uncovered deep within the Johannesburg City Council, with intelligence operatives masquerading as ordinary citizens and infiltrating all strata of civic life, gathering 'information on the activities of legitimate organizations to give to military intelligence, the security police, and the SAP at John Vorster Square.'[64]

Within the Joint Management System was the top-secret TREWITS, the Afrikaans acronym for Counter-Revolutionary Target Information Centre, founded in 1985. It brought representatives of the Security Branch (SB), SADF MI, the NIS, and the SADF Special Forces to monthly meetings where they identified activists to be killed, and made plans to kill them. In his testimony to the TRC, President FW de Klerk denied any knowledge of TREWITS, insisting that its existence would have been unauthorized, and that its members' actions – 'if they actually did it' – ran counter to the NP government's policies. Yet Jack Cronje, of the North Transvaal Security Branch death squad, declared that all death squad actions were reported to SB headquarters and to the State Security Council, making it impossible for the state's top civilian leadership not to know.[65]

During the 1980s, private security companies mushroomed, staffed by former soldiers and policemen who maintained close links with the security forces,[66] and South Africa's counterinsurgency efforts became enmeshed within its military-industrial complex. SADF MI also began setting up an array of front companies to facilitate its clandestine operations, ranging from surveillance and psychological warfare to murder.[67] Their 'privatization' afforded the state plausible deniability as its agents acted in a supposedly non-state capacity. In an Orwellian euphemism, SADF MI gave death squads innocuous names such as the

Civil Cooperation Bureau (CCB); internal communications referred to it as 'the corporation,' with its commander as the 'chairman.'[68] The precursor to the CCB, the 'Special Task Force' operating under the top-secret Project Barnacle, carried out targeted assassinations and other death squad activities, including the killing of hundreds of SWAPO prisoners of war, and the elimination of security force personnel 'suspected of disloyalty,' the latter in an operation named Dual. As the regime's NSMS began relying more on targeted assassinations, it also planned to kill MK military intelligence chief Ronnie Kasrils and leading ANC member Pallo Jordan, though these plans were ultimately cancelled.[69] The CCB in particular was envisioned as a network of skilled soldiers who would develop elaborate civilian business credentials as a cover to gather intelligence and orchestrate assassinations, dissolving the boundaries between government and private forces.[70] It had secret operatives embedded within South Africa's broader society, including within other branches of the security forces: according to a former CCB commander, 'CCB members worked for the police, Eskom [the national electricity utility], the Pretoria city council, the department of foreign affairs, and the National Intelligence Service.'[71] Special Forces from SADF's 'Recce' (reconnaissance commando) units were often deployed under the CCB's guise to perpetrate assassinations throughout southern Africa: 'We were the guys who did these "CCB" things,' explained SADF Special Forces veteran Guy Bawden.[72] Key death squad commanders such as Vlakplaas's Eugene de Kock also developed contacts with representatives from national armaments company Armscor who facilitated clandestine operations,[73] while the 'mystery company' EMLC provided the CCB with logistical support, including sophisticated specialized equipment.[74] This array of clandestine violent actors interwoven with profitable interests would leave legacies in the post-apartheid security forces.

One of the CCB's most well-known operations was the assassination of sociologist David Webster, killed in his suburban driveway in broad daylight while unloading his car. Initially, it seemed Webster had been targeted for his anti-apartheid activism; it later emerged that he was uncovering evidence that the SADF was secretly training African mercenaries at a camp in Kosi Bay, and was about to travel there to investigate further when he was gunned down. In November 1992, the *Cape Times* published CCB operative Ferdi Barnard's confession to killing Webster to prove that Barnard was 'acceptable and useful' to the SADF.[75]

Apartheid death squads were grafted onto conventional state structures, and the divisions between the two were highly permeable. The covert units that carried out extrajudicial killings and recruited spies also had ties to illicit smuggling networks. Government ministers were occasionally embroiled in illicit dealings facilitated by covert unit members. Ministers such as Adriaan Vlok would visit Vlakplaas to congratulate death squad members, while SAP Gen. Basie Smit visited so frequently that the death squad reserved a bottle of whisky specially for him.[76] The Vlakplaas operatives were known to celebrate successful missions with drinking parties and by roasting meat in a firepit while incinerating their victims' bodies alongside.[77] Yet the death squad members' debauchery and brutality belied their centrality to apartheid's workings, and their operations lay at the heart of the apartheid state, remaining largely buried after the transition.

Proxy Forces: Outsourcing Violence

As far back as the founding of Johannesburg in the 19th century, the government abetted criminal gangs as a means of undermining African communities.[78] In the final decade of apartheid, state security forces founded, armed and trained a variety of black militias and 'youth wings' that targeted anti-apartheid activists, including the Witdoeke in the Western Cape, the Eagles Youth Clubs in the Orange Free State, and the Ama-Afrika movement in the Eastern Cape.[79] The regime also fed IFP leader Mangosuthu Buthelezi false intelligence about ANC plots to kill him and then armed and trained Zulu militias for 'self-defence.' This set the stage for over a decade of strife between ANC and IFP activists in KwaZulu-Natal and throughout the Vaal Triangle.[80]

Hoping to weaken the ANC's power base through terror, the apartheid regime armed and trained IFP militants, deploying them against ANC strongholds with the aim of creating an ethnic rift between the Xhosa-dominated but staunchly non-sectarian ANC and the Zulu nationalist IFP.[81] In a 1986 SADF MI project authorized by the State Security Council and dubbed Operation Marion (as the IFP was to be apartheid's 'marionette'), 206 IFP militiamen were sent to Namibia's Caprivi Strip to undergo training in the use of automatic weapons, rockets, mortars, and explosives, as well as assassination and counter-surveillance techniques, and were armed by SADF Special Forces and the Vlakplaas unit. Of the various programmes to weaken the ANC through fomenting black-on-black violence, the IFP hit squads were 'by far the most effective…in breaking the power of the ANC/UDF in Natal (and elsewhere) and eliminating its leaders.'[82] Upon their return to KwaZulu-Natal they began operations on 21 January 1987, killing 13 people at the home of a UDF organizer in KwaMakutha. Any IFP militants' crimes that came to light would be investigated by the KwaZulu Police (KZP), which was itself heavily involved in counterinsurgency operations.[83] The regime aimed to provide the IFP with an independent operational capacity; to this end, it placed many of the Caprivi trainees in the KZP in 1989, with the result that the KZP, IFP impis, and askaris deployed in KwaZulu-Natal were all involved in targeting the ANC/UDF and the Self-Defence Units (SDUs) they set up. An estimated 130 Caprivi trainees went for further training in 1987 and were then 'incorporated into the SAP as special constables,' while in June 1989 a contingent of nearly 180 trainees was incorporated into the KZP.[84] Operation Marion was terminated in December 1990, as the SAP commissioner Johan van der Merwe stopped authorizing SB cover-ups for its offensive actions.[85] By then, however, the IFP's independent operational capacity was well established, and it continued to secretly receive regime weapons supplies and training until 1994. The KZP was commanded and staffed by a succession of white counterinsurgency veterans who coordinated raids on ANC strongholds, including Philip Powell. Buthelezi's second-in-command, the apartheid informer Themba Khoza, had the distinction of being on the NIS and SADF MI payrolls simultaneously.[86] Former Vlakplaas commander Dirk Coetzee described IFP leaders as 'power-hungry bastards, complete opportunists.'[87]

Such strategies afforded the regime 'plausible deniability' in the killing of activists, and fomented a wave of 'black-on-black' violence that obscured state culpability and cast cynical doubt on the viability of African self-rule by portraying black activists as chaotic elements destined to devour their own communities. Outsourcing violence 'maintained a distance between those who were physically involved in the fighting and those who ultimately benefited.'[88] The 1992 Goldstone Commission of inquiry into the regime's clandestine activities further revealed the SAP's role in sustaining criminal gangs such as the 'Black Cats' and 'Black Chain' in Ermelo.[89] Meanwhile, apartheid proxy forces such as Ama-Afrika battled the UDF in Eastern Cape, serving as a trial run for the training and deployment of the IFP in KwaZulu-Natal.[90]

Counterinsurgency and Urban Violence during Apartheid

The 1985 call by the ANC and UDF to 'make the townships ungovernable' entrenched a culture of disobedience and disorder, exacerbated by the deployment of 35,000 SADF troops in the townships, a number that would swell to 40,000 by 1987.[91] Counterinsurgency forces exploited this unrest by sowing suspicion and divisions among activists. After MK began to distribute hand grenades to attack the security forces in the townships, the SADF countered by sending askaris to distribute booby-trapped grenades modified to explode in activists' hands.[92] In several instances, owing to the suspicions sown by such agents provocateurs, MK units mistakenly killed guerrillas falsely accused of collaborating with the regime.[93] One former guerrilla also claimed that the notorious 'necklacing' technique of killing suspected collaborators – a widespread method which became the symbol of 'black-on-black' violence throughout the 1980s – was originally introduced by apartheid agents.[94] Though brutal, this method appears to have been effective: According to Henderson, by the late 1980s the SAP 'had lost most of [its] extensive informer networks in the South African townships due to black militant violence,' including by MK and township youth.[95] The Rhodesian Selous Scouts were known to employ 'false flag' operations in which counterinsurgency forces would target civilians and blame guerrillas,[96] and as violence escalated in South Africa in the late 1980s, there is evidence suggesting that some of the bombings attributed to MK were actually undertaken by the regime's forces in order to discredit the ANC. The 1988 murder of MK cadre Sicelo Dlomo was possibly a 'false flag operation, where the security forces planted false information among revolutionaries to set them against each other.'[97] Suspicions of false flag operations also shrouded some of the PAC operations during the early 1990s.

On 12 June 1986, Botha's government imposed a national State of Emergency in response to mounting protests. During this period, the NSMS oversaw the creation of clandestine units tasked with intelligence gathering and assassinations, following a 'low-intensity conflict' doctrine of denying insurgents a base in their own communities by terrorizing the populations they relied upon for support.[98] In addition to targeting guerrillas, these units kidnapped, tortured, and killed thousands of unarmed activists, including community organizers, trade unionists, lawyers, and professionals. These units reported to their superiors on a need-to-know basis, often bypassing conventional chains of command. When FW de Klerk replaced PW Botha as state president in 1989, he disbanded the NSMS.[99] Yet the elaborate counterinsurgency architecture was already firmly in place, complete with various channels for illicit self-financing; as one ex-guerrilla explained, 'those thugs were involved in car racketeering, ivory rackets, drug trafficking, even human trafficking, they would allow even Chinese coming in with people for prostitution, their intelligence was for them to enrich themselves.' To cover their tracks, 'they used to destroy, even kill informers whom they think were going to be problematic for them in the future.' As negotiations loomed, these counterinsurgency operators 'knew what was going to happen tomorrow. They knew that the politicians were thinking of negotiations with the ANC and PAC, so they wanted to get rich fast before anything could happen. So they were busy, trying to stop the fires of liberation.'[100]

Apartheid Counterinsurgency's External Dimension

Western intelligence agencies were key apartheid allies. For example, in 1962 the CIA supplied the SAP Security Branch with intelligence needed to arrest Nelson Mandela. According to CIA agent Paul Eckel: 'We gave them every detail, what he would be wearing, the time of day, just where he would be. They picked him up. It is one of our greatest coups.'[101] During this time, the CIA apparently had a 'deep cover' agent in the ANC and Communist Party structures in the Durban area.[102] It 'had worked in closest harmony' with the Bureau of State Security

(BOSS), and former station chief Gerry Gossens said CIA agents had stood 'side-by-side with the security police in South Africa.'[103] When Ronald Reagan came to power in 1980, he prioritized South Africa among the global hot-spots in which the United States would renew a vigorous covert operations agenda.[104] Signals intelligence shared with South Africa by CIA spies in Mozambique helped the SADF to pinpoint the location of the MK safe house in Matola raided by SADF commandos in 1981, causing Mozambique to expel a number of US diplomatic personnel.[105] By the late 1980s, strong evidence emerged that US intelligence agencies were sharing intelligence on the ANC with the British, who were in turn relaying it to South Africa; Neo Mnumzana, ANC representative to the UN in New York, said he wouldn't be surprised if the ANC's UN offices were bugged.[106] ANC representative Jeanette Mothobi claimed: 'the CIA has become the intelligence-gathering arm of the South African Security Department in South Africa.'[107] US, British and West German intelligence services were also instrumental in developing Advokaat, a South African signals intelligence complex that monitored southern African guerrilla groups' movements and communications.[108]

According to ex-BOSS spy Gordon Winter, Western intelligence agencies also recruited extensively within African liberation movements,[109] a claim reinforced by former MK guerrillas, who identified the CIA and British MI6 as having been particularly active in this regard.[110] These Western spy services also recruited agents within MK's Angolan bases.[111]

The avowed anti-communist Buthelezi was favoured by the Reagan and Thatcher administrations during the 1980s as a palatable black alternative to the ANC. Meanwhile, as we have seen, Buthelezi and his Inkatha militants received weapons, training, and support from both the apartheid regime and Western mercenaries. This support for Buthelezi mirrored American and, to a lesser extent, French backing for UNITA's Jonas Savimbi, an Angolan warlord who owed his longevity to his partnership with the apartheid regime.[112]

Did SADF MI dictate regime policy, or vice versa? O'Brien argues that under PW Botha, SADF MI was the principal actor in 'an intelligence picture which drove policy, rather than a policy which dictated the intelligence requirements,' thus making it 'directly responsible for the formation of Botha's extremely heavy-handed approach' to dealing with the anti-apartheid struggle. Instead of declaring successive states of emergency, O'Brien argues, the regime should have attempted to restore stability by 'more democratically equitable activities which would have enhanced the livelihoods of South Africa's people and given the government an effective solution to offer its opponents – what should be the driving force of any COIN [counterinsurgency] programme.'[113] In fact, the regime did attempt a version of this strategy in the mid-1980s by giving Africans limited (which is to say, meaningless) political representation, and seeking to create a black economic middle class as a bulwark against instability. This strategy failed miserably because South Africans aligned with the UDF, and the liberation movements rejected out of hand any attempt to put an African face on enduring white power. Thus, MK launched a violent campaign to enforce non-participation in sham local 'elections.'[114] Short of full democracy, there could be no 'effective solution' to the unrest in apartheid South Africa, certainly not one born of counterinsurgency strategy. O'Brien argues that South Africa could have begun negotiations with the ANC in the early 1980s had Botha received an accurate assessment from his intelligence agencies, thus avoiding the steady rise in violence that began in 1985. Yet regardless of the intelligence Botha might have received, there is no evidence suggesting a willingness on his part to embark in good faith on a path that would culminate in equal rights. The 1984 Nkomati Accord with Mozambique, in which Botha squeezed painful concessions from Samora Machel's government, before reneging on South Africa's pledge to stop supporting RENAMO rebels in Mozambique's civil war, underscores Botha's duplicity. Rather, Botha had charted the 'Total Strategy' even before his rise to power, remaking South Africa into a death squad regime; SADF MI, with its vast resources, ruthlessly pursued this aim. The violence and apparent disorder that characterized the late-apartheid era should instead be understood as an instrument of apartheid political control that the regime actively cultivated. When FW de Klerk finally opened negotiations with the ANC, the securocracy launched a campaign of devastating rearguard actions – the 'Third Force' – intended to weaken the opposition and violently undermine any post-transition democracy, a goal that it partly achieved.

3

APARTHEID COUNTERINSURGENCY DURING THE
NEGOTIATIONS, 1990–4

'When the government and the ANC started negotiations, there were
still skirmishes which were happening between the two armed forces and
those skirmishes were always involved with askaris, Special Units, MK
forces around the country until late 1993, before the election actually.'
— MK 'Special Ops' guerrilla Fumanikile Booi[1]

In June 1990, in the township of Ngangelizwe neighbouring Mthatha,
ANC member Sipho Phungulwa emerged from a taxi along with his
associate Luthando Dyasophu when three members of an MK 'icing
unit' opened fire on them, killing Phungulwa and wounding Dyasophu.
This incident is emblematic of the nebulous period in South African
history between the start of NP–ANC negotiations on 2 February 1990
and the country's first free-and-fair elections on 27 April 1994. During
this period, the number of deaths from political violence exceeded
14,000, more than in the entire decade preceding the negotiations.
Phungulwa's career and the story of his death have had several uses and
have been told from several different angles, highlighting the complexity
of the apartheid regime's counterinsurgency operations during this
period. Phungulwa and Dyasophu had been 'dissident' ANC members;
Phungulwa had participated in a mutiny at an Angolan MK base in
1984, had served time in the ANC's Angolan prison camps, and had

been rehabilitated.[2] At the ANC's 1989 Regional Political Committee meeting in Tanzania, Phungulwa had called for greater participatory democracy in the ANC. Having voiced this criticism of the movement, Phungulwa, Dyasophu and a group of other MK dissidents fled ANC bases in Tanzania in April 1990 and crossed overland to South Africa, claiming that they feared for their safety. Upon arrival in Johannesburg on 24 April, the dissidents were held and 'processed' by the government authorities.[3] They were then released in Johannesburg where they 'staged an impromptu press conference at which they expressed their fears of [ANC] retribution,' following which they approached ANC and SACP offices 'to expose the hardships they endured in Angola.'[4] In this process they even garnered the support of the Nobel Peace Prize laureate Archbishop Desmond Tutu.[5]

The MK team jumped Phungulwa and Dyasophu three weeks after their press conference. The apartheid regime and other critics of the ANC portrayed this as an attempt by ANC hard-line elements to silence the dissidents' calls for democracy; Trewhela likewise claims the MK 'assassins' targeted Phungulwa and Dyasophu to silence them.[6] Since then, Phungulwa's assassination has been held up by the ANC's critics as a symbol of its authoritarian and repressive tendencies, tendencies which they claim the ANC inherited from its Warsaw Pact mentors, particularly from the East German Stasi secret police.[7]

However, Sipho Phungulwa's killing must be considered within the context of the duel between MK and apartheid counterinsurgency forces that was very much under way during the 1990–4 transition era. In their August 1998 application for amnesty to the Truth and Reconciliation Commission (TRC), the MK operatives who shot Phungulwa testified that they had targeted him because he had been recruited and deployed by the apartheid regime as an askari, a claim which was accepted by the TRC.[8] The MK amnesty applicants said that Phungulwa, Dyasophu and the other dissidents in their party had become askaris in 1990.[9] In its decision to grant the MK men amnesty, the TRC noted: 'The applicants' understanding of the status of such defectors was that they were legitimate targets because they could readily identify MK operatives in the country, they were regarded as traitors who had crossed over to join the enemy, and were seen as people who sought to divide the ANC.'[10] The MK men testified that they had warned the local ANC structures in Mthatha that askaris were operating on their turf; placed the 'dissidents' under surveillance; and tracked them down. Furthermore, in the midst of political violence raging at the time, Phungulwa and Dyasophu would have been armed at all times as they ventured from Johannesburg into Transkei.[11]

There are several further aspects of the incident that raise questions about Phungulwa's true identity and purpose. Firstly, it strains credulity that upon crossing into South Africa, Phungulwa and his fellow dissidents would have favoured detention by the apartheid regime, which was notorious for torturing MK cadres, rather than facing the ANC. Indeed, it remains unheard of for genuine anti-apartheid activists of any stripe to have sought shelter at the hands of the apartheid security forces for any reason. Secondly, how is it that the regime swiftly released the dissidents when MK guerrillas falling into state custody were commonly imprisoned for years or sentenced to death? Thirdly, it is suspicious that upon their release the dissidents gained unfettered access to the media and were able to hold an 'impromptu' yet nationally televised press conference in Johannesburg in which they discredited the ANC.

In giving evidence to the TRC, Dyasophu testified that by holding the press conference, the dissidents had intended to *deny* that they were askaris – 'to indicate that they were not informers,' in the words of the commission.[12] Yet rank-and-file MK guerrillas acting on their own could not simply procure television airtime, much less with South Africa's state-owned media,[13] and the South African Broadcasting Corporation (SABC), which had broadcast the dissidents' press conference and aired their grievances, had long served as an instrument of South African Defence Force (SADF) psychological warfare operations. Indeed, until at least 1989 the SABC had been controlled directly by the State Security Council.[14] The Douglas Commission, which in 1993 began investigating human rights abuses in the ANC's Angolan camps, was likewise 'heavily funded and well covered by the SABC.'[15] The inquiries into ANC human rights abuses were also widely publicized by American right-wing organizations, while Western intelligence agencies had recruited spies in MK's Angolan camps.[16] Chris Hani explained the situation thus: 'These are the guys who are making a lot of noise here, they are calling themselves the ten exiles, they are campaigning to get…right wing American groups [involved in their cause].'[17] There was also a precedent for such disinformation operations: in 1988 Olivia Forsyth, a British national, claimed to have escaped from an ANC prison camp and was given refuge at the British embassy in Luanda; Forsyth later confessed to being a South African intelligence agent 'with orders to assist Pretoria's assassination groups.'[18]

Although the ANC in exile had undeniably violated detainees' rights in its Angolan prison camps, it had to contend with the real threat of apartheid spies in MK's ranks – several thousand by the ANC's own estimates.[19] Furthermore, the apartheid intelligence services publicized the abuses in MK camps in a carefully orchestrated operation to tarnish the ANC. Phungulwa's claim to be a peaceful dissident fearing retribution, and the portrayal of his killing as an act of internal repression by the ANC, strongly suggest an apartheid psychological warfare operation conducted in the context of the regime's dirty war. It indicates that apartheid operations to infiltrate MK ranks were intended not only to gain intelligence about the ANC, but to use spies to shape from within the ANC's very evolution as a movement, a strategy that would reach its height during the transition period and have lasting impacts afterwards.

State security services have used psychological warfare, known to the CIA as 'psy-ops' or 'psych war,' and referred to by the apartheid regime as 'Strategic Communications' ('Stratcom,' for short) or 'Communications Operations' ('Comops' or, in Afrikaans, 'Komops'), to shape domestic and international perceptions of ongoing conflict, and to sow divisions within insurgent groups. In Guatemala in 1954, the CIA operation codenamed PBSUCCESS used psychological warfare strategies, including radio propaganda and false media reports of impending rebellion, to generate widespread instability leading to the US-orchestrated coup that toppled the democratically elected president Jacobo Arbenz.[20] Two decades later, the CIA used similar tactics to destabilize the democratically elected Allende government in Chile and pave the way for Augusto Pinochet's 1973 seizure of power in a military coup. A CIA memo from that period insisted that 'the key is psych war within Chile' with the aim of 'leaving the indelible residue in the mind that an accumulation of arsenic does.'[21] Several years later,

CIA agents based at Rhodesia's Thornhill airbase, drawing on their experience from the CIA's Operation Phoenix covert assassination programme in Vietnam, advised Rhodesian forces on how to pile up dead bodies to stage photographs exaggerating body counts.[22] Such methods played an integral role in the apartheid counterinsurgency forces' clandestine war to shape South Africa's transition to democracy, and the regime had a spy network operating in major newspapers throughout South Africa and Namibia, planting false stories and transmitting sensitive information to the security forces.[23] Writing during the transition, MK cadre Rocky Williams noted: 'In addition to the "hard war" functions of' SADF Military Intelligence (MI) and the Special Forces, 'it is also important to consider the scope of its "soft war" or propaganda functions. Its extensive network of front organizations and its recourse to substantial funds via the Special Defence Account will enable it to influence the "hearts and minds" of voters in a prospective national election.'[24]

This chapter examines the apartheid regime's intensification of clandestine violence before and during the 1990–4 negotiations between the regime and the ANC. Apartheid counterinsurgency forces had sought to covertly mould political outcomes throughout southern Africa, honing their expertise during decades of clandestine warfare on the subcontinent. SADF MI in particular mastered the use of proxy warfare and special forces to destabilize hostile regimes throughout the 1980s, and then deployed these strategies domestically. The apartheid counterinsurgency forces benefited from South Africa's industrial strength and Cold War alliances for training, funding and technology. Their covert methods have made post-transition counterinsurgency legacies difficult to trace, yet it would be hard to overestimate the importance of counterinsurgency as a factor in shaping domestic and regional political processes during that period. The apartheid security chiefs had contemplated a more murderous approach to repressing dissent – what they referred to as the 'Argentine route,' in reference to that country's butchery of dissenters during its 1976–83 military dictatorship. As Security Branch veteran Craig Williamson explained in a March 1994 interview: 'If you want an Argentina, fine. Take two weeks and kill everybody in the ANC. No problem. And then what? Might give you another 10 years.'[25] The apartheid regime instead chose a more selective approach to killing, one intended to mould the transition rather than stop it altogether. In its submission to the TRC, the ANC noted that to hide its hand in the violence, the regime portrayed the 'terror campaign against black civilians' as 'political intolerance,' when in reality it was an attempt to '"manage" the transition to the advantage of the state.'[26] Ultimately, as former SAP operative Paul Erasmus described, 'his unit was told during their 1990 "Stratkom" training that a key objective was to reduce the ANC to "just another political party" by 1994.'[27] One key element in this strategy was to bolster Inkatha's political strength and capacity for violence, both to feed 'black-on-black' violence between its supporters and those of the ANC, and to diminish the ANC's political standing.

During the transition, the apartheid security force elites focused on three distinct counterinsurgency strategies: firstly, the deployment of proxy units to terrorize and destabilize ANC strongholds in particular, and African communities more generally; secondly, using psychological operations to shape perceptions of the ANC negatively at the public and elite levels; and thirdly, targeting the ANC's top leadership for recruitment or assassination. A fourth strategy was to attempt to shape the security sector reform process by retaining top military and police positions, by staffing the 'new' police and military with askaris, and by marginalizing MK fighters during the integration process.

Had the securocrats planned the Third Force attacks even before releasing Mandela and beginning negotiations with the ANC? There is plenty to suggest that they did. Although the regime released Mandela when De Klerk was at the National Party's helm, PW Botha had envisioned freeing Mandela as early as 1986. During this period, the regime had developed a strategy in line with the end of the Cold War and the apartheid security forces' return home from war in Angola and Namibia. The strategy '[refocused] the threat away from Communist-inspired subversion and onto South Africa's developmental problems.'[28] In this way, South Africa's ongoing violence could be redefined as post-colonial, framed instead as 'being part of the "Third World's poverty and instability"'; this move 'legitimated state violence and rationalised the white electorate's fear of "lowered standards."'[29]

Negotiations and Clandestine Violence

As late-Cold War developments saw South Africa withdraw its forces from neighbouring countries and decrease its support for foreign proxies, the ruling National Party replaced Botha with FW de Klerk, who initiated covert negotiations with the ANC. These led to the 2 February 1990 announcement of the release of Nelson Mandela and other ANC leaders from decades of imprisonment, and the unbanning of political movements and trade unions, ultimately culminating on 27 April 1994 in South Africa's first free-and-fair elections. Yet even as the South African government negotiated with the ANC, it unleashed its counterinsurgency forces on the liberation movements, triggering an era of unprecedented violence that would ultimately claim an estimated 14,000 lives, more than the total killed during the entire decade preceding the negotiations.[30] Amid the regime's indiscriminate violence during this period lay a programme of targeted killing: 'The [South African] Human Rights Commission also recorded the accelerating pace of assassinations of anti-apartheid figures: 28 in 1990, to 60 in 1991, and 97 in 1992.'[31]

Ellis and Klopp and Zuern, among others, have highlighted state violence as a strategy to increase government bargaining power and shape the course of South Africa's democratic transition.[32] Yet they consider apartheid counterinsurgency violence to have effectively ceased by mid-1992, when 'Third Force' massacres declined sharply, and subsequent political violence – including MK chief Chris Hani's assassination – was blamed on extremists unconnected to the state. However, evidence from archival research and interviews with ex-guerrillas indicate that the regime continued to deploy counterinsurgency tactics even after President De Klerk, responding to ANC pressure and following an internal inquiry culminating in the Steyn Report, purged his security forces of 23 high-ranking officers on 19 December 1992. Security force elites remained deeply involved in planning covert operations until at least April 1994, the month the ANC came to power, and likely afterwards. This has critical implications for understanding the impact of counterinsurgency on South Africa's democratic transition. Some of the most explosive evidence of apartheid counterinsurgency operations emerged in court cases during and after the transition, in which mid-level SADF MI officers became disgruntled and sued the SADF; in the subsequent court proceedings, astonishing details of SADF operations emerged. Such was the case with Maj. Nico Basson, who was in charge of running psychological warfare operations in Namibia prior to Namibian independence,[33] and with Jan Anton Nieuwoudt, who handled spies within the ANC for SADF MI.[34]

Foreshadowing 'Third Force': Counterinsurgency and the 1989 Namibian Election

In 1988 allied Cuban–Angolan forces gained the upper hand over the apartheid military in a showdown on the plains of south-west Angola, culminating in the decisive battle of Cuito Cuanavale. Faced with mounting white casualties, economic problems and emboldened adversaries, the National Party (NP) agreed to superpower-brokered negotiations in New York, accepting United Nations Security Council Resolution 435, which called for Namibian independence. The agreement's terms were that in exchange for SADF's withdrawal from Angolan and Namibian territory, Cuba would withdraw its forces from African soil and Namibia would gain independence, culminating in elections scheduled for 1989 that SWAPO, which enjoyed overwhelming popular legitimacy, was sure to win.

The apartheid regime launched a last-ditch counterinsurgency operation to prevent SWAPO from winning Namibia's first-ever free election. The South African objective in its former colony was strikingly similar to the strategy the NP would soon adopt in its negotiations with the ANC in South Africa proper: 'on the one hand, to try to gain as much international credit as possible for allowing the process to take place smoothly, and on the other to try to manage the transition as far as was possible in South African interests,' which meant eroding popular support for SWAPO to ensure it did not win a two-thirds majority.[35] Key details about SADF MI psychological and information operations during the transition from authoritarianism were revealed by SADF Maj. Nico Basson, former head of SADF MI Communications Operations ('Comops'), and published on 12 April 1991 by the newspaper *Vrye Weekblad*: 'Discrediting political leaders in the opposition camp is a popular strategy, especially in the army. In Namibia one of the main themes of the anti-SWAPO strategy was the discrediting of the senior leadership of the party. In South Africa this strategy has also been used with great success.'[36] In its Namibian operations, the army had spent over R1 million on just one front company devoted to disinformation, named PRO Communication Projects. SADF MI regarded the operation to discredit SWAPO in Namibia, codenamed Operation Agree, as a 'dress rehearsal' for the upcoming South African elections; Basson claimed that 'all the networks are in place.'[37] He added that a department of SADF MI, 'Komops Vyand,' had enjoyed great success for many years 'in the planting and dissemination of false information' on such leading ANC figures as Winnie Mandela. He identified SADF MI Col. Tobie Vermaak as the head of this project.[38]

Following a familiar pattern, in 1989 the Civil Cooperation Bureau (CCB) killed white lawyer and SWAPO activist Anton Lubowski in Namibia's capital Windhoek on the eve of elections. In violation of agreements, the regime continued to deploy the vicious Koevoet ('crowbar') police counterinsurgency unit in northern Namibia to intimidate voters until only weeks before the election,[39] which SWAPO ultimately won by less than 60 per cent instead of the projected 70–80 per cent.[40] As their occupation of Namibia drew to a close, the Koevoet counterinsurgency unit's final act was to kill, during the period 1–2 April 1989, an estimated 300 SWAPO fighters from a force of 600 that had crossed over from Angola. The SWAPO fighters, who were apparently planning to demobilize now that the war had formally ended, had 'neither adopted a threatening attitude nor opened fire' before the massacre.[41] Afterward, many Koevoet members returned to South Africa and brought their techniques home. Elements within the military and the NP expressed confidence that South Africa's upcoming elections could be similarly 'managed' in order to thwart the ANC at the ballot box.[42] SADF's clandestine plan to derail elections in Namibia also foreshadowed Third Force violence and disinformation in South Africa; SADF MI fed its own government's Department of Foreign Affairs bogus information on the eve of the election, sending foreign minister Pik Botha fraudulent radio messages 'purporting to come from UNTAG [United Nations Transition Assistance Group] and to concern a buildup of SWAPO fighters on Namibia's northern border.'[43] As Namibia moved closer towards independence, the plan to 'extract' counterinsurgency operations from there was spearheaded by its Rhodesian members, who had undergone a similar 'extraction' from Zimbabwe when it gained independence in 1980.[44]

Untraceable Violence: The 'Third Force'

The term 'Third Force' originated with deputy defence minister Adriaan Vlok, who on 4 November 1985 suggested to President PW Botha that the regime form a unit with a capability independent of the SAP and the SADF – 'hence, a "Third Force."' Another account holds that Mandela '[coined] the term "Third Force" in the wake of the 1990 Soweto train massacres.'[45] In the context of the 1986 declaration of a nationwide State of Emergency, which updated the regime's 'Total Strategy' to a 'Total Counterrevolutionary Strategy,' this unit would provide the regime with plausible deniability as it '[wiped] out terrorists' by using their own methods against them.[46] The regime pursued

> a RENAMO-style strategy of what [SADF chief of staff intelligence] General Van der Westhuizen called a policy of destabilization inside South Africa itself. Just as genuine ANC leaders sought to make areas inside South Africa ungovernable for the apartheid regime so that they could organize their own followers, the South African security establishment strove to make the same communities ungovernable for the ANC and its local supporters.[47]

Although State Security Council members later insisted that the unit was to be tasked mainly with riot-control duties, and strenuously denied that the regime was planning to unleash indiscriminate violence on pro-ANC/UDF communities, the creation of a Third Force came to pass much as Vlok had envisioned it. Vlok himself would assume the post of minister of law and order from 1986 to 1991, precisely the period when the regime would refine and then unleash its Third Force capacity.[48]

In July 1990, after a fruitless interrogation session in which he could not get the imprisoned Mac Maharaj to reveal the identities of

ANC moles in the Security Branch, South African Police (SAP) Gen. Basie Smit told him: 'You're going to see violence hit the country that will make all previous violence look like a picnic.' Maharaj recalls: 'when the train and hostel violence flared up to unprecedented heights in late August [1990], and the regime described it as black-on-black violence,' he understood the security forces' role.[49]

The spike in political violence during the years 1990-4 was multifaceted, with much of it being perpetrated by ANC-UDF and IFP supporters in the East Rand.[50] SADF reconnaissance commando units ('Recces') paired with IFP militants launched joint operations against ANC strongholds with the aim of creating an ethnic rift between the ANC and IFP.[51] Starting in September 1990, joint SADF–IFP forces massacred 572 black passengers on commuter trains in the Johannesburg area and launched a deadly spate of unsolved attacks on black civilians.[52] 'Then there were attacks on minivan taxis used by blacks, drive-by shootings in township streets, random bombings and machine gun attacks on bars, night clubs, and private homes. No arrests followed these terrible outbursts.'[53] Massacres erupted in Thokoza, Tembisa, Katlehong, Sebokeng and Soweto, and survivors described white and black plainclothes assailants randomly killing civilians, often from a white minibus.[54] The term 'Third Force' was widely used to describe the untraceable source of these attacks. Yet there was no doubt within the ANC about the origins of this violence: as Graham Morodi explained: 'there's no ordinary Zulu who can come and get into the train in Johannesburg, start killing everybody in that train and then get off from the train, stop and not being arrested.'[55] The violence aimed to erode ANC power and delegitimize it by exposing the ANC's inability to protect its constituents. The regime hoped the spectre of mass violence between black South Africans 'would serve to portray blacks as a violent people, incapable of bringing about peace,' yet the ANC insisted that the regime was orchestrating the violence, and 'the fact that there were no arrests at all' bore this out.[56]

In July 1991, Felix Ndimene, a sergeant in 5 Recce who was originally abducted from Mozambique, testified that members of his unit, organized into small teams, were involved in perpetrating the train massacres. 'Ndimene's testimony was partly supported by that of former Five Recce trooper Rhodesian Mervyn Malan, as well as other

Special Forces soldiers.'[57] This caused Mandela to accuse the regime of deploying a Third Force. Ndimene identified 'the Selous Scouts of Pietersburg and [5 Recce] together with members of RENAMO' and 'a Zimbabwean' as playing a role in train violence, 'particularly the Benrose massacre' of 13 September 1990. Ndimene described 'the intelligence division of [railway company] Spoornet Security' as being staffed by former Special Forces personnel who had 'orchestrated' the train violence.[58] A statement made to the TRC by Mr Xola Frank 'Jimmy' Mbane 'alleged that most of the briefings for train operations took place at Vlakplaas.'[59] Vlakplaas operatives also confirmed that on several occasions, after Third Force train massacres, IFP commanders Victor Ndlovu and Themba Khoza 'would say to the Vlakplaas men: "We hit them again."'[60] Revelations to the TRC showed that the tactic of using train violence predated the start of Third Force violence: SAP officer Wayne Hugh Swanepoel, in his amnesty application, 'stated that he and others in his unit were involved in throwing people from the trains around 1988 "in an attempt to cause the ANC and the IFP to blame each other,"' wearing balaclavas and painting exposed skin. They would later return 'to the scene of the crime "to make sure they were dead" and his own [police] unit would investigate the case.' Swanepoel declared that his unit was assisted by personnel 'paid by the CCB, and that the orders came "from inside the security police and higher up."'[61]

In a November 1990 address to the ANC's Organizing Committee national workshop, Popo Molefe noted that the upsurge of state-sponsored violence targeting 'black communities' was aimed at 'redefining the political terrain… It is linked to the longstanding strategy of apartheid to use terror to destroy democratic opposition.' Molefe noted that De Klerk had 'not distanced himself from this strategy,' pointing to the ongoing cabinet roles of minister of police Adriaan Vlok and defence minister Malan, and the recent promotion of former SADF MI chief Kat Liebenberg to SADF chief of staff.[62] An MK document from May 1990 noted the apartheid clandestine forces had 'also developed a system of automatic self-reproduction into many other extreme right-wing organs.'[63] And while De Klerk replaced the National Security Management System (NSMS) with the National Coordinating Mechanism (NCM), regime security structures continued to assassinate guerrillas as well as civic activists. Such was the case in the police killing of Meshack Bhekinkosi Kunene, targeted after a meeting by the Alexandra Advisory Committee, which had functioned as a Joint Management Committee and remained staffed by the exact same personnel as before.[64]

South Africa's assortment of white right-wing militant groups also provided useful cover for the security forces: the ANC's submission to the TRC highlights the episode of 'hunger strikers' Henry Martin and Adriaan Maritz, ostensibly members of the Orde Boerevolk organization, who fled to the UK and were exposed 'as agents of [SADF MI] with the specific brief of destabilising black communities in general and the ANC in particular: they had been responsible for the murder of Nick Cruse, an ANC-aligned computer technician, and the explosion of a bomb at a taxi rank in which many civilians had been injured.'[65] In addition to providing plausible deniability, regime violence committed in the name of right-wing elements served to 'exaggerate perceptions of the threat from the white and black extreme right in order to extract constitutional concessions from the ANC.'[66]

During this time, SADF Special Forces still maintained close ties with counterparts in several NATO armies, including 'particularly close' relations with Britain's Special Air Service (SAS), which had previously been connected to Rhodesian Special Forces. SADF Special Forces were also connected to US elite units through Maj. John Murphy, 'a former US soldier who served with South African Special Forces,' and who was 'also working with the [CIA],' and was connected to members of the influential RENAMO lobby in the United States, including former CIA deputy director Ray Cline, himself a close friend of George HW Bush.[67]

The Caprivi Trainees

SADF trained Inkatha fighters at the Hippo Base in Namibia's Caprivi Strip 'on at least one occasion,' and continued training 'Inkatha "hitmen"…at camps in KwaZulu itself.' There were also 'signs of collusion, in training and in general logistics, between these Inkatha forces and RENAMO…including suggestions that some RENAMO units may actually have been actively involved with Inkatha in recent township offensives.'[68] Senior IFP member Daluxolo Luthuli's 1995 affidavit and his subsequent disclosures were critical to unmasking the extent of the training IFP militants received from the SADF in the Caprivi Strip. In the words of SADF Maj. Johan Opperman, this training was intended to give the IFP the military capability 'to fuck up the ANC.'[69] Subsequently, the Caprivi trainees played an integral role in organizing and perpetrating targeted assassinations of ANC leaders and lay members, as well as indiscriminate massacres, abductions, rapes and murders that terrorized urban and rural populations throughout KwaZulu-Natal and Mpumalanga, a pattern that would endure well beyond 1994.[70] The Caprivi trainees, who were paid by SADF MI, operated under IFP auspices and also within the KwaZulu Police (KZP). In KwaZulu-Natal, the apartheid Security Branch and its local counterpart, the KwaZulu Police Bureau for Special Investigations, played a key role in fomenting the worst episodes of political violence throughout the region, such as the 'seven-day war' that tore through the Midlands in March–April 1990.[71] Indeed, a former KZP hit squad operative, serving several life sentences for murder, told the TRC: 'There was no difference between the KwaZulu Police, the IFP and the KwaZulu government. In my opinion they were one entity. I received instructions [to kill people] from Captain Langeni (KZP), Mr MZ Khumalo (KwaZulu government) and [Mr Daluxolo] Luthuli (IFP).'[72] In 1992, the KwaZulu Police included 'considerable numbers' of Inkatha's Caprivi trainees, as well as former Koevoet members and askaris.[73] Buthelezi himself justified the presence of the Caprivi trainees on the basis of his claim that as the ANC had escalated the 'People's War' phase of the armed struggle, 'a unit of Umkhonto we Sizwe was being trained to cross the border to assassinate [me] and to destroy the KwaZulu administration and buildings.'[74] Daluxolo Luthuli described a chain of command structured to ensure plausible deniability: after 1994, Buthelezi denied any knowledge of the Caprivi trainees' existence, and the IFP sought unsuccessfully to interdict the TRC from including the trainees' evidence in its final report.[75] In the TRC's Section 29 inquiry into Operation Marion, 'a top-secret document' emerged quoting former Security Branch commander Maj. Gen. Jac Büchner as saying: 'We must prevent the creation of a perception that they [Operation Marion members] work for us.' The Caprivi trainees themselves 'were encouraged to lie,' and Daluxolo Luthuli declared: 'It was clearly indicated that we should tell all sorts of lies so that nobody should know the truth as to what was happening.'[76] Luthuli's candour nearly got him killed: Taylor reports that Büchner and others had 'at one time' targeted Luthuli 'for assassination' because of his willingness 'to talk to investigating officers about Operation Marion.'

In 1991–2, Third Force violence reached its climax in the black townships of the Reef area ringing Johannesburg, Pretoria and Vereeniging. There, hostilities erupted between IFP loyalists, many of them living in workers' hostels, and ANC loyalists, some in workers' hostels and many more living in the surrounding peri-urban communities. The apartheid security forces organized raids against ANC strongholds by IFP militants armed with traditional Zulu spears, clubs and modern weaponry, setting in motion waves of retaliatory and pre-emptive attacks from both sides. The security forces also brought busloads of IFP impis ('traditional' Zulu warriors) from the rural heartland of Natal to Johannesburg to take part in attacks on communities loyal to the ANC, and to attack ANC rallies and demonstrations.[77] As one former MK guerrilla recalled, the political climate was already so charged during this period that the Third Force only needed to light a few sparks in order to set South Africa's black communities aflame.[78] To ensure plausible deniability, many of the arms SADF MI supplied to the IFP were taken from a US shipment of 'fifteen to sixteen containers full of modern weapons' destined for UNITA, seized by SADF MI after Resolution 435 was passed, and redirected to Durban for distribution 'to AWB and Inkatha members and a lot to underground agents who were fighting the ANC.'[79] Berkeley similarly describes counterinsurgency operative Jac Büchner organizing a convoy of fifteen tractor-trailers at the height of the violence loaded with weapons for Inkatha.[80] The IFP set up 'self-protection units' (SPUs) at Mlaba camp near the Umfolozi game reserve in KwaZulu-Natal, an endeavour that saw IFP units receive truckloads of arms from Vlakplaas stores and military training from SADF MI and Security Branch personnel.[81] Aiming to disrupt the upcoming elections, SADF elements trained 5,000 IFP members at Mlaba in northern Natal under the leadership of former Rhodesian soldier Philip Powell, who became a Security Branch officer and then an IFP senator; Mlaba camp was finally closed down in March 1994 after it was raided by representatives of the Transitional Executive Council.[82] In the run-up to the 1994 election, a shadowy group calling itself the Natal Liberation Army (NLA), composed of right-wing whites and Zulus, carried out a series of attacks, including one on the police station in the Transkei town of Flagstaff in which one policeman was killed, two were wounded, and arms were stolen.[83] The IFP also developed ties with the white far-right Afrikaner Weerstandsbeweging (AWB) militia, which coordinated attacks on the ANC with IFP militants and operated training camps for them.[84]

In KwaZulu-Natal, the police also used criminals from a variety of gangs to target ANC–UDF activists, trade unionists and ordinary civilians, in a wave of coordinated violence whose ultimate goal can only be understood as the destruction of African civil society. The regime deployed the Internal Stability Unit (ISU) amid unrest between quasi-criminal factions among Africans in Bhambayi north of Durban; the ISU provided IFP militants with direct support,[85] in what De Haas describes as a 'typical divide-and-rule strategy.'[86] Operating from police stations as well as from the communities in which they were embedded, KZP, Security Branch and SADF MI operatives – including undercover agents from front companies such as Adult Education Consultants – outsourced the targeting of ANC members to African operatives, sowed division, and distributed weaponry to encourage intercommunal violence. Amid the carnage, survivors occasionally reported seeing masked white operatives, in uniform or undercover.[87]

In this context, the IFP perpetrated massacres on ANC strongholds such as the one on 17 June 1992 in Boipatong on the Rand where 45 civilians died, sending the country to the brink of the abyss.[88] Vlakplaas also appears to have played a role in the Boipatong massacre: former Vlakplaas member Riaan Stander declared that he saw Vlakplaas operatives, still wearing disguises, returning to base shortly after the massacre and reporting to De Kock.[89] Vlakplaas veteran Corrie Goosen described a party at a Johannesburg brothel days after the Boipatong massacre, at which Vlakplaas and DCC members were present.[90] Writing on the eve of the April 1994 elections, Berkeley emphasized the danger that Buthelezi, like Savimbi in Angola, might reject the democratic process and 'take his supporters into the bush – or at least into the shadows, from which he will wage a deniable war of murder and sabotage in cahoots with reactionary white forces, including veterans of the same police, army, and intelligence groups with which he had been tacitly allied all along.'[91] This would prove prescient.

Inkathagate

The 'Inkathagate' scandal broke in July 1991 when the *Weekly Mail* obtained Security Branch documents revealing that IFP head Buthelezi had met with senior Durban policeman Maj. Louis Botha about countering the ANC's growing profile in KwaZulu-Natal. Buthelezi had voiced concerns that the ANC's popularity had been rising following Mandela's release, leading to a decline in IFP membership in its stronghold of Natal. According to the report, the Security Branch had paid over R250,000 into an IFP bank account 'for the purpose of organizing rallies and other anti-ANC activities shortly after Mandela's release.'[92] Even as 'De Klerk and Pik Botha had publicly deplored the township violence,' their government was funding the IFP as a counterweight to the ANC. The revelations exposed Buthelezi 'as being, in effect, a hired tool of the security services.'[93] Leaked Security Branch documents exposed six government special accounts 'for secret funding and covert operations' which had been used to subsidize seven anti-SWAPO parties in Namibia; details were also leaked of SADF MI's orchestration of 'Third Force' massacres, and SADF Special Forces' participation in the killing.[94] The scandal also revealed extensive covert regime support for Inkatha and its affiliate, the United Workers' Union of South Africa (UWUSA). Under Operation Omega, SADF MI had founded UWUSA to serve as a counterweight to the formation of the formidable Congress of South African Trade Unions (COSATU) in November 1985; now, it transpired that the regime had funnelled to UWUSA R5 million donated by the US trade union federation AFL-CIO 'as part of the US campaign to help fund anti-communist organizations abroad.'[95] The Inkathagate revelations also exposed 'Newslink,' an SADF MI psychological warfare operation deployed on 12 February 1990, within just days of the start of negotiations. Newslink was a '$4 million news organization created to discredit the ANC and other anti-apartheid organizations' which 'posed as a front to attend ANC meetings for intelligence gathering, and channelled 'disinformation to Europe, the United States and the world.'[96] It subsequently launched a similar organization with an identical mission and comparable budget, International Network Information; both were shut down abruptly after their existence was revealed in the Inkathagate scandal; and when their operatives sued the government, they themselves began to receive death threats.[97]

In the light of these revelations, De Klerk was compelled to remove defence minister Malan and law and order minister Vlok from their posts in August 1991; he replaced Malan with Roelf Meyer, who was in turn replaced in 1992 with former justice minister Kobie Coetsee when Meyer proved incapable of curbing the SADF's covert operations. Yet even as he ordered 41 'secret accounts and covert political projects' terminated in the wake of Inkathagate and the ongoing Harms Commission inquiry, the security forces were able to draw upon other secret accounts to fund their activities, and many covert units funded themselves through illicit revenue streams and were thus largely immune from state oversight. De Klerk even went so far as to reauthorize the psychological warfare operation Project Echoes.[98]

Inkathagate also provided details about the various government funding sources established to finance covert operations, leading De Klerk's regime to pass the Secret Services Account Amendment Act in 1992, whose purported aim was to centralize and tighten oversight of covert operations spending.[99] Although De Klerk had pledged to close down the State Security Council's Stratcom operations after they were exposed, in 1995 former security policeman Gary Pollack revealed that they were never closed down, but instead moved under deeper cover under the code-name TREWITS, which in Afrikaans stood for Counter-Revolutionary Target Information Centre.[100] According to Pollack, the directive to continue these operations under deeper cover was issued directly by Security Branch Gens. Basie Smit, Johann Leroux 'and another general,' who came to the Stratcom office and said 'the government wanted us to continue, but we would have to work differently. Before, we used to fill out forms about what we were doing; now we couldn't.'[101] Mindful of the Harms Commission and Inkathagate revelations, the Security Branch now delegated TREWITS oversight to regional commanders, 'reducing the "need to know" numbers in the SB to high-ranking officers and a select few foot-soldiers.' Pollack described the operation's parameters: 'The general strategy was that, besides arming Inkatha, more needed to be done to divide the black political parties and ensure the ANC didn't win the election. This included demonising the PAC and building the perception that Winnie Mandela, Peter Mokaba and MK "dissidents" were going to join the PAC.' To this end, Pollack's activities had included 'warning IFP hostel leaders of impending police raids,' and 'infiltrating weapons into [MK] and [APLA] in order to force their members to become informers.'[102]

Weaponizing Civil Society

Third Force elements infiltrated South African civil society to manufacture and escalate deadly rivalries seemingly unconnected to political violence. This strategy 'used the politics of personal greed, anger, and ambition as tools to destroy the social space in which community organizing otherwise took place, and it turned target communities into hostile turf for any ideologically motivated rebels.'[103] Under Rhodesian and then SADF guidance, RENAMO had used this same tactic in Mozambique: indiscriminately targeting supporters of the opposition party in order to expose its inability to protect its constituents, thus undermining the opposition's ability to organize. In South Africa, Third Force violence succeeded in disrupting the ANC's initiatives throughout the early 1990s. The regime's strategies of outsourcing violence were borrowed directly from JJ McCuen's counter-revolutionary warfare dictums, which emphasized such techniques as raising local militia units, training indigenous special constables, and recruiting vigilantes who would operate as counter-revolutionary guerrilla bands. To this end, the regime recruited *kitskonstabels* from the ranks of the unemployed, and raised gangs whose vigilante violence killed hundreds, thereby disrupting and fragmenting African communities. SADF MI trained the Witdoeke vigilantes to foment black-on-black violence against the UDF and ANC in the Western Cape; the Ama-Afrika gangs in the Eastern Cape; and the Black Cats gang in Ermelo.[104] As MK cadre Mzwandile Gushu told the TRC: 'It was quite apparent that the Government of the day was actively supporting the so-called Wit Doeke who were, in our opinion, merely gangsters and agents of the Government who wanted to eliminate the UDF and anyone associated with the ANC.'[105] SADF MI also ran the front company Adult Education Consultants as a means of infiltrating and shaping civil society, with the ultimate goal of undermining the ANC and eroding its electoral power by 1994. The ANC submission to the TRC noted: 'in the 1991/2 book year alone, over R21.5-million was covertly spent on these projects, aimed at countering the ANC. By this time it is believed that [covert operations] had spent over R150-million and that various regional fronts would continue to be funded at an additional cost of R20-million until 1994.'[106]

Such was also the case with the taxi violence epidemic in Western Cape, which killed 330 people at its peak in 1993. On 9 June 1991, ANC Youth League official Zola Ntsoni was assassinated in the Western Cape, and on 19 June ANC activist and taxi-conflict mediator Mziwonke 'Pro' Jack was killed. That month, 'ANC member and Western Cape Civic Committee (WCCC) chair Michael Mapongwana expressed concern that there was a sinister force orchestrating' the taxi violence sweeping through the region. Mapongwana was assassinated on 8 July 1991, giving rise to widespread suspicions of a Third Force role. Democratic Party (DP) MP Jan van Eck declared that he had 'clear evidence of the police both leading and assisting attackers,' causing him to believe that there was 'a definite attempt to destabilise the area under the guise of the taxi war.'[107] Dugard notes that the violence was designed 'to destabilise the staunchly pro-ANC communities of Khayelitsha and Nyanga in an area where the apartheid regime's usual ally, Inkatha, had little or no support.' Days after Mapongwana's murder, 10,000 Khayelitsha residents 'marched to the police station to demand adequate policing and to complain that the state was using [taxi hitmen] to orchestrate the killings of ANC leaders.'[108]

On 1 November 1991, MK deputy regional commander Mxolisi Petane and two other ANC members were arrested and charged with murder related to taxi violence. These trumped-up charges were later exposed as 'an elaborate attempt to implicate the ANC and MK in taxi violence.' Overall, the Cape Peninsula taxi violence 'disrupted community cohesion, creating fear and suspicion and causing a rift between community organisations such as the WCCC and the ANC over the ANC's inability to counter the violence.' In this case, the destabilization achieved its intended effect, as the National Party won a majority of Western Cape Provincial Legislature seats in the 1994 election.[109] Taxi violence also emerged elsewhere: in KwaZulu-Natal, 'warlord-cum-taxi operator' Kay Mtshali maintained an arms cache and strong connections to IFP Caprivi trainees, and was linked to several murders.[110]

Death Squads during the Transition

As negotiations with the ANC began, SADF MI's array of clandestine front companies accelerated their operations, ranging from surveillance and psychological warfare to murder.[111] Their 'privatization' afforded the state a layer of plausible deniability as its agents acted in a supposedly non-state capacity. Journalist De Wet Potgieter's research on the Third Force[112] purports to explain why death squads like the CCB became so violent just as the transition began. After undergoing a change of command from Maj. Gen. Joep Joubert to Maj. Gen. Eddie Webb in mid-1989, the CCB became rife with 'disorganization and chaos,' and likely 'killed agents from other military institutions without knowing they were working for the [SADF].'[113] In other words, the trigger-happy covert networks became so extensive and secretive that various units sometimes accidentally killed each other's operatives. Former CCB cell commander Pieter Botes related that under new command CCB leadership 'disintegrated' and the unit began killing indiscriminately, whereas under Joubert's 'old system' there had been 'administrative controls' such that 'where the elimination of a specific target may have had political repercussions, the approval of such a project had to be at a higher level.'[114]

Yet the mounting violence of apartheid death squads was not caused by one unit's change in command. These death squads had become notorious for their atrocities long before mid-1989, when this change of command took place, and in any case such claims also run counter to other apartheid death squad leaders' testimonies, such as those of Jac Büchner to the Harms Commission and Eugene de Kock to the TRC. According to them, top-level SADF generals and civilian decision-makers approved death squad operations and had full knowledge of them. In addition to targeting top-ranking leaders of the

ANC–UDF, other liberation movements and anti-apartheid activists, the CCB carried out 'innumerable other assassinations of lower-level officials and cadres' throughout southern Africa, elsewhere in Africa, and overseas.[115] Furthermore, the CCB section responsible for operations within South Africa was 'established together with the [units assigned to] other regions with the full knowledge and approval of [then SADF chief of staff] General Jannie Geldenhuys.'[116] It would also be gravely misleading to imply that the SAP or the regular forces of the SADF were in some way opposed to death squad activities, or committed to investigating or stopping them. Indeed, the regime tried to kill whistleblowers like Dirk Coetzee who had lifted the curtain on death squad activities.[117] On 12 February 1990, investigations into death squad activities forced the SADF to admit that the CCB was attached to its Special Forces branch, which was followed by revelations that the unit had a R28 million budget.[118] After the Harms Commission finally forced the CCB to disband on 30 July 1990, it re-emerged in the form of other front companies run by SADF MI, such as Pan-Afrik Industrial Investment Consultants (PAIIC)[119] and International Researchers–Ciskei Intelligence Services (IR-CIS), that continued to pursue counterinsurgency operations. The Directorate of Covert Collection (DCC) also secretly rehired CCB personnel after their unit's disbandment.[120] According to one report, after the CCB was shut down, many businesses established as CCB fronts '[continued] to operate as self-sustaining and often highly lucrative operations'; as the report noted: 'beneficiaries of these businesses must continue to cooperate with their former sponsors.'[121]

As former Vlakplaas commander Eugene de Kock's trial proceeded through 1995, it became clear that 'contacts between members of Vlakplaas, the CCB and the DCC range from the personal to the professional, with a significant amount of cross pollination of staff.'[122] And though SADF MI and the Security Branch carried out most Third Force operations during this period, in October 1990 'Mandela met with De Klerk to present witness affidavits' claiming that the NIS was using African 'agents provocateurs to incite township violence.' This was the first specific accusation against the NIS, whereas SADF MI, the CCB, and the SAP Security Branch 'had often been accused previously.'[123]

Based on an interview with a former SADF Special Forces officer, O'Brien writes that in addition to undermining South Africa's transition from apartheid, the CCB may have been conceived for 'an even more sinister reason,' namely 'to provide a covert counter-revolutionary capability to the existing government *following* the loss of power to a black majority government.'[124] According to O'Brien, 'the CCB was designed to provide a covert counterrevolutionary capability to the existing government following the loss of power to a black majority government'; thus its dissolution after 1990 'may not have had much impact on its individual members, who had been preparing – since 1986 – to go underground within other structures.'[125] These 'deepest-cover destabilization programmes'[126] resembled that of NATO's 'stay-behind' armies, covert right-wing paramilitary networks trained to resist invading Soviet forces across Europe, which often had links to violent crime.[127] Also designed to survive a political transition from apartheid was the NIS's ultra-secret operational unit, founded on the orders of the State Security Council and designated 'K.'[128]

Many CCB members either continued to run front SADF MI companies established during apartheid or created entirely new companies 'to carry on with either covert operations or illegal/criminal activity.'[129] These included the 'Badger Unit' run by CCB operative Staal Burger out of a Hillbrow Hotel he owned, and involving such notorious CCB operatives as Ferdi Barnard and Eugene Riley. Badger Unit was established with the approval of the Security Branch and tasked with such 'anti-terrorist' operations as 'combatting illegal gun-running and explosives'; at various points, Badger Unit operatives were deployed by the Security Branch to the black townships.[130]

Death squad operatives also received bonuses from secret funds for jobs well done.[131] Archival documents attest to the counterinsurgency operators' profit-seeking motives: for example, members of top-secret units, such as the PAIIC and CCB, received double pensions, and 'the [PAIIC] operation [in Ciskei] was probably also a justification for large-scale corruption' as operators received money from both the Ciskei government and SADF (see Chapter Five). PAIIC commander Nieuwoudt received a retrenchment package from Ciskei after IR-CIS was closed down, which the SADF told him to spend on a house; and he 'probably also double-claimed from Ciskei and SADF for his sources' payments, pocketing the difference himself.'[132] A DCC commander and former SADF Special Forces commando, Rich Verster, maintained close operational links with De Kock's Vlakplaas and with criminal underworld figures such as Ferdi Barnard, whom Verster had recruited for the DCC following Barnard's dismissal from the CCB. Verster was also involved in a range of illicit smuggling activities that he led alongside his counterinsurgency tasks.[133] These economic motivations fused with apartheid's political imperatives, and in the absence of any explicit orders to stop killing, they escalated the violence. Henderson describes the Third Force as an 'amorphous "mafia-like" network within South Africa' that brought together 'serving security forces personnel' with well-connected former personnel from the security forces and the securocrat echelons, and 'criminal elements involved in clandestine activities.'[134] After De Klerk's purge of security force ranks in December 1992, the Third Force became 'effectively privatized.'[135]

The enduring power of the Joint Management System is revealed in apartheid counterinsurgency's penetration into all facets of the state and society, including the activation of infiltrators in the electricity utility and railway systems to assist in secretly launching massacres on the East Rand and elsewhere. These operated through the CCB and other SADF MI death squad units disguised as private companies. After the Harms Commission had exposed the CCB's existence and forced its disbandment, and Inkathagate laid bare the links between the regime and the IFP's violence, apartheid counterinsurgency units were self-sufficient and equipped to operate independently at least until Mandela's 1994 election victory.[136]

Among the shocking revelations he made to the TRC and the press in 1997, former Vlakplaas askari Joe Mamasela claimed that there were seven other farms identical in purpose to Vlakplaas that were set up by the apartheid security forces, with the last farm bought by police officials in 1991.[137] These farms were privately registered under false names of senior police officials connected to death squad activity. They reflected the apartheid security establishment's shift in strategy towards clandestine violence, which could be waged with fewer constraints and greater secrecy from remote farms instead of police stations. Mamasela said that 'the farms became known as torture farms as they were situated away from the police stations,' and claimed that they had been established in each of South Africa's provinces, including some in Ladybrand in Free State, two in KwaZulu-Natal, one in Zeerust in North West, one near Randburg in Gauteng, and two in the Western Cape.[138] As with most apartheid counterinsurgency operations, the motive of profit lay not far behind. According to Mamasela, the farms were bought using SAP discretionary funds: 'as there were prospects of a new government coming in, there was an attempt to dry out some of these funds because there was a suspicion that they would now fall under the ANC government.'[139] The establishment of these farms facilitated the deployment of askaris throughout South Africa prior to the 1994 elections, 'to create panic and chaos.'[140] Mamasela's disclosure followed an order by the TRC in March 1997 to exhume the remains of Phila Ndwandwe and three other anti-apartheid activists murdered by police in KwaZulu-Natal and buried in shallow graves.

In March 1997, a former security policeman confirmed that the Eikenhof farm in the Vaal area had been used as a base by the death squads that killed hundreds of train commuters between 1991 and 1994. He told journalists that the farm's existence was kept secret by police, who had stored weapons there captured from liberation movements. Police informers in the ranks of the SDUs, including senior officials, were brought there in secret, and some were said to have helped plan the train massacres.[141] In April 1997, Mamasela alleged that 'Sam,' a former askari still employed with the John Vorster Square police force, was being closely watched by his white bosses because he could reveal details of transition-era covert operations. Along with two policemen, 'Sam' had been involved during the transition era in bombing several restaurants belonging to the Wimpy chain, attacks that were blamed on MK.[142] Another policeman from John Vorster Square, Andries van Heerden, told an inquiry that he had handled askaris 'infected with the AIDS virus' who were placed near hostels 'to infect the ANC members.'[143] Van Heerden also described how after the Goldstone Commission exposed Third Force activities in 1992, the Vlakplaas unit had conspired with the IFP leadership to attack senior ANC members at their Shell House headquarters under the cover of a Zulu march. Vlakplaas and other police units had funnelled weapons to the IFP on a weekly basis during this period, notably through IFP youth leader Themba Khoza. De Kock himself identified Khoza as a weapons trafficker and main conduit between the IFP and the regime.[144]

Regional Dimensions

Extreme right-wing rejectionists under former SADF chief Constand Viljoen approached Bantustan leaders such as Bophuthatswana's Lucas Mangope and KwaZulu's Buthelezi to form a united front against the negotiations, including the possibility of seceding from a post-apartheid South Africa. Buthelezi and the IFP threatened to secede if the ANC came to power. Meanwhile, De Kock and other death squad operatives helped the IFP build its forces; between September 1993 and April 1994, the IFP trained around 8,000 militants at secret bases throughout KwaZulu. In this, they were closely assisted by SADF MI and the Security Branch, including SAP Gens. Basie Smit and Johan van der Merwe.[145] Around 1992, the apartheid regime also planned to use a game farm in Nyawa, Zambia, as a launching pad for guerrilla-style attacks on the ANC in South Africa. Shortly after the start of negotiations, containers full of SADF MI documents were shipped to the RENAMO stronghold in Nampula, Mozambique. When RENAMO and FRELIMO achieved a peace deal in 1992, these containers were moved to the Nyawa farm. In specially designated areas of the farm, Zulu recruits were secretly trained in guerrilla warfare using weaponry including infrared sights and Soviet-made Sako 7.62 mm rifles, apparently with the secret acquiescence of Zambia's President Chiluba.[146] Many more IFP recruits received training until 1994 in various secret bases; one British mercenary claimed to have trained several hundred-strong groups of IFP militants at a farm near Heidelberg, south-east of Johannesburg, and to have selected hit squad operatives from among his trainees for taxi raids and train massacres.[147]

Even after Namibian independence and the end of South African involvement in the Angolan war, SADF MI maintained support for its external proxy forces: UNITA in Angola and RENAMO in Mozambique. After the start of negotiations with the ANC, the clandestine apartheid military structures continued to supply and arm their surrogate foreign forces for several years. This secret alliance persisted in Mozambique until 1991 and continued in Angola until at least 1992. The strategy was calculated to afford South Africa the means to instantly resume violence against neighbouring states friendly to the ANC in the event that negotiations should fail.[148]

South African foreign policy during the transition period must be situated in terms of the broader context of ongoing apartheid violence which unfolded alongside the regime's negotiations with the ANC. Retired chief of SADF MI Gen. Tienie Groenewald related that as a representative of Gen. Constand Viljoen's Afrikaner Volksfront, he had flown in a light plane to meet UNITA chief Jonas Savimbi at a village near Huambo, Angola. Groenewald sought Savimbi's assurances that UNITA would support the extreme right-wing rejectionist Volksfront if they started an insurrection against the NP government, to which Savimbi replied: 'Tell Gen. Viljoen that everything I and UNITA own are at his disposal.' In this scenario, which, according to Groenewald, nearly transpired, UNITA-controlled territory in Angola would have served as a rearguard base for extreme right-wing SADF soldiers poised to launch combat operations against the NP government to subvert any compromise with the ANC.[149] This underscores the ongoing centrality during the transition years of the apartheid regime's outsourcing of violence to the Frontline States. The regime's proxy allies such as UNITA and RENAMO stayed connected to its counterinsurgency strategy and, with SADF assistance, remained at war with the governments of Angola and Mozambique. Thus hardliners such as Viljoen and Groenewald laid plans predicated on support from their old ally, Savimbi. Meanwhile, in Mozambique, SADF MI stored containers full of sensitive documents in territory controlled by RENAMO, underscoring the strength of their mutual bond even after the Total Strategy years had given way to negotiations in both countries. RENAMO also apparently carried out a biological warfare assault on a Mozambican military camp in 1992, in the midst of negotiations with FRELIMO; this would have been entirely beyond RENAMO's capabilities were it not for the SADF's close assistance.[150]

Meanwhile, far-right elements convened under former SADF chief of staff Constand Viljoen and backed by former SADF MI chief Tienie Groenewald were poised to trigger a violent insurrection as late as early 1994. Groenewald also asserted that this right-wing rejectionist front could rely on the support of what he referred to as the 'heavies,' meaning elite units such as the CCB and SADF Special Forces which would align themselves against the De Klerk government and any moderate white elements willing to compromise with the liberation movements. Groenewald further claimed that the US ambassador to South Africa was aware of these contingency plans for a right-wing coup, and had given them his approval.[151] Apartheid death squads also continued launching targeted assassinations in neighbouring countries after negotiations began: On 22 April 1990, four members of the Chand family and a security guard were killed in Botswana by Vlakplaas for their role is assisting APLA guerrillas crossing into South Africa; and on 28 April 1990, white leftist Father Michael Lapsley was killed at his home in Harare, Zimbabwe by a parcel bomb apparently sent to him by the NIS.[152]

4

MK'S WAR IN THE SHADOWS, 1990–4

'It is our unceasing struggles — in the prisons, in mass campaigns, through the armed struggle — that has brought the regime to the negotiating table. And those negotiations are themselves a site of struggle. It is not a question of armed struggle or negotiations. Armed struggle brought about negotiations.'
— Nelson Mandela, speaking at Chris Hani's funeral,
19 April 1993

On 6 July 1990, MK cadre Fumanikile Booi met with MK chief of staff Chris Hani to discuss security arrangements during Hani's stay in Cape Town and the nearby township of Gugulethu. Negotiations with the De Klerk government were under way, and in the context of the Groote Schuur talks, MK's role was to protect the ANC leadership. Hani was scheduled to give a public address in Cape Town the following day, and he appointed Booi commander of an MK Special Ops unit tasked with protection, because 'police, Special Units and askaris' were 'out there to derail the negotiations' and 'they're armed and they're dangerous, they're out to kill.' Booi enquired about procedures should his unit be stopped by police; Hani responded that the ANC depended on a strong MK presence inside South Africa, and the cadres would need to defend themselves. Hani briefed the unit about 'information that there are askaris which have been instructed to assassinate [him] before his address in Gugulethu at NY49, while he's in Cape Town.' Booi's unit's mission was 'to counteract those askaris, if possible to kill them when I met with them.'

By night, Booi's four-man team drove along the streets of Nyanga township in the midst of light traffic, but as his vehicle passed a van parked in the shadows 'they put on their lights and immediately [followed] us.' Booi wondered, 'have these people been waiting for us all along?' The van followed the MK team around several corners, then overtook them in an uninhabited area and cut them off to prevent escape. 'Immediately' Booi recalled his briefing about 'the askaris' who were known to be 'travelling around with police vans' and 'clad in police uniforms.' He ordered his men to be combat ready. As armed white policemen wearing fatigues approached the car, Booi and his men opened fire, killing one: 'I shot at him first because I know if I couldn't shoot first, I would be killed on the spot with the [car's other] occupants.' Booi testified that this was undoubtedly a death squad, as 'ordinary police don't use conventional arms in a normal urban area.' Their 'sub-machine guns [were] a clear indication that this is part of the Special Force which will be assembled to assassinate and delay the talks inside the country.'[1] After ensuring that there were no police reinforcements coming, the MK team fled the scene.

Hani cited the incident the following day during his speech in Cape Town, declaring that since negotiations had begun 'we're repeatedly saying that askaris, some police force members, special units who were against the negotiations, were keeping on assassinating our comrades.' Hani insisted the Nyanga shootout was 'not an isolated incident.' According to Booi, 'the skirmish itself actually sent a clear message that MK is inside the country and it is advancing its military wing because it is the first time that the police could report a high number of highly trained MK "terrorists" being in the same operation at the same time.' He also pointed out that 'the government has promised that there won't be any further assassination on MK members and its leadership inside the country, but there was a continuity.' Booi attributed Hani's own assassination in 1993 to the same death squad networks, testifying that 'some of those sinister forces are actually those who participated in assassinating Comrade Chris Hani.' While Booi's unit managed to repulse the anticipated attack, other MK cadres during the 1990–4 transition era were less fortunate. Vuyisile Baloyi was killed in Gugulethu in 1990. Welile Salman and Motlatsi were 'lured to their death' in Mafikeng, Bophuthatswana, in October 1990: after crossing the border in a kombi at Zeerust, the cadres, who were armed with pistols, were stopped at a roadblock, ordered to get out, and mowed down.[2]

A former MK commander described narrowly avoiding a similar ambush while serving in a security detail for a prominent ANC leader in Pretoria several months after negotiations began. During their night off, his group of five MK guerrillas was driving beyond the city limits in a red Mercedes-Benz when, at one cadre's suggestion, they spontaneously took a detour off the main road to visit his cousin's shebeen. They later learned from intelligence sources that further along their planned route the security forces had prepared an elaborate ambush with heavy firepower for the MK team, including armoured vehicles and ambulances to evacuate any wounded from the anticipated shootout.[3] Many other ANC and MK operatives during this period were either assassinated or killed while in custody after being identified by Askaris.[4]

Origins of Operation Vula

ANC operative Tim Jenkin recalls that in the late 1980s, 'there was very little to show for the years of struggle, only hundreds of activists in the enemy's jails and the loss of tons of precious weaponry'; although MK managed to infiltrate many cadres, they faced great logistical problems, and the 'attrition rate was extremely high.'[5] In describing his own arrest by the regime in the mid-1980s, Jenkin provides a key insight into cadres' vulnerability inside South Africa: prior to their detention he and his compatriots 'were aware of surveillance but could do nothing, for our communications were too slow to be used as a tool for seeking guidance.' MK's lack of a command-and-control network inside South Africa meant that 'only the number of actions could increase but, because there were no generals on the spot, these could never be coordinated to achieve any strategic objective.' The MK leadership determined that the armed struggle was being hampered by weak communications networks, which prevented cadres from communicating 'with their leaders and between themselves,' with the result that the 'People's War never became a reality.'

To address this, in 1986 the ANC began planning Operation Vula (short for 'Vulindlela,' meaning 'open the way' in the Nguni languages). Following the ANC's 1985 Kabwe conference, the National Executive Committee (NEC) adopted a secret resolution in 1986 authorizing Vula's launch under ANC president OR Tambo's direct purview, with knowledge of the operation's existence 'restricted to a "need-to-know" basis within the ANC.'[6] Vula aimed to establish the authority of the NEC and the Politico-Military Council (PMC) on the ground to resolve the lack of an overarching ANC authority within South Africa, a problem which undermined coordination between the political structures and MK. The ANC had kept its mass action, underground, and armed struggle pillars largely separate for greater security, 'so that enemy penetration on the armed side did not lead to the destruction of the political or the mass side, or vice versa,' but now it was time to synchronize these programmes.[7] By early 1987, ANC president Tambo and Joe Slovo had chosen Mac Maharaj and Chris Hani to infiltrate South Africa, and eventually added Jacob Zuma to the command structure. Siphiwe Nyanda (code-named 'Gebuza'), commander of MK's Transvaal urban military force, would be Maharaj's deputy and Vula's military commander.[8] Jenkin credits Maharaj with the key realization that 'nothing serious could happen in the underground' until MK established a reliable communications network inside the country. To this end, Maharaj himself, along with MK Military Intelligence chief Ronnie Kasrils, was to infiltrate South Africa and implant an elaborate, unprecedented command-and-control network. Preparations involved maximum secrecy to conceal Vula from spies: only Tambo and a handful of others were aware of them. Meanwhile, Maharaj and Nyanda departed from ANC headquarters in Lusaka under the cover of alibis, flying circuitous routes from Zambia via the USSR, 'where their appearances and identities would be radically altered,' and Eastern Europe, before ultimately entering South Africa through Swaziland.[9] There are indications that Joe Modise, despite being overall MK commander, was kept in the dark about Operation Vula. Henderson finds this improbable,[10] since Modise would have noticed key MK figures being reassigned to Vula; nonetheless, it is telling that the ANC leadership would not have trusted Modise.

As the United Democratic Front (UDF) gained prominence within South Africa, the ANC began encouraging prospective MK recruits to remain in the country and to assist in setting up structures to receive trained guerrillas infiltrating from abroad. Though this strategy succeeded in some instances, it fell well short of the revolutionary war its planners envisioned.[11] Spontaneous youth uprisings, which had rendered some townships ungovernable, could not serve as a stand-in for MK operations.[12] Vula represented a breakthrough, as the ANC set up Vula structures throughout Natal and the Witwatersrand between August 1988 and May 1990. Over two years, the operation established a more extensive underground network in South Africa than the ANC had managed in the previous thirty years: an elaborate web of informer networks, arms caches, cells of operatives, and other features. Nyanda's priority was training 'MK cadres for a people's army – not for immediate deployment on the ground.'[13] Vula also gave the ANC the potential to escalate its armed insurgency in the event that talks with the regime should fail.[14] The ANC had devised a highly sophisticated computer encryption system to relay communications from South Africa to Lusaka, often routed through London. This enabled MK cadres to organize like never before: 'Details of meetings could be arranged more or less instantaneously, complete with legends and passwords. If anything went wrong at the last moment both sides could be informed timeously and take the appropriate action.'[15] According to Maharaj, the computer-based communications system functioned almost in 'real-time.'[16] As the Vula networks expanded, so did the requests for weaponry from cadres inside the country: Jenkin describes receiving encrypted requests at his office in London for 'AKM automatic rifles, TNT, detonating cord, hand grenades, RPG rocket launchers and rifle silencers,' and more. In concert with ANC members already underground, Maharaj and Nyanda 'established an internal Vula overall leadership committee (OLC) with members responsible for political mobilization and liaison, communications, logistics, military operations, intelligence and counterintelligence, and other matters'; the OLC then expanded its 'network of safe houses, communications posts, arms caches,' supply points, and intelligence networks.[17] Ultimately, Vula channels would strain under the expanding supply of 'operatives, equipment, and weapons' being smuggled into the country, forcing the ANC to improve its cross-border smuggling techniques.[18] This culminated in the establishment of MK arms caches in major urban centres and training operations for new recruits inside South Africa.

In 1989, the ANC called for the armed struggle to be intensified. The Politico-Military Council ordered that MK's leadership structures should be moved into South Africa, and that regional politico-military councils be established throughout the country.[19] While ANC officials from the Department of National Intelligence and Security (NAT) held clandestine negotiations with the apartheid National Intelligence Service (NIS), the ANC also launched major intelligence operations inside South Africa, including the NAT's Operation Bible, a highly successful attempt to recruit moles and double agents within the apartheid security structures.[20] A senior Security Branch official, watching his compatriots torture MK cadre Yunus Shaik in Durban in 1985, was so driven by 'disgust, shame, and remorse' that he became a spy for the ANC.[21] Yunus's younger brother, Moe Shaik, trained in East Germany as an MK intelligence operative, was given command of 'Vula's intelligence activities, including its intelligence gathering and counterintelligence procedures' in 1988,[22] and became the Security Branch mole's sole handler. This operation reported directly to Jacob Zuma, who ran ANC operations out of Mozambique and was then appointed chief of ANC intelligence. This gave MK 'extensive access' to Security Branch files, which revealed just how much the ANC was itself infiltrated with apartheid spies.[23] The mole was code-named 'Nightingale,' and to promote his career within the Security Branch, MK helped him to recruit informants. Yunus Shaik recalled: 'We came to learn of the SB's techniques, its tactics and strategy, competition for title and promotion, the tension between SB and other organs of state, but most importantly, we were able to scope its knowledge of our activities and deployment. Armed with this information, we could then act with impunity.'[24] According to several Vula participants, the ANC established 'a number of well-placed moles' within the police, defence force, and the Bantustan armies, and gained 'access to top-secret government intelligence reports, including [NIS] files.'[25]

Operation Bible's infiltration of various regime agencies also enabled its cadres to obtain documents that made it possible for MK operatives to travel directly by air via Johannesburg, a valuable complement to the circuitous overland routes.[26] It featured as well an elaborate system of shell companies and other money-laundering ventures to help fund MK's expanding networks. The regime apparently failed to detect Vula or penetrate its networks.

The apartheid regime's recruitment of spies within the ANC was so extensive that the ANC ruthlessly sought to weed them out 'with the assistance of its own moles in the [Security Branch],' which inevitably led to innocent cadres being accused and punished.[27] This ruthlessness ran counter to the ANC's ethos, but the cadres who spearheaded the armed struggle 'were not fazed' by the Truth and Reconciliation Commission's subsequent revelations of ANC human rights abuses during the late-struggle era: 'In a dirty war everyone plays dirty; you do not pause to consider the moral niceties when your survival is at stake.' Mac Maharaj further explained the dangers facing MK cadres from the regime's death squads: 'We were in a very dirty war. We didn't allow the possibility of being unfair to someone or mislabelling them as enemy agents to endanger our survival. We didn't have the luxury of checking and double-checking information that we plucked from the state's security files. We took what we got and did our best with it.'[28]

Yet if MK was ruthless in dispatching suspected spies, it used violence only sparingly against regime targets. As Vula evolved, its cadres reconnoitred security force targets inside South Africa and found many that were vulnerable to attack, but Tambo insisted that Vula operatives resist the temptation to launch such 'short-term actions,' and remain focused on the longer-term struggle. Instead, Vula continued smuggling and stockpiling arms, training cadres inside South Africa, and selecting candidates for more extensive training 'outside,' preparing the ground for a more elaborate and systematic phase of the struggle.[29] To maintain their low profile, Vula elements were forbidden by their command structures to intervene on behalf of other MK units operating in South Africa at the time; this posed an especially difficult challenge in KwaZulu-Natal, where by August 1988 the fighting between Inkatha and the UDF had reached new heights.[30]

Genesis of Negotiations

As popular uprising surged throughout the townships in the mid-1980s, Oliver Tambo had emphasized that the 'ANC's main objective was not "a military victory but to force Pretoria to the negotiating table."'[31] For the ANC, negotiations were the logical culmination of a struggle that stood no realistic chance of defeating apartheid on the battlefield. For the regime, negotiations afforded an opportunity to outmanoeuvre the ANC: in 1987, NIS chief Niël Barnard had written a report arguing that the ANC was 'unbeatable' as long as it remained in exile, but that by unbanning it, the regime could draw it into a 'protracted negotiations process' during which its power could be sapped, forcing it into a coalition government in which its revolutionary aims could be blunted.[32] It is unclear exactly when the ANC met with representatives of the regime for the first time. The earliest contact may have been as far back as 1984, when, in the aftermath of the Nkomati Accord between South Africa and Mozambique, the regime may have deemed it worthwhile to establish diplomatic contacts with the ANC.[33] There were definitely contacts between the regime and the ANC in 1986, and in 1987 ANC president OR Tambo and ANC International Department head Thabo Mbeki met with Afrikaner academics and Broederbond members in the UK in a series of contacts that would continue until 1990. This led to the ANC meeting with NIS chiefs in Lucerne, Switzerland; under what it codenamed Operation Flair, the NIS sent its chief director of operations Maritz Spaarwater and deputy director Mike Louw, who were later joined by NIS chief Barnard, while the ANC sent Mbeki and NAT deputy director Jacob Zuma, with NAT director Joe Nhlanhla joining afterward.[34] Between 1986 and Mandela's release in February 1990, 'at least 48' meetings were held between the regime's team, led by Barnard, and the ANC.[35] In July 1988, the NIS 'piloted a resolution through the State Security Council about secret talks between the regime and the ANC.'[36] Upon assuming the presidency of the country, De Klerk, who had been opposed to talks with the ANC, was incensed to learn that the NIS had proceeded behind his back, whereupon the NIS leadership 'respectfully brought' the resolution 'to his attention.'[37]

The NP had also initiated a dialogue with Mandela while he was still in prison: with President PW Botha's approval, Barnard, justice minister Coetsee, and Louw, along with commissioner of prisons Johan Willemse and director general of the Prisons Department Fanie van der Merwe met with Mandela repeatedly over a three-year period beginning in 1986, discussing his political and economic outlook. As early as 1989, Barnard had identified Mandela not only as the most powerful ANC figure, but also as the eventual future president of South Africa.[38] The NP team met with Mandela separately from his fellow ANC members in prison, and from ANC leaders in exile, for 'two clear reasons': firstly, it gave NIS an opportunity to try to drive a wedge between the ANC in exile and its structures within South Africa, and secondly, it allowed NIS to evaluate what Mandela knew about the ANC's leadership in exile, and whether any splits existed between them already.[39] One of Vula's greatest achievements – what Jenkin calls its 'ultimate coup' – was the establishment in April 1989 of a secret channel that enabled Tambo and the ANC leadership in exile to communicate with Mandela while he was still in Victor Verster prison. In addition to his meetings with apartheid officials, Mandela met with representatives of the Mass Democratic Movement, but his every move was under close surveillance, and he was reluctant to stake out clear positions in his dialogue with the regime so long as he could not consult with the broader movement. Now, through one of Mandela's lawyers, the ANC transmitted and received messages in 'books with secret compartments in their covers,' a tactic that originated in the days when much of the movement's leadership was imprisoned on Robben Island.[40] Unbeknown to it, the NP was negotiating with a unified ANC leadership.

MK on the Eve of Negotiations

On 22 December 1988, Cuba, Angola and South Africa signed a tripartite agreement that brought an end to South Africa's war in Angola and laid the ground for Namibia's independence. The agreement's terms also mandated that the ANC close MK bases in Angola. On 8 January 1989, the ANC leadership issued a statement that the ANC was going to pull out of Angola. Ngculu writes that 'this came as a shock to the rank and file because it was totally unexpected'; OR Tambo called on MK fighters not to lose heart and emphasized that 'this was not a cease-fire.'[41] The loss of MK's Angolan bases posed a double challenge to the movement: it greatly complicated the infiltration of cadres into South Africa, and it also forced the relocation of MK forces to bases in Tanzania and Uganda, undermining discipline and eroding morale. This forced relocation drew MK units even further from striking distance, and guerrillas designated for deployment within Vula's expanding structures 'were moved thousands of kilometres further away from their infiltration targets.'[42] Some of MK's heavier weaponry, such as Soviet-supplied armoured personnel carriers that had been used in the running war against UNITA, was impossible to transport and had to be abandoned. The ANC leadership chartered six aircraft to transport MK personnel from Angola to East Africa.[43] This move disrupted immensely the ANC's ability to organize operations or maintain command and control of units in the field.[44]

On 8 January 1989, Chris Hani explained MK's loss of momentum in that year: MK faced logistical problems related to the closing of its Angolan bases and the relocation to Tanzania and Uganda, along with infiltration by askaris.[45] In October 1989, the apartheid regime released key ANC leaders from imprisonment on Robben Island, including Harry Gwala, Ahmed Kathrada, Raymond Mhlaba, Wilton Mkwayi, Andrew Mlangeni, Elias Motsoaledi, Oscar Mpetha, and Walter Sisulu. At an event at the Mulungushi Centre in Lusaka, the first major ANC event in exile attended by Walter Sisulu, Govan Mbeki, Harry Gwala, Raymond Mhlaba and other ANC stalwarts after their release from prison, 'a contingent of MK cadres' that were 'marooned' in Lusaka loudly condemned the ANC leadership in exile, particularly Joe Modise, prompting a shaken Sisulu to step forward and assure the assembly that the ANC would be pursuing negotiations and armed struggle simultaneously.[46] Speaking in Lusaka on 18 January 1990, ANC secretary-general Alfred Nzo accidentally read to the international press corps a statement that had been intended as an address to a closed ANC gathering, in which Nzo, after emphasizing that the ANC's armed struggle 'must continue' in the absence of a negotiated end to hostilities, conceded: 'Looking at the situation realistically, we must admit that we do not have the capacity within the country to intensify the armed struggle in any meaningful way.' Nzo went on to note: 'It may therefore be that the main military task that we should pay attention to is precisely the building up of that capacity within the country…[to] both be able to fight effectively should the need arise, and to have sizeable forces at the moment when a new South African Army is formed.'[47] Nqakula notes that Nzo's blunder caused ANC cadres to ceaselessly mock him thereafter as 'Comrade No-Capacity.'

On the eve of negotiations, MK, though it could not defeat the apartheid regime in battle, likewise remained unvanquished. Its armed actions inside South Africa had steadily mounted throughout the 1980s, and Vula's goal of establishing an MK presence inside South Africa, by caching arms, infiltrating cadres, and recruiting its own spy network within the regime, was partly realized. Vula also deepened the ANC's capacity to sustain armed struggle even after losing the USSR's superpower sponsorship. Despite all the challenges facing MK by 1990, Chris Hani proclaimed: 'we are an army which has had a steady growth… At the moment MK has got soldiers, and has got material, and still commands a lot of sympathy and support among the oppressed youth in Soweto, KwaMashu, Gugulethu, and other places.'[48] In January 1990, Hani reiterated his vision of MK as a defender of the masses: 'The regime will have to give consideration to MK…MK is not there because the ANC is a banned organization. It is an answer to the violence of the regime. So, I believe that the armed struggle will continue even if the ANC is unbanned.' Hani anticipated the likelihood of violence amid negotiations, predicting that 'the regime will still use violence, the regime will still resort to its military and security forces… Do you think overnight now the regime will stop beating up the workers, shooting workers, dispersing demonstrations? Will it stop raiding homes? Will it stop using its security laws to ban and detain people?'[49] An MK publication from the 1990–4 period emphasized this mass strength and resilience as one of MK's primary assets: 'We have the numbers, we have a highly politicized community with a lot of creativity and initiative.'[50] After Mandela was released from prison and assumed full leadership of the ANC, 'he authorized that Vula continue its clandestine operations even though the ANC was then legal.'[51] In a December 1990 interview, Nyanda described how, after negotiations started, Vula began integrating newly returned cadres into its newly 'viable military structures,' while other members also participated in 'propaganda work'; however, he took care to downplay the true extent to which Vula had expanded MK military networks.[52]

MK cadre Cyril Groep recalled that as cadres prepared for the ANC leadership's release, they 'were briefed that there [were]... going to be some political changes within the country; but we had to intensify the struggle, we should increase our numbers, especially combat units within the country.'[53] Groep had amassed an arms cache after his involvement in 'raiding police stations, disarming policemen,' and was instructed to 'keep arms' to distribute to MK cadres returning from exile in 1991. That year, a surge of volunteers joined MK in the Western Cape in response to Ciskei strongman Gqozo's crackdown on the ANC; Groep established a firing range at a quarry on a farm near East London where he trained 600 cadres 'right up to 1994' to counter threats from 'the right-wingers' and ensure that 'we had to go through elections.'[54] The ANC continued to smuggle weapons into South Africa and cache them until the 1994 elections.[55] It also continued to send its cadres for training abroad even after the start of negotiations. Although East Germany and other Warsaw Pact countries which had previously been destinations of choice were no longer available by 1990, several cadres were sent to the USSR even at this late date.[56] In March 1990, Soviet representative Vasili Solodovnikov joined ANC and South African Communist Party (SACP) leaders to greet Mandela upon his arrival in Lusaka; Solodovnikov repeatedly told the movement's leadership not to abandon the armed struggle, but said 'they could not expect Soviet backing in the future.'[57]

War amid Negotiations

Mandela's release from prison and the ANC's unbanning on 2 February 1990 caught all but the highest-ranking MK cadres by surprise.[58] Jenkin recalls: 'most of us were extremely sceptical and carried on as if nothing had happened. It was too difficult to trust a regime that had always acted with such duplicity.'[59] Nonetheless, MK cadres remained loyal to their political leadership virtually across the board. The ANC's political unity withstood the tremendous stresses of the negotiated transition and the dramatic escalation in regime violence, which accounted for most of the 3,500 people killed by political violence in

1990.[60] As African communities throughout the country came under siege, instances of violent excesses by armed units loyal to the ANC, especially the less disciplined Self-Defence Units (SDUs), inevitably arose.[61] Yet overall, MK discipline held fast, and despite any discord that existed between ANC elites and MK, no political or military factions splintered off. The onset of negotiations and legalization of the ANC and SACP overtook MK's efforts to infiltrate senior leadership into the country or establish armed networks there. Nonetheless, key MK leaders, especially Hani, Kasrils and Maharaj, insisted that these structures be maintained and MK's arms caches be kept hidden 'in case the political negotiations ultimately failed.'[62]

Although MK made important advances in the late 1980s during Operation Vula, it nevertheless remained 'questionable what commitment the externalized ANC leadership had to utilize those gains.'[63] As far back as the ANC's 1969 Morogoro conference, the main line of cleavage between the ANC's elites and its rank and file, particularly the MK cadres, was discord over the movement's commitment to armed struggle (see Chapter Two). An MK document published several months after Mandela's release noted: 'We have to boldly admit that had it not been for maladministration and improper coordination between our structures we would have been much further [along].' The document noted the disjuncture between MK cadres' high motivation and capabilities, and the inconsistent and neglectful political leadership guiding its operations.[64] The start of negotiations introduced a period of ambivalence within MK about its role amid the regime's mounting violence. After De Klerk's watershed declaration on 2 February 1990, the ANC responded the following day from Lusaka to emphasize that 'the notion of the ANC unilaterally abandoning armed struggle is out of the question,' and that the movement would abide by the position it had outlined in the 1989 Harare Declaration: 'any ceasing of hostilities will have to be negotiated and will arise out of a mutually-binding cease-fire.'[65] There was nevertheless resistance among MK cadres towards compromise with the regime. One MK cadre, 'who felt that something was "drastically wrong,"' described how the armed wing's leadership was 'summoned [by the political leadership]…and they told us there was no way the ANC would just go into talks. In 1988 the rumours surfaced again, and we were again told that there would be no talks.'[66]

After the ANC was unbanned, MK struggled to repatriate as many of its cadres as possible in an orderly fashion. MK cadres could only enter South Africa legally if they had received indemnity for the 'crimes' of illegally leaving the country and receiving military training, of which all MK cadres were by definition guilty; others who had been involved in operations inside South Africa were also wanted for other offences. The regime granted indemnity fairly readily to the movement's top leadership, with a few notable exceptions, such as Chris Hani. But for MK operatives in the forward areas trying to infiltrate and consolidate MK's position inside South Africa, waiting for the ANC office in Lusaka to submit their applications for indemnity was a laborious process that forced them to surrender initiative to the regime and also put them in danger. In his autobiography *Long Walk to Freedom*, Nelson Mandela recounts visiting 25 MK political prisoners during the negotiations to try to persuade them to accept the government's offer of amnesty and leave Robben Island. These guerrillas were 'fiercely opposed' to the negotiations and 'maintained that they would leave only after victory on the battlefield,' demanding unconditional amnesty instead of having to enumerate their crimes to receive indemnity. Mandela wrote that he 'could sympathize with' the MK cadres' arguments, 'but they were being unrealistic...such a victory was out of reach. The struggle was now at the negotiating table.' He persuaded them 'to accept the government's offer.'[67]

After a round of talks held from 2 to 4 May 1990 in Cape Town, both sides issued a joint communiqué, the Groote Schuur Minute. One key point of tension between the ANC leadership and its rank and file was that in negotiations with the NP over indemnity, the former omitted mention of ANC underground and MK cadres operating clandestinely within the country. During a meeting in May 1990, Mac Maharaj, as one of Vula's commanders, castigated Joe Slovo for failing to explicitly mention these cadres and ensure their safety in the Minute's text. Slovo insisted that these cadres' protection was 'implied' in the statement's wording, to which Maharaj retorted: 'De Klerk is not going to protect us by implication.'[68] Maharaj's concerns would be borne out, as he and Siphiwe Nyanda were arrested by the Security Branch and detained before the ANC leadership's intervention to secure their release. In the case of the MK rank and file deployed inside South Africa, however, there was no understanding or agreement to prevent the regime from arresting, or assassinating, MK cadres.

Although MK guerrillas were ostensibly granted indemnity from prosecution in exchange for renouncing violence,[69] the apartheid security forces faced no comparable restrictions. Armed might was the regime's main field of leverage as the trade unions and political organizations, now unbanned, launched mass actions, paralysing South Africa's economy and giving the ANC the upper hand in negotiations. Despite the ongoing negotiations, 'to all intents and purposes, South Africa remained in a state of civil war.'[70] The transitional period created a political and legal grey zone between negotiations and violence. During this time, MK forces were caught in limbo: they were now legally permitted to be in South Africa, but they were frequently stopped or arrested by the apartheid security forces, which continued to strike covertly at the ANC's leadership and security capacities. According to several ex-guerrillas, until 1994 it was still 'open season' for the regime to target guerrillas, and apartheid death squads roamed the land.[71] Sipho Binda relates that when the negotiations began, the MK cadres imprisoned on Robben Island saw this turnabout as the result of 'our struggle. Was not because of change of heart but at the same time we said, gosh, we need to be careful. They are unbanning us so as to clobber us...we know that there are special forces' and askaris 'out to murder, assassinate us and destabilize the whole process.'[72] MK veteran James Ngculu recalls, 'there were concerns that by returning to South Africa we were entering a slaughterhouse,' and MK operatives questioned whether the ANC leadership had given this issue sufficient thought.[73] Cadres entering South Africa without indemnity risked arrest or assassination at the hands of the security forces, which had stepped up screening and surveillance at the border crossings and continued to compare travellers against the police album of known MK operatives. Ngculu crossed the border in disguise, keeping as low a profile as possible, because transit hubs such as Mmabatho and Mafikeng were known to be 'infested with askaris at the time.'[74] Manong describes being 'very nervous about returning to South Africa so soon after the unbanning of the ANC, especially after reading a lot of stories in the newspapers about the sudden disappearance of ex-MK cadres immediately after their arrival in the country, only to find their dead bodies dumped somewhere in an isolated and open veld.'[75] Apartheid death squads were deployed throughout South Africa and also in the Bantustans; Vlakplaas officer Lucas Ras testified to the TRC that after negotiations began, Vlakplaas was 'already working in Bophuthatswana' where it assisted local security forces 'with the arrest of ANC and PAC members.'[76] Just before Maharaj's arrest on 26 July 1990 under the Internal Security Act, Charles Nqakula's ANC network 'picked up the presence in Cape Town of former MK cadres who were askaris,' forcing them to conduct 'impeccable' counter-surveillance to avoid capture: 'We reported the enemy manoeuvres and the askari presence in our area and were advised to leave the Western Province and go into hiding' in Transkei. Nqakula recalls that Kopman, an MK cadre who was his section commander at MK's Pango base in Angola, was assassinated in 1992.[77]

The ANC also sought its own opportunities to strike. O'Malley writes that shortly after Mandela's release, Jacob Zuma was approached by a Security Branch member who was part of a team selected to assassinate Mandela; to prove his sincerity, the informant turned over to the ANC a rifle with a sniper scope that was to be used in the hit. Through Operation Bible, the Vula leadership had become aware of a vicious turf war between two Security Branch commanders. Maharaj and Nyanda contemplated sowing chaos by using the sniper rifle to assassinate one of the commanders, as the weapon would be traced to the regime's own arsenal; however, the opportunity never presented itself.[78]

Vula Exposed

On 7 July 1990, Vusi Ninela, an askari working for the Security Branch in Durban, arrested MK guerrilla Charles Zakhele Ndaba.[79] Ndaba, who went by the travelling name 'MK Zwelake,' had been a former commander in MK's Natal wing and had infiltrated South Africa in February via Swaziland to play a key role in Operation Vula. He had been personally selected by Vula commander Siphiwe Nyanda; according to Port Natal Security Branch intelligence unit chief Hendrik Botha, Ndaba was already working as a double agent inside MK. Botha claimed the ANC was experiencing intense paranoia about being infiltrated by spies during this period, which actually made his work easier, as he told the TRC: 'when I approached Ndaba he had two choices: firstly, to go and tell of my approach and run the risk of being suspected of being an informer or secondly to keep quiet and play along.'[80] Ndaba supposedly chose the second option and cooperated with the Security Branch, which proceeded to unravel his MK cell: the same day, they seized at gunpoint Vula operative Mbuso Shabalala after the latter met Ndaba at a rendezvous point near the deserted Greyville racecourse. Shabalala had been 'a teacher and a legend in the [Durban] area for his work in the UDF,'[81] before becoming Vula's combat department chief; Ndaba and Shabalala were tasked with training 'ANC activists in the use of weapons in the African townships around Durban.'[82] After his arrest, Ndaba also 'gave addresses of the Vula operation's safe houses in Durban, compromising the entire operation.'[83] On searching Ndaba and Shabalala, 'the police discovered several apparently non-encrypted computer diskettes containing, among other information, listings of ANC underground operatives, safe houses, arms caches, meeting places, and contact telephone, modem, and beeper numbers.'[84] Acting on this information, police also seized arms caches consisting of various small arms as well as 122 mm rockets, high explosives, and a surface-to-air missile. On 12 July, the SAP apprehended Nyanda and ANC stalwart Rayman Lalla in Kenville, a Durban suburb.[85] It was a sizeable blow to MK's ongoing secret operations.

According to former Durban Security Branch policeman Casper van der Westhuizen, after their arrest both Ndaba and Shabalala were unlawfully detained and assaulted. 'They were taken to a safe house in Verulam where they were questioned about ANC and Umkhonto we Sizwe operations.'[86] Van der Westhuizen told the TRC that Ndaba cooperated with his captors, while Shabalala did not. At the time, the SAP denied having detained Ndaba and Shabalala, despite widespread suspicion within the ANC that they were in the regime's custody; as with many other details of apartheid covert operations, their fates were only revealed by Eugene de Kock during his trial after the transition.[87] Ndaba became agitated after learning of Nyanda's arrest on 12 July.[88] Botha told the TRC that 'Ndaba had become "uncertain of his future" and it was recommended that he [undergo] plastic surgery as his informer status had been compromised.' According to Van der

Westhuizen, Ndaba 'became very depressed' and 'started acting irrationally,' threatening to return to the ANC and 'report back to them that he was an informer for the Security Branch' and also to make public the details of Shabalala's abduction.[89] According to Botha, since Ndaba had been an informer, his defection to the ANC would have endangered the Security Branch's broader network of informers within the liberation movement. 'There was a great possibility that Ndaba had realised that there were other police informers in Operation Vula, which was, indeed, the position. If he had conveyed these suspicions to the ANC, the ANC would have started a witch-hunt and the informers' lives would mean nothing.'[90] Botha explained: 'that's when I decided he should be eliminated along with Shabalala, who could [not] be released or charged lawfully anyway.'[91] Because the regime had already denied having Shabalala in custody, releasing him would have embarrassed the government, 'and he would have told the ANC about his unlawful abduction and detention.'[92]

Based on the former Security Branch officers' testimonies to the TRC, Dumisa Ntsebeza, the chairperson presiding over the amnesty hearing for Ndaba's and Shabalala's killing, raised doubts about whether Ndaba had indeed been a spy. Addressing Van der Westhuizen during his testimony to the TRC, Ntsebeza noted that although Ndaba had supposedly been recruited as an agent in 1988, he had no contact with his Security Branch handlers until May 1990, and after being detained he had been accorded no special privileges while in police custody, being held alongside Shabalala from the moment of their arrest until their deaths. This led Ntsebeza to draw an entirely different conclusion about Ndaba's status: 'I put it to you that Ndaba in fact wasn't an informer and the way that you treated him indicated that he, like Shabalala, had been picked up and he was treated in exactly the same way as Shabalala was, and in that sense the probabilities are that he wasn't an informer.'[93] Furthermore, according to Van der Westhuizen, during Shabalala's time in custody the Security Branch made no attempt to 'turn' him as an informer or an askari. Ndaba might also have 'acted in a double capacity as an ANC/MK "infiltration agent" while posing as a police informant.'[94]

Towards midnight on 12 July,[95] Security Branch policemen took Ndaba and Shabalala, bound and blindfolded, telling them that they were being moved to a second safe house, this time in northern Natal.[96] The policemen secretly took both men to the banks of the Tugela River where they shot them dead, weighted their bodies with rocks, and dumped them into the water. They then took Shabalala's Toyota Corolla, in which he had been detained, doused it with petrol and incinerated it. Van der Westhuizen acknowledged that the murders had been illegal but insisted they had 'happened in a war situation, where the rules of normal warfare are not relevant.' He also claimed: 'These actions were necessary to prevent embarrassment to the government and to help the National Party succeed in their negotiation process or position.'[97]

Following Ndaba's and Shabalala's arrest, the SAP appointed Col. Zen de Beer to head a national team to investigate Operation Vula; this quickly sought the whereabouts of the two recently arrested high-ranking MK operatives.[98] Yet SAP Gen. Steyn and Col. Botha later testified to the TRC 'that they actively concealed the whereabouts and the information, or the arrest of [Ndaba and Shabalala] and their whereabouts, from their superiors and also from Zen de Beer's investigative team.'[99] In March 1997, deputy defence minister Ronnie Kasrils noted that according to emerging evidence, information about Ndaba's and Shabalala's murders had reached the highest levels, underscoring the National Party's complicity: 'The record shows that De Klerk was closely briefed by his security police chiefs immediately after the disappearance of Ndaba and Tshabalala... The discovery of those bodies is the strongest evidence of the double-track strategy that De Klerk was following at the time of the negotiations.'[100]

Operation Vula had gone into high gear as the negotiations began, with Ronnie Kasrils infiltrating South Africa on 23 March to coordinate operations from inside the country. As the networks broadened, the ANC underground maintained brisk communications with headquarters in Lusaka, and 'vast amounts of encrypted data flowed along the wires,' coordinating operations inside the country and sending intelligence reports to prepare the ANC's leadership in exile to deal with the realities on the ground in South Africa.[101] MK also continued to bring vast quantities of weaponry into the country. The operation reached its peak in mid-1990, just prior to its leadership being detained on 14 July. After arresting Ndaba and Shabalala, the

Security Branch then lay in wait at a prearranged meeting place for the arrested cadres and other MK operatives, whom they detained in turn. According to O'Brien, a Security Branch mole inside the ANC tipped them off to Vula's existence, leading to the arrest of many undercover ANC operatives inside the country. However, the regime's claim that its moles had infiltrated Vula could have been an 'attempt to save face' in the light of the extensive underground network the ANC had managed to establish under the securocrats' noses: it seems just as likely that having arrested Ndaba, the Security Branch then stumbled upon the wider network by chance.[102] Vula operatives had carelessly violated the rule of keeping the computer-based communication system's various components separate, and so provided an intelligence bonanza for the regime. Nonetheless, Jenkin writes that the ANC's communications system was 'so sophisticated by this stage that it took but one day to repair the damage.' Maharaj and Kasrils rushed to Durban and found that although Vula had been compromised, with four cadres legally in South Africa and six more undercover cadres having been arrested, nonetheless 'the structures were developed enough to contain the damage and prevent any further arrests and police penetration,' and the underground network established by Vula continued to function smoothly.[103] Shubin claims that Vula's underground machinery 'remained largely intact' after the arrests, and ANC headquarters was able to 're-establish contact with the machinery a week later.'[104]

On 18 July 1990, in an emergency meeting with Maharaj following Mandela's return from a six-week global tour, the latter learned about Nyanda's and Shabalala's arrest, as well as 'the observation and surveillance' surrounding Maharaj, prompting Mandela to call De Klerk directly and tell him: 'I've got to meet you.'[105] Also, on 18 July, Chris Hani addressed 3,000 students at the University of Transkei in Umtata, declaring that 'the ANC might have to "seize power"' if the regime did not negotiate seriously with the ANC, and that 'the struggle still goes on. We are still deploying our cadres inside South Africa and that's no secret.' Hani insisted that the ANC needed to negotiate from a position of 'political and military strength,' prompting De Klerk to announce that he intended to raise the issue during his next meeting with Mandela, as Hani's speech 'militated against the words and the spirit of the Groote Schuur Minute.' Hani's response came on 20 July, when, dressed in an MK uniform and carrying an AK-47, and flanked by bodyguards wielding AKs, he addressed a crowd of ANC loyalists at an Mthatha rally, 'saying he has no regrets about his statement, while he expresses hope that the comments will not be used by the regime as a "red herring" in the next rounds of talks.' Hani emphasized that the Groote Schuur Minute did not commit the ANC to abandoning the armed struggle: 'I said we must prepare ourselves and Umkhonto we Sizwe in such a way that if this government decides to go back and push back the present momentum, then Umkhonto we Sizwe is duty-bound to mobilize itself and continue with operations.'[106]

Vula operatives benefited from an SAP misstep. After making the initial arrests on 12 June, the Durban Security Branch did not notify their Johannesburg counterparts until 16 June, apparently because the Durban police were still tracking down MK safe houses and arms caches and had not wanted to raise the alarm. This delay helped dozens more MK cadres to evade capture.[107] Nonetheless, on 25 July the Security Branch arrested Mac Maharaj, prompting Kasrils to return underground. Maharaj appeared in court along with seven others, facing charges of 'terrorism'; they were accused of '[conspiring] to create an underground network the task of which would be to recruit, train, lead and arm a "people's" or "revolutionary" army between July 1988 and July 1990, to be used to seize power from the government by means of an armed insurrection,' smuggling in weapons, establishing safe houses, modifying vehicles to conceal weapons and equipment, and compiling intelligence on police and army installations and officers who could be targeted.[108] The Security Branch would claim to have discovered over 15 Vula safe houses 'in Durban and Johannesburg alone.'[109]

From the regime's perspective, Vula's discovery was a 'nightmare scenario,' the trigger for a 'revolutionary war inside South Africa,' following which the NP accused the ANC of developing a 'terrorist network' and 'negotiating in bad faith.'[110] The regime seized the opportunity to launch a Stratcom operation designed to drive a wedge between the ANC and SACP and to blame the incipient Third Force violence on an alleged MK plan for armed insurrection. On 21 July, Adriaan Vlok phoned Mandela to warn him that the next day's papers would lead with news about an SACP conspiracy. This news blitz was followed by statements by Vlok's spokesman, Peet Bothma, and by an anonymous police source, blaming the uptick in violence on the SACP and alleging that the Vula operatives detained in Natal, Transvaal and elsewhere and numbering 'up to forty,' constituted a unit 'so secret that not even MK's conventional command structure knew of it.'[111] This unit was allegedly under the command of a parallel structure within the ANC's NEC that thought the negotiations would fail and were secretly preparing to launch an armed uprising in that eventuality. The Security Branch also released ANC communications it claimed to have seized alleging that Maharaj and Zuma were planning to assassinate Mandela, 'then accuse the regime and mobilize the fury of the masses to overthrow the government and seize power.'[112] Vula's discovery gave the securocrats leverage to pressure De Klerk to take a hard line with the ANC in negotiations on security matters.[113] Yet as the regime sought to transform its intelligence haul into political leverage against the ANC, 'the police [overplayed] their hand,'[114] releasing allegations that were demonstrably false: in a meeting with Mandela, De Klerk alleged that among the 2,000 pages of documents seized by the SAP were minutes of secret SACP meetings in which Joe Slovo, the plan's alleged mastermind, predicted the talks would fail and encouraged planning for an armed uprising. But when Mandela confronted Slovo with the allegations, the latter insisted that the regime had 'distorted' the documents' actual contents, which made it 'clear that the Communist Party agrees with negotiations' and that the documents even 'compliment Mr De Klerk for having the courage to come out openly and call for a change of the political system.' Slovo then gave Mandela 'a copy of the documents so he [could] see for himself.'[115] Henderson notes that De Klerk and his cabinet may also have doubted whether the Security Branch's claims of a widespread communist plot were true, especially after SADF MI had misled the government in October 1989 about a non-existent SWAPO plot to violate agreements and seize power by force in Namibia.[116]

The ANC then demonstrated its mastery of the political sphere, when Mandela told a gathering of foreign ambassadors on 28 July that the regime was trying to drive a wedge between the ANC and SACP, but that Slovo would participate in the negotiations 'whether De Klerk likes it or not.'[117] The following day, Mandela, Slovo and Hani addressed a rally at Soccer City Stadium in which Mandela insisted that the ANC was not a communist organization and warned that the regime's allegations against Slovo and the SACP were 'an insult manufactured by the enemies of democracy.'[118] In turn, Slovo and Hani addressed the assembled crowd, highlighting the regime's duplicity and emphasizing that the ANC and SACP must remain united and vigilant. Ultimately, as would repeatedly occur during the negotiation process, Mandela and De Klerk defused the latest crisis by making conciliatory statements and concessions at a meeting in Pretoria, culminating in the ANC's renunciation of armed struggle on 6 August 1990. The regime released most of the Vula detainees for lack of evidence, but Maharaj and seven other triallists remained imprisoned. When, on 20 August, the government announced that indemnity for certain offences had been granted for 41 ANC and SACP figures, Hani, Kasrils and Maharaj were not among them. Hani was granted indemnity one month later, while Maharaj remained imprisoned and Kasrils was still hunted by police.[119]

The remaining Vula triallists were ultimately released on 8 November 1990 on R300,000 bail after their propaganda value to the regime expired; it had become clear that the regime would not succeed in using Vula to play the ANC and SACP against each other during negotiations. But the regime continued its hunt for four suspects whom it dubbed 'armed and extremely dangerous' – 'Ronnie Kasrils, Janet Love, Charles Ndaba and Christopher Manye – in connection with the illegal importation of arms, ammunition and explosives.'[120] Jenkin notes that the timing of the SAP's announcement about these fugitives, coming four months after the Vula operatives' arrest, seemed calculated to cover up the Security Branch's killing of Ndaba and Shabalala, whose fates remained unknown at that point. Meanwhile, the Security Branch continued to hunt for underground Vula operatives; the assassination of computer technician Nic Cruse with a 'sophisticated' parcel bomb on 2 October 1990 was apparently linked to 'the search for additional Vula operatives still in hiding.'[121]

On 22 March 1991, in keeping with the understandings reached in the Pretoria and Groote Schuur Minutes, the nine Vula triallists and Kasrils were finally indemnified against prosecution. The remaining Vula detainees were finally released in April; on 22 June, 12 Vula operatives who had been in hiding to elude police were finally indemnified and 'unmasked' by Mandela at his Johannesburg home. That same day, the Inkathagate scandal broke (see Chapter Three), and accusations that the ANC had negotiated in bad faith were overshadowed by explosive evidence that the NP was doing the same.

Operation Vula lasted until February 1991, as the ANC recognized the need to remain vigilant vis-à-vis the regime, and to maintain structures and weapons caches that could be activated should the need arise. Although Vula is remembered largely for the underground ANC structures that were compromised when the regime uncovered them, Jenkin insists that it actually gave the regime 'a major shock' that 'shattered' its 'complacency' when the NP realized the ANC had become far more powerful and sophisticated, including in its capacity to recruit spies: 'when they discovered that their security apparatus was thoroughly infiltrated with "moles" who were passing confidential information to the ANC via Vula they must have felt very unsafe indeed.'[122] Vula also had symbolic power: although its structures would have faced a steep challenge in any general insurrection against regime forces, 'the operation and its participants attained the same respected status that World War II resistance movements in France, the Netherlands, and other European countries have been given for their efforts against wartime Nazi occupation.'[123] After the Security Branch uncovered Vula, De Klerk's government admitted that its counter-intelligence units had discovered multiple ANC moles within the SAP 'and were hunting an additional seven "codenames" described as "low level" infiltration.' The SADF was also conducting a 'spy hunt' of its own, 'with no indication of the numbers or level of infiltration.'[124] Moreover, Vula had established 'a penetration network of over twenty secret facilities,' and a year after the transition, Henderson described the ANC's recruitment of moles in the intelligence services as 'resulting in a major and possibly ongoing "mole hunt."'[125] However, Vula's exposure also raised questions about collaboration from within MK. According to Maharaj, the Security Branch accessed so much key information because Nyanda had left disks unencrypted, 'a severe breach of discipline.'[126] Subsequently, Maharaj realized that many of the details that the Special Branch had gleaned about Vula safe houses could only have been divulged by Nyanda during his interrogation while in custody; it then emerged that

Nyanda had helped his interrogators decipher Vula communications. Under different circumstances, Nyanda's extensive disclosures to the police during interrogation and in court 'might have been construed as turning state witness,' but the broader direction of negotiations overshadowed such considerations.[127]

Renouncing Armed Struggle

At an SACP conference in Natal on 19–20 May 1990, Nyanda announced that the ANC would sign an agreement with the government to suspend armed operations. Nyanda underscored that MK would still need to maintain a military capability to defend itself from groups such as the Afrikaner Weerstandsbeweging (AWB) and Inkatha, which would not be bound by this agreement.[128] Then, in talks held at the Union Building on 6 August, Mandela, joined by Slovo and Joe Modise, announced a suspension of the ANC's armed struggle, declaring 'a cease-fire with immediate effect' and an end to 'the infiltration of men and arms into South Africa.'[129] This was the key stipulation contained in a memorandum that would become known as the Pretoria Minute. Simpson notes that the regime would have expected the ANC's announcement 'given the intelligence acquired during the suppression of Operation Vula.'[130] According to one ANC leader, suspending armed struggle served to advance negotiations and also gave the ANC the moral high ground vis-à-vis the regime in the eyes of the international community.[131] Yet the ANC's renunciation of its armed struggle 'came as a shock to MK cadres,' who had been preparing 'to exploit the new conditions of legality to build the people's army, open up better communication, and intensify armed actions as a strategy to expedite the negotiations with the regime.'[132] The ANC's 1989 Harare Declaration had stipulated: 'any suspension of the armed struggle would have to come through a negotiated "mutually binding cease-fire."'[133] MK chief of operations Lambert Moloi described addressing a meeting of about 600 cadres in Lusaka following the renunciation of the armed struggle. The cadres wanted to continue fighting but Moloi told them that attacking without a plan or logistics would be 'playing into the hands of the enemy. And the enemy was ready for us. They were waiting for it.'[134]

Many MK cadres felt marginalized during the negotiations not because they were unwilling to negotiate with the enemy – a development they had expected – but because the ANC had risked 'the fruits of revolution' by unilaterally ending the armed struggle.[135] Illustrating the disconnect between ANC elites and MK, Mathews Phosa recalled that the day before 'the Pretoria discussions...there was a headline in the morning saying the ANC suspends the armed struggle. There was nothing as bad as going to the negotiations with the enemy knowing what you are going to concede... That was killing us when we were in those negotiations. But we went as disciplined cadres of the movement and engaged in a dignified way.'[136] Interviewed in 1993, Lerumo Kalako insisted that the decision to suspend armed struggle would have needed to 'involve the membership of the ANC' and 'especially the army, MK.' The leadership would have had to explain negotiations, so the rank and file could 'understand politically the importance, why you have to suspend armed struggle. Because that is one element that starts to disgruntle people even within our own ranks.' Once the leadership had made the decision, claimed Kalako, 'immediately the MK was started from then [on] to be neglected completely.' This marginalization of MK harmed the ANC's position overall because it 'tended not to tally with the reality of the situation. Because if you remember, we started all this process at the time when there was a very high level of violence in the country. So, people couldn't understand why we are negotiating despite that or why we are not giving orders to MK [to safeguard ANC strongholds].'[137]

The ANC's suspension of armed struggle was followed immediately by 'an "unprecedented wave of violence"' that 'centred around Johannesburg's townships, in which over 500 people died within a 10-day period.'[138] The onslaught posed an existential threat to ANC structures within South Africa: Kalako emphasized the need to address 'this violence' – 'how our people have been killed by Inkatha' in KwaZulu-Natal and around Johannesburg – as a key priority 'for our structures to survive.'[139] Suspending the armed struggle thus restricted MK's ability to defend itself and communities loyal to the ANC. In much of the country, MK activity was limited mainly to training poorly armed, loosely organized Self-Defence Units instead of using their superior training and weaponry to defend communities themselves.

Meanwhile, the ANC leadership aimed to 'remove all obstacles in the way to democratic consolidation.'[140] The ANC nevertheless rejected the regime's attempts to impose further conditions that would have ended MK recruitment and training, disbanded underground formations, forced the ANC to disarm and cease forms of mass mobilization such as strikes, boycotts, and work stayaways.[141] On 9 August, speaking on the ANC's behalf at a press conference, Mathews Phosa stressed that the ANC would nonetheless not 'surrender weapons, now and even in the future. Those structures, arms, and men are to remain where they are.'[142] Chris Hani counterbalanced the latest ANC concession by reiterating MK's posture of vigilance: in an address to the annual conference of the National General Council of the Congress of South African Students in Umtata on 12 August, Hani declared that MK would maintain a state of readiness and would actually increase training and recruitment.[143] Following the Pretoria Minute, MK began preparing to integrate into the new security forces, even as the police and military waged a counterinsurgency campaign.[144] The concessions were an important step towards avoiding outright civil war, but in the immediate term the ANC had de-clawed its armed wing at the precise moment when the regime escalated its campaign of clandestine violence in KwaZulu-Natal and in the Reef around Johannesburg. In particular, the illegality of MK's automatic weapons, and the ban on the military training of new recruits within South Africa, were aspects that hamstrung MK's capacity to defend itself.

The DF Malan Accords

On 12 February 1991, Mandela and De Klerk met at Cape Town's DF Malan airport to follow up on the understandings laid down in the Pretoria Minute. The meeting resulted in the DF Malan Accord, in which the ANC agreed that suspending the armed struggle was a step towards finding a peaceful solution and committed itself to ceasing the following activities: armed attacks; infiltration of cadres and weapons; forming underground structures; inciting violence or threatening armed action; and the military training of cadres within South Africa. For its part, the apartheid regime allowed that MK was a legal organization to which ANC members could belong, without violating the Pretoria Minute; it accepted the existence of MK cadres and weaponry inside South Africa, and MK's ongoing right to recruit and train cadres outside South Africa; it prepared to legalize some of MK's non-automatic weaponry; allowed the ANC's and MK's 'existing underground structures'; and conceded that some MK cadres could be indemnified.[145] The NP and the ANC also agreed that MK need not be disbanded until South Africa's democratic transition was complete, and that in the interim the NP would tolerate MK instead of regarding it as an illegal 'private army.' In return, MK would provide the government with an inventory of the weaponry it possessed, which 'would be placed under the joint control of a transitional authority once an interim government was formed.'[146] An MK communiqué noted that the armed wing had 'made a major contribution and sacrifice' towards the progress of negotiations 'by having steadfastly observed the ANC directive in terms of the agreements with the government to suspend armed operations,' a restraint born of 'the strong discipline of our cadres and their deep-seated commitment to peace, freedom, and the establishment of democracy in South Africa.'[147] MK operative Rocky Williams likewise noted: 'MK commanders have upheld the importance of subordinating military activities to those of the political leadership,' maintaining such discipline despite the regime's ongoing predation.[148] On 9 August 1991, Nelson Mandela told MK members gathered at a conference in Thohoyandou, Venda, that despite the ANC's suspension of armed struggle, 'it is precisely because of our keen awareness of the dangers inherent in the minority regime's determination to cling on to power that we dare not relax our vigilance and we dare not permit this MK to disintegrate or wither away.' Mandela told the assembled cadres that the ANC and MK needed 'to assist the masses in devising the appropriate response to state-sponsored and vigilante violence' ravaging ANC strongholds.[149] Yet the contrast was stark between the ANC's official statements about MK's role and its unresponsiveness in the face of Third Force violence. Indeed, after the ANC unilaterally renounced armed struggle, its top leadership maintained little contact with and exercised minimal leadership over its armed wing. They also refused to implement MK contingency plans to protect ANC strongholds ringing Johannesburg and Pretoria that were beset by waves of political violence: as Somadoda Fikeni described, the MK fighters 'had seen during negotiations the [Third Force] killings in the township of Boipatong and they said, we could take up arms and defend – they were stopped [by the ANC leadership].'[150]

Fumanikile Booi told the TRC that after the ANC was unbanned, MK operations during this period took place in the context of a tenuous arrangement with the NP government: 'Ourselves and the government had a mutual understanding that [MK cadres] are inside the country, we are armed, the police had that knowledge. They had instructions that when you arrest MK cadres, they will proceed to the police and we'll inform our own commanders and then that will be a negotiation between them.' If the police charged MK cadres for possession of firearms they would be 'breaching the agreements' because the NP 'government knew that we are armed, and we are inside the country.'[151] Nonetheless, it remained difficult for cadres to obtain firearm licences, and the regime continued to detain or arrest them for possessing firearms. In such instances, the ANC leadership was not always willing to intervene on their behalf, as Hani would do after Booi's arrest in January 1992 for his involvement in the Gugulethu incident described above. Booi was refused bail, prompting Hani himself to appear in court in July 1992 to secure Booi's release. '[Hani] actually told the magistrate that he is there in the court because I was on a political mission, under his command and his instruction, and he believed whatever we've done was under the political blanket of the ANC and the liberation movement Umkhonto we Sizwe.'

But Hani's advocacy on cadres' behalf during this period was the exception within the ANC leadership. At an ANC consultative conference in December 1990, Mandela reassured cadres that he had 'warned the regime that the ANC's suspension of armed struggle was conditional,' adding that the ANC would 'constantly test the validity of' the armed struggle option 'against the government's actions.'[152] At its July 1991 Durban conference, the ANC had made four resolutions concerning MK. Firstly, it should remain combat ready; secondly, 'the ANC accepts full responsibility for cadres arrested and tried in the execution of their duties while defending the people'; thirdly, the ANC would establish and expand 'MK structures at all levels including the opening of offices'; and fourthly, 'The ANC would maintain and develop MK until a democratic constitution was adopted and a new defence force was created into which MK cadres would be integrated.'[153]

Yet Lerumo Kalako highlighted the discrepancy between the ANC's revolutionary statements during this period and its reluctance to actually deploy MK to safeguard besieged communities: 'At that time there was a tendency [for] the leadership of the ANC to actually call for people to arm themselves…going on slogans saying MK is around, [yet] knowing very much that MK is disarmed by the very agreement of the negotiations…[the DF Malan Accord] and other accords which couldn't do anything' to stop the ongoing violence. The ANC leadership knew 'very well that this had opened us to imprisonment if you're starting [to defend communities against regime violence]. So, we have on our side to tell people that no, forget it, those are slogans… If you want to defend yourself, you can organize yourself in the areas and ask us to help you.' Furthermore, while MK cadres helped to organize local communities' Self-Defence Units, under the terms of the negotiations they were largely powerless to arm them against well-equipped assailants: 'Don't expect us MK and ANC won't give you any arms… We left our arms in the armoury there.' Even MK units which maintained secret arms caches could not access them 'because there's no one who will want to take out arms, AKs, and after that [get] arrested.' Kalako underscored the ANC leadership's unresponsiveness to MK cadres who had been arrested while protecting ANC strongholds: 'And what was worst, comrades [who had been] helping communities who are under attack trying to defend them were arrested and no, ANC didn't want to take responsibility to try to defend those comrades. They are serving sentences. They are treated as criminals. So that is one other element.'[154] Another MK cadre, Fraser Delisa Shamase, compared MK's situation during the transition with that of the SWAPO fighters killed by Koevoet on the eve of Namibian independence (see Chapter Three), claiming that MK's resolve to defend against regime depredations was hampered by a lack of access to weaponry: 'We are not expecting South Africa to be afraid like Namibia. Because in Namibia 200 [SWAPO] soldiers died, were killed [while] simply waiting for the United Nations [to intervene]. In our situation, how are we going to guard the gains of our revolution? We've got the army, we've got MK, but how many of them are armed? You can't get a licence for a pistol.'[155]

The Self-Defence Units

After the DF Malan Accord, as Third Force violence escalated, the ANC released its guidelines for assembling Self-Defence Units, contained in a 31-page pamphlet titled *For the Sake of Our Lives: Guidelines for the Creation of People's Defence Units*, authored by the SACP's Jeremy Cronin. The ANC had determined 'that MK cadres will lead in the formation of Self-Defence Units' (SDUs).[156] Recognizing that the ANC's failure to defend its supporters 'will inevitably lead to a loss of confidence in the ANC and the liberation movement,' the guidelines called for 'MK cadres, particularly ex-prisoners and those due to return from exile,' to 'play a leading and active role in the establishment of the defence.' Cronin's pamphlet called for MK cadres to support the SDUs, and MK fighters were often at the forefront of setting them up. Due to the urgency of the crisis, SDU cadres' level of training rarely exceeded a crash course of several weeks.[157] Training varied from unarmed military-style drills to handling armaments. Cadres also became involved in fighting, 'irrespective of any agreements that were signed calling for a cease-fire or suspension of the armed struggle.'[158] The ANC would further elaborate on the formation of SDUs during its July 1991 conference held in Durban. Speaking to reporters, Chris Hani emphasized: 'we need to ensure there are good command and control structures to prevent them from degenerating into vigilantes and lynch mobs.'[159] Command and control of the SDUs fell to 'the communities, not MK; the duty of MK was to provide military expertise.'[160]

It became impossible to enforce strict discipline within SDU ranks, and violence perpetrated in the ANC's name became more indiscriminate than ever before, even as the ANC leadership blamed the regime for the chaos engulfing South Africa.[161] MK cadres also sought, 'with varying degrees of success, to instill control and discipline' among the SDUs,[162] but the discipline that was inculcated in MK's most highly trained personnel was inevitably diluted. One ex-guerrilla explained that within MK 'there was a culture of discipline, regarding observing standing rules. Regarding punctuality. Orders were obeyed.

131

But then, when somebody disciplined has to work with raw, untrained people, anything could happen.'[163] MK Special Ops commander and logistics chief Aboobaker Ismail noted that the 'SDUs were assisted by MK cadres but the military headquarters deliberately took a decision that they would not get directly involved in the SDUs but that certain members of headquarters and members of MK were told: "Do what you have to do amongst the communities."'[164] Gear contrasts the SDU cadres' ad hoc training within South Africa and the 'thorough political education provided to' MK guerrillas at their bases 'in exile.'[165] Crash-course trainees in particular were prone to using indiscriminate violence: 'Some people got excited by being involved and do all sorts of things in the name of the movement, some of which was uncalled for, even though this person believes he is doing something in the name of liberation, but some people died who were never supposed to have died.'[166] One SDU member in Transkei whose team had killed a white civilian in his car testified to the TRC that during that era SDUs were largely autonomous: 'The ANC deployed well-trained MK members in our respective areas. Those people trained us as Self-Defence Units and then at times they left the area. Then the people who were trained had a right to take the decision on their own.'[167]

As the violence intensified during the transition years, local youths who had not originally been recruited into the SDUs 'saw an opportunity to exert power and influence' by joining them. These became known as comtsotsis: 'they were comrades (belonging to and associating with youth organizations and their members) and at the same time tsotsis (retaining their trade as thugs).'[168] Their impact was to weaken discipline and democratic procedures within SDUs and ANC-affiliated organizations, while fusing politically motivated violence with criminality. When the regime imprisoned thousands of UDF members in the late 1980s, this also left a vacuum in local structures which the comtsotsis filled.[169] Rivalries then arose among various SDUs, which in some cases threatened the very communities they were supposed to protect.[170] The TRC ultimately held the ANC responsible for mass human rights violations because of the deployment of SDUs and their enabling of violence by distributing arms into communities.[171]

The proceedings of an MK conference held at Kanyamazane, Venda, in September 1993 noted the SDUs were 'the only line of people's defence' for most African communities during the transition, and sought to ensure that they abided by MK's own strict disciplinary standards. It found that 'where [SDUs] have been used for criminal, factional, or covert state activities this has resulted from our own failure to perform the necessary role in their creation and supervision.'[172] Hani had also warned of the danger of the SDUs turning to criminality by becoming 'hijacked by criminal elements who want space for themselves so they can continue their criminal activities.' He further claimed that the apartheid government 'has infiltrated our defence units and in certain cases the government infiltrators push the defence units towards carrying out actions against the people. The government wants society to blame the ANC.'[173] Meanwhile, Inkatha, claiming to be the victim of ANC violence, set up its own 'Self-Protection Units' (SPUs), which, along with the SDUs, became involved in vigilantism and a variety of criminal enterprises.[174]

At MK's Kanyamazane conference, cadres decried 'the escalation of violence against our people and the fact that despite repeated resolutions of various ANC and MK conferences, the crucial issue of self-defence has generally been left to spontaneous, haphazard and uncoordinated initiatives of our beleaguered communities.'[175] This ongoing lack of armed protection for African communities targeted by Third Force violence was primarily due to the ANC's unwillingness to authorize MK to organize it. As late as 1993, MK was calling for 'additional MK cadres' to 'be employed on the full-time basis to work with SDUs in all major flashpoint areas,' but the ANC provided no support for these endeavours. MK also resolved to remind the ANC 'to accept full responsibility for cadres arrested and/or detained in the course of their activity in defence of the people.'[176] This was plainly a call for the ANC to honour its commitments to MK made over two years earlier at the Durban conference, underscoring the disconnect between the ANC's negotiators and MK, which was still struggling to protect African communities from state-sponsored violence. At a workshop in King William's Town in the Eastern Cape, Chris Hani acknowledged the ANC's lack of preparation, stating: 'the demand for self-defence has caught us flat-footed. It has come at a time when our underground and MK face serious problems that require far-reaching reorganization and the setting up of strong logistics. If these problems are not attended to promptly, the call for self-defence will degenerate into sheer rhetoric.'[177] As the township violence escalated in 1992 and 1993, the war between SDUs and the IFP featured everything from traditional weaponry to assault rifles and, sometimes, light machine guns, grenades, mortars and rockets.[178]

MK's War against Inkatha

KwaZulu-Natal was the most violent region during South Africa's transition, with approximately 10,000 people killed in political violence between 1990 and 1994, out of a countrywide total of about 14,000.[179] The violence between the ANC–UDF and Inkatha had been raging for years before the negotiations began, nurtured by the regime's strategy of fomenting 'black-on-black' violence (see Chapter Three). For its part, the ANC's operations in KwaZulu-Natal were largely directed by Natal Midlands ANC chief Harry Gwala, a self-described Stalinist who was released from Robben Island in November 1988 and who promptly declared a scorched-earth policy against Inkatha, earning him the reputation of a quasi-warlord. O'Malley insists that in KwaZulu-Natal, 'as in all conflicts, the blame for the carnage rests with all sides'; yet pulling the ANC–UDF and MK into the cycle of killing was precisely the regime's objective, adding fuel to the fire at the opportune moment, then standing back as it scorched everything.[180]

Although MK operations in KwaZulu-Natal during this time were largely coordinated by local ANC leaders, Chris Hani weighed in as well, occasionally deploying MK elements from Transkei to arm MK units and strike Inkatha targets there.[181] In addition to Inkatha militants, MK had to contend with criminal gangs abetted by the regime to destabilize ANC communities. In July 1990, Chris Hani met with three mid-level MK operatives, John Mndebele, Nicolas Zwane and Silos Nkonyane, at the ANC's Shell House headquarters in Johannesburg. The cadres reported that in Wesselton, Ermelo's satellite township some 200 kilometres east of Johannesburg, the SAP, along with Inkatha and its proxy gangs the Black Cats and Black Chain, was terrorizing communities aligned with the ANC and UDF, as well as the population at large.[182] This included Black Chain's attack on schoolchildren in Mbalendle, Secunda.[183] At least 17 people were killed, and scores wounded in the conflict between the Black Cats and the ANC in Ermelo.[184] Hani advised the cadres to set up SDUs and 'do what is necessary to quell the violence.'[185] In 1992, the Goldstone Commission would reveal what the ANC already knew: in Ermelo, the Black Cats were receiving support from the SAP.[186] The Goldstone Commission also heard from two members of the Black Cats who claimed SADF MI had trained them as a hit squad.[187]

In July 1990, MK cadre Mzwandile Gushu joined the ANC chief in Wesselton, Jabi Mkhwanazi, to assist MK 'in normalising the situation which prevailed in Ermelo, Piet Retief and Secunda area.' In Ermelo, the Black Cats were even housed at the local police station.[188] In Gushu's words: 'I could never allow ANC members or the Communist Party to die just like that. I was trained to protect them.'[189] As a well-trained guerrilla, Gushu targeted enemy leaders and also oversaw SDUs' operations and training. These guerrilla operations had decentralized command and control, and cadres would await the opportune moment to strike. As MK cadre Paulos Nkonyane explained: 'You may look for the person and not get him, or you may find that the place where you have to attack the person is not a safe place.'[190] Gushu told the TRC that MK cadres 'tried to get arms in our own way. The [security forces] would take our firearms saying that we were banned.' Gushu had to arm the SDUs and figure out 'how I get those firearms or the money to purchase them,' which included 'armed robbery,' as Gushu said the ANC was unwilling to subsidize arms purchases and 'lived on solidarity all the time.'[191]

On 31 October 1990, a two-man MK team composed of Sipho Motaung and Sibisi Nhlanhla received the order from their commander, 'Mandla,' to kill IFP Midlands leader Lolo Lombo. After tracking Lombo to a department store in Pietermaritzburg, Nhlanhla shot him with a pistol, killing him. The MK team escaped unscathed from the scene, but as they fled in a getaway vehicle along with two other MK operatives, they were apprehended by police.[192] On 1 July 1991, a four-man MK team was stopped by police on their way from Port Shepstone, leading to a shootout in which one was killed, another wounded, a third captured, and a fourth, Joel Makhanya, managed to escape by hiding under a bridge, before making his way to Transkei.[193]

In July 1991, Gushu killed Black Cats leader and Caprivi trainee Jwi Zwane with an AK-47 at a convenience store, wounding Zwane's accomplice.[194] Gushu also participated in killing Advice Gwala, an Inkatha and Black Chain leader in Secunda who had killed ANC members. In late 1991, Gushu met with ANC Youth League chairperson Sithule Hleza in Piet Retief to discuss the war against the IFP. Hleza briefed Gushu, telling him that the township mayor, Alpheus Msibi, was an IFP loyalist who was guarded by askaris and IFP members 'trained at Mpuzwa camp' and based at his house, from which they launched missions to kill local ANC and SACP members. On 12 December, Gushu and Hleza ambushed Msibi outside a bottlestore, wounding him and killing his bodyguard, Themba Mlangeni.[195] On 12 April 1992, Gushu carried out another hit, this time in Wesselton township, killing Chris Ngwenya, assistant to Black Cats leader Jwi Zwane, and IFP Women's League member Lindiwe Nkosi with an AK-47.[196] On 6 July 1992, Gushu was finally wounded in a shootout as he and a colleague sought to seize weaponry hidden on the grounds of the Giwi construction company, whose white owners were training and arming IFP and Black Chain militants. Gushu killed an assailant and wounded another before being shot in the leg; he was taken to hospital and arrested by police.[197]

Inkatha chief Buthelezi regarded MK as a direct threat during the negotiations: on 14 September 1991, he joined Mandela and De Klerk in Johannesburg to negotiate 'a code of conduct for political parties and organizations in the country,' as almost 2,000 IFP supporters protested outside, brandishing traditional weapons and firearms.[198] The IFP's main concern at the meeting was MK and 'its hidden arms caches,' and while the ANC agreed to include in the agreement's final wording the passage 'no private armies shall be allowed or formed,' it insisted that MK 'was a people's army, not a private army.' After the signing ceremony, Mandela declared to the press: 'MK will not be dissolved "now or in the future."' Buthelezi was critical of the negotiations, declaring in an interview two days later: 'How can one talk about peace when there are caches of arms hidden all over the country?'[199] Inkatha's fear of MK was summed up in the words of one IFP supporter to journalist Bill Berkeley: 'MK has been trained to kill the ANC's political enemies. So we fear that if MK is joined with the army, then the Inkatha leadership will be eliminated.'[200]

To support MK operations, ANC chairman for southern Natal Jeff Radebe met with Chris Hani and MK ordnance chief in Maputo Edwin Dlamini in February 1992 to discuss the large-scale smuggling of weaponry through the Golela border post between Mozambique and South Africa. This incident would reveal the tensions between the ANC's top leadership and its mid-level commanders, as well as between the centralized command in Johannesburg and the various regional commands: in this case, when Dlamini sought support from MK Ordnance Department head Aboobaker Ismail (travelling name 'Rachid'), the latter told Dlamini that MK had sufficient quantities of weaponry within South Africa and reminded him that 'Joe Modise [had] instructed that no arms be brought into the country in violation of agreements reached with the South African government.'[201] Nonetheless, Radebe proceeded to coordinate the smuggling of arms into southern Natal for distribution to SDUs in embattled communities there, delegating the task of arms distribution to MK chief of staff for southern Natal Sipho Sithole.[202] This unauthorized initiative ultimately led to 'the unravelling of MK's southern Natal structure,' as on 1 February 1993 border policemen arrested two MK operatives driving a car through the Golela border post carrying arms concealed in a hidden compartment; using intelligence gathered from the interrogation of the arrested MK operatives, on 3 February police arrested Sipho Sithole at the ANC office in Durban. In response, the ANC conducted an internal inquiry in which it found that the southern Natal regional command had organized at least five unauthorized cross-border arms transfers from Maputo to South Africa, suggesting an extensive network maintained without higher-level oversight, and drawing harsh condemnation from the regime.[203]

As ANC and NP regime elites conducted negotiations, MK forces inside South Africa during the transition experienced a high level of fragmentation and dislocation. The ANC's top leadership lacked a cohesive response to Third Force depredations, and in instances where MK guerrillas successfully protected ANC members or targeted enemies during this period, they did so at the behest of local structures or under Chris Hani's leadership. Instead of deploying MK units, the ANC responded to Third Force violence by setting up SDUs. This may have helped to prevent a further escalation of violence between MK and the apartheid security forces, but it worsened indiscriminate violence by ANC loyalists, thus further destabilizing communities.

5

INSURGENCY AND COUNTERINSURGENCY IN THE BANTUSTAN OF TRANSKEI, 1988–94

'The Transkei, show-place of the Bantustan scheme, could well be the first battlefield on which apartheid will be defeated.'
— Govan Mbeki, *The Peasants' Revolt* (1964)

With this prophetic observation, leading ANC member Govan Mbeki concluded his book on Transkei's mass resistance to apartheid rule and the imposition of the Bantustan system. As the first Bantustan to gain independence, Transkei was indeed the 'show-place' of the National Party stratagem of outsourcing the administration of South Africa's black majority to authoritarian rulers loyal to the apartheid regime. As the Bantustan regimes of Transkei, Ciskei, Bophuthatswana, and Venda hardened into self-governing territorial units by the early 1980s, they developed elaborate 'defence' forces to repress domestic unrest. In addition to their own security forces' repression, the Bantustans were exposed to panoptic surveillance and intervention by the South African Defence Force (SADF) and the South African Police (SAP). Although the apartheid regime sought to preserve the illusion of Bantustan sovereignty, the SADF and SAP played important advisory roles in the Bantustan forces, which were trained and often commanded by white officers seconded from South African Military Intelligence (SADF MI).

The apartheid strategy of outsourcing colonial governance to surrogate black authorities must itself be understood through the prism of counterinsurgency. Outsourcing coercion afforded the regime the double benefit of dividing black communities against themselves the more easily to rule them, while also minimizing white combat casualties. Setting up Bantustans as 'independent' entities also gave the apartheid regime a further layer of cover under which to clandestinely deploy its full range of police, military and intelligence forces against insurgents.

Yet the ANC and its armed wing, Umkhonto we Sizwe (MK), actively resisted apartheid counterinsurgency, and although these organizations enjoyed legitimacy in many regions and communities across South Africa, there was a veritable groundswell of popular support for them in Transkei. This was because a significant number of ANC and MK leaders hailed from Transkei and were connected to each other through kinship ties that gave MK deep operational and recruitment networks there – what Gibbs calls its 'social hinterland.'[1] Transkei became especially important to MK after Transkei Defence Force (TDF) Gen. Bantu Holomisa seized power in 1988 and soon began to display an increasingly overt affinity with the ANC and MK.

This chapter's focus is two-fold: it sheds important new light both on MK's armed insurgency and on the apartheid regime's counterinsurgency programme in Transkei in the years leading up to and during South Africa's democratic transition. If, as Barrell asserts, 'ANC armed activity was clearly foundering in the late 1980s,' and the ANC never succeeded in integrating its 'popular political base' with its military struggle, then MK's operations in Transkei during this period represent a crucial case of both its military success and its ability to rally mass support.[2] MK thrived in Transkei as its guerrillas were afforded a secure operating base in socially and geographically hospitable terrain bordering South African territory. This reveals MK's important – and thus far largely unrecognized – role in resisting the apartheid regime's counterinsurgency operations at a critical juncture during South Africa's transition from apartheid. With Holomisa offering its cadres a safe haven, MK was able to operate with far greater freedom than it had enjoyed elsewhere in South Africa, organizing, training and deploying openly even before the February 1990 start of negotiations between Pretoria and the ANC. Whereas MK's inability to sustain a military presence in the rest of South Africa largely confined it to a supporting role alongside the United Democratic Front (UDF) during this era, MK's guerrilla operations were a key component of the ANC's anti-apartheid resistance in Transkei. Indeed, under MK chief of staff Chris Hani, Transkei became MK's centre of gravity even as the start of negotiations saw the ANC move its headquarters to Johannesburg. Apartheid counterinsurgency operations in Transkei intensified from 1988 onward, in parallel with MK's consolidation there.

MK guerrillas were instrumental in thwarting the SADF-engineered November 1990 coup attempt to overthrow Holomisa and install in his stead a dictator sympathetic to the apartheid regime. This represents a rare military victory in MK's history of armed struggle against apartheid, which was greatly facilitated by MK's ability to operate freely on Transkeian territory with the local government's support – a luxury it enjoyed on only one other occasion, in northern Angola's Malanje province, where MK also acquitted itself well in battle, in this case against apartheid-proxy UNITA forces.[3] Rather than being forced to live and operate undercover, MK fighters in Holomisa's Transkei could instead operate openly in a 'liberated zone,'[4] in one of the rare instances in which the ANC's armed wing achieved its objective of 'the setting up of autonomous administration in areas which are under our control or where the enemy, for one reason or another, has forfeited control.'[5] After the beginning of negotiations, the Bantustan of Venda also became sympathetic to MK as the local strongman, Brig. Gabriel Ramushwana, aligned himself with the ANC shortly after its unbanning. However, although MK held a national conference in Venda in 1991 and in 1993, Venda did not become a hub for armed struggle activity as did Transkei.

The apartheid security forces launched numerous clandestine operations to destabilize the Bantustans of Transkei and neighbouring Ciskei, which intensified during the transitional years of 1990–4. These operations included the recruitment of askaris, informers and mercenaries for various coup attempts against leaders in both homelands.

The ANC and MK's Popular Legitimacy in Transkei

The vast majority of the African population rejected Transkei's 'independence' in 1976 and chafed under the rule of Transkeian chief minister and president Kaiser Matanzima.[6] Insulated from the international condemnation of apartheid by their ostensible sovereignty, Matanzima and other Bantustan dictators paradoxically had more leeway to repress their African populations than did the white regime itself. The Matanzima regime's clampdown on dissidents earned it a reputation for brutality rivalling that of the apartheid regime. Indeed, several interviewees attributed the late arrival in Transkei of popular movements such as the UDF not to the unfavourable conditions for political mobilization among the African population, but rather to the Matanzima regime's harshness, which did not allow for such movements to take root.[7]

The apartheid regime respected Bantustan sovereignty to the extent that this suited its domestic and foreign policy objectives. However, the tentacles of the South African military and police counterinsurgency apparatus were entrenched in every aspect of Bantustan politics, and maintained unfettered access to Bantustan territory, from which it regularly seized suspected activists.[8] As the Bantustans increasingly became integrated into South Africa's military and political 'total strategy,' their leadership answered to the top echelons of the apartheid security forces.[9] Furthermore, the Bantustan regimes would often retain the services of 'consultants' working for South African intelligence services who would shape policy decisions to Pretoria's liking.

While the apartheid regime made international headlines with its 1960 massacre of peaceful protesters at Sharpeville, in a far less publicized campaign it simultaneously moved to crush the Pondoland Revolt, a series of rural rebellions against the regime's consolidation of power through the cooptation of traditional chieftainships.[10] From then onward, the mostly rural Transkei region provided a steady flow of recruits to the ANC and PAC. In 1979, ANC leader in exile Oliver Tambo called for resistance by the people of Transkei against the Matanzima regime, swelling the cohort of youth fleeing into exile to join MK's ranks.[11] Yet even as the Bantustan government's juridical autonomy gave it freer rein to suppress black revolt, this autonomy could also cut the other way, as government officials and military officers developed links with the outlawed ANC. In response, the Matanzima regime increased political repression. ANC dissident Tennyson Makiwane, one of the leaders of the Group of Eight that broke away from the ANC in 1975 and sharply criticized its leadership and strategies, ultimately joined Kaiser Matanzima's Bantustan government in Transkei and was killed in Mthatha by MK forces in June 1980. By the early 1980s, MK attacks in Transkei began steadily increasing.[12]

Indeed, MK had elaborate support networks throughout Transkei, and while it enjoyed widespread support in many parts of South Africa, in Transkei MK guerrillas could truly move among the population as fish among water, to use Mao's dictum about guerrilla warfare. In this they were greatly assisted by King Sabata Dalindyebo, the Thembu monarch who hailed from the Madiba clan, the same royal lineage as Nelson Mandela. King Sabata would use his palace situated some forty kilometres from Mthatha, known as the Great Place, to shelter guerrillas and hide weapons caches.[13] Matanzima would eventually send King Sabata into exile in Zambia, where he joined the ANC, giving a rousing address in support of armed struggle at its landmark 1985 Kabwe conference. While in exile, King Sabata's son and heir to the throne, Buyelekhaya, joined MK in turn.[14]

MK Recruitment and Combat Operations in Transkei

Transkei's landscape was ideal for MK's armed struggle: its lush, rolling hills provided natural cover for guerrilla manoeuvres, while its border with Lesotho, an independent state landlocked by South African territory, was MK's most reliable infiltration route into the country from 1974 onward.[15] Although apartheid forces recruited many spies to combat MK in Lesotho, 'the Lesotho regime had no resources to counter us,' and the ANC had many sympathizers within the regime. Transkei also provided MK with a rear base for operatives throughout South Africa, as people from other regions 'would run to Transkei and we would harbour them from police. The terrain is favourable, and there are many places to hide.' Another advantage was that 'roads were not as accessible. You could see a car coming from five kilometres and you know those are policemen,' giving guerrillas plenty of time to flee. The Bantustan militaries were also not as well equipped as the SADF, and 'they didn't have resources like helicopters for backup.'[16]

As one former guerrilla recalled: 'Chris [Hani] came to Lesotho [to organize guerrilla formations], because there were no activities in the Eastern Cape, even Western Cape, so Transkei had to service all these areas in terms of infiltration, in terms of arming, because most bases, arms caches, we brought here from Lesotho.'[17] Transkei became a hub for MK, and guerrillas 'from Natal used to come here and stay here before being infiltrated out, maybe via even Swaziland, but arranged logistically.'[18] Arms cached in Transkei were likewise smuggled out for operations throughout South Africa 'in various ways: false bottom, trucks, buses, cars, suitcases, taking from the armouries.'[19] MK used its foothold in Transkei to begin establishing structures in Natal.[20]

From the perspective of the combatants themselves, Transkei was a natural site of MK activity largely because Chris Hani and a great many guerrilla field commanders hailed from there, including 'daring ones' who led raids into South Africa and often perished, such as 'Mpilo Maqekeza, Zola Dubeni, a lot of them.'[21] While apartheid's architects made it progressively harder for Africans to get more than a rudimentary education, a disproportionately large number of ANC and MK members from Transkei 'were also educated, [they] went to universities [at] Fort Hare, Durban, Wentworth,' making them ideal candidates for training as guerrilla commanders.[22] In Transkei, MK capitalized on the elaborate web of social and kinship ties that placed its members in close proximity to the Transkei authorities and increasingly afforded MK clandestine access to the Bantustan's corridors of power.[23] Beyond these ties, MK's focus on Transkei was part of a broader strategy concentrating on the Bantustans as an untapped source of support for MK. In a 1988 interview, Hani emphasized the indicators of instability plaguing the various Bantustans, including coup attempts, the strongmen's chronic unpopularity, and their unwillingness to declare full independence from South Africa lest this incur the masses' wrath. This 'situation of crisis,' Hani argued, constituted 'a favourable climate for the ANC and also for Umkhonto we Sizwe,' which aimed to establish itself increasingly in rural areas throughout South Africa, and to capture local popular imagination through its armed actions.[24]

Brutal though the Matanzima regime was, the ranks of the Transkei government, especially the security forces, were ripe with recruitment opportunities for the ANC. One former guerrilla described how many

Transkei Defence Force (TDF) personnel had been to school with ANC members 'and they wanted to show us that they're not on the other side but they're just working to feed their families. So we had to conscientize them. Recruit more, especially those who are working on strategic points so that we know when there are going to be roadblocks, cordon-and-search operations.'[25] Infiltrating the TDF enabled MK to hit apartheid police and military targets; as one former guerrilla explained: 'we never touched those Mickey Mouse soldiers [from the TDF] – our fight was with the apartheid regime.'[26] The TDF was also far more useful to MK intact, since MK would regularly steal weaponry from TDF armouries for its operations, and even use TDF bases to train its cadres.[27] These intelligence networks also protected MK's Transkei operations in contrast to those in other regions: according to one ex-guerrilla, the main reason Transkei-based guerrillas evaded capture more often than those infiltrating from Swaziland was that apartheid intelligence services had infiltrated MK's Swazi leadership, leading to many betrayals of guerrillas as they embarked on their missions.[28] MK's Transkei leadership, conversely, was more impregnable, and Transkei soon became a key refuge and transit point for MK guerrillas.[29]

Kinship networks in the Transkei hinterland sympathetic to the ANC competed and overlapped with networks loyal to the Bantustan regime, which had been incorporated into Pretoria's omnipresent surveillance apparatus. Guerrillas risked betrayal at the hands of traditional authorities, and infiltrating the Transkei's rural hinterlands could be especially dangerous, as one ex-guerrilla explained:

> It was worse with rural [populations], the masses, peasants: they are very conservative. And those days even the headmen were taught to check anyone who visits, anyone must be reported to the king or chief of the village, who was incorporated into the apartheid system. All those structures were under the State Security Council under those Joint Management Centres. It was not even known by the government.[30]

Several former guerrillas described Matanzima's harshness as a strong factor in their decision to join MK; two described their fathers' repeated arrests for political activity, and one related how his father was banished to a remote rural area and forced to live in a roofless hut, shattering his health.[31]

In addition to their networks of influence within the Bantustan regime, the ANC and MK benefited from widespread loyalty among other groups within society. The interviews quoted here attest to a broad range of recruitment processes. According to one former MK guerrilla who was active in Transkei, infiltrators from MK used to hide among students at Fort Hare University residences and pretend they too were students:

> At that time you never knew who was coming back from exile or who is inside. There used to be crash courses at Lesotho or Swaziland, so somebody could leave the country for three months without anyone noticing, somebody could think he's at school yet he's gone outside to undergo a crash course, and then come back to operate. So my ex-schoolmates from Fort Hare used to come around with messages from such people, 'this is what has to happen,' so we used to do that underground work. So that's how I got connected with MK, working that way.[32]

MK's crash-course trainees were tasked mainly with attacking the property of Matanzima's Transkei government, such as the 'burning of government installations, burning government cars, and anything that' would sabotage the working of government,' while avoiding inflicting casualties on lower-ranking Bantustan state personnel. MK also carried out increasingly elaborate strikes on Transkeian territory:

> The operations that we carried out here in Mthatha were very successful in terms of lobbying support, or demonstrating the way the enemy was incapable of protecting its own institutions. Among the places that were attacked was the fuel depot [on 25 June 1985], the main power station just this way, and at the dam [Mthatha's main water supply] a dummy [bomb] was put there just to show that we could have damaged this thing but we know that the whole community could be affected. So nobody was killed in those operations, but they just demonstrated that the enemy is asleep.[33]

These guerrilla operations reflected the objectives adopted at the ANC's 1985 Kabwe conference, which aimed to combine the political and military elements of the struggle by tasking MK with hitting targets that were the object of mass grievance, thereby increasing the armed struggle's visibility and relevance to the masses.[34] The 25

June 1985 bombing of the Mthatha fuel depot caused it to burn for days, embarrassing the Matanzima regime; the same day, an MK bomb attack on Transkei's main power station caused a week-long blackout throughout the Bantustan.[35] Transkei also served as a launching pad for attacking mainland South Africa: one former guerrilla told of stealing plastic explosives manufactured by South Africa's Armscor from a TDF armoury and using them to blow up an empty municipal building in Kokstad in support of a workers' strike.[36]

Another spectacular operation, the 29 July 1986 attack on Transkei's main police station near Mthatha, was also carried out in response to popular grievances against the Matanzima regime: 'People went out [of Transkei] and asked [MK commander] Chris [Hani] because there was suppression, martial law, curfew, roadblocks, so they said MK must do something. So, comrades were ordered to attack the police station, straight.' The station was operated by the SAP, which 'roved, mingled, it was everywhere.' MK forces had intelligence from a guerrilla who 'was playing for the police soccer club. He was staying with them in the police barracks.' The guerrillas attacked with rifles and grenades, killing eight security policemen and wounding five,[37] following which the SAP 'started putting sandbags around police stations now, but we were going to overrun all police stations if we wanted to.'[38] The apartheid regime also deployed teams of askaris throughout Transkei that hunted MK guerrillas and activists.[39] On 21–22 January 1987, a lone MK guerrilla, Mbulelo Ngono (MK name Khaya Kasibe), assisted by Mpilo Maqekeza, held off the combined forces of the TDF, the Transkei Police Force (TPF), and the SAP in a 36-hour shootout, then managed to escape.[40] Ngono, Maqekeza and a third guerrilla, Thandwefika Radebe, all of whom had participated in the attack on the Mthatha fuel depot, regrouped in Lesotho, where they were attacked by regime forces. Radebe was killed; Ngono fled and later disappeared after he was abducted in an attempt to 'turn' him into an askari; and Maqekeza was wounded and admitted to hospital in Maseru. While recovering, he was mysteriously transferred to a bed directly beneath a window, from which apartheid agents murdered him on 15 March 1987.[41] 'He saw his killers,' a former guerrilla related. Other MK guerrillas were trapped and killed at roadblocks and in shootouts during this period, and several civilians accused of assisting them were arrested and tortured.[42] Yet despite the constant threat of arrest or assassination by the Transkei and South African security forces, Transkei afforded MK unprecedented opportunity to train and operate within striking distance of the apartheid regime.

The Militarization of Transkei and Changing Allegiances

Fearful of the ANC's growing foothold in Transkei, the apartheid regime relied increasingly on a military response. To this end, in 1986 SADF MI concocted a strategy intended to undermine the wave of UDF–ANC uprisings in the Eastern Cape.[43] Dubbed 'Operation Katzen,' it aimed to create an organization called the Xhosa Resistance Movement (XWB, or Iliso Lomzi in Xhosa) that would oppose the ANC's and PAC's growing power in the Eastern Cape, Transkei and Ciskei. The plan was to assassinate Ciskei strongman Lennox Sebe and to consolidate Transkei and Ciskei into a single Xhosa ethnic 'homeland' under the Matanzima brothers' control that would afford fewer opportunities for the liberation movements to infiltrate and operate.[44] This homeland would become a Xhosa version of KwaZulu.[45] SADF's Eastern Cape commander (and, later, SADF MI chief) 'Joffel' van der Westhuizen wrote in June 1986 to the State Security Council that 'this XWB must in nature – and even extent – be similar to Inkatha and must together with our security forces form a counter-revolutionary front.'[46] However, the XWB would never achieve anything near the success of Inkatha, and the regime would resort in short order to manipulating the Ciskei and Transkei Bantustan regimes from within as the chief means of achieving its counterinsurgency goals. To this end, SADF MI created a Special Forces branch of the TDF under the control of Gen. Ron Reid-Daly and 26 other officers formerly of the Selous Scouts, a notoriously brutal Rhodesian counterinsurgency unit, who had been hired by the Matanzima regime in 1980 after Zimbabwean independence.[47] Operation Katzen's attempts to destabilize Ciskei and Transkei were ultimately futile, but the precedent had been set: henceforth the apartheid regime's policies towards the Bantustans would increasingly be shaped by counterinsurgency doctrine, and managed by SADF MI.

Meanwhile, winds of change began blowing through Transkeian politics. The apartheid regime acquiesced when a TDF force rounded up and deported the former Rhodesian Special Forces.[48] Kaiser Matanzima's brother George, serving as Transkei's prime minister, released TDF Brig. Holomisa from custody, where he had been held for expressing TDF troops' resentment of the Selous Scouts. The Matanzima brothers feuded over political power while corruption allegations and discontent within the military weakened both their positions, leading to the eventual appointment of Stella Sigcau to the premiership in September 1987. With South African support, Kaiser Matanzima, who had lost power following an inquiry into corruption in his administration, orchestrated Holomisa's overthrow of Stella Sigcau three months later because of corruption allegations.[49] The apartheid regime approved Sigcau's overthrow, as she had incurred their displeasure by sending a diplomatic delegation to meet with the ANC in Lusaka.[50]

In the power vacuum that ensued between Sigcau's overthrow and Holomisa's consolidation of power, the SAP tracked down and killed several MK guerrillas throughout Transkei, jeopardizing MK's Transkei operations.[51] Holomisa rose to power with the apartheid regime's blessing, and Pretoria initially approved his crackdown on Transkei's rampant corruption. But he would soon make an about-face: by 1988 Holomisa began to develop strong ties with the ANC. In November 1989, Holomisa granted permission for the reburial of King Sabata, whom KD Matanzima had sought to dishonour posthumously by refusing him a royal burial. Because of King Sabata's allegiance to the ANC, tens of thousands flocked to his reburial, which turned into a political rally where several ANC delegates urged the masses to regard Holomisa's rule favourably. Within a week of King Sabata's reburial, Holomisa had released six MK cadres from prison and reprieved two others awaiting execution,[52] including Mzwandile Vena, the sole survivor of the MK unit that had bombed the Mthatha fuel depot.[53] Several weeks later, and three months ahead of the De Klerk regime, Holomisa unbanned the ANC, PAC and several other opposition groups.[54]

Transkei's importance became magnified in the context of the ANC–NP negotiations, as the National Party sought to form alliances in the Bantustans and to deny the ANC the ability to organize and rally support there.[55] In his address to an MK conference in Venda on 9 August 1991, Holomisa insisted, 'our resolute stand and our proclaimed intention to unban ANC and PAC caused the [Republic of South Africa] President to fly down to Umtata on 11 January 1990 to express concern over the unilateral decisions we have taken.'[56] In 1992, as new waves of violence engulfed South Africa, Holomisa released to the media a collection of documents and recordings proving that top South African ministers and generals had sanctioned the murders of dozens of anti-apartheid activists in the Eastern Cape.[57]

Holomisa was prescient in anticipating the reforms that would result from South Africa's overtures to Mandela and the ANC. But his own precocious overtures to the liberation movements seemed to be motivated as much by ideology as by opportunism; after all, by openly embracing the ANC, he was exposing himself to the apartheid regime's inevitable backlash, which eventually came in the form of a coup attempt. For a time, Holomisa became extremely popular among his constituency by rallying to the side of the ANC. He joined Mandela, Tambo and Chris Hani in a victory parade in Mthatha immediately after Mandela's February 1990 release from prison, and openly provided MK with a platform in Transkei, even placing several MK soldiers in TDF ranks.[58] Holomisa clearly intended to contrast his security forces' mandate and behaviour with those of the apartheid regime when he insisted that:

> in the political scene [the TDF's] role is very circumscribed: they have to guard against selfish reactionaries who want to destroy the present order. We do not cherish the prospect of employing them in the destabilization and weakening of political rivals. We also abhor their use in the orchestration and fomenting of violence among competing political parties and organizations.[59]

By 1990, on Holomisa's order, certain MK fighters in Transkei could even walk freely in uniform carrying their trademark Soviet-made AK-47 rifles. One former guerrilla recalled that Transkeian locals were jubilant at the sight of MK soldiers openly brandishing their weaponry.[60] If the apartheid regime had used Holomisa's rise to power as an opportunity to crack down on MK, now it was the guerrillas' turn: MK's priority during the late 1980s was to 'eliminate' informers within its ranks,[61] and with Holomisa's assent, MK forces killed or wounded several askaris in Mthatha and the neighbouring township of Ngangelizwe (see Chapter Five).[62] From his base in Mthatha, Chris Hani dispatched an elite MK 'icing unit' to target askaris and collaborators as far afield as Johannesburg; Hani named this unit after Zola Dubeni, the MK guerrilla killed by police in a shootout in Cape Town in March 1987. From Transkei, MK also targeted apartheid-proxy Inkatha militants based in Natal, contributing to the spiralling violence there between IFP and ANC militias.[63]

The November 1990 Coup Attempt on Holomisa

In July 1990, Holomisa granted asylum to MK chief Chris Hani after the South African government withdrew Hani's indemnity from prosecution. Meanwhile, the onset of negotiations between the state and the ANC triggered a surge in regime-sponsored violence against ANC strongholds throughout South Africa. In this context, Transkei became the epicentre of MK operations under Hani's command. As 'Third Force' operations ravaged African communities in the Pretoria–Witwatersrand–Vereeniging region, ANC and PAC members became the prime targets of the apartheid security forces' clandestine operations. After the ANC's unbanning, Mthatha was a haven for MK cadres, and the apartheid security forces targeted them accordingly: two MK cadres, 'Monwabisi (Welile Salman) and Motlatsi (MK name),' were detained while making their way to Mthatha, and their 'brutally disfigured bodies' were discovered three months later.[64] The security forces even went so far as to divert a passenger aircraft bound for Mthatha, forcing it to land in East London because they suspected that an MK cadre was aboard. Ngculu describes the briefing he received from Chris Hani upon his arrival in Transkei: 'We had to build and organize the various units of MK. It was stressed that, in that difficult and trying period, members of MK should be well briefed and organized to avoid degeneration into uncontrollable groups.'[65]

Holomisa used his knowledge of South African counterinsurgency doctrine to 'provide Chris Hani's MK with vital support,'[66] and his links to MK likewise brought Holomisa unprecedented public legitimacy and bolstered his security forces. Many MK guerrillas based in Transkei had been trained in the USSR and other Warsaw Pact countries and had seen combat against South Africa-backed UNITA forces in Angola. These MK veterans' training, experience and ideological commitment to the anti-apartheid struggle made them a formidable force alongside the TDF.[67]

The South African regime grew increasingly infuriated with Holomisa's pro-ANC leanings, and in particular with his sheltering of Hani. Yet despite its indignation, South Africa now became trapped by its own rhetoric about Bantustan sovereignty; with the world watching after Mandela's release, it could not so easily impose a military solution. Meanwhile, the unbanning of the ANC and PAC, and the lifting of the State of Emergency which had granted the security forces sweeping powers of arrest and detention, gave SADF greater incentive to target the liberation forces through clandestine violence. The Bantustans became the lynchpin of this strategy, culminating in an attempted coup on Holomisa on 23 November 1990. The coup's primary aim was to uproot the MK formations that had established themselves in Transkei, underscoring the extent to which the SADF had come to regard MK as a threat. Indeed, by mid-1991 SADF regarded the ANC and PAC militants who were gathering under Hani and Holomisa in the Transkei as their main adversary.[68]

To maintain plausible deniability about its involvement in the coup attempt, the SADF deployed a force under the command of TDF Military Intelligence chief Col. Craig Duli, an SADF MI agent, consisting of TDF collaborators along with mercenaries from the defunct Lesotho Liberation Army, itself created in the 1970s by the apartheid regime to destabilize Lesotho.[69] The LLA was commanded by Lesotho national Ntsu Mokhehle, who 'used a base [in Transkei] supported by apartheid, a terrorist organization,'[70] to destabilize the pro-ANC Lesotho government of Leabua Jonathan.[71] 'Others [members of Duli's force] were ex-SADF,' explained an MK veteran who participated in the fighting. Duli's team also included 'askaris recruited from the liberation movements, including MK.'[72]

A favourite South African counterinsurgency strategy was to set up ostensibly civilian-owned front companies that were staffed and controlled by the intelligence services (see Chapter Two). Just as South

Africa had sought to outsource apartheid by creating the Bantustans, so it outsourced its dirty war to clandestine units, affording the state plausible deniability. Of these, one of the most notorious was the Civil Cooperation Bureau (CCB), responsible for killing many anti-apartheid activists. Within months of the CCB's July 1990 disbandment, after its activities were revealed by the state-appointed Harms Commission, SADF MI set up International Researchers– Ciskei Intelligence Services (IR-CIS) as a 'consulting' company in Ciskei, a Bantustan whose strategic importance to the SADF lay in its shared border with Transkei. Although SADF MI controlled IR-CIS, it funded this private company 'from an unknowing Ciskei government – [which] was completely separate from the SADF.'[73] On 4 March 1990, the apartheid regime toppled Ciskei President Lennox Sebe and installed Brig. Oupa Gqozo, himself allegedly on SADF MI's payroll.[74] SADF MI promptly took over all security-related aspects of Ciskei's governance, installing counterinsurgency veteran Cmdt Anton Nieuwoudt as Gqozo's senior intelligence advisor.[75] The archival sources note the 'immediate and perfect harmony between Nieuwoudt's organization and the [South African] Security Police and other [apartheid] elements,' as well as Nieuwoudt's 'uncanny ability to deploy SADF forces at very short notice without the request being formulated by the Chief of the [Ciskei Defence Force].'[76] IR-CIS's existence was exposed by Ciskei Military Intelligence officer Lt Ntantiso Kleinbooi, who claimed that the three IR-CIS chiefs – Jan Anton Nieuwoudt, Clive Brink, and Ted Brassell – were controlling Ciskei politics, with Nieuwoudt manipulating Gqozo, who was 'easily influenced... The three guys [Nieuwoudt, Brink, and Brassell] are the people who are telling Gqozo what to do, and they are doing that in the interest of South Africa through its foreign department. His change of attitude towards the people and organizations started after the establishment of this International Research.'[77]

A report from a special session of the Truth and Reconciliation Commission (TRC) details the arrest on 9 April 1990 of 25 men in Queenstown, from where they were planning a coup attempt in Transkei. They were convicted in a Port Elizabeth court and sentenced to six years in prison for illegal possession of a vast quantity of arms, yet, 'in an extraordinary step, were released on bail pending the outcome of the appeal after the Queenstown security police assured the court they would watch over the accused.'[78] While they were out on bail they amassed another arms cache. Duli then approached Gqozo for support, while Nieuwoudt and the notorious 'Vlakplaas' death squad commander Eugene de Kock – the two were 'understood to have close links' – busied themselves preparing for the coup.[79]

On 22 November 1990, this force crossed into Transkei and attempted to seize Holomisa's offices in Mthatha's Botha Sicgau administrative complex, fanning out to seize radio and television stations and other key buildings. Before they could secure control, a combined force of MK and TDF soldiers repulsed them. Craig Duli and his bodyguard Boetie Davies were killed, while the ex-LLA forces, according to an MK soldier who took part in the fighting, were 'butchered like hell.'[80]

MK fighters, better trained and more highly motivated than the TDF, were instrumental in repulsing the mercenaries. One former MK guerrilla who helped to beat back the coup attempt recalled: 'At the time I was training, jogging at the [Mthatha] stadium. So I saw soldiers running, then I became alarmed. I asked what is happening. They said, oh, they are shooting, it's a coup!' According to him, 'there wasn't advance intelligence about it,' because although the MK leadership 'knew something was going to happen,' the attempt came without any prior coordination from within the TDF, 'so it was like an invasion, like a raid.' Although certain TDF elements initially rallied to the invaders' side, prompt action by MK guerrillas soon turned the tide:

> they became afraid when they saw us MK with our [RPG-7] grenade launchers, because they didn't have such arsenals in their base, so when we took from our [arms caches], some, it was their first time seeing AK-47, so they thought, Hey! [whistles] AK! It can kill us all! Then they just became disillusioned about joining those bastards.[81]

In the heat of battle some TDF soldiers lost their nerve, only to be brought back onside by the disciplined MK fighters: 'some were running, some were hiding, stripping their uniforms, but when they saw us, they came back.' MK guerrillas on the scene also convinced their TDF counterparts not to defect, by explaining the political context of the violence, 'boosting their morale against the coup and explaining that the coup is not a progressive one, it's Boers, so they can't now join such a thing. That era had passed!' Duli and some of his henchmen managed to penetrate the Botha Sigcau complex of government buildings and hunted down Holomisa, but were soon overpowered by TDF and MK cadres; several raiders were wounded and the others, including Duli himself, were killed. After the coup attempt was thwarted, MK fighters immediately launched 'a cordon and search' operation aimed at 'uprooting all bad elements within,' only to find that all the attackers had already been captured or killed. To obscure the apartheid regime's hand, the attackers had 'used guns captured from ANC guerrillas, AK-47s – even the grenades were F1s from Russia.'[82]

According to this ex-guerrilla, it was imperative to quash the attempted coup before nightfall, since SADF forces were massed at entry points along the Transkei border waiting to invade under the pretext of restoring order.[83] The SADF had a call-up in nearby East London 'planned some months earlier, for the four days starting on November 22,' indicating that the coup attempt was planned well in advance and that the SADF had been 'geared to intervene.'[84] Archival documents reveal that SADF MI operatives based near Transkei maintained radio contact with Duli's team and were dismayed when they realized that South African forces were not going to intervene on behalf of the ill-fated coup plotters, further indicating that such an intervention had been agreed upon and planned beforehand.[85] According to Vlakplaas operative Lucas Ras in his testimony to the TRC, Vlakplaas policemen and askaris gathered at a Security Branch safe house where they 'followed the proceedings on the radio with regard to the coup.'[86] Had the coup succeeded, this force would have entered Transkei 'to assist with the identification of ANC and PAC persons who resided in Transkei and worked from there, with the exclusive purpose of arresting them and handing them over to the Transkei Security Police at that stage.'[87]

Recognizing that the threat was not over, the Transkei government, assisted by the ANC, organized a mass rally in Mthatha as a show of support for Holomisa. As one ex-guerrilla explained, 'the masses were told to come in numbers and demonstrate against the coup.'[88] Tens of thousands strong, this rally was calculated to deter SADF intervention in support of the coup attempt by demonstrating that any such move would be met with mass unrest that would attract international attention.[89] This rally displayed MK's skill at using political actions to deflect the full force of the apartheid war machine; it served to avert a much bloodier scenario, as one former guerrilla explained: 'it was going to be a long battle. Us digging in, attacking again as guerrillas. It was going to be a mess, so we had to stop it [the SADF intervention] before they came.'[90]

MK chief Chris Hani had been in Johannesburg at the time of the coup, and MK's Transkei regional commander called him, warning him to stay away from Transkei until the conflagration had died down.[91] The SADF MI operation was thwarted as MK fighters, familiar with the terrain and keenly aware of the high stakes, routed the mercenary force. Indeed, one former MK guerrilla insisted that the coup attempt's ultimate target was MK formations in the Transkei – 'they wanted MK, at the end of the day' – and that toppling Holomisa was merely the opening move.[92] This argument is borne out by archival documents indicating that MK formations operating in Transkei became the South African defence establishment's chief priority from 1990 onward, as illustrated by this mid-1990 statement by SADF MI Cmdt Anton Nieuwoudt:

> The main target, and it was very clear at this time, was the Transkei, you must understand that the ANC had begun to return from exile and many of the agents had come back to the [Republic of South Africa], and they had begun to group together with the PAC in the Transkei, and what concerned the intelligence community the most at that stage was the militants, a militant wing, come let's call it by its name, the militant ANC's and the militant PAC's which grouped together under Chris Hani together with Holomisa, and this matter was discussed at the highest level, it was a great worry, because they expected trouble from that grouping in the Transkei.[93]

Nieuwoudt's insistence that this clandestine plan 'was discussed at the highest level' suggests that FW de Klerk's administration was aware of these operations as they unfolded.[94] This echoes De Kock's 1997 testimony to the TRC in which he claimed to have received direct orders from the state for his death squad activities.[95] Furthermore, the collaboration between Nieuwoudt and De Kock in the coup attempt points to an 'operational link between SADF MI covert operations and Vlakplaas,' which, along with ballistic tests indicating that weapons for the coup were supplied by SADF, indicates a highly coordinated counterinsurgency strategy that would have required top-level authorization from within the military, if not from the civilian leadership.[96]

Ongoing Apartheid Counterinsurgency and Subsequent Plots in Transkei

The record of SADF MI counterinsurgency operations in Transkei and Ciskei reveals that even as top-level negotiations between the NP and ANC proceeded, the apartheid security forces devoted great resources to striking covertly at the ANC's leadership and security capacities, using Bantustan 'sovereignty' to add another layer of plausible deniability. In a television broadcast on the day of the coup attempt, 23 November 1990, South African foreign minister 'Pik' Botha described Holomisa as 'the African National Congress's strongest supporter in the whole of Africa'.[97] In the light of the copious evidence pointing to the regime's complicity in this affair, Botha's televised statement seems to have been coordinated with the coup attempt and intended as a justification for it. The apartheid regime thus signalled that it was prepared to reap the benefits of the coup should it succeed, while taking no responsibility for the operation. On 23 August 1991 the South African Police 'admitted they knew of the planned military takeover of Transkei. This follows an admission by the Department of Foreign Affairs that they knew of the existence of the plans.'[98]

The archival sources indicate that 'When Hani's indemnity was temporarily withdrawn in 1991, he fled to Transkei and stayed there as Holomisa's guest. This intensified SADF fears that Transkei was being used as a haven for guerrilla activity, and made it even more crucial for the SADF to maintain control of [neighbouring] Ciskei.'[99] Attacks on ANC targets in Ciskei meanwhile prompted the South African Communist Party to claim that 'there was a well-coordinated plan to weaken the ANC in the region.'[100] Thereafter, SADF MI maintained contingency plans to kill Holomisa and Hani in Transkei using surrogate forces. According to Nqakula, there were 'at least five attempts' by askaris and LLA members 'to assassinate Holomisa.'[101] One plan for 25 April 1991 detailed ongoing plots to overthrow Holomisa by SADF MI, which 'allegedly involved the assassination of Bantu Holomisa and MK's Chris Hani and suggested the possibility of a coup using SADF. Some initial planning took place in [Brig. Oupa] Gqozo's office.'[102] The plan called for Holomisa and Hani to be assassinated by the 'Transkei Group,' consisting of Kaiser Matanzima and his loyalists, who were assembled by SADF MI. Following the assassinations, SADF forces would be immediately deployed in Transkei: 'This would take place under the pretext that they had been asked to maintain law and order and search for MK bases. They would have further justified their presence by spreading disinformation about planned attacks on civilians by MK soldiers. They would also suggest that MK intended disrupting talks between the ANC and government by attacking civilians.'[103]

The plan called for the SADF to supervise the TDF while the 'Transkei Group' consolidated its power, and the askari Vulindlela Mbotoli would succeed Holomisa. In preparation for this, the askari Nkosekhaya Gobingca[104] was given the task of collecting intelligence, 'and ordered to confirm the exact location of MK bases in Transkei and the presence of any sophisticated weapons that might have been brought in.'[105] MK forces assisted the TDF in thwarting this plot by kidnapping Mbotoli from South African territory and bringing him to Transkei, where he was tried and imprisoned.[106] In 1993, 17 people were tried and convicted in Transkei for their role in the attempted 1990 coup.[107]

If authorizing the reburial of King Sabata had improved Holomisa's image in Transkei, the coup attempt greatly boosted his popularity, as 'he was regarded as having stood up to the [South African] government, which was widely regarded in Transkei as having been behind the coup attempt.'[108] In a move calculated to boost the image of the much-hated Brig. Gqozo in Ciskei, IR-CIS apparently engineered a 'coup attempt' on Gqozo and its 'subsequent "putting down"' in the hope that this might endear Gqozo to the Ciskeian population – a ploy which 'failed dismally.'[109] Indeed, as the chief of Ciskei Defence Force (CDF) Military Intelligence Col. 'Gerrie' Hugo alleged after he 'fled to Transkei and spoke out about IR-CIS' activities there, 'Nieuwoudt had total control over Gqozo' and claimed that 'as [IR-CIS's] existence depended on the existence of threats against Gqozo, the unit actively fabricated evidence of threats' emanating from 'both the ANC and from within Transkei' to justify its existence. 'The threat is always kept alive.' Nieuwoudt laid the groundwork for Operation Cable, a planned joint CDF–SADF operation targeting MK guerrillas, which was ostensibly the subject of a phone call from Nelson Mandela to Gqozo in 1991. The military build-up in Ciskei included an influx of weaponry to CDF bases, and an attack on the CDF leadership in which several officers were killed to pave the way for IR-CIS to consolidate its control over the Ciskeian military.

While SADF MI planned further strikes against Holomisa and drew up a hit list of ANC members in Ciskei, the unprecedented CDF military build-up continued apace, including the creation of a paratroop battalion commanded by SADF 32 Battalion veteran Jan Breytenbach, whose only possible purpose was to strike at Transkei.[110] This build-up was apparently in preparation for an attack on MK guerrillas based in Mdantsane township, near East London.[111]

In August 1991, South African director general of foreign affairs Neil van Heerden emphasized that there was no connection between the SADF and IR-CIS, saying that 'chief of the SADF Kat Liebenberg would have told Brig. Gqozo to disband the unit as it was an embarrassment, "because there are continued allegations that a connection exists and I can assure you no connection exists."'[112] Meanwhile, SADF MI front companies proliferated, including Multi-Media Services, a company with right-wing links headed by former SADF MI chief Tienie Groenewald and Riaan van Rensburg, who 'was linked to Ciskei activities and also claimed he had been hired by the IFP to train a task group.' Multi-Media Services supplied AK-47s to Gqozo's regime in November 1992.[113] SADF MI later funded a political party created by Gqozo, the African Democratic Movement, whose members clashed frequently with the ANC in the run-up to the April 1994 elections. Gqozo eventually contested the elections through the ADM, but did not gain a single seat.[114] Like many SADF MI operations during the period approaching the elections, this raises the question whether and to what extent these counterinsurgency initiatives were calculated not only to give the regime the upper hand in negotiations, but to shape the post-transition era.

SADF MI plans during this period reveal a sophisticated psychological operations component to spread disinformation about the SADF's attempts to uproot MK. After the failed coup attempt, the SADF had planned to justify its hunt for MK forces in Transkei on the pretext that the Transkeian government had asked it to maintain law and order; the fig leaf of Bantustan sovereignty remained essential to the SADF's counterinsurgency strategy. The SADF also intended to claim that MK had been planning to attack civilian targets, despite the apartheid regime's own record of indiscriminate killing. Indeed, on 8 October 1993 an SADF commando raid on a purported PAC safe house in Mthatha's North Crest suburb killed five African teenagers in their sleep, an attack which De Klerk himself authorized and publicly defended even as the details of the massacre came to light.[115] However, perhaps the greatest misinformation was the SADF's plan to justify an invasion of Transkei by alleging that MK had intended to disrupt the post-1990 negotiations. This reveals the regime's attempt to drive a wedge between MK and the ANC by portraying the guerrilla wing as radical extremists compared to the political leadership, whereas in reality MK subordinated itself to the ANC leadership's command, and took few initiatives without ANC authorization.[116] SADF MI's plans to kill Chris Hani along with Holomisa in Transkei are also interesting in the light of the finding that there was no broader complicity in Hani's assassination in Johannesburg in April 1993 (see Chapter Seven).

Of course, SADF counterinsurgency's chief aim was to weaken the ANC as much as possible, and its 'Third Force' massacres would push the nation to the brink of the abyss more than once during the course of negotiations. The National Party had wanted the Bantustan leaders to sit at the negotiating table, and knew that if they toppled Holomisa, they could count on his replacement to serve as a vital ally against the ANC.[117] Should the negotiations between the ANC and the NP have failed, Transkei would undoubtedly have become even more strategically important to both the ANC and the PAC, especially if open hostilities had resumed; the regime would have then redoubled its efforts to topple Holomisa and eradicate MK from its Transkei strongholds.

Archival documents mention that 'the SA security police were unhappy about the plans because of the timing of the coup and the effect it might have on President FW de Klerk in his dealings with the ANC'; combined with Mbotoli's abduction, this 'ended the coup plans.'[118] However, another equally compelling explanation for SADF MI's hesitation to launch another coup is that the MK forces entrenched in Transkei had already repulsed one attempt and, with their weaponry and training, were formidable enough to deter any others. As SADF intelligence officers themselves indicated, after the onset of negotiations in 1990 MK formations in Transkei became the SADF counterinsurgency programme's top priority. Although South Africa had originally created the Bantustans as a political and territorial periphery, Transkei ultimately came to lie at the heart of the regime's counterinsurgency strategy, as MK used Transkei's favourable political climate to capitalize on its popular legitimacy and challenge apartheid hegemony.

The ANC, MK, and the Coup Attempt's Aftermath

After thwarting the coup attempt, MK continued to thrive in Transkei until the eve of the transition to democracy and the dissolution of the Bantustans. For his part, Holomisa played an active role in envisioning MK's role during and after the transition, as evidenced by his address to the MK conference on 9 August 1991 in Venda.[119] At the conference, Holomisa downplayed the very strong ties his regime had developed with MK, denying that Transkei was 'integrating MK soldiers into the TDF,' and insisting that the 'co-operation' between MK and TDF 'is confined to giving our permission to these cadres to protect their leaders when they visit Transkei.'[120] Nonetheless, during this period MK forces became ever more closely allied to the TDF, to the point where MK assumed command of the TDF Special Forces base at Port St Johns on the Wild Coast. A former MK guerrilla recounted that Chris Hani had given 'the orders to go and join with the Transkei Defence Force,' and that the camp was renamed Chris Hani Camp in the former MK chief's honour after his assassination.[121]

MK had infiltrated the camp years before the start of negotiations, and during that era 'there were even some officers from TDF who [were sent abroad] for training under the wing of the ANC, MK. So there was that underground long before. But it was not known to the intelligence [services] of South Africa.'[122] Though it was the army of a quasi-independent state, the TDF did not compare to MK in terms of training and professionalism. The TDF supplied MK with 'another wing' of its camp 'to open up to train locals, ANC members.' The regimen included 'instilling discipline, instilling perseverance, to have patriotism and love for the country, for the masses, for the elders, and to show them the military tactics. It was a crash course but we [also] did a commando's course.'[123] The former MK guerrilla recalled Hani visiting the Port St Johns base for an inspection and saluting uniformed MK units marching in formation – a far cry from MK's underground operations in mainland South Africa. Hani's assassination came just before 'he was going to visit the camp for a march-past parade,' which was planned as an elaborate show of force for the ANC's armed wing.

The apartheid regime eventually 'sent their people infiltrating' at the base, which MK discovered when 'we were doing intelligence work within them, screening them. Because we had information that Boers wanted to attack there and they had people inside there. We didn't trust first some from TDF, so we had to start cleaning within our formations. We uprooted about five of them, they confessed,' but rather than take punitive measures against them, MK sought to rehabilitate these recruits, who were young and 'had no experience, so we had to mobilize them now for the good, to show them the right direction.'[124]

In preparation for the imminent transition, MK sought to train as many guerrillas as possible at the base, eventually turning out several hundred trainees in 'three or four groups,' a handful of whom 'went to integration, some were absorbed as captains' in the new armed forces, including TT Matanzima, Kaiser Matanzima's nephew and future chief of the post-transition South African Navy. 'So we were very proud because we produced very disciplined units from Port St Johns.' By this point, the SADF was watching the MK base intently and was fully aware of the activities there. 'No, they knew. But we were armed to defend, so they didn't want any problems, because [an attack] was not going to be sanctioned at the top [by the South African government].'[125] The link between MK and the TDF became further strengthened when a contingent of TDF soldiers was sent to train at an MK base in Uganda. This course concluded with a ceremony in December 1992 in which TDF soldiers participated prominently, wearing their own distinctive uniforms and following their own chain of command.[126] Thus although the ANC insisted on dismantling the Bantustans as part of the negotiated transition, it nonetheless exploited this opportunity to consolidate its strategic position by forging an alliance with the military of its ostensibly sovereign ally while strengthening MK's influence over the TDF. MK's evolution in Transkei into a semi-conventional army attests to the movement's readiness to assume a security force role in a free South Africa. Yet in contrast to the power that MK enjoyed during this period, South Africa's liberation brought mainly disarray for MK fighters, many of whom were either excluded from the post-transition armed forces or marginalized within them (see Chapter Eight).

As the apartheid regime dismantled the legal barriers to ANC mobilization in South Africa proper, the Bantustan puppet rulers – with the exception of Transkei's Holomisa and Venda, under the ANC-aligned strongman Gabriel Ramushwana – clung to power, prohibiting mass organization. Bophuthatswana's Lucas Mangope proved particularly steadfast in his rejection of national elections and the dissolution of the Bantustans. Thus, on 7 September 1992, when ANC protesters in the Ciskei capital of Bisho began marching on Gqozo's presidential palace, the Ciskei Defence Force, commanded by white SADF MI officers, opened fire, killing 28 and wounding over 200.[127] Holomisa had warned of precisely such an outcome in an address he made on 25 January 1991 in Venda: 'We have also to be wary of South African security personnel seconded to certain Homelands who might be inclined to encourage police behaviour similar to the one that has led to the Sebokeng killings.'[128]

The Bantustans that still opposed the democratic transition – all of them except Transkei and Venda, under the ANC-aligned strongman Gabriel Ramushwana became essential to the assorted Afrikaner extremists under the leadership of retired SADF Gen. Constand Viljoen. These rejectionists sought to forge an alliance with Gqozo and Mangope to resist the transition by force if necessary.[129] This culminated in the 11 March 1994 'Battle of Bop,' in which white-supremacist militiamen crossed into Bophuthatswana to link up with Mangope's forces, many of them firing indiscriminately at black

163

civilians. Bophuthatswana Defence Force (BDF) soldiers returned fire, killing three extremists, and mutinied against Mangope. The coalition collapsed, enabling the peaceful elections of April 1994 and the reabsorption of the Bantustans into South Africa. This endgame underscores the strategic centrality of the seemingly peripheral Bantustans to the violent power struggles leading up to the transition. Ultimately, the ANC was able to outmanoeuvre the National Party by concentrating power at the negotiating table away from the Bantustans. Meanwhile, Transkei served as an MK military stronghold and an ANC electoral power base even as the apartheid regime schemed to discredit the ANC among black people, who were soon to be given the franchise for the first time.

Legacies: Violence and Insecurity

After the April 1994 election, as a result of which Holomisa became a deputy minister under the ANC's banner, the new ANC government incorporated Transkei and Ciskei into the Eastern Cape province and dismantled the Bantustan administrative structures. Mthatha has since been plagued by high levels of violent crime, which can be traced in large part to the legacies of insurgency and counterinsurgency. Many of the weapons in circulation after the transition in the Eastern Cape and throughout South Africa originated from MK's arms caches, TDF armouries, and especially from the flood of guns which the regime brought into African communities for counterinsurgency purposes.[130]

Archival documents reveal the continuity between weapons smuggled into the region by CCB, IR-CIS, and other counterinsurgency units during the years 1990–4 and ongoing arms smuggling operations in the region post-1994. The front companies set up by the apartheid regime to facilitate covert infiltration and obscure its role in the violence made it so much more difficult to trace the flow of these weapons. Many of these arms were supplied to vigilantes such as the ADM activists in Ciskei, many of whom turned to criminality after the transition.[131]

At the same time, several taxi and bus companies had employees 'with known links to covert operations' who used their vehicles to smuggle weapons.[132] According to one former guerrilla, the taxi violence that swept much of South Africa during the late 1990s and early 2000s, in which rival taxi companies competing for routes attacked each other's staff and passengers, had its roots in Third Force violence, killing 20–30 people in Mthatha (and hundreds more elsewhere) at its height.[133] SADF MI had also set up several security companies that doubled as hit squads, trafficked in weapons, and had access to state armouries, especially in Ciskei where they 'protected' strongman Gqozo. An array of weapons also went missing from various South African military armouries before and after the April 1994 election, many of which were never found.[134]

Beyond these legacies of decentralized violence, it is important to consider the full historical import of the duel between MK and SADF MI in Transkei during South Africa's transition. Considering the state's strategy of enlisting the Bantustans to dilute the ANC's political power, the transition may well have proceeded differently had SADF MI's November 1990 coup attempt succeeded in overthrowing Holomisa. This outcome would have given the regime more leverage vis-à-vis the ANC at a crucial point in the transition, and emboldened those within the state's political and military echelons who favoured using violence to erode the ANC's electoral advantage. It certainly would have led to pitched battles between MK forces and the SADF in Transkei and perhaps elsewhere, which would have claimed many casualties and triggered a larger invasion of the sort that SADF forces had already prepared in support of the coup attempt. Viewed in this light, MK's ability to thwart apartheid counterinsurgency in Transkei must itself be regarded as a turning point in the transition, one that has thus far been largely obscured. The Transkei case also reveals another dimension of the apartheid regime's counterinsurgency programme forged within the top military echelons, and possibly with the connivance of its political leadership, aiming to shape South Africa's democratic transition through clandestine violence.

6

SPY RECRUITMENT AND THE STEYN REPORT

'Those people who were sellouts, high position people, they did their best so that MK must be insignificant in both the army and the police force, [the integration] initiative must never materialize. Because we were integrated into the South African forces, so it's [the apartheid forces] who determined who must be where.'
— Ex-combatant, Mthatha, December 2009

The April 1994 court case involving SADF MI Commandant Jan Anton Nieuwoudt was held in camera 'as Nieuwoudt's job had included the recruitment of sources, the interrogation of as many as 2,000 guerrillas, and the identification of targets for overt and covert operations.' His 'lawyers stressed the need to prevent exposure of current covert military operations, meaning clandestine operations underway the month the elections were being held.'[1] In the mid-1980s, along with Craig Williamson, Nieuwoudt had identified ANC and PAC targets outside South Africa for SADF MI's Department of Covert Collection (DCC), many of which would then be hit in cross-border raids such as the one on Gaborone in 1985.[2] Nieuwoudt was also one of the SADF MI officers fired in De Klerk's December 1992 purge following the Goldstone Commission's raid on DCC offices one month earlier. Seeking compensation, Nieuwoudt brought a civil suit against the SADF, submitting as evidence a bundle of military documents proving that until his abrupt termination he was a full-time operative whose work was authorized and valued by his superiors. In his civil case, Nieuwoudt testified that 'just before the [16 November 1992] Goldstone raid, the DCC was busy recruiting 'a very senior member of the intelligence service of the ANC'.'[3] The suit 'went to court in early April 1994 and was settled out of court just after the elections.'[4] At the time he was fired, Nieuwoudt was an MI officer first class, Internal Sub-Theatre Western Front.

The documents relating to Nieuwoudt's case shed light on the extent to which SADF MI apparently infiltrated the ANC. They included a section about 'the Joe Modise connection,' referring to MK chief Joe Modise. They also referred to secret documents that mentioned 'a very senior person' which the DCC under the command of Brig. Botha 'was in the process of recruiting "just before the State President closed us down."'[5] According to the documents, 'this unnamed person was allegedly open to being blackmailed into being recruited as he was involved in illegal activities. He is a very senior member of the intelligence service of the ANC.'[6] SADF MI's efforts were based on an assessment that Modise 'was willing to smash the ANC–SACP alliance in order to secure his own position under a future government.'[7] The plan was outlined in a top-secret memo – of which only four copies existed – sent to the DCC director. He sent the memo to his superior officer, Col. At Nel, and DCC commander Brig. 'Tolletjie' Botha, both of whom De Klerk fired two months after the memo was drafted. The memo, drafted by Nieuwoudt, described an alleged split between 'militants' led by Hani and 'moderates' led by Modise, which SADF MI could exploit by recruiting 'agents of influence' within the ANC. It then declared: '"Agent 241/222 is prepared to have a secret meeting with the Defence Force, along with: J Modise (MK commander), L Moloi (chief of operations), MK Zakes (regional commander PWV), MK Maincheck (commander of MK outside South Africa) and J Mnisi (commander Pretoria)." Elsewhere in the document, "Agent 241/ 222" is referred to as an MK regional commander.'[8] The ANC's submission to the TRC argued that Nieuwoudt's 'court action' indicated that the DCC and the front company Pan-Afrik Industrial Investment Consultants (PAIIC) 'may have been involved in a range of covert actions considered crucial to the strategy of the De Klerk regime during the negotiations phase,' and 'may also have taken over many functions of the CCB [Civil Cooperation Bureau], including operations beyond the borders of South Africa.'[9]

The court documents describe a memo, dated September 1992, which referred to 'a secret meeting between Modise, Moloi (head of MK Ops, now senior man in SANDF),[10] three named others [see above] and MI. MI clearly viewed this meeting as one with already recruited sources or with possible sources. This meeting was organized by a paid MI source (one of the five ANC members could be the source).' In note form, the document continues: 'Memo notes how much support Modise has within MK; says the meeting could be the first step towards "neutralizing the SACP/Hani/Kasrils faction" [referring to Ronnie Kasrils, then chief of MK Intelligence] and winning votes in a later election; says the MK five involved in the secret meeting do not want to fight with the old SADF unlike Hani.' The document goes on to cite a passage in Afrikaans which it translates thus: 'This discussion is also with people who want to promote their own agenda (assuring own positions), but who are also prepared to break the ANC/SACP backbone.'

Finally, the document frames this disclosure within a larger political context:

> 'This reference to Modise et al. should be seen in context of the rest of the memo: the memo discusses how SADF can keep upper hand with election looming; refers to three options open to SADF of (1) discrediting the militants within SACP and ANC, (2) "recruiting agents of influence," and (3) "exploiting the rift within MK" (encouraging the recruitment of ANC sources).'[11]

The memo noted that Modise and other moderates 'do not wish to fight with the SADF,' whereas 'Hani and his young militant guard want to fight.' This view was consistent with apartheid disinformation operations during this period that sought to divide the ANC and portray Hani as a radical planning to resort to violence, a claim for which no evidence exists. However, unlike those disinformation operations, the memo's intended audience was not National Party politicians or the South African news media, but the chief of the DCC, a unit actively trying to recruit spies in the ANC during this period.

The memo noted: 'the options which could come out of such a meeting are legion,' including 'the incorporation of moderate [MK guerrillas], the empowerment of compromised witnesses against the militants,' and 'the utilisation of own ANC members as instruments at street level.' The memo further noted the desirability of sending a 'powerful delegation' from the SADF to meet with Modise and the others, 'to ensure exploitation, shock action, mobility, and good communication in the final phase of this objective.'[12]

Nieuwoudt also '[talked] before the elections about his agents among the MK members who would be part of the SANDF: "They are already identified, we already know what ranks they will be appointed to, which of them will be generals, which of them are going to be brigadiers, and a great many of them are going to be lieutenant-colonels."' The document also mentions 'references to plenty of others recruited as moles from MK who are now in the security forces.'[13] Notorious CCB and DCC agent and convicted murderer Ferdi Barnard had likewise 'boasted to journalists about the effectiveness of his plan [to subvert MK]:

> The ANC is deeply infiltrated by the security forces. From my experience I would say that the ANC has been infiltrated very much, all departments, including the intelligence department and at the very high level. I recruited certain MK commanders as informants of mine. I started strengthening links again with Mandrax smuggling networks operating between here, Zambia, and Maputo, which had very good contacts with certain MK commanders.[14]

Barnard's mention of drug smuggling networks to compromise MK commanders is all the more interesting in the light of the 'very senior person' in the ANC previously cited, very likely Modise, who was 'open to being blackmailed into being recruited as he was involved in illegal activities.'

In a second top-secret DCC memo, dated September 1992 and included in the bundle of court documents, 'Nieuwoudt outlines to Nel plans to close down some sources and to go ahead with others. One of those sources, described as "in place (ANC) and going ahead," was agent 241/222.' The DCC also maintained key sources inside the PAC.[15] Nieuwoudt produced a third top-secret document, 'again the sole official copy in existence' and dated 9 December 1992, which noted how 'Fox' (Nieuwoudt) had 'efficiently executed his duty as a principal agent controlling eight handlers and their respective source networks in the Witwatersrand area' and had produced 431 intelligence reports; the 'memo urged retaining "Fox's" services into 1993.' SADF chief of staff Gen. Kat Liebenberg was so determined to prevent the public disclosure of these documents and their contents that he 'wrote to the Minister of Defence in March and then again in April 1993, asking for authority to pay Nieuwoudt' the difference between 'what the Supreme Court ruled the military should pay him and Nieuwoudt's own demand' of R400,000.[16]

Though it was not known 'whether any of the [ANC] group approached were indeed recruited,' the journalist Louise Flanagan noted that after the transition 'at least two' held 'senior positions': Modise as minister of defence and Lambert Moloi, 'one of the so called "Modise moderates," who in June 1994 'was promoted to Major General and made chief of the Service Brigade.' For his part, Modise told the *Mail & Guardian*: 'I want to state clearly that I never attended [that] meeting… It follows from that, that I have no information relating to the other questions you have raised.' Subsequently, deputy defence minister Ronnie Kasrils attempted to discredit the allegation as 'sloppy journalism' that 'uncritically' regurgitated apartheid disinformation. Kasrils condemned as 'preposterous' Nieuwoudt's assertion that SADF MI had already identified which among its moles in MK would occupy higher ranks in the SANDF, because MK 'at the time of the memo [September 1992] had no ranks'; yet it is obvious that the future ranking of moles could already have been determined even if they did not hold a specific rank in MK at the time. In her riposte, Flanagan noted that her reporting was based not on Nieuwoudt's assertions but on court papers that 'illustrated the MI campaigns which were being run against the ANC in the runup to the elections,' and on the basis of which 'the SADF settled the claim.' This raised the question why the ANC government, in seeking to discredit her, would 'wish to protect officers from the old SADF who were involved in illegal campaigns against legal political organisations in the runup to the elections?'[17]

These documents paint an astonishing portrait of a counter-insurgency programme led by top-ranking SADF officers seeking to shape the outcome of the transition by advancing a secret military agenda distinct from the ongoing political negotiations. Although 'Third Force' violence had become increasingly decentralized and fragmented by 1993,[18] evidence of Military Intelligence operations continuing into April 1994, the month of Mandela's election to power, indicates an ongoing counterinsurgency programme calculated to shape its crucial military and political aspects. Indeed, this agenda – to marginalize the ANC's left-wing faction, and to ensure that the *ancien régime* maintained control of the post-transition military – seems to have largely materialized in the immediate post-transition era. After the 1994 elections, Joe Modise was named Mandela's defence minister, while in the 'new' military General Georg Meiring, one of the architects of Project Echoes, a secret operation to discredit the ANC during the transition by falsely linking MK to the Irish Republican Army and the Palestine Liberation Organization,[19] became chief of staff of the new SANDF. Former MK commander Siphiwe Nyanda replaced Meiring in 1998. Modise was a key player in the 'arms deal' scandal that still roils South African political waters; he and Nyanda featured prominently in 'the odd new [post-transition] militarist alliance of white officers from the apartheid army and black guerrillas from the anti-apartheid struggle.'[20] In addition, according to one ex-MK source, an MK commander who used to betray guerrillas to SADF MI also rose to prominence in the post-transition military.[21]

To be sure, this 'odd alliance' of personnel from the ANC and the NP regime also existed in the post-transition police, the intelligence services and many other state institutions, and reflected the nature of the negotiated compromise. Furthermore, the influence of apartheid-era personnel in the security forces was counterbalanced by the appointment of ANC and MK figures such as Ronnie Kasrils, Steve Tshwete and Mosiuoa Lekota to leadership positions within the new security establishment. O'Brien notes that the ANC managed to fill all major security-related positions in the post-transition cabinet with its own personnel.[22] Nevertheless, the sources cited above demonstrate that within this context of compromise, counterinsurgency forces pursued a clandestine agenda to shape the new security forces by means of agents recruited beforehand. In 1996, Kynoch observed that former MK guerrillas needed to undergo evaluation and training before joining the post-transition military, a process from which apartheid soldiers were exempt; he further noted that whereas the new military's top brass and officers' corps included several former MK commanders, 'the SANDF remains a formal, conventional military dominated by an experienced corps of Afrikaners.'[23] This development takes on new meaning in the light of Nieuwoudt's assertions that SADF MI had seeded the post-transition security forces' ranks in advance with scores of moles recruited beforehand.

Recruiting spies within the ANC and MK was a top priority for the apartheid security forces, including the SAP's elite Security Branch, SADF Military Intelligence, and the civilian National Intelligence Service (NIS). Former SAP Security Branch Col. Lucas Ras related that he was tasked with recruiting MK informants upon his returning from serving with the SAP's Koevoet counterinsurgency unit in Namibia in 1989; he then 'operated from a safe house and within six months managed to recruit 14 MK informants' in South Africa and abroad.[24] These included an injured MK cadre abducted from his hospital bed and 'turned,' and an agent in MK's communications department in Lusaka who channelled 'all orders for infiltration during that time, the routes, the names of the people who were going to infiltrate, their orders, sabotage assignments, everything we know beforehand before they infiltrate the country.'

Of the various branches involved in intelligence recruitment, SADF MI was the most successful, with vast material and human resources at its disposal, and many ruthless covert units specializing in intelligence gathering and assassination, such as the CCB and DCC. The DCC 'would act against opponents of the state through both counter-intelligence operations and pro-active intelligence gathering operations (meaning the use of political violence, including planning assassinations, to obtain and implement intelligence).'[25] Project Coast, the regime's secret chemical-biological weapons programme, also contributed directly to 'intelligence-led targeting efforts.' It is unclear when the DCC – what O'Brien calls the 'most dangerous' of SADF MI's sub-units, 'established in the darkest of shadows' – was founded. It aimed to replicate in South Africa the sort of programmes that SADF MI had launched in Namibia and Angola, including 'intelligence collection, pseudo-operations, and the elimination of the opponent.'[26]

Investigators of the Goldstone Commission, appointed to investigate the June 1992 Boipatong massacre of ANC supporters, inadvertently stumbled upon the DCC's headquarters in a Pretoria office building on 16 November 1992, uncovering a trove of information about MI counterinsurgency programmes then still very much under way.[27] Files seized from the DCC headquarters showed that CCB operative Ferdi Barnard was on the SADF MI payroll until December 1991, despite official denials. Barnard's role was to conduct psychological operations to discredit MK by 'linking it to criminal acts and crime syndicates by using members of the Returned Exiles Committee, networks of prostitutes, homosexuals, and drug dealers.'[28] The Goldstone Commission report found that Barnard also hired spies to install computers at ANC headquarters.[29] According to Barnard's ex-lover, who was involved in setting up a brothel, this served as a venue to 'entertain' ANC members who had been recruited, and also for their SADF MI handlers to debrief them; gangsters associated with Barnard would also plan robberies there.[30] Even after being sacked from the CCB in December 1991, Barnard remained in SADF MI's employ, where he worked to discredit the ANC and gathered intelligence on APLA forces in Transkei. He had a high-level PAC informant based in Umtata codenamed 'Mr B,' who was involved in drug smuggling and had close ties with PAC president Clarence Makwetu. Barnard was also involved in attempts to discredit Winnie Mandela by leaking details to the press about her affair with an attorney.[31] Based on the Goldstone Commission's findings, De Klerk ordered the DCC to be shut down in November 1992.

In the context of the regime's spy recruitment, it is interesting to note how Detective Warrant Officer Drummond Hammond, formerly of the SAP's organized crime intelligence unit in Pretoria, described the nature of the ANC's role in transnational drug smuggling networks:

> we never picked up information that the ANC per se were smuggling, but individuals did, that was for their own gain. We all used the same routes, the smugglers, the South African intelligence services, all of them together and the ANC... They were fighting a revolutionary war but they weren't smuggling. There were individuals that we identified and targeted for smuggling purposes but that was only for personal gain.[32]

The Steyn Report

Two key disclosures in mid-1992 put President De Klerk under great pressure to rein in his security forces: First, the revelation in May 1992 that in June 1985 Gen. 'Joffel' van der Westhuizen had given the 'death signal' order to assassinate ANC activists Matthew Goniwe, Fort Calata, Sparrow Mkhonto and Sicelo Mhlauli, who became known as the Cradock Four. André de Villiers, a white farmer who informed the ANC about the 'Hammer' death squad that had murdered the activists, was himself killed in August 1992 outside his home near Port Elizabeth, a death which the SAP tried to blame on MK.[33] Then, the London-based *Independent* reported that on 17 April 1992 two SADF MI operatives, Pamela du Randt and Leon Flores, had been arrested in London and deported by the British Anti-Terrorist Squad for attempting to recruit Ulster Loyalist paramilitaries to assassinate former Vlakplaas commander Dirk Coetzee.[34] Du Randt and Flores had travelled under the pretext of investigating alleged MK–IRA links.[35] These revelations dealt a blow to the NP regime's image abroad and to its relations with the UK.[36] Coetzee had become a prime regime target since he had defected to the ANC and supplied information on apartheid death squads, whereupon he fled to London and lived under Scotland Yard protection. A March 1990 *New York Times* article quoted Coetzee as saying: 'The responsibility for the death squads goes right to the top.'[37]

A report from June 1992 described De Klerk as 'an almost immobilized captive of a powerful clique of securocrats, aided by upper echelons of [SADF MI],' who were 'determined to obstruct his political initiatives for a phased transition.'[38] The report noted that De Klerk had instructed the NIS, under its new director Mike Louw, 'to make an in-depth study of how elements within the security forces appear to be undermining his political initiatives' and to determine 'how best to deal with them.' Under Louw, the NIS became De Klerk's most trusted agency – 'and perhaps the only one he can trust in identifying "third force" elements and containing the influence of [SADF MI], the Special Forces and remnants of the old Security Branch.' Yet the NIS was 'helpless' to prevent its informants from being 'ensnared by the pervasive network' of SADF MI, 'which uses its position to limit the scope of investigations into the "Third Force."' At this point, Third

Force elements remained a 'semi-autonomous and powerful force inside the security forces, able to call on its own supplies of arms and ammunition (smuggled in from Mozambique, captured from ANC arms caches, and smuggled from former military bases in Namibia).'[39]

In November 1992, the Goldstone Commission raided the offices of the Africa Risk Analysis Consultancy (Pty) Ltd (ARAC), the front for DCC headquarters.[40] The Goldstone Commission's discovery of the DCC made it impossible for the De Klerk government to deny any longer the Third Force's existence. Displeased with the commission's public release of its findings yet alarmed by the apparent extent to which the security forces were subverting the negotiations, in November 1992 De Klerk appointed South African Air Force Lt Gen. Pierre Steyn to further investigate Third Force activities. By 10 December, Steyn, assisted by SADF Counter-Intelligence, had 'started to uncover what appeared to be a veritable rat's nest of unauthorized and illegal activity within Military Intelligence.'[41] Steyn briefed De Klerk and his cabinet about a number of units within the security forces that were 'actively pursuing their own political and criminal agendas.' Steyn divided these actors into three categories: 'those in command positions' who could not cease their involvement in anti-ANC activities; 'those in command positions who could be discredited by the activities of their subordinates; and those who were following their own agendas against the interests of the state.'[42] Of course, it seems likely that these motivations often overlapped. Elements within the security forces actively blocked attempts to further verify Steyn's findings, and only after the transition did various revelations from the TRC corroborate them. Nonetheless, the Steyn Report confirmed what ANC intelligence had always suspected regarding security force complicity in Third Force violence.

After Steyn delivered his findings, De Klerk fired 23 senior military officers, including two generals, on 19 December 1992 for their involvement in political violence.[43] All 23 of those fired had worked for the front company Pan-Afrik Industrial Investment Consultants (PAIIC); these operatives were paid out 18 months' salary. The government also made noises about prosecuting some of these fired officers, but never followed through on this threat. Deputy minster of defence Gene Louw told the press that some of these officers 'might have acted out of political convictions, but in the majority of cases these were people who were following their own agenda under the influence of actions that demand disciplinary steps, be they criminal or in the form of reprimands.'[44] Though many apartheid covert operators were indeed following their own agenda and had committed prosecutable offences, as we have seen, the nature and extent of the knowledge they possessed made most of them virtually untouchable. Thus, the regime hurried to reach a settlement with DCC agent Jan Anton Nieuwoudt, who won a R220,000 payout from the SADF shortly before the 27 April 1994 election. Another DCC officer, Commander Jack Widdowson, successfully sued the SADF for unfair dismissal after being sacked as part of De Klerk's purge of officers in December 1992.[45] In both cases, the payments were intended to buy these agents' silence regarding the extent of SADF MI operations; indeed, SADF Gen. Kat Liebenberg had secured authorization from the minister of defence to pay Nieuwoudt more than the amount of his claim.[46] In this context, it is also worth recalling SADF MI operative Gerrie Hugo's assertion, after defecting to the Transkei Defence Force in 1991, that the regime's intelligence services had so much evidence of NP corruption and wrongdoing that they were effectively immune from being held accountable (see Chapter Five). The journalist De Wet Potgieter characterized De Klerk's move as 'panicky measures by an insecure leader' following the 'bungled probe' carried out by Steyn, 'an over-ambitious' general.[47] Yet the DCC was at the heart of apartheid security elites' attempts to shape the transition by recruiting spies within the ANC leadership. It would appear that after the Goldstone Commission's findings De Klerk appointed Steyn to probe further because the initial discoveries were so explosive that they needed to be investigated within the military to maintain adequate secrecy and control. 'I am shocked…disappointed, but I'm also resolute,' De Klerk said.[48] He denied the existence of a Third Force as such, but conceded: 'I think I can say, yes, that the findings will lead to the conclusion that some of the activities did lead to the death of people.' He claimed to be an 'innocent bystander' of the clandestine violence, saying: 'The activities which have now come to my attention point to a process in which political office bearers were not fully informed or, very often, were misled.'[49]

The full scope of the Steyn Report long remained unknown, as Steyn, who began to receive threats, was 'said to have briefed the State President on the basis of a series of written reports rather than to have handed over a finished document.'[50] Steyn's main sources of information were the SADF counter-intelligence branch and the NIS.[51] He was also limited to investigating SADF MI 'rather than SADF's overall intelligence operations or those of the [SAP] and the other state security services.'[52] Although De Klerk fired or forcibly retired key SADF MI personnel in his December 1992 purge, afterwards Steyn expressed his concern at the investigation's lack of progress, and found that the SAP and SADF 'were spending more time on cover-ups and identifying leaks than gathering evidence,' and had destroyed key documents about destabilization operations by the DCC and other elements.[53] After the Steyn Report was submitted and Steyn himself took early retirement in 1993, the Goldstone Commission continued its investigation, issuing several interim reports followed by a comprehensive final report submitted on 18 March 1994. This final report, based on extensive interviews with serving security force personnel, uncovered 'a great deal of evidence to indicate that former and serving members of the police and the defence forces had become engaged in covert paramilitary activities aimed at destabilizing the settlement process, as well as in attempts to seek revenge against former colleagues.'[54]

Select portions of the Steyn Report emerged in 1996: they allegedly affirmed that there had been no SADF plot to overthrow De Klerk's government,[55] and revealed previously hidden dimensions of the SADF's nuclear, biological and chemical warfare programme, codenamed Project Coast, which was dismantled in 1993–4.[56] Yet this hardly explained De Klerk's firing of 23 officers, including two generals, after receiving the report or, for that matter, the post-transition refusal of the Mandela and Mbeki governments to reveal the report's full contents. In January 1997, the TRC determined that De Klerk had lied about the Steyn Report, whose existence he denied during a televised debate with Nelson Mandela in 1994 and in subsequent media interviews. Although 'technically speaking,' there had been no formal report, Steyn had given De Klerk and senior cabinet members a verbal briefing, substantiated by a 'staff report' submitted to De

Klerk 'comprising written notes and a diagram.'[57] More details about the Steyn Report emerged in 1997, when President Mandela, who had received the report as an oral briefing in 1994, gave a summary of it to the TRC. Mandela had considered the report's revelations to be so explosive that he did not release its details, lest they jeopardize the post-1994 transition.[58] Until then, the report had been kept secret by De Klerk, Mandela, and two attorneys general who had access to its contents. The information given by Mandela's office to the TRC included details about the apartheid regime's covert operations that corroborated claims by ex-apartheid assassins such as Joe Mamasela and various archival documents. This information portrayed a range of apartheid military and police covert operations designed to sustain violence that would undermine the transition.

More complete details finally emerged when a document summarizing the Steyn Report was compiled by TRC investigators and leaked to the press. The summary indicated that SADF Special Forces units, specifically the commandos of 1 Recce and 5 Recce (referred to in the report summary as 'Reconnaissance Regiments One and Five'), had been responsible for the train massacres across the Witwatersrand that began shortly after the start of negotiations, in an operation known as Project Pastoor. In this, they were assisted by the railway company's Spoornet intelligence network, which was composed of old SADF Special Forces and CCB operatives. Several senior Special Forces members were loaned to the Spoornet intelligence programme and helped to mastermind the violence under its auspices. Three of them later resigned. The ANC 'seemed to have information linking the military to the killings but had not used it.'[59] Vlakplaas and the SADF's 7 Medical Battalion were also involved in such missions, and ex-Rhodesian Selous Scouts were alleged to have been involved in the train massacres as well. In addition to such 'seemingly random violence,' these units engaged in other 'activities' such as 'targeted assassinations' and involvement in 'inter-organizational conflict.'[60] The summary also noted that despite the absence of concrete evidence, 'monitoring of conversations, movement, and transport' indicated that under Project Pastoor, the Recces were involved not only in the East Rand violence, but were also deployed in KwaZulu during this period, 'raising the possibility that they may be involved in activities there.'[61]

The Steyn Report gave details of training camps within South Africa set up by the DCC to train RENAMO and IFP militants, camps which were active at least into the early 1990s. After DCC offices in Durban had coordinated their training, the IFP forces were then armed by private security companies 'with strong ex-Rhodesian links.'[62] In addition to IFP forces, the DCC also trained Ciskei forces (see Chapter Five). Apartheid forces established arms caches and training bases for right-wing paramilitary forces in game reserves in both South Africa and neighbouring countries, and also stockpiled weapons in countries including Kenya, Zambia and Mauritius – there was even mention of stockpiles in Portugal – which could then be used as 'springboards' to topple African governments, and destabilize post-transition South Africa. The plan to cache weapons abroad was known as the Palmeira Project. Under its auspices, Project Pastoor shared an office with the DCC in Malawi.[63]

The revelations also further exposed the extent to which the IFP was a creature of the regime. The report found that the DCC had used SADF-run private security firms as fronts to train IFP personnel and, according to several sources in the report, organized an infrastructure whereby IFP forces could deploy 24,000 armed Zulus in the PWV (Pretoria-Witwatersrand-Vereeniging, the former name for Gauteng province) area within 24 hours. At the political level, the DCC also had full control of the 'Zulu faction's participation in talks with the government.'[64] Other arms conduits were established between South Africa and Mozambique: channels that the SADF had previously used to supply RENAMO were now being used to bring untraceable weapons into South Africa. In this way, weapons were brought through the Kruger National Park into the PWV area, while the Durban police imported AK-47s from Mozambique to arm IFP militants. Other weaponry was believed to have been funnelled from Mozambique to Afrikaner Weerstandsbeweging (AWB) extremists. The report further detailed the existence and location of arms caches near Pretoria, and the SADF's support for right-wing organizations. It confirmed that a right-wing coup was being planned. Steyn had urged the release of this information during the TRC proceedings, when certain details of the report came to light; later, the TRC itself wanted to release the report, but top-ranking members of the old military establishment insisted that they were unproven allegations which the NIS had released because it had been involved in a turf war with the SADF.[65]

The Steyn Report also discussed the activities of the SADF's notorious 7 Medical Battalion, which supplied poisons to SADF death squads and which was implicated in the use of chemical weapons against FRELIMO forces in Mozambique in the late 1980s. It discussed the chemical and biological warfare programme headed by Dr Wouter Basson, which was still under way during the transition; this programme, known as Project Jota, was being privatized to ensure its continued existence after the transition.[66] According to the Steyn Report, SADF Special Forces also 'probably' possessed a chemical and biological weapons programme; according to O'Brien, 'Steyn noted that the qualifier "probably" had to be used due to the "extensive destruction of documents" and other evidence, alongside fears by investigators that "those implicated would resort to murder if they felt threatened."'[67]

According to the report, during the transition high-ranking SADF officers met at the Loftus Versfeld rugby ground in Pretoria to discuss the creation of a new, CCB-type organization, after the CCB itself had been disbanded in 1992. This organization brought together veterans of SADF Special Forces units including 32 Battalion and paratroop battalions (the 'parabats'). Indeed, as we have seen, CCB personnel were reassigned among other secret units such as the DCC and PAIIC, which remained active at least until the month of the ANC's ascent to power. The TRC refused to release the document from Mandela's office because much of it consisted of 'untested allegations'; however, the TRC investigative team that drafted the summary of the Steyn Report noted that Steyn himself had described the allegations as 'corroborated' or 'probably true.'[68] The report discussed 'destabilization' as 'encompass[ing] a variety of actions broadly designed to destabilize the internal and external situations. There seems to be some suggestion that there was an intention of creating sufficient disorder to enable the military to step in credibly to create order.'[69] As we have seen, this same goal, albeit on a smaller scale, was envisaged by SADF MI as the final objective of its destabilization operations in Transkei and Ciskei during this period.

In 2006, more details about the Steyn Report came to light when the government declassified a key report. This further confirmed the full extent of the SADF's involvement in the unprecedented violence during the transition. In the case of the train massacres, Special Forces collaborated with the railways parastatal Spoornet, thereby showing apartheid counterinsurgency's seamless integration across institutions of state and society. The report also highlighted the SADF's role in the hostel violence on the East Rand. The Steyn investigation drew these conclusions after monitoring 'telephone conversations, evacuations, and transfers.'[70] The report attributed most of the Third Force violence to a secret SADF programme known initially as Operation Phantom, and then renamed Project Pastoor, which was said to have deviated from its original objectives – which were never specified – and to have become unaccountable to and uncontrollable by the top military and political echelons. These senior leaders and officials were found by the report not to have been responsible for the violence.[71] Instead, the operation's personnel, sourced from SADF Special Forces and the CCB, were said to have abused their positions and exceeded government policy. Yet the Steyn Report had recommended firing some of the highest-ranking officers in the SADF, including chief of the army Gen. Georg Meiring, chief of staff Gen. Kat Liebenberg, and SADF Military Intelligence chief Joffel van der Westhuizen.[72] This would suggest a level of complicity at the SADF's highest ranks. De Klerk and Roelf Meyer both had a positive relationship with Liebenberg,[73] who, as commander of SADF Special Forces, 'had presided over the military destabilization of Mozambique and Angola,' a strategy the security forces were still implementing in South Africa itself.[74] Although Steyn recommended sacking Liebenberg in 1992, De Klerk worried that this could disrupt the transition; instead, he kept Liebenberg on board, leaving him 'well situated to continue covert actions against the NP's enemies, should he have chosen to do so.'[75] De Klerk himself later recalled that he considered firing Liebenberg and several other top generals but decided against it because he lacked 'indisputable evidence' of their involvement, and because alienating the SADF further could sink the negotiations process altogether. According to De Klerk, 'the SADF represented the government's ultimate power base and was the final guarantor of the constitutional process that we had initiated,' and there were several possible scenarios that could sink that process: the ANC attempting to seize power, the secession of KwaZulu-Natal, or a right-wing rebellion.[76]

Plausible deniability aimed not just to hide the regime's responsibility: it was also intended to protect individual military and political elites. Instead of being dismissed, Liebenberg and van der Westhuizen retired after overseeing the ANC's transition to power and the SADF's conversion to the SANDF; meanwhile, Gen. Meiring, who denied any knowledge of the covert activities described in the Steyn Report, was appointed the first SANDF chief of staff. In compiling his report, Steyn's reliance on the SADF's department of counter-intelligence and on the NIS[77] indicates that during this murky period certain intelligence units were more committed than others to following the regime's civilian leadership, even as they all remained implicated to a greater or lesser degree in the shadow war against the ANC.

The 2006 report also revealed several new dimensions of the regime's counterinsurgency programme for the first time. These included revelations that the SADF had given orders to kill two detained Portuguese operatives; the regime trained paramilitary 'resistance movements' in neighbouring states; the SADF ordered PAC elements to kill ANC members in Transkei; and senior officers in the SADF 'were involved in framing contingency plans for a right-wing coup.'[78] The revelation about SADF-controlled PAC elements corroborates Chris Hani's assertion, made shortly before he was murdered, that the PAC's spiralling violence bore the hallmarks of apartheid false-flag operations. De Klerk's spokesman, Dave Steward, repeated the claim that at the time Steyn had briefed De Klerk verbally but had not submitted a written report. He called the revelations 'horrifying,' and emphasized that in taking action De Klerk 'had to rely on the very security force personnel who were being accused.' Once Steyn briefed De Klerk, 'the shutters went down and there was no way to know who on the list was deeply involved or not,' Steward said.[79]

It is difficult to overstate the Steyn Report's importance in revealing the full extent of apartheid counterinsurgency operations. Yet there is reason to believe that the disclosures about the mysterious report, which gradually came to light, stopped short of exposing its full contents. Earlier literature has mentioned 'that after mid-1992 senior SADF commanders, including the Chief of Staff (Intelligence), had a series of discreet bilateral meetings with leaders of the ANC and its armed wing.'[80] Yet these contacts appear to have been more sinister than a mere parley between counterparts from opposing sides, especially when viewed against the backdrop of counterinsurgency operations ongoing at that time, and considering that the documents cited above suggest a deliberate strategy to recruit spies in the ANC and to marginalize Hani and other committed leftists within the ANC and MK. Archival documents speculate that the alleged meeting between SADF MI and Modise's MK contingent may have been at the heart of the Steyn Report, and their mention of SADF MI operations underway in April 1994 reinforces this hypothesis. When Nieuwoudt designed the SADF plan to use Ciskei as a base from which to monitor Transkei, he was a member of the DCC, working directly under Col. Nel and director of the DCC Brig. Botha. This operation was approved all the way up the SADF chain of command, from SADF MI chief Rudolph 'Witkop' Badenhorst and his deputy, Joep Joubert. When the Ciskeian front company IR-CIS's cover was blown by the Goldstone Commission, SADF Chief Liebenberg and minister of defence Kobie Coetsee 'were aware of it and considered paying Nieuwoudt to shut him up (and probably did). This meant IR-CIS was not merely an intelligence gathering unit but also operational.'[81] According to Nieuwoudt, the PAIIC included SADF members 'who needed good covers because they operated internationally,' as well as operatives from the SAP and the NIS. It both gathered intelligence and launched operations; this was identical to the way the CCB operated.[82] Well after the Third Force violence had begun to recede, then, SADF MI was still clearly engaged in ultra-sensitive operations that the regime went to great lengths to hide: it seems clear that these were the recruitment and handling of prominent spies within the ANC.

In an interview with the author, former MK intelligence operative Barry Gilder suggested that Barnard's and Nieuwoudt's claims to have recruited spies extensively within the ANC and MK should be attributed in part to 'boastfulness.'[83] Yet although the apartheid intelligence operatives may have been prone to bravado, the actions of the NP government and its ANC successors speak loudest on this matter. Ferdi Barnard continued his criminal activities with impunity until well after the ANC came to power, and was not tried for his self-proclaimed role in the 1989 murder of David Webster until

1998; meanwhile, on the eve of elections, the National Party made massive payouts to Nieuwoudt, Joe Mamasela and other death squad and intelligence operatives to ensure their silence, while the ANC made no attempt to prosecute them or compel them to testify to the TRC. Mamasela openly speculated that this was because he could name apartheid spies within the new ANC government (see Chapter Ten). In addition to the massive payout given to Nieuwoudt, in April 1993 President De Klerk and his cabinet authorized a R17.5 million payout to be divided among 83 Vlakplaas operatives, with R1 million designated for their commander Eugene de Kock. De Klerk 'rejected any insinuation' that the payouts were intended to buy the death squad operatives' silence, and argued in parliament that he was disbanding Vlakplaas since many of these operatives were former ANC and PAC members who would be targeted by the ANC when it came to power.[84]

How Much Did De Klerk Know?

One analysis of Third Force violence from April 1992 insisted there was 'no secret army with a hidden chain of command going to the top of the [SADF] with De Klerk's secret encouragement.'[85] However, on the cusp of transition, scholar John Saul noted that De Klerk might be 'more actively complicit in security force undertakings' than was apparent in the light of available evidence, since De Klerk stood to gain politically by balancing the right-wingers' violence against the ANC's demands, causing him to interpret 'anything that weakens the ANC' as 'pure gain.' Hence he seemed 'prepared, *in furtherance of his own purposes*, to grant both his security arm and Buthelezi's vigilantes room for manoeuvre.'[86] De Klerk had denied the existence of the Steyn Report when Mandela raised the issue with him in a televised debate in 1992; he denied it again when the newspaper *New Nation* asked him about it subsequently. But in January 1997, the TRC revealed that De Klerk had lied, having received a series of verbal briefings and a 'staff report' consisting of written notes and a diagram. As details emerged during TRC proceedings of apartheid 'death farms,' high-ranking ANC members claimed it was impossible that De Klerk and the National Party leadership did not know about the death squad operations. Azanian People's Organization spokesman David Lebethe said he found it strange that De Klerk was still free after prima facie evidence had emerged 'implicating him in the discovery of the remains' of Charles Ndaba and Mbuso Shabalala: 'As head of state, then, he knew of all the activities surrounding political activism, especially to do with the liberation movements.'[87] In response, De Klerk denied any knowledge of death squad operations, and threatened legal action against ANC spokespersons, including deputy defence minister Ronnie Kasrils.[88] O'Brien notes: 'it remains unclear – to this day – just which covert operations [De Klerk] was aware of (both during his presidency and previously as a co-opted member of the SSC [State Security Council]), and how much he knew about those operations.'[89] According to Henderson, De Klerk had only limited control over the intelligence services he inherited, which threatened his control over the apartheid parliament and the negotiation process. These forces hid many of their covert operations from him, and De Klerk only asserted control when 'forced to by public "smoking gun" evidence, such as leaked or uncovered security services' files ordering unauthorized covert operations.'[90] However, former security force personnel were adamant that they had perpetrated atrocities with the government's full knowledge. In August 1995, Dries van Heerden, a 'Vlakplaas operative turned [state] witness, said after the unit blew up the headquarters of the South African Council of Churches in 1988,' police minister Adriaan Vlok 'went to the farm to congratulate them.' Dirk Coetzee, whom the Security Branch had tried to kill with a bomb embedded in a portable cassette player after he defected to the ANC, 'said it was "obvious" from this that Mr De Klerk must have known more than he has acknowledged. "Did Vlok lie to the leader of his party?" he said. "Can De Klerk really be that stupid?"'[91]

Another Vlakplaas commander, Eugene de Kock, has written: 'the person who sticks most of all in my throat is former State President FW de Klerk…because…he simply did not have the courage to declare: "Yes, we at the top levels condoned what was done on our behalf by the security forces. What's more, we instructed that it should be implemented."'[92] De Kock also pointed out that De Klerk had sat in on the State Security Council meetings and 'could have found out if he wanted to.'[93] The spirit of denial in the regime's upper echelons is characterized by Gen. Malan travelling to Durban in January 1990 to discuss a 'sensitive matter' with De Klerk, which Malan himself claimed to have just discovered: the existence of the CCB, which, according to De Klerk's autobiography, 'had been using totally unacceptable methods and strategies against the ANC and other revolutionary organizations.'[94] In November 1990, the Harms Commission exonerated Malan as defence minister from responsibility for the CCB's death squad activities.

De Klerk's officers' purge reinforces the thesis of a counterinsurgency agenda distinct from the National Party's political agenda, while raising the possibility that the outcome of the negotiations reflected a state compromise not only with the ANC to its left, but also with the security forces to its right. In the March 1992 state budget, 'half the defence budget of Rand 4.380 million (US$893.8 million) was earmarked for the SADF's clandestine Special Defence Account,' ostensibly to prevent security force elites from becoming too restive; De Klerk was also working to ensure that secret operatives would obtain immunity from prosecution under any future government.[95] Indeed, in 1992, SADF MI Col. Gert Hugo revealed in an interview that the SADF had 'contingency plans for a military takeover if the government appeared to be losing its grip on the ANC and its communist allies,' explaining that the military elite had 'so much dirt' on De Klerk's cabinet 'that they had become virtually untouchable.'[96] In an analysis from November 1992, *The Economist* reported the Goldstone Commission's findings that CCB operative Ferdi Barnard, 'a former policeman who has already been convicted of murder,' had been hired by SADF MI 'to conduct a smear campaign against the ANC' with authorization from top generals.[97] This new evidence proved De Klerk was either 'insincere and devious, or he has lost control of the security forces, especially the "special forces" of the army.' The analysis noted: 'An insincere De Klerk is less frightening than one who has lost control,' and emphasized that although 'ANC propagandists' had capitalized on revelations of regime dirty tricks, the ANC 'feared a collapse of his administration even more,' as De Klerk was their only viable negotiating partner. During his in camera testimony at the inquest into the 1989 murder of David Webster, former CCB chief Joe Verster reportedly told the judge that De Klerk 'had assured the bureau that there would be no witch-hunt, and that he accepted it had acted in good faith against enemies of the state.' These assurances were most likely intended as much 'to appease' the generals 'as to protect them.'[98] Even De Klerk's limited purge in December 1992 would strain his administration's relations with the SADF almost to the breaking point.

After negotiations began, the regime had reconfigured its 'securocracy' to make it appear more innocuous and reinforce plausible deniability. In March 1990, one month after the start of negotiations, the regime altered its existing procedures for approving covert operations in order to better conceal them. The ANC submission to the TRC detailed 'a top-secret document' outlining 'plans to change the accounting procedures governing "sensitive defence activities" funded through the Special Defence Account, dated 13/03/90.' This memo was sent by SADF chief of staff Gen. Jannie Geldenhuys to defence minister Malan, and 'was co-signed by the Minister of Finance Barend du Plessis.' According to the memo, De Klerk had been 'briefed on a broad spectrum of sensitive projects' and had 'in principle' given his approval to ongoing and new 'Stratkom projects,' even proposing to establish 'a central controlling body for such operations.' The document specified that 'covert Stratkom projects are controlled and managed by the Secretary of the SSC,' which 'receives decisions and orders in this regard from the State President' and designates tasks and funds to 'Departments,' noting that 'Project Marion was one of over forty covert projects being funded at this time from the Special Defence Account.'[99] This evidence indicates that covert operations in the early transition period were indeed highly centralized, with a well-established chain of command leading to De Klerk himself. Security Branch and DCC spy Craig Williamson described to the TRC how within the apartheid state 'the operational procedures were designed by people who knew the law, in order to circumvent proof of legal responsibility for the deed by the upper echelon.'[100]

De Klerk had reorganized political and security institutions to diminish SADF MI's power in favour of the NIS, and to increase the cabinet's decision-making powers vis-à-vis the securocrats; to this end, he also disbanded the State Security Council in favour of the National Security Committee, precursor to the post-transition National Intelligence Coordinating Committee (NICOC). Yet despite its diminished brief, SADF MI remained very powerful because it retained control over the clandestine units carrying out Third Force violence and the Bantustan security structures. Meanwhile, De Klerk came increasingly to rely on NIS to keep him informed about far-right elements within the military and police that were working to undermine negotiations with the ANC.[101]

Counterinsurgency and the Fragmentation of State Decision-Making

The apartheid security apparatus was so deeply entrenched that the civilian NP government had to contend with extremist security force elements during its negotiations with the ANC. Sparks suggests that De Klerk was forced to tolerate destabilizing Third Force activities by elements within his security forces precisely because, 'never sure of his control over Botha's old securocrat establishment, [he] never wanted to put it to the test.'[102] Even if one assumes that De Klerk genuinely wanted to put a stop to the Third Force activities, it seems likely that he could not. In an interview at the onset of the transition, Mandela himself gave his negotiating partner the benefit of the doubt while painting a portrait of Third Force activities that historical hindsight has vindicated: 'I still regard De Klerk as a man of integrity, and I think he feels the same about me. We have developed an enormous respect for each other… But he has a problem with elements of his government – especially his security establishment, which is riddled with right-wingers who are not with him at all – and he is not being frank with me about that.'[103]

Pointing to pervasive racist attitudes in the security forces, Mkhondo surmised: 'De Klerk seemed to lack the executive and operational muscle to contain police excesses and the security forces escaped effective control… [He] faced a huge dilemma: he would have liked to establish political control over the security forces but, on the other hand, he needed them as an insurance policy in case negotiations failed.'[104] All the same, even after the limited purge 'all the [military intelligence] structures remain[ed] essentially in place. The notorious General Joffel van der Westhuizen (associated with the Goniwe "death signal")' remained 'head of MI.'[105] At the same time, South African military spending continued apace into 1993–4, with De Klerk's parliament voting in a defence budget of R3.7 billion for a military whose activities often remained clandestine.[106]

Recent evidence suggests that the security establishment repeatedly sought to shape the transition through psychological warfare operations that included feeding government decision-makers with false information about the ANC. Although we may never know the exact extent or provenance of these counterinsurgency operations, we can identify their contours in the light of archival documents from the transition era. It is known that De Klerk's attempts to investigate the full extent of these operations was subverted from within his own security establishment: in 1992, SADF MI's ultra-sensitive DCC, acting on an informer's tip-off, concealed or destroyed key evidence of ongoing operations before the state-appointed Goldstone Commission could uncover it. The informer, former head of the Pretoria murder and robbery squad Henk Heslinga, alerted SAP Gens. Le Roux and Van der Merwe of the commission's impending searches. Heslinga said: 'I copied a lot of documents in the evenings and over weekends and made sure that General Le Roux and General Van der Merwe received the information. I am today very proud that I acted as a double agent. It was for a good cause and I provided all the information to the police.'[107]

There is also strong evidence that during the transition, elements within the apartheid security forces attempted to manipulate government decision-makers by providing them with false intelligence indicating that an extremist faction within the ANC planned to undermine the negotiations through violence. In April 1990, an NIS official distributed to the right-wing Conservative Party a secret intelligence report purporting to describe an ANC plan to assassinate right-wing leaders.[108] Over the coming months, the security forces continued to claim that the ANC was planning to launch a 'general insurrection,' and in December 1990 'the senior security chiefs reportedly briefed De Klerk's inner cabinet ministers on what they claimed was the ANC's "four-year hidden agenda to seize power."'[109] Beginning in September 1992, the NIS had received reports about an operation codenamed Operation Mayibuye involving Chris Hani, Ronnie Kasrils, Mac Maharaj and Siphiwe Nyanda, whose aim was to organize an extremist faction of the SACP, while other reports from the Western Cape emerged about a similar SACP operation under Tony Yengeni's command, codenamed Operation Snowball.[110] After Hani's murder in April 1993, the NIS received intelligence in the form of a detailed report about yet another conspiracy by ANC extremists, codenamed Operation Sunrise, which was allegedly organized by a veritable who's who of the ANC and SACP: Joe Slovo, Ronnie Kasrils, Tokyo Sexwale, Winnie Mandela, Siphiwe Nyanda, Harry Gwala, Rapu Molekane, Peter Mokaba, Tony Yengeni, and Blade Nzimande.[111] According to reports obtained by the NIS in June 1993, this extremist group was alleged to have organized an armed faction independent of regular ANC and MK leadership structures. The document claimed this faction had planned attacks on the IFP leadership as well as other violent acts intended to sabotage the ANC–NP negotiations, after which it planned to install a 'Transitional Executive Council' and assassinate moderate ANC leaders such as Cyril Ramaphosa. The report also claimed the group had already smuggled AK-47s and RPG-7s to MK and Self-Defence Unit members on the East Rand.[112] After obtaining the document, NIS director Niël Barnard ensured that some agents corroborated this information independently of each other, then circulated it to De Klerk and several government ministers.

The journalist De Wet Potgieter has asserted that if the document about Operation Sunrise was in fact a fabrication to misinform South Africa's civilian leaders, 'it was a damn good one' because it succeeded in duping 'top spies' such as Barnard and national police commissioner Johan van der Merwe.[113] Yet despite these men's apparent certainty about the report's authenticity, it remains entirely consistent with a string of earlier SADF MI psychological operations calibrated to sow division within the ANC and to alarm policy-makers and the broader public about the ANC's supposed hidden motives. There are further signs that this document was in fact a forgery most likely circulated by elements within SADF MI and intended to fool not only South Africa's civilian leadership but also the NIS's intelligence networks. The document explained the alleged ANC faction's shift toward violence as being based on 'a recent assessment by Slovo that the ANC is unlikely to win over 50 percent of the vote in an election [which] has prioritized consideration of an insurrectionary perspective, spearheaded by *Operation Sunrise*.'[114] Yet by 1993 the ANC had good reason to believe that it would win a comfortable majority in a free-and-fair election, as it eventually did, and it is implausible that Slovo would have miscalculated so badly – or planned to violently divide the ANC as a result – on the eve of victory. Rather, the apartheid security establishment had been maligning Slovo since long before the transition began,[115] and the document echoes the regime's attempts in an earlier era to portray Slovo as a communist mastermind. For example, in 1990 a disinformation campaign allegedly based on captured SACP documents claimed that Joe Slovo, although he publicly endorsed the negotiations, secretly planned to undermine them with violence, causing De Klerk to demand that Mandela expel Slovo from the ANC negotiations team (see Chapter Four).[116] Again, in this case, the regime's civilian leadership may have been duped by elements within their own security forces who sought to undermine the negotiations. On the other hand, it is plausible that De Klerk and his cabinet knew the intelligence was fabricated but feigned a sincere reaction to it because to do so advanced their agenda during the negotiations; they would have been naive to take this intelligence at face value when distorted information had been such a key feature of their own regime's propaganda for so long. Indeed, apartheid intelligence services had misled the political leadership with false intelligence before, notably during Namibia's 1989 transition when SADF MI fabricated intelligence that SWAPO militants were massing in violation of negotiated agreements.[117]

Furthermore, aside from such apparent misinformation, there was never any breakaway faction of MK or any other rejectionist front within the ANC seeking to subvert a negotiated transition. The only kernel of truth that the Operation Sunrise document likely contained was its allegation of arms smuggling to MK and SDU formations in Thokoza, Soweto and the East Rand. However, during this period violence still raged between the ANC and various regime proxies, and in this context the ANC's efforts to arm its loyalists were widely known. Hence evidence of ANC arms smuggling does not suggest the emergence of an extremist ANC faction, especially since the ANC's top leadership had openly authorized the formation of the SDUs.[118] It seems more likely that SADF MI manufactured the information about this 'revolutionary faction' that was 'building up an independent underground armed capability' in order to goad the De Klerk government into a pre-emptive military response that would very likely sink the negotiations and trigger fresh waves of violence.

There were also several precedents for SADF MI using sophisticated operations to spread misinformation of this sort. These included the campaign to erode SWAPO's electoral majority in Namibia, and the false police report from 1993 that Hani and Sexwale had been involved in bank robberies (see Chapter Seven). Other archival documents also reveal an SADF MI strategy from 1991 to invade the Transkei, kill strongman Bantu Holomisa and Chris Hani, and eradicate MK units there on the pretext that MK itself was planning attacks on civilian targets to disrupt the ANC–NP negotiations (see Chapter Five).[119] Finally, the Operation Sunrise document mentions: 'MK Commander, Joe Modise, is excluded from the operation, and is believed to have no knowledge of it.'[120] It seems doubtful that the MK commander could have been unaware of such an elaborate operation involving so many key ANC and MK members. Rather, the document's explicit insistence that Modise was excluded from the plot seems telling in the light of the evidence discussed above that Modise may have been recruited as an informer by SADF MI.

The apartheid intelligence services' warnings about Operation Sunrise and other alleged intelligence plots during the transition foreshadowed the myriad post-transition accusations and leaks regarding informers and secret cliques within the government and opposition that were plotting to destabilize or overthrow the ANC government. Some of these plots, and the documents purporting to reveal them, are more convincing than others. It is entirely plausible, for example, that the ANC's intelligence apparatus should have contemplated blackmailing members of the De Klerk cabinet, using intelligence at its disposal (see below). Moreover, some of these plans may not have been authorized from the top: in mid-1992, for example, reports alleged that the ANC Security Department's operations were not fully transparent to the ANC's top leadership, as 'ANC security men' still loyal to former Security Department commander Jacob Zuma were said to 'starve' Mandela and his new choice of ANC Security Department chief, Mosiuoa 'Terror' Lekota, of information. Zuma had been named ANC deputy secretary-general and was 'said to be on cordial terms with' former Security Branch chief Gen. Basie Smit.[121]

As negotiations with the ANC advanced, the NP leadership received threats in a letter dated 16 March 1992 and addressed to law and order minister Hernus Kriel from the 'Central Command Cell' of the 'Inner-Circle' group, which described itself as 'a well-structured group of former members of the South African Defence Force, Military Intelligence, Special Forces, South African Police Task Force, former Security Police and of the National Intelligence Service.'[122] The 'Inner-Circle' group's profile is consistent with the limited information available elsewhere about Die Organisasie ('The Organization'), which comprised hardline rejectionists who were mid- and high-ranking personnel within the SADF and SAP. The Inner-Circle threatened to 'hunt down and destroy' NP cabinet ministers and their families should they continue negotiations with the ANC, and to trigger a civil war in South Africa; the apartheid regime's own record of striking at overseas ANC targets lent these threats some credence. Ellis also mentions the Binnekring ('Inner Circle') organization, founded by former CCB operatives, which '[combined] drug-trafficking and gun-smuggling for profit with activities designed to bolster opposition to the ANC.'[123] 'Inner Circle' was also alleged to have been involved in the Chris Hani assassination [see Chapter Seven].

For its part, MK intelligence had also infiltrated its regime counterparts, especially within the Security Branch and the NIS.[124] Near the end of the transition period, the ANC appears to have attempted to use intelligence at its disposal as leverage against key civilian and military decision-makers in the De Klerk regime. In a letter dated 31 March 1994, the so-called ANC Working Group claimed to have 'in our midst members and ex-members of the security forces, which puts formidable means at our disposal.'[125] The letter detailed a plan to blackmail the National Party leadership based on a range of sensitive information in its possession; this included a conspiracy to kidnap and murder 'Ishmael Ebrahiam,' an apparent reference to Ebrahim Ismael Ebrahim, then a member of MK and the ANC's National Executive Committee. The document alleged NIS director Niël Barnard had ordered his agents to kidnap Ebrahim 'with the explicit understanding that he should be killed after interrogation in order to protect the NIS operative Thami Zulu [an MK commander] in Swaziland.'[126] Following Lt Gen. Joubert's objections, however, the police were 'eventually forced to charge comrade Ebrahim and bring him before a court of law.' The letter further claimed to be investigating NIS 'atrocities' and contemplated offering apartheid intelligence operatives 'indemnity,' which had been 'guaranteed' by 'comrade Mandela' in exchange for their cooperation. It claimed to have enlisted the cooperation of such high-ranking figures as 'Gen. Jaap Joubert, Brig. McIntyre, Brig. Paul Abrie, Botes (ex-CCB)' who had 'access to information and operations, the contents of which will by far excel the revelations made to the Goldstone Commission.' The letter further claimed to have enlisted the cooperation of Judge Goldstone himself, and that its authors possessed the ability to 'completely destroy' a long list of NP leadership members, which would 'effectively nullify the National Party and its present election campaign.' The list included FW de Kerk, Pik Botha, Gerrit Viljoen, Dawie de Villiers, Kobie Coetsee, Adriaan Vlok, Roelf Meyer, Hernus Kriel, Johan van der Merwe, Mike Louw, Niël Barnard, and SADF chief of staff Kat Liebenberg. The document cited evidence in the Working Group's possession that would compromise these figures, including proof that Liebenberg, Van der Merwe and Barnard were involved in 'a project to kill so-called radical political leaders'; proof that De Klerk and Coetsee knew about the CCB's existence and its operations before the Goldstone Commission investigation; proof that while he was in power PW Botha had ordered Barnard's NIS to assassinate foreign minister Pik Botha; and the allegation that 'the telephones of various senior government officials are being wiretapped by NIS on the explicit instructions of Kobie Coetsee. Full details are available.' The document's authors also claimed to have proof of sexual escapades of various prominent NP members that could be used to blackmail them. It debated whether to use this information to expose NIS chief Barnard, or to 'persuade' him instead to 'make a clean break with the present government and associate him openly with the efforts of the ANC to rid the Security Forces and NIS of maverick elements.' It further outlined a plan whereby Mandela and other top ANC officials could present this information at a press conference, and rebut NP leaders' denials by challenging them to take a polygraph test. The document exuded a bravado that the ANC leadership very likely did not endorse; in the event, none of these cloak-and-dagger tactics was required for the ANC to trounce the NP at the polls. Nevertheless, the ANC Working Group document provides a window into the ANC's perception of regime operations, scarcely a month before the elections; as for its authenticity, Potgieter notes it 'was in fact torn out of a top-secret file from the then-Commissioner of Police, Johan van der Merwe's database.'[127]

The apartheid regime's wide-ranging programme of clandestine violence shaped many of the critical aspects of South Africa's negotiated transition, including pact-making between ANC and NP elites, and security sector reform. It also affected post-apartheid relations between state and society, undermining public trust, particularly in the security forces. Because these counterinsurgency operations have remained shrouded in secrecy, they have left a legacy of unanswered questions that cut to the heart of South Africa's transition: How far up the chain of command were the orders for Third Force violence given, and who knew about them beforehand? Which ANC and MK members were recruited by apartheid intelligence agencies, and in what manner did they collaborate? The following chapters examine the role of apartheid counterinsurgency in inhibiting the thoroughgoing transformation of the security forces during South Africa's security sector reform process, and the legacies of apartheid-era spy controversies in post-transition South African politics.

7

KILLING HANI

'"You can kill a revolutionary, but you can't kill the revolution." It's what we wanted to believe, but that didn't make it true.'
— Jeffrey Haas on the 1969 murder of Chicago
Black Panther leader Fred Hampton (*The Assassination of Fred Hampton*, 2010)

'Identify and eliminate the revolutionary leaders, especially those with charisma.'
— Strategy outlined in State Security Council meeting,
24 January 1987

On 10 April 1993 Chris Hani was killed in the driveway of his home in a suburb of Boksburg, close to Johannesburg, by Janusz Waluś, a white racist whom police apprehended almost immediately. Waluś was soon linked to Conservative Party member Clive Derby-Lewis, who had supplied Waluś with the murder weapon, a Z88 pistol traced to a weapons cache stolen from a South African Air Force armoury months earlier and linked to white racist Piet 'Skiet' Rudolph. Waluś was arrested in a red Ford Laser with the murder weapon still smoking on the back seat, 'a mere twelve minutes after the murder.'[1] Upon his arrest, Waluś claimed that the murder weapon 'had been "planted."'[2] According to the police docket, Waluś admitted to police that he had been in the suburb Dawn Park, 'but had said that others had placed the incriminating evidence, the gun and the gloves,' in his car, even as he acknowledged that police could 'prove that it was me' because he had Hani's blood on his shoes.[3] Waluś then maintained a 'stony silence' throughout his time in custody and while on trial. Police quickly ruled that the murder was not the result of a broader conspiracy. He and Derby-Lewis both received the death sentence, later commuted to life imprisonment. Despite widespread calls for reopening the inquest into Hani's murder, no post-transition government has dared to do so.

Yet Hani had previously been the target of regime surveillance and several assassination attempts. An ex-MK guerrilla who had received special forces training in East Germany and Yugoslavia and regularly served as Chris Hani's bodyguard related a harrowing near miss which occurred only months before Hani was killed. The former bodyguard said that after Hani's return to South Africa from exile in 1990, 'Chris used to be surveilled. When we were still together we used to tell him hey, let's [do] counter-surveillance, we are being followed.'[4] Even after the ANC dismissed this ex-guerrilla from Hani's retinue, Hani would still occasionally call on him for additional security. On this particular occasion in January 1993, 'the mission was to go and wait for Chris.' Hani had 'boarded a plane in Johannesburg, which was going to land at seven o'clock in East London.' As he waited for Hani's plane to arrive, the MK operative 'discovered that there were askaris inside the airport, almost a platoon. I recognized three askaris. One I knew because of his involvement in killing MK comrades in roadblocks and raids.' Recognizing the danger, he returned to his car, then discreetly re-entered the airport, 'but armed now, with two F1 grenades and a Makarov [pistol].' Ominously, the usual airport security team was nowhere to be found: the askaris 'were manning everything.' The guerrilla 'took cover next to a pillar' and instructed his partner to go and inform Hani of the threat. Hani replied, 'command, Commander!' implying that the MK operative must seize the initiative. Scanning the airport, he noticed the askaris' command post on the upper floor and realized: 'if I took them by surprise, disarmed them, then Chris comes to where I am, their mission will be over.' The guerrilla went upstairs and 'confronted' the askaris 'carrying a grenade and a pistol, so there was no other option for them because I was going to shoot them. Right straight in the airport! Then fight my way out with two grenades.' Knowing the askaris would avoid inflicting casualties among white civilians at the airport, especially since their operation 'was not sanctioned by the De Klerk government, this was dirty work of the CCB,' the MK guerrilla successfully neutralized the apparent trap.[5] After escorting Hani out of the airport, he discovered that Hani had been sent without any bodyguards accompanying him on the flight, contrary to MK security procedures, supposedly due to a 'mistake' at the ANC offices in Johannesburg.[6] This left several glaring questions about the askari team's mission at the airport, and the planning that left Hani unguarded, 'because there are no coincidences like that, you know? And I'm trained in intelligence, I've been a security man for a long time.'[7]

This unresolved incident has convinced the ex-guerrilla that Waluś 'was not a lone ranger.' The speed and precision of the assassination itself suggested an elaborate surveillance operation of the sort that the ex-guerrilla himself had previously detected while serving as Hani's bodyguard. He suspects that Hani's assassins were managed as an intelligence cell to conceal a broader network. The fact that Hani had been on the flight unguarded suggested some coordination between elements within the ANC's Johannesburg office who booked Hani's flight and the askaris waiting at the airport that evening. Furthermore, during the ensuing investigation into Hani's death, 'no one ever came to us as Chris Hani's ex-guards when they were investigating, maybe to ask what we know or what we saw. I mean when someone is killed suspiciously, you go even to a servant, even to a garden boy, and get facts and follow leads. So, it didn't happen to us, as you are the first one asking me.'[8]

This chapter discusses the assassination of MK commander and South African Communist Party (SACP) leader Chris Hani on the eve of South Africa's transition to democracy. It theorizes the impact of assassinating anti-colonial struggle leaders, suggests that Hani's killing was the result of a broader conspiracy rather than the work of a lone gunman, and considers the impact of Hani's assassination on post-transition South Africa. Hani's assassination encapsulates quintessential aspects of 'sharp' counterinsurgency in terms of questions of ultimate responsibility and plausible deniability. Assassinating the leader of an anti-colonial struggle bears an incalculable impact on social movements and insurgents, leading to fragmentation, silencing, and shifting the political terrain inexorably rightward, thereby closing off options for real transformation. Such assassinations especially destroy the legitimacy of anti-colonial movements by killing beloved leaders with a reputation for incorruptibility. As De Witte writes about the impact of Lumumba's January 1961 assassination in Congo at a critical juncture in African decolonization: 'his downfall was a sign that a neo-colonial counteroffensive was already gaining ground,' a counteroffensive that set back the progress of decolonization and signalled the colonial forces' readiness to safeguard their wealth and position through clandestine violence even as African countries gained their independence.

The history of anti-colonial struggles for independence is strewn with the bodies of struggle leaders killed by colonial counterinsurgency forces and their collaborators. The exact details of these assassinations have typically been shrouded by circumstances calculated by the colonial authorities to ensure plausible deniability. Indeed, even after the exact details of certain assassinations have finally emerged, the conventional narrative – backed by what some scholars refer to as the 'colonial archive' – preserves the veil of ambiguity that casts lasting doubt on competing modes of evidence,[9] thus ensuring plausible deniability. In so doing, this narrative also casts doubt upon the testimony of those from whom competing evidence has been derived, thereby reinforcing colonial power relations and a 'grammar of domination' that preserves the subaltern status of the anti-colonial struggle and its participants even well after formal independence and the transfer of power have been achieved. The 'evidentiary procedures' that arise from the colonial archive problematize the very 'foundational character of evidence,'[10] as the colonial state's security institutions, in investigating the assassination, assert their power to decide which evidence is admissible or relevant, thus shaping for posterity the record of what happened, and why.

Consider, for example, David Lemke's 2007 characterization of Patrice Lumumba's assassination as having occurred in 'unclear circumstances': in fact, by Lemke's time of writing, archival research and the testimonies of Lumumba's assassins and their co-conspirators had revealed the exact details of the joint operation by the Belgian secret services, the CIA, and Congolese and Katangese officials that killed Lumumba.[11] Yet the original narrative of plausible deniability about Lumumba's murder has left an imprint of ambiguity that continues to perpetuate itself even though the full details of the assassination have unambiguously come to light.

Survivors are then left to cope with wreckage, and surviving leaders are often forced to compromise or face the possibility that they themselves may be targeted. The case of Cameroonian independence leader Félix-Roland Moumié, assassinated by the French SDECE intelligence service at a conference in Geneva on newly independent states on 3 November 1960, illustrates this perfectly: Moumié's predecessor in the Cameroonian independence movement Union des Populations du Cameroon (Cameroon Peoples' Movement), Ruben Um Nyobé, had himself been assassinated by the French in September 1958 near his home village in Cameroon. Moumié, who took up the struggle, was subsequently poisoned with thallium.

The colonial state's ability to covertly orchestrate such assassinations represents the ultimate symbol of its power. The ability to locate a target and strike it by bullet or explosion, with all the surveillance and intelligence gathering required to prepare for the event, is the ultimate mark of the state security forces' counterinsurgency proficiency. Political assassinations shatter the possibility for politics by highlighting the degree of stances and micro-gestures that will not be tolerated. It thus destroys what Durkheim has called 'the social life of the psyche.' In response to Gayatri Spivak's question, 'Can the subaltern speak?' we can answer no, not when the subaltern, standing on principle, has been murdered. We can also better understand the impact of such assassinations by considering the leader as an embodied figure in a political struggle. These leaders' bodies, having absorbed and reflected a whole series of postures, gestures and behaviours over time, become historical sites that have accumulated acts of resistance. These acts have destabilized the fabric of the surveillance state, whose coercive organ is intended to curtail micro-behaviours of resistance. These leaders' defiance has put in relief the kinds of behaviour normally controlled in myriad subtle ways by the surveillance state, and, in doing so, reveals the fabric of the surveillance state and the degree of its control. Thus, the state employs political assassination to ensure the subaltern's silence.

In many cases, where details of assassinations have been contradictory or incomplete, the colonial archive's narrative of events has gone virtually unchallenged. This has blunted the full impact of the assassination upon the historical currents in which it was set, and especially in terms of how it was designed to restrict the possibility of true post-colonial transformation. As De Witte writes, 'once Lumumba's government was ousted, an attempt was made to deprive the Africans of the true story of his overthrow: not only had Lumumba been physically eliminated, his life and work were not to become a source of inspiration for the peoples of Africa either.'[12] In Mozambique, Eduardo Mondlane, founder and leader of the Mozambican liberation movement FRELIMO, was killed in 1969 by the Portuguese intelligence services with intelligence supplied by FRELIMO defectors.[13] His successor, Samora Machel, would live to become president of independent Mozambique before perishing in 1986 on his way back from a summit with southern African leaders when his plane crashed into South Africa's Lebombo mountains, leaving no survivors aboard. There is strong evidence that the crash was the result of foul play by the South African security forces, who are alleged to have planted a beacon designed to mislead the aircraft's crew and cause them to misjudge their altitude and coordinates.[14]

Psychological Operations and Plots

As MK commander and SACP chief, Chris Hani had been second only to Mandela in popularity among South Africa's masses; his death triggered massive protests and riots that threatened to derail the peace negotiations and plunge the country into violence. Only Mandela's urgent televised address, in which he pleaded with black South Africans to consider their shared destiny with whites, averted total chaos.[15] In the aftermath of Hani's killing, as the dialogue between the regime and the ANC hung in the balance, the finding that Hani had been the victim of extremist loners was crucial to rallying the South African masses' support for continuing negotiations. Yet Hani had been, as we have seen, the target of several previous assassination attempts and of a sophisticated psychological warfare campaign by the regime to defame him.

Hani had been at the top of the apartheid regime's hit list for a long time: it had repeatedly tried to kill him when he was commanding MK forces from Lesotho, bombing his house in early 1980,[16] blowing up his car and narrowly missing him in June 1980, then launching a 1982 commando raid on ANC offices in Maseru: 'But then I was in Lusaka when this happened. They went for the flat where I was staying, my family, my wife and my three kids were there. But for some reason they hid next door with a Lesotho family'[17] (see Chapter Two). According to Dirk Coetzee, the Vlakplaas death squad commander who defected to the ANC in 1989, Hani 'was on the "hit list" of a secret security police death squad' (presumably Vlakplaas) for years afterward.[18] Upon his return from exile, Hani initially stayed at his brother-in-law's house in Orlando East, Johannesburg, where he 'started getting anonymous letters from a Major who said [Hani's] bodyguard was being targeted by the security forces.' The letter advised Hani to 'change his bodyguard.' Hani 'ignored the first letter,' but others soon followed, and MK 'began to take the threat seriously,' especially as the letters made it clear 'that the anonymous Major was following Chris's every movement.' Hani's bodyguard was ambushed one evening near his residence in Orlando, but 'was able to repel the attack and get away safely.' However, Hani was now obviously in danger, and MK headquarters decided to 'allow Chris to move to the Transkei until the situation was clear.'[19] Asked at a 6 July 1990 press conference in Cape Town how he felt 'about being identified by far-right groups as an assassination target,' Chris Hani jokingly referred to the alleged price on his head: 'I feel very disappointed that the right-wing feels that I am only worth R20,000.'[20] His popularity was in evidence at an SACP rally held on 29 July 1990 at the FNB soccer stadium in Johannesburg, and thereafter 'reports appeared in the foreign and local media in which Hani was defined as a threat' to the negotiations. According to these planted stories, Hani 'had an army of MK soldiers waiting for his command to scupper the negotiations.' Nqakula recalls that many cadres 'found it rather odd' that the ANC 'did not tackle the regime on Hani's behalf' regarding this disinformation.[21]

During Hani's stay in Transkei under the auspices of Bantu Holomisa's pro-ANC government, SADF MI hatched several plots to kill Hani and Holomisa, to be followed by an SADF intervention to destroy MK elements under the pretext of restoring order in Transkei.[22] These schemes culminated in the failed November 1990 coup attempt on Holomisa, and several subsequent SADF MI plots focused on destabilizing the Transkei (see Chapter Five). After Hani's arrival in Mthatha, ANC intelligence operative Ronnie Watson briefed Nqakula and Hani that the ANC would rise to power, but that 'some of the leaders of the movement would have their characters assassinated, and if the vilification did not lead to them being marginalized, they would be targeted for elimination.'[23] In late 1990, the apartheid regime withdrew Chris's indemnity, which led to a great public outcry and intervention by the ANC leadership, following which it was reinstated. As MK chief of staff, Chris Hani moved from Transkei to Johannesburg to oversee MK military headquarters (MHQ).[24] As ANC–NP negotiations progressed, plots to kill Hani evolved from military raids on the Transkei borderlands to intelligence operations targeting a high-profile political leader in the urban heart of South Africa. The assassination attempts were combined with operations intended to defame Hani and tarnish MK so as to weaken the ANC as elections approached.

A series of sinister, little-publicized incidents prior to Hani's assassination reveal the psychological warfare campaign intended to defame and discredit Hani as a way to lay the groundwork for his elimination. In the aftermath of the assassination, an article titled 'Who Killed Hani?' in the *African Communist* astutely analysed the purpose of such psychological operations: 'Part of the disinformation war is to create first and frequent impressions. The allegations need have no substance, and they may even be mutually contradictory (Hani was at once meant to be trying to take over MK and launch a separate renegade army, for instance).'[25] Key details about SADF MI psychological and information operations during the transition were revealed by SADF Maj. Nico Basson and published on 12 April 1991 by the *Vrye Weekblad*: 'Discrediting political leaders in the opposition camp is a popular strategy, especially in the army. In Namibia one of the main themes of the anti-SWAPO strategy was the discrediting of the senior leadership of the party. In South Africa this strategy has also been used with great success.'[26] Basson added that a department of

SADF Communications Operations ('Comops'), 'Komops Vyand,' had enjoyed great success for many years 'in the planting and dissemination of false information' on such leading ANC figures as Winnie Madikizela-Mandela. He named SADF MI Col. Tobie Vermaak as the head of this project.[27] The *African Communist* article pointed to the activities of the Returned Exiles Committee, composed of ANC members, including Sipho Phungulwa (see Chapter Three), who masqueraded as MK operatives who had become disgruntled after being imprisoned in ANC camps in Angola but who, in reality, had been recruited by SADF MI. The most prominent figure of this committee was Patrick Dlongwana, also known as Hlongwane or Harvey Maringa, who had been arrested in 1987 in Lusaka for attempting to infiltrate the ANC, as he was 'a notorious security policeman' who 'confessed to a lengthy and brutal career as an agent.'[28] Shortly before the July 1992 attempt on Hani's life, Dlongwana made an appearance on SABC television in a pre-recorded interview in which he threatened that the Returned Exiles Committee would assassinate ANC and MK leaders. Dlongwana was never brought to account for issuing these threats, nor was the SABC for broadcasting them. Thus, the motive for an ostensible lone assassin to kill Hani had been established in the public eye – on national television – prior to this failed attempt.[29] This is all the more striking considering the SABC's role in publicizing other supposed rifts within the ANC and MK which the apartheid security forces were keen to exploit (see Chapter Three).

Then, in July 1992, there was an attempt to assassinate Hani 'in broad daylight in central Johannesburg.'[30] As Hani walked downtown, discussing a sensitive matter with ANC stalwart Skenjana Roji,[31] a 'young black male' stalked Hani along Marshall Street on his way towards the SACP headquarters.[32] The would-be assassin then stepped into a women's hair salon, where he drew the suspicion of its employees as he 'fiddled with an object concealed in a windbreaker.' The shop employees were convinced that he was trying to cock a gun, and followed the young man back outside, where they recognized Hani half a block away and ran over to warn him.[33] Panicked, the would-be assassin ran across the street in heavy traffic and was nearly struck by oncoming vehicles; he then 'hurried over to a Toyota Cressida that had been hovering on the far side of the road, and spoke to two white males in the front. He then sprang into the back seat, and the car moved off at high speed.'[34] The Cressida 'later turned out to have false registration plates.'[35] The South African Police (SAP) were unwilling to investigate the incident, claiming they could not do so because no charges had been filed, even though the SACP held a well-publicized press conference within one hour of the event. When the SACP's lawyers laid formal charges, the police replied that an investigation was impossible because the vehicle's licence plate was false and therefore untraceable. The witnesses from the hair salon, and Hani himself, were never questioned in relation to the incident.[36]

Another incident with all the hallmarks of an SADF MI psychological operation was the widely publicized trial on 26 March 1993, two weeks before Hani's assassination, of alleged bank robber Solomon Mqanqeni and two accomplices. Facing charges in the Rand Supreme Court, the three men were alleged to be Self-Defence Unit members with MK connections. The confession that police extracted from Mqanqeni – who claimed he had been coerced – alleged that Hani and MK member Tokyo Sexwale had masterminded and profited from a series of bank robberies in 1991, distributing weapons to the robbers and receiving a portion of the loot at the ANC offices in Johannesburg's Shell House.[37] As the scandal emerged, minister of law and order Hernus Kriel 'accused MK of being nothing but criminals' and, referring to the ANC call for joint control over all armed formations in South Africa, cast doubt on MK's legitimacy: 'We are not interested in joint control over criminals…we have declared war against war-mongers and criminals.'[38] The SAP issued a statement implicating Hani and ANC member Tokyo Sexwale in the robbery,[39] yet they never once questioned, let alone contacted, Hani or Sexwale over their alleged involvement in these very serious crimes.[40] On the day that Mqanqeni and his accomplices gave their testimony in court, the three mysteriously escaped from Diepkloof prison, driving out of the prison's open front gates in the very truck in which they had entered. Five days later, the SACP issued the following statement: 'On the very evening of the statement being presented to court, Mqanqeni and his alleged accomplices mysteriously escaped from prison. Although we have no knowledge of the individual…we fear for his safety. Having usefully served a purpose, he may now well be an embarrassment to those who have used him.' [41] In a statement, Hani himself expressed concern for their safety: 'having served a useful purpose, I am worried that they might now be eliminated. In the past, fabricated escapes have been used to eliminate individuals.'[42] The regime's counterinsurgency forces were notorious for 'disappearing' collaborators who they feared might expose them. Indeed, Mqanqeni was killed by police during his alleged escape attempt.[43] In a statement following this incident, which happened only two weeks before Hani's murder, the SACP declared: 'As we move into an election campaign we can expect dirty tricks operations, directed against leading ANC-alliance figures, to move into top gear.'[44]

In the lead-up to Hani's assassination, the apartheid security forces, in concert with the NP government, intensified its programme to discredit Hani by portraying him as a black nationalist and radical leftist who was using the negotiations with the South African government to plan violence. Thus on 9 October 1992 NP minister of justice Kobie Coetsee warned: 'The ANC would be well advised to sever its links with the Communist Party and especially one Mr Hani.'[45] An 18-page disinformation document circulated by SADF MI and the NIS in late 1992, titled 'New Political Development: The South African People's Party (SAPP),' claimed that Hani and Winnie Madikizela-Mandela planned to form a breakaway faction of the ANC called the South African People's Party. This new party was said to include a secret military wing, the 'Black People's Army,' formed to attract militants from the ANC, PAC and SACP who were disenchanted with the ANC–NP negotiations, and who were undergoing training at secret bases in Zimbabwe while awaiting the cue for a mass invasion of South Africa. Minister of law and order Hernus Kriel was responsible for circulating the document. Yet it came to embarrass De Klerk's government nine days after Hani's assassination when Conservative Party MP Schalk Pienaar, who had taken the information contained in the document at face value, demanded to know why the South African government, which was keeping quiet in the aftermath of Hani's death, was not instead taking action against these dissident formations and proclaiming the truth about Hani's extremist activities prior to his assassination: 'Pienaar, obviously referring to a confidential security briefing he had received, presumably from De Klerk's securocrats, wanted to know why the government was not telling the public about Hani's South

African People's Party, "formed in a neighbouring territory... Why did the government not tell South Africa what Chris Hani was busy with in the last few months?"[46]

The document's release followed a typical pattern of SADF MI trying to destabilize South Africa's peace process through operations designed to pin the blame on alleged MK extremists. This strategy is especially interesting in the light of SADF MI's plan, described above, to cause a rift within the ANC between its paid informers and what it regarded as the hard-line communist 'Hani–Kasrils faction.' Further disinformation about Hani appeared in several media outlets in the months prior to his assassination, organized around the by-now familiar theme of Hani as an ANC renegade with a violent agenda: on 12 October 1992, *Rapport* said that Hani was planning to seize command of MK and the future South African army, and on 31 January 1993 the London *Sunday Times* claimed that Hani and Winnie Mandela were planning to split from the ANC. The Johannesburg correspondent for the London *Sunday Times*, Richard Ellis, was instrumental in the disinformation campaign, publishing stories about Hani with such outrageous headlines as 'South Africa's Saddam Stakes His Claim.'[47] Then, six days before Hani was killed, on 4 April 1993, *Rapport* ran a story that Hani and other senior MK members had held several secret, unauthorized meetings with the PAC's armed wing APLA in South Africa and Transkei 'aimed at securing mutual cooperation so as to derail the negotiations process.'[48] The next day, 5 April 1993, *The Citizen* reported that SAP spokesperson Capt. Craig Kotze had claimed: 'the government could confirm such meetings had taken place and also had information that dissident MK members had joined APLA.'[49] As with other statements made by members of De Klerk's government, Kotze's confirmation of the emergence of this fictitious radical faction raises the question: was South Africa's government itself duped by misinformation spread by the security forces, or was it participating in counterinsurgency operations including the one that culminated in Hani's murder? In any case, this disinformation campaign was clearly a systematic attempt to defame Hani and could draw upon vast resources and personnel in the South African government and the different branches of the security forces, as well as journalists who seemed willing to perpetuate these distortions.

Hani himself recognized the ominous pattern of disinformation as it unfolded. Ironically, he had deplored the wave of attacks on white civilians, and condemned what he perceived to be the PAC's and APLA's tolerance of anti-white terrorism.[50] In a piece published the day after Hani's death, South African journalist Sekola Sello related: 'two weeks ago, Chris Hani told me that the recent spate of black-on-white killings was part of a smokescreen to create the right climate for leading anti-apartheid activists to be killed.'[51] In an interview only twelve days before his assassination, Hani himself said the ANC had 'begun to detect these tricks,' and described the regime's disinformation strategy, which included 'attacks and vilification from many quarters, from the regime, from elements in the security forces, from a lot of disinformation back in Namibia.' He claimed the security forces 'will go for personalities, they have already started attacking me, linking me with a lot of evil things, and we must expect that to happen. This is a filthy group in the government. And they've got the resources.'[52]

Muddying the Waters

An ANC press statement dated the day of Hani's killing pointed to lingering questions about the circumstances of the assassination, and to the regime's lack of professionalism and urgency in handling the case. It complained: 'the waters around the assassination of Chris Hani are being muddied,' noting that 'before an investigation had commenced, Deputy [Police] Minister Myburgh had already pronounced on the case, claiming it to be the work of a lone gunman without political motive.' Furthermore, the minister of law and order Hernus Kriel blamed the ANC for the failure to guard Hani, even though the regime had only recently refused Hani's bodyguards permits for carrying weapons. SAP spokesman Capt. Kotze, who weeks earlier had confirmed Hani's alleged involvement in a plot to foment anti-white violence, had 'again demonstrated his gross insensitivity and partisanship by arrogantly calling the ANC leadership "irresponsible."' The ANC statement emphasized key unsolved aspects of the case, including 'the investigation of a second car reported to have been at the scene of the crime.'[53] Several eyewitnesses reported two cars leaving the scene of the murder; 'Captain Meyer of the Boksburg police who had first addressed the press' on the day of the assassination 'had spoken of two killers as well.'[54] Disinformation continued after Hani's assassination, with Richard Ellis running a concocted story in the London *Sunday Times* on 18 April 1993 titled 'Winnie Mandela Links ANC with Assassination of Hani.' Ellis further approached various South African politicians to raise the allegation in parliament, finally succeeding with Conservative Party MP Schalk Pienaar.[55]

As well as announcing within hours of the assassination that the killing was 'the act of a lone gunman without political motive,'[56] the SAP appointed Brig. Frans Malherbe as the official spokesperson for the Hani assassination investigation. Malherbe had previously served as the spokesperson for the investigation into the murder of David Webster, an anthropologist at the University of Witwatersrand who was murdered in broad daylight near his home in suburban Johannesburg in circumstances similar to Hani's.[57]

The police investigation discovered that Janusz Waluś was a member of the extreme-right Afrikaner Weerstandsbeweging (AWB).[58] He was also reported to have belonged to another right-wing organization, the Orde Boerevolk.[59] More recently, it has emerged that Waluś was connected to the sinister South African Institute for Maritime Research (SAIMR), a highly secretive organization that engaged in mercenary operations, and possibly in biological warfare, in various African states.[60] Walus was also an informer for the NIS.[61] Yet Waluś was no trained assassin, and the focus on his background and extreme right-wing ideology may well have served to divert scrutiny from his role as a bit player in a much more elaborate operation. Although he already owned four guns, Waluś had insisted on acquiring an additional gun from Conservative Party member Clive Derby-Lewis – the pistol that was then identified as the murder weapon – which was traced to a consignment of small arms stolen from a South African Air Force armoury several weeks before the assassination.[62] This established the link between Waluś and Lewis, and cemented the official explanation for Hani's murder, which was that it had been a plot by an isolated white-supremacist fringe.

In March 1997, SACP deputy general secretary Jeremy Cronin noted that the trial court heard testimony that the murder weapon in Hani's killing, a Z88 pistol, had changed hands five times before Waluś received it. But the investigators failed to follow up on who the five persons were and what role they may have played in the assassination. The SACP also questioned the role of former *Citizen* journalist Arthur Kemp, who had supplied Gaye Derby-Lewis, Clive Derby-Lewis's wife, with a list of addresses including those of Chris Hani, Joe Slovo and Nelson Mandela. During the murder trial, Kemp admitted to giving this list to Derby-Lewis but testified that he had been unaware of her intentions. Kemp subsequently moved to Britain and tried to sell the story of Hani's assassination to the *Sunday Times* for £10,000, prompting Cronin to insist that Kemp should come clean about any larger role he may have played. Kemp, a white supremacist, remained linked to the Hani assassination, and later resurfaced as an activist for the far-right British National Party.[63] Also, in early 1997, a London newspaper reported that elements within the ANC had colluded with Walus and Derby-Lewis in Hani's murder, and named Winnie Madikizela-Mandela as its source; Madikizela-Mandela, however, denied making the claim and 'distanced herself from the report.'[64]

Evidence of a Broader Conspiracy

Immediately after Hani's assassination, journalist Jon Qwelane, who lived down the road, visited the scene and heard United Nations observers 'talking of more than one type of ammunition cartridge found.' No such evidence was introduced at the trial. Another visitor at the scene was ANC intelligence chief Joe Nhlanhla, who found a 'soft-drink tin and two cigarette stubs' behind a neighbour's wall, as well as what appeared to be a bullet hole next to Hani's garage 'consistent with a shot having been fired from beyond the neighbour's wall,' raising Nhlanhla's suspicions that there had been a second gunman. The hole was never proved to have been from a gunshot, but ANC personnel remained suspicious.[65] According to ANC official Ronnie Watson, 'the ANC had received a phone call on the day Chris Hani was shot, by someone who said that the murder had been plotted by a number of people at the weapons shop Bentel Arms'; according to Watson, the SAP had initially agreed with the ANC's findings that there had been two cars and two assassins, before settling on the lone-gunman narrative. The ANC had information indicating that the second gunman was a swarthy figure with security force connections known as 'Alex the Greek,' but Watson's efforts to track him down were thwarted by the SAP, which had put Security Branch Gen. Basie Smit in charge of the investigation.[66]

Dutch journalist Evelyn Groenink investigated the police docket containing the evidence from Hani's murder – which was subsequently tampered with – and found several pieces of evidence suggesting a broader conspiracy: the role of Peter Jackson, 'a chemicals transporter with arms trade connections,' who was Janusz Waluś's employer at the time of the assassination and who 'seemed to have been telling Waluś what to do.' The Security Branch, which led the investigation, instructed the Brixton Murder and Robbery Squad team which participated in the investigation 'not to bother exploring [Jackson] or his arms trade and secret service contacts,' even though the docket contained files on other arms industry figures, such as Armscor representative Colin Stier. Security Police Capt. JH de Waal, who led the investigation, issued written instructions that explicitly blocked the team from following these leads: 'Information about Jackson will not be followed up.' Another memorandum from the Security Police states: 'Jackson is cooperating fully and does not need to be questioned.'[67] Waluś's agenda book, which contained several reminders to 'phone Peter' in the lead-up to the assassination, disappeared from the docket, and the copy that remained was missing the pages that corresponded to the week of the murder; it also contained contact information for several other individuals linked to the arms industry, SADF MI, and the NIS. Meanwhile, Janusz Waluś's brother, Witold, was himself involved in the arms industry, selling used military vehicles.[68]

Brixton Murder and Robbery Squad chief inspector Michael Holmes was strangely uncurious about these missed leads, telling Groenink in an interview: 'We didn't need to look at all the evidence because the Security Police put everything we needed in a box for us to work with.' Groenink also interviewed 'witnesses who identified a second man on the scene of the crime, a man with actual secret service and gun runners [sic] links,' but these witnesses were intimidated into silence, as one told her: 'But police came at night to scare the children, mess up my place and tell me that I should stay away from trying to testify. I gave up after that.'[69] This echoes the ANC statement cited above that referred to the failure to investigate a second vehicle seen fleeing the scene. Furthermore, according to Groenink, the murder scene was 'professionally shielded' by an NIS agent who happened to live 'right opposite' Hani, and who confirmed that he was the first person to arrive at the murder scene only seconds after the shooting, which would have given him sufficient time to tamper with any evidence that did not match the official story. This agent continued working for the NIS's successor, the National Intelligence Agency, after the transition.[70]

In April 1997, journalist Stefaans Brümmer uncovered a series of intelligence reports dating from early April 1993 and prepared by Eugene Riley for the NIS, warning of Hani's impending assassination. Riley was connected to the CCB and DCC and had originally been recruited by Ferdi Barnard. His reports described a conspiracy featuring ANC operatives, and cited 'internal ANC squabbles and Hani's "own agenda" as the motive.'[71] Riley claimed to have got this information from an ANC intelligence officer named 'Ramon,' later identified as Mohammed Amin Laher. The ANC denied that Laher had ever worked for it; however, the *Mail & Guardian* was able to locate Laher, who claimed 'that the assassination was a joint project by "both sides of the spectrum,"'[72] the ANC and the government security apparatus.[73] Laher had been recruited by the NIS, and claimed to have given documents about the assassination plot to Riley, his handler.[74] Riley was murdered at his home eight months after Hani's death (see Chapter Nine).[75] Laher refused to testify to the Truth and Reconciliation Commission (TRC) about Hani's death, but divulged certain details to journalists in 1997. These findings corroborate documents cited above indicating collusion between the highest echelons of ANC and apartheid security establishments. Riley's report for the NIS contained several uncorroborated allegations, but it named the correct date of the assassination plot and mentioned 'a Polish member of the strike unit.'[76] The report identified by their noms de guerre the key ANC operatives alleged to have spearheaded the conspiracy: the leader of the 'strike unit' and a senior ANC security figure 'who, according to the document, would have ordered the assassination.' Remarkably, after the report emerged, the *Mail & Guardian* located the '"leader of the strike unit," an ex-special forces soldier who joined the ANC,' who confirmed having known Riley and maintaining contact with notorious CCB operative Ferdi Barnard, 'but said the document contained "disinformation."'[77]

Riley had also authored a report for the NIS, dated 15 May 1993, alleging a plot by the same hit team to assassinate Joe Slovo. This time, there was no evidence of ANC involvement, but a plot to assassinate Slovo was indeed uncovered shortly thereafter: a group of right-wing extremists planned to shoot Slovo from a water tower near his home, prompting the ANC to assign him a bodyguard detail. This exposed once again the De Klerk government's willingness to negotiate with ANC leaders, while insisting on leaving them unguarded: although the government had granted Slovo temporary indemnity against apartheid-era charges of terrorism, so he could participate in the negotiations, the SAP 'used the pending charges to refuse him a firearm licence.'[78]

The NIA Report

An even more dramatic revelation emerged with the release of an investigative report compiled by the National Intelligence Agency (NIA) in late February 1997 and leaked to *New Nation* after its completion in March of that year. According to this report, known formally as the Covert Intelligence Report, there had been a second gunman at the scene of Hani's assassination, who was named in the report, along with Waluś. This report found that altogether about twenty other people were involved in the final conspiracy to kill Hani, including a police general, various well-known Military Intelligence operatives, agents in the Boksburg traffic department, and various Vlakplaas (C10) operatives.[79] The report also identified senior members of the security police, a Holiday Inn security officer, and members of the post-transition national parliament as being part of the conspiracy. According to the report, the Holiday Inn security officer, who had apparently 'tipped off Hani's killers on the morning of the assassination, was subsequently hired by the ANC.'[80]

At the time, *New Nation* noted: 'A full investigation into the claims made in the report could for the first time explain where Waluś's logistical support came from, who financed the operation and why the disinformation which preceded the murder was so vigorously peddled. It could also for the first time help locate the assassination within the framework of a political context.'[81] It mentioned 'evidence that the decision to assassinate Hani was a carefully planned operation with high decision-makers involved.'[82] The NIA report called for a new investigation into Hani's assassination, and the interrogation of 'senior generals, politicians, and policemen who could shed light on the conspiracy.'[83] In response, ANC legal head and Mpumalanga premier Mathews Phosa, who had been involved in the ANC's internal investigation at the time of the assassination, expressed hope that the revelations contained in the NIA report could help confirm his own 'long-held suspicion that there was a wider conspiracy' behind Hani's murder.[84] For its part, *New Nation* was advised by its lawyers not to name fifteen people who had not previously been linked to Hani's assassination but whom the new report named with the recommendation that they be fully investigated; their names have never emerged. None of the NIA report's recommendations was ever heeded, and the report itself was buried.

According to the report, 'suspicions of a second gunman were raised several times during the initial investigation [immediately after Hani's murder].' This second gunman was a former policeman who worked undercover as a manager for a private security company on the East Rand which served as a front for SADF MI. He was a former SADF Special Forces officer with 'strong right-wing connections,' who took part in the storming of the World Trade Centre by a group of right-wingers in 1993 with the aim of disrupting the multiparty talks under way there.[85] The security company itself, which was run by a commandant in the SADF's Witwatersrand Command, played a critical role in the reconnaissance and intelligence-gathering phase of the operation to kill Hani.

The NIA report stated that 'between January 1993 and April 10 [the day Hani was killed], [this undercover manager] played a very significant role in Chris Hani's assassination. He gathered most of the information on Hani's schedules, and personal life. He did most of his observations from the safety of the patrol vehicle and under the flag of the security company.'[86] This second gunman also accompanied Walus on reconnaissance missions five days before the assassination. 'It is this investigator's conclusion from evidence gathered that he was the second gunman, shooting from behind the wall' adjoining Hani's house. During the initial investigation, police had found footprints behind the wall, as well as cigarette stubs and an empty soda can left on the wall, but had not pursued these leads.[87] The report also found that during the operation's reconnaissance phase, Waluś and the second gunman were also accompanied by 'well-known' CCB operatives and the SADF MI commandant who ran the security front company.

This second gunman was also linked to assassination attempts on leading ANC figures Winnie Madikizela-Mandela and Peter Mokaba, and continued his clandestine activities after Hani was killed. According to a former Vlakplaas agent who provided much of the information for the report, the second gunman had been waiting to ambush Winnie Madikizela-Mandela inside her house when Peter Mokaba arrived unexpectedly. 'He said he was not ready to kill Peter and therefore allowed him to leave without making his presence known.'[88] The second gunman was allegedly working from the list of addresses of ANC leaders compiled by the former *Citizen* journalist and alleged SADF MI spy Arthur Kemp. He was also responsible for blowing up the offices of Sherino Printers in Benoni, which had printed ANC posters and pamphlets. The agent who compiled the report for NIA claimed to have warned the printers of the imminent threat, and also to have warned the ANC of impending attempts on Mokaba's life. Indeed, plots to kill Mokaba were widely reported around the time Hani was killed.[89]

The alleged second gunman's involvement in right-wing circles is consistent with Waluś's and Derby-Lewis's own affiliations with the Afrikaner Weerstandsbeweging ('Afrikaner Resistance Movement,' or AWB) and the Conservative Party, respectively. In the apartheid regime's final years, its intelligence services were known to have thoroughly infiltrated right-wing paramilitary groups such as the AWB, the Wit Wolwe ('White Wolves') and other white supremacist outfits. By infiltrating these quasi-Nazi groups, the security forces ostensibly sought, in the name of national security, to keep tabs on their extremist activities. Yet this infiltration served a dual purpose: it also provided the apartheid security forces with plausible deniability, which would have allowed units like Vlakplaas, SADF MI, and the CCB to pursue their own violent operations while blaming them on fringe racists.[90] Meanwhile, hardcore right-wingers were ideal as patsies; Groenink notes that the 'sophisticated echelons in the [apartheid] secret services loved using' right-wingers for their operations because they were wholly committed 'fanatics' who were 'very often also not that clever.'[91]

The NIA's report found that planning for this assassination attempt began in July 1992, when a warrant officer serving at Vlakplaas was tasked with gathering information about Hani's movements in Transkei, where Hani had already been the target of several assassination plots (see Chapter Five). There, the intelligence on Hani was gathered by a well-placed apartheid spy within the Transkeian Defence Force (TDF) Military Intelligence. This spy had access to TDF Military Intelligence Col. W. Zwayiba and to Bantu Holomisa, and it was he who disclosed the plot's details to the NIA in 1997, 'linking the entire apartheid security establishment to the killing.'[92] These intelligence-gathering activities then formed the basis for an elaborate plan orchestrated by Vlakplaas. The Vlakplaas warrant officer handling the agent in Transkei allegedly told him that 'an operation to kill Hani was planned by "head office," meaning police headquarters in Wachthuis [Pretoria].'[93] A week later, another high-ranking officer from Vlakplaas gave the agent R10,000 for the intelligence and for providing the names of possible assassins. Soon after, the agent was told that a police general 'had other plans for Hani' and the Transkei-based operation was cancelled. This correlates with information about SADF MI plots on Hani's life in Transkei in 1992 that were ultimately shelved (see Chapter Five). It also makes sense that the apartheid security forces, having perceived an opportunity to kill Hani in Johannesburg, would choose this option over an assassination attempt in Transkei, where the presence of MK forces and the coup attempt on Holomisa would make surprise difficult and deniability implausible. In Johannesburg, the apartheid forces were on home turf, as it were, and could more seamlessly gather intelligence for the assassination. During this same meeting between the Transkei-based agent and his handlers, the Vlakplaas warrant officer disclosed that 'a killer had already been recruited,' mentioning that he was a 'mover' and a Polish immigrant: namely, Waluś.[94] From then on, the operation was 'carefully managed' by a select 'inner circle' composed of Vlakplaas, South African and former Rhodesian special forces operatives.[95] According to the NIA report, this 'inner circle' had been organized in August or September 1992, soon after security force elites decided to 'eliminate the ANC leadership before it was too late.'[96] Vlakplaas's Transkeian agent was then arrested on trumped-up charges after he unwittingly revealed to Eugene de Kock that he was aware of an SADF MI gun-running racket; the agent was then imprisoned until after Hani's death, ensuring that he could leak no details of the assassination plot beforehand.[97]

Another key operative identified in the NIA report, who had previously been involved in the killings of several ANC activists, was tasked with providing the money needed for the operation.[98] Once the funding and logistics for the plot had been organized, it entered its second phase; now, the individual identified as the second gunman, using the cover of his private security firm, began conducting surveillance of Hani, monitoring his 'moves, schedules, habits, and personal life.'[99] This information was then relayed to a Vlakplaas policeman and several others, who were named in the report but whose identities were not disclosed. Of the 20 conspirators, the report especially recommended the investigation and questioning of the second gunman, a Military Intelligence commandant, and other key players in the assassination, including a traffic policeman 'known to many Third Force operatives and to the second killer,' who had attempted to have Waluś released after his initial arrest by two junior constables: 'He was far too quickly on the scene and was obviously expecting something of this nature. He should be investigated.'[100] The report also concluded: 'it is very clear that [former SAP] Gen. ——[name redacted by *New Nation*] gave the order to kill Chris Hani. He should be called in and interrogated.' Finally, the report recommended investigating another Vlakplaas policeman who had provided Waluś with his vehicle and other logistical support in preparation for the assassination.[101]

As already noted, the NIA report claimed that a range of non-clandestine operators was involved in the Hani murder plot, including a hotel security agent and members of the Boksburg traffic police force. These various assets could be coordinated by means of the remnants of the regime's Joint Management System, which featured a web of secret networks embedded within conventional state institutions – such as local police forces – and integrated into a clandestine chain of command. Such spy structures ensured that complex counterinsurgency operations could receive seamless and untraceable logistical and intelligence support, from networks that could be activated and then deactivated as the need arose. The conspiracy described by the NIA report could also have included the complicity of elements within the ANC, though none was mentioned.

Nqakula tells of an MK cadre he knew from the Pango camp in Angola, John Itumeleng Dube, who had been captured and tortured by the regime, became an askari, and was acting as a double agent secretly informing Hani of security force designs to kill him. According to Dube, 'the Boers' wanted Hani 'dead by any means possible.'[102] In April 1997, former Vlakplaas operatives claimed that most of Chris Hani's correspondence, including handwritten messages and other directives, had been intercepted by their unit. These operatives had been tasked with conducting surveillance on Hani from 1992 until his assassination, and a former Vlakplaas officer living in Pretoria, as well as a black policeman still serving in the post-transition police force, claimed to have in their possession some documents authored by Hani, including a map that Hani drew for an MK operative.[103] According to them, two former askaris and an informer, along with their white handlers, developed an elaborate surveillance operation to infiltrate Hani's office and monitor his communications. Hani's correspondence was leaked by an MK operative who had been recruited by Vlakplaas; this MK operative was based in Transkei from mid-1992 until 1993, and was an active member of the post-transition South African National Defence Force (SANDF) in 1997. *New Nation* journalist Jimmy Seepe wrote that his 'attempts to obtain copies of the map and other Hani correspondence drew a blank. The [former Vlakplaas] operative promised to give us the copy for verification once he has obtained clearance from his former bosses.'[104] It is striking that as late as 1997 the former death squad's chain of command was apparently still intact.

Another piece of the puzzle fell into place with *New Nation*'s revelation of an apartheid-era document labelled 'Top Secret' and dated September 1992, which noted: 'this conversation can be instrumental in neutralizing the current SACP/Hani/Kasrils factions. It can also be used to win votes in a future election if the SACP participants can be neutralized.'[105] *New Nation* did not provide the context of the 'conversation' in question, but, as we have seen, the same document was cited during Directorate of Covert Collection (DCC) member Jan Anton Nieuwoudt's trial, which described a meeting between members of DCC and several key MK leaders, notably Joe Modise, featuring the same passage about 'neutralizing the SACP/Hani/Kasrils faction.' In the *Mail & Guardian*, Brümmer noted that Nieuwoudt's document suggested a 'serious split' emerging between Modise and Hani, and that while Modise denied ever having been approached by SADF MI, Nieuwoudt 'ominously' discussed 'exploitation of the split' and 'a final phase to this goal.'[106]

The secret document named several DCC senior officers who were forcibly retired from the SADF after they were named in the Steyn Report, which linked the DCC to Third Force activity and led to FW de Klerk's officers' purge. Among these officers was the head of the DCC, Brig. JJ 'Tolletjie' Botha, and senior staff officer Col. At Nel, who was identified in the secret document as being responsible for the SADF's 'Internal Subtheatre,' an SADF MI structure that dealt with domestic security threats. The document, drawn up by an operative at the rank of lieutenant colonel and known only as 'Fox' (this was Jan Anton Nieuwoudt), was written at the height of the Kempton Park negotiations between the NP and the ANC, and was copied to Brig. Botha and Col. Nel for comment. 'Fox' wrote that 'the purpose of this memorandum is to inform you about the current conditions inside Umkhonto we Sizwe (MK) and to either make or ask for recommendations and guidelines to exploit this situation to the advantage of the current government.'[107] As we have seen, the 'conditions inside MK' that could be exploited referred to the alleged willingness of high-ranking members of MK leadership to be recruited by SADF MI.

The document revealed a close working relationship between the police based at John Vorster Square and the DCC, and suggested that the decision to 'neutralize' Hani and Kasrils came after the 1992 massacre of pro-ANC protesters at Bisho in Ciskei, at which time Nel and Nieuwoudt, under the guise of the Pan-Afrik Consultants front company, were both overseeing the Ciskei Defence Force under strongman Oupa Gqozo, and exploiting the opportunities this afforded them to target MK (see Chapter Five). The document also gave the code names of police agents 241/153 and 241/222, who had infiltrated the ANC and MK leadership; agent 241/222, in particular, was described as being 'instrumental in infiltrating MK leadership,' and as frequently accompanying MK leaders within South Africa.[108] *New Nation* journalists contacted Joe Mamasela, the notorious askari attached to the Vlakplaas unit, who confirmed that Vlakplaas had been involved in the preliminary stages of the plot to kill Hani, and that he 'did not doubt that other people were called into the plan' as it progressed.[109]

Meanwhile, the NIA report's mention of ANC members of parliament who were involved in the plot stands out especially in the light of the reference to SADF MI's plans to 'neutralize the SACP/Hani/Kasrils' faction in the ANC. As we have seen, these plans developed after a meeting between DCC officers and very high-ranking members of the MK leadership who were open to being recruited as apartheid spies. One of the MK leaders at this meeting was Joe Modise, who was South Africa's minister of defence when *New Nation* published the findings in 1997. In this way, *New Nation*'s coverage of the covert NIA report – which no other media outlet reported on at the time – reinforces evidence suggesting that elements within the ANC had been recruited by SADF MI and were privy to, if not actively involved in, the plan to kill Hani. Moreover, the SADF MI memo's stated objective in 'neutralizing' Hani's power – to 'win votes in a future election' – is noteworthy because it reinforces the perspective put forth in this book: that clandestine apartheid counterinsurgency operations during the transition period did not aim to derail negotiations with the ANC entirely, but rather to violently shape the outcome of a future election to the regime's advantage. This, in turn, raises the question of how high up the chain of command operations like the Hani assassination were authorized. By the time this latest plan to assassinate Hani had reached its final stages, De Klerk had already received the Steyn Report and purged SADF MI officers. Such spy recruitment provided the regime's security forces with the intelligence they needed in order to undertake operations like the Hani killing. Yet these covert operations clearly persisted after De Klerk's purge. Meanwhile, Hani's killing weakened the mass power of the left within the ANC in precisely the manner the 'neutralization' memo intended. Although in the end Hani's death did not diminish the ANC's popularity in the 1994 elections at all – if anything, like other Third Force violence, it only gave the ANC momentum – nonetheless, killing Hani dealt an immense blow to the leadership and representation of MK veterans, to the SACP, and to the mass elements of the ANC's power base. Therefore, whether or not National Party elites authorized Hani's killing, they were certainly among those who stood to benefit from it the most.

The Arms Deal Connection

A further angle from which to understand the Hani assassination relates to his apparent objection to the infamous R70 billion arms deal, a scandal now woven into the very fabric of South Africa's transition (see Chapter Ten). Maverick ANC intelligence operative Bheki Jacobs, the original whistleblower on the arms deal, claimed that Hani was killed for his opposition to the deal. Jacobs himself died in 2008 at the age of 46 from illness in what many consider to be 'mysterious circumstances.'[110] The journalist Groenink wrote that MK operatives close to Hani had told her that Hani refused to let MK become corrupted through involvement in the arms procurement programme; he thus became an obstacle that needed to be removed. The arms deal originates even before the start of South Africa's transition, when several European defence establishments that enjoyed long-standing connections with the apartheid regime, notably those of France and the UK, began to approach the ANC on the eve of negotiations. Thus in 1989 the ANC's Aziz Pahad announced: 'This is where we have tea with MI6. Of course, they are looking to talk with us. The future is very close and we have to prepare.'[111] Western intelligence agencies were only too eager to develop contacts with the ANC and MK in order to promote their countries' economic interests in the new South Africa and shape the transition to their benefit. To this end, Alain Guenon, a Frenchman with links to French intelligence and SADF MI, helped to coordinate the construction and purchase of new housing in Dawn Park, Boksburg, for ANC figures returning from exile, and had connected MK members such as Tokyo Sexwale to various business ventures. This raises the prospect that SADF MI sought to shape the ANC exiles' return, the better to surveil and entrap them.[112]

Guenon had also travelled with Sexwale to Paris in 1991 and again in 1992 to examine weapons systems that the French government was hoping to sell to South Africa once sanctions were lifted, including electronic upgrades for the Air Force's Mirage jets; Hani had refused to join those trips and had 'expressed concern about the French contacts.' MK logistics chief and former Special Ops commander Aboobaker Ismail insisted these visits violated ANC principles because the French had 'been among the biggest collaborators with apartheid.'[113]

'Nomsa,' an MK cadre interviewed by Groenink, related that 'Western arms dealers,' including representatives of weapons giant British Aerospace, were present at the 1991 MK conference in Thohoyandou, Venda. According to her, MK cadres had been 'shocked to see how close [the arms dealers] were to our leadership,' particularly Joe Modise. Top MK officials explained that the arms dealers were there to assist in projects that would provide jobs for rank-and-file MK cadres, and that the delegation from the British Aerospace 'was interested in helping unemployed veterans start new lives.'[114] Yet an MK veteran who was present recalled that the assembled guerrillas 'couldn't understand why it was so secretive; why these men were only meeting Joe Modise and his friends. We were told this information could not be brought into the open because we were still sometimes perceived as "terrorists" and these people didn't want to be seen helping us,'[115] raising suspicions about their true motives.[116] Meanwhile, the British delegation treated Modise and other officials in the MK High Command to lavish dinners and outings, and although these meetings were ostensibly intended to organize the integration of MK into South Africa's defence force, 'there was something fishy' about them, and Hani remained suspicious. Nomsa summed up the fear, widely shared among MK cadres at the time, that Modise 'was selling us out.'[117]

In 1993, nearly five months before the terms of MK's integration into the South African military were finalized, Modise travelled to the UK along with future Armscor chairman Tielman de Waal as guests of Britain's Defence Exports Services Organization (DESO).[118] Modise and his assistant, Fana Hlongwane, continued to maintain a close relationship with representatives of the British defence and finance sectors until well after the transition and the conclusion of the arms deal. Modise would also strengthen his contacts with South

African arms manufacturer Armscor, which, during the era of the anti-apartheid arms embargo, had 'made alliances in the murky world of illegal arms trading.'[119] Hani was known to have had a long-standing rivalry with Modise, dating back to Hani's harsh criticism of Modise in his 1969 memorandum, and Modise's consequent attempts to have Hani shot as a traitor (see Chapter One). In 1993, Modise was alleged to have sold off an ANC arms cache worth R2.5 million for personal profit; Hani is said to have confronted Modise about this only two weeks before he was killed.[120]

As part of their inquiry into Hani's killing, TRC researchers investigated the possibility that NATO countries' intelligence services were complicit in Hani's assassination.[121] Hani's widow, Limpho Hani, who never believed Waluś was a lone assassin, recalled interacting immediately after the murder with British investigators from Scotland Yard.[122] Lekwane notes that British and German experts who came to assist in the investigation 'would have had an interest in ensuring that this connection was not exposed or explored further.'[123] These countries' intelligence agencies, which had enjoyed long-standing ties with the apartheid security services, had begun cultivating relations with the ANC in anticipation of the impending transition, and in his 2014 testimony to the Seriti Commission of Inquiry, Terry Crawford-Browne alleged that Waluś had ultimately been working for British Aerospace, having been recruited by Rhodesian and Zimbabwean arms dealer John Bredenkamp, who received lavish bribes from the arms manufacturer for his role in brokering the arms deal (see Chapter Ten).[124] Furthermore, as noted in Chapter Three, some of the right-wing US groups that sought to discredit the ANC very likely had ties to the CIA, which was active in southern Africa during the late Cold War period.[125] According to Groenink, the security forces' top leadership had briefed US intelligence operatives in South Africa about Hani's assassination.[126]

Code-Switching and Framing Hani's Murder

Hani's murder foreshadowed the epidemic of post-conflict violent crime in South Africa and signalled the switch from political to 'ordinary' violence that accompanied the transition to democracy.

Here I borrow from Ellen Moodie the concept of 'code-switching' in the context of transitions from civil war where 'meanings of violent acts were in flux and knowledge of how the world worked was shifting.'[127] Moodie focuses on the 25 October 1993 murder of mid-level FMLN commander Francisco Velis by gunmen on motorcycles, which occurred after El Salvador's civil war but bore the hallmarks of a targeted assassination; the post-transition government insisted that Velis' killing was a non-political, common crime. Likewise, the very ordinariness of Hani's murder – he had bought a newspaper and was returning to his home in a predominantly white suburb when he was shot dead – evokes the crime wave that struck post-apartheid South Africa, where murders in residential driveways and home invasions became commonplace. Hani's death, though politically motivated, was portrayed as the desperate act of fringe extremists, unrelated to broader politics. After his assassination, both the SAP and the ANC tried to frame the phone call to police by Hani's Afrikaner neighbour, Reetha Harmse, who witnessed the fleeing getaway car, as embodying a new spirit whereby former enemies lived side by side and tried to help each other regardless of race. Indeed, in his televised speech to the nation on the night of 10 April, Nelson Mandela pointed to Harmse's actions as evidence of the post-racial society that lay ahead if South Africa's black masses could only restrain their anger over Hani's murder.[128]

Although the apartheid forces had been trying to kill Hani for decades, the mainstream narrative now implicitly framed Hani – dressed in slacks and a white shirt, unarmed and unguarded when he was killed – as a private citizen. Hani's murder during such an unguarded moment, despite his long history as a revolutionary leader, showcased the supposed ordinariness of post-apartheid life. According to this narrative, Hani was already inhabiting a place of pan-racial, middle-class normality even before the transition was completed: 'an individual withdrawn into himself, into the confines of his private interests and private caprice.'[129] This framing implied that if South Africa could only manage to get past Hani's murder, it could strive for this same promise of normality, removed from the racial and class inequalities that Hani had died fighting to abolish. This normality, which the NP and ANC jointly manufactured by framing

Hani's murder as privatized violence, can be understood as the 'state of unexception' that was intended to represent a break with South Africa's previous state of war, and that would now define South Africa's new democracy.

Nelson Mandela's speech at Hani's funeral at the FNB stadium on 19 April 1993 gave voice to popular suspicions about the regime's hand in the assassination: 'When Chris Hani criticized the theft of weapons from the Air Force base, and said those weapons were not stolen, but were taken to be used in covert operations, he too was ridiculed. Guns from those same stolen weapons were used to kill him.' Mandela went on to highlight the broader context of these covert operations, at a time when the success of negotiations was far from certain: 'This secret web of hit men and covert operations is funded by our taxes. While we remain without homes, without food, without education, almost nine billion Rand was spent in the last two years on these secret operations.'[130] Mandela's speech minces no words in linking Hani's killing to apartheid covert operations. Yet the ANC would subsequently buy into the official story that Waluś and Derby-Lewis had acted alone, leaving key questions unanswered. At the time of Hani's death, official ANC and SACP statements, as well as those made by individual members of both organizations, unanimously blamed the regime for Hani's death. Meanwhile, the ANC was completely excluded from the SAP investigation into the murder, its leadership limited to making indignant pronouncements from the sidelines. Within a matter of hours, the official investigation into Hani's death concluded that there was no broader conspiracy. Despite the investigation's shortcomings, the ANC accepted this verdict, validating the SAP's methods and, in a dramatic reversal, vouching for its impartiality and professionalism.

The SAP's finding that Waluś and Derby-Lewis were isolated extremists dissociated Hani's killing from apartheid violence, 'signify[ing] rupture rather than continuity.'[131] The official verdict that Waluś and Derby-Lewis had acted alone established a symbolic break between late-apartheid political violence and the depoliticized, 'privatized' nature of post-apartheid violent crime. Waluś, despite his nebulous right-wing ties, was portrayed as a deranged racist whose actions represented the last gasp of a doomed extremist agenda. Meanwhile, the state's security organs, still unreformed, used their own power and resources to imbue their investigation with the aura of professionalism, whitewashing their own complicity in the ongoing dirty war. The SAP now portrayed itself as a suddenly impartial force that could be trusted to investigate political crimes. It had made the switch from punitive to investigative policing that signalled authoritarianism's demise. At the time of Hani's death, battles still raged between Self-Defence Units and the IFP; MK forces who had regarded Hani as their leader remained armed. In this climate of insecurity and uncertainty, the SAP's performance of an ostensibly impartial investigation was a way to claim the state's monopoly on the legitimate use of force, downplaying its own links to apartheid covert operations. This narrative established the SAP's ostensible neutrality and affirmed its suitability to carry out the investigation and, by implication, the policing tasks that awaited it in a new democratic era. Its ruthless efficiency as a counterinsurgency force served precisely as the basis for its new image of competence at investigating crime; it could 'get the job done.' Through this prism, the SAP burnished its new image by performing the Hani investigation, swiftly catching the perpetrator and determining that he had acted alone. Indeed, the lead police investigator in the Hani case was afterward widely celebrated for his contribution to a peaceful post-apartheid society.[132] Likewise, although the British and German experts who assisted the investigation belonged to agencies that had abetted apartheid for decades, their countries' democratic status now stood for impartiality and professionalism, whitewashing Cold War allegiances and colonial histories just as South Africa was taking its seat at the global table.

By accepting the SAP's findings, the ANC facilitated its own transformation into a party shorn of its revolutionary claims and ready to govern in a neoliberal democracy. Hani's death was the entrance fee for this new reality. His assassination represented the point at which the South African state 'switched codes.' It is remarkable that both the counterinsurgent and insurgent forces – that is, the apartheid-era securocrats and the ANC – were able to agree on a shared explanation of Hani's assassination. In doing so, they transformed the incident into a watershed event that, once the nation had pulled back from the brink of war, actually propelled negotiations forward. Even before the transition was finalized, the contours of the post-transition landscape were already becoming apparent: it was to be one in which political freedom was traded for economic continuity, and the capitalism that had been previously fettered by domestic unrest and international sanctions would now be unleashed. Hani's assassination – not only his permanent removal from society, but the very process of manufacturing the narrative of his murder as an isolated incident – reinforced this post-transition reality of privatization and rampant crime, a reality that had taken root in other post-Cold War, post-civil war contexts. As Moodie writes about El Salvador, 'the state, now dominated by a new transnational faction of elites hitching themselves to capital's latest, savage mode of accumulation, was trying to fabricate a sense of normality in this new form of insecurity.'[133]

To accomplish this, it became necessary to suppress any challenges to the established explanation of isolated responsibility for Hani's murder. The colonial state now marginalized the voices and the evidence that called into question its security forces' explanation of the killing, leaving a colonial imprint on the post-colonial South African state. Much like the state authorities at the time of Hani's death, the scholarship on South Africa's transition has largely avoided examining the likelihood and implications of a broader conspiracy in Hani's assassination. One exception to this has been Aubrey Lekwane's chapter in the first edition of the volume *The Hidden Hand: Covert Operations in South Africa*, titled 'Chris Hani: Political Assassinations – Who Benefits?' In the book's second edition, Lekwane's chapter was replaced by Robert Brand's 'The Chris Hani Assassination,' in which Brand acknowledges circumstantial evidence and claims of a broader conspiracy before dismissing them and concluding that no such conspiracy existed.

Impacts

In the immediate term, the ANC actually leveraged Hani's death to strengthen its position at the negotiating table, as the prospect of sustained protests and the atmosphere of popular anger shook the government and spurred a new round of compromise.[134] Yet the impact of Hani's death on South African politics cannot be overstated. It left a gaping void in the MK and SACP leaderships. It silenced the voice that South Africa's impoverished black masses most trusted and relied upon to speak on their behalf. It extinguished the brightest star among the generation of black leaders succeeding Mandela. Hani, second only to Mandela in popularity at the time of his death, would have been a prime candidate for the posts of defence minister 'or even Deputy President,'[135] and, as the ANC's leading light from his generation, may well have succeeded Mandela as head of state.

As both MK and SACP chief, Hani embodied the ANC's armed struggle and the class aspects of the anti-apartheid struggle. His biography reads like a summary of MK's history, from the Wankie and Sipolilo armed incursions into Rhodesia, through training, recruitment and combat operations in Lesotho, Botswana, Zambia, Mozambique, and Angola, until MK units assembled in the Transkei following the transition's onset. Hani's career spanned the combat history of MK in which he often participated as both combatant and commander. When the MK command was restructured in 1987, Hani became both MK chief of staff and political commissar, 'in effect, making him the "gatekeeper" for all MK activities.'[136] In addition to commanding MK forces in battle in Angola, Hani also infiltrated South Africa several times, and when MK adopted the tactic of targeting the apartheid border patrols with mines, Hani led 'the first unit planting limpet mines in the Eastern Transvaal.' Hani would also cross South African territory overland 'to Lesotho to meet leadership of the commanders, to issue some orders,' and set an example for physical fitness: 'We used to run with him. Fit! Fit! Very disciplined. Hey! Too much. Yeah, he was a true soldier. He cared for everyone.'[137]

Another former MK guerrilla recalled meeting Hani for the first time 'in Lesotho, he used to like me, just after chatting for some few minutes he tells me he knows my family, and told me I'd be leaving for Angola very soon.' Hani would reappear to brief MK guerrillas training in the USSR, and then, 'when we were starting to operate against UNITA in the early stages, he was there.'[138] In an interview shortly after Hani's death, Ntsaluba summed up Hani's incalculable contribution to the armed struggle and the ANC underground inside South Africa: 'I always say to comrades that I am not sure, you know, looking back at some of the things that one ended up doing subsequently, if one would have had the guts and the motivation to do those things had one not been exposed to comrade Chris right at the beginning.'[139] Murray contends that Hani could have served as a leftist counterweight to the mainstream ANC and captained the SACP 'into a critical role as a key political power broker with which the first post-apartheid government would have been forced to make deals.'[140] Although it is debatable whether Hani would have taken such a leftist stance, it is certain that no South African leader in the post-transition era has approached Hani's popular legitimacy and reputation for incorruptibility. Hani embodied the sometimes tenuous nexus between MK and the ANC. As the ANC relinquished armed struggle in negotiations, it largely sacrificed the class aspects of its struggle, and Hani was killed just as this was happening. In this way, he became a symbol of the transformation that never was. Hani had been active in trying to convince the South African masses to accept the economic compromises the ANC was trying to make, but he was also envisioning ways of mobilizing communities around a redistributionist ideology at a local level: Kalako recalled that right before Hani was killed, he had urged community groups and trade unions in the Western Cape to unite 'because he was starting to think about new ways of implementing socialism in South Africa.'[141]

Hani had articulated a clear vision for South Africa's security sector reform. He had been emphatic about MK guerrillas' central role in the post-transition security forces, insisting that 'having fought for democracy,' MK 'are going to be the core of a new South African army, a new South African security force, and they have got a duty to make our leaders negotiate…from a strong position.'[142] A statement released by MK the day after Hani's killing blamed 'the South African Regime' for the murder 'in the final analysis,' and noted that the SAP was focused on suppressing MK while giving free rein to right-wing elements: 'It is precisely because of such conduct that MK maintains that the present security forces are illegitimate and will continue to be so until a democracy is established and a new police and defence force representative of the new South Africa is created.'[143] As one ex-guerrilla said: 'If Chris Hani was never murdered, things would be very different; there would be a completely different culture [within the security forces].'[144] The security sector instead became a venue for corruption that would endure long after the transition.

Hani's Legacy and Further Evidence

Hani's tremendous legitimacy, and the importance of his legacy, are evidenced by the post-transition ANC and SACP invoking his assassination in speeches and at rallies. The controversy over who killed Hani has been resurrected periodically by ANC elites as a way of claiming his mantle, causing struggle-era narratives to resonate even well after the ANC assumed power. These very public pronouncements by prominent leaders have also served to continue the discussion about whether there was indeed a broader conspiracy to kill Hani, and who the conspirators were. Widely publicized as these pronouncements are, they have stood in contradistinction to the official legal narrative endorsed by the post-apartheid state insisting that there was no broader conspiracy. Although invoking Hani's assassination has had obvious political value as a means of rallying the ANC and SACP faithful, it has also been informed by the lingering suspicion, widely held throughout South Africa, of a broader conspiracy. ANC stalwart Mathews Phosa related that according to KwaZulu-Natal leader Sifiso Nkabinde, Leonard 'Nceba' Radu perished in a suspicious car crash in the midst of his investigation into Hani's death (see Chapter Nine). In a 1996 appeal to the TRC, the ANC pointed out that new evidence was likely to arise during amnesty applications by Hani's killers, Janusz Waluś and former Conservative Party MP Clive Derby-Lewis. On 4 April 1997, the ANC issued a statement pointing to new evidence about Hani's assassination published in the newspaper *New Nation* that now vindicated its call a year earlier for the TRC to reopen the investigation of the incident.[145] In its statement, the ANC emphasized that it had never doubted that the murder was the 'result of a wider network than meets the eye.'[146]

On 11 April 1997, Hani posthumously received the Freedom of Boksburg from SACP general secretary Charles Nqakula at an award ceremony. In his address, 'Nqakula said Hani's friends and supporters were not the only ones keeping a concerned watch on Waluś and Derby-Lewis' amnesty application. There were others who had been involved in keeping surveillance on Hani. They had helped plot the killing and had supplied Waluś with the gun and Hani's address.'[147] According to Nqakula, unseen forces were worried that Waluś and Derby-Lewis – 'who had remained silent during their trial' – would begin to reveal details of the broader conspiracy. These same unseen forces, furthermore, had leaked disinformation to the media 'attempting to suggest the assassination trail led back to Hani's rivals within the African National Congress.' Nqakula's words created an atmosphere of anticipation that details of the broader conspiracy would soon come to light: 'each day brings further clues as to where the real culprits were located. It was not in the extreme rightwing, not in the Third Force, but in the heart of the old apartheid first force itself. Sooner or later, the full facts of this case will emerge.'[148]

The 'disinformation' to which Nqakula alluded is reflected in the testimony to the TRC of amnesty applicant Derrick Skosana in Nelspruit on 12 June 1997 'that former African National Congress Mpumalanga secretary Joe Nkuna told him that Hani had ordered the execution of a number of "enemy agents"' who were prominent ANC politicians at the provincial level, including finance chief Jack Modipane, public works chief Jackson Mthembu, and ANC treasurer Johannes Shabangu.[149] Skosana claimed to have been a member of the hit squad 'sent to eliminate the alleged double agents'; it had attacked Shabangu's house where six ANC members were assembled on 11 November 1992, and also narrowly missed killing Modipane, who was not at home when the hit squad passed by his house. Skosana, serving a five-year prison term, expressed regret for his actions and maintained he never would have participated in the attack had Nkuna not told him 'that the instructions came directly from Hani, and that Hani had asked for a progress report on the elimination of double agents.'[150] Skosana and Nkuna could have both been apartheid agents; they could have been loyal ANC members receiving orders from a regime spy; or Nkuna could have been an agent whose instructions Skosana believed came from Hani.

Two years later, with no further details of a conspiracy, Hani's assassination remained a provocative topic for the SACP, as its new general secretary Blade Nzimande called for the national director of public prosecutions Bulelani Ngcuka to reopen the investigation, at a rally in North West province on 11 April 1999.[151] Among the thousands attending the rally were Hani's widow, Limpho, President Nelson Mandela, and his wife, Graça Machel. Nzimande declared: 'We are not asking for a reinvestigation because we are being vindictive, but only because we want the real truth to come out, as the only basis for taking our country forward.' Nzimande directly addressed Waluś and Derby-Lewis, telling the audience: 'We would like to say to them that we know that there was a wider conspiracy in the murder of Chris Hani.' According to Nzimande, both men had been set up by a wider ring of conspirators who had now 'dumped' them and left them to take sole blame for the assassination. Now, according to Nzimande, Waluś and Derby-Lewis were being denied amnesty by the TRC 'as a way to ensure their silence behind bars.'[152] Nzimande also used Hani's mantle to condemn political opportunism and careerism within the ANC, noting that Hani had campaigned vigorously against this.

In 2016 Lindiwe Hani, the youngest of Hani's three daughters, bravely confronted Clive Derby-Lewis and Janusz Waluś in face-to-face meetings which formed the basis for her poignant memoir, *Being Chris Hani's Daughter*. Derby-Lewis, who by then was stricken with late-stage cancer, described to Lindiwe his motive for orchestrating her father's death: as a leading Conservative Party (CP) figure, Derby-Lewis thought negotiations with the ANC were a travesty and sought by all means to derail them and avert the prospect of true democracy in South Africa. Waluś had attended CP events and declared to Derby-Lewis his support for such drastic action; Waluś was willing to serve as the triggerman to 'get rid of the communist threat.'[153] Waluś then found Hani's address from a list prepared by Clive's wife, Gaye, and Clive Derby-Lewis supplied Waluś with the gun. Clive Derby-Lewis told Lindiwe that after his conviction, several ANC figures had visited him in prison to enquire whether Thabo Mbeki or any other ANC leader had colluded with him; nobody had. He died in November 2016.

Was the Hani conspiracy so simple? Based on the evidence presented in this chapter, had ANC members been involved in the plot they would have conspired with SADF MI, not Derby-Lewis. Groenink quotes Elmie Eksteen, who had first-hand knowledge of South Africa's white right-wing scene from the 1980s onwards, describing Derby-Lewis thus: 'He is a doddering old fool. I always thought that's what I'd do if I wanted to kill someone like Hani. I'd use such a person [as a patsy].'[154] Here it is instructive to recall Hani's former bodyguard describing the likelihood that shadowy forces had managed Derby-Lewis and Waluś as an unwitting cell within a broader intelligence network; Waluś had fortuitously appeared on the scene when Derby-Lewis was looking for a gunman. When Lindiwe Hani faced Waluś, she asked him about his relationship with Peter Jackson; the signs of a second gunman; the mysterious absence of bodyguards that day; and other suspicious evidence. Waluś denied knowing anything about others' involvement, but admitted it was a possibility.

Post-transition calls from within the ANC and SACP to reopen the investigation into Hani's murder highlight the unresolved tension between the ANC's official line – reinforced by the ANC's own internal post-transition inquiry – that Hani's death was the work of an isolated right-wing fringe, and the recurring doubts about this explanation that have lingered with many South Africans, including many within the ANC and SACP leadership. If Chris Hani's assassination was indeed the product of a broader conspiracy, would this not merely reinforce what is already known: that the apartheid regime often murdered its opponents? In presenting evidence that Hani had been killed while trying to stop the arms deal, Evelyn Groenink has asserted: 'it matters because the story of freedom fighters who stumbled upon corruption and wanted to stop it is worth telling.'[155] The implications of a broader conspiracy also go much further, leaving an unhealed wound at the heart of South Africa's transition. And in the light of the ANC's post-transition silence surrounding the assassination, it leaves unanswered questions about who within the ANC might have known about the plot in advance. Indeed, one assessment of South Africa's fragile democracy pointed out that popular mistrust of Thabo Mbeki's administration was partly rooted in allegations of Mbeki's involvement in the plot to kill Hani.[156] This even gave rise to a song titled 'Thabo Mbeki, Tell Us Who Killed Chris Hani,' which the SACP's newly elected chairperson, Gwede Mantashe, sang along with assembled members at the party's 2007 congress.[157] The lingering controversy over who killed Hani, and why, has persisted as a central feature of South Africa's incomplete transition. It is emblematic of the perception widely shared among South Africans that many of the fundamental inequalities and injustices of apartheid remain violently and firmly in place, even while the mechanisms giving rise to them are concealed.

8

MK'S MARGINALIZATION IN SOUTH AFRICA'S 'NEW' SECURITY FORCES

'It was mentioned on the news that the agreement signed by the participants at Lancaster House, including the nationalist leaders, contained clauses entrenching the rights of the Rhodesian forces and the minority whites. What about us, the liberators? Nothing was said about safeguarding us. Nothing about our pensions for the many painful years we had spent in the bush, away from our beloved wives and children.'

— ZIPRA commander Nicholas Nkomo

On 2 May 1994, problems arose at the Wallmansthal base near Pretoria when a contingent of about 200 MK soldiers, allegedly drunk and dissatisfied with their pay, protested and 'stoned the cars of MK officers who tried to mediate.' The protest 'was quelled after Siphiwe Nyanda called on South African Defence Force (SADF) troops to restore order,' and when the incident was over, SADF military police had detained about 170 guerrillas.[1] In October 1994, thousands of MK cadres at Wallmansthal, 'aggrieved by what they perceive to be shabby treatment and squalid conditions they encountered upon integration into the still largely white-led South African army,' went AWOL (absent without official leave), refusing to serve until their grievances had been addressed. All told, a majority of the approximately 6,800 ex-guerrillas at various assembly points went AWOL to protest 'grievances relating to living conditions, racism encountered in relations with white officers, non-payment of salaries, and delays in being processed.'[2] On 18 October, a group of 150 MK veterans protested 'outside the President's office in Cape Town,' 'demanding free transport north,' prompting President Mandela to declare that 'he had no plans to reward indiscipline.' Mandela travelled to Wallmansthal on 20 October, 'and, after lending a seemingly sympathetic ear to their complaints, informed the rebels that their choice was a simple one: either they adhere to the rules of military discipline or they were out on the street.' He also threatened to discharge 3,000 cadres who had gone on leave earlier in October and had 'refused to return' to barracks.[3]

Several former guerrillas recounted how in his harangue Mandela accused them of indiscipline and of being not soldiers but murderers and rapists. The ANC's top leadership, including Mandela and defence minister Joe Modise, denied MK veterans' allegations of racism in SANDF. MK soldiers at Wallmansthal suspected that Modise and [MK commander Siphiwe] Nyanda had 'sold out' to the apartheid regime. They jeered at Modise when he showed up to try and calm the unrest, and they stoned Nyanda and set his car alight,[4] observing that Modise and Nyanda 'had become all too cozy with former SADF generals.'[5] One ex-guerrilla described how, suspecting his collaboration with the apartheid regime, outraged cadres burned Nyanda's car when he arrived at the base, and reacted to Mandela's ensuing speech with despair and fury: 'The comrades were very angry. There was chaos. They burned the car, chased [Nyanda] away, they wanted Mandela, who came guarded by the Boers with rifles, dogs, all that,' so that the cadres, who were 'a mix of MK officers and SDU [Self-Defence Unit] members,' were 'surrounded.' Mandela 'addressed them, you know, "you are a bunch of robbers, criminals, rapists, you don't deserve to be in this army…."' The assembled cadres 'responded with bad words to him, saying that no, you are not Mandela, Mandela died in prison, you are just a dummy of Mandela, how can you say this whereas you see that we are being swallowed here, there is no integration here, you see other comrades here are being taken at night, never seen again.'[6] By November 1994, the ANC-led government began to take 'a hard line' against 'dissent by former guerrillas who have been complaining about harsh discipline and poor living conditions as they are assimilated into the SANDF [South African National Defence Force].' This culminated in defence minister Joe Modise's dismissal of over 2,000 MK guerrillas awaiting integration.[7]

Another former guerrilla pointed to both their isolation from the ANC leadership and the presence of counterinsurgency forces facing MK fighters at the assembly points:

> While being in Wallmansthal we never integrated into the army, there were problems in trying to link with other departments, having contacts. In terms of being kept up to date by the ANC, there was not that link. There are so many forces involved, powerful forces in the political setup, a very dangerous game. Third Force can crop up, fertile ground.[8]

One ex-guerrilla who had considered joining the post-transition military explained his decision to steer clear of the demobilization points: 'Yeah, ooh, I never went there, sure, because I could hear the stories… Getting to understand that some of the top military brass were sellouts – it broke my morale, and that's when I said no, I am no more going to the army.'[9] This history must be considered in the light of evidence (see Chapter Six) that SADF MI operations were ongoing even during the month of Mandela's election to power, and of SADF MI operative Jan Anton Nieuwoudt's claim that the top ranks of the post-transition military would be staffed with MK and APLA double agents recruited beforehand by the apartheid counterinsurgency forces. As integration continued into 1995, distrust remained high between former SADF personnel and former MK and APLA members, which led to friction over security arrangements at the assembly points. Meanwhile, groups of unruly cadres from the liberation armies were imprisoned after summary trials.[10]

Former guerrillas' testimonies about the insecurity and hidden violence awaiting them at the Wallmansthal base in 1993–4 serve to highlight the colonial violence that has remained concealed in historical accounts. Previous literature has noted the chaos and disillusionment that prevailed among MK cadres at Wallmansthal but does not mention the presence of askaris at the base or the disappearance of MK fighters there.[11] These details gleaned from ex-guerrillas shift the meaning of the security sector reform process and the transition itself, suggesting a clandestine programme to undermine MK guerrillas at assembly points, killing some of them. In this context, MK cadres' suspicions that Modise and Nyanda were 'selling out' went beyond mere concern that they had compromised too much in negotiations.

Predation by colonial regimes at guerrilla assembly points has been a key feature of liberation army demobilization in southern Africa. In 1989 in Namibia, apartheid counterinsurgency forces killed hundreds of SWAPO soldiers who believed the war was over and were headed for demobilization points (see Chapter Three). During the demobilization process in newly independent Zimbabwe in 1979–80, ZIPRA and ZANLA cadres were often victimized by Rhodesian military units that remained intact and operated with impunity long after Robert Mugabe's ZANU-PF government assumed power.[12] ZIPRA commander Nicholas Nkomo, who led his unit to its designated assembly point in good faith, discovered upon arrival a situation that was echoed by MK veterans' description of Wallmansthal: 'We were ordered never to take our weapons with us when going outside the camp, while forces of the old colonialist regime did so with impunity… They were even free to kill us around our assembly points because according to the Lancaster House agreement they were responsible for security around the enemy camps.'[13] Guerrillas from the Zimbabwean liberation armies also faced ambushes by Rhodesian forces as they made their way to assembly points; several were shot when they showed up at assembly points after curfew; and a bus full of demobilizing ZIPRA guerrillas was even strafed by a Rhodesian plane.

This chapter examines the ANC's haphazard approach to returning MK exiles; the apartheid regime's clandestine attempts to shape the security sector reform (SSR) process; and the incomplete integration of MK into the 'new,' post-transition security forces. Successfully reforming state security institutions is critical to democratic consolidation. The detailed and politically sophisticated vision for transforming South Africa's military, police and intelligence services described in ANC and MK documents, and by individual MK cadres, belies the regime's portrayal of MK as unequipped to take charge of state security institutions. Instead, this research portrays the ANC's armed wing as an organized, disciplined group primed for the challenges of security sector reform. In its 1992 'Ready to Govern' policy statement, the ANC emphasized: 'The challenge is to address not only the security institutions and their composition, but also to go deeper and address the very nature of security policy itself.'[14] In a policy document, MK cadre Rocky Williams noted that the security forces, more than any other state institution, were destined to be a key 'arena of political and ideological contestation,' and that 'SADF officers acknowledge that MK enjoys considerable legitimacy in the eyes of the country's majority.'[15] Yet the apartheid regime shaped the security sector reform process in ways that not only inhibited the transformation of those institutions but also defined the new regime's approach to both domestic and external security, with far-reaching impacts. In the words of one former guerrilla commander, MK was marginalized during South Africa's SSR process – 'out, last in everything.'[16] The apartheid security elites sought to preserve their power throughout the process. The ANC's own leadership, after relinquishing the armed struggle at an early stage in negotiations, largely abdicated command and control over its underground structures. This left thousands of MK guerrillas unmoored during the transition process in the midst of escalating political violence. This lack of transformation stands in stark contrast to the well-articulated vision, held within both the ANC and MK, of the post-transition security landscape.

In March 1990, minister of defence Gen. Magnus Malan claimed MK didn't 'qualify to belong to any defence force in South Africa' because 'SADF produces [military] technology while [MK] only uses that technology.'[17] Malan then proposed a combat skills contest between his men and the liberation forces to determine which were more qualified to serve. Although Malan was demoted after the 1991 Inkathagate scandal, his vision of SADF supremacy was reflected in the security force reform process. Malan insisted: 'the matter of so-called integration of armies is not on the table,'[18] and 'remarked dismissively in parliament: "we are not on the road to using the army to keep employment off the streets."'[19] Malan's claims about MK appeared calculated to 'demoralize, undermine, and neutralize the confidence of MK and its members prior to their inevitable and eventual incorporation into a restructured Defence Force.'[20]

In the later stages of the transition, apartheid security force elites justified guerrillas' exclusion from the new forces because of their supposedly inadequate training and lack of professionalism.[21] Yet even in the transition's early stages, MK elements had already noted that it was the SADF that lacked 'proper political education in their training,' insisting that the apartheid regime's repressiveness disqualified it from participating in legitimate 'post-liberation' security forces. 'While the SADF may have the technology and the personnel, it has always been a tool for repression… All its personnel need re-education, others even rehabilitation before they can be considered as having a role to play in the defence of the future [South Africa].' One MK officer noted: 'our training prepares us not only for the pre-liberation phase, but also the post phase.'[22] Another insisted that, according to statements and policy documents of the ANC and the Mass Democratic Movement, 'MK has in fact been, and still is, the champion of a democratic order in South Africa.'[23] At the onset of negotiations between the ANC and NP, an MK policy document titled 'MK and the Future' noted: 'On the question of integration, our army commander [Chris Hani] has stated that we are not proposing to join the SADF but there will be a need to create a brand new defence force. This seems like the most logical outcome of the current process of consultation with the enemy.'[24] This perspective did not account for the SADF's power to shape the process of reforming South Africa's security institutions. In reality, the SADF's old guard proved capable of subverting change in the new military, and the integration process for MK combatants during and after the transitional era was characterized by insecurity, marginalization and occasional violence.

Background to Integration

As early as 1985, MK military headquarters had decided that MK forces should begin preparing for integration into the post-apartheid security forces. The USSR, India, Tanzania and Nigeria offered assistance and 'by the time the ANC was unbanned the nucleus of a regular army was in place.'[25] Speaking in a closed-session meeting, Joe Modise noted that 'steps have been taken to train our men in ground, air, and naval forces,' and emphasized the importance of 'training in those areas in which we lag' so that MK as a 'liberation movement' could 'be present in the future South African defence apparatus.' To this end, MK's leadership had determined that it urgently needed to '[build] an officers' corps' and MK cadres were receiving such training in Tanzania and Uganda, with other countries soon to assist.[26] Many MK cadres had also received 'outstanding' officers' training in various Eastern European countries.[27] In December 1990, an ANC delegation sent to Moscow 'asked the Soviets for supplies of arms and for assistance with the training of large groups of MK members for the future regular army,' telling the Soviets that at that stage 200 to 300 'young people were leaving South Africa every week to join MK.'[28] However, the Soviets advised the ANC delegation that while they should continue to build their armed formations, no further assistance would be forthcoming from the USSR.[29]

Shortly after negotiations began, a May 1990 conference in Lusaka on the 'Future of Security and Defence in South Africa' brought together some sixty representatives from MK and the ANC with a delegation of South African soldiers, academics and policy-makers. The ANC side featured prominent figures such as Chris Hani, Joe Nhanhla and Steve Tshwete, while the South African delegation, led by Frederik van Zyl Slabbert, included SADF Gen. Wally Black. Black announced that most South African whites considered a political settlement with the ANC to be desirable and held views more moderate than the regime's positions; he also claimed that many SADF officers disagreed with Gen. Malan's contention that there would be no integration of MK cadres into the security forces, instead regarding such integration as desirable and inevitable. The conference reached a consensus that the ANC should be recognized, and that MK should be integrated into the future security forces. Ngculu recalls how SADF disdained MK 'terrorists' before discovering 'that the members of this "rag tag" army were quite knowledgeable and articulate… Many of us had received sophisticated guerrilla training in a number of countries, while our political training equipped us better than members of the SADF.'[30]

MK's military code at its founding stated: 'When we have liberated our country, Umkhonto will constitute the basis of the defence forces of our country and the revolution.'[31] MK commander Chris Hani himself was emphatic about the need to prepare the guerrillas to assume a central role in forging new state institutions: 'we must tell our cadres that we must also improve their quality because as far as I'm concerned having fought for democracy they are going to be the core of a new South African army, a new South African security force, and they have got a duty to make our leaders negotiate…from a strong position.'[32] Following the February 1990 Pretoria Minute, an MK document written by an anonymous, apparently mid-level officer imagined 'a successful insurrection…with lots of jubilation, a victorious parade of our combatants on APCs [armoured personnel carriers] and Katyushas [mobile rocket launchers], ready to take up the position of a new defence force.'[33] The document acknowledged that negotiations precluded this triumphant scenario, but underscored MK's readiness to assume control of the post-transition security forces. Another document written by an MK cadre during the transition maintained: 'MK sees itself as an important pillar in the struggle to set up in South Africa a non-racial democracy in a unitary state.'[34] Once negotiations began, the armed wing's leadership wasted no time in planning for this: 'Our army commander [Chris Hani] has recently emphasized the need to speedily build and convert MK into a regular army… We have also seen comrades being sent for long-term courses in the military academy.'[35] MK also proved resilient in adjusting to the pressures of sudden political change, even as it dealt with ongoing regime depredations and the repatriation of its cadres from foreign bases in Angola, Tanzania, Uganda and Zambia to South Africa, with limited infrastructure to receive them.

The negotiations between the ANC and NP included a 'sunset clause' that preserved important elements of the apartheid military and police as a form of 'side payment' to avert the possibility of rebellion or an attempted coup. However, apartheid intelligence recruitment played a sinister role in negotiations between ANC and NP elites.[36] The apartheid counterinsurgency forces also sought to exploit and deepen the cleavages that arose within the ANC at the start of negotiations, as attested to by SADF MI's attempt to recruit Joe Modise and several other high-ranking ANC military and intelligence officials (see Chapter Six). An SADF MI document described the meeting with Modise and the others as a crucial step towards breaking the backbone of what it referred to as the 'SACP/Hani/Kasrils faction' within the ANC. SADF MI's apparently successful recruitment of ANC decision-makers raises pointed questions about the extent of apartheid counterinsurgency's influence on the negotiations process. Although the sunset clause most directly affected the security forces during the first ten years of the transition, these were also the most critical years in terms of the potential to transform them. By the time the sunset clause expired, many ex-guerrillas had already ruled out a career in the new defence force. One MK veteran recalled that although it was 'normal' for the two sides to negotiate an end to the war, 'the compromise is too much, you know. Because our people joined the army and they felt discriminated, so they opted out, so that's why I say the situation was not conducive.' The ex-guerrilla noted: 'Even some [ANC] leaders have told us that we are not up to [safeguarding the country], but our guys have been trained in big places, so what do you mean that we don't have soldiers good enough to take responsibility, so better the people from the previous regime, which we were fighting?'[37] Another ex-guerrilla described how, even after the transition, MK veterans 'got nothing to show that we are comrades. No recognition at all.'[38] Several other studies have noted widespread bitterness among former MK and APLA guerrillas rooted in their socio-economic marginalization, including many who resigned or who were discharged from the new security forces because of pervasive racist attitudes.[39]

Armed Struggle and Compromise: Guerrilla Visions of Security Sector Reform

As Third Force violence raged, an MK policy document noted the inevitability of apartheid attitudes enduring in the security forces; it emphasized that the ANC's and MK's inferior 'bargaining power as influenced by our political and military strength, as well as other factors locally and internationally, tend[s] to dictate' the terms of security sector reform.[40] Three months after Mandela's unilateral renunciation of armed struggle, the document noted the imbalance between the regime and the ANC on this front: 'Our pronouncements on the future of the SADF have been more conciliatory than those of the enemy.'[41] As negotiations advanced, Ngculu recalls that the SADF 'was intent on stifling and frustrating integration' and remained opposed to integration 'with the armies of the liberation movements.' MK at this time was 'dispersed and disorganized,' and Military Headquarters

(MHQ) was 'in a state of flux' as it sought to establish itself within South Africa: several key members were still in exile, while others had not received indemnity. Meanwhile, cadres still based in Uganda, Tanzania and Zambia 'felt abandoned and disillusioned,' and this in turn began 'to undermine their confidence' in MK leadership.[42] In mid-1991, MK forces assembled in Transkei received instruction from ANC headquarters in Johannesburg that they were all to apply for indemnity.

The ANC leadership encouraged MK cadres to assume a role in organizing and participating in the ANC's watershed July 1991 conference in Durban. In response to widespread calls within MK for it to assert its central role in the ANC during the transition, MK assembled a delegation to represent the movement's armed wing. MK cadres also insisted that the ANC take a strong stance vis-à-vis the regime with regard to SDU and MK members arrested by the security forces as they organized defences for besieged African communities.[43] The Durban conference passed a resolution affirming that although armed activities had been suspended, the armed struggle had not been abandoned. It resolved that the ANC would 'maintain and develop MK until the adoption of a new constitution and the creation of a new defence force into which cadres of MK will be integrated'; the ANC would not surrender its arms to the regime until then. The ANC also undertook to 'popularise the demand for a single military force that will uphold and defend the values of democracy' in South Africa, and the resolution called on the National Executive Committee to 'take full responsibility for the transferring of funds to regions for the maintenance, development, and general welfare of all MK cadres, both inside and outside the country, and that proper and appropriate binding mechanisms be established to ensure this.'[44] At the Durban conference, the ANC also laid plans to organize an MK conference, to be held in August 1991 at the University of Venda in Thohoyandou.

On 9 August 1991, the conference opened in Thohoyandou, with over 500 delegates attending. Mandela gave the opening address, in which he called for MK to be 'restructured in a way that enables its cadres to join the armed forces of a democratic South Africa.'[45] Chris Hani also addressed the conference, discussing the state of MK following its 1989 relocation from Angola to bases in Tanzania and Uganda. Hani noted: 'from the very beginning MK encountered serious logistics, accommodation and transport problems' in Tanzania and Uganda. MK had been forced to abandon most of its vehicles in Angola, and the ones it brought over 'were not very serviceable and there was also the problem of spare parts.'

In delivering the keynote address at the Thohoyandou conference, Mandela announced that Chris Hani would be assuming the role of South African Communist Party chief, which meant that Hani 'would no longer serve…as Chief of Staff of MK.' Simpson notes, 'the conference reflects a high degree of confidence within the ANC that whatever concerns they may have about the activities of the "hidden" or "third" force, the negotiations will probably see a generally peaceful transition to majority rule.' Hani himself anticipated that, 'short of a major disaster,' the transition was 'very likely to be relatively peaceful,' which 'would mean we inherit a fully-fledged SA Defence Force, Transkei Defence Force, Venda Defence Force, Bophuthatswana Defence Force, Ciskei Defence Force et al.'[46] The Thohoyandou conference envisioned the road ahead for MK, calling for vigilance in the face of ongoing security threats, as well as preparations for participation in the new security forces. It also served as a forum for MK cadres to air their grievances. Chris Hani set the tone for this in his address, in which he argued that the lessons from the 1984 MK mutinies at several Angolan bases, and the grievances that triggered them, had not been sufficiently internalized and disseminated.[47] The commission on the restructuring and reorganization of MK further criticized the haphazard 'manner in which MHQ redeployed from Lusaka to Johannesburg.' Overall, MK's 'external and regional structures were in disarray and comrades had been left without clear guidance and information,' but the Thohoyandou conference restored MK cadres' confidence in the ANC leadership and 'dispelled any notion' that the ANC had sidelined them. The regime was keen to capitalize on any potential dissatisfaction or schism within MK, and after the conference 'a suspicious and cleverly crafted document was circulated, suggesting that some ANC leaders viewed MK as an "albatross" around the neck of the movement.' It also suggested that by marginalizing MK, the ANC would strengthen its credibility as a party in peace negotiations. The document 'created some tensions, suspicions and finger-pointing within the ranks of the

ANC and MK' until they determined that it was part of an apartheid 'Stratcom' operation designed to create divisions and confusion.[48]

'Ready to Govern,' the comprehensive May 1992 document expressing the ANC's vision for South Africa's democratic institutions, also sought to affirm MK's centrality. The section titled 'Peace and Security' proclaimed: 'the South African security institutions themselves developed a racist, closed, secretive, undemocratic structure lacking legitimacy in the eyes of the people. The process of democratization underway in our country will not be complete without addressing this problem.' The ANC document then contrasted this with MK – 'the People's Army – [which] represented the cutting edge in the struggle for a non-racial and democratic society. Viewed by the majority of South Africans as a liberating force, its popular support was demonstrated at countless rallies, marches, and demonstrations.'[49]

At its September 1993 Kanyamazane conference in Venda, MK released a press statement declaring: 'we are confident MK will play a significant role in the process of levelling the political playing field.'[50] This demonstrated an acute awareness that the balance of military forces in South Africa both reflected and shaped the political 'playing field' on which the negotiations unfolded. An imbalance favouring the government security forces was the surest indication of the ANC's disadvantageous bargaining position. Emphasizing the state security forces' role in fomenting violence, MK called for the SADF to 'be confined to barracks, while the SAP's task should be confined to fighting crime.'[51] At the conference, MK further called for the strengthening of its leadership through the creation of a military council, and for securing more funds to 'strengthen regional and zonal MK structures.'[52] Thus despite the lack of resources available to MK fighters returning from exile, and despite their alienation from the ANC elites, MK strove to remain organized and responsive to South Africa's shifting political terrain. Its main goals were, in the immediate term, to provide security for communities targeted by Third Force violence, and, in the longer term, to ensure the transformation of South Africa's security institutions according to democratic ideals; in establishing these goals, it was to prove prescient in identifying key challenges to South Africa's democratization.

In its 'general resolutions,' the MK conference membership, 'noting i) that there are forces intent on derailing and sabotaging the negotiation process,' and 'ii) the increase of war talk and violence,' further resolved 'to urge our leadership and negotiators to ensure that the negotiation process is speeded up,' even while remaining 'vigilant and combat ready.'[53] There was also a sense of urgency that MK would soon be bypassed by political developments in South Africa even though its key priorities remained unresolved: 'This conference is of particular importance in that this may possibly be the last opportunity MK will have to discuss these issues at a national level.'[54] Indeed, MK fighters would hold no further conferences qua MK, nor would they have another opportunity to assemble or to make further policy recommendations. Even as MK sought to address the security shortcomings in the negotiations, it remained steadfastly loyal to the ANC leadership, '[reiterating] its unequivocal support for the democratization process and the ANC's participation in the negotiation process.'[55] No extremist faction split from MK, and cadres' discipline held. They regarded the negotiations as the culmination of the ANC's strategy.[56] One MK veteran who joined the post-transition security forces suggested that MK cadres' discipline prevented its members from splintering off into rejectionist factions during and after the transition: 'That's why you don't have rebellion here. Because we understood what we are fighting for.'[57]

MK's Bases Abroad, 1989–94

The need to abandon its Angolan bases hit MK quite hard. According to one report from September 1989, the ANC's leadership in exile was 'struggling to maintain its cohesion in the face of severe setbacks' since MK's relocation to Uganda and Tanzania.[58] While Third Force violence raged in South Africa, in Tanzania MK faced difficulties adjusting to its new reality: the Tanzanian army was responsible for camp security, and proximity to local villages led to desertions. MK cadres' idleness and lack of deployment further undermined morale. A similar decline in morale took hold among MK cadres in Zambia, many of whom had been 'waiting for deployment long before the legalization of the ANC.' By contrast, Hani reported that 'the situation in Uganda was generally favourable.'[59] After 1990, MK cadres continued their training in Uganda, while others were sent to Ghana, India, Zambia and Zimbabwe to train for integration into the regular army, and a high-level MK delegation travelled to Zimbabwe to examine how in ten years the country had transformed guerrillas into 'world-class officers' in the Zimbabwe National Army.[60]

Video footage of a December 1992 ceremony held at the Kaweweta MK base in Uganda shows hundreds of tightly organized MK female and male cadets graduating from their training course and receiving individual distinctions. The proceedings were attended by a visiting ANC delegation that included such high-level representatives as Cyril Ramaphosa, Siphiwe Nyanda, and regional MK commander Andrew Masondo. Joe Modise, as MK chief of staff, addressed 'military officers and police officers, soldiers of the TDF,[61] commanders and soldiers of Umkhonto we Sizwe.' There were three 'passing out' parades to mark MK soldiers' completion of their training and celebrate their imminent integration into the new South African security forces. In his address, Modise told the assembled MK cadres:

> today, you are passing out not as the irregulars who have done so much to bring us to where we are, but you are passing out as regular soldiers that will form the nucleus of a new army, an army in South Africa that is going to defend the democratic norms of our country. You are going there to build an army that will know no colour, an army that will be based on the policy of peace.[62]

The rare footage taken in this video – as a security precaution, cameras were almost never allowed on MK bases[63] – shows highly organized MK recruits performing battle drills with weaponry ranging from small arms and machine guns to rocket-propelled grenades, mortars, rockets, field artillery, and anti-aircraft guns.

In November 1992, it emerged that over the previous several months 'the ANC had dispatched more than a thousand "raw recruits" to receive military training in Uganda,' with one group of 320 recruits sent in September and another group of over 640 dispatched in October. In each case, the groups were assembled and briefed in South Africa before being flown by chartered flights to Uganda, where they were to receive 'six months' basic training before being sent out of Uganda for specialized training.' Calling the move 'totally unacceptable,' NP constitutional development minister Roelf Meyer declared: 'One party can't go on with its own separate so-called army.'[64]

Several months before the April 1994 elections, the ANC sent a battalion-sized MK force, about 800 strong, for military training at a base in the Zambian Copper Belt near Kabwe.[65] The soldiers got to vote in the South African elections, but, strangely, 'when we arrived in Zambia, the government didn't know about our presence, nor the minister of defence.' Meanwhile, 'South African radios and newspapers published [reports] about a unit' based abroad 'that the ANC is refusing to comment about'; although the ANC claimed 'there are no units outside,' in reality 'there were units in Ghana, Zimbabwe, Angola.' The MK cadre speculated: 'maybe they were trying to sacrifice us. We voted in Zambia, but there was no logistical support for us there, it was trouble. We were just struggling, like as if we were in Angola those days.'[66] This stint was ostensibly meant to prepare MK soldiers for integration into the SANDF, but after completing their five-month training course, most of them were not integrated. It is unclear whether this was mainly due to the ANC's disorganization, or whether the apartheid old guard blocked these MK forces' integration; a third possibility, suggested by a former MK commander, is that the ANC leadership wanted to disperse its own fighters lest they disrupt the transition process out of a sense of having been marginalized by it.

Returning from Exile

MK cadres returning to South Africa from exile had to worry about their own welfare and survival; at the Kanyamazane conference, personnel present called upon the ANC to '[recognize] the serious resettlement and integration problems faced by thousands of returning exiles and MK cadres in terms of both psychological stress and disability as well as unemployment, homelessness, and destitution.'[67] Many MK soldiers 'had to wait in their homes for a long period for the outcome of negotiations,' where most lived in conditions of deprivation and could not be provided for by the ANC.[68] The poverty and alienation experienced by many MK cadres upon returning from exile underscore the split between ANC elites and masses during this phase, and the failure of many former combatants to reintegrate into society was largely due to the fact that demobilization was implemented without proper planning.[69] MHQ established a special projects department, led by Tokyo Sexwale, to assist MK cadres and support those still in the underground in Transkei and across the country,[70] but the ANC's resources were stretched thin. In a January 1993 interview, Chris Hani noted: 'Exiles and soldiers who had expected to return home as conquerors are standing in the unemployment lines.'[71] This was the opposite of the vision Hani had articulated on the eve of the transition, when he emphasized that the ANC leadership would send cadres back into South Africa from exile 'in an organized manner, [such that] when those cadres go back, they are already deployed, they have got tasks of our movement. They are deployed. We are not going back as returning refugees.'[72]

In contrast, one former MK commander described the widespread lack of resources and disorganization facing guerrillas who returned to South Africa from their bases in exile:

> When we reached the country, everyone went home, so integrating again, coming together again was not an easy thing. Even to brief each other, because there is this MKVA [MK Veterans' Association] but it's just for certain individuals who are corrupt, it's not reaching the rank and file down there. It was not easy to organize and to have one voice calling to be integrated into police [and military]. No one cared for us. The problem was that you woke up at your house, you don't know what you're going to eat. So it changes now, it becomes a survival issue for you. So if you waste your time going to ANC offices, asking for help, you become a nuisance. So most comrades became disillusioned, their morale became very low. Some died as paupers.[73]

The former MK commander went on to describe the suicide of an ex-guerrilla following a domestic dispute: 'Because a child was crying, the other one washing clothes, so the mother of the child started shouting at this fellow: you are sitting here, where is this ANC of yours? You went to exile, now you are here I'm feeding you… And the other one said, you want to know, I'll show you. Went inside and hanged himself.'[74] The local MK comrades had to pool their money to pay for a proper burial, as none was forthcoming from ANC channels 'to bury cadres, especially one who hanged himself...we buried him in a community hole. We had no place to bury him. The landlord refused permission to bury him in his yard.'[75]

However, according to another ex-guerrilla, the ANC did its best to support its cadres, and provided employment for some. Furthermore, with the return of guerrillas from exile, he believed a degree of marginalization – or at least social alienation – was inevitable: 'When we came back, the ANC took care of us.' But reintegrating guerrillas into society was a challenge because these veterans had left home in their youth; now, they 'have got this gap – they don't know money, their friends who were left behind are married, they've got children. You don't have anything. You left your parents' house; your sisters have their own children. Now you're the uncle that must sleep somewhere.'[76]

At the Kanyamazane conference, Nelson Mandela, addressing the assembled cadres, lamented that after all the sacrifices they had made, they 'should find themselves back in South Africa unemployed and without support or the means to sustain yourself,' and announced that the ANC had 'managed to raise an amount which we have allocated to MK, and with which we hope to start the process of catering for your needs.'[77] The ANC offered housing and education and had pledged R10 million for demobilized MK returnees, but had limited infrastructure to distribute it.[78] A flyer dated 14 September 1993 and issued by MK headquarters called on 'those comrades who are in need of relief' to 'report to the Regional Commands without delay.'[79] Many ex-combatants never received their payouts,[80] and for those who did, the money evaporated quickly in the context of African communities' widespread poverty.

The National Peacekeeping Force

In June 1993, MK and SADF reached an agreement on the formation of a peacekeeping force, consisting of between 7,000 and 12,000 men drawn primarily from the SADF, the SAP and MK, but also from the Bantustan militaries and APLA.[81] At its September 1993 conference at Kanyamazane, MK affirmed its commitment 'to the establishment of the National Peacekeeping Force (NPKF).'[82] The ANC and NP had jointly envisioned the NPKF as a neutral force incorporating 10,000 combatants from both sides, as a formal trust-building step. The force was seen as being 'of critical importance' because it would have 'the necessary legitimacy to replace discredited components' of the SAP's 7,000-strong Internal Stability Units, which were associated with apartheid repression.[83] It was also hoped the NPKF would be more effective in combating widespread political violence; nonetheless, there were 'grave doubts about the cohesion of its disparate parts.'[84] Chris Hani, an outspoken critic of the security forces' failure to protect black lives, had been 'one of the initiators' of the NPKF.[85] By 24 January 1994, 'contingents from the SADF, MK and the armed forces of Ciskei, Venda, and the Transkei,' numbering over 3,600 men, commenced a six-week course of training at De Brug army base near Bloemfontein 'before being deployed to mainly black areas to curb violence in the build-up to the elections.'[86] Yet MK troops that assembled to join the NPKF claimed they faced discrimination at the hands of the SADF and hazardous conditions at assembly points; according to Ngculu: 'Most of the officers of the SADF were not ready to accept MK officers as equals, largely because they came from an irregular army.'[87] The NPKF troops gathered at De Brug were in chaotic disarray just two weeks after being assembled, characterized by 'a collapse of discipline, mass desertions and widespread drunkenness,' including an incident in which 600 MK soldiers, many of whom were drunk, 'allegedly began toyi-toyiing and singing "One settler, one bullet" and "Down with FW,"' and demanding 'one dead SADF and one dead SAP member before sunrise.' An SADF instructor for the NPKF told a journalist: 'At this stage, the SADF is carrying MK. While we're still in training, this is okay. But once the force is deployed, it's going to be a no-go situation. When the SADF and police are withdrawn and we're left to sort out the problems, there's going to be serious shit.'[88] A report from March 1994 described scenes of camaraderie between SADF and MK soldiers in the NPKF, but also quoted an SADF officer who gestured towards soldiers from the liberation armies and said: 'Look at these people. They're nothing but baboons. We call them JACK – "just another confused kaffir." Still, you've got to admit, they make helluva good soldiers. The best.'[89]

On 18 April 1994, the NPKF was sent into the roiling violence of Thokoza township, one of the most violent flashpoints between

ANC and IFP loyalists during the transition period. In the ensuing gun battle between NPKF forces and IFP loyalists, one journalist covering the event was killed and another wounded; after this incident, 'the writing was on the wall' and the unit was dissolved.[90] After the transition, Joe Modise commented that the NPKF 'never had a chance, really. It was originally planned to train them for nine months, but in effect they were trained for eight weeks.'[91] The NPKF had other fundamental problems, including serious 'internal divisions' and arguments over 'who should have command over the force'; a failure to instill 'a measure of unity between the SADF and the liberation armies'; opposition and distrust on the part of SADF MI and the SAP; and the inability 'to gain any measure of legitimacy in the conflict-torn townships east of Johannesburg where it was deployed.'[92] Ngculu insists that the securocrats and regime security forces resisted the NPKF from the outset, and waged 'a vicious campaign' against it, with some security force elements 'already making plans for its demise.'[93] This foreshadowed similar challenges surrounding security force integration after the April 1994 transition.

Integration and Unrest in the Post-Transition Security Forces

A contemporary paper titled 'Military Forces during the Transition Period' by MK cadre Keith Mokoape emphasized that 'the means by which units of MK return to bases inside South Africa is one of the central problems facing us in the transition period,' and declared that assembly points for demobilizing guerrillas such as had been set up a decade earlier in newly independent Zimbabwe would not be acceptable, since such points 'rely on the presence of an outside monitoring force, isolate the guerrillas from the transition process, and leave them extremely vulnerable to attacks or polarized confrontations that could hinder or totally disrupt the transition period.'[94] Foreseeing the dangers awaiting MK cadres, the September 1993 Kanyamazane conference resolved: 'ANC negotiators should ensure total security for MK members when they get to the assembly points and also ensure remuneration for the soldiers at assembly points.'[95] Echoing earlier MK statements on the inadmissibility of clandestine units in the reformed security forces, it also demanded: 'all those with CCB and other "dirty

253

tricks" structures connections should not be allowed to sign up.' None of these stipulations would be met; instead, MK cadres found themselves at a disadvantage in the integration process. Ultimately, the SANDF that emerged from the transitional negotiations reflected the apartheid regime's position of relative power: MK and APLA cadres were merely integrated into the SADF's pre-existing structures, causing 'considerable resentment among the non-statutory forces, as rank-and-file cadres were not party to the decisions and compromises made at the Transitional Executive Council (TEC) and by their military commanders in the bi-lateral negotiations between SADF and MK.'[96]

In parallel negotiations starting in 1993, the ANC and NP agreed to create the South African National Defence Force (SANDF), a new national military incorporating all former armies. The total number of liberation movement combatants was unknown, so MK and APLA had to compile Certified Personnel Registers (CPRs) in order for their guerrillas to be integrated;[97] MK initially compiled a CPR with 83,000 names, which it pared down to 27,801 after the 1994 elections.[98] The number of cadres excluded from the CPRs is unknown. Compiling the CPRs required a level of transparency from the guerrilla movements that would have hitherto constituted a fatal security breach: guerrillas in exile had used *noms de guerre*, but pseudonyms would not be accepted for the purpose of integration. Combatants were reluctant to submit their real names because the process began in 1992 in 'a context of ongoing political violence during which some APLA and MK combatants feared for their lives.'[99]

On 28 March 1994 the first press conference was held of the new Joint Military Coordinating Council (JMCC) in Pretoria, featuring MK's Siphiwe Nyanda and SADF chief of operations Wessels Kritzinger. In a press release, they outlined the procedure for combining the forces of MK, SADF, and the Bantustan armies, which included the establishment of three assembly points for MK cadres at existing SADF bases: 8,000 cadres were to assemble at Wallmansthal near Pretoria, and 2,500 and 1,500 respectively at Bourke's Luck and Hoedspruit in the Eastern Transvaal.[100] At the conference, Nyanda told the assembled press that out of over 20,000 MK troops he only expected 16,000 or so to be integrated, and that there was no place in South Africa to accommodate the thousands of cadres still housed at bases in Tanzania and Uganda, so these would be repatriated to South Africa after the elections when camps for them would be ready.[101]

MK cadres began assembling at Wallmansthal on 28 March 1994. Journalists covering the process were told by MK commander at the base Petros Shecheshe that cadres had arrived there from across South Africa, and from Tanzania and Uganda, and that 'despite what happened in the past we were received with open arms by the army. Most of us didn't expect it.' His observation was seconded by SADF base commander Col. Terence Murphy, who said that 'no problems have arisen.'[102] This was in stark contrast to other descriptions of the conditions MK cadres faced at the assembly points, as we have seen; within a few months, hundreds of MK cadres would be deserting the base and protesting to highlight their grievances with the integration process. As one ex-guerrilla related, Mandela's visit to Wallmansthal 'didn't solve anything, things got worse. We were just swallowed. They used us, really.'[103] Another ex-guerrilla summarized the integration process: 'We compromised a lot during integration, it was hell. Look, even now, I cannot be treated at military hospital. But I was a soldier, a fighter. What's that? That's why I say it was just a total anarchy. The whole process served individuals rather than the whole MK fighters.'[104]

In its resolution on integration into the new security forces, MK resolved at the Kanyamazane conference: 'ranking must take place as soon as possible, taking into consideration training, experience, and years of service.' Yet guerrillas who chose integration into the new military or police experienced discrimination from their white counterparts and superiors, their ranks being frequently downgraded, which the SADF justified by claiming that the ranks earned in a guerrilla army were not equivalent to those in South Africa's conventional army, thereby dismissing the guerrillas' own training and experience. A related problem with the integration of MK guerrillas was the devaluing of their experience and training under the pretense that they had not been trained as a conventional army:

> There are few [MK veterans] who want to go to the army. Because that hatred is still there. Even now those guys who are with the army, they complain that Hey! we are treated there second class. When it came to ranks they undermined our training. They said it's guerrilla warfare, and

they did conventional, so their ranks should be higher than ours. And knowing that after eighteen years' fighting for this country, there's a young boy there, he's got two years' experience in the military, but he's going to be *my senior* – so we said no. We said if they want us to train conventional, we can do it but with *our* ranks, which we deserve! And by then there was nobody to stand for us.[105]

This testimony illustrates cadres' sense of abandonment by the ANC leadership, the absence of anyone to 'stand for' the guerrillas and exercise democratic civilian control over the security institutions that were the site of such systematic discrimination. Meanwhile, askaris 'were better treated than [MK veterans] because they got money when they resigned, given firearms, houses – a lot!'[106] An earlier study of the integration of ex-combatants into South Africa's new security forces also cites MK respondents' vexation that collaborators received government jobs while guerrillas continued to languish in poverty: 'We have worked hard for the ANC… But, now what is surprising is that the very ANC takes those *amalumpere*[107] [informers, askaris] who were killing people in the location, and gives them jobs.'[108]

The official numbers at integration into the new SANDF comprised 85,000 SADF troops, 17,000 MK and 6,000 APLA guerrillas, a handful of guerrillas from the tiny Azanian National Liberation Army (AZANLA, the armed wing of the Black Consciousness movement), plus 11,000 soldiers from the Bantustan armies. Gear defines demobilization in the South African context as 'the specific process of discharging former MK and APLA cadres either because they did not meet the requirements for integration into the SANDF, or because they did not wish to follow a career' in the security forces.[109] The new South African military excluded many ex-guerrillas on the pretext that they were uneducated, unmotivated or infirm, perpetuating racist stereotypes that portrayed blacks as unfit for complex roles, while discrediting the training of thousands of MK fighters in Angola, the Warsaw Pact countries, and elsewhere.[110] One ex-guerrilla in the post-transition security forces insisted that a lack of formal schooling disadvantaged many inductees: '[comrades] were de-ranked, given lower ranks, all those things. And you must understand something –

these people left the country not educated, not even having matric.'[111] Cadres at the 1991 Thohoyandou conference had anticipated that many guerrillas' lack of formal education would be a major point of contention between MK and the SADF during integration, and a vocal contingent argued that if educational qualifications were used as a basis for recruitment and integration into the new security forces, Africans, who had systematically been denied opportunities under apartheid, would yet again face discrimination.[112] Many veterans also reported inconsistencies and lapses in the administration and processing of assessments during the integration process, giving rise to suspicions that the screening process was rigged by the old SADF.[113] Ngculu recalls:

> Comrades were sent from course to course with no end in sight and were often failed on dubious grounds. Some received lower ranks in the SANDF despite their senior positions in MK. Others were left waiting for long periods for placement. Some were charged for being AWOL and subsequently dismissed from the army. The military justice system was also unfair and victimized most of the people who saw no end to their frustrations.[114]

Motumi notes that 'by the time integration began in earnest, from 27 April 1994, more than three years had elapsed after the return of the majority' of MK cadres 'from exile or release from prison.'[115] The ANC launched a comprehensive programme to prepare MK cadres and leadership for integration, and to reconfigure the new security forces to respect democratic norms and principles. Nonetheless, 'it was not an easy process. Many of our comrades fell victim to marginalization, frustration and general harassment by ex-SADF members in the new security forces.' Although the Mandela government 'was not unaware of these problems,' it 'had to approach their solution in a manner that encouraged reconciliation and trust.'[116] One former MK commander explained the difference between guerrilla training and the SADF's conventional military training: 'There you are trained specifically as a rifleman. Then you go up ranks, and maybe you join that artillery unit, or you are an infantryman, or you belong to engineering regiment. But as a guerrilla you are versatile, you train in all those fields. So that was our advantage.'[117] However, not all MK guerrillas had received such comprehensive training. MK was formally disbanded in December 1994.[118]

Under the supervision of the British Military Advisory and Training Team (BMATT) assisting with the transition, the ex-guerrillas who wanted to join the new forces had to take a compulsory written exam, which many of them failed; SADF soldiers did not undergo any screening.[119] One former MK commander declared that part of the blame for MK's marginalization lay with the BMATT, which supervised South Africa's security sector reform process as a supposedly impartial observer: 'I blame them because they were the ones overseeing everything, smooth running of the whole thing. As you know, the British were part of the whole [counterinsurgency] machinery.' Frankel portrays the BMATT as an impartial advisory team that helped to ensure a smooth and balanced transition, yet the British had previously trained apartheid military, intelligence, and Special Forces units (see Chapter Two), and one former MK cadre insisted: 'Once a colonizer, always a colonizer. They knew, they've invested here, so they had to compromise us for the sake of the minority.'[120] Barry Gilder also told me cryptically that the BMATT had played a key role in marginalizing MK cadres during the integration process, but was unwilling to elaborate.[121] The BMATT trainers favoured the APLA cadres coming in for integration over their MK counterparts, even though the former typically had less training and combat experience: 'the APLA leader group arriving [for integration] at De Brug [military base] in August 1994 was labelled by BMATT as "smarter, better-disciplined, and more political-oriented" than MK.' A very large proportion of the APLA cadres was accepted into the SANDF, raising the ire of MK, which 'generally appeared to fit far less comfortably into [SANDF] structures than did their PAC counterparts.'[122] It should also be remembered that according to the Steyn Report, APLA had been very thoroughly infiltrated by the regime (see Chapter Six).

Apartheid Continuities and Instability

In the months before the April 1994 election, violence continued to rage across several flashpoints, and the regime deployed its forces in ways that drew accusations from the ANC of an ongoing counterinsurgency agenda. The SADF was still operating in Gauteng's Katorus township to counter the violence raging between SDUs and Inkatha's SPUs,[123] and, right until it ceded power, the apartheid regime continued deploying military units to police black townships, including the notorious 32 'Buffalo' Battalion, which had also been deployed in Natal province since 1988,[124] where it fuelled the violence that raged there throughout the transition era.[125] Comprising Angolan mercenaries commanded by white officers, 32 Battalion was ostensibly used for peacekeeping, but Morodi perceived its deployment as sinister: 'they are following us. They are people who were killing people in their country [i.e., Angola and Namibia]. When Namibia got rid of them' upon gaining independence, the SADF 'brought here and they give them citizenship. They brought the Koevoet[126] here and gave them citizenship and they are using these people to go and kill' South African civilians.[127] The 1992 Goldstone Commission had recommended that 32 Battalion be withdrawn because it was exacerbating political violence.[128] Battalion 32 was also deeply implicated in transition-era counterinsurgency operations in the Bantustans, as its commander, Jan Breytenbach, had been tasked with setting up a paratrooper unit in the Ciskei Defence Force (see Chapter Five), while another officer, Col. Ockert Swanepoel, was appointed chief of Ciskei's Military Intelligence branch.[129] In a 1992 interview, Chris Hani emphasized that in its negotiations with the NP, the ANC had 'complained about 32 Battalion and said this unit should never be used for peace-making operations in this country…it is making a mess and should be withdrawn.'[130] As late as 1995, Mandela still deployed 32 Battalion against SDUs that refused to disarm.[131] Meanwhile, several SADF officers who only months earlier had been running counterinsurgency operations in Ciskei were now overseeing the forces' transition.[132] One was SADF Brig. Marius Oelschig, who had commanded the Ciskei Defence Force at the time of the massacre of unarmed ANC protesters at Bisho on 7 September 1992,[133] before being appointed head of the military integration process.[134] Another Military Intelligence officer from the SADF MI front company IR-CIS, At Nel, stayed in Ciskei for several months and then joined Army Headquarters in Pretoria shortly after the election.[135]

Ongoing Tensions

In May 1994, new defence minister Joe Modise appointed SADF Gen. Georg Meiring as SANDF chief, and on 28 June 1994 Siphiwe Nyanda, Modise's 'protégé,' was given the rank of lieutenant general and appointed acting chief of staff of the SANDF pending his completion of a three-year training course. Eight other senior MK officers were appointed at the same time as Nyanda to top ranks in various branches of the SANDF, including former Special Ops commander Aboobaker Ismail, who was given the rank of major general and appointed chief director of logistics, SANDF Headquarters. Modise made the appointments following 'bitter complaints from the public and within the Defence Force' about the conditions facing ex-guerrillas,[136] and 'objections from white generals about standards.'[137] Modise had 'been criticized for going into overdrive in implementing Mandela's reconciliation policies within the Defence Force at the expense of senior Umkhonto we Sizwe cadres waiting to be appointed to the Defence Force.'[138] During the integration talks, Modise was 'known to have built a close relationship with Meiring and other senior staff members.' Modise's critics further claimed he was 'reluctant to ruffle [Meiring's] feathers not least because he has been seduced by the status and privileges available to the minister of defence.' The week before Nyanda's appointment, some angry MK cadres 'pointed to Modise's failure to get a single senior ANC military officer appointed to the top echelons of the SANDF since taking office.'[139] The SANDF also claimed to be 'accommodating' the 'bitter complaints' emanating 'from the public and within the Defence Force' about the treatment of the non-statutory forces, noting that 'the issue of MK members being turned away when they tried to join the SANDF was a very serious one.'[140] According to Gen. Meiring, the SANDF would swell in number to 120,000 when it accommodated Bantustan armies and non-statutory forces, and would then be trimmed down over the following three years to 91,000, the number at integration.

Modise's moves did not solve many cadres' sense of having been marginalized, and in November 1994 disenchanted cadres from Wallmansthal marched forty kilometres to Mandela's offices at the Union Buildings in Pretoria, forcing the president to address their grievances by ordering an investigation into their conditions. Motumi calls this march 'the first major public indication that problems existed with the integration process in Wallmansthal.'[141] Mandela's intercession caused the SANDF to release a statement in November 1994 conceding that:

> there have been, and most likely are, shortcomings in the system, and that members of the Non-Statutory Forces (NSF) did most likely have certain legitimate grievances that have to be addressed as a matter of top priority…it would be an oversimplification to blame the lack of discipline on the part of some members of the NSF as the only contributing factor to the present situation.[142]

In February 1995, rioting MK soldiers damaged property around the Durban city centre when they protested against the SANDF high command's indifference to their condition, while in a separate incident in Durban 200 cadres marched on the SANDF's Natal Command offices and then gathered outside the ANC's Durban office demanding inclusion within the SANDF. A further 100 cadres marched to the national parliament and the ANC's Cape Town offices to protest against 'their exclusion from the SANDF integration process.' One of the protest leaders insisted the ANC 'used us for their political gains and then threw us into the dustbins,' while others said they had 'been traumatized by being turned away from the SANDF,' and demanded that Mandela address their plight.[143] On 21 August 1995, Modise announced the demobilization of almost 10,000 SANDF soldiers, all of them from MK and APLA, following hunger strikes and attempted mutinies launched in response to perceived 'racism,' the slow pace of integration, and 'poor conditions at the assembly areas, notably at Wallmansthal.'[144] Chairman of the Parliamentary Committee on Defence and former MK guerrilla Tony Yengeni told Siphiwe Nyanda in a meeting that the slow pace of integration 'was completely unacceptable.'[145] Even some of President Mandela's bodyguards went on strike in 1995, demanding higher rank in the new police service; they were threatened with loss of their jobs if they failed to return to work.[146] *The Economist* noted: 'If the government wants the army's racial composition to match the population, it is white soldiers who must lose their jobs. That would indeed test reconciliation.'[147] Following

Modise's decision to demobilize almost 10,000 SANDF soldiers from the liberation armies, an SANDF initiative to provide demobilized liberation movement soldiers with civilian skills faced serious setbacks, with only 1,000 participating out of the 'tens of thousands expected'; many ex-guerrillas distrusted the initiative.[148]

Modise's appointment of eight MK officers to top SANDF positions in June 1994 did little to change the composition and dynamics in the new defence force. In March 1997, 'disgruntled' MK cadres incorporated into the SANDF were calling for the integration process to be 'scrapped because former guerrillas are being discriminated against and persecuted.'[149] Top-level MK officers promoted to 'brigadiers and generals' in the SANDF had circulated among them a document titled 'Going Back to the Drawing Board,' which they also shared with Modise, calling for a meeting to 'address a long list of grievances' with the highest-ranking MK officers in the SANDF, Lt Gen. Siphiwe Nyanda, Lt Gen. Lambert Moloi and Maj. Gen. Andrew Masondo. A senior MK soldier who refused to be named described the reform process: 'This is a complete capitulation. There was no integration but absorption. We at the top are excluded from important decisions and our members are frustrated and when they come complaining we can't do anything for them.'[150] The document claimed that ex-MK personnel in the SANDF had been subject to 'an avalanche of courts martial'; that 'SADF soldiers are preferred for promotion'; and that many MK personnel had not had their initial two-year contracts in the SANDF renewed, or were choosing to leave the SANDF because of systemic discrimination. The situation caused one MK officer to observe, 'this is like wartime,' while another 'said the MK soldiers were fighting a war with the SADF of which the public and politicians were unaware.'[151]

Tensions within SANDF eventually reached boiling point, and in March 1997 a 'major revolt' by former liberation army cadres was 'averted at the eleventh hour' by the intervention of deputy chief of staff Siphiwe Nyanda. The black SANDF members had been dissatisfied with the pace of appointments to high-level positions and especially with defence minister Joe Modise's approach. They prepared a memorandum addressed to President Mandela and the ANC's National Executive Committee; according to one: 'we seem to be taking three steps backward every time there is a step ahead.'[152] They complained that 'three years after the integration of the armed forces, Modise was still unable to appoint former liberation force members to senior positions,' with only 12 of 28 new high-level appointments going to them. At the time, Lt Gen. TT Matanzima, former chief of the Transkei Defence Force, was rumoured to be favoured by the SADF old guard to succeed Georg Meiring as supreme commander of the SANDF, drawing the ire of former MK cadres, who wanted a commander hailing from their own forces. Modise had originally appointed Nyanda to head the SANDF's Gauteng Command, and only reversed this after facing internal pressure, ultimately appointing Nyanda to replace outgoing chief of staff Gen. Meiring.[153]

By 1998, former non-state forces personnel (overwhelmingly deriving from MK and APLA) composed 23 per cent (15,539) of the 67,859 members of the SANDF.[154] The SANDF incorporated progressively fewer members of the former liberation armies the further one moved up in rank, as only 11 per cent of personnel above the rank of major came from the liberation armies, including only 8 out of 57 lieutenant generals and major generals, and 19 of 156 brigadier generals. Of the 2,297 colonels and lieutenant colonels, only 164 originated from MK or APLA. This pattern held in lower ranks as well, where only 3,616 (12 per cent) of the 30,749 personnel with the rank of warrant officer, sergeant or corporal were from MK or APLA. Only in the mid-level ranks of captains, lieutenants and second lieutenants was the percentage of officers from MK and APLA slightly higher, at 20 per cent.[155]

Long after the transition, integration remained a laborious and controversial process that saw the continuous exclusion of MK and APLA cadres from SANDF ranks, with discrepancies and variations in the lists of liberation force personnel to be integrated, personnel whose names were missing from these lists, and successive delays in processing incoming cadres. In 1999, five years after the integration process was supposed to be complete, some MK and APLA cadres still awaited integration. Meanwhile, discrimination by former SADF personnel against former liberation forces members within SANDF remained a serious problem a decade later.[156]

Since the transition, African soldiers in general and particularly former MK and APLA fighters in the SANDF often faced discrimination within the forces, 'oppressed by the white minority who are working in the defence force, causing them to resign.'[157] An earlier study on ex-combatants' integration also notes the 'stigmatization and marginalization' of ex-guerrillas in the SANDF, some of whom mentioned persistent harassment, even beatings, causing them to resign or be dismissed; their complaints to the Defence Ministry were ignored.[158] Gear describes a post-transition incident related by a former MK cadre who, along with other ex-guerrillas in the SANDF, was 'lured to a shebeen' outside their base in the Eastern Cape, then ambushed with grenades, apparently by black soldiers hired by white SADF officers.[159] Such persecution triggered incidents like the rampage in late 1999 by SANDF Lt Sibusiso Madubela, a former APLA cadre, who shot and killed seven white officers and a white civilian at the Tempe military base.[160] According to MK veterans serving in SANDF, Madubela had been severely mistreated, particularly by a white officer who 'was a menace to black recruits and black non-commissioned officers, he would charge them, put their morale at the lowest level.'[161] One ex-guerrilla emphasized that racism remained systematic among white officers towards blacks in the army, 'and black officers were not talking, they were not defending anything. No, they just get their salaries, move the other way, they are afraid to talk, no solidarity, never.' According to another ex-guerrilla, post-transition incidents of whites abusing and even killing blacks in the military were not uncommon, though they were seldom reported. He related how one of his friends in the SANDF was killed: 'It started with these white soldiers being drunk, under the influence of cocaine sometimes, one drove an armoured personnel carrier straight into some [black] soldiers who were just sitting there, killing one whom I know from Angola, and it just appeared and it just disappeared.'[162] To this day, 'there's been so many incidents that indicates that there's a serious problem of the exclusion of some of the progressive forces, of black people in particular, and also the persecution of some black officers in the army.'[163] In 2006, another former liberation fighter 'decided to kill white officers in the defence force and then kill himself.'[164] One former MK commander insisted: 'even today, I'm telling you, there is still racism, both in the [police] and army. It's too much, it's rife. It's just exploding bit by bit. It will burn one day.'[165]

Several observers have also noted the persistence of a divide-and-rule approach towards blacks in the SANDF: 'The Boers [Afrikaners], they try always to cause a wedge between Ciskei, Transkei, Venda, PAC, MK. That's how they manage them. They manipulate them by dividing them. Reminding them of who they are. And the stupid bastards now fall prey of that every time.'[166] Gear cites an ex-guerrilla in the SANDF who claimed that his military base was divided into mutually hostile MK, APLA and SADF camps.[167] An African soldier from the Eastern Cape serving in the SANDF Special Forces described strong animosities even between ethnic Xhosa soldiers from Gauteng and Xhosas from the Eastern Cape.[168]

Lack of MK Integration into the Police

During apartheid, South Africa's military, police and intelligence forces became inextricably interlinked, and cooperated closely in repressing the liberation movements. In its policy statements leading up to and following the transition, the ANC clearly stated its aim to transform the police forces along with the military, and many MK cadres planned to assist in creating a new, democratic police force. Yet the number of fighters from the liberation forces who were integrated into the police was negligible, and no known figures exist to track this aspect of the transition.[169] Several ex-guerrillas described police training they had received, or were scheduled to receive, in preparation for this. One explained that many MK cadres 'went even to police academies outside' South Africa. 'When we came, they told us we are going to be integrated into the police, with my other comrades. But it never happened. We even got documentation, but it never materialized.'[170] Another former MK cadre explained: 'those people who were sellouts, high position people, they did their best so that MK must be insignificant in both the army and the police force, the [integration] initiative must never materialize. And the police force continued to be the old police force, and they were the former SAP.'[171]

In 1996, the new government launched an initiative to integrate SDU members from the Katorus area, near Johannesburg, into the police force. Although several SDU members did join, many of them remained involved in gangsterism, in part as a result of apartheid agents provocateurs who had been sent to destabilize them. Surprisingly, however, the new government made no effort to integrate MK cadres into the police, even though they were far more trained and disciplined than the SDU cadres, and most had many more years' experience.[172] Meanwhile, 2,000 militants from the IFP-aligned Self-Protection Units (SPUs) were incorporated into the SANDF 'despite the fact that they "never qualified in terms of the statutes because when Buthelezi was approached about their inclusion he said that the IFP did not have any paramilitary forces."'[173] A further 1,000 SPU members were integrated into the SAP.

According to one former MK fighter, the number of MK cadres integrated into the police was extremely small: 'I knew very few [cadres] who were given political appointments, but from rank and file, very, very few, if there are. No attempts were made to integrate them.'[174] Another ex-guerrilla mentioned that during the transitional period, there were plans to send an MK contingent to be trained as a police force in India:

> But that never happened, and it was going to be a great move. Now, with the training that we have, with the fitness that we have, with the political education that we had, we were going to make up a good police force for South Africa. Because the police force that was there was a corrupt police force, a brutal police force, which was unwelcome to the people. So it was going to be good if in the army there was a visible number of MK soldiers, and also in the police force a visible number of ex-freedom fighters. But now, that never happened, and it is a well-known fact that some amongst us were sellouts, so double agents had their own effect [at the] top level.[175]

A former MK commander explained that MK veterans, many of whom remained jobless and mired in poverty for years after the transition, enrolled as policemen because 'we wanted some money to feed our families. We registered, we went for interviews, we went to the doctor, everything was perfect, we signed all those forms, we waited for them to call us for training. But nothing happened till today [in 2009]. That was three years back. There was never' an organized initiative to integrate MK cadres. The MK veteran added: 'I think we can contribute a lot. Because our training is more advanced than what the police have. So through experience fighting, I think our guys can stand up to these criminals. So now, the training [the South African Police Service have] got, it's not enough, that's why there's still such crime.'[176] Indeed, the MK veterans' struggle-era combat experience and high legitimacy among South Africans attest to the contributions they could have made to the post-transition police. Fikeni describes how for many MK veterans, 'the sense of bitterness, the sense of betrayal became so high. So, every compromise has demonstrated that in that sense blacks gave more than they received.'[177] Although after the transition a number of MK veterans came to 'occupy prominent positions in both government and the corporate world' and to 'play visible and fundamental roles in society,' most ex-combatants from the liberation movements were relegated to obscurity following the struggle.[178] A coterie of ANC members benefited greatly from the ANC's post-transition Black Economic Empowerment (BEE) initiative, which allocated shares in top companies to a select few, catapulting them into conspicuous wealth. Speaking of a key BEE beneficiary, one ex-guerrilla emphasized: 'Tokyo Sexwale is a billionaire while others are suffering.'[179]

Along with the units it had maintained in various African states leading up to the 1994 elections, MK also cached a substantial arsenal throughout southern Africa. MK had prepared for a situation where negotiations deteriorated into a conflagration with rejectionist militants from the white right-wing and IFP; if this occurred, MK, orphaned by the USSR's dissolution, would have to fend for itself. In October 1994, the new SANDF launched a project codenamed Operation Rollerball to retrieve arms cached by MK throughout South Africa and in neighbouring countries. Most of the weaponry was stored in areas of the former Transvaal that were known to be strongholds of right-wing Afrikaner activity, and in KwaZulu-Natal near key flashpoints between the ANC and IFP. The SANDF's operation to recover the weaponry came to light when the SAPS's Security Branch, which remained largely intact after apartheid, tipped off journalists in an attempt to embarrass the SANDF. This move was typical of what South African journalist De Wet Potgieter called 'the political turmoil and backstabbing in those early days of the country's newfound democracy, where the term "us" and "them" was still rife in the security forces.'[180]

Aboobaker Ismail, former MK logistics commander, gave the army all the maps and directions to access the arms caches, and defence minister Joe Modise dispatched former MK cadre and SANDF officer Winston Harper to inspect MK arms caches in Botswana, where they were still being guarded by MK operatives. Apparently, the governments of Botswana, Swaziland and Mozambique had been unaware that MK had stashed huge quantities of arms and explosives on their soil. Other weaponry was cached in Angola, Zambia, Uganda and Tanzania; the arms and explosives, mainly of Eastern Bloc origin, included pistols, AK-47s, sniper rifles, rocket-propelled grenades, heavy machine guns, anti-aircraft guns, anti-tank missiles, and portable SAM-7 anti-aircraft missiles, as well as a range of mines and explosives.[181]

MK and South Africa's Post-Apartheid Institutions

An MK document from November 1990 drew attention to 'Namibia, Zimbabwe, Angola, Nicaragua, Cuba, Vietnam,'[182] all countries with successful national liberation movements. By contrast, Somadoda Fikeni notes that South Africa was 'a last comer' to independence, such that MK cadres 'had seen the integration of forces in Zimbabwe, in Namibia, and so forth; then they realized that their conditions were worse off than those other forces. So, to that extent they felt betrayed.'[183] In November 2009, defence and military veterans minister Thabang Makwetla warned that over 20,000 surviving veterans, mainly from MK, 'need to be taken care of, not only because of the personal sacrifices they had made for the country, but because they could form a renegade force or use their professional skills in criminal activities.'[184] While apartheid military and police veterans' pensions and benefits continued uninterrupted during and after the transition, guerrilla veterans for decades received no pensions or benefits, save a few who qualified and received under the Special Pension Act of 1996.[185] One MK veteran emphasized that he could not get free treatment at a hospital, whereas the apartheid policemen who had tortured him in prison today enjoy full veterans' benefits.[186] Former guerrilla Shirley Gunn describes how since the transition, 'the people who did the work have never been honoured... Yet, on the other hand, there is all sorts of handshaking, back-patting, ladder-climbing and moving above everyone else, creating this huge distance between [ANC and MK elites] and the foot soldiers on the ground.'[187] Another ex-guerrilla insisted that the ANC leadership 'don't want us near their offices – never,'[188] an experience corroborated by informants from Gear's study of South African ex-combatants. In December 2001, the ANC founded the MK Military Veterans' Association (MKMVA) to ensure ex-guerrillas' welfare.[189] A few months later, a former MK commander emphasized: 'The ultimate goal [of MKMVA] is to teach [veterans] skills and get them out of crime-related tendencies and highlight the role that they can play in fighting crime with the skills they acquired while they were still active MK members.'[190] Indeed, the post-transition economic and political options facing former MK combatants continued to be shaped by the inequalities of apartheid economics.

As one academic explained: 'When the MK cadres feel that they are being marginalized, they are deciding to involve themselves in these anti-social and criminal activities. So that's another critical aspect of the exclusion of the MK members.'[191] Mashike also points to the use of military tactics during robberies as evidence of ex-guerrillas' involvement.[192] Yet Gear notes: 'the extent to which ex-combatants are involved in, and responsible for, [crime] is unclear and contested. While anecdotal evidence clearly suggests some level of involvement, no statistical data or detailed overview of the situation is available.'[193] In 1998, Gavin Cawthra noted the 'failure to integrate a sizeable number of MK fighters into either the [SANDF] or, beyond that, the wider community,' commenting: 'If you put combatants onto the streets, they will put their skills to use in crime.'[194] Yet according to data compiled in 1998 by the SAPS Special Investigative Unit, out of over 80 people arrested 'on suspicion of involvement in cash-in-transit heists, only two have been positively identified as former MK combatants.'[195] One ex-guerrilla claimed that post-apartheid criminal activities blamed on former cadres, 'such as highway heists and bomb attacks on ATM machines,' were in fact the work of foreign ex-combatants, especially from Mozambique. Fikeni underscores that ex-combatants' involvement in crime must be understood in the broader context of the entire region's violent history.[196]

Meanwhile, ex-guerrillas' legitimacy largely endures in many South African communities, which have 'sometimes looked to former combatants to provide leadership in the fight against crime.'[197] Indeed, many private security companies established during and after the transition were founded and staffed by former MK combatants.[198] In August 1993, MK cadres established a private security company that would employ 200 jobless cadres, who had returned to South Africa from exile after 1990, to patrol 'the Kew, Marlboro and Wynberg industrial zones' in Johannesburg where mounting crime had driven away businesses, threatening the livelihood of people living in nearby Alexandra township.[199]

Frankel maintains that in the military integration process, the ANC and MK succeeded in outflanking the apartheid-era security elites because 'history, fuelled by its own logic, was loaded to the advantage of MK.' According to him, although the ANC lacked the SADF leadership's conventional military expertise, the ANC elites had a broader perspective that encompassed the 'critical interface between military and political affairs' and surpassed that of the SADF generals, 'locked as they were by years of total strategy within the strict boundaries of traditional military ideology.' Though the SADF held the upper hand in the short term, the ANC elites perceived that the ex-apartheid old guard would soon be 'swept aside by postdemocratic history.'[200] By keeping their eyes on the ultimate prize – the political kingdom – Frankel claims that MK and the ANC thus transformed the very terrain on which the old security elites stood. Yet although the ANC did gradually cement its hold on political power, the unreformed security forces remained an important source of instability for South Africa's new democracy. Writing during the transition, Seegers noted: 'A functional interpretation of state ideology is still valid, being reinforced by continuing views that "military things are better," notably because of the need to justify "control, hierarchy and power."' Even after the transition, the post-transition military would value 'unqualified commitment to the job, the shortest possible distance between a problem and its solution, control by command, and institutional simplicity,'[201] even as these were bundled with authoritarian and racist legacies.

Counterinsurgency legacies bore hidden dangers for MK cadres and a malignant impact on the transition and its aftermath. This emerged alongside a discriminatory culture on the part of white SADF personnel towards former liberation force cadres in the SANDF.[202] Institutional racism pervaded the military, triggering numerous complaints by black personnel and several violent incidents. As Somadoda Fikeni explained: 'in the army, resisting change was a way of resisting transformation,' and the 'exclusion of black people' was rampant 'in all sectors' of the new state, 'including the military.' This has included widespread 'persecution of black officers within the army.'[203] Another South African academic insisted 'that we are still having problems of Third Force, there's a Third Force that is really emerging, and as a result, some MK veterans and members were excluded, and deliberately so. Because there are people who are really still against transformation.'[204]

The security forces were also key sites of contestation in which the apartheid regime sought, just as ANC stalwart Popo Molefe predicted at the transition's onset, to shift the 'ideological terrain by depriving the national democratic struggle of its national liberation character.'[205] This counterinsurgency narrative, in which violence and power are hidden, thus reinforces the political outcome it served to shape, embodying what Guha calls 'the prose of counterinsurgency': 'the discourse of history, hardly distinguished from policy, ends up by absorbing the concerns and objectives of the latter. In this affinity with policy, historiography reveals its character as a form of colonialist knowledge.'[206] As Beverley points out, this knowledge, in turn, serves 'to construct the bureaucratic and academic discourses…that purport to represent these…insurgencies and place them in a teleological narrative of state formation.'[207] According to this narrative, the ANC needed to sacrifice its more revolutionary goals in order to ascend to power.

Considering Alternative Paths to South Africa's Security Sector Reform

After unilaterally renouncing the armed struggle, the ANC failed in its negotiations with the regime to rectify inequalities in the security forces by securing a future role for its own soldiers. A lack of agency on the part of the ANC was a major factor contributing to the institutional continuity within the security forces. The ANC had political leverage and held cards such as its ability to mobilize mass action and strikes in order to extract greater concessions from the government. According to Fikeni, the lack of reform in the security forces is attributable to three factors: 'one, lack of political will. Two, overestimation of white power. Three, lack of imagination when you allow yourself to be absorbed into existing power structures with the hope that you will transform them once inside. And you can see what it is: they were never transformed. Virtually nothing.'[208] Williams, invoking the Tsarist army's transformation into the Soviet Red Army, likewise notes that 'a high level of mass action can decisively neutralize the political direction of the armed forces regardless of the technical power that they possess.'[209] On the other hand, the apartheid security elites remained a formidable force that would have been very difficult to dislodge, and some powerful security force figures such as Constand Viljoen and Tienie Groenewald had already outlined plans to seize power (see Chapter Three). The leverage of mass struggle, which the ANC is widely accused of having failed to use in order to force thoroughgoing transformation of the state,[210] might not have been brought to bear so easily upon the security forces.

Apartheid security elites continued to exercise a grip on power within the military, police and intelligence services, and would have very likely interfered violently had the ANC insisted on having its armed wing take control of the police and military. Nor does it appear that the NP elites, had they sought to do so, could have pushed the security forces to compromise much further following De Klerk's officers' purge of 1992. The seeds of South Africa's institutional continuity were therefore contained within its military stalemate and the resulting negotiated transition, and the ANC lacked the leverage to reform these institutions through political pressure. It is also important to distinguish between the factors constraining the ANC's ability to force thoroughgoing security sector transformation and the marginalization of MK veterans within the ANC's own structures, which was far more avoidable. This latter outcome reflected, in part, the elitism that pervaded the ANC as it came to embrace the economic status quo. Most cadres were bypassed by this process, and their grievances were overshadowed by neoliberal pragmatism. According to one report, Mandela's hard line with MK dissenters, notably at Wallmansthal, stemmed from his fear 'that the perception of lawlessness and instability created by the likes of the Umkhonto rebels and rogue SDUs will inhibit local and foreign investors.'[211] In this sense, the cadres' broad political and socio-economic marginalization represents a missed opportunity to mobilize a population of politically trained activists on behalf of post-transition civic causes. In a similar vein, Suttner emphasizes that the elaborate UDF structures that mobilized activists across much of South Africa in support of the ANC were simply abandoned after the transition, squandering grassroots networks with enormous potential as channels for social transformation.[212]

Two ready counter-arguments present themselves: firstly, that allowing the regime to control security sector reform was simply the 'entrance fee' the ANC had to pay for a peaceful transition; and secondly, that the apartheid regime held the upper hand militarily and could plunge the country into bloodshed if its leadership was dissatisfied with the course of negotiations. National Party elites also worried that the powerful apartheid military could stage a coup d'état if the generals felt the government was conceding too much.[213] Yet in paying this 'entrance fee' to power, the ANC relinquished key aspects of its revolutionary political and economic platforms and diluted its representation of its mass constituencies. Ultimately, the ANC's calculus in its compromise on security sector reform stemmed partly from its fear of the apartheid forces' propensity for violence, as reflected in an MK policy document during the transition: 'we need to ask ourselves whether it would not create a greater danger for a future South Africa if we had a lot of unrehabilitated racist ex-servicemen roaming around idle and demoralized.'[214] This raises the point that although Third Force violence ultimately harmed the NP politically, it may have strengthened the old-guard security force elites during the transition and, in the words of one MK cadre's analysis, afforded 'the enemy' an ability to 'influence the rate at which the country is moving.'[215] The SADF, outmanoeuvred politically but undefeated in battle, largely dictated the terms of security sector reform, limiting the number of cadres that could be integrated and subjecting many to discrimination. Faced with this reality, the ANC chose marginalizing thousands of its own combatants over demobilizing and setting loose tens of thousands of unemployed, disgruntled SADF veterans.

9

POST-TRANSITION VIOLENCE AS A
COUNTERINSURGENCY LEGACY

'The old trick of divide and rule is still very valid today. Our experts should work day and night to set the Black man against his fellowman.'
— PW Botha in a speech to his Cabinet, 1985

'At issue is not whether South Africa will explode but whether it will continue to burn.'
— Bill Berkeley, 'The Warlords of Natal' (1994)

In December 2009, I had an astonishing glimpse of South Africa's post-apartheid policing as former guerrillas showed me a video recording of their 2006 attempt to turn in struggle-era weaponry to the police before an amnesty deadline. In an attempt to reduce the volume of guns circulating in society, the police were offering amnesty to any who would hand their weapons in. The former guerrillas went to a police station in Mthatha to surrender a massive quantity of weapons they had buried in 1989 in an arms cache, or 'dead-letter box,' in the Eastern Cape. The cache included Semtex plastic explosives, hand grenades, fuses, limpet mines, and AK-47 magazines and rounds, and the ex-guerrillas used their orienteering skills to find the exact spot where the weapons were buried. They filmed the lengthy process of digging up the arms cache and delivering it for the amnesty deadline to the regional police station, where one of them declared they were handing in the weapons for the sake of their children's future. As the MK veterans stood by for many hours waiting, police employees and passersby alike stood gawking in amazement at the arsenal arrayed on the station floor. Despite the amnesty deadline for that day, the video documents an on-duty policeman – a former askari, according to the ex-guerrillas – vainly attempting, in a series of phone conversations in both isiXhosa and English, to locate someone to process the incoming munitions. Although they had entered the station in the early afternoon, the ex-guerrillas ultimately had to take their weapons home with them late at night, returning the following day to finally hand them in. Armaments cached during the struggle era were notoriously difficult to retrieve during security force integration and afterward, and many combatants never handed them in; as one group of ex-combatants declared: 'There are DLBs [dead-letter boxes] that still exist.'[1]

The proliferation of weaponry from the liberation movements and the regime forces, along with pervasive corruption, weak security institutions, and high levels of violence, has been a factor undermining South Africa's democratic transition.[2] This incomplete transition is closely linked to apartheid counterinsurgency legacies, which include lack of reform in South Africa's security institutions and military-industrial complex; ongoing spy intrigues; links between criminal networks and the security sector; the persistence of chronic urban violence; and low levels of public trust in the South African security forces. Post-transition violence has not merely been the result of civil war legacies such as the abundance of weaponry within society, or former combatants engaging in crime: it is also the result of the apartheid regime's initiative to destabilize African communities with so-called black-on-black violence. The regime's strategy of outsourcing political violence sought to ensure that violence would reproduce itself within these communities into the future. There is a clear continuity between transition-era violence and violence after the 1994 elections. At this point, counterinsurgency legacies took on different forms in various regions and institutions throughout the country: violence persisted especially in the townships ringing Johannesburg and Pretoria, and in KwaZulu-Natal, which had previously been the key flashpoints of Third Force violence; killings in the taxi industry continued unabated, with abundant evidence of police involvement and the apparent persistence of Third Force elements; corruption and racism were rife in the 'new' security forces; weapons smuggling proliferated, often featuring actors previously linked to the apartheid regime's security forces and their Bantustan affiliates; and assorted figures with security force connections continued to die mysterious deaths. This clandestine violence was a key factor in shaping post-transition South Africa. When queried about the persistence of Third Force violence after the transition, one ex-guerrilla working in the private security field explained: 'If there is peace in an area, they will make sure that they divide the people according to their political affiliations, or according to their own tribalistic ways. Dividing Xhosas and Zulus.' According to him, even after the transition 'there was always this element of Third Force, you know, it was not gangsterism. A gangster cannot just kill people for nothing. He kills to rob. So why should you see someone spraying people with AK [assault rifle] whom you don't even know firsthand. So sure, sure, sure, it's Third Force.'[3]

Mysterious Deaths

The last major political assassination in South Africa was the 1993 killing of Chris Hani. Yet individuals connected to the liberation movements and security forces continued dying mysterious deaths in the months leading up to the April 1994 elections, and then for years afterward. These deaths have been the source of intrigue and suspicion and have underscored the presence of the parallel state in modern South African politics. As the transition approached, several apartheid intelligence agents turned up dead as the result of alleged suicides, in a pattern suggesting that they knew too much and were being 'mopped up' before their secrets might be unearthed. This pattern of unsolved deaths continued well after the ANC came to power, indicating that elements of the old regime, along with their pre-transition agenda, remained active within the post-apartheid dispensation. For example, DCC agent Eugene Riley, who 'died under mysterious circumstances' in 1994, had told a journalist that the Chris Hani assassination was the result of collusion between the apartheid regime and elements of the ANC. Riley had been recruited by death squad operative Ferdi

Barnard, who ran an elaborate international drug-smuggling network, and had himself been appointed as a 'chief agent' in the DCC in August 1991 by SADF Gen. Rudolph 'Witkop' Badenhorst after the CCB was disbanded.[4] Barnard's unit was tasked with 'find[ing] embarrassing information on ANC leaders by using prostitutes, homosexuals, and drug dealers'[5] (see Chapter Six). Riley, meanwhile, was a convicted murderer who belonged to a ring of drug and weapons smugglers and diamond thieves with long-standing links to SADF MI, whose members worked for the DCC. In January 1994, Riley was found dead in his home with a gunshot wound in the face and a revolver lying next to him. The police initially labelled the death a suicide, even though secret documents in Riley's possession had disappeared, and his girlfriend subsequently received death threats.[6]

The DCC had employed several askaris, including Chris Makgopa, who originally worked for the Vlakplaas unit under the command of Eugene de Kock, and Glory 'September' Sedibe, who also 'died under mysterious circumstances.'[7] Sedibe and fellow MK cadre Chris Mosiane had been abducted from a Swazi jail by De Kock's Vlakplaas unit in 1986; both were 'turned' as askaris, working initially for Vlakplaas before being transferred to the DCC.[8] As Sedibe had been the most prominent of all the regime's askaris (see Chapter Three), his death on 20 March 1994 garnered much attention and controversy: Ngculu echoed the ANC's position that Sedibe had very likely been poisoned by the apartheid security forces. De Kock claimed that the regime poisoned Sedibe with a toxin that mimicked the effects of hepatitis B,[9] while Pauw attributes Sedibe's death to a heart attack; in an interview with Jacob Dlamini, Sedibe's widow attributed his death to alcoholism.[10] In the weeks before his death, Sedibe, who was uniquely positioned to expose the apartheid regime's spies in the ANC, was planning to meet with ANC intelligence chief Joe Nhlanhla.[11]

Other askaris who died mysteriously include Petrus Kwagadhi, apparently from suicide; Xolelwa Norma Sosha, who was assassinated; and Silulami Mose, who, like Glory Sedibe, officially died of a heart attack.[12] In its submission to the Truth and Reconciliation Commission (TRC), the ANC emphasized that the apartheid regime 'did not hesitate to get rid of its own agents when it appeared they were about to change sides or give the ANC damaging information.' The submission suggested that 'both Solly Smith and Francis Meli' – two members of the ANC based in London known to have been recruited as apartheid spies, and who were alleged to have died of alcoholism – 'were poisoned' to prevent them from speaking out; it points to other mysterious deaths immediately before and during the transition era, such as Sedibe, Thami Zulu, and 'the death of "Fear" (Edward Lawrence) in 1988,' noting that the regime was skilled in killing with poisons that left no trace. The ANC voiced its strong suspicion 'that some of those cadres and activists who died of "natural causes" may have in fact been victims of poisoning or other chemical agents.'[13] In 1997, it emerged that Vronda Banda, a former MK cadre who joined the National Intelligence Agency (NIA), had spied for the regime. Banda led a group of MK cadres that defected to the regime months before the 1994 elections, claiming that an ANC government would lead South Africa into 'anarchy.' After Banda's death in April 1994, it emerged that the ANC's Department of National Intelligence and Security had been on the verge of exposing him as a spy at the time of his defection.[14]

International arms smuggler and intelligence operative Dirk Stoffberg was killed along with his wife at his home near Pretoria on 20 June 1994. Stoffberg claimed to have been involved in the 1988 assassination in Paris of Dulcie September, the ANC's chief representative in France, and apparently worked for the Adler Group, an intelligence organization that 'specialized in assassinations, blackmail, arms smuggling, and money laundering,' and whose services SADF MI increasingly solicited in the late 1980s.[15] Its members were involved in circumventing the international arms embargo against the apartheid regime, and Stoffberg claimed they had links to the CIA.[16] One of Stoffberg's handlers, Col. At Nel, ran him as an agent for the NIS but simultaneously worked as a commander at the DCC.[17] Stoffberg kept a trove of documents in a safe under his house, which disappeared when he was murdered. Don Lange, another arms dealer with connections to Stoffberg, was murdered at his home in Durban on 1 June 1994.[18] A former askari by the name of Nzimande testified against Eugene de Kock at the TRC and turned up dead shortly thereafter alongside his wife and a man he suspected of being her lover, ostensibly in a murder-suicide.[19] A former SADF soldier insisted that the suicide of a former member of his unit in the late 1990s was stage-managed by elements from the old security forces who wanted to prevent him from testifying to the TRC about apartheid-era atrocities.[20] Even Eugene de Kock feared that security force elements might attempt to silence him during his trial; in 1995, while in prison, he suffered a near-fatal blood clot that his family attributed to poisoning, and he 'vehemently opposed a recommendation by doctors treating him that he be transferred' to a military hospital out of fear that 'if he goes there security force members who want him dead will have easy access to him.'[21] De Kock had 'spread anxiety' throughout the ANC and NP by '[hinting] he might also identify' ANC officials 'who collaborated or informed.'[22]

On 6 November 1994 Johan Heyns, an influential Afrikaner churchman and Broderbond vice-chairman who had criticized apartheid, was murdered in his home with a large-calibre rifle. No one claimed responsibility, 'but suspicion fell on South Africa's far right' and security was tightened after evidence emerged that assassins had been hired to target several politicians, including Deputy President De Klerk, whose role in the new government of national unity was seen as a betrayal. Police 'were said to be convinced' that Heyns was murdered by assassins who had 'been hired in Europe by right-wing extremists who have drawn up a hit list of men they regard as traitors.' Others on the alleged list included Roelf Meyer, Joe Slovo and Jay Naidoo.[23]

In October 1995, Jerry Lukhele was tried for his involvement in at least three separate attempts to assassinate Mpumalanga premier and ANC stalwart Mathews Phosa. Lukhele divulged that he had been trained at an SANDF camp along with seven other men to kill Phosa and safety and security MEC Steve Mabona. Lukhele, who had previously been charged with the murder of a 'top ANC activist in Piet Retief,' implicated senior provincial police officials in the plot to kill Phosa. Suspicions were heightened as police 'appeared to be dragging their feet to investigate the matter.'[24] Lukhele told investigators that right-wing politicians and senior police officials had orchestrated the plot. When a police team was finally dispatched, Lukhele 'was shocked to find the investigating team consisting of the same policemen he had implicated in the plot.' While in prison, he survived an apparent poisoning attempt.[25] Phosa himself strongly criticized the police's handling of Lukhele's case;[26] Phosa's security detail was subsequently beefed up as the South African Police Service (SAPS) Crime Intelligence Division received a document, based on SANDF intelligence, that detailed a plot by AWB militants to sabotage his vehicle.[27] Phosa had also been the target of an Inkatha Freedom Party (IFP) assassination attempt in 1990.[28]

On 7 October 1995, chief of the NIA security directorate and former APLA commander Muziwendoda Mdluli was found dead in his car near Pretoria's botanical gardens with a bullet wound to the head. Mdluli was 'alleged to have committed suicide after visiting his girlfriend in a Johannesburg hotel'; earlier that day, he had told his lover that he was going to have a meeting with police.[29] Although the police initially ruled the death a suicide, most of Mdluli's colleagues believed he had been assassinated. In his testimony to the inquiry into Mdluli's death, pathologist Dr Stefaans Hofmeyr said that it was 'extremely unusual' for a person to commit suicide by shooting himself in the forehead, and that it was far more likely that Mdluli, who was right-handed, would have shot himself on the right side of the head.[30] The PAC and Mdluli's own family claimed that he had been murdered, and his wife, Cleopatra Mdluli, said that a few days before his death, he had received 'calls from an unknown person with an Afrikaans accent, which appeared to alarm him.'[31] The inquest heard from NIA counsel that on the night of his death, Mdluli left his briefcase at home and told his wife he was going to Swaziland, though he was actually going to liaise with a lover in Johannesburg. Mdluli told his wife the briefcase contained documents about apartheid hit squads and gun-smuggling to Rwanda.[32] An NIA director told the *Independent* newspaper that 'the agency believed Mdluli had been killed after making a breakthrough in an inquiry' that investigated involvement by former NIS agents, now working for the NIA, in a failed coup attempt in the Comoros several days earlier, led by French mercenary Bob Denard.[33]

In a similar incident, SAPS assistant commissioner and head of internal security Gen. Leonard 'Nceba' Radu was killed in a mysterious car crash in March 1997. Radu had been involved in the ANC's investigation into Chris Hani's assassination and was said to have been following several new leads in this case at the time of his death; he had also been making headway in investigating the 1995 disappearance of

INSURGENCY AND COUNTERINSURGENCY IN SOUTH AFRICA

Soweto mandrax kingpin Rocks Dlamini. Radu, favoured to replace outgoing police commissioner Wouter Grové, had been a 'thorn in the side' of the apartheid-era leadership in the post-transition SAPS, and they had opposed Radu's rise within the security forces.[34] Among Radu's colleagues, suspicions arose that his vehicle had been tampered with prior to the fatal crash; one former colleague refused to accept that it had been a 'plain accident,' claiming that a driver of Radu's calibre was unlikely to get into a fatal crash after the 'mere 30 minutes he had travelled when he met his death.'[35] According to police, Radu was killed when his car veered across the highway and was hit by an oncoming truck. Radu's anonymous former colleague said: 'I do not think that we need to just fold our arms and suggest that this was just a plain accident.'[36] Radu also reportedly possessed a list of apartheid spies in the ANC.[37]

The ANC also had its share of post-transition secrets, particularly regarding the torture and abuse of prisoners at Angolan camps such as Quatro. In 1998, a former Quatro detainee alleged that a struggle-era campaign to suppress ANC dissidents was still under way: 'Even today we live in fear. Since 1980, 57 former Mbokodo [MK's security branch] have been assassinated and seven former Quatro inmates – who is killing them? We believe they are being killed because of what they know about those who are in power now.'[38] Subsequently, there would be widespread speculation over the deaths of prominent figures within the post-apartheid security establishment. In 2003, as the details of the arms deal scandal revealed a widening web of corruption, Joe Modise's 'right-hand man,' Puso Tladi, a former MK commissar, disappeared and his fate was never discovered. Tladi had left the SANDF after Modise's death, and was 'said to have taken with him arms deal documents' that belonged to Modise; Tladi's last business meeting had been with Patrick Mothibe, who also disappeared in 2003 and who was found dead in a Lesotho mortuary.[39] In 2014, journalist Terry Crawford-Browne told the Seriti Commission of Inquiry, convened by President Jacob Zuma to investigate the arms deal, that intelligence operator Bheki Jacobs had told him six weeks before Modise's 2001 death that Modise was being poisoned, and that his death would be blamed on cancer. Crawford-Browne further told the commission that, according to Jacobs, Chris Hani had been on the verge of exposing Modise's involvement in the arms deal when he was assassinated in 1993 (see Chapter Seven).[40] Jacobs, a Soviet-trained ANC intelligence operative who returned to South Africa in November 1994, had founded a private intelligence company named Congress Consultants which served as a private intelligence service for Thabo Mbeki during his presidency (the fact that Mbeki engaged a private intelligence unit reporting directly to him suggests that he did not trust the state intelligence organs; this seems to have presaged the rift between Mbeki and Zuma, which later became the ANC's most important internal division). Jacobs then became a whistleblower who exposed corruption within the post-transition government, and was alleged to have been the original source of the arms deal revelations. He died of liver cancer in 2008 aged 46. Under these circumstances, Jacobs's untimely death was itself widely regarded as suspicious.

Gun-running and Organized Crime

As the ANC gradually consolidated power, there were fears that it would wield the security forces as an instrument to persecute enemies and critics,[41] in a manner resembling the Zimbabwean military's reign of terror in Matabeleland in the 1980s. Yet a more notable feature of the post-apartheid landscape would be the presence of apartheid remnants working to undermine the ANC's governance. Much of the crime that has characterized the post-apartheid era has had little to do with poverty or social inequality, but has stemmed rather from criminal networks within the security sector.[42] After the transition, and as late as 1999, the new ANC government would blame, 'sometimes with great justification and evidence, continued violence or domestic opposition in the post-transition era on lingering elements from the apartheid security forces.'[43] One ex-MK fighter described his arrest in the late 1990s 'for that very same offence which I was tried for [during apartheid].' His arrest prevented him from going to the TRC, where he could have revealed that 'the police who arrested me were involved in criminal activities and I knew about them. So they were in fear that I might blow the whistle. In fact, the unit that arrested me was later dissolved because it was found to have been [involved in organized crime].'[44] Elements within the post-apartheid police service also attempted to discredit the TRC by coercing a witness into giving false testimony implicating Dumisa Ntsebeza, a TRC commissioner, in a 1993 massacre by APLA of white civilians.[45] In a key example of post-transition continuity with the apartheid security forces, in 1995 the SANDF destroyed the weapons used by SADF commandos in their October 1993 raid on PAC operative Sigqibo Mpendulo's house in Mthatha in which five African teenagers were killed in their sleep, and which the SADF had claimed was an APLA safe house (see Chapter Five). The SANDF also destroyed the weapons that the SADF commandos had allegedly captured in the raid. When this surfaced in September 1995, the lawyer for the families of the five teenagers, Dumisa Ntsebeza, declared: 'The news that these weapons have been destroyed is absolutely outrageous and amounts to what one can consider concealment of evidence that would obviously be crucial in any criminal proceedings.'[46]

The apartheid counterinsurgency forces had engaged in a wide range of illegal activities and developed close links with existing organized crime networks as a means of concealing and funding their operations. These links and networks persisted after the transition, and constituted one of the most important counterinsurgency legacies. Illicit profit-seeking within South African state institutions boomed after apartheid, and MK veterans' suspicions about apartheid agents enduring after the transition, focus on their links to apartheid-era organized crime networks. These networks had afforded secrecy to apartheid counterinsurgency operations by making them self-financing, and they proved very resilient in the post-transition era. Many continued to flourish, in one form or another, within the bazaar of governmental and private security agencies, themselves largely staffed by former security force personnel.[47] The post-apartheid security forces were implicated in colluding with organized crime and subverting political change. One former guerrilla insisted that if more MK cadres had been integrated into the police, 'the crime that is here now wouldn't have been there.' He claimed post-transition crime 'was initiated by the police, it was done to undermine, to disorganize the country. Some left the police force to form private security companies, which were also involved in robberies, bank robberies, heists, it was intended to bankrupt the state.' He connected this to the role of 'sellouts amongst [the ANC]' who 'manoeuvred themselves into high positions. They were in fact promoted by the [old guard in the security forces],' who 'took the people whom they knew, their operatives, put them in high positions so that they know they are doing what they like.'[48] According to this ex-guerrilla, apartheid security elites' influence over the security forces endured well after the transition: 'it happened during the Mandela era, right into the Mbeki era, it is only now that it is being addressed.'[49]

The 1994 White Paper on Intelligence noted that as transition-era political violence abated, there 'has been an increase in common criminal activities.'[50] After the transition, 'organized crime had grown substantially and seemed to contain a direct and purposeful challenge to the new state's ability to effect its transformation initiatives.'[51] One former MK commander related an incident in 1993 that highlights the overlap between counterinsurgency and organized crime immediately prior to the transition from apartheid: his MK unit noticed a robbery and smuggling network establishing itself in his region and 'thought they were just amateurs, but when we tracked them, followed them, surveilled them, I saw three of them, I trained them in Angola and I knew they were askaris. They were sent here, but we disorganized them.'[52] He described repeated post-apartheid attempts by ex-askaris to blackmail or bribe former MK cadres:

First they wanted to blackmail us as if we were involved in these heists, these robberies. But it was exposed that [the actual criminals] were Zimbabweans, they had never been [MK] comrades. They were promoting crime themselves, the Third Force. They came to me, tried to recruit me many times. Robberies, stealing cars, all such things. So some comrades were trapped [into cooperating with criminals].[53]

In its submission to the TRC, the ANC pointed to several instances of apartheid agents turned to criminality during the transition era. These included Jose de Souza, who 'apparently became involved in gang violence' in Eersterus after being released from ANC detention in 1991, then died mysteriously before he could be tried on charges of murder and attempted murder; and death squad member Patrick Dlongwana, who took part in the 'Returned Exiles Committee' Stratcom operation (see Chapter Six) and then became involved with the warlord Thomas Shabalala.[54]

In the twilight days of apartheid, Vlakplaas commander Eugene de Kock tried to reinvent himself as an arms smuggler. He founded an import-export company called Honeybadger Arms and Ammunition (fashioned after the Vlakplaas unit emblem, which featured a honeybadger), which dealt in various small arms, and travelled in 1990 to Central and Eastern Europe to meet with dealers there. De Kock even claimed to be on the verge of closing a deal to sell South African G5 long-range artillery to Serbia when the UN imposed an arms embargo there.[55] Former Vlakplaas operative Charlie Chate was implicated by the Goldstone Commission in buying weapons from Eugene de Kock's front company, Honeybadger Arms, in 1992, and in manufacturing weapons and organizing weapons training for the IFP in early 1994. In March 1995, police seized a cache of weapons including plastic explosives and large-calibre ammunition in a raid at the home of former Vlakplaas operative Maj. Piet Snyders near Pretoria; these weapons were traced to a November 1994 theft from a police training centre at Verdrag in Limpopo. The next day, following another lead on former Vlakplaas operatives, police uncovered an even larger arms cache, 'the most sophisticated' yet, on a farm near Bronkhorstspruit.[56] Another former Security Branch operative, Brian 'Cassie' Kruger, was allegedly involved in smuggling operations in the Hamburg area of the Eastern Cape until 1996.[57] As late as June 1997, former Vlakplaas and SADF MI operative Ferdi Barnard was still running guns and a brothel from the back of an illegal casino in Johannesburg, where Jacques Pauw found him 'in deep conversation with a man who he later told me represented one of the gangs on the Cape Flats and wanted to buy weapons from him.'[58] Barnard clearly enjoyed protection from within the post-transition security establishment, as a leak in Attorney General's Office in 1997 helped Barnard fight charges against him related to his death squad activities.[59] Barnard was finally convicted in 1998 for the 1989 murder of David Webster. In January 1997, Wouter Basson, the SADF chemical warfare mastermind who had strong links to Vlakplaas and SADF MI, was arrested with 1,000 capsules of Ecstasy in his possession, and remained embroiled in controversy surrounding the alleged post-transition proliferation of apartheid-era chemical and biological weapons technology.[60]

Transkei and Ciskei, which were counterinsurgency hotbeds during the transition (see Chapter Five), remained focal points of gun-running and organized crime for years after 1994. According to archival documents: 'It's believed that a lot of weapons used illegally originated in the [Bantustan] armouries.' This made these weapons, supplied to apartheid proxies such as Oupa Gqozo's African Democratic Movement, far more difficult to trace. The SADF had also used the Bantustans as way stations for weaponry destined for UNITA and RENAMO. By the same token, the Bantustan security forces, and especially Holomisa's in the Transkei, issued and distributed weaponry to the liberation movements. This included not only MK but also APLA; many of these weapons subsequently made their way into the hands of criminal networks. Arms smugglers within the apartheid security forces also favoured sending shipments through ports, and 'the Cameron Commission of Inquiry [into illegal arms smuggling] heard that Armscor had shipped out weapons through the Port Elizabeth harbour with forged end-user certificates' because outgoing cargo 'was never checked in Eastern Cape harbours.' Queen Data Brokers, another apparent SADF MI front company, sold weapons to Pierre Bezuidenhout, a member of the Johannesburg City Council spy ring, whose members sat on the council while also spying for the Joint Management System. Bezuidenhout stockpiled weapons while running campus security at the University of Transkei in Mthatha (renamed Walter Sisulu University after the transition). Queen Data Brokers sold 700,000 rounds of ammunition to the Transkei government in May 1993, and remained in operation after the transition, using cars with false registration numbers. Various taxi and bus companies were also known to be linked to gun smuggling by covert unit members. In particular, Chilwan's Buses in the Eastern Cape was said to employ 'three people with known links to covert operations,' including one with links to violence in the Western Cape and to Oupa Gqozo's Ciskei hit squads, one with links to Craig Duli and the coup attempts on Holomisa, and one who had been a spokesman for the Matanzima government in Transkei and had helped lay the groundwork for SADF's Operation Katzen. After the transition, there were also several askaris in the Eastern Cape taxi industry with known or suspected links to SADF MI who were suspected of involvement in gun-running.

In Ciskei, Oupa Gqozo set up hit squads to target ANC members in the months before the elections, commanded by Titus Mcoyiyana, an African Democratic Movement (ADM) member. During Gqozo's rule, a number of private security companies emerged with known links to his regime and the ADM, including one known as Peace Force, which used Ciskei Defence Force bases to train Ciskei 'auxiliary' units as well as Mcoyiyana's hit squads during the years 1993–4.[61] Former police informer Nzuzo Matiwane claimed that previous members of the apartheid security forces were involved in hit squad activities in the former Ciskei well into 1995.

It is difficult to trace the evolution of SADF MI front companies after the April 1994 elections, but there is evidence that at least some of them remained operational. Ellis noted that front companies established by intelligence services 'are difficult to trace and difficult to close, not least since their existence may be quite legal and their formal ownership may be no longer vested in the state, but in nominees who cannot legally be dispossessed by administrative decree.' These companies could then rename themselves but continue their previous operations, 'as a snake sheds its skin.'[62] One instructive example is Adult Education Consultants (AEC), established by the DCC. Though it was dissolved in October 1992, one of its co-founders, Dr Johan van der Westhuizen, 're-emerged in January 1994 as one of the founders of the African Christian Democratic Party (ACDP).' The other co-founder, Louis Pasques, 'received lucrative contracts from the De Klerk government's Nutritional Development Programme, and by 1992 he had set up new consultancies, one of which purported to offer communication skills and training in "nation building" to governments in neighbouring states.'[63] Noting that these developments had 'direct relevance to the security of the [post-transition] democratic order,' the ANC pointed out that 'many of the operatives in such covert structures as AEC, the CCB, Vlakplaas and others were not only given golden handshakes, but "disappeared" with the infrastructure responsible for the violence in the post-1990 period,' highlighting the importance of subterranean actors in the post-transition phase.[64] After the transition, the ANC 'strongly suspected that some of [these front companies] are still in operation in KwaZulu-Natal; others are part of the criminal network; yet others are involved in taxi violence.' Furthermore, after the transition, elements of this shadowy network, 'which included journalists and "agents of influence" in a range of organisations and institutions,' were considered 'most certainly' to be 'still in operation; some of them continue to serve the interests of their previous masters, and it cannot be ruled out that others may be activated at some time in the future.'[65] In 1997, based on intelligence that 'there continued to exist in part of the country networks of former security organs that were actively destabilizing' Mpumalanga, ANC intelligence operative Barry Gilder visited a regional NIA office there. At the meeting where Gilder delivered his findings, a former NIS agent in charge of intelligence gathering in Mpumalanga argued: 'there are no such networks in the province. What we do have are networks of "unrehabilitated terrorists" [i.e. MK and APLA personnel] in the province. In fact, we have such "unrehabilitated terrorists" in the agency itself.'[66]

After the transition, as the ANC tackled 'apartheid's socioeconomic legacy of poverty, violence and crime,' Dugard notes that taxi violence, 'echoing other post-1994 modes of enterprise and violence,' became 'largely de-linked from formal politics.' These taxi wars originated during the transition era as a form of Third Force violence (see Chapter Three), and escalated after 1994, killing 258 people in 1999.[67] The warring taxi factions were known to deploy highly trained hitmen who perpetrated indiscriminate shootings and targeted assassinations while evading capture.[68] In October 1995, northern Transvaal police arrested an ex-MK, ex-SANDF soldier for his role in local taxi violence.[69] Rival taxi companies employed 'professional assassins' with backgrounds in the liberation movements and apartheid forces, and set up training camps for hitmen; in 1997, it emerged 'that "hundreds" of former askaris, who were retrenched by the apartheid government in its final years, [were] employed as taxi hit men' after the transition. In January 1997, a combined NIA–SAPS team was tasked with neutralizing several rural training camps for taxi hit squads.[70] According to the police, some of the hitmen had been recruited from Zimbabwe and Mozambique, along with 'former members of APLA, MK and the former Ciskei security forces and askaris.' Yet in North West province, a spokesman for the Lehlabile Taxi Organization challenged the police's contention that taxi companies were the ones training the hitmen, pointing out that several reports blamed policemen involved in the taxi industry for much of the violence. The spokesman further noted that the NP regime had designated Lehlabile as a reintegration hub for over 200 askaris, 'who were disbanded under a veil of secrecy,' and he demanded to know whether they had been 'redeployed in other police units.'[71] This raised the spectre of askaris, repurposed for a new era, playing a key role in post-transition taxi violence. SAPS personnel also widely profited from and participated in the taxi violence, drawing a rebuke in 1996 from President Mandela.[72] Such hit squad tactics also surfaced elsewhere in civil society: for example, in October 1995, the National Union of Metalworkers accused the Dorbyl company of hiring a former policeman to 'assassinate trade union leaders and destabilize the organization.' The policeman had allegedly written a document titled 'Covert Operations in Port Elizabeth and Letaba.'[73]

The post-transition disbandment of SDUs and SPUs left African populations across several provinces awash with weaponry and young men who had come of age in the midst of the apartheid regime's campaign to destabilize their communities. Similarly, for the first five years after independence, much of the violence in Gauteng province, and particularly on the Witwatersrand, was inflected with the grievances – and inflicted with the weapons – that endured since the particularly bloody 1990–4 period.[74] In Thokoza township, the site of some of the heaviest Third Force violence, 'gunmen armed with AK47 assault rifles executed 12 residents' just three days after Nelson Mandela's presidential inauguration, underscoring the continuity between apartheid and post-apartheid urban violence.[75] According to one estimate, by the end of 1997 there were 4 million illegal firearms in South Africa, a figure which would have only increased in subsequent years.[76]

After the transition, right-wing militants faded to the margins but still occasionally surfaced to launch deadly attacks. In January 1997, a group calling itself the Boere Assault Troops (BAT) launched a series of pipe bombings in North West and the Western Cape, killing four and wounding two, sparking fears of a new 'Third Force.'[77] In February 1997, the intelligence services found that right-wingers from the AWB and like-minded outfits were attempting to regroup, stealing weapons from SANDF armouries and establishing underground cells.[78] In 2002, the Boeremag militia launched a similar bombing campaign against black targets, and plotted to overthrow the ANC government, though they were quickly neutralized. A former MK commander explained: the 'right-wingers and people within intelligence circles of SADF were not doing one thing. They had different agendas. One seeking profit and others motivated by racist hatred.'[79]

Post-Transition Violence in KwaZulu-Natal

Of the various post-apartheid counterinsurgency legacies, by far the bloodiest was the political violence between the ANC and the IFP in KwaZulu-Natal. The province had been a key focus of regime counterinsurgency operations from the mid-1980s onward (see Chapter Three), and it was there that the strategy of outsourcing violence to African groups was most effective. The post-transition violence in the province persisted into the next millennium in patterns reminiscent of the apartheid era: hit squads, targeted assassinations, intelligence intrigues.

The violence continued in large part due to the flood of weaponry introduced to KwaZulu-Natal during the 1990–4 period; Pauw has noted that Eugene de Kock's 'arming of Inkatha' in his capacity as Vlakplaas commander 'may be the greatest legacy left behind by his command of the police counter-insurgency unit.'[80] After the transition, apartheid-era smuggling networks originally established by the ANC to arm SDUs were still funnelling weaponry from Mozambique into KwaZulu-Natal, fuelling the ongoing violence there.[81] In KwaZulu-Natal, local-level ANC and IFP structures continued to fight turf battles for control of neighbourhoods. The ongoing violence was traced to the highest echelons of regional leadership, as, in April 1995, 'self-confessed members of an IFP hit-squad' claimed to have received their orders from Chief Mangosuthu Buthelezi's 'top lieutenants,' including Prince Gideon Zulu, provincial minister for social welfare, and the Reverend Celani Mtetwa, minister for safety and security.[82] The magnitude of ongoing violence in KwaZulu-Natal in the transition's aftermath led newly elected President Mandela to deploy the SANDF and various national and provincial police units to sites of ongoing unrest in the Western Cape, Gauteng, Eastern Cape and KwaZulu-Natal in March 1995. These operations focused especially on establishing stability in KwaZulu-Natal and seizing weapons caches.[83]

In September 1995, KZN welfare and pensions MEC Gideon Zulu was investigated for his role in a conspiracy to murder a KwaZulu Police (KZP) officer.[84] That same month, national safety and security minister Sydney Mufamadi announced an investigation into over a dozen active KZP officers, including two brigadiers, for 'their links to hit squad networks' before and during the transition era, involving among other things the assassination of local ANC leaders. Many of these officers were among the Caprivi trainees.[85] Although the government charged some of them with murder, it did not bring charges against senior KZP and SAPS officials who, according to the inquest magistrate, had covered up some of the killings.[86] Yet in October 1995, KZN attorney general Tim McNally said 'he believes hit squads have existed and still exist,' criticizing the KZP for not conducting proper investigations.[87] That month, three witnesses in the murder trial of an IFP regional chief were seized by the Umfolozi Internal Stability Unit and reported being tortured with rubber tubes by white policemen. The IFP chief had been arrested along with two other IFP militants, one of whom had been trained at the Mlaba camp, in a context of surging violence by SPU members.[88] In October 1996, SAPS spokesman Superintendent Strini Moodley confirmed 'that at least 55 Caprivi trainees' were serving in the SAPS – 'most of them in areas of KwaZulu-Natal which have suffered or continue to suffer from outbreaks of political violence.'[89] A further eight Caprivi trainees, who had supposedly resigned in 1988, were based at Sundumbili police station 'in strife-torn Mandini,' while 19 'Caprivis' were serving with the police in Ulundi, most of them reportedly in Col. Leonard Langeni's 'notorious VIP protection unit'; Langeni had previously been implicated in multiple instances of hit squad activity. As of late 1996, other 'Caprivis' were still serving in some of the most violent regions of KwaZulu-Natal, including four in Nongoma; three in the Durban Point Road Public Order Policing Unit; three in Mpumalanga township near Durban; two each in Nkandla, Newcastle and KwaMashu and the Vryheid Firearm Unit; and one each in Ndwedwe, Ubombo, Plessislaer, Bhekithemba, Nqutu, Esikhawini, Umlazi, Ezakheni, Mahlabatini, and Izingolweni.[90]

The cycle of violence led to the flight of 600 ANC loyalists from their dwellings near Port Shepstone in early 1995. When the ANC encouraged them to return in July 1995, IFP incursions began almost immediately, culminating in the 24 December 1995 'Christmas Eve massacre' of 19 ANC members at Shobashobane. Using a pincer manoeuvre known as 'horns of a bull' that had been pioneered in the 19th century by King Shaka, the attackers, armed with rifles, pistols, spears, knives, and two-way radios, mowed down women and children, injuring dozens and destroying scores of homes. The militants targeted regional ANC leader Kipha Nyawose, who had been involved in efforts to establish peace between the ANC and IFP. Nyawose, who had already lost a dozen family members to IFP attacks, led the local ANC Self-Defence Unit, which had successfully repulsed two busloads of IFP militants brought from Durban in July. A week prior to the Christmas attack, standing in the charred ruins of a home in which eight of his family members had perished in a previous IFP attack, Nyawose told a documentary film crew that he slept in a different location every night to avoid being targeted. 'Actually, I don't know what's a good reason for why these people come to attack us,' he said. 'But they always attack us.'[91] This time, he was the first to be killed.[92] Along with several other massacres in the preceding and subsequent days, the total death toll in one week of violence in KwaZulu-Natal amounted to 189.

Subsequently, investigations revealed that the KZP had foreknowledge of the attack almost a month in advance and had done nothing to stop it. Indeed, a few days before the massacre, local ANC leaders who had got wind of impending trouble approached the police station in nearby Izingolweni to ask for protection; in response, the police, still commanded mainly by right-wing white officers, raided Shobashobane to confiscate weapons from ANC members, leaving the community defenceless when the IFP militants attacked.[93] Once the attack was under way, the police took hours to respond. There were reports that the SAPS and SANDF had been complicit at Shobashobane, 'and, indeed, the National Police Commissioner George Fivaz admitted that some policemen were identified as suspects in the massacre'; at least seven policemen, including three officers from Izingolweni police station, were implicated but only four were arrested and none convicted. At the victims' funeral, Deputy President Thabo Mbeki blamed the 'Third Force' for the killings, while KwaZulu-Natal Safety and Security Portfolio Committee chairperson Bheki Cele 'openly accused the police of being responsible for the murders.'[94]

According to observers, the IFP's assaults were calculated to help it achieve greater regional autonomy from the ANC-dominated national government, and to reinforce the IFP's standing in the lead-up to local elections scheduled for March 1996. Meanwhile, right-wing whites sought to destabilize the province to undermine the ANC. Natal University anthropologist and violence monitor Mary de Haas noted: 'there is an old-boy network still engaged in destabilization. It is driven by a right-wing ideology that likes Buthelezi because it sees him as its creation. It believes that if you can control KwaZulu-Natal, with its ports and harbours, you can control South Africa.'[95] De Haas argued that in the post-apartheid era, the violent networks that had previously been mechanisms of the regime had now been privatized 'by those formerly involved,' and were receiving support from right-wingers who remained in the police force.[96] De Haas warned that there were still right-wing elements within the local police force, noting that the Durban-based National Investigating Task Unit (NITU) under Superintendent Danie Malan was 'unfit' to police the area, and that several key witnesses of the recent violence had been killed while under the NITU's protection, indicating that 'somebody in the unit is leaking information.' Both De Haas and local ANC ward councillor Sibenjwa Nyawose complained that a policeman in the area was known to be a 'Third Force' member.[97]

The violence in KwaZulu-Natal reached a climax in February 1996, when 69 people were killed in clashes between the ANC and IFP; in June, 51 more people died.[98] The crisis between the ANC and IFP in KwaZulu-Natal required a continued security force presence. ANC loyalists insisted that the IFP had brought in 'outside warlords' to fight them. To investigate local police complicity, the SAPS assembled a team of investigators from outside the province. After two years of investigating, the team issued 96 arrest warrants, and when a convoy of police went to make arrests, it was ambushed. In the end, only 18 were arrested, and of the 13 found guilty, 5 had their sentences overturned on appeal.[99] This investigation, and subsequent trials, suggested that a 'Third Force' was responsible for ongoing destabilization operations in the province.

In February 1997, ANC provincial treasurer Zweli Mkhize pointed to a 'Third Force element' in the political violence that rocked

Dambuza, an ANC stronghold in Pietermaritzburg, noting that a 'white policeman' had been implicated.[100] By 1997, the ANC had labelled the Richmond district in the KZN Midlands a 'concentration camp,' due to the frequent targeted killings of its members there. In May 1997, ANC councillor Rodney van der Byl was assassinated after a series of phone messages warned him to abandon his position and leave the area; the ANC considered him and others to have been 'Third Force' targets, and called on the police to explain their strategy for the Midlands.[101] Meanwhile, when the ANC's provincial leadership in KZN sought to forge a peace deal with the IFP, it was rejected by Buthelezi, who claimed that it exonerated the killers of more than 430 IFP office-bearers.[102] The ANC insisted that the 'Third Force' was destabilizing KwaZulu-Natal, and on 3 August 1997, speaking to a crowd of hundreds at the funeral of five ANC members killed on 22 July, President Mandela was unequivocal: 'We are not dealing here with an individual or just a small group of criminals. We are dealing with experienced political criminals in command of huge resources – finances, weaponry, communications networks and connections at key positions.' Mandela claimed this was a 'highly coordinated network of people deployed in state organs, such as the army and police' who were 'driven by the desperate attempt to arrest the democratic transformation of our country and turn back the clock of history.' Mandela declared that arrests would follow and called on security force members to identify those in their ranks who were responsible: 'We want to know why and who decided to withdraw the security forces, especially the soldiers, from this area on the day of the massacre.'[103]

One case that embodies the post-transition counterinsurgency legacies in KwaZulu-Natal is that of Sifiso Nkabinde, an ANC leader connected to many killings before and after 1994, who was ultimately expelled from the ANC in April 1997 for having been an apartheid spy, and who was assassinated in January 1999. Nkabinde was elected the ANC's provincial deputy secretary in 1992; his mentor Harry Gwala had forced cadres to vote for him and dismissed evidence that Nkabinde was a spy. Nkabinde cultivated Richmond as a 'virtually unassailable powerbase,'[104] deploying its SDU as a personal militia to terrorize the population. He oversaw assassinations within and outside the ANC, including that of Skhumbuzo Ngwenya, rival candidate for the deputy secretaryship, killed in 1992. The ANC leadership had known since 1992 that Nkabinde had been recruited by the Security Branch, but had 'chosen to shield him to avoid losing votes,' going so far as to quash a 1994 plan by disgruntled local ANC cadres to kill Nkabinde and Gwala.[105] Nkabinde had been recruited by the Pietermaritzburg Security Branch in 1988, registered as an agent, and given the pseudonym Derrick Nene; his phone calls listed in the Nene file were made from Harry Gwala's phone.[106] In 1993, based on a tip from Nkabinde, the Security Police apprehended a Richmond IFP leader who had approached Richmond ANC youth leader Mzwandile Mbongwa with a plan to defect to the ANC and bring an IFP weapons cache with him; the IFP leader 'was subsequently killed.'[107] Nkabinde's SDU killed Mbongwa in March 1994. After his expulsion from the ANC, Nkabinde joined the United Democratic Movement (UDM) and oversaw further violence. With the death toll rising in Richmond, 'once again there was evidence that shadowy security forces were fuelling the flames,' as a team of 'credible' detectives, after making arrests linked to dozens of deaths, saw the dockets 'removed from it by the newly established [crime-fighting] unit which was to become known as the Scorpions.'[108]

After Nkabinde's assassination, it emerged that he and IFP warlord David Ntombela had been handled as informers by the same Security Branch officer, Sgt Shane Morris; Morris was only transferred out of the province by minister of safety and security Mufamadi in April 1998.[109] Ntombela was known to have links with the security forces and allegedly participated in the December 1988 Trust Feed massacre.[110] Nkabinde 'maintained contact with his handlers until shortly before his death,' and they even 'visited his house' in late 1998;[111] he was also known to maintain 'a close relationship' with other police officers.[112] At a press conference, an SAPS spokesman dodged the subject of Nkabinde's informer status: 'the question of informers is a very emotive issue in South Africa because of our past. However, informers shouldn't be looked down upon because they are important in solving crimes. Due to the threat posed by criminals, the issue of informers is handled with utmost secrecy.'[113] After Nkabinde's death, violence monitor Jenny Irish noted: 'There are elements interested in destabilising [KwaZulu-Natal]. Some are in political parties and didn't support the peace process. Some are in the police and security services. There are the criminal elements, gangsters and the like. And there are individuals on the right wing.'[114] The TRC ultimately blamed the ANC for its failure to expel Nkabinde, creating a 'climate of impunity' and contributing to the escalating violence. After Nkabinde's death, Bruce Mhlongo, an alleged NIA agent, claimed that he had received R200,000 to assemble and command the hit team that killed Nkabinde.[115]

White Inkatha MP Philip Powell was deeply involved in planning IFP violence during the transition years; Powell had also been named for an alleged role in the 1986 assassination of Swedish prime minister Olof Palme.[116] All told, from 1992 to 1994, Powell trained 1,200 IFP militants and remained implicated well after the transition.[117] The TRC accused him of 'gross violations of human rights' for arming thousands of men to fight for Inkatha in the run-up to the 1994 election, yet he was eventually nominated as an IFP senator. As late as 1999, Powell still trained and armed militias, 'but [claimed] they work for private security companies.'[118] Meanwhile, Henry Beavon, head of the KZN police's Organised Crime division, had previously worked with Vlakplaas.[119]

By 1999, violence in KwaZulu-Natal had become more calibrated: 'There are still some massacres but there are also many more individual assassinations or gang violence which targets local councillors.'[120] 'Paramilitary training' continued in some areas of KwaZulu-Natal, police continued to arm IFP supporters, Caprivi trainees still served in prominent police roles, and patterns of ongoing violence indicated that 'sinister forces continued to operate.'[121] De Haas estimated that about 4,000 people died in politically motivated murders in the province between 1994 and 1999.[122] She spoke out about destabilizing elements within the security forces: 'It's the old mafia network still in control in the police. You might say there are now blacks in senior positions but most of them came from the homelands [i.e., Bantustans]. They owed their position there to the fact that they never stood up to apartheid,' and many were 'directly involved' in political violence 'by providing weapons and providing information and protection.' Addressing the nexus of ex-apartheid and ex-KZP security personnel in the post-transition security forces in KwaZulu-Natal, ANC stalwart Bheki Cele conceded: 'It's true that a lot hasn't changed. They're agitating violence, they're corrupt, they are responsible for a lot of problems. Some go far beyond being anti-ANC. They are anti-African, they are anti-blacks ruling the country.'[123] In Nongoma – a 'no-go' area for the ANC in which it declined to campaign in the 1994 elections – over twenty people, including IFP and ANC officials, fell victim to cycles of targeted killings perpetrated by hitmen with IFP and SDU links from 1999 to 2002. Among the dead were IFP regional leader Joseph Sikhonde, who doubled as an organized crime kingpin and hit squad commander; IFP youth leader Israel Ngcobo; and Prince Cyril Zulu, an ANC-affiliated member of the Zulu royal family. Cyril Zulu's widow, Gloria Zulu, asserted: 'Many murders of ANC supporters have been successfully covered up here.'[124]

Deadly grievances between the ANC and IFP have persisted in KwaZulu-Natal: provincial and municipal officials as well as ordinary citizens have been targeted, and political and criminal motivations have become increasingly intertwined. In comparison with its apartheid-proxy contemporaries, the IFP, unlike UNITA or RENAMO, has never assumed a prominent role in national-level politics in post-conflict South Africa. Instead, its history of clandestine training and support from the apartheid regime has left legacies of localized, decentralized post-transition violence.

Racism and Corruption in the Forces

Since South Africa's democratic transition, its security institutions have remained plagued by significant levels of corruption, violence and racism.[125] In the first decade of transition, the 'sunset clause,' a key aspect of the ANC–NP pact that left most state institutions intact, contributed to the retention of apartheid-era personnel in the security forces.[126] As systemic violence gripped South Africa, its security institutions largely remained part of the problem. Racist attitudes persisted in the post-transition security forces; as one report described: 'the police, who for 40 years were used to enforce apartheid, retain their racist attitudes towards black people,' leading to growing 'tensions between the South African police and the country's new black-dominated government,' despite 'Mandela's personal intervention.'[127] In the decade following the transition, torture by police and deaths in police custody remained widespread in South Africa, while a government inquiry into SAPS racism initiated by safety and security minister Sydney Mufamadi was never released.[128] Instances of such racism could be stark: for example, in January 1995, black policemen barricaded themselves in the SAPS's Orlando station to block the return of three white colleagues who had been transferred elsewhere after being accused of racism. In response, white officers from the Johannesburg Internal Stability Unit assaulted the Orlando station, killing one black policeman and wounding several others. During the raid white policemen could be heard uttering racial epithets over their radios.[129] This incident became a major embarrassment for the ANC and Mufamadi.

Despite its much greater relative levels of economic development and political freedom, South Africa's police ranked 11th out of 12 African countries in a 2005 survey of trust in state institutions; at 35 per cent, the police were also trusted least out of any institution in the country.[130] Counterinsurgency practices entrenched within the police remained in evidence after apartheid as racism persisted within police ranks and between white policemen and black civilians. Shaw mentions a white former apartheid policeman who applied for amnesty to the TRC for killing four ANC cadres; he 'remained on in the police and was [in 2001] alleged to be involved in a series of cases of police brutality where black people were the victims.'[131] Many believed that the former Security Branch, now renamed the Crime Intelligence Division, 'continued to perform its former function under the previous government.'[132] Security Police Col. Vic McPherson, who took part in a mission to bomb the ANC's London headquarters in 1982, remained a senior officer in the post-transition police.[133] In February 1997, the Northern Province chairperson of the National Police and Public Civil Rights Union (NAPPCRU) questioned the loyalty of former Security Branch operatives in the SAPS, which he argued was 'being controlled by former Security Branch personnel.'[134] In 1997, police arrested anti-apartheid activist Mzwakhe Mbuli, a year after an attempt on his life; Mbuli was convicted despite strong indications that the police had fabricated the case.[135] De Haas notes that in the years following the transition, 'whatever changes had taken place in the police were only cosmetic and, while presenting themselves as "transformed," their bureaucratic culture had not changed,' and that 'many senior SAP staff' who 'were politically far to the right of the NP government' had retained their positions; she further describes the new government's 'reluctance' to 'take constructive action against the old order,' including 'failure' to 'take action against police' still serving after the transition despite being named by the Goldstone Commission and in court cases.[136]

In 1997, former death squad operative Joe Mamasela revealed that Stanza Bopape, a Mamelodi Civic Association activist who disappeared in 1988, had been killed by police at the John Vorster Square police station, and claimed that he helped dispose of Bopape's body. According to Mamasela, the officers responsible for killing Bopape – a sergeant and a warrant officer – were still serving in the post-transition police and had sought to conceal the details of the case rather than apply for amnesty.[137] Mamasela also claimed that senior security police personnel who had been involved in setting up seven other Vlakplaas-style farms across South Africa were very likely still serving in the post-transition SAPS.[138] Mamasela himself was still employed by the state as late as 2002.

Police corruption and complicity in crime were staggeringly high at independence: in 1995–6, 8,000 police in Gauteng alone were reported to have committed crimes of one kind or another.[139] In Johannesburg, according to the divisional police chief interviewed in 1996, four police a week were suspended for corruption and 1,076 policemen nationally were under investigation for corruption that year, an increase from 89 investigations in 1995, 56 in 1994 and 32 in 1993–4.[140] Corruption also ran deep in the new intelligence services: from 1994 to 1999, 115 state intelligence agents were implicated in crimes 'ranging from smuggling platinum and illegal dealing in gold to murder.'[141] National police commissioner and Interpol chief Jackie Selebi's 2010 conviction for links with organized crime, accepting bribes, and covering up murder, revealed pervasive corruption in the highest echelons of the post-apartheid police.[142] One former guerrilla pointed to the scandal's impact on the police rank and file: 'They can see the head of Interpol was getting money from gangsters, so why him and not me?'[143] The scandal that felled Selebi epitomizes the corruption that has penetrated all levels of the SAPS.[144]

10

SKELETONS AND GHOSTS
SPY SCANDALS IN POST-TRANSITION SOUTH AFRICA

*'We want to know who [the spies] are, not necessarily because we want
to take action against them but because, if they had been informing
on behalf of the apartheid regime, there is the likelihood that they are
doing that today.'*
  – South African president, Nelson Mandela, March 1997

'Once a spy, always a spy.'
  – Ex-combatant, Mthatha, December 2009

At an official unveiling ceremony in September 2014, head of the
Umkhonto we Sizwe Military Veterans' Association (MKMVA) and
deputy minister of defence Kebby Maphatsoe accused South African
public prosecutor Thuli Madonsela of being a CIA spy. Madonsela
had found President Jacob Zuma to have 'benefitted unduly and acted
unethically' in spending tens of millions of rands in public money
on extravagant upgrades to his family compound in the KwaZulu-
Natal village of Nkandla. Since then, Madonsela had been dogged
by criticism from a host of ANC officials and allies, which climaxed
with Maphatsoe's accusation. In a subsequent statement, Maphatsoe
declared that if Madonsela 'feels more powerful and above the
constitution, she should tell the country who her handlers are?'[1] In

response, US ambassador to South Africa Patrick Gaspard lodged a formal diplomatic complaint.

This incident embodies a number of central themes in post-apartheid South African politics: rampant corruption among political elites; campaigns to defame and delegitimize critics of this corruption; and accusations that government officials have been secretly working to destabilize South Africa by spying for remnants of the apartheid regime or for the regime's former allies. Maphatsoe then backpedalled, insisting that he had made the comments in his capacity as MKMVA chief, and not in his capacity as deputy minister of defence. He retreated into vague language, while describing international spying mechanisms: 'We know how foreign intelligence works,' he said. 'They create their own person and popularize him or her. That's how they work. They create you, including in the media... That's what they've created now.'[2]

Since 1994, persistent rumours and speculation about who spied for the apartheid regime have undermined public confidence in the new government. In the post-transition era, the self-sufficient networks that had taken root in the apartheid counterinsurgency apparatus were able to adapt with little difficulty, continuing their involvement in crime and destabilization. Former apartheid intelligence figures such as ex-NIS chief Niël Barnard joined the private sector.[3] Meanwhile, private, illicit incentives to prosper proliferated. This ongoing destabilization helped to compromise democratic South Africa's fledgling state institutions. It has also, in many cases, borne the hallmarks of the apartheid regime's psychological warfare operations, including intelligence leaks, illegal surveillance, the dissemination of false information, and a host of other methods that were the apartheid intelligence services' stock-in-trade, and have now become regular features of post-transition political life. Spy intrigues have become an intractable feature of mainstream South African politics: journalist Terry Bell called the question of who was an apartheid spy 'a suppurating cancer buried deep within the body politic that could damage the lives and careers of innocent and guilty alike.'[4] Yet, unlike in East Germany or the former Czechoslovakia, where government informers were exposed after the transition, in South Africa the identities of former spies have never been revealed. Spy intrigues rooted in the apartheid era have resurfaced at jagged moments in ways that have accelerated the fragmentation of South Africa's politics and diluted its democracy. And of course, accusations such as Maphatsoe's would have less traction had the ANC throughout its history not actually been infiltrated by hostile intelligence services.

'Spy Fever' and the Democratic State

Recruitment of apartheid spies within ANC ranks was a constant source of paranoia and instability within the ANC and MK throughout the movement's history. Reno has noted that in the Namibian context, the 'tactical effectiveness of South African military pressure became manifest in SWAPO leadership's obsession with the threat of spies and traitors.'[5] The same problem prevailed in the ANC, and no case better embodies the controversies and divisions that spy recruitment generated than that of Muziwakhe Ngwenya (MK name Thami Zulu, known as 'TZ'). The debate about whether Thami Zulu was a spy remains shrouded in mystery and competing narratives, and it foreshadowed debates about spies within ANC ranks that would persist well after the transition. After the transition, and during the Truth and Reconciliation Commission (TRC), Zulu's family demanded answers from the ANC but failed to obtain greater clarity on the case.[6] Zulu had been a prominent, charismatic MK commander in Angola and a senior member of the ANC's security department. By 1987 he was poised to ascend to MK's high command, which had vacancies that year after Joe Slovo resigned and Cassius Maake was murdered by apartheid agents. One report contends that Zulu was 'hotly favoured' by Chris Hani, then MK commissar, 'to replace Slovo as [MK] Chief of Staff,' until Hani realized that 'many in the high command' preferred Siphiwe Nyanda – who was apparently 'a protégé of army commander Joe Modise' – for the post, whereupon Hani himself assumed the chief of staff position and appointed Steve Tshwete – described as 'ill-equipped' – as MK commissar.[7]

In September 1989, the ANC was said to be 'conducting a major security sweep' targeting apartheid agents and 'suspected wrong-doers' within MK, the ANC's treasury department, and the South African Communist Party (SACP).[8] In this context, Zulu was detained. Suspicions arose after the operations which Zulu ran from Swaziland as head of MK's Natal Machinery (operating from Swaziland and Mozambique) 'suffered many casualties.'[9] In 1988, the operations chief of MK's Natal Machinery, 'Comrade Cyril,' who had been under Zulu's command 'for several years,' killed himself when he was uncovered as an apartheid spy. The subsequent investigation led by ANC Department of National Intelligence and Security (NAT) veterans Joe Nhlanhla and Iscor Chikane uncovered more spies; Zulu and others were detained. Zulu hailed from a wealthy background and seems to have grown complacent in his high rank; he also had a 'reputation for brutality' as an MK base commander in Angola, where he would leave comrades tied to trees overnight as punishment.[10] But many in the ANC could not believe that he was actually an enemy agent. Hani himself was said to be deeply upset by Zulu's imprisonment and subsequent fate.[11] Nonetheless Zulu was accused of shielding Cyril and his associates as the ANC security men tightened their net.[12] Suspicions about Zulu had intensified when several MK operatives spotted four Security Branch policemen playing golf at a Swazi hotel, and decided to assassinate them; Zulu was dispatched to retrieve the MK team's guns, but returned claiming he could not find them. In 1989, a senior NAT man met Eugene de Kock and the askari Glory Sedibe at a hotel in Vienna, Austria. The meeting was organized by SADF MI's Directorate of Covert Collection (DCC) for the purpose of recruiting the NAT agent as an apartheid spy; he took the opportunity to ask De Kock if Thami Zulu had spied for the regime. De Kock said Zulu had not, and the NAT man said in that case the ANC had 'made a terrible mistake.'[13] Of course, De Kock would have had reason to lie about which ANC operatives were apartheid spies, both during the meeting and later, in his testimony to the TRC.

Zulu was released from detention by the ANC in Zambia on 11 November 1989 'a frail and unrecognizable' man; he died five days later at the University Teaching Hospital in Lusaka. The ANC submitted to the TRC a report indicating that Zulu was HIV-positive and also suffered from tuberculosis. However, the TRC Report notes that Zulu's 'death was brought about by poisoning which must have been taken in within a day or at most two days prior to his death.'[14] Medical analysis conducted at the Lusaka hospital showed traces of the pesticide diazinon in Zulu's blood and stomach, and someone who saw

Zulu days before his death had given him three bottles of beer, in which diazinon is soluble.[15] O'Malley claims the Security Branch had 'fed the ANC misinformation about Thami Zulu…in the knowledge that Zulu would be recalled to Lusaka and arrested by NAT.'[16] Yet archival documents suggest that Zulu had actually been recruited as an NIS spy (see Chapter Six), raising the possibility, as the ANC submission to the TRC suggests, that the regime had killed him to prevent him from being exposed.[17] The ANC's own commission of inquiry concluded that enemy agents had poisoned Zulu 'either to silence TZ before he gave the game away or to provoke enmity between the ANC's military and security branches.'[18]

In other contexts, when the ANC identified spies within its ranks, especially at the senior levels, its strategy was not necessarily to punish them; when Padraig O'Malley asked Jacob Zuma why the ANC had not dealt harshly with a member of the National Executive Committee (NEC) suspected of spying, Zuma 'smiled and said, "that's not how we operated."'[19] In some cases, this approach may have been the ANC's best option, as the goal of apartheid spy recruitment was to cause the ANC's top echelons to tear themselves apart, and the ANC may have calculated that staying intact gave it the best chance of prevailing in the political realm. But whether the ANC punished suspected spies or sought more subtle means of dealing with them, the spy problem persisted.

In March 1994, former Security Branch chief Johann Coetzee had reported that some of his spies within the ANC were 'still somewhere,' but refused to elaborate.[20] After the transition, key ANC members faced rumours and allegations that they were apartheid spies. Likewise, various ANC members aggravated party infighting by accusing rivals of having been apartheid spies. Throughout Mandela's tenure as president, the ANC also had to contend with the real threat that former apartheid security force personnel could pose to the country's stability should they face prosecution or lose their jobs in a restructuring process. Meanwhile, the mushrooming private intelligence agency sector was largely staffed with ex-apartheid personnel 'who were not only suspected of fomenting the [post-transition] "Third Force" violence but also retained ties into the new intelligence structures.'[21] Furthermore, operations of unknown provenance, but bearing the imprint of the apartheid regime's 'Stratcom' programme, have continued to destabilize post-transition South African politics, mainly in the form of 'information peddling' by shadowy operators, with allegations abounding of conspiratorial cliques, impending coups d'état, and collusion with unnamed foreign intelligence agencies. The post-transition intelligence services have had little success tracing the origins of these operations. Yet in the post-apartheid era, the veracity of the allegations is of secondary importance; it is their very existence and proliferation that make it increasingly difficult to distinguish fact from fiction, eroding trust in the ANC government, and undermining civilian rule.

Several former MK personnel have insisted that clandestine elements from the former apartheid security forces have been mounting disinformation campaigns to destabilize post-transition South Africa. MK intelligence operative Barry Gilder, who became deputy chief of the new South African Secret Service, has suggested that apartheid-era spies could still be at work in the post-transition era. He raised the possibility that these spies' former handlers could be blackmailing them, using proof of their spying as leverage, in order to destabilize the country. Gilder pointed to the constant 'information peddling' in South Africa's government and intelligence services that has made it nearly impossible to sort fact from fiction. This has combined with a huge private security industry composed of ex-apartheid personnel, unwilling to serve under an ANC state and working to undermine the transformational agenda.[22] A former MK commander explained his perception of enduring clandestine networks:

'Even now, I would call those spies who were not exposed "Third Force." Because, surely, they are not serving the government of the day. They are destabilizing, sabotaging every efforts that are being done, any progress. Once a spy, always a spy. Even now former [MK] cadres are under surveillance, surely, bugging of phones. I know. [They] check what you are doing now, why were you not in the [SANDF] integration, how are you surviving.'[23]

In this sense, many South Africans understand the corruption affecting the highest levels of their government in terms that transcend mere greed, with persistent suspicions that elements within the state answer not to the elected government but to still-active hidden forces. Meanwhile, the rumours about some current ANC members having been spies led to speculation that clandestine forces have peddled this information in the post-transition era in order to sow divisions and undermine public trust.[24] Thus the question of which ANC members were apartheid spies remains volatile, not only because exposing these spies would shed light on past betrayals but because of suspicions that these agents continue to undermine democratic change. More than one ex-guerrilla expressed the belief that counterinsurgency remnants still endure today: 'The networks may not be operational, but they may be waiting to strike whenever the chance may be.'[25]

Turmoil in the Post-Transition Intelligence Services

In the post-transition Government of National Unity, 'all ministerial positions relating to security were given to ANC personnel': Joe Modise became defence minister; Sydney Mufamadi, safety and security minister; Dullah Omar, justice minister; and Alfred Nzo, minister of foreign affairs.[26] Yet, as housing minister Joe Slovo emphasized, in the mid-1990s the ANC was 'in government' but not yet 'in power,'[27] and the old securocrats still exerted great influence and possessed great power to destabilize the country, as did the explosive question of regime spies persisting in the ANC.

The question of which ANC members were regime intelligence assets had first arisen during the ANC–NP negotiations. Both sides agreed to postpone addressing the issue as each had recruited informers in the other's camp, and launching a spy hunt in the midst of negotiations could have badly undermined the transition and the resulting Government of National Unity.[28] However, the choice to leave this stone unturned would prove to have its own destabilizing consequences. As spy intrigues carried over into the post-transition era, secrecy and misinformation prevailed against the norms of democratic openness. This was particularly egregious in the case of the 'PAIIC Group,' composed of former members of SADF MI's ultra-sensitive DCC, who had been operating under a civilian front company named Pan-Afrik Industrial Investment Consultants (PAIIC) when they were sacked by FW de Klerk in December 1992 (see Chapter Six).

The PAIIC had been responsible for the recruitment and handling of spies within the ANC and PAC and their respective armed wings, and these former intelligence operatives, who had been summarily fired, possessed a wealth of extremely explosive information. The DCC was partially dismantled, but nevertheless remained intact and operational after the transition.[29] According to TRC investigator Jan-Ake Kjellberg, Nigel Barnett, suspected to have been involved in the 1986 murder of Swedish prime minister Olof Palme, was still employed by the DCC when Mozambican police arrested him in Maputo in 1997 – 'three years into the Mandela government!'[30] Apartheid-era secrecy prevailed over democratic openness as new minister of defence Joe Modise 'moved to interdict' the press from publishing further details about the DCC, claiming this was necessary to prevent agents from exposing their 'fellow officers and their sources.'[31] SANDF chief of staff Gen. Meiring justified the gag order on the media by claiming in court papers it was necessary to keep intelligence agents' identities secret. SANDF also censored information on the DCC front companies Africa Risk Analysis Consultancy (ARAC) and PAIIC; the latter had been integral to SADF MI counterinsurgency operations in Transkei and Ciskei during the transition era (see Chapter Six), and the SADF had issued assurances a year earlier that PAIIC had been dismantled.[32] After the transition, the SANDF continued to restrict 'access to the public files on Arac and PAIIC,' and in June 1994 the *Mail & Guardian* reported: 'more ominously, PAIIC appears to be operating despite official SADF claims that it closed down in February 1993.'[33] In June 1994, the unemployed former PAIIC officers petitioned President Mandela, arguing that they had been used as scapegoats by the previous regime, and asking either to be given back their jobs or to be given 'a better deal in recognition of their long service.' According to one intelligence analyst, the former SADF MI officers threatening to divulge the information were 'too junior to have run or even had knowledge of really senior ANC figures working as agents for the other side.'[34] Yet one of the group's spokesmen, Clive Brink, had been involved in a wide range of covert operations on behalf of both the DCC and Vlakplaas (see Chapter Nine).

Brink and the group's other spokesperson, DCC operative Gerhard Jansen van Rensburg, claimed that SADF MI chief Lt Gen. Joffel van der Westhuizen had been aware of all their operations, and that there was nothing illicit or criminal about them. Van Rensburg asserted that the apartheid government, 'through its intelligence agencies, had sustained the ANC. Intelligence operatives had paid ANC sources well and even provided them with equipment, such as laminating machines and vehicles.'[35] Although it would have strengthened van Rensburg's hand to exaggerate the extent to which his unit had infiltrated the ANC, his assertion makes a remarkable claim about the collaboration and eventual interdependence between SADF MI and some of its spies within the ANC. The PAIIC Group balanced this appeal to kinship with a threat: it 'created some panic within the ranks of the new [SANDF] and newly elected ANC government when they made veiled threats of revealing the names of ANC members who worked as sources and spies for the old regime.'[36]

SANDF chief of staff intelligence Gen. Dirk Verbeek, responded with threats of his own, warning that the SANDF might take legal action against members of the PAIIC Group 'should they reveal names and sources in "an effort to blackmail the SANDF"'; he told the press that these threats could have 'serious consequences' and that the SANDF would take all measures at its disposal to prevent any of this information from being leaked. According to Verbeek, Modise 'was considering the group's demands,' as a result of which on 13 June 1994 he dropped the interdict he had imposed four days earlier to prevent any media outlet from reporting on this process. Modise's statement declared: 'I have examined information made available by former military intelligence officers of the Directorate of Covert Collection (DCC) concerning allegations that certain members of the ANC alliance, the PAC, and others had acted as informants of the apartheid state.' Modise's statement announced that he had lifted the interdict 'having satisfied myself that such information does not pose a threat to the democratic transition.'[37] Of course, the information posed no such threat only because it was not going to be released. Modise's interdict is all the more interesting considering that he himself may well have been recruited by the DCC during the transition (see Chapter Six). The ANC later 'strongly criticized' Modise 'for his attempt recently to muzzle newspaper reports about "dirty tricks" carried out by the former South African Defence Force.'[38]

Modise's 'aborted attempt' to impose censorship on the issue of spies also revealed a 'titanic struggle' between Modise and SANDF chief Gen. Meiring over control of the armed forces, in the course of which former SADF MI officers claimed to have information that would 'compromise individual ANC leaders.'[39] According to sources 'close to the Ministry of Defence,' Meiring convinced Modise to censor the *Mail & Guardian* over 'the threat of major political damage to the ANC and the government through the revelation of highly placed South African moles in the ANC, dating back to its period in exile,' which could give the military's old guard 'a hold over some ANC leaders, including ministers and deputy ministers.'[40] According to government and intelligence officials, the apartheid intelligence services ran a 'decades-long' programme seeking to penetrate the ANC using 'false flag' operations in which South African agents posed as operatives of American, British, Soviet or Israeli intelligence services 'and won over ANC leaders sympathetic to those governments.' The agents would then reveal to their sources that they had been supplying intelligence to the apartheid regime, leaving them compromised and 'forcing them to continue supplying material.' The operation allegedly succeeded such that 'at least one cabinet minister and one deputy' in the ANC government had been recruited; the *Mail & Guardian* possessed their names but refused to divulge them in the absence of definite proof.[41]

The PAIIC Group then de-escalated the situation by assuring Modise that they had no 'hidden agenda' and did not intend to reveal the names or identities of sources, nor to blackmail the new government for money.[42] In a formal statement released on 14 June, the PAIIC declared:

> No information was given to the press which, in our belief, constitutes a breach of the Official Secrets Act. Contrary to the allegations contained in the SANDF's application for the interdict, we have not revealed the names or identities of sources, collaborators, or informers of former colleagues, neither is it our intention to do so now or in the future.[43]

That same month, President Mandela appointed former MK intelligence chief Ronnie Kasrils as deputy minister of defence amid growing concerns within the ANC that Modise was 'not up to the job' and unable to exert authority over Meiring.[44]

The NIS had amassed intelligence on the ANC by means of moles and other forms of surveillance,[45] but in July 1994 transport minister and former Operation Vula chief Mac Maharaj released three volumes of secret NIS files that the ANC had taken during Operation Vula, 'dated 1980 and packed with information about what NIS knew about ANC underground networks.'[46] Maharaj declared: 'I am aware that files are being destroyed and tampered with to make the ANC afraid of the [forthcoming] Truth Commission,' and claimed he was 'signalling that we have the capacity to compare information and know what they have'; former regime operatives should thus not attempt to 'blackmail us and believe we are scared of the truth.' He also claimed the ANC had 'more volumes,' though he had been surprised by 'how little information they had [about the ANC] and how inaccurate it was.' Maharaj gave the documents to the Mayibuye Centre at the University of the Western Cape.[47]

The DCC resurfaced on 13 July 1995 when Wally Wilsenach, another former PAIIC member and its provisional spokesman, appealed to President Mandela to clear their names 'in view of the renewed awareness surrounding the need to reconcile our broken nation via the truth.' Wilsenach further appealed to Mandela, 'as the highest authority in the country, to call for the contents of the so-called Goldstone and Steyn reports and review our situation.' Mandela did not respond. Wilsenach and any other PAIIC member who felt aggrieved could have testified to the TRC and revealed details of the DCC's activities.[48] Wilsenach also declared that his unit's members had been exposed in a turf war between intelligence agencies, and that the Counter-Intelligence Directorate, another branch of the old SADF, 'had information about DCC members' links to MI6 and to the Zimbabwean CIO [Central Intelligence Organization], as well as information about illicit diamond deals and fraud.'[49]

The ex-PAIIC members then sought to refute a report claiming that in a press conference on 16 June 1994 these disgruntled former Military Intelligence members had threatened to take action against their former colleagues in the new Defence Force, including 'surveillance and harassment of DCC, illegal telephone tapping of serving members, threats to fabricate false evidence against senior Intelligence Division officers, actions to obtain information regarding

DCC to sell to the press and foreign intelligence services, phone calls to foreign intelligence services designed to sabotage DCC,' and 'threats designed to sabotage the political transition process.' The former members stated that 'in the past, Military Intelligence, in smear campaigns, could allege almost anything as it was never expected of them to provide the evidence or to prove their allegations,' and went on to note that 'it appears as if MID [Military Intelligence Department] are still up to their old habits, even in post-apartheid South Africa.'[50]

This was a remarkable attempt by former SADF MI operatives to reinvent themselves and disavow their involvement in precisely the 'old habits' for which De Klerk had fired them on the eve of the transition. The pattern of allegations and denials, which first emanated from the intelligence community only months after the ANC came to power, would soon become an intractable aspect of South African politics more broadly. Regardless of whether this particular group of former SADF MI operatives had in fact engaged in surveillance, communications operations or intelligence-peddling operations after the transition, as reports alleged, these sorts of covert, illicit activities would quickly develop into a permanent feature of the post-apartheid South African landscape. Meanwhile, 62 members of the DCC were integrated into the SANDF, including operatives who had been gathering intelligence on the ANC and PAC as late as March 1994. Henri van der Westhuizen, a DCC agent who had monitored the ANC and was still working for the unit after the transition, assaulted a former SADF officer who he believed had provided information about the DCC to the media.[51]

Several government sources insisted that the debacle around the Modise interdict was conclusive proof that a Truth Commission needed to be established soon; according to one, it would 'create an ordered framework for dealing with the past and reduce the risk of blackmail to the government or leading political figures.'[52] Yet the TRC ultimately failed to tackle the issue of spies, leaving open the possibilities for blackmail and instability. One government source insisted Modise needed to ask Mandela to release the full Steyn Report in order to lift the veil of secrecy around the DCC's activities. In a televised debate with De Klerk before the April 1994 election, Mandela had 'angrily told viewers' that the former had refused to divulge to him the Steyn Report's contents; yet once in power,

Mandela himself would not release it, either.[53] Although the details of the Steyn Report that eventually emerged painted a detailed picture of apartheid counterinsurgency operations (see Chapter Six), they did not address SADF MI spy recruitment within the ANC, even though this had been one of the DCC's primary tasks. This raises the question whether there was a section in the Steyn Report on spy recruitment that was kept secret.

Spies and the TRC

The failure of the post-transition criminal justice system to compel the truth from top-ranking apartheid elites or to hold them accountable was laid bare in a 1999 court appearance of key regime and IFP figures, including former SADF defence minister Magnus Malan and IFP Chief Buthelezi's personal secretary, MZ Khumalo. They were being tried for their involvement in ordering the 1987 massacre of 13 ANC supporters at KwaMakhutha in KwaZulu-Natal, and the trial was crucial in establishing that Third Force violence had originated at the most senior levels of the regime.[54] Yet despite an abundance of evidence linking the triallists to the formation and instruction of the IFP's Caprivi trainees, and their subsequent unleashing to foment violence, Malan and his fellow generals refused to provide any details about this massacre or any others and were not compelled to reappear in court to offer any further testimony; they were ultimately acquitted in October 1996.[55] The SANDF remained similarly guarded about its apartheid-era personnel's involvement in covert operations, inhibiting the TRC from unearthing key evidence.[56] The TRC, which offered former combatants from all sides the opportunity to obtain amnesty in exchange for testifying about the political violence they had perpetrated, was widely celebrated for promoting national healing, but top apartheid leaders dodged the TRC or, as in the case of PW Botha, refused to testify to the TRC altogether. Yet nowhere were the TRC's shortcomings more evident than in its inability to address the issue of who had been a spy. This unwillingness contradicted the commission's mandate to bring to light the truth about the struggle against apartheid. The ANC requested that the TRC investigate 'which agents of the former government were reintegrated into networks of the state when the ANC resumed a legal profile in SA and what activities they were involved in.'[57] This question would have proven explosive, as the allegations and counter-allegations about who had been a spy – and the possibility of exposing existing spies – could have been disastrous for the fragile new democracy.

Thus former askari Joe Mamasela, who was believed to have personally killed over 40 people, was paid R400,000 by the National Party government immediately before the ANC came to power, and was never convicted, imprisoned or even summoned before the TRC. According to Mamasela: 'They gave me too much money. I think it was to shut my big mouth up.'[58] His enduring impunity may well have been linked to his public announcement on 7 March 1997 'that he knew, but would not name, five ministers in the first post-apartheid cabinet who were apartheid agents.'[59] After making this claim, Mamasela began receiving anonymous death threats, prompting him to go underground because he felt there were forces who were trying to 'shut [him] up so that the past should never be known.'[60] Though the threats came from people claiming to belong to the ANC, he believed they were 'people posing as ANC members, who might be coming from the previous security establishment.'[61] Mamasela claimed that some of the alleged spies within the ANC had been directly on the Vlakplaas payroll, and that he and other death squad operatives had personally delivered payments to them. According to him, the spies had been recruited as early as 1981, and some of these unnamed ANC ministers were still spying as late as 1993, during the high-level ANC–NP negotiations at Kempton Park.[62] These five spies played an integral role 'in helping the police deal with the [MK] guerrillas who used to infiltrate the country,' and would be flown to Vlakplaas by helicopter for payment and debriefing. Mamasela claimed to have travelled to Botswana and Swaziland to pay the spies, to whom the NIS and DCC also had access. He also claimed to have given the ANC names of former spies holding important positions in the SANDF and NIA in 1996, which dovetails with Jan Anton Nieuwoudt's claim that SADF MI had placed many moles within the post-transition SANDF (see Chapter Six).[63] Roelof du Plessis, the lawyer for five former Security Branch policemen testifying to the TRC for the murder of ANC activists, likewise told the commission that his clients knew the names of five ANC ministers who had been apartheid spies. The TRC amnesty committee 'ruled against the disclosure of the informants' names despite a request not to do so by Deputy President Thabo Mbeki.' The ANC sent a high-level delegation to meet with TRC chairperson Archbishop Desmond Tutu to push for the names to be disclosed.[64]

Mamasela's allegations had a widespread impact within the ANC at the national and provincial levels, as ANC structures in Gauteng, North West, Eastern Cape, Western Cape, KwaZulu-Natal and Free State provinces all 'disclosed that they were holding both formal workshops and informal discussions' to ensure the 'smooth management' of the controversy these allegations would unleash.[65] Various branches of the ANC prepared in their own way for the spies' unmasking: for example, the ANC provincial secretary for KwaZulu-Natal, Sipho Gcabashe, called upon former spies 'to approach relevant ANC formations' and confess to their 'double roles' during apartheid; those who did not confess should be unmasked by the TRC, he said. However, Gcabashe also emphasized the importance of differentiating between true spies and others who had given information under duress: 'For instance, a person who breaks down during interrogation cannot be labelled as a spy.' On the other hand, the ANC Youth League's national spokesperson Thabo Masebe discouraged discussion of the topic because 'the rumours originated from persons like Mamasela and other discredited former security cops,' and the spying allegations were themselves likely to be part of a destabilization operation.[66] For his part, President Mandela was understood to have in his possession the names of three ANC members who were allegedly spies, but his office indicated that he would leave the naming of the spies to the TRC.[67] According to O'Brien, 'there is evidence that President Mandela was informed in 1994 that up to five senior ANC officials' had spied for the apartheid regime.[68]

In 1986, MK Special Ops commander Solly Shoke narrowly escaped assassination at his home in Mbabane, Swaziland, when, armed with an axe, he repulsed askaris coming through the door. At the TRC, Eugene de Kock, who had commanded the operation, 'agreed to tell' Shoke the name of the informer in MK who had betrayed him, but 'the amnesty committee asked [Shoke] not to divulge it.'[69] Shoke kept his word. Although exposing spies might have been salutary for the ANC, the spy allegations that gripped the country in the early post-transition years also sowed distrust and disorder. Such was the case with the accusations levelled in 1997 against ANC deputy minister Peter Mokaba, dating from the period when he had been incarcerated by the regime. According to these allegations, Mokaba had broken down under interrogation and collaborated with the security police, and divulged intelligence during a personal interrogation by NP law and order minister Adriaan Vlok. In his rebuttal, Mokaba demanded that his name be cleared, claiming that his interrogator had asked him about his views regarding the South African Youth Congress's response to the negotiations, and Mokaba 'told him to talk to our leadership which was in exile.' Mokaba, who had been cleared by the ANC of all suspicion in three successive statements issued during the transition era, further addressed the accusations that had surfaced against him: 'What is shocking here is that this information is used as so-called evidence that I am a spy.'[70] In a pattern that would become familiar, Mokaba said that though he initially believed that the ANC had played no part in spreading the allegations against him, he had become convinced that certain ANC members were active in a campaign to defame him. These unidentified ANC members, he alleged, belonged to a 'cabal' – possibly working in concert with apartheid security police remnants – that took part in what Mokaba called 'a disinformation campaign aimed at controlling Africans.'[71]

In March 1997, in response to Mamasela's claim to know former spies within the ANC cabinet, TRC deputy chairperson Alex Boraine announced that the commission did not intend to launch a large-scale investigation to 'sniff out' alleged informers.[72] Boraine claimed: 'we have neither the resources, the time, nor the inclination to do this. We are determined not to allow this issue to become a political football.'[73] He qualified this by saying that the TRC would take action if, in the midst of a hearing, allegations were made that a specific informer had been involved in committing gross human rights violations: 'In these cases, we are bound to investigate the allegation just as we would any other allegation of direct involvement in a gross violation.'[74] As spy allegations generated a furore in the South African media, Boraine underscored 'the critical importance' of '[keeping] in mind that we are dealing with allegations which will need to be corroborated before any public announcement is made.'[75] Yet in a context where most apartheid security force archives had been destroyed, where mistrust and rumours were rife, and where many TRC witnesses feared for their lives, corroboration was a near-impossible standard to achieve. Boraine's insistence on it signalled the exclusion of apartheid spy recruitment from the TRC's purview altogether.

A few days prior to Boraine's statement, the TRC's amnesty committee had ruled that 'it was not appropriate for former security policeman Capt. Jacques Hechter to name' the informers he allegedly ran.[76] This resulted in a widespread outcry and prompted the ANC to send a high-level delegation to the TRC to pressure them to make the informers' names public. Boraine responded: 'We informed the ANC that we had already set in motion procedures to obtain the identities of alleged informers.'[77] The TRC wrote to Hechter's lawyers and those of four other former security policemen who had applied for amnesty, threatening to subpoena the policemen if they did not provide the informers' names.[78] Nonetheless, the names were never made public, and the TRC's leaders chose never to address the issue of intelligence recruitment. During his testimony to the TRC in 2000, when pressed to give the name of a single police informer whose identity would have been compromised had the Security Branch released Operation Vula operative Charles Ndaba instead of murdering him and Mbuso Shabalala, former Security Branch officer Casper van der Westhuizen refused: 'No, I can't do that, Chairperson, I cannot make known the names of the informers.'[79] Nonetheless, van der Westhuizen claimed to know 'about other informers who were also connected in that area, in the regions and positions [that] Ndaba was in.'

The Spy Intrigues Deepen

The TRC had set a precedent by refusing to investigate whether KwaZulu-Natal politician Sifiso Nkabinde had been an apartheid spy (see Chapter Nine).[80] The intrigue surrounding apartheid spies also played out in more local contexts: Dlamini describes meeting an ANC municipal councillor in a township outside Piet Retief who boasted of having brought MK insurgents across the nearby border fence with Mozambique as a member of the underground. Unbeknown to her, Dlamini had already interviewed a former askari who revealed that the municipal councillor herself had been on the apartheid security forces' payroll.[81]

In seeking to identify who was a spy, one key problem was that the various apartheid intelligence services had systematically destroyed their records. The TRC reported: 'the urge to destroy [archival records] gained momentum in the 1980s and widened into a coordinated endeavour, sanctioned by the Cabinet and designed to deny the new democratic government access to the secrets of the former state.'[82] In 1992, the state-appointed Goldstone Commission began investigating clandestine apartheid operations in earnest, prompting SADF MI and the Security Branch to begin destroying files; in 1993, the NIS alone destroyed approximately '44 tons of paper and microfilm records.'[83] The TRC's final report notes that in 'July 1993, the Security Secretariat advised government offices to destroy certain categories of classified records.' Their destruction ultimately bore 'a severe impact on South Africa's social memory. Vast amounts of official documentation, particularly around the inner workings of the state's security apparatus, have been obliterated.'[84] This wholesale destruction of files prevented a definitive list of apartheid spies from emerging.

Since the transition, lists of apartheid spies, and rumours of such lists, have repeatedly surfaced in South African politics. One such list of apartheid spies in the ANC was said to have disappeared during the TRC proceedings in 1997, shortly before it was to be made public.[85] Gilder asserts that he 'had heard rumours of such a list, but I have never seen the list,' casting doubt on its existence.[86] Mandela himself was understood to have 'received an extensive counterintelligence briefing by the ANC's security department prior to choosing his cabinet'; according to one report, 'sources refused to divulge what the president was told, but said "[Mandela] is a lawyer. You must be careful not to come to him with circumstantial evidence, he demands proof."'[87]

In October 1997 Enoch Zulu, a former APLA guerrilla, repeated on television his struggle-era accusation that in 1961 PAC cadre Stanley Mogoba, then imprisoned on Robben Island, had given evidence against Zulu while serving as a state witness at Zulu's trial.[88] As a result, Mogoba, an MP for the PAC, was grilled for six hours by the NIA while being vetted to serve on the parliamentary intelligence committee. This primed the country for a debate in parliament in

October 1997, when PAC MP Patricia de Lille shocked the nation by naming seven ANC members whom she claimed were on a list of 12 apartheid-era spies given to President Nelson Mandela and Deputy President Thabo Mbeki. The purported spies were minister of defence Joe Modise, minister of public enterprises Stella Sigcau, minister of minerals and energy Penuell Maduna, deputy minister of intelligence services Joe Nhlanhla, deputy minister of environmental affairs Peter Mokaba, Mpumalanga premier Mathews Phosa, and Eastern Cape premier Arnold Stofile. None of them commented on de Lille's allegation. The ANC denied the existence of such a list, and challenged de Lille, who had been speaking under parliamentary privilege, to repeat her allegations outside parliament.[89] Mandela declared that de Lille's accusations were 'mere politicking.'[90]

The controversy deepened when Bantu Holomisa, responding to Mandela's assertion that he had no list of spies, claimed that Mandela had 'on more than one occasion reprimanded executive members of the [ANC], saying he has their files and knows who among them are spies.'[91] Holomisa had belonged to the ANC's National Executive Committee, and alleged that in a January 1996 meeting in Cape Town, Mandela told a 'stunned' NEC that 'they should not forget that he now has access to their files. He reminded us that we shouldn't talk too much because he knows some of us were working for the [apartheid] state.' Holomisa said Mandela repeated the threat several times over the course of the meeting. 'He could not just have said that. It means Madiba knows.'[92] In a reply to the ANC's challenge to de Lille a week earlier, Holomisa declared: 'I challenge the ANC to deny that Mandela has never told them about his knowledge that some National Executive Committee members were apartheid agents.'[93]

Despite his denials of having ever seen a list of spies, in March 1997 Mandela reacted to allegations of apartheid spies in his government, declaring: 'We want to know who [the spies] are, not necessarily because we want to take action against them but because, if they had been informing on behalf of the apartheid regime, there is the likelihood that they are doing that today.'[94] At the very highest decision-making levels, then, the post-apartheid leadership was openly concerned about the enduring impact of apartheid intelligence recruitment on the new democracy. Note Mandela's concern that informing 'on behalf of the apartheid regime' might be ongoing, even after the transition. This reinforces perceptions of a cabal comprising elements within the security forces, along with private and external actors, still collaborating to destabilize the ANC.

In his address to the ANC's 50th National Conference on 16 December 1997, Mandela pointed out 'the former ruling establishment's' refusal to cooperate with the TRC, 'especially with regard to telling the truth about' the National Security Management System (NSMS), 'including the informers, agents and operatives who were such an important part of this system.' Mandela insisted that this group – whom he dubbed 'the counter-revolution' – now awaited the opportunity to 'activate this counter-insurgency machinery,' consisting of 'elements of the former ruling group' seeking 'to establish a network which would launch or intensify a campaign of destabilisation' to weaken the ANC and use 'crime to render the country ungovernable.' He claimed this 'counter-revolutionary network' was 'already active' in the government and other sectors and was 'capable of carrying out very disruptive actions' to weaken the democratic order. According to Mandela, since the transition the network's activities had included 'the encouragement and commission of crime'; 'the weakening and incapacitation of the state machinery, including the theft of public assets, arms and ammunition'; 'the hiding of sensitive and important information from legal organs of state'; and 'the building of alternative structures, including intelligence machineries as well as armed formations.' Mandela also mentioned evidence that these elements had 'established or are maintaining a variety of international contacts,' including 'neo-fascist groupings' and the regime's former allies.[95]

Instability in the Post-Transition Intelligence Services

The National Intelligence Agency (NIA) and South African Secret Service (SASS) came into being on 1 January 1995 after the formal termination of the NIS, with the SASS becoming South Africa's foreign intelligence arm. These agencies brought together 4,000 personnel from the NIS, the ANC's security department, the various Bantustan intelligence services, and a small contingent from the PAC's Pan-African Security Services (PASS), with 2,130 of these hailing from the

NIS, and 910 from the ANC.[96] O'Brien highlights a paradox of South Africa's post-transition intelligence services: the NIA's raison d'être as a domestic intelligence service in a newly democratic country was inherently tenuous, considering the apartheid regime's history of spying on its citizens. Meanwhile, the newly minted South African Police Service (SAPS), which would ordinarily hold the brief of domestic intelligence, was itself a direct carry-over from the apartheid-era SAP, and in the immediate post-transition security landscape the ANC government did not fully trust it.[97] The ANC had several reasons for wanting to retain apartheid-era structures and personnel from the NIS: the NIS, having played a key role in arranging talks with the ANC, held 'a far more enlightened attitude' than did personnel from SADF MI or the Security Branch, and possessed 'assets and capabilities that the ANC would not want to lose, including sources, information on both the white right-wing and extremists in parties such as the IFP, technological capabilities, and greater professional training than those in the ANC.' The NIA's first chief was former ANC head of security Sizakele Sigxashe, while NP intelligence veteran Mike Louw headed the SASS. By the mid-2000s the NIA would become increasingly drawn into the infighting within the ANC between sitting president Thabo Mbeki and his challenger, Jacob Zuma.[98]

In September 1995, the government established the Joint Standing Committee on Intelligence (JSCI), which established a civilian oversight mechanism for the intelligence services in a dramatic break from apartheid-era procedures. Nonetheless, the new Intelligence Services Control Act of 1994 governing the committee's activities allowed for the intelligence services to conceal from their political bosses 'information which could reveal the identity of a source, or any knowledge of intelligence or counter-intelligence methods carried out by any service if that information could also reveal a source.' This represented yet another way in which the existence and identity of spies were concealed in the post-transition era: the 'absolute protection of sources' was established precisely because 'both sides prior to the 1994 elections engaged in espionage activities against the other,' and thus it was 'assumed that each side had (and may have continued to maintain) sources in the other camp.' This was considered so sensitive that any revelation about spies and intelligence sources could seriously disrupt the negotiated compromise that had led to the creation of the new agencies and the oversight procedures governing them in South Africa's new democracy. The JCSI also ran into problems related to lingering counterinsurgency legacies, as several committee members 'were deeply implicated (to varying degrees) in allegations of links to "Third Force" and other destabilizing activities aimed at the new democratic process.'[99]

By 1995, the NIA employed 3,000 agents and had a budget of R600 million, yet it struggled to provide the Government of National Unity with intelligence on violence in KwaZulu-Natal and throughout the country. The NIA's classified reports were 'leaked on more than one occasion to Inkatha Freedom Party officials who have been linked to destabilization operations,' such as IFP senator Philip Powell, who 'tabled a leaked NIA report in Parliament' to prove the NIA was biased against Inkatha.[100] The NIA also employed several key Vlakplaas operatives until the late 1990s, including Dirk Coetzee, who was appointed as the NIA's director of counter-terrorism, as well as several who had served under Eugene de Kock at Vlakplaas.[101] In October 1995, De Klerk stated that had he wanted to, he could have preserved apartheid for another ten years with the security forces' backing, prompting one journalist to reflect, 'what is there to suggest that he could not use [the security forces] to advance his own party agenda now?'[102] In its 1995 assessment of the Government of National Unity, the ANC argued that the NP was still trying to destabilize the ANC, using 'networks built within and outside the country during the years of apartheid rule for the counter-insurgency "total strategy."' The assessment noted that during the struggle years, the security forces recruited 'many criminals…to work against the liberation movement,' and asked: 'What has happened to this network and to what extent are some of them involved in the current wave of violent crime as part of a deliberate strategy of destabilization?'[103] The report noted that if the NP and IFP were to 'claim any clout beyond their numbers in elected bodies, it should be expected that they will seek to mobilize' security and intelligence forces 'behind them,' asking: 'given all these factors, to what extent can we expect the loyalty of those forces?'[104] The document further noted the recent 'South African Police Union (SAPU) strike,[105] difficulties in obtaining information from intelligence structures, [and] mindset problems in the SANDF' as evidence that the post-transition security forces were not loyal to the ANC government. The report recommended forming 'highly professional, mobile, and loyal units that will defend the democratic order in the event of crises,'[106] units that could bypass official channels to expedite intelligence reports and avoid leaks.[107] However, this step would ultimately undermine confidence and deepen intrigue within the increasingly labyrinthine post-apartheid intelligence landscape.

To bypass leaky and cumbersome official channels, NIA agents in the field began sending intelligence reports directly to Mandela and Deputy President Thabo Mbeki. This practice in turn threatened to overload Mandela's staff with 'untested data and possible misinformation about the country's security situation.' ANC officials were particularly worried by the prospect that intelligence passing through the National Intelligence Coordinating Committee (NICOC) was being 'compromised' in the hands of the Department of Military Intelligence, which was 'still heavily staffed with agents schooled in the military's old dirty-tricks campaigns.'[108] Despite these setbacks, ANC MP Lindiwe Sisulu, who sat on committees overseeing the reform of the military, police and intelligence services, asserted that the process of integrating agents from the regime, ANC, PAC, and Bantustan services in the NIA 'has worked better than similar processes in the police and military.'[109]

A further complication was that the Freedom Front and IFP, both of which had been linked to 'clandestine efforts at derailing South Africa's transition to democracy,' were 'represented on the committee' and had 'access to sensitive security reports.'[110] It was particularly troubling that deputy safety and security minister Joe Matthews served as the IFP representative on the parliamentary oversight committee, even though he, along with Powell, was linked to Inkatha's efforts to build its own clandestine intelligence structure.[111] In early 1996, it emerged that the NIA and SAPS were engaged in a rivalry in which 'each agency was spying on not only [the] other but the various political parties as well.'[112]

'Communication Operations' and the McBride Affair

In the first decade after the transition, reports proliferated about secret networks of apartheid political, military and intelligence personnel lurking in the shadows, waiting patiently for an opportunity to destabilize or overthrow the ANC government.[113] The intelligence reports during the transition that repeatedly warned of an extremist ANC faction splintering off and attempting to disrupt negotiations were now replaced by rumours of well-connected white-supremacist networks aiming to unseat the ANC government. These rumours themselves had a destabilizing effect, even as they repeatedly proved to have no basis in fact. They could tend towards the fantastic: for example, in 1995 South African and British journalists published *The Mini-Nuke Conspiracy: Mandela's Nuclear Nightmare*, alleging that the regime had not dismantled all of its nuclear warheads before the transition; that some 'low-yield' warheads might have fallen into right-wing extremists' hands; and that a secret police unit still possessed one warhead.[114] In 1997, Mandela convened the intelligence service chiefs at his residence and ordered them to investigate a report he had received concerning an Afrikaner organization, the Verligte Aksie Groep (VAG, or 'Enlightened Action Group'), which had stolen state funds and taken them abroad during the transition years, and which now aimed to use these funds to destabilize the government by financing organized crime in South Africa, along with other operations. The investigation yielded little new information about the VAG, which eventually proved to be spurious.[115]

This threat and others were traced to 'information peddlers,' most of whom had served with the former apartheid security services and then founded their own private security and intelligence companies as the transition unfolded. Whereas the new security and intelligence services struggled to integrate former enemies into their ranks and make themselves answerable to a democratic government, these new security companies faced few such constraints. They attracted highly trained and experienced personnel and stayed very well connected to agents from the apartheid-era services who remained in the new security agencies, as well as in 'other government departments, the private sector, and the telecommunications service providers.'[116] Gilder asserts that the continuous rumours of plots to undermine or overthrow the ANC government 'by 1999, by 2004, by 2009' originated from within these shadowy formations, and argues that 'conspirators may have been within [the new security forces]' in the form of 'former apartheid agents still in the closet and working with our old enemies and their old handlers to foment just such a conspiracy.'[117] Mandela himself had claimed in a speech he gave to the NIA and South African Secret Service that 'there were elements in South Africa's spy services working alongside "sinister forces" to undermine the country's democracy,' accusing the services of incompetence and collusion with the 'Third Force.'[118]

These post-transition rumours of right-wing plots to overthrow the ANC government were supplemented in February 1998 by rumours of a left-wing plot with a similar objective, in the form of a report concocted by SANDF's Intelligence Division and personally delivered by SANDF chief of staff Gen. Georg Meiring to Mandela. The report's contents came to light on 19 March, and became known as the 'McBride Affair' as its allegations were linked to the arrest of ANC operative and MK veteran Robert McBride. McBride was serving as director of Asian affairs in the South African Department of Foreign Affairs and also in the ANC's security department when he was arrested on 10 March in Mozambique for illegally possessing a firearm. At the time, McBride was in Mozambique investigating arms-smuggling networks run by gangs allegedly comprising 'disgruntled ex-MK soldiers' who were hijacking cash-in-transit vans in South Africa.[119] According to Mozambican police, McBride was 'caught "red-handed" following a "sting" operation by their security services,' in which the authorities 'found an arms cache containing AK-47 assault rifles, machine guns and grenade launchers at Polana Canico refugee camp' in Maputo.[120] As the scandal unfolded, it emerged that McBride was secretly working for the NIA, tasked with identifying the mafia bosses behind the heists, and was also the Department of Foreign Affairs representative on the National Intelligence Coordinating Committee (NICOC). On 16 March, SANDF officers approached SAPS assistant commissioner 'Suiker' Britz with allegations that McBride was 'involved in an "anti-government plot"'; the following day, the SANDF Intelligence Division gave Britz documents supporting these allegations. Britz then repeated SANDF intelligence claims that McBride had been procuring weapons for a secret organization within the ANC plotting to overthrow Mandela's government. However, by 20 March, key ANC figures were speculating that McBride had been framed by ex-apartheid elements in the security forces who wanted to undermine the ANC and avenge McBride's role in MK operations during the 1980s, notably the deadly 1986 Magoo's Bar bombing in Durban. Moreover, these ANC figures alleged that McBride was on the verge of exposing the ties of ex-apartheid personnel to organized crime networks at the time of his arrest.[121]

McBride had been accompanied by Vusi Mbatha, who was arrested while purchasing weapons from a Mozambican arms dealer but not charged; it turned out that Mbatha 'had a long history of working with' SADF MI 'as well as being a police informer.' On 26 March, Britz proclaimed that McBride was 'definitely involved in smuggling guns,' leading to IFP claims that the cash-in-transit hijackers were actually stealing money to line ANC coffers.[122] It then emerged that one of the SAPS officers sent to assist the Mozambican police in their investigation, Frans Labuschagne, had been a Third Force operative during the transition era[123] and was also involved in the July 1987 assassination of Cassius Maake in Swaziland; Maake was the highest-ranking MK operative killed by the regime during the struggle years.

According to the SANDF report, the renegade faction was called FAPLA, the 'Front African People's Liberation Army'[124] – and was planning to murder judges and 'occupy Parliament, broadcasting stations and key government institutions,' and though the alleged list of conspirators reached 130, the security forces never provided the Joint Standing Committee on Intelligence with their names, unlike in cases where ANC members were accused of being apartheid informants.[125] McBride was alleged to be in charge of weapons procurement for FAPLA, which had ostensibly amassed a cache of automatic rifles, grenades, and pistols of Warsaw Pact origin under the auspices of Winnie Madikizela-Mandela, with Siphiwe Nyanda, SANDF Gen. Lambert Moloi and Bantu Holomisa being among the other key coup plotters. Even when it became clear that McBride had become entangled in a broader disinformation plot, the ANC government did not rush to assist or exonerate him, and Deputy President Thabo Mbeki appeared unaware that McBride had in fact worked as an agent and informant for both the NIA and South African Secret Service, a claim borne out by subsequent investigations.[126] McBride was still imprisoned in Mozambique in August 1998 when new details emerged highlighting the complicity of senior Mozambican government and security officials in smuggling arms to South Africa; it appeared that McBride was being detained precisely because he threatened to expose these officials' role. Furthermore, money Mbatha paid to arms dealer Alex Mamba went to the chief of Mozambique's Police Intelligence Services, who had ties to old-guard personnel in the SAPS. O'Brien notes: 'The fact that members of the Mozambican security forces' were still 'acting in collusion with members of South Africa's security forces appears to indicate that old covert networks established by the apartheid security forces continue to be used in a variety of forms,' including weapons smuggling, which ex-apartheid personnel had originally used to sustain and fund covert operations and which had now become central to their 'transition from security guarantors of the state to the organized crime operators that many of them became.' Meanwhile, a joint South African–Mozambican police task force launched an operation to seize and destroy over sixty arms caches 'identified and mapped' throughout Mozambique, apparently based on the intelligence McBride had gathered.[127]

As the McBride controversy widened, the details of the previous month's SANDF Military Intelligence report delivered by Gen. Meiring to Mandela were leaked to the media. The report alleged that a radical faction within the ANC, which included Winnie Mandela, Bantu Holomisa, Ronnie Kasrils, and various former MK members in the new military, including SANDF deputy chief Siphiwe Nyanda, was planning to assassinate Mandela and overthrow his government ahead of the 1999 elections. The report implicated 'more than 100 public figures, military personnel and international figures' in the plot.[128] Mandela responded by appointing a commission of inquiry, which found the report to be 'utterly fantastic.' A *Mail & Guardian* editorial noted: 'Military intelligence, left largely unscathed by the activities of the [TRC], is clearly little more than a home for unreconstructed reactionaries and conspirators from the *ancien régime*,' while the NIA – a 'supposedly "elite" body' – was 'in fact nothing more than the proverbial nest of vipers.'[129] The parallels with SADF MI's transition-era psychological warfare operations, such as Operation Sunrise, were unmistakable. Moreover, Meiring had circumvented established channels by handing the report to Mandela directly instead

of going through NICOC and the cabinet Committee on Security and
Intelligence, raising questions about Meiring's own role. Furthermore,
the report was based on information supplied by a single source:
former SADF MI operative Mbatha. The subsequent inquiry revealed
that Mbatha had been in contact with several senior old-guard police
officers, including Labuschagne, and that the report was overseen
by Hendrik Christoffel Nel, 'a former [CCB and DCC] officer' who
became head of the SANDF's counter-intelligence unit.[130] As a result,
Meiring, who in January 1997 had been implicated by the TRC in the
apartheid regime's dirty tricks campaign against the ANC, was forced
to resign in May 1998, along with several other apartheid hold-overs
serving in the SANDF. Nyanda became the SANDF's first chief of staff
from the ranks of MK, and the plot convinced the ANC to monitor
and control the security service transformation even more closely,
convening the Moerane Commission to oversee the transformation of
Defence Intelligence.[131]

On the heels of the McBride Affair came a similar scandal in
which old-guard policemen, who had been appointed to replace the
discredited 'Suiker' Britz by police national commissioner George
Fivaz, released a report in June 1998 alleging that MK and APLA
veterans had formed a militant organization called Mkapla. This radical
group, the report claimed, was responsible for stealing weaponry
from SANDF bases in a series of thefts and was planning to disrupt
the 1999 national elections. But there was no such group as Mkapla,
and the policemen who wrote this report were found to have got all
their information from one source: former SADF MI operative Vusi
Mbatha.[132] ANC officials described this incident as another 'right-wing
plot to destabilize the country through disinformation,' and a source
inside the Defence Ministry stated: 'They want to suggest that MK
and APLA cannot be trusted, or entrusted with the responsibility of
defending the country, so that when their conspiracy starts swinging
into action, people should blame APLA and MK.'[133]

In late 2001, a remarkable document began circulating in South
African political and intelligence circles, titled 'Report to the
Honourable Patricia de Lille of the Independent Democrats,' and
signed by the 'Concerned Patriotic Intelligence Community Loyal to
the Constitution of the Republic of South Africa.' The report outlined

a conspiracy to unseat Thabo Mbeki as state president and replace him with a cabal, led by Jacob Zuma, which included Mac Maharaj, Moe Shaik, Jackie Selebi and others. The cabal's ostensible aim was to destabilize South Africa in order to increase its members' opportunities for power and profit, working in conjunction with former apartheid figures as well as foreign multinationals and intelligence services.[134] The report further alleged that in 1985, at the start of MK's Operation Vula, Moe Shaik had been captured and 'turned' by the NIS, thus enabling the NIS to thoroughly infiltrate the ANC's intelligence services and to manipulate Operation Vula from afar, capturing MK agents and ensuring that the ANC and MK would negotiate with the regime from a position of weakness. The report claimed that in 1994, upon being tasked with integrating ANC intelligence directorate personnel into the post-transition NIA, Shaik 'made sure that the NIS [double] agents in Vula as well as the NIS operatives were put in control of the new intelligence services of the democratic South Africa.'[135] It further alleged that the NIS killed Charles Ndaba and Mbuso Shabalala to protect Shaik's identity as a double agent. The decision to submit the report to de Lille was noteworthy, as she had been the first politician in the democratic era to raise the issue of apartheid spies in the new government.

The report was also striking because it corroborated an earlier accusation levelled at Mac Maharaj and the ANC leadership, alleging that they had not disclosed everything they knew about Shabalala's and Ndaba's deaths. In 1997, details of the two MK cadres' deaths had surfaced during evidence given to the TRC by six former security policemen who testified about their role in killing 12 people in KwaZulu-Natal. This prompted Mbuso Shabalala's brother Vuso to accuse transport minister Mac Maharaj of having failed to conduct a satisfactory investigation into their deaths. Vuso Shabalala claimed that Maharaj and Moe Shaik had 'been part of efforts to suppress the truth,' charging that 'the truth about the fate of Mbuso would have been established long ago if the relevant ANC leaders and commanders of Operation Vula had lent their weight to the investigations.'[136] Vuso Shabalala deplored the fact that the six security policemen would in all likelihood receive amnesty for testifying, even though they 'have not told everything they know. They have said very little.' Several years later, Bheki Jacobs would allege that Shaik had played a role in betraying the two cadres to the apartheid security forces.[137] In this context of rampant spying accusations, the TRC further muddied the waters of the post-transition era through its resolute refusal to address the issue of who had been spies.

Spy controversies and rumours would persist in South African politics, with 'continuing rumours and suspicions swirling around' Thabo Mbeki's presidency, including suspicions of coup attempts, and 'growing tensions within the post-apartheid security apparatus and political leadership.' In response Mbeki appointed the Hefer Commission, which would ultimately lead to his resignation and the quashing of corruption charges against Jacob Zuma, 'clearing the way for him to become President.'[138] Beginning in 1997, the ANC government had sought to deploy its intelligence services in the fight against organized crime, aiming to develop a comprehensive strategy. This resulted in the formation of the Organized Crime Task Force, which brought together the heads of the various security forces and the prosecuting authorities, and ultimately the launch in September 1999 of the Scorpions crime-fighting unit, formally known as the Directorate of Special Operations (DSO). The Scorpions operated separately from the police and reported directly to the national public prosecutor. On several occasions, they halted government activity as they deployed from helicopters to raid administrative buildings and seize files and hard drives as evidence of government corruption.[139] The unit conducted several high-level investigations into ministers charged with corruption, including Zuma himself, who disbanded the Scorpions shortly after Thabo Mbeki's removal from the presidency. Some observers accused Zuma of having weakened the state's ability to fight crime for the sake of partisan politics.[140] Yet many of the Scorpions' investigators and prosecutors had originally worked for the apartheid regime, and within the ANC the Scorpions were regarded as an unwieldy force lacking oversight that sometimes appeared to be pursuing its own agenda. Although they answered to National Prosecuting Authority chief and ANC veteran Vusi Pikoli, the Scorpions frequently leaked 'as yet unproved corruption allegations' against prominent and respected leading cadres of the struggle against apartheid.[141] The Scorpions also removed dockets from police forces gathering evidence against IFP warlords in KwaZulu-Natal, thwarting efforts to prosecute them[142] (see Chapter Nine). As the rift grew between President Thabo Mbeki and his challenger Jacob Zuma during 2005, many ANC members 'could not shake the feeling that there were subterranean forces who, at the very least, sought to feed the divisions between the two most senior leaders of party and government.'[143]

These suspicions led the Mbeki government to appoint the Khampepe Commission of Inquiry into the Scorpions. Judge Khampepe presented her findings to Mbeki on 3 February 2006, in which she criticized the Scorpions for leaking information about ongoing investigations to the media, and found that the Scorpions were conducting illegal surveillance operations.[144] Soon afterwards, the Scorpions, in a move that echoed apartheid psychological operations, delivered a report on an alleged conspiracy by key ANC members, such as Saki Macozoma, Bulelani Ngcuka, Pumzile Ngcuka, Joel Netshitenzhe, Frank Chikane and others, to discredit Zuma, carried out through email correspondence and chat-rooms. Although the government's inspector-general of intelligence found the messages to have been fabricated, many ANC members remained convinced of their authenticity. This occurred against the backdrop of numerous attempts by former apartheid security force personnel in the post-transition era 'to feed fabricated intelligence into the security services, government, and the media.'[145] In 2006, after NIA chief Billy Masetlha was fired for criminal activities, minister of intelligence Ronnie Kasrils convened the Ministerial Review Commission on Intelligence under Joe Matthews. The Matthews Commission found that the NIA had become 'politicized' and had developed a 'very troubling' and 'inappropriate' tendency to covertly monitor and report on developments within government departments and political parties.[146]

Perhaps the greatest episode of post-transition spy intrigue arose from the so-called Browse Mole Report. This began on 12 July 2006, when Scorpions investigators submitted to their head Leonard McCarthy and national director of public prosecutions Vusi Pikoli an intelligence report named *The Special Browse Mole Consolidated Report*; neither the report's contents nor any statements accompanying its release explained this bizarre title. The report claimed to have uncovered a plot by Jacob Zuma to unseat President Thabo Mbeki. In this, the report alleged, Zuma was backed by a group of former MK guerrillas, and had received financial support from Libyan strongman Muammar Gaddafi, Angolan president Eduardo dos Santos, and a variety of other domestic and external backers. The report further alleged that Zuma's supporters were planning a coup against Mbeki should Zuma be convicted on the corruption charges he was then facing.[147]

On 7 May 2007 a copy of the report was anonymously faxed to the general secretary of COSATU, prompting a complaint by the SACP, which triggered an investigation in June 2007 by the parliamentary Joint Standing Committee on Intelligence (JSCI). The plot thickened when the NIA investigated the report on the basis of 'spy tapes' it had gathered, further widening the distrust between South Africa's various security agencies. In July 2007, the National Security Council's task force on the Browse Mole Report gave a briefing to the JSCI and the media on their findings thus far. According to this investigation, the report bore the hallmarks of 'information peddling,' which was becoming a key feature of post-transition politics; it found that the Scorpions had been duped into taking the information of the 'peddlers' at face value; that the 'peddlers' disseminated their information through 'facilitators,' and may have had direct access to key figures within the ANC; that the report, having initially been ignored by the state's law enforcement agencies, was then leaked to ensure it had the greatest possible impact on South African politics; that the 'peddlers' sought to create divisions within the ANC; and, lastly, that 'these pedlars have links to foreign governments including foreign intelligence services.'[148]

As an ever-greater volume of information has been leaked into the post-transition political realm regarding conspiracies within South African politics and intelligence agencies, its impact has been to erode the unity of the ruling ANC and the quality of South African democracy. These conspiracy allegations, however outlandish, have fed doubts and mistrust within the state, as well as mistrust of the government within society. They have spurred the ever-greater involvement of the intelligence and security agencies in the political realm, compromising the attempts of post-apartheid legislators to establish clear democratic controls and restrictions on the security forces' power. Meanwhile, the sources of these allegations have remained largely untraceable, causing the ANC government to appear paranoid and eager to abuse its power as it has ordered repeated investigations and attempted to broaden its powers to impose secrecy.

The tension that has characterized the post-apartheid state's relationship with its security forces demonstrates the persistence of counterinsurgency legacies. In 2005, ANC veteran Saki Macozoma complained to intelligence minister (and former MK intelligence chief) Ronnie Kasrils about being under NIA surveillance. In response, Kasrils ordered an investigation, whose mandate he then widened to include the growing rift between the Mbeki and Zuma factions, and the surge in popular protest against the government that year regarding the absence of service delivery.[149] In ordering the investigation, Kasrils blamed these political disruptions on '*agents provocateurs*, whom he sought to fish out.'[150] As in the arms deal scandal, state elites deflected corruption charges with allegations that their accusers had been apartheid spies. To this day, allegations of secret cliques nested within South African state institutions persist. Even as they undermine public trust in the state, such allegations echo the transition-era intrigue surrounding apartheid intelligence recruitment within ANC ranks. Hence during the trial of former national police commissioner Jackie Selebi, former director of police intelligence Mulangi Mphego 'dropped a bombshell...alleging that Selebi's prosecutor is part of a "judicial mafia" trying to subvert the state.' Mphego claimed that 'intelligence revealed the involvement of no less than 45 people and seven private entities,' including the prosecutor and lead investigator in Selebi's case.[151] Gumede noted the danger of the 'collapse of proper boundaries between party and State,' including the National Prosecuting Authority and 'State intelligence agencies.'[152]

Although blaming spies for triggering popular uprisings against the state, or for levelling charges that threaten elite interests, is a trusted tactic of authoritarian regimes – indeed, the apartheid regime itself routinely blamed black protest on communist or Soviet influence – it is far less common for democracies to resort to this tactic. In this sense, Kasrils's casting of blame on saboteurs whom he vowed to root out must be understood as a direct legacy of Third Force destabilization, when anonymous agents executed the orders of hidden forces, domestic or external, located in the state, quasi-state or private realms. Whether

ANC officials like Kasrils actually believed such sinister forces were at work, or whether they were resurrecting struggle-era rhetoric to distract public attention from their own shortcomings, their statements reflect the enduring suspicion and mistrust that form the apartheid counterinsurgency's toxic legacy.

This same perspective can also be found from below, as it were. Addressing widespread popular suspicions that ANC members who profited from the transition were 'sellouts,' Somadoda Fikeni declared: 'It's very easy to see an informer in every other person.'[153] Yet such suspicions have continued to shape popular perceptions and participation in South African politics. Instances of violence and disorder within society have given rise to the belief that hidden forces were fomenting unrest to prevent progress. For example, a feud at secondary schools in KwaThema township, allegedly between members of the Congress of South African Students and the Pan Africanist Students' Organization, killed several students between 1993 and 1996, prompting police to begin patrolling outside school buildings. The bloodshed 'puzzled many people' in the local community because it endured for years but lacked an obvious cause; one teacher involved in attempts to resolve the violence noted: 'one cannot rule out the involvement of a Third Force. Who is supplying these children with bullets, as they didn't run out of bullets?'[154] In his analysis of popular resistance to the ANC's privatization of service delivery, Buur notes the 'recycling' of 'past struggle narratives' about the ANC's clandestine enemies to discredit the ANC government's critics, even though 'it is no longer possible to identify with the same certainty the evil or hidden forces.'[155] This overlooks the persistent, unresolved questions about Third Force activity that continue to inform popular dissatisfaction with the pace and scope of post-transition development. It is crucial to understand that, rightly or wrongly, many South Africans believe Third Force destabilization is ongoing; they are not simply resorting to old tropes to make sense of new problems. In this way, counterinsurgency legacies remain entrenched within South Africa's state and society. Unmoored and disembodied from its original historical context, counterinsurgency has remained a self-replicating force that generates violence and undermines South African democracy.

Security–Corruption Nexus: The Arms Deal

The twin imperatives of post-conflict security and development have given rise to a burgeoning literature on the 'security–development nexus.'[156] But the massive corruption that endures in post-conflict settings, particularly within South African security force channels,[157] suggests the emergence of a 'security–corruption nexus' that threatens to overshadow post-conflict development. The notorious arms deal scandal, in which ANC elites received fabulous kickbacks from purchasing an array of exorbitant new weapons systems, epitomizes how post-transition elites have hitched themselves to the military-industrial complex's payoffs. The arms deal thus represents one of apartheid counterinsurgency's enduring legacies, as the security forces, no longer engaged in actual combat, became a prime venue for corruption. ANC elites used these networks embedded within the state to profit through the same channels that had developed during apartheid.[158]

During the high apartheid era, the Muldergate affair exposed the nexus between apartheid's counterinsurgency and military-industrial complexes, when politicians and businessmen became embroiled in a scandal centring around clandestine operations to shape news coverage of South Africa by buying media outlets and paying off journalists. In the 1980s the increasing militarization of the apartheid bureaucracy was accompanied by the militarization of South Africa's economy as it undertook to develop an indigenous arms manufacturing and export sector. This created an important post-transition legacy linking top-level corruption to the military-industrial complex. Shortly after the transition, Kynoch described worrying tendencies in the 'new' South African defence establishment: 'it adheres rigidly to political realism, supports the expansion of a massive defence industry and international arms trade, and manages to retain a budget grossly out of proportion with the legitimate security needs of the country.'[159] The purchase of these new weapons systems reflected elites' subservience to the military-industrial complex and its profits.

Well prior to the 1994 transition, European powers were courting the ANC about arms purchases – and the ANC was listening. In October 1991, the ANC sent a delegation to India to arrange for the training of MK cadres in preparation for their integration into a conventional army.[160] Curiously, the trip was arranged by Alain Guenon, a Frenchman with extensive ties to SADF MI who had 'made several propaganda films for the SADF.' Guenon had also arranged the visit of an ANC delegation to Paris in April 1991,

> where the ANC met with French arms manufacturers, senior military officials and the minister of industries, Roger Fouroux, to discuss French future arms sales to South Africa and the training of ANC military cadres. Acting as a consultant with the French military industrial company SAGEM, Guenon set up the visit to discuss the possibilities of re-establishing French military links with a post-apartheid South Africa.

ANC representatives Tokyo Sexwale and Bantu Holomisa told journalist Gavin Evans that they were untroubled by Guenon's background.[161]

The arms deal scandal tainted many post-transition politicians, who reaped kickbacks from the purchase of state-of-the-art weapons systems, including Swedish warplanes, British attack jets, helicopters, and naval frigates, corvettes, and submarines from a French-German-Italian consortium, bought despite the nonexistence of external military threats to South Africa. With the lifting of anti-apartheid sanctions, the South African military acquired cutting-edge weaponry; the indigenous arms industry also profited tremendously.[162] Ironically, British Aerospace, manufacturer of the Hawk jet, paid huge kickbacks to defence minister Joe Modise in the form of a donation to a foundation ostensibly set up to benefit destitute MK veterans, from which the veterans received not a cent.[163] Before his death, Joe Modise also served on the board of directors of BKS, 'an Afrikaner civil engineering company' which had enjoyed close ties to the apartheid regime.[164]

One South African civil servant emphasized that the 'eroding state moral authority has real consequences on the state's ability to create safety.'[165] A former MK guerrilla reinforced this comment, insisting that the 'demonstration effect' of the arms deal had led to an increase in urban violence and crime post-apartheid:

> When the arms deal came, people saw that, hey man, these people who we believe are our leaders, they are corrupt, they are thieves themselves, they are dishonest, because our country is not in a war threat, so why

buy arms with so much money, with so much billions when poverty is the main thing that needs to be addressed. And then the crime wave took over, and it became very much uncontrollable.[166]

Inevitably, from the intrigue surrounding the arms deal surfaced the skeletons of apartheid counterinsurgency's most sensitive legacy: the question of which ANC members had spied for the regime. When faced in 2003 with accusations of corruption in the arms deal scandal, South African deputy president Jacob Zuma and his ally Schabir Shaik replied by accusing national director of public prosecutions Bulelani Ngcuka of being an apartheid spy, claiming that they possessed files to prove it, and prompting President Mbeki to appoint the Hefer Commission to investigate the charge; it later proved to be baseless. Ngcuka had investigated Zuma on corruption charges in 2003, but had ultimately decided there was not enough evidence to prosecute him; he then announced that although the National Prosecuting Authority believed Zuma to be corrupt, they lacked the evidence to prove it. The ANC investigation into Ngcuka's background as an apartheid spy, following accusations by Moe Shaik and Mac Maharaj, must be understood in this context.

After facing false accusations of corruption in February 2003 and after being questioned by the Scorpions, Mac Maharaj became convinced Ngcuka was keeping files on people in South Africa's leadership circles, as FBI chief J Edgar Hoover had done in the US.[167] Maharaj also saw Ngcuka's hand in a case in which Philip Powell, about to be arrested for gun-running and murder, 'was allowed to go to the UK under an arrangement never made public.'[168] In September 2003, Moe Shaik stepped forward to disclose that MK had opened a file on Ngcuka in 1988 and by 1989 had concluded that he was 'probably a spy,' codenamed Agent RS 452. Later that same month, Shaik retracted this claim, saying that his post-1994 investigations revealed RS 452 to have been 'a white person from the Eastern Cape.' At the same time, the former Eastern Cape lawyer Vanessa Brereton, now living in London, came forward and admitted to having spied for the regime under the code name RS 452.[169] This did not put to rest suspicions that Ngcuka may have spied for the regime in some capacity.[170] The 'quarrel' arising between Ngcuka and Jacob Zuma and the concomitant spy allegations raised the spectre 'of real patriots being hunted down as enemy agents while real enemy agents urged on the hunt.'[171]

External Destabilization

The colonial powers' intelligence agencies and counterinsurgency forces mirrored the apartheid state's role in seeking to shape African countries' trajectories both during and after their struggles for independence. In Kenya, the British colonial administration fought a protracted war with the Mau Mau insurgency, which ultimately culminated in the British defeating the rebels and appointing Jomo Kenyatta as leader. Just as later with the ANC, Kenyatta's Kenyan African National Union (KANU) had been riven by an elite–mass split, and Kenyatta was known to fear and distrust the radicalism of his own movement's armed wing.[172] In Zimbabwe, Western countries had covertly provided Ian Smith's racist Rhodesian regime with extensive support. For example, in autumn 1978 two US generals visited Rhodesia and met with Smith and key Rhodesian army generals. The exact purpose of their visit was unclear, but they probably advised the Rhodesian military, and encouraged the Rhodesians – whom one general compared to 'early American pioneers' – by telling them to 'hold out against the odds until the cavalry comes.'[173] Maj. Gen. William P Yarborough, founder of the US Green Berets special forces, visited Rhodesia six times during the 1970s. Horne points out that 'many on both sides of the Atlantic' hoped that a win for Ronald Reagan in the 1980 US presidential race could turn the superpower's backing in Rhodesia's favour, much as it would ultimately do for apartheid South Africa. In the event, the British foreign intelligence service MI6 played an integral role in brokering the 1979–80 Lancaster House negotiations, which saw Robert Mugabe's ZANU take power.

Western intelligence services were similarly waiting in the wings during the final days of apartheid, evaluating how best to maximize their influence in the post-transition era while drawing ANC leaders' attention. Hence in 1988 ANC stalwart Aziz Pahad told journalist Evelyn Groenink, 'this is where we have tea with MI6,' meaning that it was time for the ANC to begin cultivating ties with Western intelligence agencies (see Chapter Seven). The true extent of the collusion of

NATO countries' security establishments with the apartheid regime's covert operations remains unknown, but available evidence suggests it was quite extensive. In his 1995 testimony on apartheid death squad activities, SAP Col. Putter claimed that assassination was an integral 'strategic communications' method used by the British, who were 'the experts in the field.'[174] During the Cold War, prominent international crime bosses had business contacts with both South African and Western intelligence agencies; it is believed that some of these organized crime rings remained active in post-transition South Africa while also maintaining their ties with Western intelligence services.[175] Tim Jenkin recalls that when he worked from London for the ANC, his team 'had no doubt that the British secret services were also keeping an eye on us and there was no reason for us to believe that they were not working hand in glove with the apartheid authorities, whom their leader, Margaret Thatcher, so dearly loved.' British elements were also complicit in spreading apartheid disinformation: in 1990 'a rightwing MP' claimed in the British parliament that Jenkin 'was working with the Irish Republican Army to make bombs' to target civilians, a claim which 'later turned out to be a coverup for the fact that the South African regime was supplying weapons to Ulster extremists.'[176]

After the transition began, the United States sought to further strengthen its influence in the region by stepping up 'its so-called development assistance to South African blacks' through a variety of funds 'for "strengthening democratic institutions"' with known links to the CIA.[177] France, which has maintained extensive economic and political interests throughout Africa since the colonial era, also had strong intelligence ties to the apartheid regime, stemming from the aftermath of Congolese independence, when South African and French mercenaries fought side by side to defend the breakaway Katanga republic. Before his death at the hands of unknown assassins, SADF MI agent Dirk Stoffberg said he had organized the 1988 killing of ANC representative Dulcie September in Paris, a crime which has remained unsolved (see Chapter Nine). Stoffberg claimed to have hired the assassins but would not reveal who had ordered the hit; he said the assassins themselves were two former French Legionnaires and that these same men were involved in a failed assassination attempt on Godfrey Motsepe, the ANC representative in Brussels.[178] These details corroborate the theory that the French intelligence services played a role in September's assassination because she was about to expose the full scope of French arms sales to the apartheid regime, including nuclear technology.[179] Shortly after September was killed, the French newspaper *Le Monde* cited French and Belgian intelligence sources claiming that Stoffberg commanded a special South African death squad in Europe, and had received assistance from Jean-Dominique Taousson, a far-right-wing Frenchman and a former OAS member who worked at the South African embassy in Paris.[180] This squad could have been a section of the CCB, whose mandate covered overseas operations, or it could have been a unit unto itself. One investigation into the 1989 assassination of SWAPO sympathizer Anton Lubowski in Windhoek also points to involvement by the French intelligence services, in conjunction with organized crime elements and SADF MI.[181]

After the onset of negotiations, and prior to the arms deal, SADF MI was busy trying to obtain advanced weapons systems, including everything from ballistic missile detection software to jet engines, over-the-horizon radar, and air-to-air and surface-to-air missile systems.[182] And, despite the formal US embargo on selling arms to the apartheid regime, the Reagan Administration until 1988, and afterward the CIA, imaginatively sought to bypass these constraints. In 1995 Robert Clyde Ivy, who was being tried in a US court for his role in smuggling missile guidance technology to the apartheid regime, argued that 'his defiance of export controls was done with the connivance' of the CIA. In his affidavit to US prosecutors, Ivy stated: 'during the six years of my meetings and discussions with the CIA, none of the agents suggested that any of our exports or shipments were illegal' (though they contravened President Jimmy Carter's 1977 ban on 'intelligence and material cooperation' with the apartheid regime), and the CIA 'encouraged the continuation of our relationship and contacts with South Africa.' The South African state arms company Armscor paid Ivy's legal costs, retaining the 'high-powered' US lawyer Brendan Sullivan, who had been counsel to US Lt Col. Oliver North during the Iran-Contra affair. Armscor also attempted to block seven South Africans from testifying in the USA during an inquiry into apartheid-era arms smuggling and fraud because, as one of the seven put it: 'Armscor is terrified that new people and companies will be named if we give evidence. That would drag in top politicians and executives from companies right across the country.'[183]

In September 1995, the IFP drew up a draft constitution that would give KwaZulu-Natal, including its own security forces, semi-autonomous status – an agenda that the newly established Constitutional Court 'rejected out of hand,' declaring that it 'appeared "intended to legitimize armed secession."'[184] The ANC then received intelligence that the IFP was using aid money from Germany's Konrad Adenauer Foundation, earmarked for development projects, to expand its paramilitary and intelligence capacities.[185] The taxpayer-funded German foundation had 'sunk tens of millions of Rand into Inkatha' since the 1980s. South African intelligence obtained information about two German citizens in KwaZulu-Natal helping the IFP rebuild an intelligence arm to replace its apartheid-era Bureau of Security and Intelligence (BSI), which had operated alongside the now-disbanded KwaZulu Police. The new intelligence unit was to feature several key figures with deep ties to apartheid-era violence, such as Philip Powell and BSI veteran Stan Armstrong, who was identified by the Harms Commission as the link between the IFP's political leadership and its clandestine militant training programme.[186]

When the TRC called on top apartheid military personnel to testify, its proceedings threatened to unmask the CIA's 'silent partnership' with the apartheid regime, which journalist Jeff Stein predicted could 'turn out to be every bit as embarrassing as disclosure of its activities in Haiti and Guatemala.'[187] The TRC ultimately shed little light on the CIA's role in South Africa, but this in no way suggests that its role was minimal. Under the 1987 Intelligence Authorization Act, the US Congress had forced the Reagan administration to limit all foreign covert actions, explicitly including those with South Africa, but these continued in secret all the same.[188] In 1985, the CIA dispatched veteran operative Millard Shirley to South Africa to train agents in techniques, including the use of prussic acid as an untraceable assassination tool. Shirley also advised Telkom, the government postal and communications agency (where deep-cover CCB agents were known to be embedded), in such techniques. In addition, the CIA trained Telkom workers in monitoring communications and placing listening devices, 'some of which it [was] still uncovering' after the transition. Telkom manager Peter Ross called this programme 'very sinister,' and suspected that in addition to assisting the regime, the CIA wanted to place its own agents to ensure lasting influence amid South Africa's uncertain political future.[189] According to former SAP officer Gerard Ludi, Shirley 'was the top CIA official in South Africa for many years'[190] before he was killed in a car crash in Swaziland. Meanwhile, Garth Barratt, a former Rhodesian SAS commander working for South Africa's electricity utility Eskom, had given lectures in the USA on behalf of the pro-RENAMO lobby organized by CIA veteran Ray Cline and supported by a Rhodesian SAS veteran living in the USA, Bob Mackenzie.[191]

Another aspect of the continuity between Third Force operations and post-transition South Africa is the lingering suspicion that many apartheid-era agents maintain Cold War-era connections with Western intelligence agencies.[192] The CIA and MI6 are known to have recruited their own spies within both the government and the ANC during the Cold War years, when their governments' interests aligned closely with those of the apartheid regime.[193] In a 1996 interview, retired former chief of SADF MI Maj. Gen. Tienie Groenewald mentioned MI6 and CIA involvement in Third Force activities, announcing cryptically: 'I know of CIA operations...supplies, financial involvement through a network of fronts.'[194] Berkeley notes Groenewald's claim is 'plausible but difficult to substantiate.' Former apartheid intelligence operative Martin Dolinchek claimed the CIA 'was involved "on the periphery" with covert aid to Inkatha,' but would not elaborate.[195] According to an ex-MK guerrilla: 'our country is not really governed by us. There is a lot of CIA activities around, foreign intelligence services, MI6. Because our intelligence services are in tatters [since the transition], so [foreign intelligence services] get in those cracks and operate there.'[196] As the end of apartheid dawned, there was a reported 'hundred-fold increase in the number of declared – let alone undeclared – foreign intelligence officers in the country between 1990 and 1994, presenting a serious challenge for protective security and counter-espionage.'[197] Despite the establishment of the National Intelligence Coordinating Committee (NICOC) in terms of the 1994 National Strategic Intelligence Act, the new intelligence services were burdened by divisions between ex-apartheid and liberation forces personnel, and by the culture of secrecy and compartmentalization between government departments inherited from the previous regime. These divisions provided British and US intelligence services with opportunities to strengthen their influence; for example, the US Federal Bureau of Investigation cultivated links with the Western Cape province's government – the only non-ANC provincial government in South Africa – under the pretext of combating terrorism. Meanwhile, the British MI6 circumvented governmental oversight by dealing with former apartheid personnel in the SAPS Crime Intelligence Division (the former Security Branch).[198]

In 2001, the FBI trained 2,000 South African police and intelligence experts, leading to suspicions that US intelligence agencies took this opportunity to recruit spies from among their trainees.[199] During his service in the post-apartheid intelligence services, Gilder describes receiving an envelope containing $5,000 from the CIA chief of station in South Africa, in the time-honoured manner of spy recruitment; Gilder immediately labelled the money as 'foreign assistance' and deposited it into his agency's coffers. Today, the apartheid regime's former Western allies are known to maintain their interest in South Africa largely because of its extensive mineral wealth, and the Anglo American and De Beers mining giants, two of the most powerful players in South Africa, are known to work 'in close conjunction with British intelligence.'[200] In 1995, former Security Branch officer Gary Pollack claimed that in addition to his counterinsurgency duties, he had spied for mining giant Anglo American during the transition, 'bugging conversations of Cyril Ramaphosa, FW de Klerk, Pik Botha and Roelf Meyer.'[201]

Though it is impossible to determine the full extent of the involvement of Western intelligence, this nevertheless adds context to the perception, widespread in South Africa, that covert elements continue to actively shape national politics. As colonial regimes collapsed across southern Africa, counterinsurgency forces first retreated from the ex-Portuguese colonies to Rhodesia, and then from Rhodesia to South Africa. In each case, these remnant forces bolstered ongoing colonial wars against African liberation movements with the assistance of Western powers (see Chapter Two). Hence the suspicion that since 1994 apartheid elements likewise have remained active, abetted by their former allies. These perceptions of external manipulation – 'our country is not really governed by us' – further undermine confidence that South Africans are capable of determining their own country's destiny.

CONCLUSION
COUNTERINSURGENCY AS HEGEMONY

'Democracy is now but a shade of its former substance. This is Cold War terror's most important legacy.'
— Greg Grandin, *The Last Colonial Massacre* (2011)

'The national middle class discovers its historic mission: that of intermediary. Seen through its eyes, its mission has nothing to do with transforming the nation; it consists, prosaically, of being the transmission line between the nation and capitalism, rampant though camouflaged, which today puts on the mask of neo-colonialism.'
— Frantz Fanon, *The Wretched of the Earth* (1961)

This book has examined the hidden histories of the insurgent and counterinsurgent forces in South Africa, exploring their aims and strategies and their roles in shaping post-transition outcomes. The ANC's armed wing, Umkhonto we Sizwe (MK), played a critical role in resisting apartheid violence, although it was mainly restricted to fighting on the regime's terms, and was never in a position to defeat it on the battlefield. Moreover, for much of its history, MK faced powerful internal divisions that were themselves largely a product of the regime's strategy to recruit spies within ANC and MK ranks. The regime violence itself preceded the ANC's decision in 1961 to develop an armed wing, but after MK's emergence, and especially after the exodus of South African youth seeking to join MK in response to the 1976 Soweto uprising, the regime's counterinsurgency strategy became more sophisticated and ferocious. With key assistance from NATO member states, the South African government developed its 'Total Strategy,' which focused on the annihilation of insurgents both armed and unarmed, and on destabilizing neighbouring states sympathetic to the ANC.

By the mid-1980s, the regime concentrated increasingly on developing various means of clandestine warfare, which included death squads within its military intelligence structures and spy networks within the ANC and PAC. By the late 1980s, the regime also focused on perfecting means of 'black-on-black' violence intended to weaken and discredit the liberation movements; shift blame for violence away from the white-minority regime; and undermine black demands for self-rule. This involved deploying askaris (guerrillas 'turned' and organized into death squads), secretly training 206 militants from the Inkatha Freedom Party (IFP) in Namibia's Caprivi Strip – the 'Caprivi trainees' – to spearhead violence against ANC and UDF loyalists in KwaZulu-Natal; arming IFP militants; and aiding and abetting various criminal gangs, such as the Black Cats, Black Chain, Witdoeke and others, as a means of weaponizing black civil society against the liberation movements. This counterinsurgency programme laid the foundation for the dramatic spike in violence that engulfed South Africa after the regime released Nelson Mandela and began formally negotiating with the ANC in February 1990.

By the late 1980s, MK was, in fact, better poised than at any previous moment in its history to attempt an armed seizure of power inside South Africa, through the clandestine structures it developed within the framework of Operation Vula. With the approval of its leader in exile, Oliver Tambo, the ANC smuggled operatives and weaponry into South Africa and established communications networks, safe houses, 'dead-letter boxes' (arms caches), and a chain of command rooted in Johannesburg and Durban. ANC intelligence also recruited moles within the apartheid security formations during this period, particularly inside the South African Police's Security Branch and the civilian intelligence agency, the National Intelligence Service (NIS). The regime discovered Vula's existence in July 1990, arresting several operatives and forcing the others underground. However, many of Operation Vula's structures remained intact.

CONCLUSION

The 1990–4 transition era was a nebulous period for MK's insurgents: its cadres and ANC loyalists were besieged by regime violence; meanwhile, as a trust-building measure in the midst of negotiations, in August 1990 the ANC's political leadership unilaterally renounced armed struggle. The ANC's ability to provide material support for its cadres returning from exile was very limited. MK cadres also risked arrest by the regime's forces for carrying weaponry, even as death squads continued to hunt them down. In the face of raging Third Force violence, the ANC lacked a comprehensive strategy for deploying its armed wing to defend communities loyal to it and MK lacked centralized command and control. MK cadres were instead largely relegated to training the Self-Defence Units, whose role as poorly trained and often ill-disciplined paramilitaries contributed to the spiral of violence during the transition years. Nevertheless, MK fighters, deployed individually and in small units, in some cases countered regime death squads, IFP militants and affiliated gangs.

The exception to this pattern was in the Bantustan of Transkei. After seizing power in 1988, strongman Bantu Holomisa developed pro-ANC leanings, and Transkei, long a hinterland for the ANC and MK by virtue of its history of anti-apartheid activism and strong kinship networks with the liberation movement, soon became a hotbed of MK activity; this intensified with MK chief of staff Chris Hani's arrival in 1990. Under Holomisa's rule, MK developed ties with the Transkei Defence Force (TDF), which assisted the ANC's armed wing and gave it access to TDF bases. This inevitably drew the apartheid security forces' attention, and in November 1990 SADF MI sent a team of askaris and mercenaries led by former TDF Military Intelligence chief Col. Craig Duli to stage a coup against Holomisa. MK and TDF forces repulsed the attempt and deterred or foiled SADF MI's subsequent clandestine forays into Transkei. Had MK not succeeded in thwarting these counterinsurgency plans, the regime's attempts to violently undermine the ANC would have been emboldened at a critical juncture during the transition. The case of MK in Transkei during the transition years demonstrates MK's military and organizational capabilities in a context where a sympathetic local government – in this case, Holomisa's regime – afforded it a favourable environment in which to operate.

'Sharp' Counterinsurgency and Transitions to Democracy

I have defined 'sharp' counterinsurgency as comprising clandestine forms of violence which include recruiting spies, sponsoring proxy militant forces, deploying death squads, and orchestrating targeted assassinations. Such operations become increasingly useful to the regime in the midst of negotiations because they afford it plausible deniability, enabling the government to maintain its credibility as a bona fide negotiating partner while simultaneously using violence to weaken the insurgent side. When the negotiations began, the apartheid regime's array of clandestine violent forces was poised to strike, using a range of 'sharp' counterinsurgency techniques. Within months, they began targeting black communities, especially in the townships ringing Johannesburg and Pretoria and in KwaZulu-Natal, with violence calibrated to expose the ANC's inability to defend communities loyal to it. IFP militants backed by soldiers and mercenaries from the ranks of the SADF's Special Forces massacred blacks on trains, at taxi stands, and in their homes, while battles raged between IFP members, typically armed with traditional weaponry, and ANC loyalists; street protests often turned violent. After the Boipatong massacre in June 1992, in which IFP militants, apparently assisted by regime forces, killed 45 ANC loyalists, the country teetered on the brink of full-scale civil war. Against this backdrop of generalized violence, the regime's death squads hunted ANC and MK operatives, ranging from civic activists to trained guerrillas. The regime's forces also engaged in elaborate psychological operations intended to discredit the ANC domestically and abroad; many of these disinformation operations falsely alleged that a faction within the ANC and MK was secretly planning to renege on agreements with the government and use the negotiations as a smokescreen to launch a general insurrection aiming to violently seize power. During this period, the regime's intelligence services intensified their efforts to recruit spies within the ANC's highest ranks, and, according to interviews and archival documents, SADF MI appears to have succeeded in this endeavour.

In November 1992, investigators from the Goldstone Commission uncovered the headquarters of MI's Directorate of Covert Collection (DCC), leading President De Klerk to appoint SADF Gen. Pierre

Steyn to investigate Third Force operations and culminating in his firing of 23 SADF MI officers in December 1992. However, 'sharp' counterinsurgency operations continued, and they powerfully undermined MK's position during the negotiations. Two key examples of this are the April 1993 assassination of long-time MK commander and SACP leader Chris Hani, and the persecution and marginalization of MK cadres at the Wallmansthal assembly point, which began in the months preceding the ANC's victory at the polls in April 1994 and persisted for several months thereafter. According to former guerrillas I interviewed, regime forces mounted an operation at the Wallmansthal base that involved askaris screening and conducting surveillance of incoming MK cadres; several MK cadres disappeared. This episode, and the subsequent mistreatment of MK guerrillas at the assembly points, which triggered mutinies, desertions and protests and compelled Nelson Mandela himself, by then the country's president, to visit Wallmansthal in October 1994 highlight the security dilemma facing rebel movements when disarming and gathering for integration or demobilization.

There is much evidence to suggest that Chris Hani's assassination was the culmination of an SADF MI strategy to recruit agents within the ANC's top ranks in order to undermine Hani and the South African Communist Party (SACP) in the negotiations. This strategy was described in court documents produced in DCC agent Jan Anton Nieuwoudt's lawsuit against the SADF for his wrongful dismissal. The court documents mention that SADF MI was still running clandestine operations during the same month that elections were being held, in April 1994; the documents also referred to SADF MI's moles within MK, whose ranks as officers in the post-transition South African National Defence Force (SANDF) had already been determined.

During South Africa's transition period, regime death squads such as SADF MI's Civil Cooperation Bureau and the South African Police's Vlakplaas unit were very active, targeting MK combatants and assisting the IFP and other militant groups to attack the ANC. Death squad personnel were determined to stop South Africa's black majority from coming to power, but they were also motivated by profit. Many had developed their own illicit revenue streams to fund their operations, especially by smuggling drugs and weapons. Some established private security companies; Vlakplaas commander Eugene de Kock launched his own arms trading company. These twin motivations – undermining black political power (in this case, the new ANC-led government) through violence, and deriving profit from criminal networks – also persisted after South Africa's April 1994 elections. The chains of command for 'sharp' counterinsurgency operations are by definition concealed to afford the regime plausible deniability, and questions persist about how much President De Klerk and other high-ranking National Party politicians knew about such operations, or whether indeed they had authorized them, after negotiations began with the ANC in February 1990. These chains of command became all the more obscure after the transition, as mid-level or high-ranking officers in the post-transition military, police and intelligence services appeared to be involved in violence, criminal networks and disinformation operations. There is evidence that the regime's top security echelons – the 'securocrats' – had designed apartheid counterinsurgency units, such as SADF MI's CCB, DCC, and their innumerable front companies, to integrate seamlessly into civil society precisely so that they could continue to function autonomously even after a transition to majority rule. In some cases, as with disgruntled DCC operatives' threat in June 1994 to unmask regime spies within the ANC, their impact could be quite overt. In other cases, former security force personnel played a more hidden or obscure role, such as Philip Powell, a former death squad operative who became a senator for the IFP and also continued training paramilitary forces after the transition.

There is much evidence indicating that authoritarian security force elements sustained 'sharp' counterinsurgency operations after South Africa's transition to democracy. This includes a string of mysterious deaths after the transition, such as the suspicious 'suicide' of NIA operative Muziwendoda Mdluli in 1995 and the death of police investigator 'Nceba' Radu in 1997. 'Sharp' counterinsurgency also persisted after the transition in the form of several untraceable disinformation campaigns intended to cause rifts within the ANC and to undermine public confidence in the new democracy. The most notable of these psychological operations was the 1998 McBride Affair, in which the post-transition SANDF chief and former apartheid general Georg Meiring personally delivered to President Mandela a

Military Intelligence report alleging that a radical cabal within the ANC was plotting an imminent and violent seizure of power.

Political violence still pitted ANC and IFP loyalists against each other in KwaZulu-Natal, claiming over one thousand lives from 1994 to 2000. Several observers alleged that a cabal of security personnel from the former apartheid regime and IFP were collaborating to destabilize the province. Many of the 'Caprivi trainees' still served in the post-transition security forces and contributed to this destabilization. Askaris and other African operatives to whom the regime had outsourced violence persisted in the post-apartheid security forces and in civil society and contributed to maintaining criminal networks that sustained high levels of violence.

Truth about apartheid counterinsurgency began to leak as the transition itself got under way, exposing ever-greater dimensions of regime violence, from the Harms Commission's inadvertent uncovering of the CCB death squad in 1990, to the Inkathagate revelations of 1991, and the Goldstone Commission and the Steyn Report findings from 1992 onward. The Truth and Reconciliation Commission (TRC) played by far the most important and transparent role in exposing the nature and extent of apartheid violence. Yet many important truths have remained buried, obscured by the regime's systematic destruction of its military, police and intelligence files, and by the ANC's unwillingness once in power to explore the question of which of its members had been spies.

The importance of counterinsurgency strategies in triggering and sustaining political violence in South Africa has long been under-estimated. Mamdani interprets the Zulu–Xhosa ethnic dimensions of the violence between the IFP and ANC in the townships around Johannesburg and Pretoria as 'the rural in the urban': ethnic nationalisms derived from the colonial project of rural black homelands clashing within South Africa's industrial heartland.[1] Yet this explanation ignores the apartheid regime's use of the IFP as a counterinsurgency tool against the ANC's power. Though ethnic animosities were combustible, the apartheid regime had doused the entire scene with fuel, as it were, and then lit the match. Kynoch points to the instrumental motivations that drove much of the violence in South Africa during the transition period, arguing that within the African population, combatants from

351

all sides took advantage of factors such as lawlessness and abundant weaponry to engage in profitable crimes disguised as politically motivated violence, setting in motion patterns of violence that persist in South Africa to this day.[2] Yet this formulation ignores the regime's strategy of unleashing Third Force violence via proxy forces embedded within society, and underestimates the vast resources at the security forces' disposal during this period. Although some perpetrators on both sides may have been seeking profit, they did so within a context of security force encouragement of black criminality in order to weaken and destabilize African communities. Outsourcing violence to African groups, some of which the regime formed from scratch, and flooding African communities with weaponry, were deliberate apartheid counterinsurgency strategies designed to accelerate 'black-on-black' violence, rather than mere by-products of nationwide unrest. Decentralization of violence was a key regime objective, intended to make terrain inhospitable for all forms of resistance to apartheid. Counterinsurgency must therefore be considered as causally prior to other factors such as ethnic hatreds or profit-seeking to explain the political violence during this era.

Evidence of the apartheid regime's counterinsurgency campaign also contributes to the historiographical debate about the nature and context of the ANC's military activities during South Africa's democratic transition. Anthea Jeffery argues that the ANC and MK orchestrated the spike in political violence during the years 1990–4 as a strategy to destabilize South Africa and weaken the National Party government's bargaining position during negotiations.[3] Writing amid the spike in violence that followed Chris Hani's assassination, John Kane-Berman argued: 'The demonization of the state and the romanticization of the behaviour of its victims – two sides of the same coin – have helped to prolong the violence.'[4] Yet during Kane-Berman's time of writing, the full extent of the regime's responsibility for violence in the transition era, though widely suspected, was not yet revealed. Instead this book demonstrates that during this period MK's use of violence was primarily a defensive response to intensifying apartheid counterinsurgency, rather than an offensive strategy to shape the transition in the ANC's favour. This reinforces previous findings about the regime's complicity in organizing and launching Third Force attacks during the transition to weaken the liberation forces through violence.[5] Other authors have pointed to the transition as a period when both the regime and the ANC began to spin out of control, as state oversight of covert operations and discipline within the ANC–UDF loosened.[6] On 6 April 1993, speaking at the reburial of Solomon Mahlangu, an MK cadre captured and executed by the regime in 1979, Nelson Mandela addressed a crowd of 4,000 in Mamelodi township outside Pretoria, declaring: 'I am not going to blame only Inkatha and the government [for political violence] – our people are just as involved.'[7] Yet the often indiscriminate violence of the ANC's Self-Defence Units and other loyal forces also suited the regime's designs for a post-Cold War order in which South African apartheid would become unexceptional against the broader backdrop of widespread civil war and disorder across Africa.[8]

Counterinsurgency and Post-Transition Violence

Political violence in South Africa remained at a high level during and after the transition. While it may be insufficient, as Taylor points out in his analysis of post-transition violence in KwaZulu-Natal, 'to reduce an understanding of political violence to a conspiracy theory involving just those old guard remnants of the apartheid era who may have remained active within the security forces,'[9] the presence of these actors remains only one counterinsurgency legacy causing post-transition violence: others include the abundance of firearms throughout the country; the persistence of criminal networks originating with security force operatives; and the cycles of 'black-on-black' violence abetted and encouraged by the apartheid regime, which persisted in various parts of the country.

Counterinsurgency campaigns seek to deprive insurgents of local communities' loyalties by using the communities themselves as battlegrounds. This destroys kinship and reproduces mistrust in new contexts removed from the struggle-era battle lines. The recruitment of askaris and informers decimated social capital networks in African communities, helping to bring post-apartheid society to a place where 'criminality has become the norm.'[10] The 'increased crime, corruption, and poverty that frequently follow democratic openings'[11] can be explained in part through the *presence* of pernicious authoritarian legacies, rather than through the absence of post-transition institutional power and organization. Although levels of violence remained high in South Africa after 1994, the political nature of violence largely receded, leaving in its wake the poverty and anomie that are apartheid's nationwide legacy. More recent waves of violence in several South African cities targeting immigrants and refugees from other parts of Africa must be understood through this lens.

The role of apartheid counterinsurgency in South Africa's democratic transition has been much wider than previously understood, bearing striking implications for the literatures on democratic transitions, security sector reform, and civil war termination, and having powerful policy implications. As previous literature has noted, democratic transitions that did not relapse into civil war have nevertheless tended towards a bloody aftermath. An analysis of counterinsurgency deepens our understanding of why this occurs. The alarming resilience of counterinsurgency programmes during democratic transitions leaves distinct legacies in the institutional, social capital and participatory realms that prevent democratic consolidation and shape 'grey zone' outcomes. At the participatory level, a study of counterinsurgency illuminates the role that state intelligence services can play in shaping pacts between incumbents and rebel elites. Spy agencies' secret efforts to recruit or kill top-ranking rebel leaders shift the terms and political terrain of negotiations to the right, restricting true political change, perpetuating authoritarian power structures, and silencing progressive forces. This splits rebel movements between powerful elites and sidelined masses, disempowering broad, racially marginalized sectors of the population and worsening their impoverishment.

Counterinsurgency legacies also give rise to political uncertainty and instability both within state institutions and between the state and civil society. Fears of conspiracies and cabals, covert political agendas, and hidden loyalties, represent a form of continuity with the authoritarian past that undermines trust and, with it, democratic consolidation. Authoritarian, corrupt and racist practices often endure in the security sector after democratization, undermining institutional legitimacy and sustaining criminal networks. Even as security institutions ostensibly pass under civilian control, counterinsurgency programmes can remain at least partly intact, compromising security sector reform effectiveness and legitimacy, and contributing to an ongoing insecurity ecology. Counterinsurgency relies heavily on informer networks and on outsourcing violence to paramilitaries to ensure 'plausible deniability,' contributing to the destruction of social capital and the atomization of society. The distrust and violence that these strategies sow among marginalized populations perpetuate themselves in the post-transition era, replacing social capital networks with privatized, securitized geographies. A history of state-sponsored political violence and copious small arms supply have left in their wake an epidemic of non-institutional violence, ranging from gang warfare, kidnapping and organized crime, to individual-level violence.

Caroline Moser provides a useful typology of urban violence that ranges from political violence (characterized by guerrilla and paramilitary conflict, and assassinations); to institutional violence (extrajudicial killings and vigilante violence); economic violence (kidnapping, armed robbery, drug trafficking); economic social violence (petty theft, small gangs, turf wars); and social violence (individual and family-level violence, sexual violence).[12] The causal relations between different categories of violence are not only contemporaneous, but also occur along a historical spectrum in which political and institutional violence leave decentralized legacies. Indeed, political violence in South Africa, as in post-insurgency, post-Cold War negotiated transitions in places like El Salvador and Guatemala, has given way to institutional, economic and social violence whose origins and impacts can be disaggregated neither from the past, nor from each other.

Better MK integration could have mitigated some of these inequalities by inculcating a higher level of professionalism within the post-transition security forces and imbuing them with greater legitimacy among the local populations. This could have aided in establishing better policing by strengthening law and order institutions, and challenged the continued racism that prevailed for years in the security forces. This might not have single-handedly averted high levels of post-transition violence, but by strengthening state institutions it would nevertheless have contributed to a more complete democratic consolidation. Instead, South Africa's post-transition security forces remained plagued by racism, corruption and ineffectiveness, and persistent low levels of legitimacy. Meanwhile, private security companies, whose numbers were already growing steadily during apartheid's final decade, mushroomed after the transition, filling a vacuum left by the new security forces' ineptitude. Since the transition from apartheid, security privatization has imitated counterinsurgency's propensity for outsourcing. Reflecting its broader embrace of privatization, the South African government has embraced 'a libertarian agenda promoting a shift from the public to the private, with the apparent loss of public accountability.'[13] Like other sectors of the post-apartheid economy, the privatization of security attracted foreign corporations, as global private security titans such as Chubb and Wackenhut have joined a burgeoning local private security market. At the foreign policy level, privatization since apartheid gave rise to the proliferation of private military companies such as Executive Outcomes, whose acceptance of natural resource wealth profits as payment from war-torn African governments represents a continuation with the apartheid-era counterinsurgency's pillaging of natural resources to fund their proxy wars.[14]

The hegemony of neoliberal economic and security paradigms shaped South Africa's transition at a broader level. The post-transition legacies of counterinsurgency programmes include the stunting of state security sector reform by preserving authoritarian tendencies and channels of corruption within these forces, thereby eroding their effectiveness and legitimacy. These compromised security institutions in turn contribute to high post-transition levels of urban violence, both through an inability to police effectively and by actively participating in certain forms of criminal activity. This strongly distorts and subverts democratic change. If, as MacGinty claims, 'the key to understanding crime in a post-peace accord context lies in the "persistence factors" through which the elements and dynamics of wartime persist into the post-peace accord period,'[15] one of the keys to understanding these 'persistence factors' lies in analysing counterinsurgency, which in turn largely explains chronic post-authoritarian violence and insecurity.

From Low-Intensity Conflict to Low-Intensity Democracy

Counterinsurgency's post-authoritarian legacies of disorder should be considered within the broader context of post-Cold War neoliberal hegemony and the phenomenon characteristic of many Global South democracies that Gills and Rocamora, punning on the US counterinsurgency doctrine of low-intensity warfare, have termed 'low-intensity democracy,' in which '"elite democracies" in effect coexist with tacit military dictatorships. Social reform agendas that could have established the basis for broader popular participation and greater social justice have been abandoned.'[16] This corresponds closely to what Oxhorn calls 'neopluralism,' 'a market-centered pattern of political incorporation' in which 'unprecedented' political rights are accompanied by narrowed 'social rights of citizenship.'[17] Mbembe has insisted on characterizing the African political transitions of democracy's 'third wave' as 'recompositions' featuring 'the co-existence, within the same dynamic, of elements belonging to warfare as to the conduct of civil politics.'[18] Counterinsurgency programmes have thus been integral to securing what McSherry calls 'the class orientation of the state.'[19]

In November 1990, nine months after the formal start of negotiations and three months after Third Force violence had exploded, the ANC held a conference at which Popo Molefe, a senior leader, identified the National Party's key strategies to make South Africa's political terrain as inhospitable as possible to the liberation forces. These included regaining 'legitimacy in the eyes of the mass of the governed and the international community'; presenting De Klerk's regime 'as a force indispensable to the process of the transition both as the manager of this process and the force best placed to secure it'; and shifting 'the ideological terrain by depriving the national democratic struggle of its national liberation character and present[ing] it as a contest between "free enterprise" and "socialism."'[20] The regime's counterinsurgency strategy already aimed to weaken and discredit the ANC, both domestically and in the international arena, along the lines Molefe described. Whether or not De Klerk's regime sanctioned Third Force violence, the violence unquestionably facilitated the regime's pursuit of its broader objective to preserve apartheid elites' ongoing influence.

Despite the ANC's rise to power, then, apartheid counterinsurgency partially achieved the objectives Molefe identified in his address. The role of the apartheid military and police structures in shaping the transition, and their enduring post-transition power, represent the manifestation of this hegemony, in which racial inequalities were abolished but class inequalities widened.

Post-apartheid racism and its economic, spatial and socio-cultural segregations also persisted in South African society at large; in this sense, the unreformed security institutions can be understood as a microcosm of the broader society. Many former apartheid counterinsurgency masterminds later sought to deny that they had been defending a racist system, claiming dispassionately that the purpose of South African counterinsurgency was to protect free enterprise and Western values from communist socialism.[21] Former SAP Special Branch chief Jac Büchner, commissioner of the Kwa-Zulu Police from 1989 to 1992, explained in a 1996 interview that he 'did not see' his role 'as upholding apartheid… In my whole working career, I spent more time with blacks than with whites.'[22] This is instructive for what it teaches us about colonialism's versatility in shedding overt racial discrimination as a way to adapt and survive after apartheid.

CLR James observed: 'The race question is subsidiary to the class question and to think of imperialism in terms of race is disastrous. But to neglect the racial factor as merely incidental is an error only less grave than to make it fundamental.'[23] MK's ideology, largely shaped by the SACP,[24] likewise regarded economic oppression as subsuming racial oppression. This understanding was exemplified by the SACP analysis of South Africa's condition as 'Colonialism of a Special Type,' that is, a domestic colonial arrangement whereby the profits of white racial domination accrued not to a distant European metropole but to a white settler population living alongside Africans. Indeed, several ex-guerrillas referred to 'CST' as the system dominating South Africa under apartheid. Pointing to the ANC's embrace of the economic status quo as negotiations with the NP progressed, Taylor situates the ANC's 'counterhegemonic' elements firmly within its socialist–communist camp, and notes: 'socialism was largely absent from the negotiations process and this disorientation suggests why counterhegemonic impulses were largely lacking from the ANC side in the transition process.'[25] These 'counterhegemonic impulses' were embodied in the socialist politics favoured by the ANC's mass base and incorporated elements borrowed from Marxist-Leninist liberation ideology that interpreted the armed struggle as one of a revolutionary army fighting apartheid's 'bourgeois army.'[26] Thus the ANC's rank and file tended to be more socialist and more militant than the elites that negotiated the end of apartheid on the basis of shared economic priorities with South Africa's white elites.

Colonialism was first and foremost a capitalist project that instrumentalized race as a tool to maximize wealth exploitation; apartheid epitomized the violence of colonialism's legal, institutional and socio-cultural racism, and the tremendous profits it brought to racial and economic elites. Corporate interests were instrumental in spearheading European colonial ventures, and privately funded expeditionary forces colonized much of Africa and other continents.[27] In some instances, those same corporate interests also spearheaded decolonization, recognizing that colonial modes of extraction had ceased to be profitable, and trading them instead for a version of the same modes of extraction outsourced to the liberation forces' elites as they assumed power. Indeed, the very nature and implementation of key apartheid institutions such as the pass laws and the establishment of the homelands system were in great part aimed at organizing both capital and labour for South Africa's industrialization.[28] It was therefore no coincidence that captains of private industry were the first to initiate dialogue with the ANC in 1986 to explore how the inevitable political shift could be managed so as to preserve corporate wealth and political privilege as much as possible.[29] This dialogue morphed into ANC negotiations with the National Party, and white elites eventually chose the pragmatism of abolishing state racism, and sharing power and revenues with their ANC counterparts, in exchange for enshrining private profiteering.

Against the backdrop of ongoing counterinsurgency operations, two closely interconnected factors contributed to South Africa's incomplete transition. Firstly, the ANC elite's growing distance from its base of mass support, which was partly a result of apartheid intelligence recruitment operations, as we have seen; and secondly, the decline and fall of the ANC's redistributionist platform, which overlaps with its elite–mass split. Situating the South African transition in the broader context of the neoliberal 'moment,' Taylor points out that 'the further involved in the negotiations the elites of the ANC became, the greater they began to identify with the hegemonic project that was being pushed by a multiplicity of actors.'[30]

Upon his release from prison, Mandela himself identified the nationalization of industries as a top priority for the ANC, alarming the politicians and captains of industry who formed South Africa's white elite.[31] Yet Mandela's discourse would soon change, and the more socialist elements within the ANC became sidelined, as the negotiated pact between elites took shape. The intelligence recruitment explanation set forth here is important to consider in contrast to Klein's portrayal of a disorganized and amateurish ANC negotiating team that withdrew its major demands for wealth redistribution after the NP easily outmanoeuvred it in negotiations.[32] Others have attributed the ANC's embrace of neoliberal economics to the greed of individual ANC leaders, who quickly became accustomed to luxury.[33] The ANC's post-transition embrace of neoliberal market capitalism gave rise to widespread accusations that the ANC's leadership had 'sold out.' These accusations must be understood not only in terms of economic compromise, but also in the light of the apartheid regime's sustained, and apparently successful, attempts to recruit spies within the ANC leadership during the transition era.

South Africa's transition ultimately protected and maximized corporate interests and profits.[34] McKinley notes a 'strategic convergence that occurred between the liberation movement and international capitalism.'[35] The 1955 Freedom Charter had reflected the compromises within the ANC, embodying its embrace of African nationalists and doctrinaire Marxists alike, calling 'for nationalization of the mines, but not for a more general challenge to basic property relations.'[36] The ANC's 1989 Harare Declaration similarly envisioned economic and land tenure reforms in only vague terms.[37] After the transition, the ANC adopted a series of progressively more right-wing economic programmes, abandoning the 1994 RDP's (Reconstruction and Development Programme) generous provisions for community development in favour of GEAR (Growth, Employment, and Redistribution) in 1996, which embraced private business on the premise that elite wealth would trickle down. Thus far, the transfer of wealth to blacks has occurred almost exclusively at the elite level, through the very narrow Black Economic Empowerment (BEE) programme, which has made multimillionaires of a handful of well-connected black South Africans, leaving tens of millions in crushing poverty, with inadequate housing and utilities.[38] While in South Africa, I more than once heard African citizens invoke the maxim: 'The boardroom table changes the black man, not the other way around.' The drastic 'Chicago school'-style economic reforms, typical only a decade earlier of authoritarian regimes such as Pinochet's Chile, were now the very reforms embraced by democratizing South Africa, further entrenching the country's wide, highly racialized gap between rich and poor.[39] By contrast, on the eve of the transition's onset, Chris Hani had stressed the importance of 'tak[ing] this question of negotiation away from the clever initiatives and manoeuvres of individuals. We want to put it squarely in the hands of the people. The people must know that negotiations is an arena of struggle.'[40] Months before his assassination, Hani had foreseen the transition's direction: 'What I fear is that the liberators emerge as elitists…who drive around in Mercedes-Benzes and use the resources of this country…to live in palaces and gather riches.'[41]

The arms deal scandal represented the military-industrial complex's triumph in the new South Africa. Although the security forces' operations and mandate had changed, a form of colonial profiteering remained embedded within South African politics. Now, the military stopped playing the same repressive role but maintained its economic role, while apartheid's erstwhile NATO allies vied to cement their influence. At the other end of the spectrum, many MK veterans – as well as the redistributionist ideology they espoused and fought for – became cut off from the security institutions they had fought to reshape and from the ANC whose vanguard they once formed.

At the international level, the USSR had been the ANC's main patron during the Cold War, and one of Mandela's primary tasks upon his release from prison was to reassure those Western leaders who felt uneasy about the ANC's communist leanings and win their support.[42] Meanwhile, the SACP, once the vanguard of the anti-apartheid struggle, has slid into irrelevance. One former guerrilla argued that previous generations of SACP leadership 'were great men [and women], we used to respect them, you know, when you see them you see your *father*. Dignified comrades!' Whereas nowadays, SACP officials are seen as corrupt: '[Now] you see a communist wearing a shoe costing twelve thousand and a shirt costing four thousand, driving a car costing seven hundred and fifty thousand, then you call yourself a communist? How? You will turn fools, not us.' Despite the changing times, he insisted: 'we grew in the ANC culture and the Communist Party culture, you cannot come and tell us things have changed… Discipline is discipline.'[43] Instead, the SACP has become a vehicle for elites to secure power and profits. The ANC has seen the demobilization and marginalization of those who fought for class transformation in South Africa, and whose rank and file internalized the ideological rationale for their fight. In an interview Dr Somadoda Fikeni underscored South Africa's widening wealth disparities since the transition, the concentration of wealth into ANC elites' hands, and their corresponding inability to understand the poor and disempowered: 'In 1991 when the ANC met in Durban for its conference, you would count the number of buses which were there. When again the ANC met in 1997, buses were half that population. When now they met in Polokwane [in December 2007], you would think it was a German car show. It tells you where the elite has gone. That's the most graphic depiction of that social distance.'[44]

Since the transition, there has been mounting tension between the ANC's championing of private wealth and the fact that it 'constantly draws on the rhetoric of the past struggle, insisting that the development of the new democracy remains a direct continuation of that history.'[45] Despite the ANC's use of struggle-era discourse as a means of shoring up its own legitimacy, after 1994 it was slow in assisting the combat veterans who spearheaded the very struggle the party invokes today. Against the backdrop of South Africa's tremendous economic inequality, many MK veterans, and the redistributionist ideology they fought for, have languished in obscurity. This has created a vacuum in South African politics that the ANC struggles to fill, leaving an opening for the anti-elite politics and incendiary rhetoric of Julius Malema's Economic Freedom Fighters, thus further weakening democracy.

In this context, counterinsurgency legacies have also manifested themselves in the increasingly militarized state responses to urban violence in South Africa, as the state has deployed special units to target law-breakers, while leaders encourage violent state responses to crime in increasingly strident pronouncements. This militarization of policing has underscored the post-transition government's willingness to use violence in defence of the economic status quo, targeting protesters who deplore economic inequalities reminiscent of apartheid. This dehumanization of law-breakers is encoded through the police's increasing willingness to 'shoot to kill.' In recent years, the military has even clashed with the police when soldiers protested against poor conditions. A police officer in Krugersdorp highlighted parallels with apartheid-era policing: 'generally, the police are trigger-happy…look at what happens when there are service delivery protests: the police shoot retreating protesters from the back.'[46] The killing of citizens protesting against inadequate delivery of basic services such as electricity and water shows the South African state coming full circle, shooting the still overwhelmingly black poor who rise up because of socio-economic grievances. These militarized state responses to post-apartheid unrest culminated in the massacre by police of 14 unarmed miners at Marikana on 16 August 2012, an episode reminiscent of the March 1960 Sharpeville massacre that had compelled ANC leaders to launch their armed struggle in the first place. The Marikana massacre epitomized counterinsurgency's post-transition legacies, as South Africa's government once again deployed its security forces to quell dissent against a backdrop of savage inequality.

NOTES

INTRODUCTION

1. Confidential interview with ex-combatant, December 2009.
2. Confidential interview with ex-combatant, December 2009.
3. Confidential interview with ex-combatant, December 2009.
4. Confidential interview with ex-combatant, December 2009.
5. Confidential interview with ex-combatant, December 2009.
6. Confidential interview with ex-combatant, December 2009.
7. For example, Minnaar, Anthony. 1998. The 'Third Force.' In *The Hidden Hand: Covert Operations in South Africa*, edited by Charl Schutte, Ian Liebenberg, and Anthony Minnaar, 2nd edn. Pretoria: Human Sciences Research Council, pp. 57-78.
8. Ellis, Stephen. 1998. The Historical Significance of South Africa's Third Force. *Journal of Southern African Studies* 24 (2), p. 293.
9. Kilcullen, David. 2010. *Counterinsurgency*. Oxford: Oxford University Press, pp. 154-5.
10. Price, David H. 2010. Soft Power, Hard Power, and the Anthropological 'Leveraging' of Cultural 'Assets.' In *Anthropology and Global Counterinsurgency*, edited by John D Kelly, Beatrice Jauregui, Sean T Mitchell, and Jeremy Walton. Chicago, IL: University of Chicago Press, pp. 245-60.
11. Mason, T David, and Dale A Krane. 1989. The Political Economy of Death Squads: Toward a Theory of the Impact of State-Sanctioned Terror. *International Studies Quarterly* 33 (2): 175-98.
12. Dlamini, Jacob. 2014. *Askari*. Auckland Park: Jacana.
13. Musah, Abdel-Fatau. 2003. Privatization of Security, Arms Proliferation, and the Process of State Collapse in Africa. In *State Failure, Collapse, and Reconstruction*, edited by J Milliken. Oxford: Blackwell Publishing.
14. Mamdani, Mahmood. 1996. *Citizen and Subject: Contemporary Africa and the Legacy of Late Colonialism*. Princeton, NJ: Princeton University Press.

15. Thomas, Martin. 2008. *Empires of Intelligence*. Berkeley, CA: University of California Press, pp. 2, 5.
16. Schlesinger, Stephen, and Stephen Kinzer. 2005. *Bitter Fruit: The Story of the American Coup in Guatemala*. Cambridge, MA: Harvard University Press, p. 251.
17. Schirmer, Jennifer. 1998. *The Guatemalan Military Project: A Violence Called Democracy*. Cambridge, MA: Harvard University Press, p. 288.
18. McSherry, J Patrice. 1997. *Incomplete Transition: Military Power and Democracy in Argentina*. New York: St Martin's Press.
19. McSherry, J Patrice. 2005. *Predatory States: Operation Condor and Covert War in Latin America*. New York: Rowman and Littlefield Publishers.
20. Ganser, Daniele. 2005. *NATO's Secret Armies: Operation Gladio and Terrorism in Western Europe*. New York: Frank Cass, p. 63.
21. Donghi cited in McSherry, *Predatory States*, p. 26.
22. McSherry, *Predatory States*, p. 28.
23. 'Vlok Is Named on "Dirty Tricks" Tape,' *Sunday Times*, 12 March 1995.
24. 'Vlok Is Named on "Dirty Tricks" Tape,' *Sunday Times*, 12 March 1995.
25. Stanley, William. 1996. *The Protection Racket State*. Philadelphia: Temple University Press.
26. Schlesinger and Kinzer, *Bitter Fruit*, p. 251.
27. Mazzei, Julie. 2009. *Death Squads or Self-Defense Forces? How Paramilitary Groups Emerge and Challenge Democracy in Latin America*. Chapel Hill, NC: University of North Carolina Press.
28. Gutierrez-Sanin, Francisco. 2010. Mechanisms. In *Economic Liberalization and Political Violence*, edited by Francisco Gutierrez-Sanin and Gerd Schönwalder. London: Pluto Press.
29. Gear, Sasha. 2002. Now That the War Is Over: Ex-Combatants' Transition and the Question of Violence: A Literature Review, www.csvr.co.za.
30. McSherry, *Predatory States*; Douek, Daniel. 2013. Counterinsurgency's Impact on Transitions from Authoritarianism: The Case of South Africa. *Politikon* 40 (2), pp. 55-75.
31. Knight, Amy W. 2000. The Enduring Legacy of the KGB in Russian Politics. *Problems of Post-Communism* 47 (4), pp. 3-15; Knight, Amy W. 2003. The KGB, Perestroika, and the Collapse of the Soviet Union. *Journal of Cold War Studies* 5 (1), pp. 67-93.
32. For example, Weinstein, Jeremy. 2006. *Inside Rebellion: The Politics of Insurgent Violence*. Cambridge: Cambridge University Press.
33. For example, Weinstein, *Inside Rebellion*; Metelits, Claire. 2010. *Inside Insurgency: Violence, Civilians, and Revolutionary Group Behavior*. New York: New York University Press.

34. For example, Collier, Paul. 2000. Rebellion as a Quasi-Criminal Activity. *Journal of Conflict Resolution* 44 (6).

35. Kalyvas, Stathis. 2001. 'New' and 'Old' Civil Wars: A Valid Distinction? *World Politics* 54 (October), p. 107.

36. Davidson, Basil. 1981. *The People's Cause: A History of Guerrillas in Africa*. Harlow: Longman.

37. For example, Howe, Herbert M. 1994. The South African Defence Force and Political Reform. *Journal of Modern African Studies* 32 (1); Kynoch, Gary. 1996. The 'Transformation' of the South African Military. *Journal of Modern African Studies* 34 (3), pp. 441-57; Cawthra, Gavin, and Bjorn Moller (eds). 1997. *Defensive Restructuring of the Armed Forces in Southern Africa*. Brookfield, VT: Ashgate.

38. Spear, Joanna. 2002. Disarmament and Demobilization. In *Ending Civil Wars: The Implementation of Peace Agreements*, edited by SJ Stedman, Donald Rothschild and Elizabeth M Cousens. Boulder, CO: Lynne Rienner.

39. Williams, Rocky. 2006. African Armed Forces and the Challenges of Security Sector Transformation. In *Security Sector Reform and Post-Conflict Peacebuilding*, edited by A Schnabel, and Hans-Georg Erhart. New York: United Nations, pp. 48, 46.

40. South African Police Service. 2008. South African Police Service Annual Report.

41. Shaw, Mark. 2002. *Crime and Policing in Post-Apartheid South Africa*. Bloomington, IN: Indiana University Press.

42. Mamdani, Mahmood. 1996. *Citizen and Subject: Contemporary Africa and the Legacy of Late Colonialism*. Princeton, NJ: Princeton University Press; Chipkin, Ivor. 2004. Nationalism as Such: Violence during South Africa's Political Transition. *Public Culture* 16 (2), pp. 315-35; Steinberg, Jonny. 2008. *Thin Blue: The Unwritten Rules of Policing South Africa*. Johannesburg: Jonathan Ball; Kynoch, Gary. 2005. Crime, Conflict, and Politics in Transition-Era South Africa. *African Affairs* 104 (416), pp. 493-514; Kynoch, Gary. 2008. Urban Violence in Colonial Africa: A Case for South African Exceptionalism. *Journal of Southern African Studies* 34 (3), pp. 629-45.

43. Campbell, Bruce B. 2000. Death Squads: Definition, Problems, and Historical Context. In *Death Squads in Global Perspective: Murder with Deniability*, edited by Bruce B Campbell and Arthur D Brenner. New York: Palgrave Macmillan, p. 9.

44. Mashike, Lephophotho. 2008. Age of Despair: The Unintegrated Forces of South Africa. *African Affairs* 107 (June), pp. 433-53.

45. Chikwanha, Annie Barbara. 2005. Trust in Institutions in Sub-Saharan Africa's Emerging Democracies. In *Trust in Public Institutions in South*

Africa, edited by S and NB Askvik. Burlington, VT: Ashgate Publishing; Steinberg, *Thin Blue*.

46. For example, O'Donnell, Guillermo, and Philippe C Schmitter. 1986. *Transitions from Authoritarian Rule: Tentative Conclusions about Uncertain Democracies*. Baltimore: Johns Hopkins University Press; Hagopian, Frances, and Scott P Mainwaring (eds). 2005. *The Third Wave of Democratization in Latin America: Advances and Setbacks*. New York: Cambridge University Press.

47. McSherry, *Incomplete Transition*.

48. Levitsky, Steven, and Lucan A Way. 2010. *Competitive Authoritarianism*. New York: Cambridge University Press, pp. 58-9.

49. Wilson, Richard. 1992. Continued Counter-Insurgency: Civilian Rule in Guatemala, 1986–91. In *Low Intensity Democracy: Political Power in the New World Order*, edited by Barry Gills and Joel Rocamora. London: Pluto Press, pp. 144-59; Farina, Luis. 2010. *No Place to Hide: Gang, State, and Clandestine Violence in El Salvador*. Cambridge, MA: Harvard University Press; Moodie, Ellen. 2010. *El Salvador in the Aftermath of Peace: Crime, Uncertainty, and the Transition to Democracy*. Philadelphia: University of Pennsylvania Press; Brands, Hal. 2011. Crime, Irregular Warfare, and Institutional Failure in Latin America: Guatemala as a Case Study. *Studies in Conflict and Terrorism* 34 (3), pp. 228–47.

50. Arias, Enrique, and Daniel Goldstein. 2010. Violent Pluralism: Understanding the New Democracies of Latin America. In *Violent Democracies in Latin America*, edited by Arias and Goldstein. Durham, NC: Duke University Press, pp. 1-34.

51. Reno, Will. 1998. *Warlord Politics and African States*. Boulder, CO: Lynne Rienner.

52. Allina-Pisano, Jessica. 2009. How to Tell an Axe Murderer: An Essay on Ethnography, Truth, and Lies. In *Political Ethnography: What Immersion Contributes to the Study of Power*, edited by E. Schatz. Chicago, IL: University of Chicago Press, p. 56.

53. Skinner, cited in Gear, 'Now That the War Is Over,' p. 35; emphasis added.

54. Lalu, Premesh. 2009. *The Deaths of Hintsa*. Cape Town: Human Sciences Research Council Press; Guha, Ranajit. 1994. The Prose of Counterinsurgency. In *Culture / Power / History: A Reader in Contemporary Social Theory*, edited by NB Dirks, Geoff Eley, and Sherry B Ortner. Princeton, NJ: Princeton University Press.

55. Confidential interview with ex-combatant, December 2009.

1. UMKHONTO WE SIZWE'S ARMED LEGITIMACY

1. The ANC's Radio Freedom, broadcast from Lusaka, was enormously popular in South Africa though listening to it was a criminal offence that carried a minimum sentence of five years; the broadcast always opened with the song 'Hamba Kahle Umkhonto we Sizwe.' This song was also used to serenade struggle heroes, especially at funerals; Berkeley describes ANC cadres chanting it at a funeral for an ANC member killed in post-independence political violence in KwaZulu-Natal (*The Graves Are Not Yet Full*, p. 151), underscoring its ubiquity as a struggle song.

2. Davis, Stephen M. 1987. *Apartheid's Rebels: Inside South Africa's Hidden War*. New Haven, CT: Yale University Press; Cock, Jacklyn. 1997. The Cultural and Social Challenge of Demilitarization. In *Defensive Restructuring of the Armed Forces in South Africa*, edited by B Moller and Gavin Cawthra. Brookfield, VT: Ashgate Publishing; Cherry, Janet. 2011. *Umkhonto we Sizwe*. Auckland Park: Jacana; Ngculu, James. 2009. *The Honour to Serve: Recollections of an Umkhonto Soldier*. Claremont: David Philip.

3. For example, Cherry, *Umkhonto we Sizwe*.

4. Williams, Rocky. 2000. The Other Armies: A Brief Historical Overview of Umkhonto we Sizwe, 1961–1994. *South African Military History Society Journal* 11 (5).

5. Wood, Elisabeth Jean. 2000. *Forging Democracy from Below: Insurgent Transitions in South Africa and El Salvador*. New York: Cambridge University Press.

6. Weinstein, Jeremy. 2006. *Inside Rebellion: The Politics of Insurgent Violence*. Cambridge: Cambridge University Press; Metelits, Claire. 2010. *Inside Insurgency: Violence, Civilians, and Revolutionary Group Behavior*. New York: New York University Press.

7. Kalyvas, Stathis. 2001. 'New' and 'Old' Civil Wars: A Valid Distinction? *World Politics* 54 (October), pp. 99-118.

8. Kynoch, Gary. 2008. Urban Violence in Colonial Africa: A Case for South African Exceptionalism. *Journal of Southern African Studies* 34 (3), pp. 629-45.

9. Shubin, Vladimir. 2009. *ANC: A View from Moscow*. Auckland Park: Jacana Press.

10. Cherry, *Umkhonto we Sizwe*, pp. 71-2.

11. African National Congress Submission to the Truth and Reconciliation Commission, Section 5.3, 'Towards People's War and People's Power, 1979–90,' August 1996.

12. Murray, Martin. 1994. *The Revolution Deferred: The Painful Birth of Post-Apartheid South Africa*. London: Verso, p. 259.

13. Sanders, James. 2006. *Apartheid's Friends: The Rise and Fall of South Africa's Secret Service*. London: John Murray Publishers, p. 223.
14. Braam, Conny. 2004. *Operation Vula*. Auckland Park: Jacana.
15. Confidential interview with ex-combatant, December 2009.
16. 'MK Comes of Age,' SAHA, Section 5.17 (Umkhonto we Sizwe).
17. 'Notes of Meeting with Chris Hani, Chief of Staff and Deputy Commander of Umkhonto we Sizwe, and Steve Tshwete, Political Commissar,' from an interview by John D Battersby, 3 June 1988, Lusaka, Zambia.
18. Lan, David. 1985. *Guns and Rain: Guerrillas and Spirit Mediums in Zimbabwe*. London: James Currey.
19. Wolfie Kodesh interview with Graham Morodi, 1993 (Mayibuye Archives).
20. Barrell, Howard. 1990. The Turn to the Masses: The African National Congress' Strategic Review of 1978–9. *Journal of Southern African Studies* 18 (1), pp. 64-92.
21. Lodge, Tom, and Bill Nasson. 1991. *All, Here, and Now: Black Politics in South Africa in the 1980s*. Cape Town: Ford Foundation.
22. Harris, Peter. 2012. *A Just Defiance*. Berkeley, CA: University of California Press.
23. Gilder, Barry. 2012. *Songs and Secrets: South Africa from Liberation to Governance*. London: Hurst Publishers.
24. Reno, Will. 2011. *Warfare in Independent Africa*. Cambridge: Cambridge University Press, p. 111.
25. Quoted in 'MK and the Future,' SAHA, Section 5.17 (Umkhonto we Sizwe).
26. Meredith, Martin. 2005. *The Fate of Africa*. New York: Public Affairs, p. 124.
27. In this operation, the American CIA played a key role in assisting the South African security forces to locate and track the ANC leadership (Weiner, Tim. 2007. *Legacy of Ashes: The History of the CIA*. New York: Doubleday, 2007).
28. *Dawn: Journal of Umkhonto we Sizwe, 25th Anniversary Souvenir Issue*, 1986, p. 12.
29. Former MK officer Commander Masala, interviewed in the film *The Luthuli Detachment* (2007, Qoma Film Productions).
30. Former MK officer and SANDF Col. Ngcobo, interviewed in the film *The Luthuli Detachment* (2007, Qoma Film Productions).
31. Former MK officer Zola Skweyiya, interviewed in the film *The Luthuli Detachment* (2007, Qoma Film Productions).
32. Williams, 'The Other Armies.'

33. 'The Wankie Campaign,' by Chris Hani. In *Dawn: Journal of Umkhonto we Sizwe,*' pp. 34-7.

34. Ngculu, *The Honour to Serve.*

35. Confidential interview with ex-combatant, December 2009.

36. Cherry, *Umkhonto we Sizwe*, p. 45.

37. McKinley, Dale T. 1997. *The ANC and the Liberation Struggle: A Critical Political Biography*. London: Pluto Press, p. 68.

38. Confidential interview with ex-combatant, November 2009.

39. Confidential interview with ex-combatant, November 2009.

40. Wolfie Kodesh interview with Graham Morodi (Mashigo), 1993.

41. Confidential interview with ex-combatant, December 2009.

42. Confidential interview with ex-combatant, December 2009.

43. Confidential interview with ex-combatant, November 2009.

44. Confidential interview with ex-combatant, November 2009.

45. Confidential interview with ex-combatant, November 2009.

46. Cock, 'The Cultural and Social Challenge of Demilitarization,' p. 120.

47. Confidential interview with ex-combatant, December 2009.

48. Confidential interview with ex-combatant, December 2009.

49. Confidential interview with ex-combatant, December 2009; though white defectors from MK were rare, Pauw mentions that South African Police (SAP) Col. Eugene de Kock's Vlakplaas death squad unit had at least one white former MK member in its ranks.

50. Confidential interview with ex-combatant, December 2009.

51. Ngculu, *The Honour to Serve*, p. 103.

52. Sparks, Allister. 2003. *Beyond the Miracle*. Chicago, IL: University of Chicago Press.

53. Confidential interview with ex-combatant, December 2009.

54. Confidential interview with ex-combatant, December 2009.

55. Will Reno, seminar at McGill University, Montreal, 13 April 2008.

56. http://www.anc.org.za/ancdocs/history/or/or80-11.html.

57. Elster, Jon. 2004. *Closing the Books: Transitional Justice in Historical Perspective*. New York: Cambridge University Press, p. 197.

58. Chabal, Patrick. 1983. *Amilcar Cabral: Revolutionary Leadership and People's War*. Cambridge: Cambridge University Press, p. 148.

59. Cherry *Umkhonto we Sizwe*, p. 10.

60. Cherry *Umkhonto we Sizwe*, p. 80.

61. Confidential interview with ex-combatant, December 2009.

62. Confidential interview with ex-combatant, November 2009.

63. Confidential interview with ex-combatant, November 2009.

64. Confidential interview with ex-combatant, December 2009.

65. Author's interview with Dr Somadoda Fikeni, 20 December 2009.

66. Confidential interview with ex-combatant, December 2009.

67. Confidential interview with ex-combatant, December 2009.

68. Confidential interview with ex-combatant, December 2009.

69. Confidential interview with ex-combatant, November 2009.

70. Smith, Janet, and Beauregard Tromp. 2009. *Hani: A Life Too Short*. Johannesburg: Jonathan Ball Publishers.

71. Paul Landau made this point during a talk on the genesis of the ANC's armed struggle at McGill University, Montreal, Canada, April 2015.

72. Davis, *Apartheid's Rebels*.

73. Houston, Gregory, and James Ngculu. 2014. *Voices of Liberation: Chris Hani*. Cape Town: HSRC Press, p. 76.

74. Houston and Ngculu, *Voices of Liberation*, p. 77.

75. Houston and Ngculu, *Voices of Liberation*, p. 80.

76. Simpson, Thula. 2016. *Umkhonto we Sizwe: The ANC's Armed Struggle*. Cape Town: Penguin, pp. 167-8.

77. Houston and Ngculu, *Voices of Liberation*, pp. 81-2.

78. Ellis, Stephen. 1994. Mbokodo: Security in ANC Camps, 1961–1990. *African Affairs* 93 (371), pp. 279-98.

79. Simpson, *Umkhonto we Sizwe*, pp. 162-3.

80. Manong, Stanley. 2015. *If We Must Die: An Autobiography of a Former Commander of uMkhonto we Sizwe*. Johannesburg: Nkululeko Publishers.

81. Manong, *If We Must Die*, p. 125.

82. Ellis, Stephen. 2012. *External Mission: The ANC in Exile, 1960–1990*. London: Hurst.

83. Manong, *If We Must Die*, p. 126.

84. Manong, *If We Must Die*, p. 169.

85. Groenink, Evelyn. 2018. *Incorruptible: The Story of the Murders of Dulcie September, Anton Lubowski and Chris Hani*. Cape Town: ABC Press, p. 261.

86. Holden, Paul, and Hennie van Vuuren. 2011. *The Devil in the Detail: How the Arms Deal Changed Everything*. Jeppestown: Jonathan Ball, p. 70.

87. Johnson, RW. 2010. *South Africa's Brave New World*. London: Penguin Books, p. 29.

88. Ellis, Stephen, and Tsepo Sechaba. 1992. *Comrades against Apartheid: The ANC and the South African Communist Party in Exile*. London: James Currey.

89. 'Hani Not Yet Laid to Rest,' *Mail & Guardian* (Johannesburg), 29 March 2009.

90. 'Notes of Meeting with Chris Hani, Chief of Staff and Deputy Commander of Umkhonto we Sizwe, and Steve Tshwete, Political Commissar,' from an interview by John D Battersby, 3 June 1988, Lusaka, Zambia.

91. Holden and Van Vuuren, *The Devil in the Detail*, p. 35.

92. Davis, *Apartheid's Rebels*, p. 123.

93. 'Notes of Meeting with Chris Hani, Chief of Staff and Deputy Commander of Umkhonto we Sizwe, and Steve Tshwete, Political Commissar,' from an interview by John D Battersby, 3 June 1988, Lusaka, Zambia.

94. Williams, 'The Other Armies.'

95. 'MK and the Future,' SAHA, Section 5.17 (Umkhonto we Sizwe).

96. Cherry, *Umkhonto we Sizwe*, p. 58.

97. 'MK and the Future,' SAHA, Section 5.17 (Umkhonto we Sizwe).

98. Before MK was disbanded, Modise expressed regret for the loss of civilian life in MK operations such as the 1983 Church Street bombing, emphasizing that the attack was aimed at the 'top brass,' not at some of the SAAF's civilian employees who were killed (Cherry, *Umkhonto we Sizwe*, p. 57).

99. 'Fuel Refineries Strategic Targets for ANC in 80s, TRC Hears' (from a hearing in Durban, 27 September 1999), http://www.justice.gov.za/trc/media/1999/9909/p9900927a.html.

100. Davis, *Apartheid's Rebels*, p. 129.

101. Minter, William. 1994. *Apartheid's Contras: An Inquiry into the Roots of War in Angola and Mozambique*. London: Zed Books.

102. Wolfie Kodesh interview with Sipho Binda, 1993.

103. Wolfie Kodesh interview with Ayanda Ntsaluba, 1993.

104. Ngculu, *The Honour to Serve*.

105. Confidential interview with ex-combatant, December 2009.

106. Davis, *Apartheid's Rebels*, p. 118.

107. 'Notes of Meeting with Chris Hani, Chief of Staff and Deputy Commander of Umkhonto we Sizwe, and Steve Tshwete, Political Commissar,' 3 June 1988, Lusaka, Zambia.

108. Gilder, *Songs and Secrets*, p. 93.

109. 'Notes of Meeting with Chris Hani, Chief of Staff and Deputy Commander of Umkhonto we Sizwe, and Steve Tshwete, Political Commissar,' from an interview by John D Battersby, 3 June 1988, Lusaka, Zambia.

110. 'Application in terms of Section 18 of the Promotion of National Unity and Reconciliation Act, No. 34 of 1995, Joseph Elias Makhura, Frans "Ting Ting" Masango, Obed Masina, and Neo Potsane: Decision.'

111. 'Notes of Meeting with Chris Hani, Chief of Staff and Deputy Commander of Umkhonto we Sizwe, and Steve Tshwete, Political Commissar,' from an interview by John D Battersby, 3 June 1988, Lusaka, Zambia.

112. Williams, 'The Other Armies.'

113. Amnesty Decision: Velaphi Sazi Favious Msane, TRC, Cape Town, 29 March 2001, http://sabctrc.saha.org.za/documents/decisions/59385. htm?t=%2Bmahlangu+%2Bsolomon&tab=hearings.

114. Interview with Chris Hani, Lusaka, 21 January 1990: Road Ahead Perspective, SAHA, Section 5.17 (Umkhonto we Sizwe).

115. Gilder, *Songs and Secrets.*

116. Confidential interview with ex-combatant, November 2009.

117. Confidential interview with ex-combatant, November 2009.

118. 'Notes of Meeting with Chris Hani, Chief of Staff and Deputy Commander of Umkhonto we Sizwe, and Steve Tshwete, Political Commissar,' from an interview by John D Battersby, 3 June 1988, Lusaka, Zambia.

119. Author's interview with Dr Somadoda Fikeni, Tshwane, December 2009.

120. Cherry *Umkhonto we Sizwe*, p. 92.

121. Davis, *Apartheid's Rebels*, p. 120.

122. 'Notes of Meeting with Chris Hani, Chief of Staff and Deputy Commander of Umkhonto we Sizwe, and Steve Tshwete, Political Commissar,' from an interview by John D Battersby, 3 June 1988, Lusaka, Zambia.

123. Confidential interview with ex-combatant, December 2009.

124. Dlamini, Jacob. 2014. *Askari.* Auckland Park: Jacana, p. 13.

125. Henderson, Robert D'A. 1997. Operation Vula against Apartheid. *International Journal of Intelligence and Counterintelligence* 10 (4), p. 425.

126. Suttner, Raymond. 2004. The UDF Period and Its Meaning for Contemporary South Africa. *Journal of Southern African Studies* 30 (3), pp. 691-701.

127. Confidential interview with ex-combatant, November 2009.

128. Confidential interview with ex-combatant, December 2009.

129. Gear, Sasha. 2002. Now That the War Is Over: Ex-Combatants' Transition and the Question of Violence: A Literature Review, www. csvr.co.za, p. 29.

130. Sparks, Allister. 1994. *Tomorrow Is Another Country*. New York: Penguin Press.

131. Lodge, Tom. 1995. Soldiers of the Storm: A Profile of the Azanian People's Liberation Army. In *About Turn: The Transformation of the South African Military and Intelligence*, edited by J Cilliers and M Reichardt. Halfway House: Institute for Defence Policy, pp. 105-17.

132. Jeffery, Anthea. 2009. *People's War: New Light on the Struggle for South Africa*. Johannesburg: Jonathan Ball Publishers.

133. Sparks, *Tomorrow Is Another Country.*

134. Bell, Terry, with Dumisa Buhle Ntsebeza. 2003. *Unfinished Business: South Africa, Apartheid, and Truth.* London: Verso.

135. Mayibuye Archives, Wolfie Kodesh interview with Lerumo Kalako, MCA 6 – 294, 6 July 1993; this suspicion was borne out by the Steyn Report's findings: see Chapter Six.

136. Foster, Don, Paul Haupt, and Marésa de Beer (eds). 2005. *The Theatre of Violence: Narratives of Protagonists in the South African Conflict.* Cape Town: Human Studies Research Council.

137. Gear, 'Now That the War Is Over,' p. 28.

138. Foster et al., *The Theatre of Violence.*

139. Shubin, Vladimir. 2008. *The Hot 'Cold War': The USSR in Southern Africa.* London: Pluto Press.

140. One important exception was the killing of four APLA cadres in a shootout with MK forces at a voter education station in Port St Johns one month before the 1994 elections; these APLA cadres were a renegade faction, however, since by this time the PAC leadership had rescinded its rejectionist stance towards the negotiations.

141. Confidential interview with ex-combatant, December 2009.

142. Manong, *If We Must Die*, p. 86.

143. Manong, *If We Must Die*, p. 256.

144. There is much controversy as to just how decisive was the Cuban-FAPLA victory over SADF at Cuito Cuanavale, a battle in which both sides claimed victory; however, Gleijeses (*Visions of Freedom: Havana, Washington, Pretoria, and the Struggle for Southern Africa*) illustrates the strategic victory scored by the Cuban side with a quote from SADF Col. Jan Breytenbach, commander of the crack 32nd Battalion: 'bloody Fidel Castro outsmarted South Africa's generals, and it became dangerous.'

145. Confidential interview with ex-combatant, December 2009.

2. THE COLONIAL ORIGINS OF COUNTERINSURGENCY

1. Hani, Lindiwe, and Melinda Ferguson. 2017. *Being Chris Hani's Daughter.* Auckland Park: Jacana.

2. Confidential interview with ex-combatant, November 2009.

3. Survivors of the Matola raid found a swastika emblazoned on the helmet of one of the dead SADF commandos (Slovo, *Every Secret Thing*).

4. Gear, Sasha. 2002. Now That the War Is Over: Ex-Combatants' Transition and the Question of Violence: A Literature Review, www.csvr.co.za, p. 10.

5. Hanlon, Joseph. 1986. *Beggar Your Neighbours: Apartheid Power in Southern Africa.* Bloomington, IN: Indiana University Press.

6. Pauw, Jacques. 1997. *Into the Heart of Darkness: Confessions of Apartheid's Assassins*. Johannesburg: Jonathan Ball Publishers.

7. 'Mozambique/South Africa: The Special Forces behind RENAMO,' *Africa Confidential* 28 (24), 2 December 1987.

8. Ellis, Stephen. 1998. The Historical Significance of South Africa's Third Force. *Journal of Southern African Studies* 24 (2), pp. 261-99.

9. ANC Second Submission to the TRC.

10. Murray, Martin. 1994. *The Revolution Deferred: The Painful Birth of Post-Apartheid South Africa*. London: Verso, p. 232.

11. 'Armscor in Tussle with Agents over Trial,' *Sunday Times*, 12 March 1995.

12. Berkeley, Bill. 2001. *The Graves Are Not Yet Full: Race, Tribe, and Power in the Heart of Africa*. New York: Basic Books; Williams, Rocky. 2000. The Other Armies: A Brief Historical Overview of Umkhonto we Sizwe, 1961–1994. *South African Military History Society Journal* 11 (5).

13. Williams, 'The Other Armies,' p. 4.

14. Ellis, 'The Historical Significance of South Africa's Third Force,' p. 266.

15. Sanders (*Apartheid's Friends: The Rise and Fall of South Africa's Secret Service*) reports that all the Rhodesian intelligence files were transferred from Salisbury to Pretoria on the day of Zimbabwean independence.

16. 'South Africa: Genesis of the Third Force,' *Africa Confidential* 32 (19), 27 September 1991.

17. According to Groenink, Burnett was not actually trying to kill Watson, but in an interview with Potgieter, former SAP officer Drummond Hammond confirmed that Burnett was arrested after 'botching' an attempt on Watson's life (SAHA AL 3283, De Wet Potgieter interview with Detective Warrant Officer Drummond Hammond, Centurion, South Africa, 25 February 2010).

18. Nqakula, Charles. 2017. *The People's War: Reflections of an ANC Cadre*. Johannesburg: Mutloatse Heritage Trust, p. 233.

19. 'Researchers Present Apartheid South Africa's Dirty Tricks Findings to TRC,' SAPA, 10 November 1997 (Johannesburg).

20. Schirmer, Jennifer. 1998. *The Guatemalan Military Project: A Violence Called Democracy*. Cambridge, MA: Harvard University Press.

21. Author's correspondence with J Patrice McSherry, June 2011.

22. 'Researchers Present Apartheid South Africa's Dirty Tricks Findings to TRC' SAPA, 10 November 1997 (Johannesburg); see also Hassan, Magda. 2009. SA Links in the Palme Murder. *Deep Politics Forum*, 16 September.

23. Davidson, Basil. 1981. *The People's Cause: A History of Guerrillas in Africa*. Harlow: Longman.

24. Cherry, Janet. 2011. *Umkhonto we Sizwe*. Auckland Park: Jacana, pp. 26-7.

25. Harris, Peter. 2012. *A Just Defiance*. Berkeley, CA: University of California Press.
26. Minter, William. 1994. *Apartheid's Contras: An Inquiry into the Roots of War in Angola and Mozambique*. London: Zed Books, p. 124.
27. Berkeley, *The Graves Are Not Yet Full*, p. 177.
28. Confidential interview with ex-combatant, November 2009.
29. Confidential interview with ex-combatant, November 2009.
30. Cabral, Amilcar. 1973. New Year's Message. In *Return to the Source: Selected Speeches of Amilcar Cabral*. New York: Monthly Review Press, p. 199.
31. Fanon, Frantz. 1961. *The Wretched of the Earth*. New York: Grove Press, p. 109.
32. Houston, Gregory, and James Ngculu. 2014. *Voices of Liberation: Chris Hani*. Cape Town: HSRC Press, p. 123.
33. Mayibuye Archives, Wolfie Kodesh interview with Lerumo Kalako MCA 6 – 294, 6 July 1993.
34. Mayibuye Archives, Wolfie Kodesh interview with Lerumo Kalako MCA 6 – 294, 6 July 1993.
35. Manong, Stanley. 2015. *If We Must Die: An Autobiography of a Former Commander of uMkhonto we Sizwe*. Johannesburg: Nkululeko Publishers, p. 92.
36. Ellis, 'The Historical Significance of South Africa's Third Force,' p. 268.
37. Pauw, *Into the Heart of Darkness*.
38. SAHA, TRC Gunrunning.
39. TRC Testimony of Enock Tshabalala, Batandwa Ndondo Matter, Mthatha, 24 August 1998, http://www.justice.gov.za/trc/amntrans/1998/98082425_umt_umtata1.htm.
40. Glory Sedibe's sister, Jackie Sedibe (see Chapter Six), rose to the rank of general in the post-apartheid SANDF, and was married to Joe Modise.
41. Pauw *Into the Heart of Darkness*, p. 73.
42. Pauw, *Into the Heart of Darkness*, p. 74.
43. Dlamini, Jacob. 2014. *Askari*. Auckland Park: Jacana.
44. Pauw, *Into the Heart of Darkness*.
45. Dlamini, *Askari*.
46. Truth and Reconciliation Commission Amnesty Hearing, 24 August 1998, Eugene Alexander de Kock, Batandwa Ndondo Matter, www.trc.co.za.
47. Fumanikile Booi, Testimony to the TRC on the death of Nicholas Johannes Els, Cape Town, 28 October 1999. Available at: http://www.justice.gov.za/trc/amntrans/1999/99101828_ct_991028.htm.
48. Confidential interview with ex-combatant, December 2009.

49. Truth and Reconciliation Commission Amnesty Hearing, 24 August 1998, Eugene Alexander de Kock, Batandwa Ndondo Matter, www.trc. co.za.

50. Confidential interview with ex-combatant, December 2009.

51. Truth and Reconciliation Commission Amnesty Hearing, 24 August 1998, Eugene Alexander de Kock, Batandwa Ndondo Matter, www.trc. co.za.

52. O'Brien, Kevin. 2011. *The South African Intelligence Services: From Apartheid to Democracy, 1948–2005*. New York: Routledge, p. 108.

53. Notes of a meeting with Chris Hani, Chief-of-Staff and Deputy Commander of Umkhonto we Sizwe, and Steve Tshwete, Political Commissar, from an interview by John D Battersby, 3 June 1988 in Lusaka, Zambia.

54. Confidential interview with ex-combatant, December 2009.

55. Gottschalk, Keith. 2000. The Rise and Fall of Apartheid's Death Squads, 1969–93. In *Death Squads in Global Perspective: Murder with Deniability*, edited by BB Campbell and Arthur D Brenner. New York: St Martin's Press, p. 34.

56. O'Brien, *The South African Intelligence Services*.

57. McCarthy, Shaun. 1996. Challenges for the South African Intelligence Community. In *South Africa's Defense and Security into the 21st Century*, edited by W Gutteridge. Brookfield, VT: Dartmouth Publishing, p. 71.

58. Sparks, Allister. 1994. *Tomorrow Is Another Country*. New York: Penguin Press, p. 158.

59. Phillips, Ian. 1998. The Eagles Youth Clubs. In *The Hidden Hand: Covert Operations in South Africa*, 2nd edn, edited by C Schutte, Ian Liebenberg, and Anthony Minaar. Pretoria: Human Sciences Research Council, p. 213.

60. O'Brien, *The South African Intelligence Services*, p. 90.

61. Ellis, 'The Historical Significance of South Africa's Third Force.'

62. Confidential interview with ex-combatant, December 2009.

63. Confidential interview with ex-combatant, December 2009.

64. 'Shock over City Council "Spy" Allegations,' *The Citizen*, 21 March 1990.

65. Pauw, *Into the Heart of Darkness*, p. 195.

66. Cawthra, Gavin. 1986. *Brutal Force: The Apartheid War Machine*. London: International Defence and Aid Fund for Southern Africa.

67. SAHA Archives, TRC Gunrunning.

68. Ellis, 'The Historical Significance of South Africa's Third Force.'

69. O'Brien, *The South African Intelligence Services*, p. 130.

70. Sanders, James. 2006. *Apartheid's Friends: The Rise and Fall of South Africa's Secret Service*. London: John Murray Publishers.

71. SAHA, AL 3283, B1.1.2.1, 'The Civil Cooperation Bureau (CCB), a Third Force.'
72. Groenink, Evelyn. 2018. *Incorruptible: The Story of the Murders of Dulcie September, Anton Lubowski and Chris Hani.* Cape Town: ABC Press, p. 231.
73. Ellis, 'The Historical Significance of South Africa's Third Force,' p. 289.
74. SAHA, AL 3283, B1.1.2.1, 'The Civil Cooperation Bureau (CCB), a Third Force.'
75. 'The South African Army and Police: Apartheid's Cannibals,' *Michigan Citizen* 15 (19), 3 April 1993. Groenink (*Incorruptible*) mentions that the SADF base near Kosi Bay had been involved in smuggling sensitive military technologies that Webster may have stumbled upon, prompting the security forces to eliminate him. The *African Communist* further mentions that on 25 May 1989, a man calling himself Van Niekerk showed up at Webster's research laboratory and sought access to his office. His colleagues, immediately suspicious, barred the stranger from entering, whereupon he left with several other men by boat. As the SAP spokesperson for the investigation of Webster's murder, Brigadier Frans Malherbe (then a colonel), claimed that Van Niekerk had indeed been a student at the University of Potchefstroom, and that there was nothing untoward about this incident; yet both Potchefstroom and Witwatersrand universities subsequently checked their records and denied that any such student had ever been registered ('Who Killed Hani?' *African Communist*).
76. Pauw, *Into the Heart of Darkness.*
77. Pauw, *Into the Heart of Darkness.*
78. Shaw, Mark. 2002. *Crime and Policing in Post-Apartheid South Africa.* Bloomington, IN: Indiana University Press; Kynoch, Gary. 2005. Crime, Conflict, and Politics in Transition-Era South Africa. *African Affairs* 104 (416), pp. 493-514.
79. Schutte, Charl, Ian Liebenberg, and Anthony Minnaar (eds). 1998. *The Hidden Hand: Covert Operations in South Africa*, 2nd edn. Pretoria: Human Sciences Research Council.
80. Berkeley, *The Graves Are Not Yet Full.*
81. Gottschalk, 'The Rise and Fall of Apartheid's Death Squads,' p. 244.
82. O'Brien, *The South African Intelligence Services*, p. 125.
83. Basie Smit testimony to Section 29 of the TRC, Durban, 9 July 1997 (SAHA, AL 2878_B01.5.75.02.21).
84. 'IFP's "Caprivis" Still on the Job,' *Mail & Guardian*, 11 October 1996.
85. O'Brien, *The South African Intelligence Services*, p. 126.
86. Sanders, *Apartheid's Friends.*

87. Berkeley, *The Graves Are Not Yet Full*, p. 174.
88. Gear, 'Now That the War Is Over,' p. 15.
89. Houston and Ngculu, *Voices of Liberation*.
90. Flanagan, Louise. 1998. Covert Operations in the Eastern Cape. In *The Hidden Hand: Covert Operations in South Africa*, 2nd edn, edited by C Schutte, Ian Liebenberg, and Anthony Minaar. Pretoria: Human Sciences Research Council, p. 196.
91. McKinley, Dale T. 1997. *The ANC and the Liberation Struggle: A Critical Political Biography*. London: Pluto Press.
92. Pauw, *Into the Heart of Darkness*, p. 47.
93. Confidential interview with ex-combatant, December 2009.
94. Confidential interview with ex-combatant, December 2009.
95. Henderson, Robert D'A. 1995. South African Intelligence under De Klerk. In *About Turn: The Transformation of the South African Military and Intelligence*, edited by J Cilliers and M Reichardt. Halfway House: Institute for Defence Policy, p. 150.
96. Backmann, René. 1980. Confession of a Dog of War. In *The CIA in Africa*. London: Zed Books, pp. 146-58.
97. Nqakula, *The People's War*, p. 301.
98. Ellis, 'The Historical Significance of South Africa's Third Force.'
99. Mkhondo, Rich. 1993. *Reporting South Africa*. Portsmouth, NH: Heinemann.
100. Confidential interview with ex-combatant, December 2009.
101. 'CIA Linked to Mandela's Arrest,' *Washington Post*, 11 July 1990.
102. 'CIA Linked to Mandela's Arrest,' *Washington Post*, 11 July 1990.
103. Weiner, Tim. 2007. *Legacy of Ashes: The History of the CIA*. New York: Doubleday, 2007, p. 362.
104. Weiner *Legacy of Ashes*, p. 377.
105. Minter, *Apartheid's Contras*.
106. 'S. Africa's Intelligence Network,' *Afro-American*, 11 April 1987.
107. 'S. Africa's Intelligence Network,' *Afro-American*, 11 April 1987.
108. 'Evidence of US Strategic Role,' *Newsday*, 2 August 1986.
109. Winter, Gordon. 1981. *Inside BOSS, South Africa's Secret Police*. New York: Penguin, p. 431.
110. Author's confidential interview with ex-combatant, November 2009.
111. Sanders, *Apartheid's Friends*.
112. Indeed, during the NP-ANC negotiations, Savimbi had pledged to assist rejectionist far-right elements under the leadership of retired SADF General Constand Viljoen as late as 1994 (De Wet Potgieter interview with Tienie Groenewald, 2009).
113. O'Brien, *The South African Intelligence Services*, p. 69.

114. 'Notes of Meeting with Chris Hani, Chief of Staff and Deputy Commander of Umkhonto we Sizwe, and Steve Tshwete, Political Commissar,' from an interview by John D Battersby, 3 June 1988, Lusaka, Zambia.

3. APARTHEID COUNTERINSURGENCY DURING THE NEGOTIATIONS, 1990–4

1. Fumanikile Booi testimony to the TRC on the death of Nicholas Johannes Els, Cape Town, 28 October 1999.
2. Phungulwa was part of the 'Group of Ten' that arrived in Johannesburg from Tanzania. In addition to Phungulwa, the group included Mwezi Twala, Vusi Shange, Diliza Mthembu, David Makhubedu, Luthando Dyasop [also rendered 'Dyasophu'], Motyatyambo Mzimeli and Patheka Sodo, 'many of whom played prominent roles in the mutiny in 1984' (Simpson, *Umkhonto we Sizwe*, p. 462).
3. Smith, Janet, and Beauregard Tromp. 2009. *Hani: A Life Too Short.* Johannesburg: Jonathan Ball Publishers.
4. Trewhela, Paul. 2009. *Inside Quatro: Uncovering the Exile History of the ANC and SWAPO.* Johannesburg: Jacana, p. 200.
5. Confidential interview with ex-combatant, December 2009.
6. Trewhela, Paul. 1991. The Killing of Sipho Phungulwa. *Searchlight South Africa* 2 (2), pp. 8-30; Trewhela *Inside Quatro.*
7. Trewhela *Inside Quatro*; Jeffery, Anthea. 2009. *People's War: New Light on the Struggle for South Africa.* Johannesburg: Jonathan Ball Publishers; Ellis, Stephen. 2012. *External Mission: The ANC in Exile, 1960–1990.* London: Hurst.
8. 'Amnesty Decisions, Ian Ndibulele Ndzamela, Pumlani Kubukeli, Mfanelo Dan Matshaya,' 18 August 1998.
9. 'Amnesty Decisions, Ian Ndibulele Ndzamela, Pumlani Kubukeli, Mfanelo Dan Matshaya,' 18 August 1998.
10. 'Amnesty Decisions, Ian Ndibulele Ndzamela, Pumlani Kubukeli, Mfanelo Dan Matshaya,' 18 August 1998.
11. Confidential interview with ex-combatant, December 2009.
12. 'Amnesty Decisions, Ian Ndibulele Ndzamela, Pumlani Kubukeli, Mfanelo Dan Matshaya,' 18 August 1998.
13. Confidential interview with ex-combatant, December 2009.
14. Powell, Ivor. 1998. Aspects of Propaganda Operations. In *The Hidden Hand: Covert Operations in South Africa*, 2nd edn, edited by C Schutte, Ian Liebenberg, and Anthony Minaar. Pretoria: Human Sciences Research Council, pp. 335-42.
15. Powell, 'Aspects of Propaganda Operations,' p. 339.

16. Sanders, James. 2006. *Apartheid's Friends: The Rise and Fall of South Africa's Secret Service*. London: John Murray Publishers.

17. Mayibuye Archives, MCH 88 no. MCA6-284, Wolfie Kodesh interview with Chris Hani, 1 April 1993.

18. 'Toll of Unsolved Killings: Opponents of Apartheid,' *The Times*, 18 November 1989.

19. http://www.justice.gov.za/trc/hrvtrans/submit/anc2.htm# Operations.

20. Cullather, Nick. 1999. *The CIA's Classified Account of Its War in Guatemala, 1952–54*. Stanford, CA: Stanford University Press.

21. Grandin, Greg. 2011. *The Last Colonial Massacre: Latin America during the Cold War*. Chicago, IL: University of Chicago Press, p. 191.

22. Horne, Gerald. 2001. *From the Barrel of a Gun: The United States and the War in Zimbabwe, 1965–1980*. Chapel Hill, NC: University of North Carolina Press.

23. 'Media Spies Warned,' *New Nation*, 20 March 1997; 'CCB Men Break Ranks,' *New Nation*, 16 May 1997.

24. Williams, Rocky. 1991. *Back to the Barracks: The SADF and the Dynamics of Transformation*. Johannesburg: IDASA, p. 46.

25. Herbstein, Denis. 1994. Old Spies Don't Die. *Africa Report* 39 (2), March-April.

26. ANC Statement to the Truth and Reconciliation Commission, Vol. 4.9 (August 1996), http://www.justice.gov.za/trc/hrvtrans/submit/anctruth.htm#4.

27. ANC Statement to the Truth and Reconciliation Commission, Vol. 4.9 (August 1996).

28. O'Brien, Kevin. 2011. *The South African Intelligence Services: From Apartheid to Democracy, 1948–2005*. New York: Routledge, p. 141.

29. Seegers, Annette. 1991. South Africa's National Security Management System, 1972–1990. *Journal of Modern African Studies* 29 (2), p. 268.

30. Klopp, Jacqueline, and Elke Zuern. 2007. The Politics of Violence in Democratization: Lessons from Kenya and South Africa. *Comparative Politics* 39 (2), pp. 1-32.

31. ANC Statement to the Truth and Reconciliation Commission, Vol. 4.9 (August 1996), http://www.justice.gov.za/trc/hrvtrans/submit/anctruth.htm#4.

32. Ellis, Stephen. 1998. The Historical Significance of South Africa's Third Force. *Journal of Southern African Studies* 24 (2), pp. 261-99; Klopp and Zuern, 'The Politics of Violence in Democratization.'

33. Powell, 'Aspects of Propaganda Operations.'

34. SAHA, A2.4.1.7 (TRC Gunrunning).

35. Saunders, Christopher. 1992. Transition in Namibia 1989-90 and the South African Case. In *Peace, Politics, and Violence in the New South Africa*, edited by N Etherington. London: Hans Zell Publishers, p. 220.

36. *Vrye Weekblad*, 12 April 1991.

37. *Vrye Weekblad*, 12 April 1991.

38. *Vrye Weekblad*, 12 April 1991.

39. Saunders, 'Transition in Namibia 1989-90 and the South African Case.'

40. Powell, 'Aspects of Propaganda Operations.'

41. Sanders, *Apartheid's Friends*, p. 251.

42. Mkhondo, Rich. 1993. *Reporting South Africa*. Portsmouth, NH: Heinemann, p. 60.

43. Saunders, 'Transition in Namibia 1989–90 and the South African Case,' p. 228.

44. O'Brien, *The South African Intelligence Services.*

45. 'South Africa: Violence in Transition,' *Africa Confidential* 33 (8), 17 April 1992.

46. O'Brien, *The South African Intelligence Services*, p. 159.

47. Reno, Will. 2011. *Warfare in Independent Africa*. Cambridge: Cambridge University Press, p. 114.

48. Reno, *Warfare in Independent Africa*, p. 161.

49. O'Malley, Padraig. 2007. *Shades of Difference: Mac Maharaj and the Struggle for South Africa*. New York: Viking, p. 373.

50. Ellis, 'The Historical Significance of South Africa's Third Force.'

51. Gottschalk, Keith. 2000. The Rise and Fall of Apartheid's Death Squads, 1969–93. In *Death Squads in Global Perspective: Murder with Deniability*, edited by BB Campbell and Arthur D Brenner. New York: St Martin's Press.

52. Gottschalk, 'The Rise and Fall of Apartheid's Death Squads.'

53. Sparks, Allister. 1994. *Tomorrow Is Another Country*. New York: Penguin Press, p. 138.

54. Mkhondo, *Reporting South Africa*, p. 56.

55. Mayibuye Archives, Wolfie Kodesh interview with Graham Morodi, MCA6 – 324, 6 July 1993.

56. Ngculu, James. 2009. *The Honour to Serve: Recollections of an Umkhonto Soldier*. Claremont: David Philip, p. 232.

57. 'South Africa: Genesis of the Third Force,' *Africa Confidential* 32 (19), 27 September 1991.

58. TRC, Vol. 2, ch. 7, p. 612.

59. TRC, Vol. 2, ch. 7, p. 613.

60. Pauw, Jacques. 1997. *Into the Heart of Darkness: Confessions of Apartheid's Assassins*. Johannesburg: Jonathan Ball Publishers, p. 130.

61. TRC, Vol. 2, ch. 7, p. 613.

62. 'African National Congress, Organizing Committee National Workshop, 6–9 November 1990: Strategic Priorities for Building the ANC: Address by Comrade Popo Molefe,' SAHA.

63. 'MK and the Future,' SAHA, p. 5.

64. Van der Westhuizen, Christi. 2007. *White Power and the Rise and Fall of the National Party.* Cape Town: Zebra Press, p. 204.

65. ANC Statement to the Truth and Reconciliation Commission, Vol. 4.9 (August 1996), http://www.justice.gov.za/trc/hrvtrans/submit/anctruth.htm#4.

66. ANC Statement to the Truth and Reconciliation Commission, Vol. 4.9 (August 1996).

67. 'South Africa: Genesis of the Third Force,' *Africa Confidential* 32 (19), 27 September 1991.

68. Saul, John S. 1993. *Recolonization and Resistance in Southern Africa in the 1990s.* Toronto: Between the Lines Press, p. 102.

69. Sithole, Jabulani. 2013. The Inkatha Freedom Party and the Multiparty Negotiations. In *The Road to Democracy in South Africa, Vol. 6 (1990–1996).* South Africa Democracy Education Trust, Pretoria: University of South Africa Press, p. 854.

70. Sithole, 'The Inkatha Freedom Party and the Multiparty Negotiations'; De Haas, Mary. 2013. Violence in Zululand: The 1990s. In *The Road to Democracy in South Africa, Vol. 6 (1990–1996).* South Africa Democracy Education Trust, Pretoria: University of South Africa Press, pp. 876-957.

71. 'Top KZP Officers Implicated in Murders,' *New Nation*, 2 May 1997.

72. TRC, Vol. 5, ch. 6, section 112, p. 230.

73. 'South Africa: Violence in Transition,' *Africa Confidential* 33 (8), 17 April 1992.

74. Magubane, Bernard. 2013. The Beginning of the End: The Garrison State Is Finally Dismantled. In *The Road to Democracy in South Africa, Vol. 6 (1990–1996).* South Africa Democracy Education Trust, Pretoria: University of South Africa Press, p. 1396.

75. Sithole, 'The Inkatha Freedom Party and the Multiparty Negotiations.'

76. Taylor, Rupert. 2002. Justice Denied: Political Violence in KwaZulu-Natal after 1994. Centre for the Study of Violence and Reconciliation, Violence and Transition Series, vol. 6.

77. Lesch, Graham Michael. 2006. *Shadows of Justice.* Durban: Roberts Printers.

78. Confidential interview with ex-combatant, December 2009.

79. Lesch, *Shadows of Justice*, p. 175.

80. Berkeley, Bill. 2001. *The Graves Are Not Yet Full: Race, Tribe, and Power in the Heart of Africa*. New York: Basic Books.

81. Pauw, *Into the Heart of Darkness*, pp. 129-30.

82. O'Malley, *Shades of Difference*, p. 396; Claude, Nicholas. 1996. Lost and Forgotten: Irregular Forces in KwaZulu-Natal. *KwaZulu-Natal Briefing* 4, pp. 13-17.

83. 'Rightists Face Murder Charges,' *New Nation*, 29 September 1995.

84. De Haas, 'Violence in Zululand,' p. 910.

85. Berkeley, Bill. 1994. The Warlords of Natal. *Atlantic Monthly* (March), pp. 85-100.

86. De Haas, 'Violence in Zululand,' p. 898.

87. Mkhondo *Reporting South Africa*; De Haas, 'Violence in Zululand.'

88. Murray, Martin. 1994. *The Revolution Deferred: The Painful Birth of Post-Apartheid South Africa*. London: Verso.

89. Pauw, *Into the Heart of Darkness*, p. 129.

90. Pauw, *Into the Heart of Darkness*.

91. Berkeley, 'The Warlords of Natal.'

92. Simpson, Thula. 2016. *Umkhonto we Sizwe: The ANC's Armed Struggle*. Cape Town: Penguin, p. 480.

93. Saul, *Recolonization and Resistance in Southern Africa in the 1990s*, p. 102.

94. Henderson, Robert D'A. 1995. South African Intelligence under De Klerk. In *About Turn: The Transformation of the South African Military and Intelligence*, edited by J Cilliers and M Reichardt. Halfway House: Institute for Defence Policy, pp. 155-6.

95. Sithole, 'The Inkatha Freedom Party and the Multiparty Negotiations,' p. 869.

96. 'The South African Army and Police: Apartheid's Cannibals,' *Michigan Citizen* 15 (19), 3 April 1993.

97. 'The South African Army and Police: Apartheid's Cannibals,' *Michigan Citizen* 15 (19), 3 April 1993.

98. O'Brien, *The South African Intelligence Services*, p. 192.

99. O'Brien, *The South African Intelligence Services*, p. 192.

100. 'Stratcom Never Died, Says Ex-Cop,' *Mail & Guardian*, 18 August 1995.

101. 'Stratcom Never Died, Says Ex-Cop,' *Mail & Guardian*, 18 August 1995.

102. 'Stratcom Never Died, Says Ex-Cop,' *Mail & Guardian*, 18 August 1995.

103. Reno, *Warfare in Independent Africa*, pp. 114-15.

104. O'Brien, *The South African Intelligence Services*, p. 125.

105. Mzwandile Gushu Amnesty Hearing, TRC, 22 July 1998.

106. ANC Statement to the Truth and Reconciliation Commission, Vol. 4.9 (August 1996).

107. Dugard, Jackie. 2001. From Low Intensity War to Mafia War: Taxi Violence in South Africa (1987–2000). Centre for the Study of Violence and Reconciliation, Violence and Transition Series, vol. 4.
108. Dugard, 'From Low Intensity War to Mafia War.'
109. Dugard, 'From Low Intensity War to Mafia War.'
110. De Haas, 'Violence in Zululand,' p. 904.
111. SAHA, A2.4.1.7 (TRC Gunrunning 1974-97).
112. SAHA, AL 3283 (De Wet Potgieter collection, featuring interviews and archival documents collected by South African journalist De Wet Potgieter).
113. SAHA, AL 3283 B1.1.2.1 ('The Civil Cooperation Bureau (CCB), a Third Force').
114. SAHA, AL 3283 B1.1.2.1. Regarding Botes's membership of the CCB, Potgieter quotes SADF Colonel Jan Breytenbach, who knew Botes, insisting that he 'can't understand how he became mixed up with things like this.' Yet Breytenbach himself had commanded the SADF paratrooper raid on the refugee camp at Cassinga, Angola, on 4 May 1978, that killed 672 Namibian refugees, about half of them children (Heywood, *The Cassinga Event*); he was also involved in training a Ciskei Defence Force paratrooper unit which was intended as a counterinsurgency unit (see Chapter Three). Atrocities perpetrated by the SADF, then, were hardly restricted to death squads.
115. O'Brien, *The South African Intelligence Services*, p. 137.
116. SAHA, AL 3283 B1.1.2.1.
117. Harris, Peter. 2012. *A Just Defiance*. Berkeley, CA: University of California Press.
118. SAHA, A2.4.1.7 (TRC Gunrunning 1974-97).
119. SAHA, AL 3283 B1.1.3.1 (Pan-Afrik Industrial Investment Consultants).
120. Henderson, 'South African Intelligence under De Klerk,' p. 161.
121. 'South Africa: Looking Through the Mirrors,' *Africa Confidential* 33 (15), 31 July 1992.
122. 'Shadowy Web of Security Force Conspiracy Begins to Emerge,' *Sunday Times*, 12 March 1995.
123. Henderson, 'South African Intelligence under De Klerk,' p. 153.
124. O'Brien, *The South African Intelligence Services*, p. 133; emphasis in original.
125. O'Brien, *The South African Intelligence Services*, p. 183.
126. O'Brien, *The South African Intelligence Services*, p. 103.
127. McSherry, J Patrice. 2005. *Predatory States: Operation Condor and Covert War in Latin America*. New York: Rowman and Littlefield Publishers.
128. O'Brien, *The South African Intelligence Services*, p. 249.

129. O'Brien, *The South African Intelligence Services*, p. 183.

130. O'Brien, *The South African Intelligence Services*, p. 183.

131. Pauw, *Into the Heart of Darkness.*

132. SAHA, A.2.4.1.07.1.1.3 (TRC Gunrunning 1974-97).

133. Pauw, *Into the Heart of Darkness.*

134. Henderson, 'South African Intelligence under De Klerk,' p. 73.

135. Ellis, 'The Historical Significance of South Africa's Third Force,' p. 293.

136. 'The Secrets of Stratcom,' *Mail & Guardian*, 23 June 1995.

137. 'Seven Other Death Farms' *New Nation*, 20 March 1997.

138. 'Seven Other Death Farms' *New Nation*, 20 March 1997.

139. 'Seven Other Death Farms' *New Nation*, 20 March 1997.

140. 'Seven Other Death Farms' *New Nation*, 20 March 1997.

141. 'Farm of Killers,' *New Nation*, 14 March 1997.

142. 'Shell House and the Mystery Wimpy Bombers,' *New Nation*, 18 April 1997. MK forces did also launch several bomb attacks on Wimpy restaurants (Cherry, *Umkhonto we Sizwe*), a plan that was hotly condemned within the ANC as running counter to its values and aims (Nqakula, *The People's War*).

143. 'Shell House and the Mystery Wimpy Bombers,' *New Nation*, 18 April 1997.

144. 'De Kock Claims Probed,' *New Nation*, 7 August 1997.

145. Pauw, *Into the Heart of Darkness*, pp. 136-7.

146. SAHA, De Wet Potgieter Collection, B1.1.5.1 Operation Nyawa.

147. 'Mercenary Claims 20 Are Buried on "Hit Squad" Farm,' *Sunday Times*, 12 March 1995.

148. Minter, William. 1994. *Apartheid's Contras: An Inquiry into the Roots of War in Angola and Mozambique*. London: Zed Books.

149. SAHA, AL 3283, De Wet Potgieter interview with SADF Gen. Tienie Groenewald, Centurion, South Africa, 12 October 2009.

150. 'Apartheid Army's Deadly Secrets,' IOL, 30 April 2006.

151. SAHA, AL 3283, De Wet Potgieter interview with SADF Gen. Tienie Groenewald, Centurion, South Africa, 12 October 2009.

152. Truth and Reconciliation Commission Final Report Vol.2 Ch.7, p.592.

4. MK'S WAR IN THE SHADOWS, 1990–4

1.   Fumanikile Booi testimony to the TRC regarding the death of Nicholas Johannes Els, Cape Town, 28 October 1999, available online at: http://www.justice.gov.za/trc/amntrans/1999/99101828_ct_991028.htm.

2.   Ngculu, James. 2009. *The Honour to Serve: Recollections of an Umkhonto Soldier*. Claremont: David Philip, p. 131.

3. Confidential interview with ex-combatant, November 2009.

4. Among others, the Truth and Reconciliation Commission named MK cadre Scelo Msomi, killed by Askaris in June 1990 after returning from Tanzania for a mission; Johannes Sweet Sambo, killed in July 1991 in Komatipoort while in police custody; and MK cadre Wellington Mbili, who died in police custody in Port Shepstone on 4 October 1993. see TRC Final Report Vol. 2, Ch. 7, p. 596-7.

5. Jenkin, Tim. 1995. Talking to Vula: The Story of the Secret Underground Communications Network of Operation Vula. *Mayibuye*, May-October. Accessed at http://www.anc.org.za/content/talking-vula.

6. Henderson, Robert D'A. 1997. Operation Vula against Apartheid. *International Journal of Intelligence and Counterintelligence* 10 (4), p. 424.

7. O'Malley, Padraig. 2007. *Shades of Difference: Mac Maharaj and the Struggle for South Africa*. New York: Viking, p. 247.

8. O'Malley, *Shades of Difference*, p. 250.

9. Jenkin, 'Talking to Vula.'

10. Henderson, 'Operation Vula against Apartheid.'

11. O'Brien, Kevin. 2011. *The South African Intelligence Services: From Apartheid to Democracy, 1948–2005*. New York: Routledge, p. 98.

12. O'Malley, *Shades of Difference*, p. 263.

13. O'Malley, *Shades of Difference*, p. 262.

14. O'Brien, *The South African Intelligence Services*.

15. Jenkin, 'Talking to Vula.'

16. O'Malley, *Shades of Difference*, p. 279.

17. Henderson, 'Operation Vula against Apartheid,' p. 431.

18. Henderson, 'Operation Vula against Apartheid,' p. 432.

19. Ngculu, *The Honour to Serve*, p. 196.

20. O'Brien, *The South African Intelligence Services*, p. 173.

21. O'Malley, *Shades of Difference*, p. 267.

22. Henderson, 'Operation Vula against Apartheid,' p. 433.

23. O'Malley, *Shades of Difference*, p. 267.

24. O'Malley, *Shades of Difference*, p. 267.

25. Henderson, 'Operation Vula against Apartheid,' p. 433.

26. O'Malley, *Shades of Difference*, p. 269.

27. O'Malley, *Shades of Difference*, p. 268.

28. O'Malley, *Shades of Difference*, pp. 268, 276.

29. O'Malley, *Shades of Difference*, p. 282.

30. O'Malley, *Shades of Difference*, p. 296.

31. McKinley, Dale T. 1997. *The ANC and the Liberation Struggle: A Critical Political Biography*. London: Pluto Press, p. 78.

32. O'Brien, *The South African Intelligence Services*, p. 168.

33. O'Brien, *The South African Intelligence Services*, p. 176.
34. O'Brien, *The South African Intelligence Services*, p. 177.
35. O'Malley, *Shades of Difference*, p. 243.
36. Nqakula, Charles. 2017. *The People's War: Reflections of an ANC Cadre.* Johannesburg: Mutloatse Heritage Trust, p. 280.
37. Barnard cited in Nqakula, *The People's War*, p. 280.
38. O'Brien, *The South African Intelligence Services*, p. 177.
39. O'Brien, *The South African Intelligence Services*, p. 177.
40. Jenkin, 'Talking to Vula.'
41. Ngculu, *The Honour to Serve*, p. 194.
42. Henderson, 'Operation Vula against Apartheid,' p. 434.
43. Ngculu, *The Honour to Serve*, p. 194.
44. O'Malley, *Shades of Difference*.
45. Simpson, Thula. 2016. *Umkhonto we Sizwe: The ANC's Armed Struggle.* Cape Town: Penguin, p. 452.
46. Simpson, *Umkhonto we Sizwe*, pp. 454-5.
47. Simpson, *Umkhonto we Sizwe*, p. 454.
48. Houston, Gregory, and James Ngculu. 2014. *Voices of Liberation: Chris Hani.* Cape Town: HSRC Press, p. 126.
49. 'Interview with Chris Hani, Lusaka, 21 January 1990: Road Ahead Perspective' (SAHA).
50. 'MK and the Future,' p. 4 (SAHA).
51. O'Malley, *Shades of Difference*, p. 262.
52. 'Operation Vula – The Facts behind the Fiction: Interview with Siphiwe Nyanda.' *Mayibuye* (Johannesburg) 1 (8), December 1990, pp. 10-12.
53. Houston, Gregory. 2013. The Re-establishment of the ANC inside the Country, 1990–1994. In *The Road to Democracy in South Africa, Vol. 6 (1990–1996).* South Africa Democracy Education Trust, Pretoria: University of South Africa Press, p. 195.
54. Houston, 'The Re-establishment of the ANC inside the Country,' p. 195.
55. O'Malley, *Shades of Difference*, p. 390.
56. One notable late graduate of the Soviet/Russian training was Bheki Jacobs, who remained in Russia until 1994 and would assume a central, intelligence-based role in South African politics under Thabo Mbeki's presidency.
57. Henderson, 'Operation Vula against Apartheid,' p. 435.
58. See, for example, Gilder, Barry. 2012. *Songs and Secrets: South Africa from Liberation to Governance.* London: Hurst Publishers.
59. Jenkin, 'Talking to Vula.'
60. O'Malley, *Shades of Difference*.

61. Mkhondo, Rich. 1993. *Reporting South Africa*. Portsmouth, NH: Heinemann.

62. Henderson, 'Operation Vula against Apartheid,' p. 435.

63. McKinley, *The ANC and the Liberation Struggle*, p. 82.

64. 'MK and the Future,' p. 6.

65. Simpson, *Umkhonto we Sizwe*, p. 459.

66. *The Star*, 28 April 1991, cited in McKinley, *The ANC and the Liberation Struggle*, p. 87.

67. Mandela, Nelson. 1994. *Long Walk to Freedom*. New York: Little, Brown, pp. 506-7.

68. Simpson, *Umkhonto we Sizwe*, p. 464.

69. Murray, Martin. 1994. *The Revolution Deferred: The Painful Birth of Post-Apartheid South Africa*. London: Verso, p. 121.

70. Gear, Sasha. 2002. Now That the War Is Over: Ex-Combatants' Transition and the Question of Violence: A Literature Review, www.csvr.co.za, p. 32.

71. Confidential interview with ex-combatant, November 2009.

72. Wolfie Kodesh interview with Sipho Binda (alias Mandla Jawara), 1993.

73. Ngculu, *The Honour to Serve*, p. 198.

74. Ngculu, *The Honour to Serve*, p. 201.

75. Manong, Stanley. 2015. *If We Must Die: An Autobiography of a Former Commander of uMkhonto we Sizwe*. Johannesburg: Nkululeko Publishers, p. 3.

76. TRC, 'Craig Duli Matter' (Day 3), MD Ras testimony, 20 April 1999.

77. Nqakula, *The People's War*, pp. 264, 267.

78. O'Malley, *Shades of Difference*, pp. 290-1.

79. Simpson, *Umkhonto we Sizwe*, p. 467.

80. 'Man Killed for Exposing Security Branch,' South African Press Association, 19 August 1999 (Durban), available at: http://www.justice.gov.za/trc/media%5C1999%5C9908/p990819a.htm.

81. O'Malley, *Shades of Difference*, p. 277.

82. Henderson, 'Operation Vula against Apartheid,' p. 434.

83. 'Man Killed for Exposing Security Branch,' South African Press Association, 19 August 1999 (Durban).

84. Henderson, 'Operation Vula against Apartheid,' pp. 418, 419.

85. Simpson, *Umkhonto we Sizwe*, p. 467.

86. 'Ex-Cop Tells How ANC Members Were Killed,' IOL News, 12 April 2000, available at: https://www.iol.co.za/news/south-africa/ex-cop-tells-how-anc-members-were-killed-34365.

87. 'TRC Investigators Find Hidden Graves,' South African Press

Association, 12 March 1997 (Cape Town), available at: http://www.
justice.gov.za/trc/media/1997/9703/s970312f.htm.

88. TRC Amnesty Hearing, Application of Botha, Du Preez, Steyn,
    Wasserman, and Van der Westhuizen, Pinetown, 11 April 2000.

89. TRC Amnesty Hearing, Application of Botha, Du Preez, Steyn,
    Wasserman, and Van der Westhuizen, Pinetown, 11 April 2000.

90. 'Ex-Cop Tells How ANC Members Were Killed,' IOL News
    (Johannesburg), 12 April 2000.

91. 'Man Killed for Exposing Security Branch,' South African Press
    Association, 19 August 1999 (Durban).

92. 'Ex-Cop Tells How ANC Members Were Killed,' IOL News
    (Johannesburg), 12 April 2000.

93. TRC Amnesty Hearing, Application of Botha, Du Preez, Steyn,
    Wasserman, and Van der Westhuizen, Pinetown, 11 April 2000.

94. Henderson, 'Operation Vula against Apartheid,' p. 445 n.

95. The TRC record dates Ndaba's and Shabalala's murders as having
    occurred on the night of 14 July.

96. TRC Amnesty Hearing, Application of Botha, Du Preez, Steyn,
    Wasserman, and Van der Westhuizen, Pinetown, 11 April 2000.

97. TRC Amnesty Hearing, Application of Botha, Du Preez, Steyn,
    Wasserman, and Van der Westhuizen, Pinetown, 11 April 2000.

98. TRC Amnesty Hearing, Application of Botha, Du Preez, Steyn,
    Wasserman, and Van der Westhuizen, Pinetown, 11 April 2000.

99. TRC Amnesty Hearing, Application of Botha, Du Preez, Steyn,
    Wasserman, and Van der Westhuizen, Pinetown, 11 April 2000.

100. 'De Klerk Accused of Duplicity,' *Irish Times*, 17 March 1997.

101. Jenkin, 'Talking to Vula.'

102. Henderson, 'Operation Vula against Apartheid,' p. 419.

103. Jenkin, 'Talking to Vula.'

104. Houston, 'The Re-establishment of the ANC inside the Country,'
     pp. 196-7.

105. Simpson, *Umkhonto we Sizwe*, p. 469.

106. Simpson, *Umkhonto we Sizwe*, pp. 469-70.

107. Henderson, 'Operation Vula against Apartheid,' p. 436.

108. Jenkin, 'Talking to Vula.'

109. Henderson, 'Operation Vula against Apartheid,' p. 429.

110. O'Brien, *The South African Intelligence Services*, p. 175.

111. Simpson, *Umkhonto we Sizwe*, p. 470.

112. O'Malley, *Shades of Difference*, p. 366.

113. Henderson, 'Operation Vula against Apartheid,' p. 436.

114. Simpson, *Umkhonto we Sizwe*, p. 471.

115. Simpson, *Umkhonto we Sizwe*, p. 471.
116. Henderson, 'Operation Vula against Apartheid,' p. 436.
117. Simpson, *Umkhonto we Sizwe*, p. 471.
118. Simpson,.*Umkhonto we Sizwe*, p. 471.
119. Henderson, 'Operation Vula against Apartheid,' p. 437.
120. Jenkin, 'Talking to Vula.'
121. Henderson, 'Operation Vula against Apartheid,' p. 452.
122. Jenkin, 'Talking to Vula.'
123. Henderson, 'Operation Vula against Apartheid,' p. 420.
124. Henderson, 'Operation Vula against Apartheid,' p. 440.
125. Henderson, 'Operation Vula against Apartheid,' p. 154.
126. O'Malley, *Shades of Difference*, p. 378.
127. O'Malley, *Shades of Difference*, p. 383.
128. Simpson, *Umkhonto we Sizwe*, p. 464.
129. Simpson, *Umkhonto we Sizwe*, pp. 472-3.
130. Simpson, *Umkhonto we Sizwe*, p. 473.
131. Houston, 'The Re-establishment of the ANC inside the Country,' p. 199.
132. Ngculu, *The Honour to Serve*, p. 213.
133. McKinley, *The ANC and the Liberation Struggle*, p. 100.
134. Houston, 'The Re-establishment of the ANC inside the Country,' p. 198.
135. Confidential interview with ex-combatant, November 2009.
136. Houston, 'The Re-establishment of the ANC inside the Country,' p. 198.
137. Wolfie Kodesh interview with Lerumo Kalako, 1993.
138. McKinley cited in Houston, 'The Re-establishment of the ANC inside the Country,' p. 200.
139. Wolfie Kodesh interview with Lerumo Kalako, 6 July 1993.
140. Ngculu, *The Honour to Serve*, p. 213.
141. Ngculu, *The Honour to Serve*, p. 214.
142. Simpson, *Umkhonto we Sizwe*, p. 477.
143. Simpson, *Umkhonto we Sizwe*, p. 473.
144. Sparks, Allister. 1994. *Tomorrow Is Another Country*. New York: Penguin Press, p. 124.
145. Ngculu, *The Honour to Serve*, pp. 214-15.
146. Sparks, *Tomorrow Is Another Country*, p. 131.
147. 'MK National Conference in Venda: Press Statement,' 1991 (SAHA).
148. Williams, Rocky. 1991. *Back to the Barracks: The SADF and the Dynamics of Transformation*. Johannesburg: IDASA, p. 30.
149. 'Address of Comrade President Nelson Mandela to the Conference of Umkhonto we Sizwe, Thohoyandou, Venda, 9 August 1991' (SAHA).
150. Author's interview with Dr Somadoda Fikeni, December 2009.
151. Fumanikile Booi testimony to the TRC regarding the death of Nicholas

Johannes Els, Cape Town, 28 October 1999, available online at: http://www.justice.gov.za/trc/amntrans/1999/99101828_ct_991028.htm.

152. Nqakula, *The People's War*, p. 283.

153. 'MK National Conference in Venda: Press Statement,' 1991 (SAHA).

154. Wolfie Kodesh interview with Lerumo Kalako, 6 July 1993.

155. Wolfie Kodesh interview with Fraser Delisa Shamase, 1993.

156. 'MK and the Future,' p. 1, SAHA, Section 5.17 (Umkhonto we Sizwe).

157. Confidential interview with ex-combatant, December 2009.

158. Ngculu, *The Honour to Serve*, p. 232.

159. Simpson, *Umkhonto we Sizwe*, p. 479.

160. Ngculu, *The Honour to Serve*, p. 216.

161. Mkhondo, *Reporting South Africa*.

162. Gear, 'Now That the War Is Over,' p. 65.

163. Confidential interview with ex-combatant, November 2009.

164. Taylor, Rupert. 2002. Justice Denied: Political Violence in KwaZulu-Natal after 1994. Centre for the Study of Violence and Reconciliation, Violence and Transition Series, vol. 6.

165. Gear, 'Now That the War Is Over,' p. 84.

166. Confidential interview with ex-combatant, November 2009.

167. Mulamisi Maxhayi testimony to the TRC, Port St Johns Incident, 5 October 1998.

168. Motumi, Tsepe. 1995. The Spear of the Nation: The Recent History of Umkhonto we Sizwe (MK). In *About Turn: The Transformation of the South African Military and Intelligence*, edited by J Cilliers and M Reichardt. Halfway House: Institute for Defence Policy, p. 97.

169. Berkeley, Bill. 1994. The Warlords of Natal. *Atlantic Monthly* (March), pp. 85-100.

170. Motumi, 'The Spear of the Nation,' p. 98.

171. De Haas, Mary. 2013. Violence in Zululand: The 1990s. In *The Road to Democracy in South Africa, Vol. 6 (1990–1996)*. South Africa Democracy Education Trust, Pretoria: University of South Africa Press, pp. 876-957.

172. 'Special Conference of MK Held at Mgwenya College of Education in Kanyamazane [Venda], from 3-4 September 1993' (SAHA).

173. Houston and Ngculu, *Voices of Liberation*, p. 269.

174. Kynoch, Gary. 2005. Crime, Conflict, and Politics in Transition-Era South Africa. *African Affairs* 104 (416), pp. 493-514.

175. 'Special Conference of MK Held at Mgwenya College of Education in Kanyamazane, from 3-4 September 1993' (SAHA).

176. 'Special Conference of MK Held at Mgwenya College of Education in Kanyamazane, from 3-4 September 1993' (SAHA).

177. Ngculu, *The Honour to Serve*, p. 216.

178. Cilliers, Jackie, and Markus Reichardt. 1995. The National Peacekeeping Force: The Triumph of Politics over Security. In *About Turn: The Transformation of the South African Military and Intelligence*, edited by J Cilliers and M Reichardt. Halfway House: Institute for Defence Policy, pp. 35-62.
179. O'Malley, *Shades of Difference*, p. 338.
180. O'Malley, *Shades of Difference*, pp. 264, 293.
181. Confidential interview with ex-combatant, November 2009.
182. Simpson, *Umkhonto we Sizwe*, p. 468.
183. Mzwandile Gushu Amnesty Hearing, TRC, 22 July 1998.
184. 'TRC Gives Amnesty to 18 and Refuses It to Five,' SAPA, 12 January 1999.
185. Simpson, *Umkhonto we Sizwe*, p. 468.
186. Houston and Ngculu, *Voices of Liberation*, p. 265.
187. Berkeley, 'The Warlords of Natal.'
188. Mzwandile Gushu Amnesty Hearing, TRC, 22 July 1998.
189. Mzwandile Gushu Amnesty Hearing, TRC, 22 July 1998.
190. Amnesty Hearing, Paulos 'Pistol' Nkonyane, TRC, Ermelo, 29 July 1998.
191. Mzwandile Gushu Amnesty Hearing, TRC, 22 July 1998.
192. Simpson, *Umkhonto we Sizwe*, p. 474.
193. Simpson, *Umkhonto we Sizwe*, pp. 478-9.
194. Mzwandile Gushu Amnesty Hearing, TRC, 22 July 1998.
195. Mzwandile Gushu Amnesty Hearing, TRC, 22 July 1998.
196. Mzwandile Gushu Amnesty Hearing, TRC, 22 July 1998.
197. Mzwandile Gushu Amnesty Hearing, TRC, 22 July 1998.
198. Simpson, *Umkhonto we Sizwe*, p. 482.
199. Simpson, *Umkhonto we Sizwe*, p. 482.
200. Berkeley, 'The Warlords of Natal.'
201. Simpson, *Umkhonto we Sizwe*, p. 486.
202. Simpson, *Umkhonto we Sizwe*, p. 487.
203. Simpson, *Umkhonto we Sizwe*, pp. 495-6.

5. INSURGENCY AND COUNTERINSURGENCY IN THE BANTUSTAN OF TRANSKEI, 1988–94

1. Gibbs, Timothy. 2011. Chris Hani's 'Country Bumpkins': Regional Networks in the African National Congress Underground, 1974–1994. *Journal of Southern African Studies* 37 (4), pp. 677-91.
2. Barrell, Howard. 1990. The Turn to the Masses: The African National Congress' Strategic Review of 1978-9. *Journal of Southern African Studies* 18 (1), pp. 64-92.

3. Confidential interview with ex-combatant, November 2009.

4. Gibbs, 'Chris Hani's "Country Bumpkins",' p. 689.

5. SAHA, Section 5.17 (Umkhonto we Sizwe), 'MK and the Future,' document dated November 1990, author unknown.

6. Southall, Roger. 1982. *South Africa's Transkei: The Political Economy of an 'Independent' Bantustan*. New York: Monthly Review Press.

7. Confidential interview with ex-combatants, November 2009.

8. Confidential interview with ex-combatants, November 2009.

9. Sanders, James. 2006. *Apartheid's Friends: The Rise and Fall of South Africa's Secret Service*. London: John Murray Publishers.

10. Mbeki, Govan. 1964. *South Africa: The Peasants' Revolt*. Middlesex: Penguin.

11. Confidential interview with ex-combatant, November 2009.

12. Southall, *South Africa's Transkei*.

13. 'X-MK Members Visit King Sabata's Graveside,' *Indabazethu* [Mthatha], 27 February 2002.

14. Author's interview with King Buyelekhaya Dalindyebo, Mthatha, December 2009; whereas King Buyelekhaya's well-documented relations with the ANC became fraught in later years, during the struggle era he completed training at an MK base in Zambia.

15. Confidential interview with ex-combatant, December 2009.

16. Confidential interview with ex-combatant, December 2009.

17. Confidential interview with ex-combatant, December 2009.

18. Confidential interview with ex-combatant, December 2009.

19. Confidential interview with ex-combatant, December 2009.

20. Wolfie Kodesh interview with Ayanda Ntsaluba, 1993 (Mayibuye Archives).

21. Confidential interview with ex-combatant, December 2009.

22. Confidential interview with ex-combatant, December 2009.

23. Gibbs, Timothy. 2014. *Mandela's Kinsmen: Nationalist Elites and Apartheid's First Bantustan*. Auckland Park: Jacana Press.

24. SAHA, Section 5.17 (Umkhonto we Sizwe), 'Notes of Meeting with Chris Hani, Chief of Staff and Deputy Commander of Umkhonto we Sizwe, and Steve Tshwete, Political Commissar,' from an interview by John D Battersby, 3 June 1988, Lusaka.

25. Confidential interview with ex-combatant, November 2009.

26. Confidential interview with ex-combatant, November 2009.

27. Confidential interview with ex-combatant, November 2009.

28. Confidential interview with ex-combatant, November 2009.

29. Gibbs, 'Chris Hani's "Country Bumpkins".'

30. Confidential interview with ex-combatant, December 2009.

31. Confidential interview with ex-combatants, November 2009.

32. Confidential interview with ex-combatant, November 2009.

33. Confidential interview with ex-combatant, November 2009.

34. SAHA, Section 5.17 (Umkhonto we Sizwe), 'Notes of Meeting with Chris Hani, Chief of Staff and Deputy Commander of Umkhonto we Sizwe, and Steve Tshwete, Political Commissar,' from an interview by John D Battersby, 3 June 1988, Lusaka.

35. Simpson, Thula. 2016. *Umkhonto we Sizwe: The ANC's Armed Struggle*. Cape Town: Penguin, p. 462.

36. Confidential interview with ex-combatant, December 2009.

37. Ellis, Stephen, and Tsepo Sechaba. 1992. *Comrades against Apartheid: The ANC and the South African Communist Party in Exile*. London: James Currey, p. 140.

38. Confidential interview with ex-combatant, December 2009.

39. Bell, Terry, with Dumisa Buhle Ntsebeza. 2003. *Unfinished Business: South Africa, Apartheid, and Truth*. London: Verso, p. 200.

40. TRC, Final Report, Vol. 2, ch. 5, subsection 23.

41. TRC, Final Report, Vol. 2, ch. 5, subsection 23.

42. TRC, Final Report, Vol. 2, ch. 5, subsection 23.

43. Sanders, *Apartheid's Friends*, p. 265.

44. TRC press release, 'Intelligence Chief Speaks Out on Operation Katzen,' East London, 6 April 1999.

45. O'Brien, Kevin. 2011. *The South African Intelligence Services: From Apartheid to Democracy, 1948–2005*. New York: Routledge, pp. 126-7.

46. Flanagan, Louise. 1998. Covert Operations in the Eastern Cape. In *The Hidden Hand: Covert Operations in South Africa*, 2nd edn, edited by C Schutte, Ian Liebenberg, and Anthony Minaar. Pretoria: Human Sciences Research Council, p. 194.

47. Southall, *South Africa's Transkei*. Former Selous Scouts commander Ron Reid-Daly had not enjoyed serving in the SADF Special Forces and so moved on to prominence in Transkei; see 'Mozambique / South Africa: The Special Forces behind RENAMO,' *Africa Confidential* 28 (24), 2 December 1987.

48. Southall (*South Africa's Transkei*, p. 4) reports that Pretoria removed Reid-Daly's Selous Scouts because the regime had come to regard them 'as a destabilizing element' in the region. However, the Rhodesians had in fact been operating directly under SADF orders, and destabilization was precisely the regime's goal. Rather, the Selous Scouts left because Holomisa and other high-ranking TDF officers had come to resent the Rhodesians' control over security matters in Transkei and kicked them out.

49. Peires, JB. 1992. The Implosion of Transkei and Ciskei. *African Affairs* 91, p. 370.

50. Confidential interview with ex-combatant, December 2009.

51. Peires, 'The Implosion of Transkei and Ciskei.'

52. Peires, 'The Implosion of Transkei and Ciskei,' p. 371.

53. TRC Final Report, Vol. 2, ch. 5, subsection 23.

54. Southall, *South Africa's Transkei*, p. 6.

55. Sparks, Allister. 1994. *Tomorrow Is Another Country*. New York: Penguin Press, p. 147.

56. SAHA, Section A2.4.1.7 (TRC Gunrunning 1974-97).

57. Mkhondo, Rich. 1993. *Reporting South Africa*. Portsmouth, NH: Heinemann, p. 74.

58. Bell and Ntsebeza, *Unfinished Business*.

59. SAHA, Section A2.4.1.7 (TRC Gunrunning 1974-97).

60. Confidential interview with ex-combatant, Mthatha, December 2009.

61. SAHA, section 5.17 (Umkhonto we Sizwe), 'Notes of Meeting with Chris Hani Chief of Staff and Deputy Commander of Umkhonto we Sizwe, and Steve Tshwete, Political Commissar,' from an interview by John D Battersby, 3 June 1988, Lusaka, Zambia.

62. Confidential interview with ex-combatant, Mthatha, December 2009; see also 'Shot "Askari" Caused Camp Deaths – Claim,' *Daily Dispatch*, 22 April 1998; Truth and Reconciliation Commission (TRC) Statement, Umtata, 13 August 1998, available at http://www.info.gov.za/speeches/1998/98814_0x6839810595.htm.

63. Jeffery, Anthea. 2009. *People's War: New Light on the Struggle for South Africa*. Johannesburg: Jonathan Ball Publishers.

64. Ngculu, James. 2009. *The Honour to Serve: Recollections of an Umkhonto Soldier*. Claremont: David Philip, p. 201.

65. Ngculu, *The Honour to Serve*, p. 202.

66. Gibbs, 'Chris Hani's "Country Bumpkins",' p. 679.

67. Confidential interview with ex-combatant, November 2009.

68. SAHA, section A2.4.1.7 (TRC Gunrunning 1974–97).

69. SAHA, section A2.4.1.7 (TRC Gunrunning 1974–97).

70. Confidential interview with ex-combatant, November 2009.

71. Hanlon, Joseph. 1986. *Beggar Your Neighbours: Apartheid Power in Southern Africa*. Bloomington, IN: Indiana University Press. The ANC withdrew from Lesotho in 1986 after Chief Leabua Jonathan was finally overthrown in an SADF-sponsored coup by Maj. Gen. Lekhanya.

72. Nqakula, Charles. 2017. *The People's War: Reflections of an ANC Cadre*. Johannesburg: Mutloatse Heritage Trust, p. 267.

73. SAHA, Section A2.4.1.7 (TRC Gunrunning 1974-97).

74. SAHA, Section A2.4.1.7 (TRC Gunrunning 1974-97).

75. SAHA, Section A2.4.1.7 (TRC Gunrunning 1974-97).

76. SAHA, Section A2.4.1.7 (TRC Gunrunning 1974-97).

77. SAHA, Section A2.4.1.7 (TRC Gunrunning 1974-97).

78. SAHA, Section A2.4.1.7 (TRC Gunrunning 1974-97).

79. SAHA, Section A2.4.1.7 (TRC Gunrunning 1974-97).

80. Confidential interview with ex-combatant, Mthatha, December 2009.

81. Confidential interview with ex-combatant, Mthatha, December 2009.

82. Confidential interview with ex-combatant, Mthatha, December 2009.

83. Confidential interview with ex-combatant, Mthatha, December 2009.

84. SAHA, Section A2.4.1.7 (TRC Gunrunning 1974-97).

85. SAHA, Section A2.4.1.7 (TRC Gunrunning 1974-97).

86. TRC, 'Craig Duli Matter' (Day 3), MD Ras testimony, 20 April 1999.

87. TRC, 'Craig Duli Matter' (Day 3), MD Ras testimony, 20 April 1999.

88. Confidential interview with ex-combatant, December 2009.

89. Confidential interview with ex-combatant, December 2009.

90. Confidential interview with ex-combatant, December 2009.

91. Confidential interview with ex-combatant, December 2009.

92. Confidential interview with ex-combatant, December 2009.

93. SAHA, Section A2.4.1.7 (TRC Gunrunning 1974-97).

94. According to SAHA documents (Section A2.4.1.7: TRC Gunrunning 1974–97), in April 1995 the South African Police finally admitted that the Duli coup plotters had used weapons supplied by the SADF. The SADF declined to say how the weapons got into the hands of the attackers.

95. Truth and Reconciliation Commission Amnesty Hearings, 1 October 1997, Port Elizabeth, Case No. 0066/96, http://www.justice.gov.za/trc/amntrans/pe/mother3.htm012.

96. SAHA, Section A2.4.1.7 (TRC Gunrunning 1974-97).

97. Peires, 'The Implosion of Transkei and Ciskei,' p. 236.

98. SAHA, Section A2.4.1.7 (TRC Gunrunning 1974-97).

99. SAHA, Section A2.4.1.7 (TRC Gunrunning 1974-97).

100. SAHA, Section A2.4.1.7 (TRC Gunrunning 1974-97).

101. Nqakula, *The People's War*, p. 269.

102. SAHA, Section A2.4.1.7 (TRC Gunrunning 1974-97).

103. SAHA, Section A2.4.1.7 (TRC Gunrunning 1974-97).

104. The TRC likewise notes 'the involvement of an MI source, Prince Nkosekhaya Gobingca, as a key player in several sites of violence in the western and eastern Cape' (TRC Final Report Vol.5, p. 238).

105. SAHA, Section A2.4.1.7 (TRC Gunrunning 1974-97). The 'sophisticated weapons' in question were likely Soviet-supplied SAM-7 shoulder-fired anti-aircraft missiles (NATO codename 'Strella'), highly portable weapons that MK guerrillas first carried on missions in the late 1980s,

and which could compromise SADF air superiority. MK commander Hani mentioned these weapons in an interview ('Interview with Chris Hani, Deputy Commander Umkhonto we Sizwe, Lusaka 21 January 1990: Road Ahead Perspective,' SAHA 5.17: Umkhonto we Sizwe; see also Chapter One), and they appear in a post-transition inventory of MK weaponry stockpiled in neighbouring southern African countries (SAHA, AL3283, B1.1.4.2, 'Movement Plan for Ex-MK Arms and Armament in Foreign Countries').

106. SAHA, Section A2.4.1.7 (TRC Gunrunning 1974-97).
107. SAHA, Section A2.4.1.7 (TRC Gunrunning 1974-97).
108. SAHA, Section A2.4.1.7 (TRC Gunrunning 1974-97).
109. SAHA, Section A2.4.1.7 (TRC Gunrunning 1974-97).
110. SAHA, Section A2.4.1.7 (TRC Gunrunning 1974-97). In the event, the Ciskei Defence Force paratroop unit met a grim fate when at least 14 paratroopers drowned in Ciskei's Fish River in August 1991 'after they were mistakenly dropped in the river during a training exercise.' An investigation found that the CDF had ignored the 'required safety regulations' and an expert's warning about the dangers of jumping near the river, and that Gqozo's Ciskei government had 'suppressed an inquiry into the matter and threatened the families of the victims.'
111. SAHA, Section A2.4.1.7 (TRC Gunrunning 1974-97).
112. SAHA, Section A2.4.1.7 (TRC Gunrunning 1974-97).
113. SAHA, Section A2.4.1.7 (TRC Gunrunning 1974-97).
114. SAHA, Section A2.4.1.7 (TRC Gunrunning 1974-97).
115. Bell and Nstebeza, *Unfinished Business*, pp. 202–3.
116. Barrell, 'The Turn to the Masses.'
117. SAHA, Section A2.4.1.7 (TRC Gunrunning 1974-97).
118. SAHA, Section A2.4.1.7 (TRC Gunrunning 1974-97).
119. SAHA, Section 5.17 (Umkhonto we Sizwe), 'The Role of the Homelands and Their Armies in the Transitional Period and Future South Africa.'
120. SAHA, Section 5.17 (Umkhonto we Sizwe), 'Office of the Military Council of Transkei: Address by Major General Bantu Holomisa to the MK Conference in Venda, 9 August 1991.'
121. Confidential interview with ex-combatant, Mthatha, December 2009.
122. Confidential interview with ex-combatant, Mthatha, December 2009.
123. Confidential interview with ex-combatant, Mthatha, December 2009.
124. Confidential interview with ex-combatant, Mthatha, December 2009.
125. Confidential interview with ex-combatant, Mthatha, December 2009.
126. *MK in Uganda* (video).
127. Sparks, *Tomorrow Is Another Country*, p. 149.
128. SAHA, Section 5.17 (Umkhonto we Sizwe), 'Office of the Military

Council of Transkei: Address by Major General Bantu Holomisa to the MK Conference in Venda, 9 August 1991.'

129. Sparks, *Tomorrow Is Another Country.*
130. Cock, Jacklyn. 1997. The Cultural and Social Challenge of Demilitarization. In *Defensive Restructuring of the Armed Forces in South Africa*, edited by B Moller and Gavin Cawthra. Brookfield, VT: Ashgate Publishing, p. 136.
131. SAHA, Section A2.4.1.7 (TRC Gunrunning 1974-97).
132. SAHA, Section A2.4.1.7 (TRC Gunrunning 1974-97).
133. Confidential interview with ex-combatant, December 2009.
134. SAHA, Section A2.4.1.7 (TRC Gunrunning 1974-97).

6. SPY RECRUITMENT AND THE STEYN REPORT

1. SAHA, A2.4.1.7 (TRC Gunrunning 1974-97).
2. O'Brien, Kevin. 2011. *The South African Intelligence Services: From Apartheid to Democracy, 1948–2005.* New York: Routledge, p. 150.
3. In early 1996, journalist Louise Flanagan reported in the Johannesburg weekly *Mail & Guardian* on Anton Nieuwoudt's memorandum about SADF MI's attempts to recruit Modise and other top MK personnel in the early 1990s. See Flanagan, 'How Military Intelligence Tried to Recruit Modise,' *Mail & Guardian*, 23-29 February 1996.
4. SAHA, A2.4.1.7 (TRC Gunrunning 1974-97).
5. SAHA, A2.4.1.7 (TRC Gunrunning 1974-97).
6. SAHA, A2.4.1.7 (TRC Gunrunning 1974-97).
7. Flanagan, 'How Military Intelligence Tried to Recruit Modise.'
8. Flanagan, 'How Military Intelligence Tried to Recruit Modise.' The documents were first released by former SADF MI officer Gerrie Hugo, who had a grievance against the SADF based on what he alleged was his unfair dismissal. Flanagan was romantically involved with Hugo, causing the ANC to allege that Flanagan's information was tainted with bias; however, Flanagan herself noted that she had never sought to hide her relationship with Hugo and had recused herself from reporting on his case.
9. ANC Statement to the Truth and Reconciliation Commission, Vol. 4.9 (August 1996), http://www.justice.gov.za/trc/hrvtrans/submit/anctruth.htm#4.
10. According to an ex-guerrilla, the apartheid regime attempted to recruit Moloi as a spy (author's confidential interview, December 2009); note also the document's mention of Moloi's high-ranking position in the post-transition military.
11. SAHA, A2.4.1.7 (TRC Gunrunning 1974-97); Trewhela ('The Killing of Sipho Phungulwa,' *Searchlight South Africa* 2 (2) 1991) also refers to a

split between an MK faction in Johannesburg commanded by Modise, and an MK faction in Transkei commanded by Hani.

12. Flanagan, 'How Military Intelligence Tried to Recruit Modise.'
13. SAHA, A2.4.1.7 (TRC Gunrunning 1974–97).
14. Mkhondo, Rich. 1993. *Reporting South Africa*. Portsmouth, NH: Heinemann, p. 86.
15. Flanagan, 'How Military Intelligence Tried to Recruit Modise.'
16. Flanagan, 'How Military Intelligence Tried to Recruit Modise.'
17. 'Where's the Truth in the Modise Recruiting Row?' *Mail & Guardian*, 1 March 1996.
18. Ellis, Stephen. 1998. The Historical Significance of South Africa's Third Force. *Journal of Southern African Studies* 24 (2), p. 292.
19. Mkhondo, *Reporting South Africa*, p. 86.
20. Kynoch, Gary. 1996. The 'Transformation' of the South African Military. *Journal of Modern African Studies* 34 (3), p. 451.
21. Confidential interview with ex-combatant, December 2009.
22. O'Brien, *The South African Intelligence Services.*
23. Kynoch, 'The "Transformation" of the South African Military,' p. 443.
24. SAHA, AL 3283, De Wet Potgieter interview with Col. Lucas Ras (Centurion, Pretoria, 26 October 2009).
25. O'Brien, *The South African Intelligence Services*, p. 115.
26. O'Brien, *The South African Intelligence Services*, pp. 115, 117.
27. Mkhondo, *Reporting South Africa.*
28. 'Who Killed Hani?' *African Communist* 132, First Quarter 1993.
29. 'The South African Army and Police: Apartheid's Cannibals,' *Michigan Citizen* 15 (19), 3 April 1993.
30. Pauw, Jacques. 1997. *Into the Heart of Darkness: Confessions of Apartheid's Assassins*. Johannesburg: Jonathan Ball Publishers, p. 280.
31. Pauw, *Into the Heart of Darkness*, p. 280.
32. SAHA, AL 3283, De Wet Potgieter interview with Detective Warrant Officer Drummond Hammond, Centurion, South Africa, 25 February 2010.
33. 'Police Hint ANC Framed Them for White's Murder; South Africa,' *The Times*, 24 August 1992.
34. 'The South African Army and Police: Apartheid's Cannibals,' *Michigan Citizen* 15 (19), 3 April 1993.
35. O'Brien, *The South African Intelligence Services*, p. 191.
36. 'South Africa: Looking through the Mirrors,' *Africa Confidential* 33 (15), 31 July 1992.
37. 'The South African Army and Police: Apartheid's Cannibals,' *Michigan Citizen* 15 (19), 3 April 1993.

38. 'South Africa: Looking through the Mirrors,' *Africa Confidential* 33 (15), 31 July 1992.

39. 'South Africa: Looking through the Mirrors,' *Africa Confidential* 33 (15), 31 July 1992.

40. 'Pan-Afrik Investment Consultants' (SAHA, B1.1.3.1).

41. De Klerk, cited in Magubane, Bernard. 2013. The Beginning of the End: The Garrison State Is Finally Dismantled. In *The Road to Democracy in South Africa, Vol. 6 (1990–1996)*. South Africa Democracy Education Trust, Pretoria: University of South Africa Press, p. 1407.

42. De Klerk, cited in Magubane, 'The Beginning of the End,' p. 1408.

43. Subsequently, two-thirds of those fired were cleared of 'illegal activities or illicit links,' and claimed that they were targeted based on inter-agency feuding between the NIS and SADF MI (O'Brien, *The South African Intelligence Services*, p. 190).

44. 'Pan-Afrik Investment Consultants' (SAHA, B1.1.3.1).

45. 'What the Generals Didn't Tell Modise,' *Mail & Guardian*, 17 June 1994.

46. SAHA, 'TRC Gunrunning in the Eastern Cape, 1974-1997.'

47. 'Pan-Afrik Investment Consultants' (SAHA, B1.1.3.1).

48. 'The South African Army and Police: Apartheid's Cannibals,' *Michigan Citizen* 15 (19), 3 April 1993.

49. 'The South African Army and Police: Apartheid's Cannibals,' *Michigan Citizen* 15 (19), 3 April 1993.

50. Ellis, 'The Historical Significance of South Africa's Third Force,' p. 290.

51. 'Shocks from the Steyn Report,' *Mail & Guardian*, 31 January 1997.

52. Henderson, Robert D'A. 1995. South African Intelligence under De Klerk. In *About Turn: The Transformation of the South African Military and Intelligence*, edited by J Cilliers and M Reichardt. Halfway House: Institute for Defence Policy, p. 161.

53. 'De Klerk Lied – TRC,' *New Nation*, 10 January 1997.

54. O'Brien, *The South African Intelligence Services*, p. 190.

55. Potgieter, De Wet. 2007. *Total Onslaught: Apartheid's Dirty Tricks Exposed*. Cape Town: Zebra Press, p. 299.

56. Purkitt, Helen, and Stephen Burgess. 2005. *South Africa's Weapons of Mass Destruction*. Indianapolis: Indiana University Press, pp. 164-5.

57. 'De Klerk Lied – TRC,' *New Nation*, 10 January 1997.

58. 'Shocks from the Steyn Report,' *Mail & Guardian*, 31 January 1997.

59. 'Apartheid Army's Deadly Secrets,' IOL, 30 April 2006.

60. 'Shocks from the Steyn Report,' *Mail & Guardian*, 31 January 1997.

61. 'Shocks from the Steyn Report,' *Mail & Guardian*, 31 January 1997.

62. 'Shocks from the Steyn Report,' *Mail & Guardian*, 31 January 1997.

63. 'Apartheid Army's Deadly Secrets,' IOL, 30 April 2006.

64. 'Apartheid Army's Deadly Secrets,' IOL, 30 April 2006.
65. 'Apartheid Army's Deadly Secrets,' IOL, 30 April 2006.
66. 'Shocks from the Steyn Report,' *Mail & Guardian*, 31 January 1997.
67. O'Brien, *The South African Intelligence Services*, p. 189.
68. 'Shocks from the Steyn Report,' *Mail & Guardian*, 31 January 1997.
69. 'Shocks from the Steyn Report,' *Mail & Guardian*, 31 January 1997.
70. 'Shocks from the Steyn Report,' *Mail & Guardian*, 31 January 1997.
71. 'Apartheid Army's Deadly Secrets,' IOL, 30 April 2006.
72. 'Shocks from the Steyn Report,' *Mail & Guardian*, 31 January 1997.
73. 'South Africa: Looking through the Mirrors,' *Africa Confidential* 33 (15), 31 July 1992.
74. Saul, John S. 1993. *Recolonization and Resistance in Southern Africa in the 1990s.* Toronto: Between the Lines Press, p. 103.
75. Van der Westhuizen, Christi. 2007. *White Power and the Rise and Fall of the National Party.* Cape Town: Zebra Press, p. 205.
76. Magubane, 'The Beginning of the End,' p. 1409.
77. 'Shocks from the Steyn Report,' *Mail & Guardian*, 31 January 1997.
78. 'Apartheid Army's Deadly Secrets,' IOL, 30 April 2006.
79. 'Apartheid Army's Deadly Secrets,' IOL, 30 April 2006.
80. Ellis, 'The Historical Significance of South Africa's Third Force,' p. 292.
81. SAHA, A.2.4.1.07.1.1.3 (TRC Gunrunning 1974-97).
82. SAHA, A.2.4.1.07.1.1.3 (TRC Gunrunning 1974-97).
83. Author's interview with Barry Gilder, Baltimore, November 2013.
84. Pauw, *Into the Heart of Darkness*, p. 135. De Kock and other death squad members also secretly negotiated a deal with the commissioner of police, Gen. Johan van der Merwe, whereby the state would cover their legal expenses should they ever be brought to trial; South African taxpayers ultimately paid over R5 million to cover De Kock's post-transition legal bills.
85. 'South Africa: Violence in Transition,' *Africa Confidential* 33 (8), 17 April 1992.
86. Saul, *Recolonization and Resistance in Southern Africa in the 1990s*, pp. 103-4; emphasis in original.
87. 'Seven Other Death Farms,' *New Nation*, 20 March 1997.
88. 'Seven Other Death Farms,' *New Nation*, 20 March 1997.
89. O'Brien, *The South African Intelligence Services*, p. 194.
90. Henderson, 'South African Intelligence under De Klerk,' p. 141.
91. Bill Keller, 'A Glimpse of Apartheid's Dying Sting,' *New York Times*, 20 February 1995.
92. *A Long Night's Damage*, cited in Taylor, Rupert. 2002. Justice Denied:

Political Violence in KwaZulu-Natal after 1994. Centre for the Study of Violence and Reconciliation, Violence and Transition Series, vol. 6.

93. Magubane, 'The Beginning of the End,' p. 1390.
94. Magubane, 'The Beginning of the End,' p. 1391.
95. 'South Africa: Violence in Transition,' *Africa Confidential* 33 (8), 17 April 1992.
96. Mkhondo, *Reporting South Africa*, p. 80.
97. 'Peace in the Balance: South Africa,' *The Economist*, 28 November 1992, p. 44.
98. 'Peace in the Balance: South Africa,' *The Economist*, 28 November 1992, p. 44.
99. ANC Statement to the Truth and Reconciliation Commission, Vol. 4.9 (August 1996), http://www.justice.gov.za/trc/hrvtrans/submit/anctruth.htm#4.
100. Memorandum by Craig M. Williamson, 'Aspects of State Counter-Revolutionary Warfare Principles and Strategy: Republic of South Africa in the 1980s,' presented to the TRC, Cape Town, 9 October 1997, Section 5.8.
101. O'Brien, *The South African Intelligence Services*, p. 179.
102. Sparks, Allister. 1994. *Tomorrow Is Another Country*. New York: Penguin Press, p. 157.
103. Sparks, *Tomorrow Is Another Country*, p. 156.
104. Mkhondo, *Reporting South Africa*, p. 79.
105. 'Who Killed Hani?' *African Communist* 132, First Quarter 1993.
106. 'Who Killed Hani?' *African Communist* 132, First Quarter 1993.
107. SAHA, AL 3283, De Wet Potgieter interview with Henk Heslinga, former head of the Pretoria murder and robbery squad, 5 October 2009.
108. Henderson, 'South African Intelligence under De Klerk,' p. 153.
109. Henderson, 'South African Intelligence under De Klerk,' p. 437.
110. SAHA, AL 3283 B1.2.2.2b ('Operation Sunrise': SACP Revolutionary Faction within the ANC).
111. SAHA, AL 3283 B1.2.2.2b ('Operation Sunrise': SACP Revolutionary Faction within the ANC).
112. The ANC had set up the SDUs in communities loyal across much of South Africa, particularly in the townships around Johannesburg and Pretoria and in Natal province, which were targeted by IFP militants.
113. SAHA, AL 3283 B1.2.2.1 ('Operation Sunrise: Was It Fact or Fiction?').
114. SAHA, AL 3283 B1.2.2.2b ('Operation Sunrise': SACP Revolutionary Faction within the ANC).

115. Slovo, Joe. 1995. *Slovo: The Unfinished Autobiography*. Johannesburg: Ravan Press.

116. Slovo, *Slovo.*

117. Henderson, Robert D'A. 1997. Operation Vula against Apartheid. *International Journal of Intelligence and Counterintelligence* 10 (4), pp. 418-55.

118. See 'For the Sake of Our Lives: Guidelines for the Creation of People's Self-Defence Units' by Jeremy Cronin, submitted as Appendix Nine of the ANC's Second Submission to the TRC, available at http://www.justice.gov.za/trc/hrvtrans/submit/anc2.htm#Operations.

119. SAHA, A2.4.1.7 (TRC Gunrunning 1974-97).

120. SAHA, AL 3283 B1.2.2.2b ('Operation Sunrise': SACP Revolutionary Faction within the ANC).

121. 'South Africa: Violence in Transition,' *Africa Confidential* 33 (8), 17 April 1992.

122. SAHA, De Wet Potgieter Collection, B1.5.4.1, 'Threats against De Klerk.'

123. Ellis, 'The Historical Significance of South Africa's Third Force,' p. 295.

124. Author's interview with Barry Gilder, Baltimore, November 2013.

125. SAHA, De Wet Potgieter Collection, B1.5.4.1, 'Threats against De Klerk'; in the foreword to this section of his archival collection, Potgieter remarks: 'it will never be clear whether documents, like the ones in this file, were merely disinformation or real threats as part of the pressure on the De Klerk regime and the ANC while they were locked in peace talks in the pre-1994 era.'

126. This section is notable for accusing Thami Zulu of being an apartheid spy; it is interesting to consider this allegation in the light of the ANC's Second Submission to the TRC, in which it suggests that Thami Zulu's mysterious death was the result of poisoning by the apartheid regime (see Chapter Ten).

127. SAHA, De Wet Potgieter Collection, B1.5.4.1, 'Threats against De Klerk.'

7. KILLING HANI

1.   Groenink, Evelyn. 2018. *Incorruptible: The Story of the Murders of Dulcie September, Anton Lubowski and Chris Hani*. Cape Town: ABC Press, p. 265.

2.   'Hints of Truth about Hani's Death,' *Mail & Guardian*, 4 April 1997.

3.   Groenink, *Incorruptible*, p. 290.

4.   Confidential interview with ex-combatant, November 2009.

5.   Confidential interview with ex-combatant, November 2009.

6.   This mirrored the circumstances of Hani's murder; a 1998 ANC

internal report found that Hani 'had spent the night before the murder with a woman at a Johannesburg airport hotel, which explained why his bodyguards had not been present when Waluś [shot Hani]' (Brand, The Chris Hani Assassination, In *The Hidden Hand: Covert Operations in South Africa*, 2nd edn, edited by C Schutte, Ian Liebenberg, and Anthony Minaar. Pretoria: Human Sciences Research Council, 1998, p. 332); according to Groenink, the ANC had given Hani's bodyguards the Easter weekend off, a decision Hani had approved (*Incorruptible*, p. 305).

7. Confidential interview with ex-combatant, November 2009.
8. Confidential interview with ex-combatant, November 2009.
9. Lalu, Premesh. 2009. *The Deaths of Hintsa*. Cape Town: Human Sciences Research Council Press.
10. Lalu, *The Deaths of Hintsa*, p. 45.
11. See, for example, De Witte, Ludo. 2001. *The Assassination of Lumumba*. London: Verso.
12. De Witte, *The Assassination of Lumumba*, p. xxi.
13. Minter, William. 1988. *Operation Timber: Pages from the Savimbi Dossier*. Trenton, NJ: Africa World Press.
14. Douek, Daniel. 2017. New Light on the Samora Machel Assassination: 'I Realized It Was No Accident'. *Third World Quarterly* 9 (38), pp. 2045-65. See, for example, Debora Patta's testimony to Section 29 of the TRC (SAHA, AL 2878_B01.5.75.01.29.04).
15. Mkhondo, Rich. 1993. *Reporting South Africa*. Portsmouth, NH: Heinemann, p. 165.
16. Truth and Reconciliation Final Report, Vol.2 Ch.2, p.105.
17. Mayibuye Archives, MCH 88 MCA6-284 (Wolfie Kodesh interview with Chris Hani, 1 April 1993).
18. 'Toll of Unsolved Killings: Opponents of Apartheid,' *The Times*, 18 November 1989.
19. Ngculu, James. 2009. *The Honour to Serve: Recollections of an Umkhonto Soldier*. Claremont: David Philip, p. 216.
20. Simpson, Thula. 2016. *Umkhonto we Sizwe: The ANC's Armed Struggle*. Cape Town: Penguin, p. 466.
21. Nqakula, Charles. 2017. *The People's War: Reflections of an ANC Cadre*. Johannesburg: Mutloatse Heritage Trust, p. 265.
22. SAHA, A2.4.1.7 (TRC Gunrunning 1974-97),
23. Nqakula, *The People's War*, p. 266.
24. Ngculu, *The Honour to Serve*, p. 216.
25. 'Who Killed Hani?' *African Communist* no.132, First Quarter 1993.
26. 'Who Killed Hani?' *African Communist* no.132, First Quarter 1993.
27. 'Who Killed Hani?' *African Communist* no.132, First Quarter 1993.

28. 'Who Killed Hani?' *African Communist* no.132, First Quarter 1993.

29. 'Who Killed Hani?' *African Communist* no.132, First Quarter 1993.

30. Lekwane, Aubrey. 1994. The Chris Hani Assassination: Political Assassinations – Who Benefits? In *The Hidden Hand: Covert Operations in South Africa*, edited by Charl Schutte, Ian Liebenberg and Anthony Minnaar. Pretoria: Human Sciences Research Council, p. 325.

31. Nqakula, *The People's War*, p. 300.

32. 'Who Killed Hani?' *African Communist* no.132, First Quarter 1993.

33. 'Who Killed Hani?' *African Communist* no.132, First Quarter 1993.

34. 'Who Killed Hani?' *African Communist* no.132, First Quarter 1993.

35. Lekwane, 'The Chris Hani Assassination,' p. 325.

36. 'Who Killed Hani?' *African Communist* no.132, First Quarter 1993.

37. 'The Mqanqeni Affair: South African Communist Party Central Committee Statement' (31 March 1993) (SAHA, 5.16 Hani's Death).

38. 'Who Killed Hani?' *African Communist* no. 132, First Quarter 1993.

39. Lekwane, 'The Chris Hani Assassination,' p. 326.

40. 'Who Killed Hani?' *African Communist* no.132, First Quarter 1993.

41. 'The Mqanqeni Affair: South African Communist Party Central Committee Statement' (31 March 1993) (SAHA, 5.16 Hani's Death).

42. 'Who Killed Hani?' *African Communist* no.132, First Quarter 1993.

43. Lekwane, 'The Chris Hani Assassination,' p. 326.

44. 'The Mqanqeni Affair: South African Communist Party Central Committee Statement' (31 March 1993) (SAHA, 5.16 Hani's Death).

45. Lekwane, 'The Chris Hani Assassination,' p. 325.

46. 'The Mqanqeni Affair: South African Communist Party Central Committee Statement' (31 March 1993) (SAHA, 5.16 Hani's Death).

47. 'The Mqanqeni Affair: South African Communist Party Central Committee Statement' (31 March 1993) (SAHA, 5.16 Hani's Death).

48. 'The Mqanqeni Affair: South African Communist Party Central Committee Statement' (31 March 1993) (SAHA, 5.16 Hani's Death).

49. 'The Mqanqeni Affair: South African Communist Party Central Committee Statement' (31 March 1993) (SAHA, 5.16 Hani's Death).

50. 'The Mqanqeni Affair: South African Communist Party Central Committee Statement' (31 March 1993) (SAHA, 5.16 Hani's Death).

51. Sekola Sello, 'Honesty Might Have Cost Chris His Life,' *City Press*, 14 April 1993.

52. Mayibuye Archives, MCH 88 MCA6-284 (Wolfie Kodesh interview with Chris Hani, 1 April 1993).

53. 'ANC Press Statement on Police Pronouncements,' 13 April 1993, Johannesburg (SAHA, 5.17 Umkhonto we Sizwe); later police attempts to identify or explain the 'second car' proved inconclusive (Smith,

Janet, and Beauregard Tromp. 2009. *Hani: A Life Too Short*. Johannesburg: Jonathan Ball Publishers).

54. Groenink, *Incorruptible*, p. 266.
55. 'Who Killed Hani?' *African Communist* no.132, First Quarter 1993.
56. 'Who Killed Hani?' *African Communist* no.132, First Quarter 1993.
57. 'Who Killed Hani?' *African Communist* no.132, First Quarter 1993.
58. 'ANC Department of Information and Publicity: MK Statement on the Assassination of Chris Hani,' 14 April 1993, Johannesburg (SAHA, 5.16 Hani's Death).
59. ANC Statement to the Truth and Reconciliation Commission, Vol. 4.9 (August 1996), http://www.justice.gov.za/trc/hrvtrans/submit/anctruth.htm#4.
60. SAHA, AL 3283 B1.3.1 (South African Institute for Maritime Research).
61. TRC Final Report Vol.2 Ch.7, p.654.
62. Smith and Tromp, *Hani*.
63. 'BNP Activist Was Linked to South Africa Murder,' *The Independent*, 9 May 2009.
64. 'Posthumous Honour for SACP Chief,' *New Nation*, 27 March 1997.
65. 'Hints of Truth about Hani's Death,' *Mail & Guardian*, 4 April 1997.
66. Groenink, *Incorruptible*, pp. 273-4.
67. Evelyn Groenink,'Dulcie, Hani, Lubowski: A Story That Could Not Be Told,' *ZAM Magazine*, 24 April 2013.
68. 'Book Troubles Brother of Chris Hani Assassin,' *Independent Online* (IOL) News, 25 February 2004.
69. Groenink, 'Dulcie, Hani, Lubowski.'
70. Groenink, 'Dulcie, Hani, Lubowski.'
71. 'Hints of Truth about Hani's Death,' *Mail & Guardian*, 4 April 1997.
72. 'Hints of Truth about Hani's Death,' *Mail & Guardian*, 4 April 1997.
73. Brand, 'The Chris Hani Assassination.' In *The Hidden Hand*, p. 328.
74. Johnson, RW. 2010. *South Africa's Brave New World*. London: Penguin Books.
75. 'What Modise Didn't Know About DCC,' *Mail & Guardian*, 17 June 1994.
76. 'Hints of Truth about Hani's Death,' *Mail & Guardian*, 4 April 1997.
77. 'Hints of Truth about Hani's Death,' *Mail & Guardian*, 4 April 1997.
78. Slovo, Gillian. 1997. *Every Secret Thing*. London: Virago, p. 205.
79. 'The Hani Conspiracy,' *New Nation*, 27 March 1997.
80. 'Hani Murder: Shocking New Evidence,' *New Nation*, 27 March 1997.
81. 'Hani Murder: Shocking New Evidence,' *New Nation*, 27 March 1997.
82. 'The Hani Conspiracy,' *New Nation*, 27 March 1997.
83. 'The Hani Conspiracy,' *New Nation*, 27 March 1997.

84. 'The Hani Conspiracy,' *New Nation*, 27 March 1997.

85. 'Hani Murder: Shocking New Evidence,' *New Nation*, 27 March 1997.

86. 'Hani Murder: Shocking New Evidence,' *New Nation*, 27 March 1997.

87. 'Hani Murder: Shocking New Evidence,' *New Nation*, 27 March 1997.

88. 'Hani Murder: Shocking New Evidence,' *New Nation*, 27 March 1997.

89. 'Hani Murder: Shocking New Evidence,' *New Nation*, 27 March 1997.

90. Some of the AWB's activities, such as its training of IFP militants at secret bush camps, appear to have been directly outsourced by the security forces' covert units, and supported the latter's objectives.

91. Groenink, *Incorruptible*, p. 255. Walus was also connected to right-wing organizations suspected to be fronts for the SAP, whose members also worked closely with CCB operative Leonard Veenendal during this period (TRC Final Report Vol. 2 Ch. 7, p.654)

92. 'Hani Murder: Shocking New Evidence,' *New Nation*, 27 March 1997.

93. 'Hani Murder: Shocking New Evidence,' *New Nation*, 27 March 1997.

94. 'Hani Murder: Shocking New Evidence,' *New Nation*, 27 March 1997.

95. 'Hani Murder: Shocking New Evidence,' *New Nation*, 27 March 1997.

96. 'Hani Murder: Shocking New Evidence,' *New Nation*, 27 March 1997. The Truth and Reconciliation Final Report, released in October 1998, also mentioned the 'Inner Circle', while noting that its role had not been conclusively proven: 'Allegations still abound that a wider conspiracy was involved in the assassination. Some of those alleged to have been involved (names withheld at this stage) have also been implicated in intelligence documents as part of the so-called 'Inner Circle' or 'Binnekring' of 67 members of special forces (mainly CCB) and MI allegedly set up in July 1990. According to the former Transkei Intelligence Service they were tasked to carry out special operations by top generals in former MI structures.' (TRC Final Report Vol. 2 Ch. 7, p. 653). This was apparently a reference to the findings of the NIA report released in 1997. However, the TRC report concludes that it was 'unable to find evidence' that Hani's murderers 'took orders from international groups, security forces or from higher up in the right-wing echelons'.

97. 'Hani Murder: Shocking New Evidence,' *New Nation*, 27 March 1997.

98. 'The Hani Conspiracy,' *New Nation*, 27 March 1997.

99. 'The Hani Conspiracy,' *New Nation*, 27 March 1997.

100. 'Hani Murder: Shocking New Evidence,' *New Nation*, 27 March 1997. Brümmer identifies the traffic policeman as a member of the Boksburg City Council civil defence department and establishes his identity and those of the SADF MI commandant and the second gunman, as well as the name of the security firm, but does not name them. Brümmer notes: 'The security firm employee this week denied he had anything to do with

the plot, but acknowledged being friends with the former MI member and the civil defence department member, as indicated in the report.' See 'Hints of Truth about Hani's Death,' *Mail & Guardian*, 4 April 1997.

101. 'Hani Murder: Shocking New Evidence,' *New Nation*, 27 March 1997.
102. Nqakula, *The People's War*, p. 299.
103. 'The Hani Conspiracy Widens,' *New Nation*, 4 April 1997.
104. 'The Hani Conspiracy Widens,' *New Nation*, 4 April 1997.
105. 'Hani's Death Warrant?' *New Nation*, 11 April 1997.
106. 'Hints of Truth about Hani's Death,' *Mail & Guardian*, 4 April 1997.
107. 'Hani's Death Warrant?' *New Nation*, 11 April 1997.
108. 'Hani's Death Warrant?' *New Nation*, 11 April 1997.
109. 'Hani's Death Warrant?' *New Nation*, 11 April 1997.
110. Marianne Thamm, 'Clive Derby-Lewis Parole Opens Renewed Speculation into Hani Murder and the Arms Deal,' *Daily Maverick*, 19 June 2014.
111. 'How Arms Dealer Got His Hooks Into the ANC,' *Mail & Guardian*, 19 January 2007.
112. Groenink, *Incorruptible*.
113. Groenink, *Incorruptible*, p. 260.
114. 'How Arms Dealer Got His Hooks Into the ANC,' *Mail & Guardian*, 19 January 2007.
115. 'How Arms Dealer Got His Hooks Into the ANC,' *Mail & Guardian*, 19 January 2007.
116. Groenink, *Incorruptible*, p. 309.
117. Groenink, *Incorruptible*, p. 309.
118. Marianne Tham, 'Clive Derby-Lewis Parole Opens Renewed Speculation into Hani Murder and the Arms Deal,' *Daily Maverick*, 19 June 2014.
119. 'How Arms Dealer Got His Hooks into the ANC,' *Mail & Guardian*, 19 January 2007.
120. Johnson, *South Africa's Brave New World*.
121. Lekwane, 'The Chris Hani Assassination.' In 2014, on the author's behalf, a mutual acquaintance approached former TRC investigator Christelle Terreblanche to see if she would be willing to discuss with me her investigation into foreign countries' complicity in the Hani assassination; Terreblanche was unwilling.
122. Groenink, *Incorruptible*, p. 266.
123. Lekwane, 'The Chris Hani Assassination,' pp. 326-7.
124. 'Chris Hani was Killed before He Could Expose Joe Modise,' *City Press*, 8 October 2014.
125. Sanders, James. 2006. *Apartheid's Friends: The Rise and Fall of South Africa's Secret Service*. London: John Murray Publishers; McKinley, Dale T. 1997.

The ANC and the Liberation Struggle: A Critical Political Biography. London: Pluto Press.

126. Groenink, *Incorruptible*, p. 304.

127. Moodie, Ellen. 2010. *El Salvador in the Aftermath of Peace: Crime, Uncertainty, and the Transition to Democracy*. Philadelphia: University of Pennsylvania Press, p. 53.

128. Sparks, Allister. 1994. *Tomorrow Is Another Country*. New York: Penguin Press. Meanwhile, Groenink (*Incorruptible*), who sought to interview Harmse about inconsistencies in her testimony about Hani's killing, suspects that Harmse herself was a key player in the regime's disinformation campaign to frame Hani's murder as the work of a lone gunman.

129. Marx, cited in Moodie, *El Salvador in the Aftermath of Peace*, p. 63.

130. Gilder, Barry. 2012. *Songs and Secrets: South Africa from Liberation to Governance*. London: Hurst Publishers, p. 143.

131. Moodie, *El Salvador in the Aftermath of Peace*, p. 54.

132. Groenink, *Incorruptible*.

133. Moodie, *El Salvador in the Aftermath of Peace*, p. 54.

134. Sparks, *Tomorrow Is Another Country*.

135. Groenink, *Incorruptible*, p. 295.

136. Henderson, Robert D'A. 1997. Operation Vula against Apartheid. *International Journal of Intelligence and Counterintelligence* 10 (4), p. 426.

137. Confidential interview with ex-combatant, December 2009.

138. Confidential interview with ex-combatant, November 2009.

139. Wolfie Kodesh interview with Ayanda Ntsaluba, MCA 6 – 344A.

140. Murray, Martin. 1994. *The Revolution Deferred: The Painful Birth of Post-Apartheid South Africa*. London: Verso, p. 128.

141. Wolfie Kodesh interview with Lerumo Kalako, Mayibuye Archives, MCA 6 – 294, 6 July 1993.

142. 'Interview with Chris Hani, Deputy Commander Umkhonto we Sizwe, Lusaka 21 January 1990: Road Ahead Perspective' (SAHA, 5.17: Umkhonto we Sizwe).

143. 'ANC Department of Information and Publicity: MK Statement on the Assassination of Chris Hani,' 14 April 1993, Johannesburg (SAHA, 5.16 Hani's Death).

144. Confidential interview with ex-combatant, November 2009.

145. 'New Info on Hani's Death Vindicates Reinvestigation Call: ANC,' Johannesburg, 4 April 1997.

146. 'New Info on Hani's Death Vindicates Reinvestigation Call: ANC,' Johannesburg, 4 April 1997.

147. 'Freedom of Boksburg Posthumously Conferred on Hani,' SAPA, 11 April 1997.

148. 'Freedom of Boksburg Posthumously Conferred on Hani,' SAPA, 11 April 1997.

149. 'Hani Allegedly Ordered Killings of Top ANC Men,' SAPA, 12 June 1997.

150. 'Hani Allegedly Ordered Killings of Top ANC Men,' SAPA, 12 June 1997.

151. 'SACP Leader Calls for Investigation into Hani Murder to Be Reopened,' SAPA, http://www.justice.gov.za/trc/media/1999/9904/s990411a.htm.

152. 'SACP Leader Calls for Investigation into Hani Murder to Be Reopened,' SAPA.

153. Hani, Lindiwe, and Melinda Ferguson. 2017. *Being Chris Hani's Daughter*. Auckland Park: Jacana, p. 185.

154. Groenink, *Incorruptible*, p. 255.

155. Groenink, Evelyn. 2013. Dulcie, Hani, Lubowski: A Story That Could Not Be Told. *ZAM Magazine*, 24 April, p. 4.

156. Mattes, Robert. 2002. South Africa: Democracy without the People. *Journal of Democracy* 13 (1), pp. 27-8.

157. 'Hani Not Yet Laid to Rest,' *Mail & Guardian*, 29 March 2009.

8. MK'S MARGINALIZATION IN SOUTH AFRICA'S 'NEW' SECURITY FORCES

1.   Simpson, Thula. 2016. *Umkhonto we Sizwe: The ANC's Armed Struggle*. Cape Town: Penguin, p. 511.

2.   Rocky Williams, cited in Mashike, Lephophotho. 2008. Age of Despair: The Unintegrated Forces of South Africa. *African Affairs* 107 (June), p. 19.

3.   'Mandela Quells Mob Rule,' *Africa Research Bulletin*, 1–31 October 1994, pp. 11626-7.

4.   'South Africa: Who Exactly Is In Command?' *The Economist*, 19 November 1994.

5.   Frankel, Philip. 2000. *Soldiers in a Storm: The Armed Forces in South Africa's Democratic Transition*. Boulder, CO: Westview Press, p. 79.

6.   Confidential interview with ex-combatant, December 2009; Kynoch ('The "Transformation" of the South African Military') and Mashike ('Age of Despair') mention Mandela's speech at Wallmansthal and the hostile reception it received from MK cadres, but do not mention the disappearance of cadres at the base. The incident does not appear in Mandela's 1994 autobiography.

7.   'ANC Fighters Dismissed,' *Africa Research Bulletin*, 1–30 November 1994, p. 11662.

8.   Confidential interview with ex-combatant, November 2009.

9. Confidential interview with ex-combatant, December 2009.

10. Frankel, *Soldiers in a Storm*.

11. For example, Frankel, *Soldiers in a Storm*; Mashike, 'Age of Despair.'

12. Alexander, Jocelyn, JoAnn McGregor, and Terence Ranger. 2000. *Violence and Memory: One Hundred Years in the 'Dark Forests' of Matabeleland*. Oxford: James Currey.

13. Alexander, McGregor and Ranger, *Violence and Memory*, p. 183.

14. 'Ready to Govern,' SAHA Archives.

15. Williams, Rocky. 1991. *Back to the Barracks: The SADF and the Dynamics of Transformation*. Johannesburg: IDASA, pp. 28-9.

16. Confidential interview with ex-combatant, December 2009.

17. 'MK and the Future,' p. 7 (SAHA).

18. 'Magnus: "No" to SADF-Umkhonto Merger,' *The Citizen*, 21 March 1990.

19. Laurie Nathan, 'Article on the IDASA-ANC Conference on the "Future of Security and Defence in South Africa ,' 23–27 May 1991, Lusaka (SAHA).

20. Williams, *Back to the Barracks*, p. 27.

21. Kynoch, Gary. 1996. The 'Transformation' of the South African Military. *Journal of Modern African Studies* 34 (3), pp. 441-57.

22. 'MK and the Future,' pp. 2-7 (SAHA).

23. 'Military Forces during the Transition Period: Paper by Keith Mokoape' (SAHA).

24. 'MK and the Future,' p. 8 (SAHA).

25. Ngculu, James. 2009. *The Honour to Serve: Recollections of an Umkhonto Soldier*. Claremont: David Philip, p. 198.

26. Simpson, *Umkhonto we Sizwe*, pp. 481-2.

27. Williams, *Back to the Barracks*, p. 37.

28. Houston, Gregory. 2013. The Re-establishment of the ANC inside the Country, 1990–1994. In *The Road to Democracy in South Africa, Vol. 6 (1990–1996)*. South Africa Democracy Education Trust, Pretoria: University of South Africa Press, p. 197.

29. Henderson, Robert D'A. 1997. Operation Vula against Apartheid. *International Journal of Intelligence and Counterintelligence* 10 (4), pp. 418-55.

30. Ngculu, *The Honour to Serve*, p. 236.

31. The military code of Umkhonto we Sizwe, ANC document, cited in 'MK and the Future' (SAHA MK).

32. 'Interview with Chris Hani, Lusaka, 21 January 1990: Road Ahead Perspective' (SAHA).

33. 'MK and the Future,' p. 2 (SAHA MK).

34. 'Military Forces during the Transition Period: Paper by Keith Mokoape' (SAHA).

35. From a document of unknown authorship titled 'MK and the Future,' dated November 1990, p. 1 (SAHA).

36. Douek, Daniel. 2013. 'They Became Afraid When They Saw Us': MK Insurgency and Counterinsurgency in the Bantustan of Transkei, 1989–94. *Journal of Southern African Studies* 39 (1), pp. 207-25.

37. Confidential interview with ex-combatant, November 2009.

38. Confidential interview with ex-combatant, November 2009.

39. Gear, Sasha. 2002. Wishing Us Away: Challenges Facing Ex-Combatants in the 'New' South Africa. Centre for the Study of Violence and Reconciliation, Violence and Transition Series, vol. 8; Mashike, 'Age of Despair.'

40. 'MK and the Future,' p. 4 (SAHA).

41. 'MK and the Future,' p. 4 (SAHA).

42. Ngculu, *The Honour to Serve*, p. 217.

43. Ngculu, *The Honour to Serve*, p. 217.

44. Ngculu, *The Honour to Serve*, pp. 218-19.

45. Simpson, *Umkhonto we Sizwe*, p. 480.

46. Simpson, *Umkhonto we Sizwe*, p. 481.

47. Ngculu, *The Honour to Serve*, p. 225.

48. Ngculu, *The Honour to Serve*, pp. 228-30.

49. 'Ready to Govern: ANC Policy Guidelines for a Democratic South Africa, 28-31 May 1992' (SAHA).

50. 'Special Conference of MK Held at Mgwenya College of Education in Kanyamazane [Venda], from 3-4 September 1993' (SAHA).

51. 'Special Conference of MK Held at Mgwenya College of Education in Kanyamazane [Venda], from 3-4 September 1993' (SAHA).

52. 'Special Conference of MK Held at Mgwenya College of Education in Kanyamazane [Venda], from 3-4 September 1993' (SAHA).

53. 'Special Conference of MK Held at Mgwenya College of Education in Kanyamazane [Venda], from 3-4 September 1993' (SAHA).

54. 'Special Conference of MK Held at Mgwenya College of Education in Kanyamazane [Venda], from 3-4 September 1993' (SAHA).

55. 'Special Conference of MK Held at Mgwenya College of Education in Kanyamazane [Venda], from 3-4 September 1993' (SAHA).

56. Confidential interview with ex-combatant, December 2009.

57. Confidential interview with ex-combatant, December 2009.

58. 'South Africa: Crackdown Hits Hani's Men,' *Africa Confidential* 30 (18), 8 September 1989.

59. Simpson, *Umkhonto we Sizwe*, p. 481.

60. Ngculu, *The Honour to Serve*, p. 231.
61. A contingent of Transkei Defence Forces troops hosted by MK was also present (see Chapter Five).
62. *MK in Uganda* (video, 1992).
63. Confidential interview with ex-combatant, November 2009.
64. Simpson, *Umkhonto we Sizwe*, pp. 494-5.
65. Confidential interview with ex-combatant, December 2009.
66. Confidential interview with ex-combatant, December 2009.
67. 'Special Conference of MK Held at Mgwenya College of Education in Kanyamazane [Venda], from 3-4 September 1993' (SAHA).
68. Motumi, Tsepe. 1995. The Spear of the Nation: The Recent History of Umkhonto we Sizwe (MK). In *About Turn: The Transformation of the South African Military and Intelligence*, edited by J Cilliers and M Reichardt. Halfway House: Institute for Defence Policy, p. 101.
69. Mashike, 'Age of Despair.'
70. Ngculu, *The Honour to Serve*, p. 216.
71. Ngculu, *The Honour to Serve*, p. 208.
72. 'Interview with Chris Hani, Lusaka 21 January 1990: Road Ahead Perspective' (SAHA).
73. Confidential interview with ex-combatant, December 2009.
74. Confidential interview with ex-combatant, December 2009.
75. Confidential interview with ex-combatant, December 2009.
76. Confidential interview with ex-combatant, December 2009.
77. Simpson, *Umkhonto we Sizwe*, p. 500.
78. 'Special Conference of MK Held at Mgwenya College of Education in Kanyamazane [Venda], from 3-4 September 1993' (SAHA).
79. Flyer dated 14 September 1993, titled 'Call to Umkhonto we Sizwe' issued 'by the Army Chief of Staff on behalf of the MHQ [Military Headquarters] of Umkhonto we Sizwe' (SAHA MK).
80. Gear, Sasha. 2002. Now That the War Is Over: Ex-Combatants' Transition and the Question of Violence: A Literature Review, www.csvr.co.za.
81. Simpson, *Umkhonto we Sizwe*, p. 499.
82. 'Special Conference of MK Held at Mgwenya College of Education in Kanyamazane [Venda], from 3-4 September 1993' (SAHA Archives).
83. 'South Africa: Partners in Policing,' *Africa Confidential* 35 (2), 21 January 1994.
84. 'South Africa: Partners in Policing,' *Africa Confidential* 35 (2), 21 January 1994.
85. Groenink, Evelyn. 2018. *Incorruptible: The Story of the Murders of Dulcie September, Anton Lubowski and Chris Hani*. Cape Town: ABC Press, p. 302.
86. Simpson, *Umkhonto we Sizwe*, p. 503.

87. Ngculu, *The Honour to Serve*, p. 232.

88. Simpson, *Umkhonto we Sizwe*, p. 503.

89. 'Old Foes Unite in Peacekeeping Force: South Africa,' *The Times*, 31 March 1994.

90. Ngculu, *The Honour to Serve*, p. 233.

91. 'Top SANDF Posts for MK Officers,' *The Citizen*, 29 June 1997.

92. Frankel, *Soldiers in a Storm*, p. 39.

93. Ngculu, *The Honour to Serve*, p. 233.

94. 'Military Forces during the Transition Period: Paper by Keith Mokoape,' p. 5 (SAHA Archives).

95. 'Special Conference of MK Held at Mgwenya College of Education in Kanyamazane, from 3-4 September 1993' (SAHA).

96. Gear, 'Now That the War Is Over,' p. 41.

97. Gear, 'Now That the War Is Over,' p. 41.

98. Frankel, *Soldiers in a Storm*, p. 82.

99. Mashike, 'Age of Despair,' p. 10.

100. Simpson, *Umkhonto we Sizwe*, p. 508.

101. Simpson, *Umkhonto we Sizwe*, p. 508.

102. Simpson, *Umkhonto we Sizwe*, p. 510.

103. Confidential interview with ex-combatant, December 2009.

104. Confidential interview with ex-combatant, November 2009.

105. Confidential interview with ex-combatant, December 2009.

106. Confidential interview with ex-combatant, November 2009.

107. This Xhosa struggle term originates from *lumpenproletariat*, reflecting MK's Marxist-Leninist interpretation of Africans who collaborated with the apartheid regime.

108. Gear, 'Now That the War Is Over,' p. 19.

109. Gear, 'Now That the War Is Over,' p. 40.

110. Kynoch, Gary. 1996. The 'Transformation' of the South African Military. *Journal of Modern African Studies* 34 (3), p. 444.

111. Confidential interview with ex-combatant, December 2009.

112. Ngculu, *The Honour to Serve*, p. 229.

113. Gear, 'Now That the War Is Over,' pp. 23-4.

114. Ngculu, *The Honour to Serve*, p. 236.

115. Motumi, 'The Spear of the Nation,' p. 101.

116. Ngculu, *The Honour to Serve*, p. 236.

117. Confidential interview with ex-combatant, December 2009.

118. Houston, 'The Re-establishment of the ANC inside the Country.'

119. Gear, 'Now That the War Is Over.'

120. Confidential interview with ex-combatant, November 2009.

121. Author's interview with Barry Gilder, Baltimore, November 2013.

122. Frankel, *Soldiers in a Storm*, p. 76.

123. Van Loggerenberg, Jan. 1996. The Katorus Task Group: A Case Study. In *South Africa's Defence and Security into the 21st Century*, edited by W Gutteridge. Aldershot: Dartmouth Publishing, pp. 54-5.

124. 'South Africa: Violence in Transition,' *Africa Confidential* 33 (8), 17 April 1992.

125. Laurie Nathan, 'Article on the IDASA-ANC Conference on the Future of Security and Defence in South Africa,' 23–27 May 1991, Lusaka (SAHA).

126. Koevoet was a South African Police counterinsurgency unit staffed with white officers and black conscripts that was stationed in Namibia until its independence in 1989, whereupon its members were brought to operate in South Africa; Eugene de Kock commanded Koevoet before being assigned to Vlakplaas.

127. Wolfie Kodesh interview with Graham Morodi, 1993 (Mayibuye Archives).

128. Houston, Gregory, and James Ngculu. 2014. *Voices of Liberation: Chris Hani*. Cape Town: HSRC Press, p. 264. The Goldstone Commission noted that 32 Battalion 'soldiers had acted in a manner "completely inconsistent with the function of a peacekeeping force and, in fact, became perpetrators of violence".' This occurred notably in April 1992 when, after a 32 Battalion patrol came under fire from unknown gunmen, it killed two civilians and injured more than 100 in the Phola Park township, also raping and assaulting several women. (Truth and Reconciliation Commission Final Report Vol. 2 Ch. 7, p.591)

129. 'Arms Control: South Africa,' *The Economist*, 19 September 1992.

130. Houston and Ngculu, *Voices of Liberation*, p. 264.

131. Reno, Will. 1998. *Warlord Politics and African States*. Boulder, CO: Lynne Rienner, p. 60.

132. SAHA, TRC Gunrunning.

133. 'Beyond Bisho,' *The Times*, 1 October 1992.

134. Kynoch, 'The "Transformation" of the South African Military,' p. 444.

135. SAHA, TRC Gunrunning,

136. 'Top SANDF Posts for MK Officers,' *The Citizen*, 29 June 1994.

137. Simpson, *Umkhonto we Sizwe*, p. 513.

138. 'The Titanic Battle for Control of the Defence Force,' *Mail & Guardian*, 17 June 1994.

139. 'The Titanic Battle for Control of the Defence Force,' *Mail & Guardian*, 17 June 1994.

140. 'The Titanic Battle for Control of the Defence Force,' *Mail & Guardian*, 17 June 1994.

141. Motumi, 'The Spear of the Nation,' p. 101.

142. Motumi, 'The Spear of the Nation, p. 102.
143. Motumi, 'The Spear of the Nation,' p. 102.
144. 'Military Veterans Pose a Problem,' *New Nation*, 1 September 1995.
145. 'Dismissal Threat to Striking Mandela Guards: South Africa,' *The Times*, 25 August 1995.
146. 'Dismissal Threat to Striking Mandela Guards: South Africa,' *The Times*, 25 August 1995.
147. 'Military Blend,' *The Economist*, 26 August 1995.
148. 'Soldiers of Misfortune,' *New Nation*, 27 October 1995.
149. 'Old-Style SANDF Officers Are Still at War with Us, MK Soldiers Tell Modise,' *Sunday Independent*, 2 March 1997.
150. 'Old-Style SANDF Officers Are Still at War with Us, MK Soldiers Tell Modise,' *Sunday Independent*, 2 March 1997.
151. 'Old-Style SANDF Officers Are Still at War with Us, MK Soldiers Tell Modise,' *Sunday Independent*, 2 March 1997.
152. 'Revolt Averted,' *New Nation*, 14 March 1997.
153. 'Revolt Averted,' *New Nation*, 14 March 1997.
154. Frankel, *Soldiers in a Storm*, p. 89.
155. Frankel, *Soldiers in a Storm*, p. 89.
156. Mashike, 'Age of Despair.'
157. Author's interview with Mr Somkoko and Mr Sonamzi, Walter Sisulu University, Mthatha, 8 December 2009.
158. Gear, 'Wishing Us Away,' p. 26.
159. Gear, 'Wishing Us Away,' p. 27.
160. Mashike, 'Age of Despair.'
161. Author's interview with Mr Somkoko and Mr Sonamzi, Walter Sisulu University, Mthatha, 8 December 2009.
162. Confidential interview with ex-combatant, December 2009.
163. Author's interview with Mr Somkoko and Mr Sonamzi, Walter Sisulu University, Mthatha, 8 December 2009.
164. Author's interview with Mr Somkoko and Mr Sonamzi, Walter Sisulu University, Mthatha, 8 December 2009.
165. Confidential interview with ex-combatant, December 2009.
166. Confidential interview with ex-combatant, December 2009.
167. Gear, 'Wishing Us Away.'
168. Confidential interview with SANDF soldier, November 2009; in her mid-twenties, this soldier was too young to have fought during the struggle era.
169. Author's interview with Dr Johan Burger, senior researcher, Crime, Justice and Politics Programme at the Institute for Security Studies, Pretoria, 9 December 2009.

170. Confidential interview with ex-combatant, November 2009.

171. Confidential interview with ex-combatant, November 2009.

172. Personal communication with Sasha Gear, researcher at the Centre for the Study of Violence and Reconciliation (Johannesburg), 13 August 2010.

173. Taylor, Rupert. 2002. Justice Denied: Political Violence in KwaZulu-Natal after 1994. Centre for the Study of Violence and Reconciliation, Violence and Transition Series, vol. 6.

174. Confidential interview with ex-combatant, November 2009.

175. Confidential interview with ex-combatant, December 2009.

176. Confidential interview with ex-combatant, December 2009.

177. Author's interview with Dr Somadoda Fikeni, 21 December 2009.

178. Gear, 'Wishing Us Away,' p. 8.

179. Confidential interview with former ANC activist, December 2009.

180. SAHA, De Wet Potgieter Collection, 'Operation Rollerball,' B1.1.4.1.

181. SAHA, De Wet Potgieter Collection, 'Operation Rollerball,' B1.1.4.1.

182. 'MK and the Future,' p. 1 (SAHA).

183. Author's interview with Somadoda Fikeni, Tshwane, December 2009.

184. 'Deputy Minister Warns That Military Veterans May Revolt,' Pretoria News, 10 November 2009.

185. Mashike, 'Age of Despair.'

186. Confidential interview with ex-combatant, November 2009.

187. Foster, Don, Paul Haupt, and Marésa de Beer (eds). 2005. The Theatre of Violence: Narratives of Protagonists in the South African Conflict. Cape Town: Human Studies Research Council, p. 223.

188. Confidential interview with ex-combatant, December 2009.

189. 'X-MK Members Visit King Sabata's Grave Side,' Indabazethu (Eastern Cape), 27 February 2002.

190. 'X-MK Members Visit King Sabata's Grave Side,' Indabazethu (Eastern Cape), 27 February 2002.

191. Author's interview with Mr Somkoko and Mr Sonamzi, Walter Sisulu University, Mthatha, December 2009.

192. Mashike, 'Age of Despair,' pp. 17-21. These findings were also reinforced in an interview by the author with R Somkoko and S Sonamzi, Walter Sisulu University, Mthatha, December 2009.

193. Gear, 'Wishing Us Away,' p. 30.

194. 'Scapegoats for the Country's Ills,' Helen Suzman Foundation, Issue 10 (Second Quarter), 1998.

195. 'Scapegoats for the Country's Ills,' Helen Suzman Foundation, Issue 10 (Second Quarter), 1998.

196. Author's interview with Dr Somadoda Fikeni, December 2009.

197. Gear, 'Wishing Us Away,' p. 64.
198. Confidential interview with ex-combatant, November 2009.
199. Simpson, *Umkhonto we Sizwe*, p. 500.
200. Frankel, *Soldiers in a Storm*, pp. 41-2.
201. Seegers, Annette. 1991. South Africa's National Security Management System, 1972–1990. *Journal of Modern African Studies* 29 (2), p. 268.
202. Mashike, 'Age of Despair.'
203. Author's interview with Somadoda Fikeni, Tshwane, South Africa, December 2009.
204. Author's interview with Mr Somkoko and Mr Sonamzi, Walter Sisulu University, Mthatha, South Africa, December 2009.
205. For Molefe's entire quote, see the Conclusion.
206. Guha, Ranajit. 1994. The Prose of Counterinsurgency. In *Culture/Power/History: A Reader in Contemporary Social Theory*, edited by NB Dirks, Geoff Eley, and Sherry B Ortner. Princeton, NJ: Princeton University Press, p. 355.
207. Beverley, John. 1999. *Subalternity and Representation: Arguments in Cultural Theory*. Durham: Duke University Press, p. 27.
208. Author's interview with Somadoda Fikeni, Tshwane, South Africa, December 2009.
209. Williams, *Back to the Barracks*, p. 36.
210. See, for example, McKinley, Dale T. 1997. *The ANC and the Liberation Struggle: A Critical Political Biography*. London: Pluto Press.
211. 'Mandela Quells Mob Rule,' *Africa Research Bulletin*, 1–31 October 1994, pp. 11626-7.
212. Suttner, Raymond. 2004. The UDF Period and Its Meaning for Contemporary South Africa. *Journal of Southern African Studies* 30 (3), pp. 691-701.
213. Sparks, Allister. 1994. *Tomorrow Is Another Country*. New York: Penguin Press.
214. 'MK and the Future,' p. 7 (SAHA).
215. 'MK and the Future,' p. 7 (SAHA).

9. POST-TRANSITION VIOLENCE AS A COUNTERINSURGENCY LEGACY

1. Taylor, Rupert. 2002. Justice Denied: Political Violence in KwaZulu-Natal after 1994. Centre for the Study of Violence and Reconciliation, Violence and Transition Series, vol. 6.
2. Darby, John. 2006. Post-Accord Violence in a Changing World. In *Violence and Reconstruction*, edited by J Darby. Notre Dame: University of Notre Dame Press; Oomen, Barbara. 2004. Vigilantism or Alternative

Citizenship? The Rise of Mapogo a Mathamaga. *African Studies* 63 (2), pp. 153-71; Hansen, Thomas Blom. 2006. Performers of Sovereignty: On the Privatization of Security in Urban South Africa. *Critique of Anthropology* 26 (3), pp. 279-95.

3. Confidential interview with ex-combatant, December 2009.
4. 'What the Generals Didn't Tell Modise,' *Mail & Guardian*, 17 June 1994.
5. Pauw, Jacques. 1997. *Into the Heart of Darkness: Confessions of Apartheid's Assassins*. Johannesburg: Jonathan Ball Publishers, p. 279.
6. Pauw, *Into the Heart of Darkness*, p. 281.
7. 'What the Generals Didn't Tell Modise,' *Mail & Guardian*, 17 June 1994.
8. TRC Final Report, Vol. 2, ch. 2, subsection 34.
9. Dlamini, Jacob. 2014. *Askari*. Auckland Park: Jacana.
10. Pauw, *Into the Heart of Darkness*; Dlamini, *Askari*.
11. Dlamini, *Askari*.
12. Pauw, *Into the Heart of Darkness*, p. 69.
13. African National Congress, Second Submission to the TRC: http://www.justice.gov.za/trc/hrvtrans/submit/anc2.htm#Operations.
14. 'MK Man Was Apartheid Spy,' *New Nation*, 2 May 1997.
15. Pauw, *Into the Heart of Darkness*, p. 297.
16. Pauw, *Into the Heart of Darkness*, p. 303.
17. Pauw, *Into the Heart of Darkness*, p. 300. In 1990, Stoffberg performed an assignment for Ciskei strongman Brig. Oupa Gqozo, which reinforces the portrayal of apartheid covert units working in concert, since Pan-Afrik Consultants, a DCC subsidiary, was heavily involved in advising Gqozo at that time.
18. Pauw, *Into the Heart of Darkness*, p. 313.
19. Pauw, *Into the Heart of Darkness*, p. 69.
20. Gear, Sasha. 2002. Wishing Us Away: Challenges Facing Ex-Combatants in the 'New' South Africa. Centre for the Study of Violence and Reconciliation, Violence and Transition Series, vol. 8, p. 116.
21. 'De Kock's Family Alleges Poison Bid,' *Sunday Times*, 9 April 1995.
22. Bill Keller, 'A Glimpse of Apartheid's Dying Sting,' *New York Times*, 20 February 1995.
23. 'Reformist Afrikaner Murdered,' *Africa Research Bulletin*, 1–30 November 1994, pp. 11661-2.
24. 'Would-Be Assassin Lives in Fear in Jail,' *New Nation*, 13 October 1995.
25. 'Would-Be Assassin Lives in Fear in Jail,' *New Nation*, 13 October 1995.
26. 'Plan to Silence Phosa's Would-Be Killer Alleged,' *New Nation*, 20 October 1995.
27. 'Cops Warn of Plot to Kill Premier,' *New Nation*, 27 October 1995.

28. 'TRC Gives Amnesty to 18 and Refuses It to Five,' SAPA, 12 January 1999.

29. '"Nceba" Radu's Death: The Mystery Deepens,' *New Nation*, 14 March 1997.

30. 'Intelligence Chief's "Odd" Gunshot,' *Mail & Guardian*, 15 October 1997.

31. 'Intelligence Chief's "Odd" Gunshot,' *Mail & Guardian*, 15 October 1997.

32. 'Intelligence Chief's "Odd" Gunshot,' *Mail & Guardian*, 15 October 1997.

33. 'Spy Chief Mystery,' *The Independent*, 8 October 1995; see also 'South African Spy Chief Probing Coup When Slain,' *Orlando Sentinel*, 9 October 1995.

34. '"Nceba" Radu's Death: The Mystery Deepens,' *New Nation*, 14 March 1997.

35. '"Nceba" Radu's Death: The Mystery Deepens,' *New Nation*, 14 March 1997.

36. '"Nceba" Radu's Death: The Mystery Deepens,' *New Nation*, 14 March 1997.

37. Radu was also reportedly investigating the 1995 death of Muziwendoda Mdluli. SAPS investigations commissioner Bushie Engelbrecht, who took possession of Radu's briefcase, admitted that it contained sensitive documents, but claimed they had been removed from the briefcase at the crash site. The briefcase and documents later disappeared. see, 'The Man Who Knew Too Much'.

38. 'The Execution of a Camp Commander,' *Mail & Guardian*, 30 October 1998.

39. 'Where Is Modise's Money Man?' *Mail & Guardian*, 23 September 2011.

40. 'Chris Hani Was Killed before He Could Expose Joe Modise,' *City Press*, 8 October 2014.

41. Kynoch, Gary. 1996. The 'Transformation' of the South African Military. *Journal of Modern African Studies* 34 (3), pp. 441-57.

42. Ellis, Stephen. 1999. The New Frontiers of Crime in South Africa. In *The Criminalization of the State in Africa*, edited by JF Bayart, Stephen Ellis, and Béatrice Hibou. Indianapolis: Indiana University Press.

43. O'Brien, Kevin. 2011. *The South African Intelligence Services: From Apartheid to Democracy, 1948–2005.* New York: Routledge, p. 186.

44. Confidential interview with ex-combatant, November 2009.

45. Bell, Terry, with Dumisa Buhle Ntsebeza. 2003. *Unfinished Business: South Africa, Apartheid, and Truth*. London: Verso, p. 341.

46. SAHA, TRC Gunrunning 1974-97.

47. Ellis, Stephen. 1998. The Historical Significance of South Africa's Third Force. *Journal of Southern African Studies* 24 (2), pp. 261-99; Ellis, 'The New Frontiers of Crime in South Africa'; Sanders, James. 2006. *Apartheid's Friends: The Rise and Fall of South Africa's Secret Service*. London: John Murray Publishers.

48. Confidential interview with ex-combatant, November 2009.

49. Confidential interview with ex-combatant, November 2009.

50. White Paper, cited in O'Brien *The South African Intelligence Services*, p. 184.

51. Gilder, Barry. 2012. *Songs and Secrets: South Africa from Liberation to Governance*. London: Hurst Publishers, pp. 186-7.

52. Confidential interview with ex-combatant, November 2009.

53. Confidential interview with ex-combatant, November 2009.

54. ANC Second Submission to the TRC, Appendix Seven.

55. Pauw, *Into the Heart of Darkness*, p. 133.

56. 'Arms Major Implicated in De Kock Trial,' *Sunday Times*, 12 March 1995.

57. SAHA, TRC Gunrunning 1974-97.

58. Pauw, *Into the Heart of Darkness*, p. 265.

59. Pauw, *Into the Heart of Darkness*, p. 266.

60. Sanders, *Apartheid's Friends*.

61. SAHA, TRC Gunrunning 1974-97.

62. Ellis, Stephen. 1996. Africa and International Corruption: The Strange Case of South Africa and Seychelles. *African Affairs* 95 (379), p. 193.

63. ANC Statement to the Truth and Reconciliation Commission, Vol. 4.9 (August 1996), http://www.justice.gov.za/trc/hrvtrans/submit/anctruth.htm#4.

64. ANC Statement to the Truth and Reconciliation Commission, Vol. 4.9 (August 1996).

65. ANC Statement to the Truth and Reconciliation Commission, Vol. 4.9 (August 1996), http://www.justice.gov.za/trc/hrvtrans/submit/anctruth.htm#4.

66. Gilder, *Songs and Secrets*, pp. 198-9.

67. Dugard, Jackie. 2001. From Low Intensity War to Mafia War: Taxi Violence in South Africa (1987–2000). Centre for the Study of Violence and Reconciliation, Violence and Transition Series, vol. 4 (May).

68. 'Cops Set to Pounce on Taxi Hitman,' *New Nation*, 22 September 1995.

69. 'Soldiers of Misfortune,' *New Nation*, 27 October 1995.

70. 'Taxi Wars Exposé: Police Set to Pounce on Taxi War Hit Squad Training Camps,' *City Press*, 5 January 1997.

71. 'Taxi Wars Exposé: Police Set to Pounce on Taxi War Hit Squad Training Camps,' *City Press*, 5 January 1997.

72. Dugard, 'From Low Intensity War to Mafia War.'

73. 'Hired Cop Accused of Death Plot,' *New Nation*, 13 October 1995.

74. Gear, 'Wishing Us Away.'

75. Neocosmos, Michael. 1998. From Peoples' Politics to State Politics: Aspects of National Liberation in South Africa. In *The Politics of Opposition in Contemporary Africa*, edited by AO Olukoshi. Stockholm: Nordiska Afrikainstitutet, p. 216.

76. Du Toit, Pierre. 2001. *South Africa's Brittle Peace*. New York: Palgrave, p. 50.

77. 'Rightwing Terror or a New Third Force?' *New Nation*, 10 January 1997.

78. 'Rightwingers Regroup,' *New Nation*, 14 February 1997.

79. Confidential interview with ex-combatant, December 2009.

80. Pauw, *Into the Heart of Darkness*, p. 130.

81. Taylor, 'Justice Denied.'

82. 'Top IFP Members May Face Hit Squad Charges,' *Sunday Times*, 9 April 1995.

83. 'Anxiety in KwaZulu Natal over Crackdown,' *Sunday Times*, 12 March 1995.

84. 'Top IFP Man Investigated,' *New Nation*, 29 September 1995.

85. 'Top Officers Named in Hit Squad Probe,' *New Nation*, 22 September 1995.

86. 'Cops Up for Murder,' *New Nation*, 22 September 1995.

87. 'A-G Criticizes KZP over Hitsquads,' *New Nation*, 13 October 1995.

88. 'Tortured,' *New Nation*, 20 October 1995.

89. 'IFP's "Caprivis" Sill on the Job,' *Mail & Guardian*, 11 October 1996.

90. 'IFP's "Caprivis" Sill on the Job,' *Mail & Guardian*, 11 October 1996.

91. 'Inkatha Raid Stirs Plot Fears,' *The Independent*, 30 December 1995.

92. 'Inkatha Raid Stirs Plot Fears,' *The Independent*, 30 December 1995.

93. 'Inkatha Raid Stirs Plot Fears,' *The Independent*, 30 December 1995.

94. Taylor, 'Justice Denied.'

95. 'Inkatha Raid Stirs Plot Fears,' *The Independent*, 30 December 1995.

96. 'Inkatha Raid Stirs Plot Fears,' *The Independent*, 30 December 1995.

97. 'Police Still Patrolling KZN Area,' *New Nation*, 25 August 1995.

98. Kynoch, 'The "Transformation" of the South African Military.'

99. 'Inkatha Raid Stirs Plot Fears,' *The Independent*, 30 December 1995.

100. 'Political Violence Rocks ANC Stronghold,' *New Nation*, 28 February 1997.

101. '"Third Force" Target?' *New Nation*, 9 May 1997.

102. 'ANC Pushes Ahead with Peace Plan,' *New Nation*, 17 January 1997.

103. 'Fears of Shadowy Force Return to South Africa,' *New York Times*, 11 August 1997.

104. 'How ANC Protected "Warlord" Spy,' *Mail & Guardian*, 7 November 1997.
105. 'How ANC Protected "Warlord" Spy,' *Mail & Guardian*, 7 November 1997.
106. Taylor, 'Justice Denied.'
107. 'Enemies Who Worked Together for the Police,' *Mail & Guardian*, 19 February 1999.
108. De Haas, Mary. 2013. Violence in Zululand: The 1990s. In *The Road to Democracy in South Africa, Vol. 6 (1990–1996).* South Africa Democracy Education Trust, Pretoria: University of South Africa Press, p. 956.
109. 'Enemies Who Worked Together for the Police,' *Mail & Guardian*, 19 February 1999.
110. Berkeley, Bill. 1994. The Warlords of Natal. *Atlantic Monthly* (March), pp. 85-100.
111. 'Enemies Who Worked Together for the Police,' *Mail & Guardian*, 19 February 1999.
112. De Haas, 'Violence in Zululand,' p. 943.
113. 'Enemies Who Worked Together for the Police,' *Mail & Guardian*, 19 February 1999.
114. 'Warlord Buried as Killing Goes On,' *Mail & Guardian*, 1 February 1999.
115. Taylor, 'Justice Denied.'
116. O'Brien, *The South African Intelligence Services*, p. 115.
117. De Haas, 'Violence in Zululand,' p. 914.
118. 'Warlord Buried as Killing Goes On,' *Mail & Guardian*, 1 February 1999.
119. 'Warlord Buried as Killing Goes On,' *Mail & Guardian*, 1 February 1999.
120. 'Warlord Buried as Killing Goes On,' *Mail & Guardian*, 1 February 1999.
121. De Haas, 'Violence in Zululand,' pp. 948-52.
122. 'Warlord Buried as Killing Goes On,' *Mail & Guardian*, 1 February 1999.
123. 'Warlord Buried as Killing Goes On,' *Mail & Guardian*, 1 February 1999.
124. Taylor, 'Justice Denied.'
125. Lodge, Tom. 1998. Political Corruption in South Africa. *African Affairs* 97 (387), pp. 157-87; Brogden, M, and P Nijhar. 1998. Corruption and the South African Police. *Crime, Law and Social Change* 30 (1), pp. 89-106; Hyslop, J. 2005. Political Corruption before and after Apartheid. *Journal of Southern African Studies* 31 (4), pp. 773-89.
126. Shaw, Mark. 2002. *Crime and Policing in Post-Apartheid South Africa.* Bloomington, IN: Indiana University Press, pp. 22-8.
127. 'ANC Fighters Dismissed,' *Africa Research Bulletin*, 1–30 November 1994, p. 11662.
128. Shaw, *Crime and Policing in Post-Apartheid South Africa.*
129. 'Nine Cops Face Rap over Shootout,' *New Nation*, 20 October 1995.

130. Chikwanha, Annie Barbara. 2005. Trust in Institutions in Sub-Saharan Africa's Emerging Democracies. In *Trust in Public Institutions in South Africa*, edited by S and NB Askvik. Burlington, VT: Ashgate Publishing.

131. Shaw, *Crime and Policing in Post-Apartheid South Africa*, p. 32.

132. McCarthy, Shaun. 1996. Challenges for the South African Intelligence Community. In *South Africa's Defense and Security into the 21st Century*, edited by W Gutteridge. Brookfield, VT: Dartmouth Publishing, p. 69.

133. Pauw, *Into the Heart of Darkness.*

134. 'Union Questions Police Allegiance,' *New Nation*, 28 February 1997.

135. Bell and Ntsebeza, *Unfinished Business*, p. 340.

136. De Haas, 'Violence in Zululand,' p. 942. In October 1998, the Truth and Reconciliation Final Report noted that while the post-transition era was beyond its scope, 'The Commission notes with concern the ongoing reports of torture and deaths in custody, which have reached alarming levels… It has been suggested that [torture] were and are routine methods in police criminal investigations and to a large degree replace routine investigative work.' (TRC Final Report Vol. 2, Ch. 7, p. 590)

137. 'John Vorster Policemen Killed Stanza Bopape,' *New Nation*, 20 March 1997.

138. 'Seven Other Death Farms,' *New Nation*, 20 March 1997.

139. Brogden and Nijhar, 'Corruption and the South African Police,' p. 93.

140. Lodge, 'Political Corruption in South Africa,' p. 22.

141. Sanders *Apartheid's Friends*, p. 356.

142. 'Judgment Day for Selebi,' *Mail & Guardian*, 1 July 2010.

143. Confidential interview with ex-combatant, December 2009.

144. Gilder points out that the corruption charges linking Selebi to mafia boss Glenn Agliotti may have arisen because Selebi thought he was running Agliotti as an intelligence source; this raises the possibility that Selebi was framed (Gilder, *Songs and Secrets*, p. 291).

10. SKELETONS AND GHOSTS: SPY SCANDALS IN POST-TRANSITION SOUTH AFRICA

1.   'Madonsela: CIA Accusation Sparks Diplomatic Row,' *Mail & Guardian*, 8 September 2014.

2.   'Madonsela: CIA Accusation Sparks Diplomatic Row,' *Mail & Guardian*, 8 September 2014.

3.   Sanders, James. 2006. *Apartheid's Friends: The Rise and Fall of South Africa's Secret Service*. London: John Murray Publishers.

4.   Sanders, *Apartheid's Friends*, p. 363.

5.   Reno, Will. 2011. *Warfare in Independent Africa*. Cambridge: Cambridge University Press, p. 104.

6.   TRC, 'Human Rights Violations, Submissions – Questions and Answers,' Mr and Mrs P Ngwenya, Soweto, Day 5, 26 July 1996.

7.   'South Africa: Crackdown Hits Hani's Men,' *Africa Confidential* 30 (18), 8 September 1989.

8.   'South Africa: Crackdown Hits Hani's Men,' *Africa Confidential* 30 (18), 8 September 1989.

9.   TRC, 'Human Rights Violations, Submissions – Questions and Answers,' 26 July 1996, Mr and Mrs P Ngwenya, Soweto, Day 5.

10. Manong, Stanley. 2015. *If We Must Die: An Autobiography of a Former Commander of uMkhonto we Sizwe*. Johannesburg: Nkululeko Publishers, p. 228. Another MK camp commander with a reputation for brutality, Kenneth Mahamba, was executed by a military tribunal in 1984 after being found guilty of spying.

11. 'Was ANC 'Spy' Poisoned in Exile?' *The Star*, 14 October 2003.

12. 'South Africa: Crackdown Hits Hani's Men,' *Africa Confidential* 30 (18), 8 September 1989.

13. Simpson, Thula. 2016. *Umkhonto we Sizwe: The ANC's Armed Struggle*. Cape Town: Penguin, p. 450.

14. TRC Report, Vol. 2, ch. 4 paragraph 146, p. 358.

15. 'Was ANC "Spy" Poisoned in Exile?' *The Star*, 14 October 2003.

16. O'Malley, Padraig. 2007. *Shades of Difference: Mac Maharaj and the Struggle for South Africa.* New York: Viking, p. 428.

17. SAHA, De Wet Potgieter Collection, B1.5.4.1, 'Threats Against De Klerk: The "ANC Working Group".'

18. 'Was ANC "Spy" Poisoned in Exile?' *The Star*, 14 October 2003.

19. O'Malley, *Shades of Difference*, p. 427.

20. Herbstein, Denis. 1994. Old Spies Don't Die. *Africa Report* 39 (2), March-April.

21. O'Brien, Kevin. 2011. *The South African Intelligence Services: From Apartheid to Democracy, 1948–2005.* New York: Routledge, p. 217.

22. Author's interview with Barry Gilder, Baltimore, November 2013.

23. Confidential interview with ex-combatant, November 2009.

24. Gilder, Barry. 2012. *Songs and Secrets: South Africa from Liberation to Governance*. London: Hurst Publishers.

25. Confidential interview with ex-combatant, November 2009.

26. O'Brien, *The South African Intelligence Services*, p. 205.

27. Slovo, Joe. 1995. *Slovo: The Unfinished Autobiography*. Johannesburg: Ravan Press.

28. O'Brien, *The South African Intelligence Services.*

29. 'What the Generals Didn't Tell Modise,' *Mail & Guardian*, 17 June 1994.

30. Groenink, Evelyn. 2018. *Incorruptible: The Story of the Murders of Dulcie September, Anton Lubowski and Chris Hani.* Cape Town: ABC Press, p. 238.

31. 'What the Generals Didn't Tell Modise,' *Mail & Guardian*, 17 June 1994.

32. 'What the Generals Didn't Tell Modise,' *Mail & Guardian*, 17 June 1994.

33. 'What the Generals Didn't Tell Modise,' *Mail & Guardian*, 17 June 1994.

34. 'The Titanic Battle for Control of the Defence Force,' *Mail & Guardian*, 17 June 1994.

35. SAHA, De Wet Potgieter Collection, B1.1.3.1, Pan-Afrik Investment Consultants.

36. SAHA, De Wet Potgieter Collection, B1.1.3.1, Pan-Afrik Investment Consultants.

37. SAHA, De Wet Potgieter Collection, B1.1.3.1, Pan-Afrik Investment Consultants.

38. 'Defense Job Widened by Mandela,' *The Times*, 27 June 1994.

39. 'The Titanic Battle for Control of the Defence Force,' *Mail & Guardian*, 17 June 1994.

40. 'The Titanic Battle for Control of the Defence Force,' *Mail & Guardian*, 17 June 1994.

41. 'The Titanic Battle for Control of the Defence Force,' *Mail & Guardian*, 17 June 1994.

42. SAHA, De Wet Potgieter Collection, B1.1.3.1, Pan-Afrik Investment Consultants.

43. SAHA, De Wet Potgieter Collection, B1.1.3.1, Pan-Afrik Investment Consultants. Curiously, the PAIIC Group released its official statements on letterhead emblazoned with the Latin motto 'Felix qui potuit rerum cognoscere causas,' with an English translation beneath: 'Blessed is he who can recognize the truth.' Judge Louis Harms, appointed by FW de Klerk to head an official inquiry into apartheid death squads and covert activities in 1990, had emblazoned this same motto on his commission's final report, which was widely regarded as a sham that enabled the National Party to wash its hands of death squad allegations, and left the regime's counterinsurgency mechanisms intact as negotiations began with the ANC.

44. 'Defense Job Widened by Mandela,' *The Times*, 27 June 1994.

45. O'Brien, *The South African Intelligence Services.*

46. Anton Harber, 'Mac Releases Captured NIS Files,' *Weekly Mail & Guardian*, 29 July 1994.

47. Anton Harber, 'Mac Releases Captured NIS Files,' *Weekly Mail & Guardian*, 29 July 1994.

48. SAHA, De Wet Potgieter Collection, B1.1.3.1, Pan-Afrik Investment Consultants.

49. 'What the Generals Didn't Tell Modise,' *Mail & Guardian*, 17 June 1994; this inter-agency turf war mirrors the SADF's Counter-Intelligence Directorate's role in supplying Pierre Steyn with information about SADF Military Intelligence during his investigation.

50. From a letter addressed to deputy defence minister Ronnie Kasrils titled 'Re: Unresolved Matters Regarding Alleged Third Force Activities,' signed the PAIIC Group, dated 17 August 1994 (SAHA, 'The PAIIC Group,' B1.1.3.14).

51. 'What the Generals Didn't Tell Modise,' *Mail & Guardian*, 17 June 1994.

52. 'The Titanic Battle for Control of the Defence Force,' *Mail & Guardian*, 17 June 1994.

53. 'The Titanic Battle for Control of the Defence Force,' *Mail & Guardian*, 17 June 1994.

54. Berkeley, Bill. 2001. *The Graves Are Not Yet Full: Race, Tribe, and Power in the Heart of Africa*. New York: Basic Books.

55. Taylor, Rupert. 2002. Justice Denied: Political Violence in KwaZulu-Natal after 1994. Centre for the Study of Violence and Reconciliation, Violence and Transition Series, vol. 6.

56. See, for example, D Douek, 'New Light on the Samora Machel Assassination: "I Realized It Was No Accident."'

57. 'Was ANC "Spy" Poisoned in Exile?' *The Star*, 14 October 2003.

58. Pauw, Jacques. 1997. *Into the Heart of Darkness: Confessions of Apartheid's Assassins*. Johannesburg: Jonathan Ball Publishers, p. 135.

59. Bell, Terry, with Dumisa Buhle Ntsebeza. 2003. *Unfinished Business: South Africa, Apartheid, and Truth*. London: Verso, p. 344.

60. 'Spies Fever Grips ANC,' *New Nation*, 4 April 1997.

61. 'Spies Fever Grips ANC,' *New Nation*, 4 April 1997.

62. 'Five ANC Ministers Spied for Nats – Claim,' *New Nation*, 7 March 1997.

63. 'Five ANC Ministers Spied for Nats – Claim,' *New Nation*, 7 March 1997.

64. 'Five ANC Ministers Spied for Nats – Claim,' *New Nation*, 7 March 1997.

65. 'Five ANC Ministers Spied for Nats – Claim,' *New Nation*, 7 March 1997.

66. 'Five ANC Ministers Spied for Nats – Claim,' *New Nation*, 7 March 1997.

67. 'Five ANC Ministers Spied for Nats – Claim,' *New Nation*, 7 March 1997.

68. O'Brien, *The South African Intelligence Services*, pp. 218-19.

69. Nqakula, Charles. 2017. *The People's War: Reflections of an ANC Cadre*. Johannesburg: Mutloatse Heritage Trust, p. 272.

70. 'I Was No Spy,' *New Nation*, 11 April 1997.

71. 'I Was No Spy,' *New Nation*, 11 April 1997.

72. 'He Walks in Fear,' *New Nation*, 14 March 1997.

73. 'He Walks in Fear,' *New Nation*, 14 March 1997.

74. 'He Walks in Fear,' *New Nation*, 14 March 1997.

75. 'He Walks in Fear,' *New Nation*, 14 March 1997.

76. 'He Walks in Fear,' *New Nation*, 14 March 1997.

77. 'He Walks in Fear,' *New Nation*, 14 March 1997.

78. 'He Walks in Fear,' *New Nation*, 14 March 1997.

79. TRC Amnesty Hearing, Application of Botha, Du Preez, Steyn, Wasserman, and Van der Westhuizen, Pinetown, 11 April 2000.

80. 'Mandela Has Files on Spies,' *Mail & Guardian*, 30 October 1997.

81. Dlamini, Jacob. 2014. *Askari*. Auckland Park: Jacana.

82. TRC Report, Vol. 1, ch. 8.

83. Gilder, *Songs and Secrets*, pp. 182-3.

84. TRC Report, Vol. 5, ch. 6, pp. 226-7.

85. Confidential interview with ex-combatant, December 2009.

86. Author's interview with Barry Gilder, Baltimore, November 2013.

87. 'The Titanic Battle for Control of the Defence Force,' *Mail & Guardian*, 17 June 1994.

88. 'PAC's De Lille Names "Spies",' *Mail & Guardian*, 23 October 1997.

89. 'PAC's De Lille Names "Spies",' *Mail & Guardian*, 23 October 1997.

90. 'Mandela Has Files on Spies,' *Mail & Guardian*, 30 October 1997.

91. 'Mandela Has Files on Spies,' *Mail & Guardian*, 30 October 1997.

92. 'Madiba' is Nelson Mandela's clan name, and is widely used in South Africa to refer to him.

93. 'Mandela Has Files on Spies,' *Mail & Guardian*, 30 October 1997.

94. Sanders, *Apartheid's Friends*, p. 339.

95. 'Report by the President of the ANC, Nelson Mandela, to the 50th National Conference of the African National Congress, Mafikeng, 16 December 1997.'

96. O'Brien, *The South African Intelligence Services*, p. 208.

97. O'Brien, *The South African Intelligence Services*, p. 209.

98. O'Brien, *The South African Intelligence Services*, pp. 209-10.

99. O'Brien, *The South African Intelligence Services*, pp. 214-15.

100. 'SA Intelligence World in Turmoil,' *Mail & Guardian*, 20 October 1995.

101. O'Brien, *The South African Intelligence Services*, p. 218.

102. 'De Klerk, Closet Generalissimo,' *New Nation*, 13 October 1995.

103. 'The ANC Takes a Long, Hard Look at the GNU,' *New Nation*, 13 October 1995.

104. 'SA Intelligence World in Turmoil,' *Mail & Guardian*, 20 October 1995.

105. This strike included some of Mandela's bodyguards – see Chapter Eight.

106. 'The ANC Takes a Long, Hard Look at the GNU,' *New Nation*, 13 October 1995.

107. 'SA Intelligence World in Turmoil,' *Mail & Guardian*, 20 October 1995.

108. 'SA Intelligence World in Turmoil,' *Mail & Guardian*, 20 October 1995.

109. 'SA Intelligence World in Turmoil,' *Mail & Guardian*, 20 October 1995.
110. 'SA Intelligence World in Turmoil,' *Mail & Guardian*, 20 October 1995.
111. 'SA Intelligence World in Turmoil,' *Mail & Guardian*, 20 October 1995.
112. O'Brien, Kevin. 1999. South African Intelligence in Chaos. *Jane's Intelligence Review* (January), p. 47.
113. Sanders, *Apartheid's Friends*.
114. 'Nuclear Nightmare,' *New Nation*, 20 October 1995.
115. Gilder, *Songs and Secrets*, p. 188.
116. Gilder, *Songs and Secrets*, p. 188.
117. Gilder, *Songs and Secrets*, p. 189.
118. O'Brien, 'South African Intelligence in Chaos,' p. 46.
119. O'Brien, 'South African Intelligence in Chaos,' p. 45.
120. Clarke, Liam, and Inigo Gilmore, 'IRA Linked to African Arms Deal,' *Sunday Times* (London), 15 March 1998; in an added twist, amid the ongoing Northern Ireland peace talks, Gerry Kelly of Sinn Fein was alleged to have visited McBride just before his arrest, fuelling 'fears that the IRA may be secretly rearming itself with foreign weapons for a potential return to violence if its aims are not met'; this was reminiscent of the transition-era SADF psy-ops 'Project Echoes,' which sought to link MK to the IRA (see Chapter Three).
121. O'Brien, 'South African Intelligence in Chaos,' pp. 45-6.
122. O'Brien, 'South African Intelligence in Chaos,' p. 46.
123. 'Leaking Another Pile of Baloney,' *Mail & Guardian*, 12 June 1998.
124. This echoed the Angolan Army's official acronym, FAPLA.
125. O'Brien, 'South African Intelligence in Chaos,' p. 48.
126. O'Brien, 'South African Intelligence in Chaos,' p. 48.
127. O'Brien, 'South African Intelligence in Chaos,' p. 49.
128. O'Brien, 'South African Intelligence in Chaos,' p. 46.
129. 'An Axe, Not a Broom, for the Spies,' *Mail & Guardian*, 9 April 1998.
130. O'Brien, 'South African Intelligence in Chaos,' p. 47.
131. Gilder, *Songs and Secrets*, p. 189.
132. 'Leaking Another Pile of Baloney,' *Mail & Guardian*, 12 June 1998.
133. 'Leaking Another Pile of Baloney,' *Mail & Guardian*, 12 June 1998.
134. Sanders, *Apartheid's Friends*.
135. Sanders, *Apartheid's Friends*, p. 393.
136. 'ANC Denies Vula Cover-up,' *New Nation*, 20 March 1997.
137. Sanders, *Apartheid's Friends*.
138. O'Brien, *The South African Intelligence Services*, p. 219.
139. Jean Comaroff, lecture at McGill University, Montreal, 29 March 2010.
140. Russell, Alec. 2009. *Bring Me My Machine Gun: The Battle for the Soul of South Africa from Mandela to Zuma*. New York: Perseus.

141. Gilder, *Songs and Secrets*, p. 242.

142. De Haas, Mary. 2013. Violence in Zululand: The 1990s. In *The Road to Democracy in South Africa, Vol. 6 (1990–1996)*. South Africa Democracy Education Trust, Pretoria: University of South Africa Press, pp. 876-957.

143. Gilder, *Songs and Secrets*, p. 267.

144. Gilder, *Songs and Secrets*, p. 277.

145. Gilder, *Songs and Secrets*, p. 274.

146. O'Brien, *The South African Intelligence Services*, p. 229.

147. Holden, Paul, and Hennie van Vuuren. 2011. *The Devil in the Detail: How the Arms Deal Changed Everything.* Jeppestown: Jonathan Ball; Gilder, *Songs and Secrets*.

148. Gilder, *Songs and Secrets*, p. 290.

149. Gilder, *Songs and Secrets*, p. 276.

150. Gumede, William (ed.). 2009. *The Poverty of Ideas.* Johannesburg: Jacana, p. 174.

151. Adriaan Basson and Sam Sole, 'Selebi Spy's Paranoid World,' *Mail & Guardian*, 4–10 December 2009.

152. Gumede, *The Poverty of Ideas*, p. 173.

153. Author's interview with Dr Somadoda Fikeni, Tshwane (Pretoria), 20 December 2009.

154. 'Third Force Suspected in Pupils' Bloody Feud,' *New Nation*, 17 January 1997.

155. Buur, Lars. 2007. The Intertwined History of Security and Development: The Case of Development Struggles in South Africa's Townships. In *The Security-Development Nexus: Expressions of Sovereignty and Securitization in Southern Africa*, edited by Lars Buur, Steffen Jensen, and Finn Stepputat. Cape Town: HSRC Press, p. 119.

156. For example, Buur, Jensen, and Stepputat, *The Security-Development Nexus*.

157. Brogden, M, and P Nijhar. 1998. Corruption and the South African Police. *Crime, Law and Social Change* 30 (1), pp. 89-106; Marks, Monique. 2000. Transforming Police Organizations from Within: Police Dissident Groupings in South Africa. *British Journal of Criminology* 40, pp. 557-73; Hyslop, J. 2005. Political Corruption before and after Apartheid. *Journal of Southern African Studies* 31 (4), pp. 773-89.

158. Holden and Van Vuuren, *The Devil in the Detail*.

159. Kynoch, Gary. 1996. The 'Transformation' of the South African Military. *Journal of Modern African Studies* 34 (3), p. 442.

160. Simpson, *Umkhonto we Sizwe*, p. 483.

161. Simpson, *Umkhonto we Sizwe*, p. 483.

162. Kynoch, 'The "Transformation" of the South African Military.'

163. Holden, Paul. 2008. *The Arms Deal*. Johannesburg: Jonathan Ball Publishers, p. 107.

164. Manong, *If We Must Die*, pp. 267-8.

165. Confidential interview with South African civil servant, November 2009.

166. Confidential interview with ex-combatant, November 2009.

167. O'Malley, *Shades of Difference*, p. 416.

168. O'Malley, *Shades of Difference*, p. 419.

169. O'Malley, *Shades of Difference*, p. 421.

170. O'Malley, *Shades of Difference*.

171. 'Was ANC "Spy" Poisoned in Exile?' *The Star*, 14 October 2003.

172. Branch, Daniel. 2009. *Defeating Mau Mau, Creating Kenya: Counterinsurgency, Civil War, and Decolonization*. Cambridge: Cambridge University Press.

173. Horne, Gerald. 2001. *From the Barrel of a Gun: The United States and the War in Zimbabwe, 1965–1980*. Chapel Hill, NC: University of North Carolina Press, p. 223.

174. 'Vlok Is Named on Secret Dirty Tricks Police Tape,' *Sunday Times*, 12 March 1995.

175. Ellis, Stephen. 1996. Africa and International Corruption: The Strange Case of South Africa and Seychelles. *African Affairs* 95 (379), pp. 165-96; Ellis, Stephen. 1999. The New Frontiers of Crime in South Africa. In *The Criminalization of the State in Africa*, edited by JF Bayart, Stephen Ellis, and Béatrice Hibou. Indianapolis: Indiana University Press.

176. Jenkin, Tim. 1995. Talking to Vula: The Story of the Secret Underground Communications Network of Operation Vula. *Mayibuye*, May-October. Accessed at http://www.anc.org.za/content/talking-vula.

177. McKinley, Dale T. 1997. *The ANC and the Liberation Struggle: A Critical Political Biography*. London: Pluto Press, p. 92.

178. Pauw, *Into the Heart of Darkness*.

179. 'On the Twisted Trail of Dulcie's Death' by Evelyn Groenink, *Mail & Guardian*, 9 January 1998.

180. Pauw, *Into the Heart of Darkness*, p. 296.

181. 'Lubowski, the French, the Mafia, and MI Links,' by Evelyn Groenink, *Mail & Guardian*, 1 October 1999; see also, Groenink's 2018 book *Incorruptible*.

182. Henderson, Robert D'A. 1995. South African Intelligence under De Klerk. In *About Turn: The Transformation of the South African Military and Intelligence*, edited by J Cilliers and M Reichardt. Halfway House: Institute for Defence Policy, p. 155.

183. 'Armscor in Tussle with Agents over Trial,' *Sunday Times*, 12 March 1995.

184. De Haas, 'Violence in Zululand,' p. 941.

433

185. 'Inkatha's Secret German War Chest,' *Mail & Guardian*, 15 September 1995.

186. 'Inkatha's Secret German War Chest,' *Mail & Guardian*, 15 September 1995.

187. 'CIA Could Face Trouble if South Africa Murder Case Throws Light on its Role,' *Baltimore Sun*, 12 November 1995.

188. O'Brien, *The South African Intelligence Services*, p. 76.

189. 'CIA Could Face Trouble if South Africa Murder Case Throws Light on its Role,' *Baltimore Sun*, 12 November 1995.

190. 'CIA Could Face Trouble if South Africa Murder Case Throws Light on its Role,' *Baltimore Sun*, 12 November 1995.

191. 'South Africa: Genesis of the Third Force,' *Africa Confidential* 32 (19), 27 September 1991.

192. Confidential interview with ex-combatant, November 2009.

193. Weiner, Tim. 2007. *Legacy of Ashes: The History of the CIA.* New York: Doubleday, 2007; Sanders *Apartheid's Friends.*

194. Berkeley, Bill. 2001. *The Graves Are Not Yet Full: Race, Tribe, and Power in the Heart of Africa.* New York: Basic Books, p. 172.

195. 'CIA Could Face Trouble if South Africa Murder Case Throws Light on Its Role,' *Baltimore Sun*, 12 November 1995.

196. Confidential interview with ex-combatant, November 2009.

197. O'Brien, *The South African Intelligence Services*, p. 184.

198. Gilder, *Songs and Secrets.*

199. Gilder, *Songs and Secrets*; confidential interview with ex-combatant, November 2009.

200. Sanders, *Apartheid's Friends*, p. 366.

201. '"Stratcom" Never Died, Says Ex-Cop,' *Mail and Guardian*, 18 August 1995.

CONCLUSION: COUNTERINSURGENCY AS HEGEMONY

1. Mamdani, Mahmood. 1996. *Citizen and Subject: Contemporary Africa and the Legacy of Late Colonialism.* Princeton, NJ: Princeton University Press.

2. Kynoch, Gary. 2005. Crime, Conflict, and Politics in Transition-Era South Africa. *African Affairs* 104 (416), pp. 493-514.

3. Jeffery, Anthea. 2009. *People's War: New Light on the Struggle for South Africa.* Johannesburg: Jonathan Ball Publishers.

4. Kane-Berman, John. 1993. *Political Violence in South Africa.* Johannesburg: South African Institute of Race Relations, p. 88.

5. Mkhondo, Rich. 1993. *Reporting South Africa.* Portsmouth, NH: Heinemann; Murray, Martin. 1994. *The Revolution Deferred: The Painful Birth of Post-Apartheid South Africa.* London: Verso; Ellis, Stephen. 1998.

The Historical Significance of South Africa's Third Force. *Journal of Southern African Studies* 24 (2), pp. 261-99; Gottschalk, Keith. 2000. The Rise and Fall of Apartheid's Death Squads, 1969–93. In *Death Squads in Global Perspective: Murder with Deniability*, edited by BB Campbell and Arthur D Brenner. New York: St Martin's Press.

6. Gear, Sasha. 2002. Now That the War Is Over: Ex-Combatants' Transition and the Question of Violence: A Literature Review, www.csvr.co.za.

7. 'Mandela Accepts ANC Blame,' *The Times*, 7 April 1993.

8. Seegers, Annette. 1991. South Africa's National Security Management System, 1972–1990. *Journal of Modern African Studies* 29 (2), pp. 253-73.

9. Taylor, Rupert. 2002. Justice Denied: Political Violence in KwaZulu-Natal after 1994. Centre for the Study of Violence and Reconciliation, Violence and Transition Series, vol. 6.

10. Author's interview with Cheryl Frank, senior researcher, Institute for Security Studies, Tshwane (Pretoria), November 2009.

11. Carothers, Thomas. 1997. Democracy without Illusions. *Foreign Affairs* 76 (1), p. 91.

12. Moser, Caroline. 2004. Urban Violence and Insecurity: An Introductory Roadmap. *Environment and Urbanization* 16 (October), pp. 3-16.

13. Baker, Bruce. 2002. Living with Non-State Policing in South Africa: The Issues and Dilemmas. *Journal of Modern African Studies* 40 (1), p. 31.

14. See, for example, Ellis, Stephen. 1996. Africa and International Corruption: The Strange Case of South Africa and Seychelles. *African Affairs* 95 (379), pp. 165-96.

15. MacGinty, Roger. 2006. *No War, No Peace*. New York: Palgrave Macmillan, p. 126.

16. Gills, Barry, and Joel Rocamora. 1992. Low Intensity Democracy. *Third World Quarterly* 13 (3), p. 501.

17. Oxhorn, Philip. 2007. Neopluralism and Citizenship in Latin America. In *Citizenship in Latin America*, edited by JS Tulchin and Meg Ruthenberg. Boulder, CO: Lynne Rienner Publishers, pp. 124-7.

18. Mbembe, cited in Joseph, Richard. 1999. The Reconfiguration of Power in Late-Twentieth Century Africa. In *State, Conflict, and Democracy in Africa*, edited by R Joseph. Boulder, CO: Lynne Rienner, p. 60.

19. McSherry, J Patrice. 2005. *Predatory States: Operation Condor and Covert War in Latin America*. New York: Rowman and Littlefield Publishers.

20. 'ANC Organizing Committee National Workshop, 6–9 November 1990: Strategic Priorities for Building the ANC. Address by Comrade Popo Molefe' (SAHA).

21. Berkeley, Bill. 2001. *The Graves Are Not Yet Full: Race, Tribe, and Power in the Heart of Africa*. New York: Basic Books.

22. Berkeley, *The Graves Are Not Yet Full*, p. 180.
23. James, CLR. 1963. *The Black Jacobins: Toussaint L'Ouverture and the Santo Domingo Revolution*. New York: Vintage Books, p. 29.
24. Ellis, Stephen. 2012. *External Mission: The ANC in Exile, 1960–1990*. London: Hurst.
25. Taylor, Ian. 2001. *Stuck in Middle GEAR: South Africa's Post-Apartheid Foreign Relations*. Westport, CT: Praeger, p. 46.
26. Confidential interview with ex-combatant, Mthatha, November 2009.
27. Rodney, Walter. 1972. *How Europe Underdeveloped Africa*. Dar es Salaam: Bogle-L'Ouverture.
28. Lodge, Tom. 1983. *Black Politics in South Africa since 1945*. London: Longman Publishers.
29. Sparks, Allister. 1994. *Tomorrow Is Another Country*. New York: Penguin Press; Klein, Naomi. 2007. *The Shock Doctrine: The Rise of Disaster Capitalism*. Toronto: Alfred A Knopf.
30. Taylor, *Stuck in Middle GEAR*, p. 38.
31. Taylor, *Stuck in Middle GEAR*.
32. Klein, *The Shock Doctrine*.
33. Author's interview with Dr Somadoda Fikeni, Tshwane (Pretoria), 20 December 2009.
34. For example, Bond, Patrick. 2004. *Talk Left Walk Right*. Scottsville: University of KwaZulu-Natal Press; Turok, Ben. 2008. *The Evolution of ANC Economic Policy*. Cape Town: New Agenda; Klein, *The Shock Doctrine*.
35. McKinley, Dale T. 1997. *The ANC and the Liberation Struggle: A Critical Political Biography*. London: Pluto Press, p. 83.
36. Marx, Anthony W. 1998. *Making Race and Nation: A Comparison of the United States, South Africa, and Brazil*. New York: Cambridge University Press, p. 199.
37. Turok, *The Evolution of ANC Economic Policy*, p. 31.
38. Turok, *The Evolution of ANC Economic Policy*; Russell, Alec. 2009. *Bring Me My Machine Gun: The Battle for the Soul of South Africa from Mandela to Zuma*. New York: Perseus.
39. Klein, *The Shock Doctrine*.
40. Interview with Chris Hani, Lusaka, 21 January 1990: Road Ahead Perspective (SAHA).
41. 'Editorial: Hani's Words Still Resonate Today,' *Herald Live*, 11 April 2018.
42. Shubin, Vladimir. 2008. *The Hot 'Cold War': The USSR in Southern Africa*. London: Pluto Press.
43. Confidential interview with ex-combatant, December 2009.

44. Author's interview with Dr Somadoda Fikeni, Tshwane (Pretoria), 20 December 2009.
45. Buur, Lars. 2007. The Intertwined History of Security and Development: The Case of Development Struggles in South Africa's Townships. In *The Security-Development Nexus: Expressions of Sovereignty and Securitization in Southern Africa*, edited by Lars Buur, Steffen Jensen, and Finn Stepputat. Cape Town: HSRC Press, p. 111.
46. Rawoot, Ilham, Sello S Alcock, and Monako Dibetle. 2009. Insecurity in the Forces. *Mail & Guardian*, 13 to 19 November.

BIBLIOGRAPHY

Archival sources

The following sections of the South African History Archive (SAHA) at the William Cullen Library, University of the Witwatersrand, Johannesburg, South Africa, were consulted on 20 December 2009. The Archive has since moved to the Women's Gaol in Braamfontein. Most documents have the author's name and date of release; some have neither.

H5.3.4 Kabwe Conference
'Political Report of the National Executive Committee to the National Consultative Conference, June 1985, Presented by the President of the ANC' –address by OR Tambo

5.5.5 Negotiations Bulletin
'"Ready to Govern": ANC Policy Guidelines for a Democratic South Africa,' 28–31 May 1992

5.16 Hani's Death
The Mqanqeni Affair: South African Communist Party Central Committee Statement, 31 March 1993
ANC Press Statement on Police Pronouncements, 13 April 1993, Johannesburg
ANC Department of Information and Publicity: MK Statement on the Assassination of Chris Hani, 14 April 1993, Johannesburg

5.17 Umkhonto we Sizwe
'MK Comes of Age'
Dawn: Journal of Umkhonto we Sizwe, 25th Anniversary Souvenir Issue, 1986
'Notes of Meeting with Chris Hani, Chief of Staff and Deputy Commander of Umkhonto we Sizwe, and Steve Tshwete, Political Commissar,' from an interview by John D Battersby, 3 June 1988, Lusaka, Zambia

439

'Interview with Chris Hani, Deputy Commander, Umkhonto we Sizwe, Lusaka 21 January 1990: Road Ahead Perspective' (interview follows extended NEC [National Executive Committee] meeting, 18–20 January 1990)

Laurie Nathan, Article on the IDASA-ANC Conference on the 'Future of Security and Defence in South Africa,' 23–27 May 1990, Lusaka

'MK and the Future,' dated November 1990 (author unknown)

'African National Congress Organizing Committee National Workshop, 6-9 November 1990: Strategic Priorities for Building the ANC. Address by Comrade Popo Molefe'

'MK National Conference in Venda. Press Statement,' 1991

'Military Forces during the Transition Period: Paper by Keith Mokoape'

'Address of Comrade President Nelson Mandela to the Conference of Umkhonto we Sizwe,' Thohoyandou, Venda, 9 August 1991

'Office of the Military Council of Transkei: Address by Major General Bantu Holomisa to the MK Conference in Venda, 1991'

Special Conference of MK Held at Mgwenya College of Education in Kanyamazane, 3–4 September 1993

'Call to Umkhonto we Sizwe' issued 'by the Army Chief of Staff on behalf of the MHQ [Military Headquarters] of Umkhonto we Sizwe,' 14 September 1993

A2.4.1.7 TRC Gun-running 1974–97

AL 3283 De Wet Potgieter Collection

A2.2.6: Interviews with General Tienie Groenewald, 12 October 2009

A2.2.6.1: English translation of the original Afrikaans transcript of the interview with General Tienie Groenewald regarding the establishment of the Volksfront (People's Front)

A2.2.6.2: English translation of the original Afrikaans transcript of the interview with General Tienie Groenewald regarding the threat of civil war at the beginning of 1994

A2.2.7.2: English translation of the original Afrikaans transcript of the interview with Colonel Lucas Ras regarding interrogation techniques used by the security police

A2.2.7.3: English translation of the original Afrikaans transcript of the interview with Colonel Lucas Ras regarding Umkhonto we Sizwe (MK) informants

B1.2.3.2: Documents on the ANC and SACP

B1.2.3.2.1: Narrative 'Selection of Documents on the ANC and the SACP from Security Branch Files'

B1: Military Intelligence and SAP Security Branch activities

B1.1: SADF

B1.1.1: Anti-ANC Propaganda

B1.1.1.1: Narrative 'Anti-ANC Propaganda'

B1.1.1.2: Disinformation publication *Face to Face with the ANC*, 1988

B1.1.2: Civil Cooperation Bureau (CCB)

B1.1.2.1: Narrative 'The Civil Cooperation Bureau (CCB), a Third Force'

B1.1.2.2: Document on Military Intelligence (MI) and CCB front organisations and dirty tricks

B1.1.2.3: CCB front organisations

B1.1.3: Directorate for Covert Collection (DCC)

B1.1.3.1: Narrative 'Pan Afrik Industrial Investment Consultants (PAIIC)'

B1.1.3.2: DCC member list

B1.1.3.8: Discussion document: Background regarding ex-PAIIC members (marked 'Secret'), 10 June 1994

B1.1.3.9: Letter from the PAIIC Group to Minister of Defence, JM (Joe) Modise, 11 June 1994

B1.1.3.10: Interdict against PAIIC, 1994

B1.1.3.10.1: Press statement released by Defence Minister Joe Modise: Withdrawal of 9 June interdict, 13 June 1994, with covering fax message 14 June 1994

B1.1.3.10.2: Press statement by the PAIIC Group: Reaction to withdrawal of interdict of 9 June 1994 by Minister of Defence, 14 June 1994, with covering fax message, 15 June 1994

B1.1.3.11: SADF press statement regarding DCC, 16 June 1994 (Afrikaans)

B1.1.3.12: Analysis of CSI statement delivered during a press conference on 16 June 1994 regarding the interdict

B1.1.3.13: Letter from PAIIC Group to President Nelson Mandela regarding 'Unresolved matters pertaining to the PAIIC Group,' 20 June 1994

B1.1.3.14: Letter from PAIIC to Deputy Minister of Defence, Ronnie Kasrils, 17 August 1994

B1.1.3.15: Letter from W Wilsenach of the PAIIC Group to President Nelson Mandela regarding 'Reports on alleged Third Force activities conducted by Justice R Goldstone and Genl. P. Steyn,' 13 July 1995

B1.1.4: Operation Rollerball

B1.1.4.1: Narrative 'Operation Rollerball'

B1.1.4.2: Memorandum regarding movement plan for ex-MK arms and armaments in foreign countries (marked 'Restricted'), 29 July 1994

B1.1.4.3: Fax document regarding the Transkei Defence Force issuing weapons to both APLA and ANC members, 20 September 1994

B1.1.4.4: Police notice regarding legislation for the gathering of arms and armaments by Operation Rollerball operatives, with covering telefax message, 24 October 1994 (Afrikaans)

B1.1.4.5: Operations instruction 61/94: Collection of former MK caches in the country, 20 October 1994 (Afrikaans)

B1.1.4.6: Operations instruction 59/94: Collection of former MK weapons and ammunition within the possession of individuals, 25 October 1994

B1.1.4.7: Supplementary instructions (marked 'Secret'), November 1994 (Afrikaans)

B1.1.4.8: Listing: Weapons from out of the country

B1.1.4.9: Correspondence regarding feedback on the progress with Operation Rollerball inside the country (marked 'Secret'), November 1994 (Afrikaans)

B1.1.4.10: SADF response on media enquiry regarding Operation Rollerball, 2 December 1994; 9 December 1994

B1.1.5: Operation Nyawa

B1.1.5.1: Narrative 'Operation Nyawa'

B1.1.5.2: Working document entitled 'Operasie Nyawa' (1993–4) (Afrikaans/English)

B1.2.2: Operation Sunrise

B1.2.2.1: Narrative 'Operation Sunrise was it fact or fiction?'

Mayibuye Archives Centre: Oral History of Exiles Project, University of the Western Cape

MCA 6 – 245 : Sipho Binda interview

MCA 6 – 257 : Josias (Sipho) Chabalala interview

MCA 6 – 284 : Chris Hani Interview

MCA 6 – 294 : Lerumo Kalako interview

MCA 6 – 305 : Abraham Lentsoane interview

MCA 6 – 321 : Jumainah Modiakgotla interview

MCA 6 – 324 : Graham Morodi interview

MCA 6 – 338 : Cleophas M Ndlovu interview

MCA 6 – 344 : Ayanda Ntsaluba interview

MCA 6 – 365 : Fraser Delisa Shamase interview

Truth and Reconciliation Commission

African National Congress Submission to the Truth and Reconciliation Commission Section 5.3, 'Towards People's War and People's Power, 1979–90' (August 1996), available at http://www.justice.gov.za/trc/hrvtrans/submit/anctruth.htm#4

African National Congress Second Submission to the TRC, Appendix Seven, available at http://www.justice.gov.za/trc/hrvtrans/submit/anc2.htm# Operations

African National Congress Statement to the Truth and Reconciliation Commission, vol. 4.9 (August 1996), http://www.justice.gov.za/trc/ hrvtrans/submit/anctruth.htm#4

'Amnesty Decisions, Ian Ndibulele Ndzamela, Pumlani Kubukeli, Mfanelo Dan Matshaya,' 18 August 1998, available at http://sabctrc.saha.org.za/ hearing.php?id=58593&t=phungulwa&tab=hearings

'Amnesty Decision: Velaphi Sazi Favious Msane,' TRC, Cape Town, 29 March 2001, http://sabctrc.saha.org.za/documents/decisions/59385. htm?t=%2Bmahlangu+%2Bsolomon&tab=hearings

'Amnesty Hearing, Application of Botha, Du Preez, Steyn, Wasserman, and Van der Westhuizen,' TRC, Pinetown, 11 April 2000

'Amnesty Hearing, Eugene Alexander de Kock, Batandwa Ndondo Matter,' TRC, 24 August 1998

'Amnesty Hearing, Paulos "Pistol" Nkonyane,' TRC, Ermelo, 29 July 1998

Basie Smit testimony to Section 29 of the TRC, Durban, 9 July 1997 (SAHA AL2878_B01.5.75.02.21)

Debora Patta's testimony to Section 29 of the TRC (SAHA AL2878_ B01.5.75.01.29.04)

'For the Sake of Our Lives: Guidelines for the Creation of People's Self-Defence Units' by Jeremy Cronin, submitted as Appendix Nine of the ANC's Second Submission to the TRC, available at http://www.justice. gov.za/trc/hrvtrans/submit/anc2.htm#Operations

'Fuel Refineries Strategic Targets for ANC in 80s, TRC Hears' (from a hearing in Durban, 27 September 1999), available at http://www.justice.gov.za/ trc/media/1999/9909/p9900927a.html

Memorandum by Craig M Williamson, 'Aspects of State Counter-revolutionary Warfare Principles and Strategy: Republic of South Africa in the 1980s,' presented to the TRC, Cape Town, 9 October 1997, Section 5.8.

Mzwandile Gushu Amnesty Hearing, TRC, 22 July 1998, available at http:// www.justice.gov.za/trc/amntrans%5C1998/98072030_erm_blacat2. htm

'Researchers Present Apartheid SA's Dirty Tricks Findings to TRC,' South African Press Association (SAPA), Johannesburg, 10 November 1997, available at http://www.justice.gov.za/trc/media%5C1997%5C9711/ s971110a.htm

'Testimony of Enock Tshabalala, Batandwa Ndondo Matter,' TRC, Mthatha, 24 August 1998, available at http://www.justice.gov.za/trc/ amntrans/1998/98082425_umt_umtata1.htm

'Testimony of MD Ras, Craig Duli Matter' (Day 3), TRC, 20 April 1999
Truth and Reconciliation Commission, Final Report, Vol. 1, ch. 8.
Truth and Reconciliation Commission, Final Report, Vol. 2, ch. 2, subsection 34.
Truth and Reconciliation Commission, Final Report, Vol.2, ch. 5, subsection 23.
Truth and Reconciliation Commission, Final Report, Vol. 5, ch.6, pp. 226-7
Truth and Reconciliation Commission, 'Human Rights Violations, Submissions – Questions and Answers,' Mr and Mrs P Ngwenya, Soweto, Day 5, 26 July 1996, available at http://www.justice.gov.za/trc/hrvtrans/soweto/ngwenya.htm
Truth and Reconciliation Commission, Press Release, 'Intelligence Chief Speaks Out on Operation Katzen,' East London, 6 April 1999.

Audiovisual resources

MK in Uganda (an undated video with no production or release credits, featuring unedited footage of daily life, training, and graduation ceremonies at an MK base in Uganda, December 1992).
MK in Tanzania (an undated video with no production or release credits, featuring unedited footage of daily life, training, and graduation ceremonies, different from the *MK in Uganda* video; despite the title, the footage is actually from an MK base in Uganda, c.1992).
The Luthuli Detachment (2007, Qoma Film Productions): features interviews with MK cadres who took part in the 1967–8 Wankie Campaign and archival photos from that era.

Books and articles

Alexander, Jocelyn, JoAnn McGregor, and Terence Ranger. 2000. *Violence and Memory: One Hundred Years in the 'Dark Forests' of Matabeleland.* Oxford: James Currey.
Allina-Pisano, Jessica. 2009. How to Tell an Axe Murderer: An Essay on Ethnography, Truth, and Lies. In *Political Ethnography: What Immersion Contributes to the Study of Power*, edited by E. Schatz. Chicago, IL: University of Chicago Press.
Altbeker, Anthony. 2007. *A Country at War with Itself.* Johannesburg: Jonathan Ball.
Arias, Enrique, and Daniel Goldstein. 2010. Violent Pluralism: Understanding the New Democracies of Latin America. In *Violent Democracies in Latin*

America, edited by Arias and Goldstein. Durham, NC: Duke University Press, pp. 1-34.

Backmann, René. 1980. Confession of a Dog of War. In *The CIA in Africa*. London: Zed Books, pp. 146-58.

Baines, Gary. 2014. *South Africa's 'Border War': Contested Narratives and Conflicting Memories*. New York: Bloomsbury.

Baker, Bruce. 2002. Living with Non-State Policing in South Africa: The Issues and Dilemmas. *Journal of Modern African Studies* 40 (1): 29-53.

Barkan, Joel D. 2002. The Many Faces of Africa: Democracy across a Varied Continent. *Harvard International Review* 24 (2): 72-7.

Barnard, Rita, and Grant Farred (eds). 2004. *After the Thrill Is Gone: A Decade of Post-Apartheid South Africa*. Durham, NC: Duke University Press.

Barrell, Howard. 1990. The Turn to the Masses: The African National Congress' Strategic Review of 1978–9. *Journal of Southern African Studies* 18 (1): 64-92.

Basson, Adriaan, and Sam Sole. 2009. Selebi Spy's Paranoid World. *Mail & Guardian (South Africa edn)*, 4–10 December 2009.

Bateman, Barry. 2009. Zuma Homage to the 'Forgotten Heroes'. *The Star*, 17 December 2009.

Bates, Robert H. 1999. The Economic Bases of Democratization. In *State, Conflict, and Democracy in Africa*, edited by R Joseph. Boulder, CO: Lynne Rienner Publishers.

Bell, Terry, with Dumisa Buhle Ntsebeza. 2003. *Unfinished Business: South Africa, Apartheid, and Truth*. London: Verso.

Berkeley, Bill. 1994. The Warlords of Natal. *Atlantic Monthly* (March), pp. 85-100.

Berkeley, Bill. 2001. *The Graves Are Not Yet Full: Race, Tribe, and Power in the Heart of Africa*. New York: Basic Books.

Berry, Sara. 1992. Hegemony on a Shoestring: Indirect Rule and Access to Agricultural Land. *Africa* 62 (3): 327-55.

Best, Heinrich, and John Higley (eds). 2010. *Democratic Elitism: New Theoretical and Comparative Perspectives*. Leiden: Brill.

Beverley, John. 1999. *Subalternity and Representation: Arguments in Cultural Theory*. Durham: Duke University Press.

Bloom, Mia. 2005. *Dying to Kill: The Allure of Suicide Terror*. New York: Columbia University Press.

Bond, Patrick. 2004. *Talk Left Walk Right*. Scottsville: University of KwaZulu-Natal Press.

Bottoman, Wonga Welile. 2010. *The Making of an MK Cadre*. Pretoria: LiNc Publishers.

Bourdieu, Pierre, Loïc Wacquant, and Samar Farage. 1994. Rethinking the State: Genesis and Structure of the Bureaucratic Field. *Sociological Theory* 12 (1): 1-18.

Bozzoli, Belinda. 2004. *Theatres of Struggle and the End of Apartheid.* Athens, OH: Ohio University Press.

Braam, Conny. 2004. *Operation Vula.* Auckland Park: Jacana.

Brainard, Lael, and Derek Chollet (eds). 2007. *Too Poor for Peace? Global Poverty, Conflict, and Security in the 21st Century.* Washington, DC: Brookings Institution Press.

Branch, Daniel. 2009. *Defeating Mau Mau, Creating Kenya: Counterinsurgency, Civil War, and Decolonization.* Cambridge: Cambridge University Press.

Brand, Robert. 1998. The Chris Hani Assassination. In *The Hidden Hand: Covert Operations in South Africa,* 2nd edn, edited by C Schutte, Ian Liebenberg, and Anthony Minaar. Pretoria: Human Sciences Research Council.

Brands, Hal. 2011. Crime, Irregular Warfare, and Institutional Failure in Latin America: Guatemala as a Case Study. *Studies in Conflict and Terrorism* 34 (3): 228–47.

Bratton, Michael. 2004. State Building and Democratization in Sub-Saharan Africa: Forwards, Backwards, or Together? AfroBarometer Working Paper 43.

Brogden, M, and P Nijhar. 1998. Corruption and the South African Police. *Crime, Law and Social Change* 30 (1): 89-106.

Buur, Lars. 2003. Crime and Punishment on the Margins of the Post-Apartheid State. *Anthropology and Humanism* 28 (1): 23-42.

Buur, Lars. 2005. Sovereignty and Democratic Exclusion in the New South Africa. *Review of African Political Economy* 32 (104): 253-68.

Buur, Lars. 2007. The Intertwined History of Security and Development: The Case of Development Struggles in South Africa's Townships. In *The Security-Development Nexus: Expressions of Sovereignty and Securitization in Southern Africa,* edited by Lars Buur, Steffen Jensen, and Finn Stepputat. Cape Town: HSRC Press, pp. 109-31.

Buur, Lars, and Stephen Jensen. 2004. Introduction: Vigilantism and the Policing of Everyday Life in South Africa. *African Studies* 63 (2): 139-52.

Buur, Lars, Steffen Jensen and Finn Stepputat (eds). 2007. *The Security-Development Nexus: Expressions of Sovereignty and Securitization in South Africa.* Uppsala: Nordiska Afrikainstitutet, and Cape Town: HSRC Press.

Cabral, Amilcar. 1973. New Year's Message. In *Return to the Source: Selected Speeches of Amilcar Cabral.* New York: Monthly Review Press.

Call, Charles T, and William Stanley. 2001. Protecting the People: Public Security Choices after Civil Wars. *Global Governance* 7 (2): 151-72.

Campbell, Bruce B. 2000. Death Squads: Definition, Problems, and Historical Context. In *Death Squads in Global Perspective: Murder with Deniability*, edited by Bruce B Campbell and Arthur D Brenner. New York: Palgrave Macmillan/St Martins Press, pp. 1-26.

Campbell, Bruce B, and Arthur D Brenner (eds). 2000. *Death Squads in Global Perspective: Murder with Deniability*. New York: St Martin's Press.

Cann, John P. 1997. *Counterinsurgency in Africa: The Portuguese Way of War, 1961–1974*. Westport, CT: Greenwood Press.

Carothers, Thomas. 1997. Democracy without Illusions. *Foreign Affairs* 76 (1): 85-99.

Carothers, Thomas. 2002. The End of the Transition Paradigm. *Journal of Democracy* 13 (1): 5-21.

Cawthra, Gavin. 1986. *Brutal Force: The Apartheid War Machine*. London: International Defence and Aid Fund for Southern Africa.

Cawthra, Gavin. 1997. *Securing South Africa's Democracy*. London: Macmillan Press.

Cawthra, Gavin, and Bjorn Moller (eds). 1997. *Defensive Restructuring of the Armed Forces in Southern Africa*. Brookfield, VT: Ashgate.

Chabal, Patrick. 1983. *Amilcar Cabral: Revolutionary Leadership and People's War*. Cambridge: Cambridge University Press.

Cherry, Janet. 2011. *Umkhonto we Sizwe*. Auckland Park: Jacana.

Chikwanha, Annie Barbara. 2005. Trust in Institutions in Sub-Saharan Africa's Emerging Democracies. In *Trust in Public Institutions in South Africa*, edited by S and NB Askvik. Burlington, VT: Ashgate Publishing.

Chipkin, Ivor. 2004. Nationalism as Such: Violence during South Africa's Political Transition. *Public Culture* 16 (2): 315-35.

Cilliers, Jackie, and Markus Reichardt. 1995. The National Peacekeeping Force: The Triumph of Politics over Security. In *About Turn: The Transformation of the South African Military and Intelligence*, edited by J Cilliers and M Reichardt. Halfway House: Institute for Defence Policy, pp. 35-62.

Clarke, Liam, and Inigo Gilmore. 1998. IRA Linked to African Arms Deal. *Sunday Times* [London], 15 March, p. 28.

Claude, Nicholas. 1996. Lost and Forgotten: Irregular Forces in KwaZulu-Natal. *KwaZulu-Natal Briefing* 4, pp. 13-17.

Cock, Jacklyn. 1997. The Cultural and Social Challenge of Demilitarization. In *Defensive Restructuring of the Armed Forces in South Africa*, edited by B Moller and Gavin Cawthra. Brookfield, VT: Ashgate Publishing.

Cock, Jacklyn. 2005. 'Guards and Guns': Towards Privatized Militarism in Post-Apartheid South Africa. *Journal of Southern African Studies* 31 (4): 791-803.

Collier, David. 1993. The Comparative Method. In *Political Science: The State of the Discipline II*, edited by A Finifter. Washington, DC: American Political Science Association.

Collier, Paul. 2000. Rebellion as a Quasi-Criminal Activity. *Journal of Conflict Resolution* 44 (6).

Cullather, Nick. 2006. *The CIA's Classified Account of Its War in Guatemala, 1952–54*. Stanford, CA: Stanford University Press.

Daley, Suzanne. 1997. Fears of Shadowy Force Return to South Africa. *New York Times*, 11 August.

Darby, John. 2006. Post-Accord Violence in a Changing World. In *Violence and Reconstruction*, edited by J Darby. Notre Dame: University of Notre Dame Press.

Davidson, Basil. 1981. *The People's Cause: A History of Guerrillas in Africa*. Harlow: Longman.

Davis, Stephen M. 1987. *Apartheid's Rebels: Inside South Africa's Hidden War*. New Haven, CT: Yale University Press.

De Haas, Mary. 2013. Violence in Zululand: The 1990s. In *The Road to Democracy in South Africa, Vol. 6 (1990–1996)*. South Africa Democracy Education Trust, Pretoria: University of South Africa Press, pp. 876-957.

De Witte, Ludo. 2001. *The Assassination of Lumumba*. London: Verso.

Diamond, Larry. 2005. *Squandered Victory: The American Occupation and the Bungled Effort to Bring Democracy to Iraq*. New York: Times Books.

Diamond, Larry, and Marc F Plattner (eds). 1996. *Civil-Military Relations and Democracy*. Baltimore: Johns Hopkins University Press.

Dlamini, Jacob. 2014. *Askari*. Auckland Park: Jacana.

Dogan, Mattei, and John Higley (eds). 1998. *Elite Crises and the Origins of Regimes*. Lanham, MD: Rowman and Littlefield Publishers.

Douek, Daniel. 2013. Counterinsurgency's Impact on Transitions from Authoritarianism: The Case of South Africa. *Politikon* 40 (2): 55-75.

Douek, Daniel. 2013. 'They Became Afraid When They Saw Us': MK Insurgency and Counterinsurgency in the Bantustan of Transkei, 1989–94. *Journal of Southern African Studies* 39 (1): 207-25.

Douek, Daniel. 2017. New Light on the Samora Machel Assassination: 'I Realized It Was No Accident'. *Third World Quarterly* 9 (38): 2045-65.

Du Toit, Pierre. 2001. *South Africa's Brittle Peace*. New York: Palgrave.

Dugard, Jackie. 2001. From Low Intensity War to Mafia War: Taxi Violence in South Africa (1987–2000). Centre for the Study of Violence and Reconciliation, Violence and Transition Series, vol. 4 (May).

Ellis, Stephen. 1994. Mbokodo: Security in ANC Camps, 1961–1990. *African Affairs* 93 (371): 279-98.

Ellis, Stephen. 1996. Africa and International Corruption: The Strange Case of South Africa and Seychelles. *African Affairs* 95 (379): 165-96.

Ellis, Stephen. 1998. The Historical Significance of South Africa's Third Force. *Journal of Southern African Studies* 24 (2): 261-99.

Ellis, Stephen. 1999. The New Frontiers of Crime in South Africa. In *The Criminalization of the State in Africa*, edited by JF Bayart, Stephen Ellis, and Béatrice Hibou. Indianapolis: Indiana University Press.

Ellis, Stephen. 2012. *External Mission: The ANC in Exile, 1960–1990*. London: Hurst.

Ellis, Stephen, and Tsepo Sechaba. 1992. *Comrades against Apartheid: The ANC and the South African Communist Party in Exile*. London: James Currey.

Elster, Jon. 2004. *Closing the Books: Transitional Justice in Historical Perspective*. New York: Cambridge University Press.

Fanon, Frantz. 1961. *The Wretched of the Earth*. New York: Grove Press.

Fanon, Frantz. 1967. *A Dying Colonialism*. New York: Grove Press.

Farina, Luis. 2010. *No Place to Hide: Gang, State, and Clandestine Violence in El Salvador*. Cambridge, MA: Harvard University Press.

Fauvet, Paul, and Marcelo Mosse. 2003. *Carlos Cardoso: Telling the Truth in Mozambique*. Cape Town: Double Storey Books.

Ferguson, James. 1994. *The Anti-Politics Machine: 'Development,' Depoliticization, and Bureaucratic Power in Lesotho*. Minneapolis: University of Minnesota Press.

Ferguson, James. 2006. *Global Shadows: Africa in the Neoliberal World Order*. Durham: Duke University Press.

Flanagan, Louise. 1996. How Military Intelligence Tried to Recruit Modise. *Mail & Guardian*, 23–29 February.

Flanagan, Louise. 1998. Covert Operations in the Eastern Cape. In *The Hidden Hand: Covert Operations in South Africa*, 2nd edn, edited by C Schutte, Ian Liebenberg, and Anthony Minaar. Pretoria: Human Sciences Research Council.

Foster, Don, Paul Haupt, and Marésa de Beer (eds). 2005. *The Theatre of Violence: Narratives of Protagonists in the South African Conflict*. Cape Town: Human Studies Research Council.

Foucault, Michel. 1995. *Discipline and Punish: The Birth of the Prison*, 2nd edn, translated by A Sheridan. New York: Vintage Books.

Frankel, Philip. 2000. *Soldiers in a Storm: The Armed Forces in South Africa's Democratic Transition*. Boulder, CO: Westview Press.

Ganser, Daniele. 2005. *NATO's Secret Armies: Operation Gladio and Terrorism in Western Europe*. New York: Frank Cass.

Gear, Sasha. 2002. Now That the War Is Over: Ex-Combatants' Transition and the Question of Violence: A Literature Review, www.csvr.co.za

Gear, Sasha. 2002. Wishing Us Away: Challenges Facing Ex-Combatants in the 'New' South Africa. Centre for the Study of Violence and Reconciliation, Violence and Transition Series, vol. 8.

George, Alexander L, and Andrew Bennett. 2005. *Case Studies and Theory Development in the Social Sciences*. Cambridge, MA: MIT Press.

Gerring, John. 2007. *Case Study Research: Principles and Practices*. Cambridge: Cambridge University Press.

Gibbs, Timothy. 2011. Chris Hani's 'Country Bumpkins': Regional Networks in the African National Congress Underground, 1974–1994. *Journal of Southern African Studies* 37 (4): 677-91.

Gibbs, Timothy. 2014. *Mandela's Kinsmen: Nationalist Elites and Apartheid's First Bantustan*. Auckland Park: Jacana Press.

Gibson, James L. 2004. *Overcoming Apartheid: Can Truth Reconcile a Divided Nation?* New York: Russell Sage Foundation.

Gilder, Barry. 2012. *Songs and Secrets: South Africa from Liberation to Governance*. London: Hurst Publishers.

Gills, Barry, and Joel Rocamora. 1992. Low Intensity Democracy. *Third World Quarterly* 13 (3): 501-23.

Glassmyer, Katherine, and Nicholas Sambanis. 2008. Rebel-Military Integration and Civil War Termination. *Journal of Peace Research* 45 (3): 365-84.

Gleijeses, Piero. 2013. *Visions of Freedom: Havana, Washington, Pretoria, and the Struggle for Southern Africa*. Baltimore, MD: Johns Hopkins University Press.

Gottschalk, Keith. 2000. The Rise and Fall of Apartheid's Death Squads, 1969–93. In *Death Squads in Global Perspective: Murder with Deniability*, edited by BB Campbell and Arthur D Brenner. New York: St Martin's Press.

Government of South Africa. 2011. *Inquiry into the 1986 Death of Mozambican President Samora Machel 1998*. Available at http://www.justice.gov.za/trc/media/pr/1998/p980518b.htm

Government of South Africa. *Hearing on the Assassination of Sipho Phungulwa*. Available from http://www.info.gov.za/speeches/1998/98814_0x6839810595.htm

Grandin, Greg. 2011. *The Last Colonial Massacre: Latin America during the Cold War*. Chicago, IL: University of Chicago Press.

Groenink, Evelyn. 2013. Dulcie, Hani, Lubowski: A Story That Could Not Be Told. *ZAM Magazine*, 24 April.

Groenink, Evelyn. 2018. *Incorruptible: The Story of the Murders of Dulcie September, Anton Lubowski and Chris Hani*. Cape Town: ABC Press.

Guevara, Ernesto Che. 1961. *Guerrilla Warfare*. New York: Vintage Books.

Guha, Ranajit. 1994. The Prose of Counterinsurgency. In *Culture/Power/History: A Reader in Contemporary Social Theory*, edited by NB Dirks, Geoff Eley, and Sherry B Ortner. Princeton, NJ: Princeton University Press.

Gumede, William (ed.). 2009. *The Poverty of Ideas*. Johannesburg: Jacana.

Gutierrez-Sanin, Francisco. 2010. Mechanisms. In *Economic Liberalization and Political Violence*, edited by Francisco Gutierrez-Sanin and Gerd Schönwalder. London: Pluto Press.

Haas, Jeffrey. 2010. *The Assassination of Fred Hampton*. Chicago, IL: Lawrence Hill Books.

Hagopian, Frances, and Scott P Mainwaring (eds). 2005. *The Third Wave of Democratization in Latin America: Advances and Setbacks*. New York: Cambridge University Press.

Hänggi, Heiner. 2009. Security Sector Reform. In *Post-Conflict Peacebuilding*, edited by C Vincent. Oxford: Oxford University Press.

Hani, Lindiwe, and Melinda Ferguson. 2017. *Being Chris Hani's Daughter*. Auckland Park: Jacana.

Hanlon, Joseph. 1986. *Beggar Your Neighbours: Apartheid Power in Southern Africa*. Bloomington, IN: Indiana University Press.

Hansen, Thomas Blom. 2006. Performers of Sovereignty: On the Privatization of Security in Urban South Africa. *Critique of Anthropology* 26 (3): 279-95.

Harber, Anton. 1994. Mac Releases Captured NIS Files. *Weekly Mail & Guardian*, 29 July.

Harris, Peter. 2012. *A Just Defiance*. Berkeley, CA: University of California Press.

Hartzell, Caroline, and Matthew Hoddie. 2007. *Crafting Peace: Power-Sharing Institutions and the Negotiated Settlement of Civil Wars*. University Park: University of Pennsylvania Press.

Hassan, Magda. 2009. SA Links in the Palme Murder. *Deep Politics Forum*, 16 September.

Henderson, Robert D'A. 1995. South African Intelligence under De Klerk. In *About Turn: The Transformation of the South African Military and Intelligence*, edited by J Cilliers and M Reichardt. Halfway House: Institute for Defence Policy, pp. 140-69.

Henderson, Robert D'A. 1997. Operation Vula against Apartheid. *International Journal of Intelligence and Counterintelligence* 10 (4): 418-55.

Herbstein, Denis. 1994. Old Spies Don't Die. *Africa Report* 39 (2), March-April.

Heywood, Annemarie. 1996. *The Cassinga Event*. Windhoek: John Meinert.

Höglund, Kristine, and I William Zartman. 2006. Violence by the State: Official Spoilers and Their Allies. In *Violence and Reconstruction*, edited by J Darby. Notre Dame, IN: University of Notre Dame Press.

Holden, Paul. 2008. *The Arms Deal*. Johannesburg: Jonathan Ball Publishers.

Holden, Paul, and Hennie van Vuuren. 2011. *The Devil in the Detail: How the Arms Deal Changed Everything*. Jeppestown: Jonathan Ball.

451

Hornberger, Julia. 2004. 'My Police, Your Police': The Informal Privatization of the Police in Inner-City Johannesburg. *African Studies* 63 (2).

Horne, Gerald. 2001. *From the Barrel of a Gun: The United States and the War in Zimbabwe, 1965–1980.* Chapel Hill, NC: University of North Carolina Press.

Houston, Gregory. 2013. The Re-establishment of the ANC inside the Country, 1990–1994. In *The Road to Democracy in South Africa, Vol. 6 (1990–1996).* South Africa Democracy Education Trust, Pretoria: University of South Africa Press, pp. 154-211.

Houston, Gregory, and James Ngculu. 2014. *Voices of Liberation: Chris Hani.* Cape Town: HSRC Press.

Howe, Herbert M. 1994. The South African Defence Force and Political Reform. *Journal of Modern African Studies* 32 (1).

Hyslop, J. 2005. Political Corruption before and after Apartheid. *Journal of Southern African Studies* 31 (4): 773-89.

Ilham Rawoot, Sello S Alcock, and Monako Dibetle. 2009. Insecurity in the Forces. *Mail & Guardian*, 13-19 November.

James, CLR. 1963. *The Black Jacobins: Toussaint L'Ouverture and the Santo Domingo Revolution.* New York: Vintage Books.

Jeffery, Anthea. 2009. *People's War: New Light on the Struggle for South Africa.* Johannesburg: Jonathan Ball Publishers.

Jenkin, Tim. 1995. Talking to Vula: The Story of the Secret Underground Communications Network of Operation Vula. *Mayibuye*, May-October. Accessed at http://www.anc.org.za/content/talking-vula

Johnson, RW. 2010. *South Africa's Brave New World.* London: Penguin Books.

Joseph, Richard. 1999. The Reconfiguration of Power in Late-Twentieth Century Africa. In *State, Conflict, and Democracy in Africa*, edited by R Joseph. Boulder, CO: Lynne Rienner.

Kalyvas, Stathis. 2001. 'New' and 'Old' Civil Wars: A Valid Distinction? *World Politics* 54 (October): 99-118.

Kalyvas, Stathis. 2006. *The Logic of Violence in Civil War.* New York: Cambridge University Press.

Kane-Berman, John. 1993. *Political Violence in South Africa.* Johannesburg: South African Institute of Race Relations.

Kasrils, Ronnie. 2004. *Armed and Dangerous: From Undercover Struggle to Freedom.* Johannesburg: Jonathan Ball.

Katznelson, Ira. 1997. Structure and Configuration in Comparative Politics. In *Comparative Politics: Rationality, Culture, and Structure*, edited by M Lichbach and Alan Zuckerman. New York: Cambridge University Press.

Keen, David. 1998. The Economic Functions of Violence in Civil Wars. Adelphi Paper 320.

Keller, Bill. 1995. A Glimpse of Apartheid's Dying Sting. *New York Times*, 20 February.

Kelly, John D, Beatrice Jauregui, Sean T Mitchell, and Jeremy Walton (eds). 2010. *Anthropology and Global Counterinsurgency*. Chicago, IL: University of Chicago Press.

Kilcullen, David. 2010. *Counterinsurgency*. Oxford: Oxford University Press.

Klein, Naomi. 2007. *The Shock Doctrine: The Rise of Disaster Capitalism*. Toronto: Alfred A Knopf.

Klopp, Jacqueline, and Elke Zuern. 2007. The Politics of Violence in Democratization: Lessons from Kenya and South Africa. *Comparative Politics* 39 (2): 1-32.

Knight, Amy W. 2000. The Enduring Legacy of the KGB in Russian Politics. *Problems of Post-Communism* 47 (4): 3-15.

Knight, Amy W. 2003. The KGB, Perestroika, and the Collapse of the Soviet Union. *Journal of Cold War Studies* 5 (1): 67-93.

Kohli, Atul. 2004. *State-Directed Development: Political Power and Industrialization in the Global Periphery*. New York: Cambridge University Press.

Kooning, Kees, and Dirk Kruijt (eds). 1999. *Societies of Fear: The Legacy of Civil War, Violence, and Terror in Latin America*. London: Zed Books.

Kramer, Mario. 2007. *Violence as Routine: Transformation of Local-Level Politics and the Disjunction between Centre and Periphery in KwaZulu-Natal*. Cologne: Rudiger Koppe Verlag.

Kramer, Mark. 2004. The Perils of Counterinsurgency: Russia's War in Chechnya. *International Security* 29 (3): 5-62.

Kritz, Neil (ed.). 1995. *Transitional Justice: How New Democracies Reckon with Their Authoritarian Past*, vol. 3. Washington, DC: US Institute for Peace.

Kurtenbach, Sabine. 2008. Social and Political Fractures after Wars: Youth Violence in Cambodia and Guatemala. *Youth Violence in Post-War Societies: Conceptual Considerations on Continuity and Change of Violence* (1), http://www.postwar-violence.de/index.php?article_id=41

Kynoch, Gary. 1996. The 'Transformation' of the South African Military. *Journal of Modern African Studies* 34 (3): 441-57.

Kynoch, Gary. 2005. Crime, Conflict, and Politics in Transition-Era South Africa. *African Affairs* 104 (416): 493-514.

Kynoch, Gary. 2008. Urban Violence in Colonial Africa: A Case for South African Exceptionalism. *Journal of Southern African Studies* 34 (3): 629-45.

Lalu, Premesh. 2009. *The Deaths of Hintsa*. Cape Town: Human Sciences Research Council Press.

Lan, David. 1985. *Guns and Rain: Guerrillas and Spirit Mediums in Zimbabwe*. London: James Currey.

Legassick, Martin. 2002. *Armed Struggle and Democracy: The Case of South Africa*. Uppsala: Nordiska Afrikainstitutet.

Lekwane, Aubrey. 1994. The Chris Hani Assassination: Political Assassinations – Who Benefits? In *The Hidden Hand: Covert Operations in South Africa*, edited by Charl Schutte, Ian Liebenberg and Anthony Minnaar. Pretoria: Human Sciences Research Council.

Lesch, Graham Michael. 2006. *Shadows of Justice*. Durban: Roberts Printers.

Levitsky, Steven, and Lucan A Way. 2010. *Competitive Authoritarianism*. New York: Cambridge University Press.

Lodge, Tom. 1983. *Black Politics in South Africa since 1945*. London: Longman Publishers.

Lodge, Tom. 1995. Soldiers of the Storm: A Profile of the Azanian People's Liberation Army. In *About Turn: The Transformation of the South African Military and Intelligence*, edited by J Cilliers and M Reichardt. Halfway House: Institute for Defence Policy, pp. 105-17.

Lodge, Tom. 1998. Political Corruption in South Africa. *African Affairs* 97 (387): 157-87.

Lodge, Tom, and Bill Nasson. 1991. *All, Here, and Now: Black Politics in South Africa in the 1980s*. Cape Town: Ford Foundation.

MacGinty, Roger. 2006. *No War, No Peace*. New York: Palgrave Macmillan.

Magubane, Bernard. 2013. The Beginning of the End: The Garrison State Is Finally Dismantled. In *The Road to Democracy in South Africa, Vol. 6 (1990–1996)*. South Africa Democracy Education Trust, Pretoria: University of South Africa Press, pp. 1371-1415.

Mahoney, James, and Dietrich Rueschemeyer (eds). 2003. *Comparative Historical Analysis in the Social Sciences*. Cambridge: Cambridge University Press.

Mamdani, Mahmood. 1996. *Citizen and Subject: Contemporary Africa and the Legacy of Late Colonialism*. Princeton, NJ: Princeton University Press.

Mandela, Nelson. 1994. *Long Walk to Freedom*. New York: Little, Brown.

Mandela, Nelson. 1997. Address to the 50th National Conference of the ANC in Mafikeng (16 December). Available at https://www.sahistory.org.za/archive/report-president-anc-nelson-mandela-50th-national-conference-african-national-congress-mafik

Manong, Stanley. 2015. *If We Must Die: An Autobiography of a Former Commander of uMkhonto we Sizwe*. Johannesburg: Nkululeko Publishers.

Mao Zedong. 1961. *On Guerrilla Warfare*. New York: Praeger.

Marais, Hein. 2001. *South Africa: Limits to Change. The Political Economy of Transition*. Cape Town: University of Cape Town Press.

Marks, Monique. 2000. Transforming Police Organizations from Within: Police Dissident Groupings in South Africa. *British Journal of Criminology* 40: 557-73.

Martin, James. 1998. *Gramsci's Political Analysis*. New York: St Martin's Press.

Marx, Anthony W. 1998. *Making Race and Nation: A Comparison of the United States, South Africa, and Brazil*. New York: Cambridge University Press.

Mashike, Lephophotho. 2008. Age of Despair: The Unintegrated Forces of South Africa. *African Affairs* 107 (June): 433-53.

Mason, T David, and Dale A Krane. 1989. The Political Economy of Death Squads: Toward a Theory of the Impact of State-Sanctioned Terror. *International Studies Quarterly* 33 (2): 175-98.

Mattes, Robert. 2002. South Africa: Democracy without the People. *Journal of Democracy* 13 (1): 22-36.

Mazzei, Julie. 2009. *Death Squads or Self-Defense Forces? How Paramilitary Groups Emerge and Challenge Democracy in Latin America*. Chapel Hill, NC: University of North Carolina Press.

Mbeki, Govan. 1964. *South Africa: The Peasants' Revolt*. Middlesex: Penguin.

McCarthy, Shaun. 1996. Challenges for the South African Intelligence Community. In *South Africa's Defense and Security into the 21st Century*, edited by W Gutteridge. Brookfield, VT: Dartmouth Publishing Company.

McKinley, Dale T. 1997. *The ANC and the Liberation Struggle: A Critical Political Biography*. London: Pluto Press.

McSherry, J Patrice. 1997. *Incomplete Transition: Military Power and Democracy in Argentina*. New York: St Martin's Press.

McSherry, J Patrice. 2005. *Predatory States: Operation Condor and Covert War in Latin America*. New York: Rowman and Littlefield Publishers.

Meredith, Martin. 2005. *The Fate of Africa*. New York: Public Affairs.

Metelits, Claire. 2010. *Inside Insurgency: Violence, Civilians, and Revolutionary Group Behavior*. New York: New York University Press.

Minnaar, Anthony. 1998. The 'Third Force.' In *The Hidden Hand: Covert Operations in South Africa*, edited by Charl Schutte, Ian Liebenberg, and Anthony Minnaar, 2nd edn. Pretoria: Human Sciences Research Council, pp. 57-78.

Minter, William. 1988. *Operation Timber: Pages from the Savimbi Dossier*. Trenton, NJ: Africa World Press.

Minter, William. 1994. *Apartheid's Contras: An Inquiry into the Roots of War in Angola and Mozambique*. London: Zed Books.

Mkhondo, Rich. 1993. *Reporting South Africa*. Portsmouth, NH: Heinemann.

Moodie, Ellen. 2010. *El Salvador in the Aftermath of Peace: Crime, Uncertainty, and the Transition to Democracy*. Philadelphia: University of Pennsylvania Press.

Moser, Caroline. 2004. Urban Violence and Insecurity: An Introductory Roadmap. *Environment and Urbanization* 16 (October): 3-16.

Motumi, Tsepe. 1995. The Spear of the Nation: The Recent History of Umkhonto we Sizwe (MK). In *About Turn: The Transformation of the South*

African Military and Intelligence, edited by J Cilliers and M Reichardt. Halfway House: Institute for Defence Policy, pp. 84-103.

Mtimkulu, Bereng. 1993. Joe Slovo Slams Cops. *City Press*, 14 April.

Mueller, John. 2000. The Banality of Ethnic War. *International Security* 25 (1): 42-70.

Murray, Martin. 1994. *The Revolution Deferred: The Painful Birth of Post-Apartheid South Africa*. London: Verso.

Musah, Abdel-Fatau. 2003. Privatization of Security, Arms Proliferation, and the Process of State Collapse in Africa. In *State Failure, Collapse, and Reconstruction*, edited by J Milliken. Oxford: Blackwell Publishing.

Nathan, Laurie. 1996. Civil-Military Relations in the New South Africa. In *South Africa's Defense and Security into the 21st Century*, edited by W Gutteridge. Brookfield, VT: Dartmouth Publishing Company.

Neocosmos, Michael. 1998. From Peoples' Politics to State Politics: Aspects of National Liberation in South Africa. In *The Politics of Opposition in Contemporary Africa*, edited by AO Olukoshi. Stockholm: Nordiska Afrikainstitutet.

Ngculu, James. 2009. *The Honour to Serve: Recollections of an Umkhonto Soldier*. Claremont: David Philip.

Nqakula, Charles. 2017. *The People's War: Reflections of an ANC Cadre*. Johannesburg: Mutloatse Heritage Trust.

O'Brien, Kevin. 1999. South African Intelligence in Chaos. *Jane's Intelligence Review* (January): 45-9.

O'Brien, Kevin. 2011. *The South African Intelligence Services: From Apartheid to Democracy, 1948–2005*. New York: Routledge.

O'Donnell, Guillermo, and Philippe C Schmitter. 1986. *Transitions from Authoritarian Rule: Tentative Conclusions about Uncertain Democracies*. Baltimore: Johns Hopkins University Press.

O'Malley, Padraig. 2007. *Shades of Difference: Mac Maharaj and the Struggle for South Africa*. New York: Viking.

Oomen, Barbara. 2004. Vigilantism or Alternative Citizenship? The Rise of Mapogo a Mathamaga. *African Studies* 63 (2): 153-71.

Orkin, Mark. 1992. 'Democracy Knows No Colour': Rationales for Guerrilla Involvement among Black South Africans. *Journal of Southern African Studies* 18 (3): 642-69.

Oxhorn, Philip. 2007. Neopluralism and Citizenship in Latin America. In *Citizenship in Latin America*, edited by JS Tulchin and Meg Ruthenberg. Boulder, CO: Lynne Rienner Publishers.

Parker, Karen F. 2008. *Unequal Crime Decline: Theorizing Race, Urban Inequality, and Criminal Violence*. New York: New York University Press.

Pauw, Jacques. 1997. *Into the Heart of Darkness: Confessions of Apartheid's Assassins*. Johannesburg: Jonathan Ball Publishers.

Peires, JB. 1992. The Implosion of Transkei and Ciskei. *African Affairs* 91: 365-87.

Pereira, Anthony W, and Mark Ungar. 2004. The Persistence of the *Mano Dura*: Authoritarian Legacies and Policing in Brazil and the Southern Cone. In *Authoritarian Legacies and Democracy in Latin America and Southern Europe*, edited by K Hite, and Paola Cesarini. Notre Dame: University of Notre Dame Press.

Phillips, Ian. 1998. The Eagles Youth Clubs. In *The Hidden Hand: Covert Operations in South Africa*, 2nd edn, edited by C Schutte, Ian Liebenberg, and Anthony Minaar. Pretoria: Human Sciences Research Council, pp. 213-28.

Potgieter, De Wet. 2007. *Total Onslaught: Apartheid's Dirty Tricks Exposed*. Cape Town: Zebra Press.

Powell, Ivor. 1998. Aspects of Propaganda Operations. In *The Hidden Hand: Covert Operations in South Africa*, 2nd edn, edited by C Schutte, Ian Liebenberg, and Anthony Minaar. Pretoria: Human Sciences Research Council, pp. 335-42.

Price, David H. 2010. Soft Power, Hard Power, and the Anthropological 'Leveraging' of Cultural 'Assets.' In *Anthropology and Global Counterinsurgency*, edited by John D Kelly, Beatrice Jauregui, Sean T Mitchell, and Jeremy Walton. Chicago, IL: University of Chicago Press, pp. 245-60.

Purkitt, Helen, and Stephen Burgess. 2005. *South Africa's Weapons of Mass Destruction*. Indianapolis: Indiana University Press.

Reno, Will. 1998. *Warlord Politics and African States*. Boulder, CO: Lynne Rienner.

Reno, Will. 2011. *Warfare in Independent Africa*. Cambridge: Cambridge University Press.

Rodney, Walter. 1972. *How Europe Underdeveloped Africa*. Dar es Salaam: Bogle-L'Ouverture.

Russell, Alec. 2009. *Bring Me My Machine Gun: The Battle for the Soul of South Africa from Mandela to Zuma*. New York: Perseus.

Sanders, James. 2006. *Apartheid's Friends: The Rise and Fall of South Africa's Secret Service*. London: John Murray Publishers.

Saul, John S. 1993. *Recolonization and Resistance in Southern Africa in the 1990s*. Toronto: Between the Lines Press.

Saul, John S. 2005. *The Next Liberation Struggle: Capitalism, Socialism, and Democracy in Southern Africa*. Scottsville: University of KwaZulu-Natal Press.

Saunders, Christopher. 1992. Transition in Namibia 1989–90 and the South African Case. In *Peace, Politics, and Violence in the New South Africa*, edited by N Etherington. London: Hans Zell Publishers.

457

Saunders, Christopher. 2016. 'Forged in the Trenches'? The ANC and SWAPO: Aspects of a Relationship. In *South Africa after Apartheid*, edited by Arrigo Pallotti and Ulf Engel. Boston, MA: Brill.

Schatz, Edward (ed.). 2009. *Political Ethnography:What Immersion Contributes to the Study of Power*. Chicago, IL: University of Chicago Press.

Schatz, Edward. 2009. Ethnographic Immersion and the Study of Politics. In *Political Ethnography: What Immersion Contributes to the Study of Power*, edited by E Schatz. Chicago, IL: University of Chicago Press.

Scheper-Hughes, Nancy. 2004. Dangerous and Endangered Youth: Social Structures and Determinants of Violence. *Annals of the New York Academy of Sciences* 1036: 13-46.

Schirmer, Jennifer. 1998. *The Guatemalan Military Project: A Violence Called Democracy.* Cambridge, MA: Harvard University Press.

Schlesinger, Stephen, and Stephen Kinzer. 2005. *Bitter Fruit: The Story of the American Coup in Guatemala.* Cambridge, MA: Harvard University Press.

Schutte, Charl, Ian Liebenberg, and Anthony Minnaar (eds). 1998. *The Hidden Hand: Covert Operations in South Africa*, 2nd edn. Pretoria: Human Sciences Research Council.

Seegers, Annette. 1991. South Africa's National Security Management System, 1972–1990. *Journal of Modern African Studies* 29 (2): 253-73.

Sello, Sekola. 1993. Honesty Might Have Cost Chris His Life. *City Press*, 14 April.

Shaw, Mark. 2002. *Crime and Policing in Post-Apartheid South Africa.* Bloomington, IN: Indiana University Press.

Shubin, Vladimir. 2008. *The Hot 'Cold War': The USSR in Southern Africa.* London: Pluto Press.

Shubin, Vladimir. 2009. *ANC: A View from Moscow*. Auckland Park: Jacana Press.

Simpson, Thula. 2009. The Making (and Remaking) of a Revolutionary Plan: Strategic Dilemmas of the ANC's Armed Struggle, 1974–1978. *Social Dynamics* 35 (2): 312-29.

Simpson, Thula. 2016. *Umkhonto we Sizwe: The ANC's Armed Struggle.* Cape Town: Penguin.

Sithole, Jabulani. 2013. The Inkatha Freedom Party and the Multiparty Negotiations. In *The Road to Democracy in South Africa, Vol. 6 (1990–1996).* South Africa Democracy Education Trust, Pretoria: University of South Africa Press, pp. 836-75.

Slovo, Gillian. 1997. *Every Secret Thing.* London: Virago.

Slovo, Joe. 1995. *Slovo: The Unfinished Autobiography*. Johannesburg: Ravan Press.

Smith, Janet, and Beauregard Tromp. 2009. *Hani: A Life Too Short.* Johannesburg: Jonathan Ball Publishers.

South African Police Service. 2008. South African Police Service Annual Report.

Southall, Roger. 1982. *South Africa's Transkei: The Political Economy of an 'Independent' Bantustan*. New York: Monthly Review Press.

Southall, Roger. 1992. Introduction: Rethinking Transkei Politics. *Journal of Contemporary African Studies* 11 (2): 1-30.

Southall, Roger. 2000. The State of Democracy in South Africa. *Journal of Commonwealth and Comparative Politics* 38 (3): 147-70.

Sparks, Allister. 1994. *Tomorrow Is Another Country*. New York: Penguin Press.

Sparks, Allister. 2003. *Beyond the Miracle*. Chicago, IL: University of Chicago Press.

Spear, Joanna. 2002. Disarmament and Demobilization. In *Ending Civil Wars: The Implementation of Peace Agreements*, edited by SJ Stedman, Donald Rothschild and Elizabeth M Cousens. Boulder, CO: Lynne Rienner.

Standing, Andre. 2006. *Organized Crime: A Study from the Cape Flats*. Pretoria: Institute for Security Studies.

Stanley, William. 1996. *The Protection Racket State*. Philadelphia: Temple University Press.

Stedman, Stephen. 1997. Spoiler Problems in Peace Processes. *International Security* 22 (Autumn): 5-53.

Steinberg, Jonny. 2008. *Thin Blue: The Unwritten Rules of Policing South Africa*. Johannesburg: Jonathan Ball.

Stott, Noel. 2002. From the SADF to the SANDF: Safeguarding South Africa for a Better Life for All? Available at www.csvr.co.za

Suttner, Raymond. 2004. The UDF Period and Its Meaning for Contemporary South Africa. *Journal of Southern African Studies* 30 (3): 691-701.

Suttner, Raymond. 2008. *The ANC Underground in South Africa to 1976*. Auckland Park: Jacana Press.

Tambo, OR. Address 1979. Available from http://www.anc.org.za/ancdocs/history/or/or79-1.html

Tambo, OR. Address 1980. Available at http://www.anc.org.za/ancdocs/history/or/or80-11.html

Tanner, Murray Scott. 2000. Will the State Bring *You* Back In? Policing and Democratization (Review Article). *Comparative Politics* 33 (3): 101-24.

Taylor, Brian D. 2003. *Politics and the Russian Army: Civil-Military Relations, 1689–2000*. New York: Cambridge University Press.

Taylor, Brian D. 2011. *State Building in Putin's Russia: Policing and Coercion after Communism*. New York: Cambridge University Press.

Taylor, Ian. 2001. *Stuck in Middle GEAR: South Africa's Post-Apartheid Foreign Relations*. Westport, CT: Praeger.

459

Taylor, Rupert. 2002. Justice Denied: Political Violence in KwaZulu-Natal after 1994. Centre for the Study of Violence and Reconciliation, Violence and Transition Series, vol. 6.

Thamm, Marianne. 2014. Clive Derby-Lewis Parole Opens Renewed Speculation into Hani Murder and the Arms Deal. *Daily Maverick*, 19 June.

Thomas, Martin. 2008. *Empires of Intelligence*. Berkeley, CA: University of California Press.

Tilly, Charles. 1985. War Making and State Making as Organized Crime. In *Bringing the State Back In*, edited by DR Peter Evans and Theda Skocpol. Cambridge: Cambridge University Press.

Tismaneanu, Vladimir. 2009. Foreword: Truth, Memory, and Reconciliation: Judging the Past in Post-Communist Societies. In *Transitional Justice in Eastern Europe and the Former Soviet Union: Reckoning with the Communist Past*, edited by L Stan. New York: Routledge.

Toft, Monica Duffy. 2010. *Securing the Peace: The Durable Settlement of Civil Wars*. Princeton, NJ: Princeton University Press.

Trewhela, Paul. 1991. The Killing of Sipho Phungulwa. *Searchlight South Africa* 2 (2): 8-30.

Trewhela, Paul. 2009. *Inside Quatro: Uncovering the Exile History of the ANC and SWAPO*. Johannesburg: Jacana.

Trinquier, Roger. 1961. *Modern Warfare: A French View of Counterinsurgency*. New York: Praeger Publishers.

Turok, Ben. 2008. *The Evolution of ANC Economic Policy*. Cape Town: New Agenda.

Twala, Mwezi. 1994. *Mbokodo: Inside MK. A Soldier's Story*. Johannesburg: Jonathan Ball.

Urdal, Henrik. 2006. A Clash of Generations? Youth Bulges and Political Violence. *International Studies Quarterly* 50: 607-29.

Van der Westhuizen, Christi. 2007. *White Power and the Rise and Fall of the National Party*. Cape Town: Zebra Press.

Van Loggerenberg, Jan. 1996. The Katorus Task Group: A Case Study. In *South Africa's Defence and Security into the 21st Century*, edited by W Gutteridge. Aldershot: Dartmouth Publishing.

Wacquant, Loic. 1999. How Penal Common Sense Comes to Europeans: Notes on the Transatlantic Diffusion of Neoliberal Doxa. *European Societies* 1 (3): 319-52.

Wacquant, Loic. 2008. *Urban Outcasts: A Comparative Sociology of Advanced Marginality*. Cambridge: Polity Press.

Walter, Barbara. 1997. The Critical Barrier to Civil War Settlement. *International Organization* 51 (Summer): 335-64.

Warren, Kay B. 2000. Death Squads and Wider Complicities: Dilemmas for the Anthropology of Violence. In *Death Squads: The Anthropology of State Terror*, edited by JA Sluka. Philadelphia: University of Pennsylvania Press.

Weiner, Tim. 2007. *Legacy of Ashes: The History of the CIA*. New York: Doubleday, 2007.

Weinstein, Jeremy. 2006. *Inside Rebellion: The Politics of Insurgent Violence*. Cambridge: Cambridge University Press.

Williams, Rocky. 1991. *Back to the Barracks: The SADF and the Dynamics of Transformation*. Johannesburg: IDASA.

Williams, Rocky. 2000. The Other Armies: A Brief Historical Overview of Umkhonto we Sizwe, 1961–1994. *South African Military History Society Journal* 11 (5).

Williams, Rocky. 2006. African Armed Forces and the Challenges of Security Sector Transformation. In *Security Sector Reform and Post-Conflict Peacebuilding*, edited by A Schnabel, and Hans-Georg Erhart. New York: United Nations.

Wilson, Richard. 1992. Continued Counter-Insurgency: Civilian Rule in Guatemala, 1986–91. In *Low Intensity Democracy: Political Power in the New World Order*, edited by Barry Gills and Joel Rocamora. London: Pluto Press, pp. 144-59.

Winter, Gordon. 1981. *Inside BOSS, South Africa's Secret Police*. New York: Penguin.

Wood, Elisabeth Jean. 2000. *Forging Democracy from Below: Insurgent Transitions in South Africa and El Salvador*. New York: Cambridge University Press.

Wood, Elisabeth Jean. 2004. *Insurgent Collective Action and Civil War in El Salvador*. New York: Cambridge University Press.

Yanow, Dvora. 2009. Dear Author, Dear Reader: The Third Hermeneutic in Writing and Reviewing Ethnography. In *Political Ethnography: What Immersion Contributes to the Study of Power*, edited by E Schatz. Chicago, IL: University of Chicago Press.

Unattributed articles

'A-G Criticizes KZP over Hitsquads,' *New Nation*, 13 October 1995.

'An Axe, Not a Broom, for the Spies,' *Mail & Guardian,* 9 April 1998.

'ANC Denies Vula Cover-up,' *New Nation*, 20 March 1997.

'ANC Fighters Dismissed,' *Africa Research Bulletin*, 1–30 November 1994, p. 11662.

'ANC Pushes Ahead with Peace Plan,' *New Nation,* 17 January 1997.

'The ANC Takes a Long, Hard Look at the GNU,' *New Nation*, 13 October 1995.

'Anxiety in KwaZulu Natal over Crackdown,' *Sunday Times*, 12 March 1995.

'Apartheid Army's Deadly Secrets,' IOL, 30 April 2006, https://www.iol.co.za/news/politics/apartheid-armys-deadly-secrets-275899

'Arms Control: South Africa,' *The Economist*, 19 September 1992.

'Beyond Bisho,' *The Times* (London), 1 October 1992.

'BNP Activist Was Linked to South Africa Murder,' *The Independent*, 9 May 2009.

'CCB Men Break Ranks,' *New Nation*, 16 May 1997.

'Chris Hani Was Killed before He Could Expose Joe Modise,' *City Press*, 8 October 2014.

'CIA Could Face Trouble if South Africa Murder Case Throws Light on Its Role,' *Baltimore Sun*, 12 November 1995.

'CIA Linked to Mandela's Arrest,' *Washington Post*, 11 July 1990.

'Cops Set to Pounce on Taxi Hitman,' *New Nation*, 22 September 1995.

'Cops Up for Murder,' *New Nation*, 22 September 1995.

'Cops Warn of Plot to Kill Premier,' *New Nation*, 27 October 1995.

'Defence Job Widened by Mandela,' *The Times* (London), 27 June 1994.

'De Klerk, Closet Generalissimo,' *New Nation*, 13 October 1995.

'De Klerk Lied – TRC,' *New Nation*, 10 January 1997.

'De Klerk Tries to Stem Natal Defections: South Africa,' *The Times* (London), 12 August 1993.

'De Kock Claims Probed,' *New Nation*, 7 August 1997.

'De Kock's Family Alleges Poison Bid,' *Sunday Times*, 9 April 1995.

'Dismissal Threat to Striking Mandela Guards: South Africa,' *The Times*, 25 August 1995.

'Enemies Who Worked Together for the Police,' *Mail & Guardian*, 19 February 1999.

'Evidence of US Strategic Role,' *Newsday*, 2 August 1986.

'The Execution of a Camp Commander,' *Mail & Guardian*, 30 October 1998.

'Farm of Killers,' *New Nation*, 14 March 1997.

'Five ANC Ministers Spied for Nats – Claim,' *New Nation*, 7 March 1997.

'Freedom of Boksburg Posthumously Conferred on Hani,' South African Press Association, 11 April 1997, http://www.justice.gov.za/trc/media/1997/9704/s970411b.htm

'Hani Allegedly Ordered Killings of Top ANC Men,' South African Press Association, 12 June 1997, http://www.justice.gov.za/trc/media/1997/9706/s970612e.htm

'The Hani Conspiracy,' *New Nation*, 27 March 1997.

'The Hani Conspiracy Widens,' *New Nation*, 4 April 1997.

'Hani Murder: Shocking New Evidence,' *New Nation*, 27 March 1997.

'Hani Not Yet Laid to Rest,' *Mail & Guardian*, 29 March 2009.

'Hani's Death Warrant?' *New Nation*, 11 April 1997.

'He Walks in Fear,' *New Nation*, 14 March 1997.

'Hints of Truth about Hani's Death,' *Mail & Guardian*, 4 April 1997.

'Hired Cop Accused of Death Plot,' *New Nation*, 13 October 1995.

'Hit Man Says IFP Made Him "a Killing Machine,"' *Sunday Times*, 26 March 1995.

'How ANC Protected "Warlord" Spy,' *Mail & Guardian*, 7 November 1997.

'How Arms Dealer Got His Hooks into the ANC,' *Mail & Guardian*, 19 January 2007.

'I Was No Spy,' *New Nation*, 11 April 1997.

'IFP's "Caprivis" Still on the Job,' *Mail & Guardian*, 11 October 1996.

'Inkatha Raid Stirs Plot Fears,' *The Independent*, 30 December 1995.

'Inkatha's Secret German War Chest,' *Mail & Guardian*, 15 September 1995.

'Intelligence Chief's "Odd" Gunshot,' *Mail & Guardian*, 15 October 1997.

'John Vorster Policemen Killed Stanza Bopape,' *New Nation*, 20 March 1997.

'Leaking Another Pile of Baloney,' *Mail & Guardian*, 12 June 1998.

'Magnus: "No" to SADF-Umkhonto Merger,' *The Citizen*, 21 March 1990.

'The Man Who Knew Too Much', *Indian Ocean Newsletter* No.759, 29 March 1997

'Mandela Accepts ANC Blame,' *The Times* (London), 7 April 1993.

'Mandela Has Files on Spies,' *Mail & Guardian*, 30 October 1997.

'Mandela Quells Mob Rule,' *Africa Research Bulletin*, 1–31 October 1994, pp. 11626-7.

'Media Spies Warned,' *New Nation*, 20 March 1997.

'Mercenary Claims 20 Are Buried on "Hit Squad" Farm,' *Sunday Times*, 12 March 1995.

'Military Blend,' *The Economist*, 26 August 1995.

'Military Veterans Pose a Problem,' *New Nation*, 1 September 1995.

'MK Man Was Apartheid Spy,' *New Nation*, 2 May 1997.

'Mozambique/South Africa: The Special Forces Behind RENAMO,' *Africa Confidential* 28 (24), 2 December 1987.

'Nceba Radu's Death: The Mystery Deepens,' *New Nation*, 14 March 1997.

'New Info on Hani's Death Vindicates Reinvestigation Call: ANC,' SAPA, 4 April 1997, http://www.justice.gov.za/trc/media/1997/9704/s970404b.htm

'Nine Cops Face Rap over Shootout,' *New Nation*, 20 October 1995.

'Nuclear Nightmare,' *New Nation*, 20 October 1995.

'Old Foes Unite in Peacekeeping Force: South Africa,' *The Times* (London), 31 March 1994.

'Old-Style SANDF Officers Are Still at War with Us, MK Soldiers Tell Modise,' *Sunday Independent*, 2 March 1997.

'Operation Vula – The Facts behind the Fiction: Interview with Siphiwe Nyanda,' *Mayibuye* (Johannesburg) 1 (8), December 1990, pp. 10-12.

'PAC's De Lille Names "Spies",' *Mail & Guardian*, 23 October 1997.

'Peace in the Balance: South Africa,' *The Economist*, 28 November 1992, p. 44.

'Plan to Silence Phosa's Would-Be Killer Alleged,' *New Nation*, 20 October 1995.

'Police Hint ANC Framed Them for White's Murder: South Africa,' *The Times* (London), 24 August 1992.

'Police Still Patrolling KZN Area,' *New Nation*, 25 August 1995.

'Political Violence Rocks ANC Stronghold,' *New Nation*, 28 February 1997.

'Posthumous Honour for SACP Chief,' *New Nation*, 27 March 1997.

'Reformist Afrikaner Murdered,' *Africa Research Bulletin*, 1–30 November 1994, pp. 11661-2.

'Revolt Averted,' *New Nation*, 14 March 1997.

'Rightists Face Murder Charges,' *New Nation*, 29 September 1995.

'Rightwing Terror or a New Third Force?' *New Nation*, 10 January 1997.

'Rightwingers Regroup,' *New Nation*, 14 February 1997.

'S. Africa's Intelligence Network,' *Afro-American*, 11 April 1987.

'SA Intelligence World in Turmoil,' *Mail & Guardian*, 20 October 1995.

'Scapegoats for the Country's Ills,' Helen Suzman Foundation, no. 10 (Second Quarter 1998).

'The Secrets of Stratcom,' *Mail & Guardian*, 23 June 1995, https://mg.co.za/article/1995-06-23-the-secrets-of-stratcom

'Seven Other Death Farms,' *New Nation*, 20 March 1997.

'Shadowy Web of Security Force Conspiracy Begins to Emerge,' *Sunday Times*, 12 March 1995.

'Shell House and the Mystery Wimpy Bombers,' *New Nation*, 18 April 1997.

'Shock over City Council "Spy" Allegations,' *The Citizen*, 21 March 1990.

'Shocks from the Steyn Report,' *Mail & Guardian*, 31 January 1997, https://mg.co.za/article/1997-01-31-shocks-from-the-steyn-report

'Soldiers of Misfortune,' *New Nation*, 27 October 1995.

'South Africa: Crackdown Hits Hani's Men,' *Africa Confidential* 30 (18), 8 September 1989.

'South Africa: Genesis of the Third Force,' *Africa Confidential* 32 (19), 27 September 1991.

'South Africa: Looking through the Mirrors,' *Africa Confidential* 33 (15), 31 July 1992.

'South Africa: Partners in Policing,' *Africa Confidential* 35 (2), 21 January 1994.

'South Africa: Violence in Transition,' *Africa Confidential* 33 (8), 17 April 1992.

'South Africa: Who Exactly Is in Command?' *The Economist*, 19 November 1994.

'The South African Army and Police: Apartheid's Cannibals,' *Michigan Citizen* 15 (19), 3 April 1993.

'South African Spy Chief Probing Coup When Slain,' *Orlando Sentinel*, 9 October 1995.

'Spies Fever Grips ANC,' *New Nation*, 4 April 1997.

'Spy Chief Mystery,' *The Independent*, 8 October 1995.

'"Stratcom" Never Died, Says Ex-Cop,' *Mail & Guardian*, 18 August 1995.

'Taxi Wars Exposé: Police Set to Pounce on Hit Squad Training Camps,' *City Press*, 5 January 1997.

'Third Force Suspected in Pupils' Bloody Feud,' *New Nation*, 17 January 1997.

'"Third Force" Target?' *New Nation*, 9 May 1997.

'The Titanic Battle for Control of the Defence Force,' *Mail & Guardian*, 17 June 1994.

'Toll of Unsolved Killings: Opponents of Apartheid,' *The Times* (London), 18 November 1989.

'Top IFP Man Investigated,' *New Nation*, 29 September 1995.

'Top IFP Members May Face Hit Squad Charges,' *Sunday Times*, 9 April 1995.

'Top KZP Officers Implicated in Murders,' *New Nation*, 2 May 1997.

'Top Officers Named in Hit Squad Probe,' *New Nation*, 22 September 1995.

'Top SANDF Posts for MK Officers,' *The Citizen*, 29 June 1994.

'Tortured,' *New Nation*, 20 October 1995.

'TRC Gives Amnesty to 18 and Refuses It to Five,' SAPA, 12 January 1999.

'Union Questions Police Allegiance,' *New Nation*, 28 February 1997.

'Vlakplaas Men Paid R17. 5m,' *Sunday Times*, 2 April 1995.

'Warlord Buried as Killing Goes On,' *Mail & Guardian*, 1 February 1999.

'Was ANC "Spy" Poisoned in Exile?' *The Star*, 14 October 2003.

'What Modise Didn't Know about DCC,' *Mail & Guardian*, 17 June 1994.

'What the Generals Didn't Tell Modise,' *Mail & Guardian*, 17 June 1994.

'Where's the Truth in the Modise Recruiting Row?' *Mail & Guardian*, 1 March 1996.

'Would-Be Assassin Lives in Fear in Jail,' *New Nation*, 13 October 1995.

INDEX

Operation Condor (1968–89), 10, 56
Operation Gladio (1956–90), 10, 56
Operation PBSUCCESS (1954), 76
Operation Phoenix (1968–72), 77
Matola raid (1981), 70
Peace Corps and, 41
Rivonia raid (1963), 69
strengthening democratic institutions, 339
TRC and, 341
Certified Personnel Registers (CPRs), 254
Chate, Charlie, 286
chemical weapons, 173, 178, 286
Cherry, Janet, 31, 39, 57
Chicago school economics, 361
Chikane, Frank, 331
Chikane, Iscor, 304
child mortality, 36
Chile, 7, 10, 76, 361
Chiluba, Frederick, 98
Chilwan's Buses, 287
China, 69
Christmas Eve massacre (1995), 293
Chubb, 356
Church Street bombing (1983), 37, 44–5
Ciskei Defence Force (CDF), 158–9
Ciskei Republic (1981–94), 112, 139, 141, 157, 158–9, 164, 181
ADM, 287, 288
Bisho massacre (1992), 163, 220, 259
Buffalo Battalion in, 259
coup (1990), 153
DCC in, 180
IR-CIS, 94, 95, 153, 158–9, 164, 184, 259

Nieuwoudt in, 95, 153, 158, 159, 184, 220
NPKF, formation of (1993–4), 252
organized crime in, 287
PAIIC in, 95, 308
Sebe assassination plan (1986), 148
weapons smuggling in, 159, 164
Citizen, The, 208, 211
Civil Cooperation Bureau (CCB), 65–6, 93–6, 100, 169, 173, 174, 288, 349, 351
Bantustans, operations in, 153, 164
De Klerk and, 186–7
disbanding of (1990), 94, 96, 153
DCC, relations with, 94, 174, 181
Hani assassination (1993), 216
Hani assassination attempt (1993), 198–9
Lubowski assassination (1989), 81
SANDF and, 253
September assassination (1988), 340
Telkom and, 341–2
train violence, 84, 179
Webster assassination (1989), 65–6, 184, 187, 210
civil society, 7, 12, 17, 19, 59, 91–3
Adult Education Consultants, 88, 92, 288
Joint Management Centres (JMCs), 63–4, 85, 96
Third Force and, 88, 91–3
class, 19, 22, 229, 230
Cline, Ray, 85, 342
code-switching, 224–8
coercive capacity, 19

Operation Marion training
  (1986), 66–7, 86–7
parliamentary election (1989),
  80–82
PLAN, 35
psychological warfare in, 80–82,
  192, 193, 204
SADF MI in, 80–82, 122, 173,
  192, 193, 204
SAP in, 54
SWAPO, *see* SWAPO
Tripartite Accord (1988), 51, 78,
  80, 109
UN Resolution 435 (1978), 87
Nampula, Mozambique, 98
Natal Liberation Army (NLA), 88
Natal University, 294
National Coordinating Mechanism
  (NCM), 84
National Intelligence Agency (NIA),
  26, 289, 320–23
Banda, 279
De Lille report (2001), 329
Browse Mole Report affair
  (2006–7), 331–2
Hani assassination report (1997),
  214–22
IFP and, 322
Macozoma's surveillance
  complaint (2005), 333
Matthews Commission (2006),
  331
McBride Affair (1998), 325–8,
  350–51
Mdluli assassination (1995), 281
Mogoba interrogation (1997),
  318
NIS, continuity in, 213, 321
SAPS, relations with, 323
spies in, 213, 314
Vlakplaas operatives in, 322

National Intelligence Coordinating
  Committee (NICOC), 188, 323,
  325, 342
National Intelligence Service (NIS),
  47, 63, 95, 289
ANC moles in, 47, 194, 346
ANC negotiations, 106, 108
CCB and, 65
De Klerk and, 175, 188, 189
De Lille report (2001), 329
destruction of files, 318
Inner Circle group, 194
K unit, 95
Khoza and, 67
NIA, continuity in, 213, 321
Operation Mayibuye report
  (1992), 190
Operation Sunrise report (1993),
  191
PAIIC members, 184
Steyn Report (1992), 178, 181,
  183
Stoffberg, 279
Third Force violence and, 94
TREWITS and, 64
National Investigating Task Unit
  (NITU), 294
National Party, 5
ANC Working Group letter
  (1994), 194–6
Bantustans, relations with,
  149–50, 160, 165
De Klerk appointed president
  (1989), 69, 79, 108
Government of National Unity,
  322
Groote Schuur talks (1990), 101,
  114, 120–21, 123
Hani assassination (1993), 225
Inner Circle group letter (1992),
  194

non-racialism, 13, 36–8, 242
Nongoma, KwaZulu-Natal, 292, 298
North, Oliver, 340
North Atlantic Treaty
   Organization (NATO), 10, 17,
   18, 56, 95, 339, 346, 361
North Crest, Mthatha, 160
North Transvaal Security Branch,
   62, 64
North West
   BAT pipe bombings (1997), 290
   Mamasela spy allegations (1997),
   315
   taxi violence, 289
   torture farms, 97
Northern Ireland, 55, 172, 175, 339
Nqakula, Charles, 111, 116, 157,
   203–4, 219, 231–2
Nqutu, KwaZulu-Natal, 292
Ntombela, David, 296
Ntsaluba, Ayanda, 229
Ntsebeza, Dumisa, 118, 284
Ntsoni, Zola, 92
nuclear weapons, 178, 324, 340
Nutritional Development
   Programme, 288
Nyanda, Siphiwe
   arrest (1990), 116, 117, 120,
   124–5
   Chief of Defence Force Staff
   (1994–6), 172, 235, 238,
   260, 261, 262, 303
   JMCC press conference (1994),
   254
   Kaweweta visit (1992), 248
   McBride Affair (1998), 326, 327
   Operation Mayibuye (1992), 190
   Operation Sunrise story (1993),
   191
   Operation Vula (1986–91), 104,
   105, 111, 116, 124–5

renunciation of armed struggle
   (1990), 125
   SANDF revolt averted (1997),
   262–3
   SANDF chief of staff (1998–
   2005), 263, 328
   Wallmansthal protest (1994), 235
Nyanga, Cape Town, 92, 102
Nyawa, Zambia, 98
Nyawose, Kipha, 293
Nzimande, Blade, 191, 232–3
Nzo, Alfred, 110, 307

O'Brien, Kevin, 70–71, 95, 120,
   172–3, 181, 186, 315, 321, 327
O'Malley, Padraig, 116, 134, 305
Oelschig, Marius, 259
Omar, Dullah, 307
'One Settler, One Bullet', 49
Operation Agree (1989), 81
Operation Bible (1986–90), 106,
   116
Operation Cable (1991), 159
Operation Condor (1968–89), 10,
   56
Operation Flair (1989–94), 108
Operation Gladio (1956–90), 10, 56
Operation Katzen (1986), 148, 287
Operation Marion (1986–90),
   66–7, 86–7, 188
Operation Mayibuye (1992), 190
Operation Omega (1985), 89
Operation PBSUCCESS (1954), 76
Operation Phantom, see Project
   Pastoor
Operation Phoenix (1968–72), 77
Operation Rollerball (1994), 267–8
Operation Snowball (1992), 191
Operation Sunrise (1993), 191–3
Operation Vula (1986–91), 103–25,
   311, 317, 329, 346

INDEX

Security Branch infiltration, 47,
83, 106, 107, 124, 194
Silverton bank shootout (1980),
40
Sipolilo campaign (1967–8), 35
Slurry attack (1989), 46
Special Operations unit, 44, 61,
73, 101, 132, 223, 260, 315
Swaziland bases, 42, 60, 268
Tanzania bases, *see under* Tanzania
in Transkei, 140–65, 229
treason trial (1988), 33, 61
Uganda bases, *see under* Uganda
Venda conferences, *see under*
Venda Republic
Voortrekkerhoogte rocket attack
(1981), 44
Wankie campaign (1967), 33, 35,
41, 42, 229
Zambian bases, *see* Zambian MK
bases
Zimbabwe bases, 248, 249
Umlazi, KwaZulu-Natal, 292
Union des Populations du
Cameroon, 201
UNITA (*União Nacional para a
Independência Total de Angola*), 32,
36, 50, 98–9
Afrikaner Volksfront, relations
with, 99
arms sales to, 43, 287
France, relations with, 70
MK, conflict with, 37, 43, 44,
110, 141, 152, 229
Modise, relations with, 43
SADF, relations with, 54, 57,
87, 98
United Democratic Front (UDF),
45, 47, 71, 82, 83, 105, 141,
273, 346, 353
Ama-Afrika, conflict with, 68

formation of (1983), 45
IFP, conflict with, 68
KwaMakutha massacre (1987), 67
necklacing, 48
in Transkei, 142
Witdoeke and, 91–2
United Democratic Movement
(UDM), 296
United Kingdom, 8, 57, 258
Advokaat, development of, 70
ANC in, 105, 299
arms deal scandal (1998–), 222,
223, 224, 336
British Aerospace, 223, 224, 336
British Military Advisory and
Training Team (BMATT), 258
British National Party (BNP), 211
carrot and stick, 58
Du Randt and Flores arrest
(1992), 175
Hani assassination (1993), 223,
227
Lancaster House negotiations
(1979–80), 235, 338
Malayan Emergency (1948–60),
55
Mau Mau uprising (1952–60),
58, 338
MI6, 70, 222, 311, 338, 342, 343
negotiations in, 108
Northern Ireland, 55, 172, 175,
339
Special Air Service (SAS), 56,
85, 342
United Nations, 70, 80
ANC representatives, 70
Hani assassination (1993), 211
Resolution 435 on Namibia
(1978), 87
Transition Assistance Group
(UNTAG), 81